Edited and designed by
Time Out Paris
100 rue du Fbg-St-Antoine
75012 Paris
Tel: +33(0)1.44.87.00.45
Fax: +33(0)1.44.73.90.60
e-mail: paris@timeout.com

Editor Natasha Edwards
Production Editor Rosalind Sykes
Research Caroline Boyce, Frances Dougherty, Lucia Scazzocchio
Index Richard Wright

Art Director Richard Joy
Ad Design Nadine Lennox

Sales & Administration Manager Philippe Thareaut
Advertising Executives Claire O'Neill, Mia Tahara Stubbs, Susanne Twerenbold

Managing Director Karen Albrecht

Marketing & Distribution Manager Jonathan Bryant

For
Time Out Guides Ltd
Universal House
251 Tottenham Court Road
London W1P 0AB
Tel: +44(0)20 7813 3000
Tel: +44(0)20 7813 6001
http://www.timeout.com
e-mail: guides@timeout.com

Editorial Director Peter Fiennes
Series Editor Caroline Taverne
Art Director John Oakey

Group Advertisement Director Lesley Gill
Sales Director Mark Phillips

Publisher Tony Elliott
Managing Director Mike Hardwick
Financial Director Kevin Ellis
Marketing Director Gillian Auld
General Manager Nichola Coulthard
Accountants Catherine Bowen, Bridget Carter

Features for the eighth edition were written or updated by:
Paris by Season Katherine Spenley. **History** Rosalind Sykes, Stephen Mudge (Royal foibles). **Architecture**
Natasha Edwards. **What is Paris?** Mark Hunter. **Islands**, **Right Bank**, **Left Bank**, **Beyond the Périphérique**,
Natasha Edwards, Susan Bell (The beautiful and the bizarre), Simon Cropper (Mystic Mr Fix-It), Jean
O'Sullivan (And God created Paris..., Rhyme, reason & the rush hour), Alan Tillier (Ghost train, Strictly
academic). **Museums** Simon Cropper, Natasha Edwards, Rosalind Sykes. **Art Galleries** Natasha Edwards.
Accommodation Katherine Spenley. **Restaurants** adapted from *Time Out Eating & Drinking in Paris Guide*,
Rosa Jackson (Flavours of the Maghreb). **Cafés & Bars** Adapted from *Time Out Eating & Drinking in Paris
Guide*, Katherine Spenley (The literary café rewritten). **Fashion** Caroline Boyce, Rowan Tomlinson, Nadine
Frey (Techy trendoids...), Julie Street (Shopping the third way). **Specialist Shopping** Natasha Edwards, Alex
Papazafiropoulos, Nadine Frey (Reinventing the grands magasins), Rowan Tomlinson (Out of Africa). **Food &
Drink** Rosa Jackson, Peter Havas (The Montmartre harvest). **Cabaret, Circus & Comedy** Natasha Edwards.
Children Natasha Edwards. **Clubs** Lucia Scazzocchio. **Dance** Carol Pratl. **Film** Simon Cropper, Toby Rose
(Aladdin's flicks, On location). **Gay & Lesbian** Toby Rose. **Music: Classical & Opera** Stephen Mudge.
Music: Rock, Roots & Jazz Anna Britten, Richard Ogier, Andil Gosine (La vie en rose...). **Sport** Rosalind
Sykes, Rosa Jackson (Rock and stroll). **Theatre** Annie Sparks. **Trips out of Town** Natasha Edwards, Sadie
Ryan, Stephen Mudge (Houses to write home about). **Directory** Katherine Spenley.

Photography by Tom Craig, Adam Eastland, Colm Pierce, Jon Perugia. **Additional photography** Brigitte
Baudesson, Philippe Cibille, Brigitte Enguerand, Nathalie Jacqualt, Eric Mahoudeau, Jean-Pierre
Maurin,Crescenzo Mazza, Dawn Moon. **Additional photos courtesy** The Bridgeman Art Library International
Ltd, Collections Photographiques du Musée Carnavalet, Opéra National de Paris, Théâtre de la Ville.
Maps p364-375 by Mapworld, p376-378 courtesy RATP.

Contents

About the Guide

The *Time Out Paris Guide* is one of an expanding series of guides that includes *London, Amsterdam, Barcelona, Berlin, Florence, Madrid, Prague, Rome, New York, Los Angeles, Sydney* and *Tokyo.* This eighth edition has been thoroughly revised and updated by staff and freelance writers resident in Paris. More than just a book for tourists, it is also for frequent visitors or long-term residents. It covers all the major sights and attractions, but also takes you to the city's more obscure and eccentric venues, as well as shops, restaurants, cafés, bars and clubs.

For events each week, see the weekly *Time Out Paris* section (in English) inside French listings magazine *Pariscope,* available at newstands. The quarterly *Time Out Paris Free Guide* is available in selected hotels, bars and visitor centres. For detailed reviews of 850 Paris restaurants, cafés and bars, buy the *Time Out Eating & Drinking in Paris Guide*. Penguin's new *Time Out Book of Paris Walks* features 23 themed itineraries by eminent writers and journalists.

PRACTICAL GUIDE

We've tried to make this book as useful as possible. Addresses, telephone numbers, transport details, opening times, admission prices and credit card details are all included in our listings.

All the information in the guide was checked and correct when we went to press, but bear in mind that arrangements can change at any time. If you want to be really sure, it's a good idea to phone ahead to check opening times, dates of exhibitions, admission prices and the like. The same applies to information on disabled access; it's wise to phone first to check your needs can be met.

EDITORIAL INDEPENDENCE

It shold be stressed that the information we give is impartial. *Time Out* maintains a strict policy of editorial independence, and advertisers are never guaranteed special treatment of any kind. No organisation or enterprise has been included in this guide because the owner or manager has advertised in our publications. Their impartiality is one of the reasons why our guides are so successful and well respected.

BOLD TYPE

Where we mention important places or events also listed elsewhere in the guide, or in detail later in the chapter, they are highlighted in **bold**.

ADDRESSES

Paris is divided into 20 *arrondissements,* which form a snail-shell spiral beginning at Notre Dame and finishing at the Porte de Montreuil on the eastern edge of the city. Paris addresses include the *arrondissement* in the postcode, which begins with the prefix 750. For example, an address in the 1st *arrondissement* would have the postcode 75001, and one in the 20th would be 75020. In this guide we have referred to the *arrondissements* as 1st, 2nd, 3rd, 4th and so on. Addresses within the area covered in the large-scale map have also been given map references, but it is often equally simple to locate a street by seeing which *arrondissement* it is in, or looking for the nearest Métro.

PRICES

The prices listed throughout the guide should be used as guidelines. We try to give the best and most-up-to date advice, so we always want to hear if you've been badly overcharged. You'll increasingly come across prices indicated in Euros (1 Euro = 6.55957F). Euro cheques are accepted in some places, but full transition to the European currency and the arrival in circulation of Euro coins and notes will take place only on 1 January 2002.

TELEPHONES

All French phone numbers have ten digits. From outside France, dial the country code (33) and leave off the zero at the start of the number.

CREDIT CARDS

Throughout this guide, the following abbreviations have been used for credit cards: **AmEx** American Express; **DC** Diners' Club; **MC** Mastercard; **V** Visa/Barclaycard. Note that shops, restaurants, cafés and museums will often not accept credit cards for sums of less than 100F.

LET US KNOW

We hope you enjoy the *Time Out Paris Guide* and that it makes your stay more enjoyable. However, if you disagree with any of our reviews, or have found somewhere you love and think should be included, let us know; your views on places you visited are always welcome. There's a reader's reply card in the book for your comments.

> The Internet site www.timeout.com offers guide information and arts and entertainment listings to Paris and 28 other cities worldwide.

Introduction

Sometimes Paris is hard to see. The city has been obscured by so many layers of myth, of people, places and events that have made its identity, that there is no reality – or, rather, no single reality. A human archaeology has been building up ever since the start: Abélard and Héloïse (the city of love), Etienne Marcel (the city of revolutions, heroes and assassins), Madame de Sévigné (socialites and intellectuals), Madame de Maintenon (back to love again), the dazzling Sun King and his court, Monet and other artistic rebels. There's the naughty *belle époque* and those cancanning Dorriss girls, Piaf singing sparrow-like in the street, Hemingway drinking everywhere. Each *quartier* – Montmartre, Montparnasse, St-Germain – evokes a different wave of associations. What is the boulevard St-Germain without Sartre and De Beauvoir, or the boulevard St-Michel without May 68? Even somewhere as apparently straightforward as the Louvre has its mysteries: a medieval castle is concealed within a Renaissance palace, and it's not just the crowds round the Mona Lisa but the very familiarity of the art icon that obscures her face.

But forget all of that. Leave the phantoms behind and venture into the Paris of today. Attempt to discover the modern Paris, a city that is neither more nor less than all the other Parises, but which is still building its identity with names we haven't yet heard of, as the current generation of artists, architects, filmmakers, writers, designers and musicians puts its stamp on it, each competing for a place in the new Paris mosaic.

The place sometimes seems like a ceaseless merry-go-round of where is in and where is out – a Ménilmontant very different from the one in Trenet's song, a Champs-Elysées making a comeback, a dynamic canal-side culture far from Arletty, a barge-party ethos down on the Seine, a St-Germain where fashion and the arts are learning to cohabit.

Paris, offering up a thousand images and as many others, is one of the world's great metropolises. Yet it is also a collection of villages, and the site of an eternal battle between grandeur and intimacy, extrovert and introvert, fashion versus intellect. Cosmopolitan, cultivated and welcoming – yet sometimes closed in on itself and self-centred – Paris is a city that is still coming to terms with itself, with its ever-changing populations and its position on the planet. But Paris is every bit as worth discovering now as then. It is self-satisfied, yes; irritating, often; fascinating, always. *Natasha Edwards.*

In Context

Coolin
I R I S H P U B

**Marché Saint Germain,
15 Rue Clement,
75006 Paris :
Tel. 44.07.00.92**

METRO ODEON - MABILLON

Paris by Season

The new millennium augurs plenty of time-related speculation, but the city also offers timeless fun and highbrow cultural treats.

While summer is the best time to do Paris on foot, the serious arts season closes down from mid-July to the end of August, resuming in the autumn with new shows and productions. But over Christmas or New Year the city keeps buzzing; theatres, museums and concert halls open as usual.

Look out for two-for-one promotions, which usually last a couple of weeks, such as 'La Mairie de Paris vous invite au concert' and 'La Mairie de Paris vous invite au théâtre' (information on 01.42.78.44.72). The *Time Out Paris* section inside *Pariscope* covers events each week. Selected museum shows are previewed in chapter **Museums,** further annual events and festivals are covered in the **Arts & Entertainment** chapters.

Public holidays

On *jours fériés* banks, many museums, most shops and some restaurants close; public transport runs as on Sunday. New Year, May Day, Bastille Day and Christmas are the most fully observed holidays. New Year's Day (Jour de l'An) 1 Jan; Easter Monday (Lundi de Pâques); May Day (Fête du Travail) 1 May; VE Day (Victoire 1945) 8 May; Ascension Day (Jour de l'Ascension); Whit Monday (Lundi de Pentecôte); Bastille Day (Quatorze Juillet) 14 July; Feast of the Assumption (Jour de l'Assomption) 15 Aug; All Saints' Day (Toussaint) 1 Nov; Remembrance Day (L'Armistice 1918) 11 Nov; Christmas Day (Noël) 25 Dec.

Spring

end Feb-early Mar: Salon de l'Agriculture
Paris-Expo, porte de Versailles, 15th (01.49.09.60.00). M° Porte de Versailles. **Admission** 55F.
Rural France comes to town to create the largest farm in the world. Farmers inspect gigantic bulls, perfectly groomed sheep and manicured pigs, then repair to the food and drink hall to sample regional produce. If there's an election in the offing, politicians will be out in force too.

end Feb-end Mar: Banlieues Bleues
Seine St-Denis and area. Information (01.49.22.10.10). **Admission** 75F-150F.
Held in the Paris suburbs, this festival draws some of the greatest and most interesting names in classic jazz, blues, R&B, soul, funk, flamenco, world and gospel. Among attractions in 2000 are Sam Rivers, Abbey Lincoln, the Art Ensemble of Chicago and the New York Art Quartet featuring Amiri Baraka.

mid Mar: La Nuit des Publivores
Grand Rex, 1 bd Poissonnière, 2nd (01.44.88.98.00). M° Bonne-Nouvelle. **Admission** 200F.
New and old ads from around the world are screened all night, with breaks for ice cream. Fave ads get applause and cheesey ones get hisses. Themes for 2000 see the inevitable Y2K, alongside Iraq and a retrospective of 20 years of Publivores.

mid Mar: Le Printemps des rues
Festival of street theatre and street performance featuring over 600 entertainers, around the Bastille, Bercy, République, Nation and La Villette.

end Mar-early Apr: Festival EXIT
Maison des Arts et de la Culture de Créteil, pl Salvador Allende, 94000 Créteil (01.45.13.19.19). M° Créteil-Préfecture. **Tickets** 40F-200F.
This avant-garde dance, theatre and performance festival has made a big impact with its radical multi-national programme, which has introduced such companies as Dumb Type to Paris. 2000 features Improbable Theatre, Granilla Syntheses and new technology art from Pierreck Sorin and Times Up.

1 Apr: Poisson d'Avril
On April Fool's Day the big joke is to stick a paper fish on some unsuspecting sucker's back. French journos pride themselves on seasonal hoaxes.

Mar/Apr: Festival du Film de Paris
Cinéma Gaumont Marignan, 27 av des Champs-Elysées, 8th (01.42.65.12.37). M° Franklin D Roosevelt **Admission** 35F/day; 150F/week.
The public can see unreleased international films and meet directors, actors and technicians. In 2000, Paris has teamed up with LA, Faye Dunaway presides over the jury; Hollywood bigwigs are promised.

mid Apr-end May: Foire du Trône
pelouse de Reuilly, 12th (01.46.27.52.29). M° Porte Dorée. **Admission** free; rides 10F-20F.
The largest funfair in France has it all: a huge Ferris wheel, haunted houses, *barbe à papa* (candy floss), plus old-fashioned fortune tellers and freak shows.

Good Friday: Le Chemin de la Croix
square Willette, 18th. M° Anvers or Abbesses. **Information** (Sacré-Coeur 01.53.41.89.00).
A crowd follows the Archbishop of Paris from the bottom of Montmartre up the steps to the Sacré Coeur, as he performs the stations of the cross.

early Apr: Marathon de Paris
starts around 9am, av des Champs-Elysées, first runners finish around 11am, av Foch. **Information** (01.41.33.15.68).

20,000 runners huff round a scenic marathon course, taking in the Bois de Boulogne and the quais.

end April-early May: Foire de Paris
Paris Expo, pl de la porte de Versailles. M° Porte de Versailles. **Information** (01.49.09.61.21). **Admission** 50F.
Paris' biggest salon is a kind of amalgam of the Ideal Home Exhibition and Food & Wine fairs. A public showcase for every sector of commerce and industry – gastronomy, tourism, multimedia – with madcap inventions and plenty to taste and try out.

1 May: Fête du Travail
Labour Day is far more ardently maintained than Christmas or New Year. All museums and sights (except the Eiffel Tower) close while unions and leftist groups stage a colourful march through working-class eastern Paris via the Bastille. Lilies of the valley are sold on street corners and given to mum.

end May: La Course au Ralenti
departs 10am, rue Lepic, arrives pl du Tertre, 18th. M° Abbesses or Anvers. **Information** (01.46.06.79.56).
Vintage cars crawl up the streets of Montmartre. Last car to sputter over the 300m course wins.

Summer

end May-early June: French Tennis Open
Stade Roland Garros, 2 av Gordon-Bennett, 16th (01.47.43.48.00). M° Porte d'Auteuil. **Admission** 45F-280F.
The international tennis circus descends on Paris for the French Grand Slam. A very glitzy event.

end May: Les Cinq Jours de l'Objet Extraordinaire
rues du Bac, de Lille, de Beaune, des Sts-Pères, de l'Université, de Verneuil, quai Voltaire, 7th. M° Rue du Bac or St-Germain-des-Prés. **Information** (01.42.61.18.77). **Admission** free.
For five days, the upmarket antique dealers of the elegant Carré Rive Gauche each showcase one item according to theme. Evening and Sunday openings.

early June-early July: Foire St-Germain
pl St-Sulpice and other venues in St-Germain-des-Prés, 6th. M° St-Sulpice. **Information** (01.40.46.75.12).
An echo of the medieval fair, with an antiques fair by the fountain, the Marché de la Poésie poetry salon, concerts and open-air theatre. For children there's a circus and miniature train.

early June: Portes Ouvertes à la Garde Républicaine
12 bd Henri IV, 4th (01.49.96.13.13). M° Sully-Morland. **Admission** free.
Polished horses, gleaming weaponry, booming brass as the presidential guard opens its doors.

June-July: Festival de St Denis
Various venues in St-Denis. M° St-Denis Basilique. **Information** (01.48.13.12.10). **Admission** 50F-250F.
Hear top classical choirs and orchestras amid the Gothic splendour of St-Denis Basilique and other nearby historic buildings.

end June-14 July: Festival Chopin à Paris
Orangerie de Bagatelle, parc de Bagatelle, Bois de Boulogne, 16th. M° Porte Maillot, then bus 244. **Information** (01.45.00.22.19). **Admission** 80F-150F.
An annual treat for piano lovers taking an aspect of Chopin's music. Evening concerts are candlelit.

21 June: Fête de la Musique
All over France. **Information** (01.40.03.94.70).
Steel bands, Celtic rock, Yiddish singers, wandering accordionists and classical string quartets all join in on the longest day of the year, when thousands of musicians give free concerts all over the city. Rising rock, ragga and fusion talent plays at place Denfert-Rochereau, Arab musicians at the Institut du Monde Arabe, but more anarchic gigs put on by cafés or by street musicians often offer the best entertainment. Classical venues include Sainte-Chapelle, Musée d'Orsay and the Palais de Justice. 2000 promises Périphérock – concerts on the Périphérique ring road.

mid-June: Feux de la St-Jean
quai St-Bernard, 5th (01.43.29.21.75). M° Gare d'Austerlitz. **Admission** free.
The feast of St John the Baptist is celebrated in France with fireworks, in Paris along the Seine.

end June: Gay Pride March
Information Centre Gai et Lesbien (01.43.57.21.47).
The parade grows more colourful by the year and draws big crowds, despite squabbling among the organisers. The route usually takes in République and the Bastille, but is subject to last-minute change, followed by an official fête and club events.

end June: Course des Garçons et Serveuses de Café
starts and finishes Hôtel de Ville, pl de l'Hôtel de Ville, 4th. M° Hôtel de Ville. **Information** (01.42.96.60.75).
A highlight of the alternative sporting year as over 500 bona fide café waiters and waitresses in uniform (bow ties, aprons, the lot) and tray and glasses in hand race over an 8km circuit via the Grands Boulevards and St-Germain-des-Prés.

end June-early July: La Goutte d'Or en Fête
square Léon, 18th. M° Barbès-Rochechouart. **Information** (01.53.09.99.22). **Admission** free.
Local and established names play raï, rap and reggae in the largely Arab and African Goutte d'Or.

1-9 July: Jazz à La Villette
211 av Jean-Jaurès, 19th (08.03.07.50.75/ 01.44.84.44.84). M° Porte de Pantin. **Admission** free-160F.
After twelve years, the Halle That Jazz festival has now colonised the entire La Villette complex. Big jazz, blues and Latin names perform in the Grande Halle, more experimental crossover types at the Cité de la Musique, and freebie events take place in smaller bar spaces or in the park itself.

Midsummer musical madness takes over town for the **Fête de la Musique**.

13, 14 July: Le Quatorze Juillet (Bastille Day)

The French national holiday commemorates the storming of the Bastille prison on 14 July 1789, start of the French Revolution and a foretaste of bloodier events to come (*see chapter* **History**). On the evening of 13 July, Parisians dance at place de la Bastille. More partying takes place at firemen's balls: the stations of rue de Sévigné, rue du Vieux-Colombier, rue Blanche and bd du Port-Royal are particularly renowned (usually 13 and 14 July). There's a big gay ball on quai de la Tournelle (5th). At 10am on the 14th, crowds line the Champs-Elysées as the President reviews a military parade from the Arc de Triomphe to Concorde. (Note: the Métro stops on the Champs are closed.) In the evening, thousands gather on the Champ-de-Mars for fireworks at Trocadéro.

14 July: Miss Guinguette Contest

Guinguette de l'Ile du Martin-Pêcheur, 41 quai Victor-Hugo, 94500 Champigny-sur-Marne (01.49.83.03.02). RER Champigny-sur-Marne. **Admission** 40F.
Contestants at this Marne dancehall are judged on dancing, dress and knowledge of guinguette culture.

14 July-15 Aug: Paris, Quartier d'Eté

Various venues. **Information** (01.44.94.98.00). **Admission** free-100F.
Proof that life does go on in Paris in August with an eclectic programme of classical and world music, dance, circus, storytelling, theatre and other offbeat entertainment, often outdoors in the Tuileries, Jardins du Luxembourg, Palais-Royal and other local parks, involving a wildly eclectic international array of participants.

mid-July-end Aug: Le Cinéma en Plein Air

Parc de la Villette, 19th (01.40.03.76.92). M° Porte de Pantin. **Admission** free.
Lie on the grass or recline in a deckchair for La Villette's tenth outdoor film festival, where movies are projected on to a huge screen. Past themes have included screen goddesses and Westerns.

end July/early Aug: Le Tour de France

finishes av des Champs-Elysées, 8th. **Information** *(01.41.33.15.00).*
Epic bike ride rocked by drugs scandals in the past finishes with a flourish at the Champs-Elysées.

15 Aug: Fête de l'Assomption

Cathédrale Notre Dame de Paris, pl Notre Dame, 4th (01.42.34.56.10). M° Cité. **Admission** free.
Notre Dame becomes again a place of religious rather than touristic pilgrimage. A procession parades around the Ile de la Cité behind a statue of the Virgin.

Autumn

Sept: Fêtes de Seine

Quais de la Seine.
Fireworks, a *brocante* and other events beside the river. In 2000, an exhibition, Nautical Fields, presents a history of all things fluvial.

mid-Sept: Fête de L'Humanité

Probably Parc de la Corneuve, Seine-St-Denis. **Information** (01.49.22.72.72). **Admission** 60F.

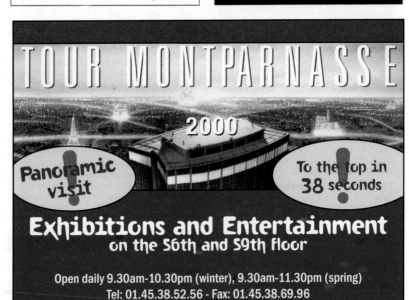

With two ministers in the Jospin government, the French Communist Party remains a rare force in Europe and the jamboree put on by its newspaper *L'Humanité* is a celebration of all things left. Expect political debate, street artistes, lots of food stalls and a busy programme of pop, jazz and world music.

mid-Sept: Journées du Patrimoine

All over France.

This is the weekend when thousands queue for hours to reach the parts the public usually cannot. Not only are government ministries usually inaccessible but many are also in beautiful historic buildings. The longest waits are for the Palais de l'Elysée (home of the President), Matignon (home of the PM), Palais-Royal (Ministry of Culture, Conseil d'Etat) and Palais du Luxembourg (Senate). If you don't like waiting, seek out the more obscure embassies, ministries or opulent corporate headquarters: the Marais and Fbg-St-Germain are particularly ripe for mansion hopping. This year's theme is citizenship. *Le Monde* and *Le Parisien* give detailed info, as does the Hôtel de Sully, 62 rue St-Antoine, 4th.

mid-Sept: Techno Parade

Route to be confirmed. **Information** (08.36.68.91.99). Techno has been drawn into the cultural fold with this big parade through Paris dreamed up by ex-culture minister Jack Lang in 1998, and inspired by Berlin's Love Parade. Drawing an estimated 200,000 revellers and floats by over 20 Parisian and provincial clubs and international guests, the fest finishes with spin-off parties all over town.

mid-Sept: FIAC

Paris Expo, Porte de Versailles. 15th. M° Porte de Versailles. **Information** OIP (01.41.90.47.80). **Admission** 70F.
Around 160 French and international galleries participate in Paris' contemporary art fair. After some staid years, the emphasis is back on the contemporary with a special section for young galleries.

15 Sept-31 Dec: Festival d'Automne

Various venues. **Information** 156 rue de Rivoli, 1st (01.53.4517.00). **Admission** 100F-250F.
A highbrow challenge to the senses as world-class performers present experimental theatre, modern opera and contemporary dance at such prestige venues as the Théâtre de la Ville, Odéon and the suburban public theatres.

Sept: La Journée sans voitures

A day without cars, or at least that's the idea, although the practice of banning cars in selected parts of Paris (and towns elsewhere in France) on the initiative of the environment minister looks suspiciously like traffic jams elsewhere.

early Oct: Fête des Vendanges à Montmartre

rue des Saules, 18th. M° Lamarck-Caulaincourt. Mairie du XVIIIème, 1 pl Jules-Joffrin, 18th. M° Jules-Joffrin. **Information** (01.46.06.00.32).
The grape harvest at the Montmartre vineyard is celebrated with great pomp in a parade from town hall to vineyard and back. Locals dress up in pseudo-historic garb, bands parade and speeches are made. *See chapter* **Food & Drink**.

early Oct: Prix de l'Arc de Triomphe

Hippodrome de Longchamp, Bois de Boulogne, 16th (01.49.10.20.30). M° Porte d'Auteuil plus free shuttle bus. **Admission** lawns free, enclosure 50F.
Le tout Paris takes its best frocks and champagne coolers out for a canter for France's premier horse race.

end Oct Salon du Chocolat

Espace Eiffel Branly, 23 quai Branly, 7th (01.45.03.21.26). M° Alma-Marceau. **Admission** 50F.
A feast of chocolate to satisfy all gluttons.

Oct: Open Studios

Bastille (11th, 12th; Artistes à la Bastille (01.53.36.06.73; Génie de la Bastille 01.40.09.84.03); Ménilmontant (11th, 20th; 01.40.03.01.61); 13ème Art (13th; 01.45.86.17.67). **Admission** free.
Open studio weekends are an interesting way to discover hundreds of painters, sculptors, engravers, photographers and designers – of wildly differing styles and standards – and the places where they work. The longest established scheme is around the Bastille, but there are others in the heavily artist-populated areas of Ménilmontant and the 13th. Information points distribute maps and dossiers.

early Oct: Mondial de l'Automobile

Paris-Expo, porte de Versailles, 15th. M° Porte de Versailles. **Information** (01.56.88.22.40). **Admission** 50F.
Next in 2000, the vast biennial, international motor show is a must for all who like fast things on wheels.

mid Oct: Salon Mix Move

Paris-Expo, porte de Versailles, 15th. M° Porte de Versailles. **Information** (01.56.88.22.40). **Admission** 100F.
Salon dedicated to all things techno. 1999's event involved over 50 labels showcasing their stuff, DJs, VJs and concerts in venues all over the city.

mid-Oct: Salon du Champignon

Jardin des Plantes, 36 rue Geoffroy-St-Hilaire, 5th (01.40.79.36.00). M° Gare d'Austerlitz. **Admission** free.
Autumn means wild mushroom season and even in the Paris area, the keen head off to the Forest of Fontainebleau to seek them out. At the salon, hundreds of specimens are on show and mycologists on hand to help identify those safe to eat.

mid-Oct: Semaine du Goût

various venues across France.
Celebrating France's culinary heritage, taste week is a foodies' dream. 99's extravanzga included tastings, demonstrations, special menus in selected restaurants and even a food film festival.

1 Nov: All Saints' Day

Although a full-blown US-style Hallowe'en has suddenly caught on, the more traditional remember the dead on 1 Nov; cemetery visiting, traditionally accompanied by chrysanthemums, is big business.

Nov: Mois de la Photo

all over Paris. **Information** Maison Européenne de
la Photographie (01.44.78.75.01). **Admission** varies.
Every two years, photo exhibitions are put on in
museums and commercial galleries all over town,
with an emphasis on contemporary art photography. The 2000 festival has Paris as its theme.

early Nov: Festival Fnac-Inrockuptibles

La Cigale and other venues. **Admission** varies.
Inrocks is the place to discover next year's next big
thing – introducing such acts as Gus Gus, Fiona
Apple, Travis and Morcheeba to Paris. In the past
couple of years, it's shifted from indie dominance to
take in trance and electronic tendencies.

early Nov: Marjolaine

Parc Floral de Paris, Bois de Vincennes, 12th.
M° Château de Vincennes. **Information**
(01.45.56.09.09). **Admission** 40F.
Alternative/green living *à la parisienne*. 450 stands
dispense organic food and wine, household, health
and beauty products and inform on environmental
groups from Greenpeace to cycling campaigns.
Lectures range from the earnest to downright odd.

11 Nov: Armistice Day

Arc de Triomphe, 8th. M° Charles de Gaulle-Etoile.
At the remembrance ceremony for the dead of both
World Wars, wreaths are laid by the President at the
Tomb of the Unknown Soldier under the Arc de
Triomphe. The remembrance flower is not the
poppy but the *bleuet* (cornflower) after the colour of
the pantalons worn by World War I infantry. *See
also Compiègne in chapter* **Trips Out of Town**.

Nov: Fête du Beaujolais Nouveau

The arrival of Beaujolais Nouveau on the third
Thursday in November is no longer the much-hyped
event of a few years ago, but wine bars and cafés are
still thronged (some from midnight on Wednesday,
but especially Thursday evening) as customers
gather to 'assess' the new vintage.

Winter

early Dec: Salon Nautique de Paris

Paris-Expo, porte de Versailles, 15th (01.41.90.47.10).
M° Porte de Versailles. **Admission** 30F-60F.
Take to the seven seas as the international boat
show shows off luxury yachts, leisure cruisers and
record-breaking cats, among displays of windsurf-
ing and other watery sports.

early Dec: Salon du Cheval, du Poney et de l'Ane

Paris-Expo, porte de Versailles, 15th (01.49.09.64.27).
M° Porte de Versailles. **Admission** 50F-65F.
Everything you'll ever need to satisfy the equestrian-
minded members of the family.

mid-Dec-early March: Patinoire de l'Hôtel de Ville

*pl de l'Hôtel de Ville, 4th (01.42.76.40.40). M° Hôtel-
de-Ville.* **Admission** free (skate hire 30F).
The outdoor ice rink is just the thing for a chilly

winter evening, surrounded by a forest of fir trees
to give the illusion that you are far from the city.

late Dec: Africolor

*Théâtre Gérard Philipe, 59 bd Jules-Guesde, 93200
St-Denis (01.48.13.70.00). M° St-Denis Basilique.*
Admission 50F.
This annual African music fest promises a melting
pot of traditional and Western-influenced sounds
from across the African continent, culminating in a
big all-night party on Christmas Eve.

24, 25 Dec: Christmas

Christmas is a family affair in France, with a dinner
(on Christmas Eve) that traditionally involves foie
gras or oysters, goose or turkey and a rich chocolate
yule log (*bûche de Noël*). On Christmas Eve, Notre
Dame Cathedral is packed for the 11pm service.

31 Dec: New Year's Eve

On the Réveillon or Fête de la St-Sylvestre, thousands
crowd the Champs-Elysées and let off bangers, while
nightclubs and restaurants put on expensive *soirées*.
More oysters, foie gras and bubbly.

1 Jan: La Grande Parade de Paris

*leaves 2pm from Porte St-Martin, 2nd. M°
Strasbourg-St Denis.* **Information** (03.44.27.45.67).
The New Year parade traditionally wound its way
round Montmartre, but in 2000 switched to the
Grands Boulevards, with over-the-top floats, march-
ing bands, giant balloon characters and more.

6 Jan: Fête des Rois (Epiphany)

Pâtisseries sell thousands of *galettes des rois*, a flaky
pastry cake with frangipane filling in which a *fève*
or tiny charm is hidden. Whoever finds the charm
dons a cardboard crown, becomes king or queen for
a day, and chooses a consort.

Jan: Commemorative Mass for Louis XVI

*Chapelle Expiatoire, 29 rue Pasquier, 8th
(01.42.65.35.80). M° St-Augustin.*
On the Sunday closest to 21 January, anniversary of
the beheading of Louis XVI in 1793, members of
France's aristocracy gather with die-hard royalists
and assorted other far-right crackpots to mourn the
end of the monarchy. Firm republicans are supposed
to mark the day by eating *tête de veau*.

Jan/Feb: Nouvel An Chinois

*Around av d'Ivry and av de Choisy, 13th. M° Porte
de Choisy or Porte d'Ivry.*
Dragon dancers snake between the tower blocks to
usher in Chinese New Year. Festivities take place on
the nearest weekend(s) to the actual date.

early Feb: Festival Présences

*Maison de Radio France, 116 av du Président-
Kennedy, 16th (01.42.30.22.22). RER Kennedy-
Radio France.* **Admission** free.
Risk the contemporary at this free festival of musi-
cal creation, by resident orchestras and guests.

*Even red giraffes start swaying to the beat
for the* **Techno Parade.**

Key Events

c250 BC Lutétia founded on the Ile de la Cité by a Celtic tribe, the Parisii
52 BC Paris conquered by the Romans
260 St Denis executed on Mount Mercury
361 Julian, Governor of Lutétia, becomes Roman Emperor
451 Attila the Hun nearly attacks Paris
496 Frankish king Clovis baptised at Reims
508 Clovis makes Paris his capital
543 Monastery of St-Germain-des-Prés founded
635 King Dagobert establishes Fair of St-Denis
800 Charlemagne becomes first Holy Roman Emperor. Moves capital from Paris to Aix-la-Chapelle (Aachen)
845-880 Paris sacked by the Vikings
987 Hugues Capet, Count of Paris, King of France

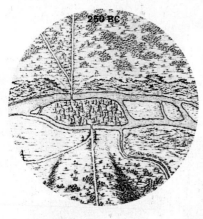

c1100 Abélard meets Héloïse
1136 Abbot Suger begins Basilica of St-Denis
1163 Building of Notre Dame begins
1181 Philippe-Auguste establishes market at Les Halles
1190-1202 Philippe-Auguste constructs new city wall
1215 University of Paris recognised with Papal Charter
1246-48 Louis IX (St-Louis) builds the Sainte-Chapelle
1253 Sorbonne founded
c1300 Philippe IV Le Bel rebuilds Conciergerie
1340 Hundred Years' War with England begins
1357 Revolt by Etienne Marcel

1364 Charles V moves royal court to the Louvre and builds Bastille and Vincennes fortresses
1420-36 Paris under English rule; 1422 Henry V of England dies at Château de Vincennes
1463 First printing press in Paris
1528 François 1er begins rebuilding Louvre
1572 23 Aug: St Bartholemew's Day massacre of Protestants
1589 Henri III assassinated
1593 Henri IV converts to Catholicism, ending Wars of Religion
1605 Building of place des Vosges and Pont Neuf, the first bridge without houses atop it
1610 Henri IV assassinated
1634 Académie Française founded by Richelieu
1643 Cardinal Mazarin becomes regent
1648-53 Paris occupied by the *Fronde* rebellion
1661 Louis XIV begins personal rule – and to transform Versailles; fall of Fouquet
1667 Paris given its first street lighting
1671 Building of Les Invalides
1672 Creation of the Grands Boulevards on line of Charles V's city wall. Portes St-Denis and St-Martin built
1680 Comédie Française founded
1682 Louis XIV transfers court to Versailles
1685 Colbert commissions place des Victoires
1700 Beginning of War of the Spanish Succession
1715 Death of Louis XIV; Philippe d'Orléans becomes regent
1720 South Sea Bubble: John Law's bank scheme collapses
1751 First volume of Diderot's *Encyclopédie*
1753 Place Louis XV (later Concorde) begun
1785 Fermiers Généraux Tax Wall built
1789 First meeting of Etats-Généraux since 1614
1789 14 July: Paris mob takes the Bastille. Oct: Louis XVI forced to leave Versailles for Paris. Population of Paris is about 600,000
1791 20 June: Louis XVI attempts to escape Paris
1792 September Massacres. 22 Sept: Republic declared. Royal statues torn down
1793 Execution of Louis XVI and Marie-Antoinette. Louvre museum opens to the public
1794 The Terror – 1300 heads fall in six weeks. July: Jacobins overthrown; Directoire takes over
1799 Napoléon stages coup, becomes First Consul
1804 Napoléon crowned emperor in Notre Dame
1806 Napoléon commissions the Arc de Triomphe
1814 Napoléon defeated; Russian army occupies Paris; Louis XVIII grants Charter of Liberties
1815 Napoléon regains power (the 'Hundred

Days'), before defeat at Waterloo. Bourbon monarchy restored, with Louis XVIII

1828 Paris given first horse buses
1830 July: Charles X overthrown; Louis-Philippe of Orléans becomes king
1836 Completion of Arc de Triomphe
1837 First railway line to St-Germain-en-Laye
1838 Daguerre creates first daguerreotypes
1848 Louis-Philippe overthrown, replaced by Second Republic. Most men get the vote. Louis-Napoléon Bonaparte elected President
1852 Following coup, Louis-Napoléon declares himself Emperor Napoléon III: Second Empire. Bon Marché, first department store, opens
1853 Haussmann appointed Prefet de Paris
1862 Construction of Palais Garnier begins. Hugo's *Les Misérables* published
1863 Manet's *Déjeuner sur l'Herbe* exhibited
1866 *Le Figaro* daily newspaper founded
1870 Prussian victory at Sedan; siege of Paris. Napoléon III abdicates
1871 Commune takes over Paris; column in place Vendôme destroyed. May: *semaine sanglante*
1874 First Impressionist exhibition in Nadar's *atelier* on boulevard des Capucines
1875 Bizet's *Carmen* at Opéra Comique
1889 Paris Exhibition on centenary of Revolution: Eiffel Tower built. Moulin Rouge opens
1894-1900 Dreyfus case polarises opinion
1895 Dec: world's first public film screening by the Lumière brothers at the Jockey Club (Hôtel Scribe)
1900 Paris' *Exposition Universelle*: Grand Palais, Petit Palais, Pont Alexandre III built. Population of Paris two million. First Métro line
1904 Pablo Picasso moves to Paris
1910 Floods in Paris
1914 As World War I begins, Germans beaten back from Paris at Battle of the Marne
1918 11 Nov: Armistice signed in the forest of Compiègne

1977

1919 Peace conference held at Versailles
1927 La Coupole opens in Montparnasse
1934 Fascist demonstrations
1936-37 France elects Popular Front government under Leon Blum; first paid holidays
1940 Germans occupy Paris. 18 May: De Gaulle's call to arms from London
1941-42 Mass deportations of Paris Jews
1944 25 Aug: Paris liberated
1946 Fourth Republic established. Women given the vote
1947 Dior's New Look
1949 Simone de Beauvoir's *The Second Sex*
1955-56 Revolt begins in Algeria; demonstrations on the streets in Paris
1957 Opening of CNIT in new La Défense business district
1958 De Gaulle president: Fifth Republic
1959 France founder member of the EEC. *Nouvelle vague* cinema: Godard's *A Bout de Souffle*
1968 May: student riots and workers' strikes in Paris and across France
1969 De Gaulle resigns, Pompidou becomes president; Les Halles market closes
1973 Boulevard Périphérique inaugurated
1977 Centre Pompidou opens. Jacques Chirac elected mayor of Paris
1981 François Mitterrand elected president; abolition of the death penalty
1986 Musée d'Orsay opens
1989 Bicentenary of the Revolution celebrated: Louvre pyramid and Opéra Bastille completed
1992 Disney theme park opens outside Paris
1995 May: Jacques Chirac elected president
1996 Dec: Opening of new Bibliothèque Nationale François Mitterrand
1997 General election: Socialist government elected under Lionel Jospin
1998 July: France wins football World Cup at Stade de France

1792

History

Sort your Celts from your Gauls, your Valois kings from your Bourbon monarchs, and your 'sans-culottes' from your 'soixante-huitards'.

PRE-HISTORY

Traces of habitation in the Paris basin have been found from the fourth and second millennia BC in Montmorency and Villejuif. Within Paris, Neolithic canoes, evidence of early river traffic, were discovered at Bercy in the early 1990s. Bronze age tombs and artefacts have also been discovered.

250BC: CELTIC PARISII

In about 250BC a Celtic tribe called the Parisii, probably driven from lands further east by the more powerful Belgae, established a fishing settlement on the Ile de la Cité. Sited on a route between Germany and Spain at the confluence of the Seine and the Marne, it was a natural crossroads. The Celts were canny traders, and grew prosperous – witness the hoard of gold coins from the first century BC in the **Musée des Antiquités Nationales**, St-Germain-en-Laye.

ROMAN CONQUEST

Its strategic position also made the city a prime target. By the first century BC the Romans had arrived in northern Gaul. Julius Caesar mentions the city of the Parisii, on an isle in the Seine, known as Lutétia, in his *Gallic Wars*. In 53BC when the Celtic tribes, the Senones and the Carnutes, refused to send delegates to the Assembly of Gaul at Amiens, he ordered the assembly to keep watch over the rebellious tribes. In 52BC, the Celt Vercingétorix spearheaded a revolt, joined by Camulogenus, who took control of Lutétia, while his army camped on Mons Lutetius, now site of the Panthéon. Caesar's lieutenant Labienus crushed the rebels at Melun, and marched downstream, camping in an area now occcupied by the Louvre's Cour Carrée. In a brief battle by the Champ de Mars, Camulogenus and his army were massacred, and Vercingétorix captured; thereafter the Parisii tribe and Gaul were under Roman rule.

Lutétia thrived. The Roman town centred on what is now the Montagne Ste-Geneviève on the Left Bank. Many of its villas were of masonry, brick and mortar, some embellished with frescoes and mosaics. A model of the ancient city, along with architectural vestiges, is on view at **Musée Carnavalet**. Around AD50-200 Lutétia acquired its grandest public buildings. The remains of a forum have been uncovered on rue Soufflot, a trio of bathing establishments, parts of the city wall and a hypocaust (heating system) at the Crypte Archéologique de Notre Dame. There was also a temple to Jupiter, where the cathedral now stands. Only the **Arènes de Lutèce**, where Romans saw Christians slaughtered by lions, and the **Thermes de Cluny** reflect any of this former glory today.

CHRISTIANITY & ST-DENIS

Christianity appeared in the third century AD, when Athenian St-Denis, first bishop of Lutétia, was sent to evangelise its people. Legend has it that in 260, he and two companions began to knock pagan statues off their pedestals. They were arrested and decapitated on Mount Mercury, thereafter known as Mons Martis (Mount of Martyrs), later Montmartre. Plucky Denis picked up his head and walked away, chanting psalms. He finally fell north of Paris, where a pious Christian woman buried him. A sanctuary was later erected on the spot, since replaced by the **Basilique St-Denis**.

Roman power weakening, Lutétia (renamed Paris in 212) was under increasing attack from barbarians from the east. Many inhabitants retreated to their ancestral island, and a wall was built around the Cité. In 313 Emperor Constantine effectively made Christianity the new religion of the Empire.

357-363: EMPEROR JULIAN

In 357, a new governor, Constantine's nephew Julian, arrived in Lutétia (as he still called it). He improved the city's defences, and sought to return to Platonic ideals in opposition to what he saw as the brutality of Constantine and subsequent Christian emperors. In 361, after victories over the barbarians, his army declared him Roman Emperor in Paris. Condemned by Christian historians as 'Julian the Apostate', he could do little to turn back the new faith, or the decline of Rome; he was killed in battle in 363.

STE-GENEVIEVE & ATTILA THE HUN

By the early fifth century, Roman rule had effectively collapsed in northern Gaul, its cities left to fend for themselves. In the ensuing chaos, the exemplary life of Ste-Geneviève – and the threat of war – helped confirm many converts in the new faith. As the legend goes, in 451 Attila the Hun and his army were approaching Paris. Its people prepared to flee, but Geneviève told them to stay, saying the Hun would spare their city so long as they repented of their sins and prayed with her. Miraculously, Attila did not attack but moved off to the south. Geneviève was acclaimed saviour of Paris.

*Together at last in a neo-Gothic tomb in Père Lachaise cemetery: **Abélard and Héloïse**.*

CLOVIS & THE MEROVINGIANS

It was only a temporary reprieve. In 464 Childéric the Frank attacked Paris, and in 508 his son Clovis made it his capital, seated at the old Roman governor's palace on the Ile de la Cité. The now-aged Geneviève converted the new king to Christianity; he was baptised by St-Rémi in **Reims**, 496. Clovis (ruled 481-511) began the Merovingian dynasty, of 'Long-haired kings' (they never cut their hair, apparently). On the Left Bank he founded the abbey of St-Pierre et St-Paul (later Ste-Geneviève), where he, queen Clotilde and Geneviève could be buried side by side. The **Tour de Clovis**, within the Lycée Henri IV, is a last relic of the basilica. Ste-Geneviève, who died about 512, remains the patron saint of Paris; a shrine to her and relics are in the church of **St-Etienne-du-Mont** (originally adjoining the abbey). Clovis' son and successor Childéric II founded the equally renowned abbey of St-Germain-des-Prés. Not that the Merovingians were especially pious: under their law an inheritance had to be divided equally among heirs. This led to regular bloodletting and infanticide between royal princes, dowager queens and uncles, and the eventual snuffing-out of the line in 751.

CAROLINGIANS V VIKINGS

Next came the Carolingians, named after Charles Martel ('the Hammer'), credited with halting the spread of Islam with his victory over the Moors at Tours in 732. In 751 his son Pepin 'the Short' was proclaimed King of all the Franks. His heir Charlemagne extended the Frankish kingdom and

was made Holy Roman Emperor by the Pope in 800. As his capital he chose Aix-La-Chapelle (Aachen), entrusting Paris to a hereditary count.

After Charlemagne, the Carolingian empire gradually fell apart, helped by famine, flood and marauding Vikings (the Norsemen or Normans), who sacked the city repeatedly between 845 and 885 and looted wealthy abbeys like **St-Germain-des-Prés**. When Emperor Charles II the Bald showed little interest in defending the city, Parisians sought help from Robert the Strong, Count of Anjou. His son Eudes (Odo), succeeded him as Count of Paris, and led the defence of the city in a ten-month-long Viking seige in 885, sharing the throne 893-898 with Charles III the Simple. The feudal lords thus came to outpower their masters. In 987, the Count of Paris, Hugues Capet, great-grandson of Robert the Strong, was elected King of France by his peers at **Senlis**, and made Paris his capital. A new era was beginning.

THE CAPETIANS

The ascension of Hugues Capet, founder of the Capetian dynasty, is the point from which 'France' can be said to exist. For a long time, however, the kingdom consisted of little more than the Ile-de-France. Powerful local lords – in Normandy, Burgundy, the south, and later the possessions of the Kings of England – would defy royal authority for centuries. 'France' would largely be created through the gradual extension of Parisian power.

Paris continued to grow in importance, thanks to its powerful abbeys and the fairs of St-Germain and

St-Denis. By the twelfth century, three distinct areas were in place: religion and government on Ile de la Cité, intellectual life around the Left Bank schools, and commerce and finance on the Right Bank.

ABBOT SUGER

A major figure in this renaissance was Suger, Abbot of St-Denis and minister to a series of weak monarchs, Louis VI (the Fat) and Louis VII (the Younger). The latter unwisely divorced the first of his three wives, Eleanor of Aquitaine, who then married Henry II of England, bringing a vast portion of southwest France under English control. Suger did much to hold the state together and give it an administration; as priest, he commissioned the new **Basilique St-Denis** in 1136, to house pilgrims flocking to the shrine. Considered the first true Gothic building, St-Denis set the style across France and northern Europe for four centuries. In 1163, Bishop Sully of Paris began building **Notre Dame**, embodiment of the High Gothic aesthetic.

ABELARD & HELOISE

Paris was developing a reputation as a centre of learning. The abbeys had kept scholastic traditions alive and, by the eleventh century, the Canon school of Notre Dame was widely admired. By 1100, scholars began to move out from the cathedral school and teach independently in the Latin Quarter. One such was Pierre Abélard, a brilliant logician and dialetician who had rooms in the **rue Chanoinesse** behind Notre Dame. He would be forever remembered for his part in one of the world's great love stories, a star-crossed saga of forbidden sex, castration and classical philosophy.

In 1118, at 39, Abélard was taken on by Canon Fulbert of Notre Dame as tutor to his 17-year-old niece Héloïse. The pair began a passionate affair, but were found out by the Canon. Twice he enjoined them to celibacy, twice they disobeyed him. Following an illegitimate pregnancy and a secret marriage, the enraged father had Abélard castrated and his daughter consigned to a monastery. Abélard went on to write refined works of medieval philosophy, while Héloïse continued to send tormented, poetic missives to her lost lover. The two were reunited in death at the Paraclete, the oratory-cum-convent which Abélard had himself established and given to Héloïse, who became a famous abbess, and her nuns. In 1817 their remains came to rest in a fanciful neo-Gothic tomb in **Père Lachaise cemetery**.

In 1215 the Paris schools combined in a more formally organised 'university' under papal protection. The greatest medieval thinkers attended this 'New Athens': German theologian Albert the Great, Italians Thomas Aquinas and Bonaventure, Scot Duns Scotus, Englishman William of Ockham. Most famous of the schools was the **Sorbonne**, founded in 1253 by Robert de Sorbon, Louis IX's chaplain.

PHILIPPE AUGUSTE

The first great Capetian monarch Philippe II (Philippe Auguste 1165-1223) became king in 1180. He won Normandy from King John of England and added Auvergne and Champagne. The first great royal builder to leave a mark on Paris, he built a new, larger fortified city wall, chunks of which can still be seen in **rue des Jardins-St-Paul** in the Marais and **rue Clovis** in the Latin Quarter. He began a new fortress on the Right Bank, the **Louvre**, but his main residence was still on Ile de la Cité (*see* **Conciergerie**). In 1181, he established the first covered markets, Les Halles, on the site they occupied until 1969; food merchants, drapers and other trade corporations followed. He also sought to do something about the city's mud and foul odours, ordering the paving of streets, and closing the most pestilential cemeteries.

LOUIS IX (ST LOUIS)

Philippe's grandson Louis IX (1226-70) was famed for his extreme piety. When not on crusade, he put his stamp on Paris, commissioning the **Sainte-Chapelle**, convents, hospices and student hostels. But it was his grandson, Philippe IV (Le Bel, 1285-1314) who transformed the fortress on the Cité into a palace for a king, with the monumental Salle des Gens d'Armes in the **Conciergerie**. The end of his reign, however, was marred by insurrection and riotous debauchery. In suspiciously quick succession, his three sons ascended the throne. The last, Charles IV, died in 1328, leaving no male heir.

THE VALOIS KINGS

All this proved irresistible to the English, who claimed the French crown for young Edward III, son of Philippe IV's daughter. The French refused to recognise his claim, as Salic law barred inheritance via the female line. Philippe de Valois, the late king's cousin, claimed the crown for himself (Philippe VI, 1328-50), and thus began the Hundred Years' War.

The Black Death arrived in Europe in the 1340s and, in Paris, outbreaks of the plague alternated with battles, bourgeois revolts, popular insurrections and bloody vendettas between aristocratic factions. In 1355, Etienne Marcel, a rich draper, *prévôt* of the Paris merchants (a kind of mayoral precursor) whose house was on the site of the future Hôtel de Ville and member of the *Etats-généraux* (it had met for the first time in Paris in 1347), seized Paris. His aim was to limit the power of the throne and gain a constitution for the city from Dauphin Charles (then regent, as his father Jean II had been captured by the English). In January 1357 Marcel declared a general strike and armed his merchants, speaking out against corrupt royal counsellors and demanding the release of Charles 'The Bad', King of Navarre, direct descendant of the Capetians, ally of the English – and prisoner of the French king. The Dauphin grudg-

François 1er: *grand, grander, grandeur.*

ingly accepted the *Etats'* extended powers but, after Charles of Navarre escaped prison and received a glorious welcome in Paris, offered to defend the city only if the *Etats* footed the bill. The city was divided; treachery and murder ensued until, in 1358, the Dauphin's supporters retook the city, and Marcel and his followers were executed. France's first popular revolution died with its leader.

CHARLES V (1364-80)
The former Dauphin distanced himself from the Paris mob by transferring his residence to the Louvre. He further extended the city walls and had a new stronghold built on the eastern edge of Paris, the **Bastille**. Despite political turmoil, the arts flourished. Parisian artisans produced peerless miniatures, tapestries and manuscripts, together with gold, silver and carved ivory *objets*.

1420-36: ENGLISH RULE
After the battle of Agincourt in 1415 the English, in alliance with Jean, Duc de Bourgogne (*see chapter* **Right Bank**, **Tour Jean Sans Peur**), seemed to prevail. From 1420 to 1436 Paris was under English rule (as was most of France), with the Duke of Bedford as governor. In 1431, Henry VI of England was crowned King of France in Notre Dame. But the city was almost constantly besieged by the French, at one time helped by Joan of Arc. Eventually, Charles VII (1422-61) retook his capital.

RENAISSANCE & HERESY
Booksellers Fust and Schöffer brought printed books to the city in 1463, supported by wily Louis XI (1461-81) against the powerful scribes' and booksellers' guilds. In 1470, Swiss printers set up a press at the Sorbonne. By the end of the sixteenth century Parisian printers had published 25,000 titles.

In the last decades of the fifteenth century the restored Valois monarchs sought to reassert their position. Masons erected Flamboyant Gothic churches (*see chapter* **Architecture**), as well as impressive mansions commissioned by nobles, prelates and wealthy bourgeois, such as **Hôtel de Cluny** and **Hôtel de Sens**. The city's population tripled over the sixteenth century.

FRANÇOIS 1ER
The ost spectacular Valois was François 1er (1515-47), epitome of a Renaissance monarch. He engaged in endless wars with great rival Emperor Charles V, but also built sumptuous châteaux at **Fontainebleau**, **Blois** and **Chambord**, and gathered a glittering court of knights, poets and Italian artists, such as Leonardo da Vinci and Benvenuto Cellini. He also set about transforming the Louvre into the palace we see today, where he hung his Titians, Raphaels and the *Mona Lisa*.

François 1er's grandeur, however, was unable to prevent the advance of Protestantism, even if ever more heretics were sent to the stake. Huguenot (French Protestant) strongholds were mostly in the west; Paris, by contrast, was a citadel of virulent, often bloodthirsty Catholic orthodoxy, complicated by interwoven aristocratic squabbles between the factions of the Huguenot Prince de Condé and the Catholic Duc de Guise, supported by François 1er's successor Henri II (1547-60).

THE WARS OF RELIGION
By the 1560s, the situation had degenerated into open warfare. Henri II's scheming widow Catherine de Médicis, regent for the young Charles IX (1560-74), was the power behind the throne. Savagery was seen on both sides, and paranoia was rife. In 1572, a rumour ran round that Protestant Huguenots were plotting to murder the royal family and sack the city; in anticipation, on 23 August, St-Bartholomew's Day, Catholic mobs turned on anyone suspected of Protestant sympathies, slaughtering over 3000 people. When Henri III (1574-89) sought a compromise between the two sides, Paris turned on its sovereign and forced him to flee the Louvre. In August 1589 he was assassinated by a fanatical monk, so ending the Valois line.

HENRI IV & THE BOURBON DYNASTY
Henri III had recognised his ally Henri of Navarre, a Huguenot, as heir. He in turn proclaimed himself King Henri IV, founding the Bourbon dynasty. Fervently Catholic Paris continued to resist in a siege that dragged on for nearly four years. Its

inhabitants ate cats, rats, donkeys and even grass. Henri IV agreed to become a Catholic in 1593, and was received into the church at St-Denis, declaring that 'Paris vaut bien une messe' (Paris is well worth a mass). On 22 March 1594, he entered the city.

Aided by minister Sully, Henri IV undertook to unify the country and re-establish the monarchy's power. In Paris, he set about changing the face of his ravaged capital. He commissioned **place Dauphine** and Paris' first enclosed, geometrical square – the place Royale, now **place des Vosges**. But he never got round to improving the city's congested streets, habitually clogged with pedestrians, horses, donkeys and coaches. In 1610, after at least 23 other assassination attempts had failed, the King was stabbed to death by a Catholic fanatic while caught in a bottleneck on the **rue de la Ferronnerie**. The *ancien régime* began as it would end: with regicide.

LOUIS XIII & CARDINAL RICHELIEU

On Henri's death son Louis XIII (1610-43) was only eight years old, and Henri's widow, Marie de Médicis, became regent. She commissioned the self-aggrandising **Palais du Luxembourg**, and a series of 24 panels glorifying her role painted by Rubens, now in the Louvre. In 1617 Louis XIII, still only 16, was encouraged to take over. But the real power lay with Cardinal Richelieu, who in 1624 became the king's chief minister.

Richelieu won the confidence of tormented Louis XIII, who stuck by his minister through numerous plots hatched by his mother, wife Anne of Austria, assorted princes and disgruntled grandees. A brilliant administrator, he created a strong, centralised monarchy, paving the way for the absolutism of Louis XIV and steadily grinding down what he perceived as the two major enemies of the monarchy: abroad, Spain, and the independence of the aristocracy (especially the Huguenots) at home. A great architectural patron, he commissioned Jacques Lemercier to build him a palace, which became the **Palais-Royal**, and rebuilt the **Sorbonne**. This was the height of the Catholic Counter-Reformation,

In good times, Parisians shopped at the market: in bad times, they ate cats, rats, even grass.

and architects were commissioned to create such lavish Baroque churches as the **Val-de-Grâce**.

The literary lights of the *Grand Siècle* often found their patrons in the elegant Marais *hôtels particuliers*, where salons hosted by lettered ladies like Mlle de Scudéry, Mme de la Fayette, Mme de Sévigné and the erudite courtesan Ninon de l'Enclos, rang with witty asides and political intrigue. By comparison, Richelieu's Académie Française (founded 1634) was a fusty, pedantic reflection of the establishment.

CARDINAL MAZARIN & LA FRONDE

Richelieu died in 1642. Next year Louis XIII died, leaving five-year-old Louis XIV as heir. Anne of Austria became regent, with Cardinal Mazarin (a Richelieu protégé whose palace is part of the **Bibliothèque Nationale Richelieu**) as chief minister.

In 1648 the royal family was made to flee Paris by the **Fronde**, a rebellion of peasants and aristocrats led by the prince de Condé against taxes and growing royal power. Parisians supported the revolt at first but soon tired of anarchy. When Mazarin's army entered Paris in 1653 with the boy-king, they were warmly received. Mazarin died in 1661, shortly after Spain had been decisively defeated, leaving France stronger than ever, with military capacity to spare.

LOUIS XIV, THE SUN KING

This was the springboard for Louis XIV's absolute rule, with the classically megalomaniac statement 'L'Etat, c'est moi' ('The state is me'). Military expansion was essential to Louis XIV's concept of greatness, and France was engaged in continual wars against the Dutch, Austria and England.

An essential figure in Louis' years of triumph was minister of finance Jean-Baptiste Colbert. He amassed most of the other important ministries over the 1660s and determined to transform Paris into a 'new Rome', with grand, symmetrical vistas – a sort of expression of absolute monarchy in stone. In the 1680s, he commissioned the finely proportioned **place des Victoires** and **place Vendôme** to glorify the king, and opened up the first boulevards along the line of Charles V's wall, with triumphal arches at **Porte St-Denis** and **Porte St-Martin**.

Louis XIV took little interest in Colbert's schemes. Such was his aversion to Paris that from the 1670s he focused on **Versailles**, whither he transferred the court, and into which he poured vast wealth. A place at court was essential for a successful career.

The arts flourished. In 1659 Molière's troupe of actors settled in Paris under the protection of the King, presenting plays for court and public. After the playwright's death in 1673, they became the **Comédie Française**. Favoured composer at Versailles was the Italian Lully, granted sole right to compose operas (in which the King often appeared). Rameau and Charpentier also composed, while the tragedies of Racine were encouraged.

Despite Colbert's efforts, endless wars left the royal finances in permanent disorder, reflected in growing poverty, vagrancy and a great many crippled war veterans. The **Invalides** was built to house them on one side of town, the **Salpêtrière** on the other to shelter fallen women. Colbert died in 1683, and the military triumphs of earlier years gave way to the grim struggles of the War of the Spanish Succession. Life at Versailles soured under dour Mme de Maintenon, Louis' last mistress, whom he secretly married in 1684. Nobles began sneaking away to the modish **Faubourg-St-Germain**.

PHILIPPE D'ORLEANS

Louis XIV had several children, but not long before his own death, both his son and grandson died, leaving five-year-old great-grandson Louis XV (1715-74) as heir. The Regent, Philippe d'Orléans, an able general and diplomat, speedily returned the Court to Paris. Installed in the Palais-Royal, his lavish dinners regularly degenerated into orgies. The pleasure-loving courtiers and the Parisians who aped them spawned a large service population of dressmakers, jewellers, hairdressers, decorators and domestic servants. Tales of country youths corrupted by the city where they came to seek their fortune inspired writers from Marivaux to Rousseau, Restif de la Bretonne to the Marquis de Sade: Paris was the *nouvelle Babylone*, the modern Sodom.

1720: THE SOUTH SEA BUBBLE

The state remained chronically in debt, though the Regent sought to avoid further military entanglement. Taxation came mainly in duties on such commodities as salt. Collection was farmed out to a kind of private corporation, the *Fermiers généraux*, who passed an amount to the state and kept a proportion for themselves. This system bore down on the poor, was riddled with corruption and never produced the required resources; nevertheless none of the *ancien régime*'s ministers was ever able to abolish it. The Regent thought he had a remedy with Scottish banker John Law's investment scheme in the French colonies, which inspired a frenzy of wheeler-dealing. But in 1720, a run on the bank revealed that very little gold and silver was on hand to back up the paper bills. Panic ensued. Law was expelled from France, and the Regent, and to some extent royal government, were deeply discredited. The South Sea Bubble had burst.

LOUIS XV & THE ENLIGHTENMENT

As soon as he was his own man, Louis XV left Paris for Versailles, which again saw sumptuous festivities in its new opera. But in the Age of Enlightenment, Paris was the real capital of Europe. 'One lives in Paris; elsewhere, one simply vegetates,' wrote Casanova. Paris salons became the forum for intellectual debate under renowned hostesses like the Marquise du Deffand on rue de Beaune and Mme Geoffrin on rue St-Honoré. The King's mistress, the Marquise de Pompadour

(1721-64), was a friend and protectress of Diderot and the *encyclopédistes*, of Marivaux and Montesquieu, and corresponded with Voltaire. She encouraged Louis XV to embellish his capital with monuments, such as Jacques Ange Gabriel's **Ecole Militaire** and place Louis XV (**place de la Concorde**). Intellectual activity was matched by a flourishing of fine arts with painters like Boucher, Van Loo and Fragonard setting the style.

LOUIS XVI

The great failure of Louis XV's reign was the defeat in the Seven Years' War (1756-63), in which France lost most of its colonies in India and Canada to Britain. As his grandson Louis XVI (ruled 1774-91), began his reign, France was expanding economically and culturally. Across Europe, people craved Parisian luxuries. In the capital, roads were widened, lamps erected, gardens and promenades created. Nobs indulged in horse racing (a taste acquired from the English) at **Vincennes** and the **Bois de Boulogne**. On boulevard du Temple, all classes watched dancers, singers, acrobats and trained monkeys. The city was obsessed with the new, from ballooning (begun by the Montgolfier brothers in 1783) to the works of Rousseau. Even royal princes flirted with the new sensibilities, as Louis-Philippe d'Orléans developed the **Palais-Royal** as a kind of open house for different classes, entertainments and ideas.

But France's intervention in the American War of Independence drove finances further towards bankruptcy. In 1785, at the behest of the *Fermiers généraux*, a tax wall was built around Paris, which only increased popular discontent (*see chapter* **Architecture**). Louis XVI's only option was to appeal to the nation; first through the *parlements* or regional assemblies of lawyers and, if all else failed, the *Etats-généraux*, the representation of the nobility, clergy and commoners, which had not met since 1614, and which would inevitably alter the relationship between society and a monarchy that believed it had an absolute right to command. Louis XVI continued to prevaricate, as 1789 began.

EARLY 1789

The spring of 1789 found Louis XVI increasingly isolated as unrest swept through France. In Paris, the people were suffering the results of a disastrous harvest, and there were riots in the Faubourg St-Antoine. The king finally agreed to convene the *Etats-généraux* at Versailles in May. The members of the Third Estate, the commoners, aware that they represented a far larger proportion of the population than nobility and clergy, demanded a system of one vote per member. Discussions broke down, and a rumour went round that the King was sending troops to arrest them. On 20 June 1789, at the Jeu de Paume at Versailles, the Third Estate took an oath not to separate until 'the constitution of the

kingdom was established'. Louis backed down, and the *Etats-généraux*, newly renamed the **Assemblée Nationale**, set about discussing a Constitution.

Debate also raged in the streets among the poor *sans-culottes* (literally, 'without breeches': only the poor wore long trousers). It was assumed that any concession by the King was intended to deceive. Louis had posted foreign troops around Paris, and on 11 July dismissed his minister, Jacques Necker, considered the commoners' sole ally. On 13 July an obscure lawyer named Camille Desmoulins leapt on a café table in the Palais-Royal. Likening Necker's dismissal to another St-Bartholomew's Day, he called to the excited crowd: 'Aux armes!' 'To arms!'

STORMING THE BASTILLE

On 14 July, the crowd marched on **Les Invalides**, carrying off thousands of guns, then moved on to the hitherto invincible **Bastille**, symbol of royal repression. Its governor, the Marquis de Launay, refused to surrender, but the huge crowd outside grew more aggressive. It seems that one nervous Bastille sentry fired a shot, and within minutes there was general firing on the crowd. The mob brought up cannon to storm the fortress. After a brief battle, and the deaths of 87 revolutionaries, Launay offered his surrender. He was immediately killed, and his head paraded through Paris on a pike. Inside only seven prisoners were found. Nevertheless, the Revolution now had the symbolic act of violence that marked a break with the past.

Political debate proliferated on every side, above all in the rapidly multiplying political clubs, such as the Cordeliers, who met in a Franciscan monastery in St-Germain, or the radical Jacobins, who had taken over a Dominican convent on rue St-Honoré. Thousands of pamphlets were produced, read avidly by a remarkably literate public.

But there was also real hardship among the poor. As disruption spread through the country, wheat deliveries were interrupted, raising bread prices still further. In October, an angry crowd of women marched to Versailles to protest – the incident when Marie-Antoinette supposedly said, 'let them eat cake' (*see* **Royal Foibles**, *p21*). The women ransacked part of the palace, killing guards, and were only placated when Louis XVI appeared with a revolutionary red-white-and-blue cockade and agreed to be taken to Paris. The royal family were now virtual prisoners in the Tuileries.

In the Assembly, the Girondins, who favoured an agreement with the monarchy, originally prevailed, but came under intense attack from the openly Republican Jacobins. On 20 June 1791, Louis and his family tried to leave Paris by night, hoping to organise resistance from safety abroad. They got as far as the town of Varennes, where they were recognised and returned to Paris as captives.

In 1792, the monarchies of Europe formed a coalition to save Louis and his family. A Prussian

Royal Foibles

Most people are familiar with Marie-Antoinette's agricultural whims and will visit the charming farm at Versailles, Le Hameau, based on the then village of Chantilly. The manicured pseudo rusticity showed that her animals enjoyed a suitably regal lifestyle. Apparently the Queen was content to observe the activities of the farm from afar and did not, as legend has it, enjoy dressing up as a peasant and getting her hands dirty. Less well known is her milking parlour at Rambouillet, built to cheer her up by Louis XVI, where cows could lap their milk from specially designed Sèvres porcelain troughs. Her zoological interests were obviously shared by her husband, who in 1786 set up the Bergerie Nationale, buying a flock of Merino sheep from Spain, whose famed soft wool may have played an important role in her actions. History does not record who did the knitting.

His great-grandfather Louis XIV, le Roi Soleil, had been responsible for many festive elements of town planning; parks and parties were the order of the day. It is a little-known fact that the Grands Boulevards were not the creation of Haussmann, who redesigned them in the 19th century. It was Louis XIV who tore down a central section of the city to provide a popular tree-lined alley for the strolling classes. He was particularly taken by the pleasures of the famous *nuits de Sceaux*, evenings of sumptuous fireworks and theatrical presentations among the architectural follies of Le Brun and Perrault in the château gardens of his illegitimate son, the Duc du Maine.

To celebrate the birth of his first official child, in 1662, the king organised a magnificent celebration in front of the Louvre in the area that bears the name of the event to this day, the Carrousel du Louvre. Louis was 23 at the time and was thrilled to take part in the parade, which featured the good and the great of the time dressed as Romans, Persians and Indians, and which preceded the grandest of royal jousting tournaments. Jousting had always been a popular sport of kings and poor old Henri II paid dearly for it when, during a three-day contest in 1559 at the Hôtel de Sully, rue St-Antoine, he was stabbed in the eye and died a few days later.

Other royals went in for less dangerous sports. Billiards had been played in France in various forms since the Middle Ages, but it was François 1er, a fine player on the green baize, who gave the game social respectability. Henri III, France's first outed gay monarch, created a nationwide passion for *bilboquet*, a game of ball and cup, of little obvious danger. He could not, however, stop his two favourite courtiers embarking in a dual that killed them both. On the day of their funeral in 1578 he arrived in a richly decorated royal barge, dressed entirely in black, to lay the first stone of the Pont Neuf.

Perhaps he would have been comforted by the future Louis XV's recipe for hot chocolate, which is preserved in the archives at Versailles. The method is as follows but it should be born in mind that chocolate at the time was considered a medicine:

'You put as many bars of chocolate as cups of water in a cafetière and let it simmer over a low heat. When you are ready to serve, add an egg yolk for each four cups and stir with a baton over a low heat without boiling. It is better to make it the day before to serve the next day.'

A happier gastronomic offering had come from Henri IV, who pronounced that all families in France should have a *poule au pot* (poached chicken and vegetables) on their tables on Sunday; today the dish still bears his name.

To enjoy all these sybaritic pleasures the ability to stay in power is essential and these indulgent lifestyles were in part responsible for the revolution. Royal apologists will tell you that Marie-Antoinette was an admirable politician and will argue that her infamous comment when told that the people lacked bread, 'Let them eat cake!', was in fact an astute comment. 'Cake' is the traditional translation of 'brioche', which apparently did not carry the same tax as bread and would have been more readily available. More indicative of the Queen's detachment from reality occurred on the night of their planned escape from the Louvre. Disguised in fancy dress, Marie-Antoinette left last and got lost in the narrow streets of the Carrousel du Louvre, scene of so many Royal fêtes. She arrived a full two hours late for the planned escape, a delay which was to prove fatal. A case of being hoisted on your own caprice.

army marched into France; the Duke of Brunswick threatened to raze Paris if the King came to harm. Paranoia reigned and anyone who showed sympathy for Louis could be accused of conspiring with foreign powers against the people. On 10 August, an army of *sans-culottes* demanded the Assembly officially depose Louis. This was refused, and the crowd attacked the Tuileries. The royal family were imprisoned in the **Temple** by the radical Commune de Paris, led by Danton, Marat and Robespierre.

1792-94: THE TERROR

The next month, as the Prussians approached Paris, saw the September Massacres. Revolutionary mobs invaded prisons to eliminate anyone who could possibly be a 'traitor' in a bloodletting that accounted for close to 2000 people. The monarchy was formally abolished on 22 September 1792, proclaimed Day I of 'Year I of the French Republic'. Soon after, the French citizen army defeated the Prussians at Valmy.

This was the beginning of the most radical phase of the Revolution. The Jacobins proclaimed the need to be implacable with 'the enemies within', and so Dr Guillotin's invention took its place in the *place de la Révolution* (formerly Louis XV, now Concorde). Louis XVI was executed on 21 January 1793, followed in October by Marie-Antoinette.

In September 1793 the Revolutionary Convention, replacing the Assemblée Nationale, put 'terror on the agenda', in response to demands for more decisive action against foreign spies. The Revolution, as the Jacobin St-Just said, 'devoured its own children': most of the leading Girondins, Philippe-Egalité of Orléans, and even Jacobins such as Danton and Camille Desmoulins would meet the scaffold. In the *Grande Terreur* of 1794, 1300 heads fell in six weeks at place du Trône Renversé ('Overturned Throne', now **place de la Nation**), the bodies dumped in communal graves (*see chapter* **Right Bank, Cimitière de Picpus**).

THE AGE OF REASON

Cultural transformation now proceeded apace; churches were confiscated in November 1789, made like Notre Dame into 'temples of reason' or put to practical uses. Many were vandalised; the carved bookcases from the Celestins convent were transferred to the Bibliothèque Nationale, while the Sainte-Chapelle became a storehouse for flour. All titles were abolished – *monsieur* and *madame* became *citoyen* and *citoyenne*. Artists participated in the revolutionary cause: as well as painting portraits of revolutionary figures and the *Death of Marat*, David organised the Fête de la Régénération in August 1793 at the Bastille.

THE DIRECTOIRE

The collective psychosis of the Terror could not endure. In July 1794 a group of moderate Republicans led by Paul Barras succeeded in arresting Robespierre, St-Just and the last Jacobins, who were immediately guillotined amid expressions of generalised hatred for these erstwhile popular heroes.

The wealthy, among them some Revolutionary *nouveaux riches*, emerged blinking into the city's fashionable corners. Barras and his colleagues set themselves up as a five-man Directoire to rule the Republic. In 1795, they were saved from a royalist revolt by an ambitious young Corsican general Napoléon Bonaparte, in a shootout at the **Eglise St-Roch**. France, if no longer the fire-breathing Republic of the Jacobins, was still at war with most European monarchies. Bonaparte was sent to command the army in Italy, where he covered himself with glory. In 1798, he took his army to Egypt, which he almost succeeded in conquering.

EMPEROR NAPOLEON

When he returned to France, he found a Republic in which few had any great faith, while many were prepared to accept a dictator who had emerged from the Revolution. There had always been two potentially contradictory impulses behind the Revolution: a desire for a state that would be a democratic expression of the people, but also for one that would be an effective, powerful defender of the nation. Under Napoléon, the former impulse was put on hold, while France was given the most powerful centralised, militaristic state it had ever seen.

In November 1799 Bonaparte staged a coup, and in 1800 he was declared First Consul. Between continuing military campaigns, he set about transforming France – the education system (with the *Grandes Ecoles*), civil law (the *Code Napoléon*) and administration all bear the Napoleonic stamp to this day. In 1804, he crowned himself Emperor in an ostentatious ceremony in Notre Dame. Napoléon's first additions to the city were the **Canal St-Martin**, *quais* and fine bridges, notably the **Pont des Arts**. He desired to be master of the 'most beautiful city in the world', with palaces, boulevards, monuments and temples evoking the splendour of Augustan Rome – as in the **Madeleine** and the **Bourse**. The Emperor's official architects, Percier and Fontaine, also designed the **rue de Rivoli**.

Parisian society regained its *brio*. Egyptomania swept town after Bonaparte's Egyptian campaign, seen in Empire-style furniture and in architectural details in the new area around rue and **passage du Caire**, while fashionable ladies mixed transparent Greek draperies and couture *à l'égyptienne*.

The Napoleonic epic was inseparable from military expansion. In 1805, he crushed Austria and Russia at Austerlitz. But he overreached himself in the disastrous invasion of Russia in 1812, and in 1814 Paris was occupied, for the first time since the Hundred Years' War, by the Tzar's armies. Napoléon had one last throw, with his escape from confinement in Elba, return to Paris, and the 'hundred days' that ended in 1815 with defeat by Wellington at Waterloo.

Don't start the revolution without me: Louis XVI arrives at the Louvre in July 1789.

MONARCHY RESTORED

In 1814, and then again in 1815, after Waterloo, the Bourbons were restored to the throne of France, in the shape of an elderly brother of Louis XVI, who had spent the Revolution in exile as Louis XVIII. Although his 1814 Charter of Liberties recognised that the pretensions of the *ancien régime* were lost forever, he and his ministers still sought to establish a repressive, Catholic regime that would in some way turn back the clock, hoping to find support in more conservative rural France.

Paris, however, still nurtured a strong feeling of rebellion. Over 60 years, a pattern would be repeated, already seen to some extent in 1789: Paris, especially the working-class east, was far more radical than anywhere else in the country. Its disproportionate weight in French affairs meant it was often seen as imposing its radicalism on the nation at large. At the same time, this radicalism was fed by a progressive press, liberal intellectuals – among them artists and authors Hugo, Daumier, Delacroix and Lamartine – radical students and a growing, poor, anarchic underclass. When provoked, this volatile coalition could explode into revolutionary violence.

THE 1830 REVOLUTION

Another brother of Louis XVI, Charles X, became king in 1824. He proved reactionary, aided – to his downfall – by absolutist minister Prince Polignac who on 25 July 1830 abolished freedom of the press, dissolved the Chamber of Deputies and altered election laws, all in violation of the Charter of Liberties. Next day, 5000 printers and press workers were in the street. Three newspapers defiantly published. When police tried to seize copies, artisans and shopkeepers joined the riot. On 28 July, the disbanded National Guard came out rearmed, Republicans organised insurrection committees, and whole regiments of the Paris garrison defected. Charles hid out in St-Cloud as a provisional government raised the *tricolore* at the Hôtel de Ville. There then followed three days of fighting, known as *Les Trois Glorieuses*, till Charles was forced to abdicate in favour of his heir.

1830-48: LOUIS-PHILIPPE

Another eccentric leftover of the *ancien régime* was winched on to the throne: Louis-Philippe, Duc d'Orléans, son of Philippe-Egalité. A father of eight, who never went out without his umbrella, he was eminently acceptable to the Paris bourgeoisie. But the workers, who had spilled their blood in 1830 only to see quality of life worsen, simmered with rancour and frustration throughout the 'July Monarchy'.

In the first half of the century, the population of Paris doubled to over a million, as a building boom – in part on land seized from the nobility and clergy – brought floods of provincial workers. After 1837, when France's first railway line was laid between Paris and St-Germain-en-Laye, there were stations to build too. The overflow emptied into the poorest quarters. Novelists such as Balzac, Hugo and Eugène Sue were endlessly fascinated by the city's underside, penning hair-raising accounts of dank, tomb-like hovels where the sun never shone, and of dismal, dangerous streets.

Working-class heroes: the Hôtel de Ville after it was burnt by the Paris Commune, 1871.

The well-fed, complacent bourgeoisie (mordantly caricatured in Daumier's lithographs) regarded this populace with fear. For while the Bourse, property speculation and industry flourished after 1830, workers were still forbidden from forming unions or striking. Gaslight cheered up the city streets but enabled the working day to be extended to fifteen hours-plus. Factory owners pruned salaries to the limit and exploited children, unfettered by legislation. Unemployed or disabled workers and their families were obliged to beg, steal or starve. An 1831 cholera epidemic claimed 19,000 victims, and aggravated already bitter class divisions. The rich blamed workers, beggars and immigrants for breeding disease; the poor hated the bourgeoisie who could afford to escape the city's fetid air, or move to the spacious new neighbourhoods in the 8th and 9th *arrondissements*. The stage was set for a battle.

Louis-Philippe's *préfet* Rambuteau made a pitch to win Bonapartist support, finishing the **Arc de Triomphe** and the **Madeleine**, and also initiated some projects of his own, notably the **Pont Louis-Philippe** and **Pont du Carrousel**.

1848: REVOLUTION AGAIN

On 23 February 1848 nervous troops fired on a crowd on boulevard des Capucines. Again, demonstrators demanded blood for blood and barricades covered the city. The Garde Nationale defected to the rebels' side. In the Tuileries, Louis-Philippe abdicated, abandoning palace, capital and country – just as Charles X had done eighteen years earlier.

The workers' revolution of 1848 briefly made France a republic again. The Second Republic was given a progressive provisional government, which included Romantic poet Lamartine and a mechanic – the first French proletarian to hold such a position. They abolished slavery in the colonies and the death penalty for political crimes, gave most French men (but only men) the vote, and set up National Workshops to guarantee jobs for all workers. But the capital had not counted on the reaction of the provinces. In May 1848, general elections put a conservative commission at the head of the Republic. An early official act was to disband the 'make work' scheme as too costly and allied with socialism.

Desperate workers took to the streets in the 'June Days'. And this time the insurgents got the worst of it: thousands fell under the fire of the troops of General Cavaignac, and others were massacred in reprisals after the combat had ended.

LOUIS-NAPOLÉON (NAPOLÉON III)

At the end of 1848, to widespread surprise, new elections gave an overwhelming mandate to a new President of the Republic, Louis-Napoléon Bonaparte, nephew of the great Emperor. After consolidating his position, he decided he didn't merely want to preside but to reign, seizing power in a *coup d'état* on 2 December 1851. In 1852, the Prince-Président moved into the Tuileries Palace as Emperor of France: *Vive Napoléon III*.

At home, Napoléon III combined authoritarianism with crowd-pleasing social welfare in true Bonapartist style. Abroad, his policies included absurd adventures such as the attempt to make Austrian Archduke Maximilian Emperor of Mexico. Napoléon III had grandiose plans for Paris too. His ideas included completing the **Louvre**, landscaping the **Bois de Boulogne**, constructing new iron market halls at **Les Halles**, and opening up a series of new boulevards and train stations. To carry out these daunting tasks he appointed an Alsatian Protestant named Baron Haussmann, Préfet de la Seine from 1853. Haussmann set about his programme with unprecedented energy, giving the aged, malodorous city its greatest-ever transformation (*see chapter* **Architecture**).

The new Paris was a showcase city, with the first department stores and the International Exhibition of 1867. With so much building work, there was plenty of opportunity for speculation. The world capital of sensual pleasure was again decried as a 'New Babylon'. Even Haussmann was not above reproach, forced to resign in 1869 after some of his projects were shown to be based on highly questionable accounts. The combination of sensuality and indulgent opulence of the Second Empire can well be seen in the regime's most distinctive single building, Charles Garnier's **Palais Garnier**.

1870-71: THE FRANCO-PRUSSIAN WAR

In 1870, Napoléon III was maneouvred into war with the German states, led by Bismarck's Prussia. At Sedan, on 4 September 1870, the French army was crushed, and the Emperor abdicated.

Days later, a Parisian crowd demanded and won a new Republic, proclaimed to much cheering at the Hôtel de Ville. A provisional government was formed, yet within weeks Paris was under Prussian siege. Beleaguered Parisians shivered and starved through winter. In January 1871, Prussian artillery bombarded the southern *arrondissements*. The French government negotiated a temporary armistice with Bismarck, then hastily arranged elections for a National Assembly mandated to make peace. Paris voted republican, but the majority went to conservative monarchists. The peace terms signed at Versailles on 28 January 1871 – a five billion-franc indemnity, occupation by 30,000 German troops and ceding of Alsace-Lorraine to the newly united Germany– were seen as betrayal by disgusted Parisian patriots. Worse, the new Assembly under Adolphe Thiers spurned the mutinous capital and chose to set up in Versailles instead.

1871: THE PARIS COMMUNE

Paris was marked by revolution in the nineteenth century and none proved bloodier nor more consequential than the last, which lasted nine weeks from March to May 1871 and which remains engraved in the collective memory of the left and the French working class, a revolt rivetingly portrayed in posters, prints and newspapers at the **Musée de l'Art et d'Histoire de St-Denis**.

The turning point came on 18 March 1871, when Thiers sent a detachment of soldiers to Montmartre to collect 200 cannons from the Garde Nationale, which had been paid for through public subscription to defend the city during the German siege. The abortive mission ended disastrously as insurrectionists led by heroine schoolteacher Louise Michels fended off the troops, killing two generals (a feat recorded in a plaque on rue du Chevalier-de-la-Barre, behind Sacré-Coeur).

Thiers immediately ordered all government officials and the regular army to leave Paris for Versailles, leaving the city in the hands of the poor and a wide-ranging spectrum of radicals. On 26 March, the Commune of Paris was proclaimed at the Hôtel de Ville. As Louis Blanc said: 'The Hôtel de Ville was the place chosen for the consecration of all revolutionary powers, the way Reims was formerly chosen for the coronation of kings.' The Commune's Assembly comprised workers, clerks, accountants, journalists, lawyers, teachers, artists, doctors and a handful of small business owners, who decreed the separation of Church and State, the secularisation of schools, abolition of night work in bakeries, creation of workers' cooperatives, and a moratorium on debts and rents. Yet, there was never any question of abolishing private property, since the worker's fundamental aim was to become proprietor of an *atelier*.

Even artists got swept up in Commune fever. A federation of artists established in April 1871 attracted such talents as Corot, Daumier, Manet, Millet and the caricaturist André Gill (later of the **Lapin Agile** in Montmartre). Its mission: to urge the suppression of the Academy and the Ecole des Beaux-Arts, in favour of art freed of governmental sanctions. Courbet reopened the Louvre and the **Muséum d'Histoire Naturelle**. On 12 April, the column on place Vendôme celebrating Napoléon's victories was knocked down with great fanfare.

While support for the Commune was palpable among thousands of disenfranchised workers and inflamed intellectuals, their lack of organisation and political experience proved fatal, and they were also outnumbered. It was only a matter of days when Thiers and his Versaillais troops began their assault on the city. On 4 April, the Commune's two principal military strategists, Flourens and Duval, were taken prisoner and executed. By 11 April, Thiers' troops had retaken the suburbs and dismantled forts at Issy and Vanves, which had withstood the Prussian siege.

LA SEMAINE SANGLANTE

Soon, barrages of artillery encircled the city, while inside Paris barricades of sandbags and barbed wire sprung up everywhere. Men, women and even children were caught up in house-to-house street fighting. On 21 May, in the week that would go down as the *Semaine sanglante* (Bloody Week),

Thiers' Versaillais entered the city through the Porte de St-Cloud, and occupied the prosperous west of the city, capturing Auteuil, Passy and the 15th *arrondissement*. Within three days of street fighting, more than half the city was retaken. Marquis Gallifet, 'the butcher of the Commune', did a brutal 'mop-up' job in the parc des Buttes-Chaumont. On 28 May, among the tombs of the **Cimetière Père Lachaise**, 147 Communards were cornered and executed, against the 'Mur des Fédérés', today a moving memorial to the insurrection. The final battle played itself out in a narrow square formed by the rues de Belleville, Fbg-du-Temple and Oberkampf.

An estimated 3-4000 Communards or *fédérés* were killed in combat, compared with 877 Versaillais. The Commune retaliated by kidnapping and killing the Archbishop of Paris and other members of the clergy, setting fire to a third of the city. 'Paris will be ours or Paris will no longer exist!' vowed 'the red virgin' Louise Michels. The Hôtel de Ville and Tuileries palace were set ablaze. Although the Hôtel de Ville was rebuilt, the Tuileries was not and was ultimately torn down in 1880.

During the *Semaine sanglante*, thousands of insurrectionists were singled out and shot. At the Châtelet, Mazas and Roquette prisons, the Jardins du Luxembourg, Parc Monceau, Ecole Militaire and Panthéon, at least 10,000 Communards were shot en masse, many buried under public squares and pavements. There were over 40,000 arrests and over 5000 deportations, including Louise Michels to New Caledonia for seven years.

THE THIRD REPUBLIC

The Third Republic, established in 1871, was an unloved compromise, although it survived for 70 years. The right yearned for the restoration of some kind of monarchy; to the left, the Republic was tainted by its suppression of the Commune.

Changing Paris – with its busy boulevards, railway stations and cafés – provided subject matter for the Impressionist painters, led by Monet, Renoir, Manet, Degas and Pissarro, art's avant-garde. Rejected by the official Salon, their first exhibition took place in 1874 in the *atelier* of the photographer Félix Nadar, on boulevard des Capucines.

Paris celebrated its faith in science and progress with two World Exhibitions. The 1889 exhibition was designed to mark the centenary of the Revolution and confirm the respectability of the Third Republic. Centrepiece was a giant iron structure, the **Eiffel Tower**, erected in the face of protests, such as that of writer Maupassant, who denounced it as a 'barbaric mass'.

On 1 April 1900, another World Exhibition greeted the new century. A futuristic city sprang up on the banks of the Seine, of which the **Grand** and **Petit Palais**, ornate **Pont Alexandre III** and grandiose Gare d'Orsay (now **Musée d'Orsay**) remain. In July 1900 the first line of the Paris Métro ferried passengers from Porte Maillot to Vincennes, in the unheard-of time of 25 minutes. The 1900 Exhibition drew well over 50 million visitors, who marvelled at the wonders of electricity, rode on the exciting new Ferris wheel, and drank in the heady atmosphere of Paris.

Street-fighting men, women and children during 1871's 'Semaine sanglante': thousands died.

THE DREYFUS CASE

After the defeat of 1870, many circles were obsessed with the need for 'revenge' and the recovery of Alsace-Lorraine; a frustration also expressed in xenophobia and anti-Semitism. These strands came together in the Dreyfus case, which polarised French society for years. In 1894, a Jewish army officer, Captain Alfred Dreyfus, was accused of spying for Germany, quickly condemned and sent off to Devil's Island. As the facts emerged, suspicion pointed clearly at another officer. Leftists and liberals took up Dreyfus' case, such as Emile Zola, who published his defence of Dreyfus, *J'Accuse*, in *L'Aurore* in January 1898; rightists were bitterly opposed, sometimes taking the view that even if he were innocent it was imperative that the honour of the army should not be questioned, although divisions were not always clear cut: radical future prime minister Clemenceau supported Zola, but so did the prince of Monaco. Such were the passions mobilised that fights broke out in the street; nevertheless, Dreyfus was eventually released in 1900.

THE NAUGHTY 90s

Paris of the naughty nineties was synonymous with illicit pleasures inaccessible elsewhere. In 1889, impresario Maurice Zidler opened the **Moulin Rouge**, which successfully repackaged a half-forgotten dance called the *chahut* as the can-can. In 1894, what is believed to have been the world's first strip joint opened nearby on rue des Martyrs, the Divan Fayouac, with a routine titled *Le Coucher d'Yvette* (*Yvette Goes to Bed*). At the trial of Oscar Wilde in 1895, the mere fact that he owned 'French books' was held as evidence against him.

The *belle époque* ('beautiful era', a phrase coined in the 1920s in a wave of nostalgia after World War I) – and most of all the decade before 1914 – was a time of prestigious artistic activity. When Countess Greffulhe (model for Proust's Princesse de Guermantes in *Remembrance of Things Past*) bestowed her patronage on Debussy, Mussorgsky, Diaghilev and his Ballets Russes, it was seen to be chic to favour avant-garde artists and musicians. The city was all French kisses and saucy *danseuses*, an immovable feast of oysters and champagne – at least until August 1914. But what remains now of the dizzying legend?

For one thing the restaurants. Seek out the **Train Bleu** in the Gare de Lyon, all chandeliers, dripping stucco, triumphant frescoes, deep leather settees. The irrepressible *bouillon* **Chartier** in rue Montmartre seems to have popped straight out of a Toulouse-Lautrec painting. The brasseries **Bofinger**, **Julien**, les Ministères and Grand Colbert (to name but a few) have been tastefully restored in keeping with the style of the period (*see* chapter **Restaurants**). Other remnants of the Belle Epoque (much was knocked down in the 1920s-30s in the name of rectilinear good taste) include the

Pride of Paris

Millennium? What millennium? For the men and women who run the Paris Métro, the year 2000 is, above all, a centenary. They've unleashed a flurry of festivities – some rather fanciful – ranging from websites, books, conferences and exhibitions to the transformation of stations into virtual reality playgrounds.

Until the launch on 19 July 1900 of the first Métro line (35 years after the London Underground opened) the project was a mire of controversy. The collaboration between engineer Fulgance Bienvenüe (commemorated at M° Montparnasse-Bienvenüe) and the Art Nouveau architect Guimard would destroy *vieux* Paris, said detractors. Socialists denounced it as a capitalist plot and, looking at the massive marketing machine behind the current celebrations, one might wonder if there is some truth to this. But by the end of the year such was its success that 18 million passengers had been transported 10km across Paris in a mind-boggling 25 minutes.

Today the Métro boasts 14 lines, the latest being the post-postmodern Météor, its seven stations echoing the grandiose design ethos of the earliest ones. There are 370 stations, 570 trains circulating at peak times – and countless bedraggled bodies struggling to preserve a sliver of personal space amid rush-hour hordes.

But – recent rubbish collection strikes apart – the Métro is clean, punctual and utterly indispensable. Beloved, even. It is admired worldwide, having served as the model for subways from Cairo to Chile. In that spirit, four stations have been chosen to 'incarnate' foreign counterparts, though judging by the effort at Invalides, dressed up as Moscow (makeshift papier mâché cupolas, assorted blini tastings), 'vaguely evoke' might be a more accurate term. There is a whiff of the naff, too, about the nine stations being 'honoured' with virtual installations that reflect their locations: St-Germain-des-Prés will be turned into a huge literary revue, while Carrefour-Pleyel (commemorating piano-maker Ignaz Pleyel) becomes – don't ask how – a musical instrument.

More practical endeavours include improvements to some 200 stations – lighting, furnishings, facilities – and the restoration of 86 listed Art Nouveau entrances by Guimard. These are heartening moves. Parisians don't want anything fancy – just keep the trains running on time, and maintaining a service that Londoners can only dream about.

Elysée Montmartre concert hall and the **Lapin Agile**, haunt of the then avant-garde. Department stores such as **Samaritaine, le Printemps, les Galeries Lafayette** still boast cupolas, mosaics and spectacular vistas atop historic staircases.

THE GREAT WAR

On 2 August 1914, France learned that war with Germany was imminent. Many Parisians rejoiced, for it seemed simply that the long-awaited opportunity for 'revenge' had finally come. However, the Allied armies were steadily pushed back. Paris filled with refugees, and by 2 September the Germans were on the Marne, just 15 miles from the city. The government took refuge in Bordeaux, entrusting the defence of the capital to General Galliéni. What then occurred was later glorified as the 'Miracle on the Marne'. Troops were ferried to the front in Paris taxis. By 13 September, the Germans were pushed back to the Oise; Paris was safe. In the trenches battles raged on, and Paris industrialised to produce weapons and chemicals.

After the catastrophic battle of Verdun in 1916 had inflicted appalling damage on the French army, a strong current of defeatism emerged. Parisian spirits were further sapped by a flu epidemic and the shells of 'Big Bertha' – a gigantic German cannon levelled at the city from 75 miles away. The veteran Clemenceau was made prime minister in 1917 to restore morale. On 11 November, the Armistice was finally signed in the forest of **Compiègne**. Celebrations lasted for days, but the war had cut a swathe through France's male population, killing over 1 million men.

THE INTERWAR YEARS

Paris emerged from the War with a restless energy expressed in an artistic scene that was more dynamic and more cosmopolitan than ever. The city's continuing fascination with the new was seen in its enthusiastic embrace of Art Deco. Artistic life centred on Montparnasse (*see chapter* **Left Bank**), a bohemian whirl of colourful emigrés and daring nightclubs and cabarets. Cars became more frequent in the capital and the cinema a popular pastime, with the construction of grand picture palaces like **Le Grand Rex**.

The Depression did not hit France until after 1930, but when it arrived, it unleashed a wave of political violence. On 6 February 1934, Fascist and extreme right-wing groups demonstrated against the Republic and tried to invade the Assemblée Nationale. Fire hoses and bullets beat them back. Fifteen were killed, 1500 wounded. Socialists and Communists united in the face of Fascism and the economic situation to create the Popular Front. In 1936, socialist Léon Blum was elected to head a Popular Front government. In the euphoric 'workers' spring' of 1936, workers were given the right to form unions, higher salaries, a 40-hour

week and, for the first time, paid holidays.

By the autumn, debates about the Spanish Civil War had split the coalition, and the economic situation was deteriorating. Blum's government fell in June 1937. France seemed within an inch of revolution. The working class was disenchanted, and right-wing parties grew on the back of fear of Communism, which to many seemed a far more immediate threat than Hitler. Tragically, each camp of a France that was divided into right and left feared the enemy within far more than the real enemy that was waiting on its doostep.

THE SECOND WORLD WAR

Britain and France declared war on Germany in September 1939, but for months this meant only the *drôle de guerre* (phoney war), characterised by rumour and inactivity. On 10 May 1940, the Germans invaded France, Belgium and Holland. By 6 June, the French army had been crushed and the Germans were near Paris. A shell-shocked government left for Bordeaux, archives and works of art were hurriedly hidden or bundled off to safety. Thousands of Parisians threw belongings into cars, carts, prams and bikes and began their own exodus south. Overnight the city emptied out. Whereas the population of Greater Paris in 1936 was 4.96 million, by the end of May 1940 it was 3.5 million, and by 27 June, stood at about 1.9 million.

Paris fell on 14 June 1940 with virtually no resistance. The German Army marched along the **Champs-Elysées**. At the Hôtel de Ville, the *tricolore* was lowered and the swastika raised. The French cabinet voted to request an armistice, and Maréchal Pétain, an elderly hero of the First War, dissolved the Third Republic and took over the government. The Germans occupied two-thirds of France, while the French government moved south to Vichy. A young, autocratic general, Charles de Gaulle, went to London to organise a Free French movement in open opposition to the occupation.

The Nazi insignia soon hung from every public building, including the Eiffel Tower. Hitler visited Paris only once, on 23 June 1940, taking in the Palais Garnier, Eiffel Tower and Napoléon's tomb at the Invalides. Leaving the city, he observed: 'Wasn't Paris beautiful?... In the past, I often considered whether we would not have to destroy Paris. But when we are finished in Berlin, Paris will only be a shadow. So why should we destroy it?'

THE OCCUPATION

For most Parisians, the occupation meant going without creature comforts. For the Germans, Paris was their western headquarters, and a very attractive assignment compared to, for example, Russia. They lapped up luxury goods, and swamped Paris' best nightspots, restaurants and hotels. There was no shortage of Parisians who accepted them, and warmed to an enemy who offered a champagne

The Train Bleu restaurant epitomises the splendour and decadence of the **Belle Epoque**.

lifestyle and sustained Paris' traditional glitter. In the entertainment world, Maurice Chevalier and the actress Arletty were later condemned for having performed for, or having still closer contacts with the Germans, as was couturier Coco Chanel.

Private cars were banned and replaced with horse-drawn carriages and *vélo-taxis*, carts towed behind a bicycle. Bread, sugar, butter, cheese, meat, coffee and eggs were rationed. City parks and rooftops were made into vegetable gardens and a substitute for coffee, dubbed *café national*, was made with ground acorns and chickpeas.

Occupied Paris also had its share of pro-Vichy bureaucrats who preferred to work with the Germans than embrace what many saw as a futile opposition. There were also *attentistes* (wait and see-ers) and black marketeers, who became rich on the back of Nazi rationing. Even so, many were prepared to risk being hauled off to the Gestapo torture chambers at rue des Saussaies, avenue Foch or rue Lauriston. By the summer of 1941, the first executions of French underground fighters by the Germans had begun, in response to the activities of the patriots, organised from Britain.

DEPORTATION OF JEWS

There was also the rounding-up and deportation of Jews, in which the role of the Vichy authorities remains a sensitive issue to this day. On 29 June 1940, Jews were ordered to register with the police; on 11 November, all Jewish businesses were required to post a yellow sign. The wearing of the yellow star was introduced in May 1942, soon followed by regulations prohibiting Jews from restaurants, cinemas, theatres, beaches, and most jobs.

The first deportations of Jews (most foreign-born) took place on 14 May 1941. In August, 6000 Jews were rounded up in the 11th *arrondissement* and interned in the suburb of Drancy, before being sent on to Auschwitz. In July 1942, 12,000 Jews were summoned to the Vélodrome d'Hiver (the winter cycling stadium) in Paris. The Vichy Chief of Police ensured that not only Jews aged over 18, but also thousands of young children not on the original orders, were deported in what is known as the Vél d'Hiv. A monument commemorating the event was commissioned by the French government and installed on the quai de Grenelle in July 1994, near where the Vélodrome once stood.

Still, not all Parisians stood for the persecution of the Jews. Many Jews were hidden during the war, and a number of government officials tacitly assisted them with ration cards and false papers. While one-third of French Jews were deported and killed in concentration camps during the war, the remaining two-thirds were saved, largely through the efforts of French citizens and the Résistance.

THE LIBERATION

In June 1944, the Allies invaded Normandy. German troops began to retreat east, and Parisians saw a real opportunity to retake their city. On 10 to 18 August there were strikes on the Métro and of public services. There was no radio broadcasting, but people began to sense that liberation was at hand.

On 19 August, a *tricolore* was hoisted at the

Hôtel de Ville, and the Free French forces launched an insurrection, occupying several buildings. On 23 August, Hitler ordered Von Choltitz, the German commander, to destroy the French capital. Von Choltitz stalled, for which inaction he would later be honoured by a grateful French government. On 25 August, General Leclerc's French 2nd Armoured Division, which had been carefully put at the head of the US forces approaching Paris in order that it would be French troops who would first enter the city, made their way into Paris by the Porte d'Orléans. The city went wild. There were still snipers hidden on rooftops, but in the euphoria of the moment no one seemed to care. Late in the afternoon, De Gaulle arrived to make his way down the Champs-Elysées to the Hôtel de Ville. 'We are living minutes that go far beyond our paltry lives,' he cried out to an ecstatic crowd.

DE GAULLE & THE POST-WAR YEARS

In the immediate postwar years, those who had led the fight against Vichy and the Germans felt that now was the time to build a new society and a new republic. The National Resistance Council's post-war reform programme was approved by most parties from left to right, and De Gaulle was proclaimed provisional President. At first vigilante justice prevailed: accusations of collaboration began to fly, mock trials were set up, and severe punishments were doled out to *collabos*, but many former Vichy officials escaped trial and rose within the administration.

As the economy began to revive, postwar Paris became a magnet for thousands of French men and women for whom the capital represented a new opportunity. The population rose dramatically: in 1946, there were 6.6 million inhabitants in greater Paris, but by 1950 that number had increased by 700,000. In response, the state built *villes nouvelles* (new towns) and low-income housing.

THE ALGERIAN WAR

De Gaulle relinquished office in 1946, and the Fourth Republic was established. Thereafter, French troops were constantly engaged in a losing battle to save France's disintegrating Empire. Vietnam was lost in 1954, but after revolt broke out in Algeria in 1956 Socialist prime minister Guy Mollet sent in almost half a million troops. Algeria also became a major issue for intellectuals, and it was only a matter of time before the battles were reflected in Paris. Mutinous army officers, opposed to any 'sell-out' of the French settlers or *colons* in Algeria, took over government headquarters in Algiers. It was time, decided the Fourth Republic, to admit defeat and wheel the old demagogue out of retirement. In May 1958 De Gaulle came back, with the understanding that he was to be allowed to rewrite the constitution and give France the republic he thought she deserved.

The liberation of Paris, August 1944.

DE GAULLE & THE FIFTH REPUBLIC

De Gaulle appeared to promise one thing to settlers in Algeria, while negotiating with rebel leaders for their country's independence. On 17 October 1961, the pro-independence FLN demonstrated in Paris, and police shot at the crowd. Officially only three were killed, but recently released archives show that over 300 bodies were fished out of the Seine alone. In 1962 Algeria was proclaimed independent, and some 700,000 embittered colonists came straggling back to France. De Gaulle beamed down from his presidential throne like the monarch he wasn't. He commanded foreign policy, intervened in domestic policy, and reported to the nation by means of carefully orchestrated press conferences or appearances on television.

The state was again under pressure to provide housing. Radical urbanisation plans were hastily drawn up for Paris. Although historic areas were considered sacrosanct, large areas succumbed to the ball and chain: the 'Manhattanisation' of Paris was underway. André Malraux, Minister of Culture, however, undertook a major series of measures to ensure the preservation of the historic Marais.

The post-war mood of crisis was over, and into the breach thundered a sharp, fresh 'new wave' of cinema directors, novelists and critics – Truffaut, Melville, Godard and Resnais were among the filmmakers who gained international status.

MAY 1968

By 1968, youth chafed against their yokes, as their numbers swelled the over-stretched French educational system. Dissatisfaction was widespread, not just with education, but also with the authoritarian nature of the state, in contrast to the 60s mood of counterculture. In early May the students took to the streets. On 3 May, paving stones were torn up, perhaps inspired by the Situationist group's slogan 'sous les pavés, la plage' ('beneath the paving stones, the beach'). By mid-May, workers and trade unions at Renault and Sud-Aviation had joined the protest and, by 20 May, six million people were on strike across France. After negotiations failed, De Gaulle's proposal for a referendum was rejected with the worst night of violence. But by 30 May, the tide began to turn with an anti-strike demonstration on the Champs-Elysées. By 5 June, workers began to go back to their factories.

Even today, barely a week goes by without you hearing a French person evoke *soixante-huit*. If not a political revolution, May '68 was a cultural and social uprising that shook the institutions and the ruling classes, forcing an attitude of open debate and forming a new generation, many of whom constitute the French establishment, especially the media, today. After losing a referendum in early 1969, De Gaulle retired to his provincial retreat, where he died in 1970.

1970: GEORGES POMPIDOU

Georges Pompidou or Pom-Pom – as De Gaulle's successor was often called – didn't preside over any earth-shattering political developments. What Pompidou (a Conservative) did do was begin the process that radically changed the architectural face of Paris, implanting an uncompromisingly avant-garde building, the **Centre Pompidou**, in the heart of one of the city's oldest neighbourhoods. He also built the expressways along the Seine and gave the go-ahead to the redevelopment of Les Halles.

VALERY GISCARD D'ESTAING

Valéry Giscard d'Estaing became president in 1974, on the sudden death of Pompidou. He made clear his desire to transform France into an 'advanced liberal society'. Notable among his decisions were those to transform **Gare d'Orsay** into a museum, and the creation of a high-tech science museum in the vast abattoirs at **La Villette**.

FRANÇOIS MITTERRAND

In an abrupt political turnaround, the Socialists, led by François Mitterrand, swept into power in 1981. The mood in Paris was initially electric, although after nationalising some banks and industries, Socialist France of the prosperous 1980s turned out to be not wildly different from Gaullist France. In Paris, the period was defined politically by the ongoing feud between Mitterrand and Jacques Chirac, Paris' right-wing mayor since 1977.

From the very beginning of his presidency, Mitterrand cherished ambitions for transforming Paris: the *Grands Projets*. His first operation was the most daring: open-heart surgery on the Louvre.

The **Louvre Pyramid** in turn carried with it a corollary, the transfer of the Ministry of Finance to a new complex at **Bercy**. If the **Grande Arche** gave a monument to La Defénse in the west, Bercy was part of a vast programme for the renewal of eastern Paris along with **Opéra Bastille**. Last and most controversial *Grand Projet* was the **Bibliothèque Nationale François Mitterrand**, completed after Mitterrand's death in January 1996.

Despite policies of decentralisation, Paris remained the intellectual and artistic hub of France, helped by the rivalry between left-wing government and the right-wing Mairie de Paris, which saw Paris-funded exhibitions at the Petit Palais and Musée d'Art Moderne de la Ville de Paris rival the national Grand Palais and Centre Pompidou.

THE CHIRAC ERA

The last years of the Mitterrand era were marked by the President's ill health, and a seeping away of his prestige. The start of the presidency of Jacques Chirac, elected in May 1995, was marked by social strife, with strikes in autumn 1995, terrorist attacks, corruption scandals and a prime minister, Alain Juppé, whose unpopularity exceeded even that of previous record-holder – France's only woman PM, Edith Cresson. In May 1997, in a massive strategic miscalculation, Chirac called a general election a year early. A Socialist coalition under Lionel Jospin won by a landslide, leaving Chirac sidelined into a largely ceremonial role in the *cohabitation* and the Gaullist party in total disarray. The Socialist coalition (which includes Greens and Communists) started its reign with a record number of leading female ministers and unprecedented popularity.

At the end of 1999, after two years in power, the government no longer appeared as squeaky clean as at first, but with Jospin cleverly distanced from scandal, the right splintered into factions and the far right finally neutralised since the split between Le Pen and former cohort Bruno Mégret, it doesn't appear to be under any real threat.

While refuting charges of Blairite 'liberalism', many former state companies (BNP, France Telecom) have been wholly or partially privatised. The economy of the fourth-richest nation is booming – seen in falling unemployment, Bourse records, rising property prices and thriving luxury areas like avenue Montaigne and the Champs-Elysées.

Jean Tiberi, Chirac's successor as Paris mayor, involved in rumours of corruption, is highly unpopular, but he is determined to fight the next mayoral election in 2001. Paris remains largely immune from the main demonstrations (hunting rights, agriculture) and the social strife and violence that plague the suburbs. *Grand Projets* have gone out of fashion, but development goes on in the huge ZAC Rive Gauche and in local projects for the impoverished Goutte d'Or.

Architecture

From the grandiose concepts of Louis XIV, Napoléon and Haussmann to Mitterrand's Grands Projets, Paris has always been about show.

Whether by way of walls, squares and boulevards or *Grands Projets*, Paris has developed through periods of conscious planning: its apparent homogeneity stems from use of the same materials over the centuries: local yellow limestone and slate – later zinc – roofs. It was only early this century that brick became widely used and, with a few exceptions like the Eiffel Tower, only since the war that large-scale use of glass, concrete and steel have created more obtrusive landmarks.

The Romanesque

The medieval city was centred on the Ile de la Cité and the Latin Quarter. The main thoroughfares of the medieval – and even the modern – street plan of the area, in the rue St-Jacques and rue Mouffetard, followed those of Roman Paris. Paris had several powerful Romanesque abbeys outside the city walls, but existing remains of this simple style are sparse. The tower of **St-Germain-des-Prés**, although topped by a later spire, still has its rounded arches, while some decorated capitals survive in the typically solid-feeling nave.

Gothic Paris

It was in the **Basilique St-Denis**, begun in 1136, under the patronage of the powerful Abbot Suger, that the Gothic trademarks of pointed arches, ogival vaulting and flying buttresses were combined for the first time. Gothic vaulting allowed buildings to span large spaces and let light in, bringing with it an aesthetic of brightness and verticality. A spate of building followed with cathedrals at **Chartres**, Sens and Laon, as well as **Notre-Dame**, which incorporated all the features of the style: twin-towered west front, soaring nave, intricate rose windows and buttressed east end.

Shortly after work on Notre-Dame had commenced, in the 1190s, King Philippe-Auguste began the building of the first **Louvre**, with a solid defensive keep, part of which can be seen within the Louvre today. In the following century, ribbed vaulting became ever more refined and columns more slender, in the Rayonnant or High Gothic style. Master mason/architect Pierre de Montreuil continued work on St-Denis with the rose windows. His masterpiece, the 1246-48 **Sainte-Chapelle**, takes the Gothic ideal to its height. The stained glass windows of the upper chapel virtually create a wall of glass and reduce the stone tracery to a minimum.

The later Flamboyant-Gothic style saw a wealth of decoration. **Eglise St-Séverin**, with its twisting spiral column, is particularly original. The pinnacles and gargoyles of the early sixteenth-century **Tour St-Jacques** and the porch of **St-Germain-l'Auxerrois** are typical. The **Tour Jean Sans Peur** is a rare fragment of an early fifteenth-century mansion, while Paris' two finest medieval mansions, the Hôtel de Cluny (now **Musée National du Moyen-Age**) and **Hôtel de Sens**, were both urban palaces for powerful abbots. With living quarters at the back of an enclosed forecourt, Cluny is a precursor of the domestic style of the Marais *hôtel particulier*.

The Renaissance

The influence of the Italian Renaissance came late to Paris, and was largely due to the personal impetus of François 1er. He installed Leonardo da Vinci at **Amboise** and brought over Primaticcio and Rosso to work on his palace at **Fontainebleau**. It was not until 1528 that he set about updating the **Louvre**, with the Cour Carrée, by Pierre Lescot. The pretty, hybrid church of **St-Etienne-du-Mont** shows that Renaissance style remained a largely superficial effect: the structure is Flamboyant-Gothic, the balustrade of the nave and the elaborate roodscreen (possibly by Delorme) are Renaissance. A heavier hybrid is the massive **St-Eustache**. The **Hôtel Carnavalet**, altered by Mansart next century, and the **Hôtel Lamoignon**, both in the Marais, are Paris' best remaining examples of Renaissance mansions.

The *Ancien Régime*

France's first Bourbon king, Henri IV, had great plans for modernising his capital. He built the **Pont-Neuf** and **place Dauphine** on the Ile de la Cité and **place des Vosges** in the Marais. Both followed a symmetrical plan, with vaulted galleries and steeply pitched roofs.

The seventeenth century was a high point in French power; the monarchy desired buildings that reflected its grandeur, a need satisfied by the Baroque style. Great architects emerged under court

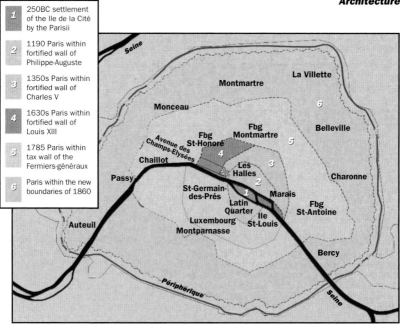

1	250BC settlement of the Ile de la Cité by the Parisii
2	1190 Paris within fortified wall of Philippe-Auguste
3	1350s Paris within fortified wall of Charles V
4	1630s Paris within fortified wall of Louis XIII
5	1785 Paris within tax wall of the Fermiers-généraux
6	Paris within the new boundaries of 1860

Paris *through the ages, as successive ramparts and ring roads have spread from the centre.*

patronage: Salomon de Brosse, François Mansart, Jules Hardouin-Mansart (his nephew), Libéral Bruand and Louis Le Vau, decorator Charles Lebrun and landscape architect André Le Nôtre. Even at **Versailles,** Baroque never reached the excesses of Italy or Austria. French architects followed Cartesian principles of harmony and balance.

The **Palais du Luxembourg,** built by de Brosse in Italianate style for Marie de Médicis, combines classic French château design with elements of the Pitti Palace in Marie's native Florence. Counter-Reformation churches like the **Eglise St-Paul-St-Louis** or the **Chapelle de la Sorbonne** followed the Gésu in Rome. The **Eglise de Val-de-Grâce,** designed by Mansart, and later Jacques Lemercier, is one of the grandest examples of Baroque architecture in Paris.

Nouveaux-riches flocked to build mansions in the Marais and the Ile-St-Louis. Those in the Marais follow a symmetrical U-shaped plan, with a secluded courtyard: look through the archways to the *cour d'honneur* of the **Hôtel de Sully** or **Hôtel Salé,** where facades are richly decorated, in contrast with their street faces. In contrast, along **rue du Faubourg-St-Antoine,** a working district, the buildings where the furniture-makers lived and worked in were tall, with arches leading from the street to cobbled courtyards lined with workshops.

Under Colbert, Louis XIV's chief minister, the creation of stage sets to magnify the Sun King's power proceeded apace. The Louvre grew as Claude Perrault created the sweeping west facade, while Hardouin-Mansart's **place des Victoires** and **place Vendôme,** an elegant octagon of arches and Corinthian columns, were both designed to show off equestrian statues of the king

Rococo & Neo-Classicism

In the early eighteenth century, the Faubourg-St-Germain overtook the Marais in fashion. Most of the mansions there are now ministries or embassies; today you can visit the Hôtel Bouchardon (**Musée Maillol**), which has some original carved panelling.

Under Louis XV, the severe lines of the previous century were softened by rounded corners and decorative detailing, such as satyr masks over doorways, at the Hôtel Chenizot (51 rue St-Louis-en-l'Ile) and Hôtel d'Albret (31 rue des Francs-Bourgeois). The main developments came in interior decoration, with the frivolous French Rococo style. The best example is the **Hôtel de Soubise,** with panelling, plasterwork and paintings by decorators of the day including Boucher, Restout and Van Loo.

From the 1750s geometry was back as Ancient Rome inspired another monument to royal majesty, Jacques Ange Gabriel's Neo-Classical **place de la Concorde;** and Soufflot's domed **Panthéon** on a Greek cross plan was inspired by the one in Rome. One late addition by the *ancien régime* was the tax wall, the *Mur des Fermiers Généraux*, built around the city in 1785. Utopian Claude-Nicolas Ledoux's **toll gates** played games with pure geometrical forms; circular at Parc Monceau and La Rotonde de la Villette, and rectangular pairs at place Denfert-Rochereau and place de la Nation.

The Nineteenth Century

The Revolution largely confined itself to pulling buildings down. Royal statues bit the dust along with the Bastille prison, and churches became 'temples of reason' or grain stores. Napoléon, however, soon brought Paris back to a proper sense of its grand self. Land confiscated from aristocracy and church was built up. A stern Classicism was preferred for the **Arc de Triomphe**, the Greek-temple inspired **Madeleine** and Brongniart's **Bourse**.

By the 1840s Classical style was under challenge from a Gothic revival led by Eugène Viollet-le-Duc. Critics accused him of creating a romanticised notion of the medieval; his use of colour was felt to pollute these monuments. Judge for yourself in the choir of Notre-Dame and the Sainte-Chapelle or visit the castle he (re)built largely from scratch at **Pierrefonds**. Historical eclecticism ruled, though, with the Neo-Renaissance **Hôtel de la Païva**, **Hôtel de Ville** or **Eglise de la Trinité**. Hittorrf chose Antique polychromy in the **Cirque d'Hiver**, while Byzantium and the Romanesque made a comeback from the 1870s.

Engineering innovations made the use of iron frames in buildings increasingly common. Henri Labrouste's reading room at the **Bibliothèque Ste-Geneviève** (1844-50), in place du Panthéon, was one of the first to use iron for the entire structure. Stations like Hittorrf's **Gare du Nord** (1861-65) and such apparently massive stone structures as the Galerie d'Evolution (**Muséum d'Histoire Naturelle**) and **Musée d'Orsay** are but shells around an iron frame, allowing spacious, light-filled interiors. The most daring, emphatic iron structure of them all was the **Eiffel Tower**, built in 1889, then the tallest structure in the world.

Baron Haussmann

Few figures in Paris history have had a worse press than Georges-Eugène Haussmann (1809-1891). First, he's charged with the glitzy *Grands Boulevards* – which have existed since Louis XIV – and then he's blamed for destroying Paris. Yet much of Paris as we know it is due to his transformations under the Second Empire.

Appointed Napoléon III's *Préfet de la Seine* in 1853, Haussmann was not an architect but an administrator. Aided by architects and engineers including Baltard, Hittorff, Alphand and Belgrand, he set about making Paris the most modern city of its day. Broad boulevards were cut through the old

city. Ile de la Cité was decimated, but some old districts were left unaltered. An estimated 27,000 houses were demolished and some 100,000 built.

The boulevards were in part anti-revolutionary measures against the politically volatile working classes, forcing them to move to the outer *faubourgs* and making construction of barricades more difficult, but they also answered real communication and health problems in a city that had grown from 500,000 in 1789 to 1 million in 1850.

Haussmann constructed asylums (Hôpital Ste-Anne, 14th), prisons (Prison de la Santé, 14th), new schools, churches (**Eglise St-Vincent de Paul**), hospitals, and the water and sewage systems. He landscaped the Bois and other parks, and gave Paris its new market pavilions at **Les Halles**. Here Haussmann proved he could also be an innovator, persuading Baltard to build the pavilions not in stone but using a visible iron structure. It was such a success that Verlaine described the ten pavilions as 'the lace of Vulcan', and the style was soon copied in local markets, like the **Marché St-Quentin**, across the city.

Haussmann financed his vision by some dubious credit operations, which ultimately led to his downfall as he was forced to resign in 1869 after exposure of highly questionable accounts. Amid the upheaval, one building epitomised Second-Empire style. Charles Garnier's sumptuous **Palais Garnier** opera of 1862-75 perfectly expresses the ambition of mid-century Paris. The city also acquired the Haussmannian apartment block, which has lasted until well into this century. It's a form that has been adaptable to different styles, budgets and sites.

The Twentieth Century

Paris has always been about show and the twentieth century began with an outburst of extravagance for the 1900 *Exposition Universelle*. Laloux's Gare d'Orsay (now **Musée d'Orsay**) and the Train Bleu brasserie were ornate examples of the heavy Beaux-Arts floral style of the period.

Genuine Art Nouveau architecture in Paris is quite rare, although some fine interiors exist, such as the **Bouillon Racine** or eateries like **Julien**. Art Nouveau at its most fluid and flamboyant can be seen in Guimard's Métro stations and his 1901 **Castel Béranger**, the entrance to the luxury apartment block by Jules Lavirotte at 29 avenue Rapp, or in shop 2 of **La Samaritaine**, built 1905-10 by Frantz Jourdain, with its whiplash-style staircase, *verrière* and peacock-adorned fresco.

It was all a long way from the roughly contemporary work of Henri Sauvage, innovative but too

*Rebirth of the Renaissance: the **Hôtel de Ville** was rebuilt in Neo-Renaissance style.*

eclectic to be identified with any movement. After the geometrical **Cité Commerciale Argentine** flats (1904), his tiled apartment block at **6 rue Vavin** (1911-12) was the first to use stepped-back terraces as a way of getting light into the different storeys. He went to a bigger social housing project in rue des Amiraux, tiled artists' studios-cum-flats in rue La Fontaine, and the more overtly Art Deco 1920s extension of La Samaritaine. Social housing began to be put up citywide, funded by philanthropists, such as the Rothschilds in rue de Prague.

The Modern Movement

After World War I, two names stand out for their innovation and influence – Auguste Perret and Le Corbusier. A third, Robert Mallet-Stevens, stands unrivalled for his elegance. Paris is one of the best cities in the world for Modern Movement houses and studios (often in the 16th and western suburbs like Boulogne and Garches), but also in a more diluted form for public buildings, such as town halls, low-cost public housing and in numerous schools built in the socially minded 1930s.

Perret stayed largely within a classical aesthetic, but his use of reinforced concrete (which he had used less visibly for the **Théâtre des Champs-Elysées**) gave scope for more varied facades than traditional walls. Most interesting is his **Conseil Economique et Social** at place d'Iéna, a circular pavilion with an open horseshoe staircase.

Le Corbusier tried out his ideas in private houses, such as the **Villa La Roche** and **Villa Savoy**. His Pavillon Suisse at the **Cité Universitaire** and **Armée du Salut** hostel in the 13th can be seen as an intermediary point between these villas and the mass housing schemes of his *Villes Radieuses*, which became so influential and so debased in projects across Europe after 1945.

Other notable Modern buildings include Adophe Loos' house for Dadaist poet Tristan Tzara in avenue Junot, supposedly the epitome of his maxim 'ornament is crime', Chareau's influential Maison de Verre (31 rue St-Guillaume, 7th, not visible from the street), houses by Lurçat and Perret near Parc Montsouris, Pierre Patout's steamboat-style apartments (3 bd Victor, 15th) and Studio Raspail at 215 bd Raspail by Elkouken.

The love of chrome, steel and glass found its way into Art Deco cafés and brasseries like **La Coupole**, or the Comédia theatre and **Grand Rex** cinema.

Postwar Paris

The aerodynamic aesthetic of the 1950s saw the 1958 **UNESCO** building, by Bernard Zehrfuss, Pier Luigi Nervi and Marcel Breuer, and the beginnings of La Défense. The *bidonvilles* or shanty-towns that had sprouted around the city, many occupied by immigrant workers, cried out for a solution. In the 60s and 70s, tower blocks sprouted in the suburbs

and new towns: Sarcelles, Mantes la Jolie, Cergy-Pontoise, Evry, Melun-Sénart and Créteil. Redevelopment inside the city was limited, although new regulations allowed taller buildings, noticeably in Montparnasse and in the 13th and 19th. Piano and Rogers' high-tech **Centre Pompidou**, opened in 1977, was the first of the daring prestige projects that have become a trademark of modern Paris.

The 1980s & Beyond

Mitterrand's *Grands Projets* dominated the 1980s and early 90s as he sought to leave his stamp on the city with Nouvel's **Institut du Monde Arabe**, Sprecklesen's **Grande Arche de la Défense**, as well as Ott's more dubious **Opéra Bastille**, Perrault's **Bibliothèque Nationale** (a curious throwback to the 60s) and Chemetov's Bercy finance ministry. Stylistically, the buzz word has been 'transparency' – from IM Pei's **Louvre Pyramid**, and Nouvel's **Fondation Cartier** with its clever slices of glass, to Armstrong Associates' new **Maison de la Culture du Japon** – while also allowing styles as diverse as Portzamparc's **Cité de la Musique**, with geometrical blocks round a colourful internal street, or Richard Meier's neo-Modernist **Canal+** headquarters. The city also privileged public housing: of note are the human-scale housing round Parc de la Villette and Parc André-Citroën, Piano's red-tile-and-glass ensemble in rue de Meaux (19th), La Poste's apartments for young postal workers designed by young architects such as Frédérick Borel (rue Oberkampf), or housing in the suburb of Clichy by Fuksas.

Curiously, some of the most impressive buildings of the late 1990s have been either sacred or sporting. It's not easy to develop a new religious vernacular; Architecture Studio at Notre Dame de l'Espérance in the 15th and Botta at the new **Evry Cathedral** have responded with more or less successful geometrical solutions. Sports facilities have been boosted by Henri and Bruno Gaudin's streamlined Stade Charléty and Zublena and Macary's **Stade de France**. The Métro has also made a return to style not seen since Guimard's station entrances, with Antoine Grumbach's and Bernard Khon's stations for the new Météor line.

At the end of the 90s, the age of the *Grands Projets* is over, although a competition for Chirac's Musée des Arts Premiers is underway. Paris has gained two new footbridges: the passerelle de Solférino by French architect-engineer Marc Mimram and the future passerelle de Bercy by young Austrian architect Dietmar Feichtinger. Although construction continues apace in the ZAC Rive Gauche (around the new Bibliothèque Nationale) and ZAC Alésia-Montsouris, issues of conservation and conversion of the existing urban fabric seem to be on the agenda for the city rather than gleaming pleasure domes.

Regrets, we've had a few…

Paris has never quite got it together as far as the city's industrial heritage is concerned. Thirty years after the now-regretted demolition of Les Halles in 1969 – in the name of progress – it still manages to knock down former industrial buildings with barely a whimper, until it's too late. Keener to promote its image as city of fashion, food and culture, it forgets that it was also the city of Citroën, Renault, tobacco processing, light industries from silver to glasswares, not to mention all the associated transport and warehousing and more ancient craft workshops (furniture along Faubourg St-Antoine, tapestries at Les Gobelins). The debate surfaced again in 1999 with the last-ditch attempt by architect Jean Nouvel to save the massive Renault factory at Boulogne-Billancourt.

A few buildings have survived, often as the result of private initiative, to find new life, generally in the arts domain. Espace Electra, an electricity substation, is now used for temporary exhibitions (*see chapter* **Museums**); a former printworks has become La Ménagerie de Verre dance and theatre venue in a beautiful conversion by Faloci; while the celebrated Cartoucherie de Vincennes complex (*see chapter* **Theatre**) occupies an impressive long line of brick pavilions with glass and iron roofs, once a cartridge-making factory. Also in the suburbs, La Manufacture des Tabacs at Issy-les-Moulineaux, a huge state cigarette factory in use until

1978, has been converted into, among other things, the stylish La Manufacture restaurant (01.40.93.08.98). At Ivry-sur-Seine, the Manufacture des Oeillets (01.46.71.71.10), a metal rivet factory built in 1935 under the inspiration of the Chicago School, has been renovated and converted into theatre, gallery and studios.

Although the Bercy docks area has changed out of all recognition, there are a few signs of hope. Les Chais Lheureux, wine and spirits warehouses, have been preserved as the Pavillons de Bercy (Musée des Arts Forains and Salons Vénitiens, fairground and carnival collections), while the string of 42 brick warehouses on Cours St-Emilion are slowly coming back to life as wine bars and cafés.

Across the river in the ZAC Rive Gauche, a cluster of industrial buildings still face an uncertain future. Les Frigos (91 quai Panhard et Levassor, 13th), former concrete SNCF refrigerated warehouses, with dramatic freezer pipes running across ceilings and massive iron doors, became artists' and musicians' studios in the 1980s, but are nonetheless struggling to keep their place in the masterplan. Just beyond them, the Grands Moulins de Paris, a series of grandiose flour mills, were damaged recently in a fire but could survive as part of a future university complex; while near the Périphérique, the Compressed Air Building awaits a purpose – perfect for an art exhibition space perhaps?

What is Paris?

Within a couple of decades the city's social and cultural fabric has altered radically, leaving Parisians to wonder – is it still Paris?

October 12, 1999, was the day that the Printemps department store proudly declared on Métro posters that it had 'legalised shopping by men', a quaint notion in a city where the dictates of chic apply to anyone who can afford them. It was also the seventeenth anniversary of my arrival in Paris, for what was supposed to be a month-long visit. The Socialists had just taken power, promising to eliminate unemployment, to open a country closed in on itself and, most important, to 'change life'. What they changed can be felt, and sometimes seen, all over Paris.

Part of it is the internationalisation and abrupt modernisation of what was then, in many ways, a provincial city, self-sufficient in its grandeur, convinced by a quarter-century of Gaullist rhetoric that it could cut its own proud path in the world. Since the Single European Act made Europe a reality in 1985, foreign investment has skyrocketed, sowing profit and unease everywhere from the auction rooms of Drouot – now exposed to competition from Sotheby's and Christie's – to corporate boardrooms. American cinema, which in 1981 held what was considered a scandalous 30 per cent of the French market, now sells about two out of three tickets in the country. Paris is grander, richer and busier than ever, yet the natives wonder if it still belongs to them.

They have lived through a profound shift in values in a very short time. Parisians complain about the 'materialisation' of life, and the reduction of *élégance*, previously a matter of manners and presence, to the scale of a bank account. They struck back in the public service strikes of December 1995, the biggest protests in Paris since May 68, whose subtext, documented by stupefied pollsters, was the glaring divide between a privileged elite and the public it milks.

The Paris we saw through the down-and-out eyes of Orwell and Hemingway is mostly legend now; hardly anyone still lives on what a French proverb calls 'love and cold water'. The canaries in this coal mine were the *clochards*, neighbourhood bums who were fed with leftover soup from bistros and allowed to sleep off their hangovers in doorways. Unlike the Anglo-American vagabond, the *clochard* had a face and a history, and every one in the *quartier* knew both. In the late 1980s, as unemployment shot past the 3 million mark, he was overshadowed by the anonymous SDF (*sans domicile fixe*), the twin brother of the Reaganite

homeless, who invaded the streets and the Métro.

More than anything else, the *Grands Projets* (Great Projects) – the *Grand Louvre*, the Grande Arche de la Défense, the Cité des Sciences et de l'Industrie at La Villette, the Opéra Bastille, the Musée d'Orsay, the Institut du Monde Arabe, the imposing bunker of the Ministry of Finances at Bercy and the Bibliothèque Nationale François Mitterrand – altered the fabric of Paris. They made this city, once again, the cultural capital of Europe, as the late President François Mitterrand dreamed. But their operating costs and the drive for profitability that ensued sapped the egalitarian notion that the best things in Paris are free. For the first time, the renovated Louvre stopped offering a weekly free day (after an outcry, it restored one per month). As a prominent figure on the right proclaimed: 'The Louvre is our very own Disneyland.' Paris became a machine that generates increasingly expensive fun.

The *Grands Projets* also drew the rich into the remaining 'popular' neighbourhoods of the city's east and north – the Marais, Bastille, Porte de Pantin. About two-thirds of the one-star hotels that served as way-stations for expats like myself have disappeared, bought out by speculators and upgraded, along with thousands of *chambres de bonne* (maids' rooms) and rent-controlled apartments. This is one reason that half a million people have moved out of Paris in the past decade, making it an older, richer place.

That upwardly mobile process continues. Even the Goutte d'Or, the medieval winemaking centre which, by the early 1980s, more closely resembled Casablanca's casbah than Paris, has been redeveloped. This is not necessarily bad: the Thieves' Market on the boulevard de la Chapelle was a great place to lose your wallet or your blood, and the Halle St-Pierre museum at the foot of Sacré-Coeur champions artists excluded by the icy contemporary collections of the state. Likewise, the Canal St-Martin, where Arletty fashioned her whore's fantasies around Louis Jouvet in *Hôtel du Nord*, is less sinister since the *branché* (hip) crowd discovered it. The question is whether you prefer comfort to local colour, with all the dangers it contains.

Café society survives, though in a profoundly altered form. Bookshops and the landmark Drugstore at the heart of St-Germain, where you could find cigarettes or someone you knew on a Sunday, have been turned into fashion emporia and hair salons. The intellectual scene is still there, but you have to run harder, further and later to keep up with it. People work longer hours now – evening rush in the Métro starts around six and often continues till nine – and their average daily commute has grown from five kilometers in the 1960s to 30 today.

Walk along the rue du Faubourg St-Denis, where the passage Brady serves as the nerve centre for the city's Indian and Turkish populations. There are more beauty shops here for African women than for Frenchwomen, and the best deals on chicken are found in Islamic butchers. The renewal of the Parisian working classes comes from these people.

Since 1981, they have been defined as the 'Immigrant Problem', the central motif of French politics. Not all foreigners pose a problem, of course. Folks like me – educated refugees from Reaganism, Thatcherism, Sovietism, Pinochet and Peking – were assiduously courted by the Socialists. But while rebel Chinese students were prominently featured in the 1989 bicentennial parade, and the Chinese artist Chen Zen represented France at the last Venice Biennale, the government's servile appeasement of Peking is the subject of disgusted commentary in *Le Monde*. Likewise, the honours that former Minister of Culture Jack Lang showered on foreign artists obscured the hypocrisy of official 'multicultural' policies. At the end of the 1980s, while car-burning riots exploded amid the housing towers of the decayed immigrant cités, French rockers were more worried about collecting subsidies than out-clashing the Clash.

The other five million immigrants in the country – a plurality from Iberia, the East after Berlin lost its Wall, the Maghreb and Francophone Africa, Tamils and Kurds – have been cruelly used by both left and right. In 1981 the Socialists legalised hundreds of thousands of 'clandestine' immigrants, then ordered prosecutors to crack down on foreigners in time for elections. They also took calculated steps – guaranteed media time, changed voting rules – to ensure that the neo-fascist National Front, which took a measly 0.18 per cent of the vote in 1981, would get into the National Assembly by feeding on the Gaullist electorate. In 1986 the Gaullists legislated the Pasqua Act, which provided for expeditious and often arbitrary expulsion of immigrants, and when the Socialists took back power in 1988, they enforced it. Not until 1998, when the World Cup was won by a French team whose heroes included Africans and Arabs, did politicians begin to realise that the public was no longer scared of foreigners. That was already obvious to anyone who listens to radio; since 1994, *raï* and rap have climbed the charts that were topped by *variété* a decade earlier.

Meanwhile, you felt Le Pen and his Front like the dregs of a nightmare. From 1987-92 they won a solid block of seats in the regional council of the Ile-de-France, which includes Paris. In 1995 the Front captured three cities in sweet Provence, and attained 40 per cent of the vote in Melun. It isn't that the French are racist; more important, the Front claimed a monopoly on the issues of cutting taxes and fighting corruption, as left and right raised the state's share of national wealth to a current 45.3 per cent, and their leaders were hauled to court for soliciting bribes and enriching their relatives. By 1997, the Gaullists were cutting open deals with the FN to hold the Regional Councils. Miraculously, the Front shattered in an internal power struggle in December 1998, one of the best Christmases in memory.

The anxiety that clung to immigrants survives the Front, but its object is *les Anglo-Saxons*, seen as the new, unchallenged masters of the world. Anglo-American feminism is upheld as the model to avoid in sexual relations, Anglophone corporations are fingered as closet totalitarians, and the English-language media has been conceptualised as weapons against the French mind. There is something real behind these charges: France is unique, and the French want it to stay that way. The irony is that it will, anyway, if Paris is any indication. It is not what it was when I got here, but it isn't like any place else. *Mark Hunter*

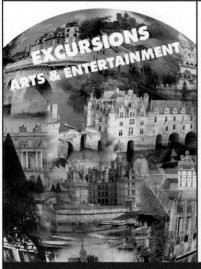

Sightseeing

48-Hour Paris

Two days in the city? Ten musts for making the most of your visit.

Classic Paris

• Begin where it all started on Ile de la Cité, with a visit to **Notre Dame** and the **Sainte-Chapelle**.
• Admire the Cour Carrée before entering the **Louvre** through IM Pei's Pyramid, for a sampling of the treasures in the art museum to beat all art museums.
• Walk through the Marais – with the intimate **place des Vosges**, the **Musée Carnavalet** and the works of the master in the **Musée Picasso**.
• Immerse yourself in Monet's waterlilies at the **Musée Marmottan – Claude Monet**.
• Catch up on culture with a night at the opera or ballet in the glamorous marble halls of **Palais Garnier** or a Molière classic at the **Comédie Française**.
• Brave the crowds at the **Grands Magasins**.
• Be tempted at the **Marché Mouffetard**, one of the best food markets in Paris.
• Stroll in the **Jardins du Luxembourg**, the quintessential Paris park, with its statues, joggers, pony rides and the French Senate.
• Play at café society with the literati at the **Café de Flore** before shopping in the elegant fashion, furniture boutiques and art galleries of St-Germain-des-Prés.
• Feast on oysters at a classic brasserie: **Bofinger**, **Gallopin** or **La Coupole**.

Alternative Paris

• Tog yourself out in fleamarket *frippes* at the Marché Malik in the **Marché aux Puces de Clignancourt** (Sat-Mon) or at **Antik Batik**.
• Stock up on organic food – and wine – at the **Marché Biologique Raspail** (Sun morning).
• Be dazzled by Moreau's jewel-like symbolist paintings at the **Musée Gustave Moreau** or wonder at the mystical *Lady and the Unicorn* at the **Musée National du Moyen Age (Cluny)**.
• Join multi-ethnic Paris – Arab, African, Chinese, Jewish – at the market along **boulevard de Belleville** (Tue, Fri mornings).
• Study the New Age literature, 60s plastic and record stores on **rue Keller** and rue de Charonne.
• Soak at the *hammam,* followed by mint tea in the Moorish tea room at the **Mosquée de Paris**, then keep up the theme with an exhibition or classical Arab music at the **Institut du Monde Arabe**.
• Commune with the spirits at **Cimetière du Père Lachaise** – and say hello to Jim Morrison, Oscar Wilde and medieval lovers Abélard and Héloïse.
• Eat a wholesome veggie meal at **La Ville de Jagganath** or **Aquarius**.
• Take in an alternative circus at the **Espace Chapiteaux** at La Villette, dance *à deux* at Le Bal (fortnightly) at the **Elysée Montmartre**.
• Have a nightcap at hippy throwback **Polly Magoo**.

Trendy Paris

• Walk through the Marais with its beautiful buildings and succession of offbeat clothes, design and gift shops; pose over tea at **Le Loir dans la Théière** or for coffee (and sci-fi loos) at **L'Etoile Manquante**. Stop off for the latest photo show at the **Maison Européenne de la Photographie**.
• Visit the reopened and reinvigorated **Centre Pompidou**: the artworks of the Musée National d'Art Moderne, temporary exhibitions, film series, debates and the aerial escalator view.
• People spot over lunch at the **Pause Café** or a drink at the **Barrio Latino** at the Bastille.
• View hip young artists at the galleries on **rue Louise-Weiss**, then sway to DJs, live bands and art exhibits on board the **Batofar**, moored in front of the **Bibliothèque Nationale François Mitterrand**.
• Check out fashion and design essentials at **Colette** and have a drink in the basement water bar.
• Browse the new **Antoine et Lili** by the Canal St-Martin, before tapas **Chez Prune**.
• Down a Mojito on bar-filled **rue Oberkampf**.
• Forget the Arc de Triomphe, get the modern view from the top of the **Grande Arche de la Défense**.
• Head to the Champs-Elysées (yes, it's in again) for dinner at **Food, Spoon & Wine** or **Man Ray**, before dropping in (if you can get past the door) to check out the excess at **Queen**.

Kids' Paris

• Start at the top, go high up the **Eiffel Tower**, then in circles on the Champ de Mars merry-go-round.
• See the flora and fauna at the **Jardin des Plantes**, with live beasts in the **Ménagerie** and stuffed specimens and skeletons in the **Muséum National d'Histoire Naturelle**.
• Take to the river on a Seine **boat trip** for an instant panorama of the riverside sights (Louvre, Musée d'Orsay, Eiffel Tower, Institut de France).
• Take the funicular up the *butte* Montmartre, for **Sacré Coeur** and the street artists in place du Tertre.
• Lick an ice cream from **Berthillon**.
• Mummies please: visit the Egyptian department at the **Musée du Louvre**, with its whole chamber of embalmed cats and dogs.
• Descend into the gloomy entrails of the **Catacombes** for legions of skulls and crossbones.
• Dine at kitsch Chinese restaurant **Le Président** or **New Nioullaville** in Belleville.
• Explore **La Villette** with its Chinese dragon slide, red *folies*, **Géode** IMAX cinema and the **Cité des Sciences et de l'Industrie**.
• Brave the African masks and smiling crocodiles at the **Musée des Arts d'Afrique et d'Océanie**.

In Perspective

We have divided the city – as Parisians traditionally do – into Right Bank (*Rive Droite*) and Left Bank (*Rive Gauche*), with the Seine and its islands running through the middle. Each has its own image and many Parisians – although they may live one side and work on the other – are passionately attached to their Left or Right Bank identity. The Right Bank has long symbolised commerce and entertainment, clubs and cabaret. The Left Bank is more literary and intellectual, with its universities, famous cafés and arthouse cinemas.

The divisions are, of course, more complex, with the grand and the intimate, the old and the new, the sacred and the profane all mingling on both sides of the river. On the Right Bank, the Faubourg-St-Antoine, with its craftsmen's alleyways and tradition of working-class revolt, is a very long way from the bourgeois, residential 16th, itself light years from gaudy Pigalle, while even the business-dominated area near the Bourse shifts imperceptibly into the rag trade of Sentier, or south with the quiet passages surrounding the Palais-Royal.

Indeed, one can argue for an east-west division of Paris: the bourgeois, businessy west versus the working-class east with its immigrant mix. Here again, there's a grain of truth and plenty of exceptions. What you will find everywhere is a lived-in city made up of distinctive *quartiers*: it's not just a question of monuments, but the people who throng there, that make the different districts fascinating to explore.

The city continues to evolve, in both planned developments (the Seine Rive Gauche development around the new Bibliothèque Nationale) and a more organic process (the oddball bars around the Canal St-Martin). Bookshops and cinemas still line the Latin Quarter, students still pour out of the

Sorbonne, but smart fashion groups associated with Faubourg-St-Honoré and avenue Montaigne have colonised St-Germain-des-Prés, in a sometimes uneasy relationship with its more bohemian intellectual past. Artists and students have moved on to the cheaper, anarchic bars of Ménilmontant, philosophers argue it out at the Bastille, while the Marais, known for its museums and historic mansions, also hosts Paris' ever-more visible gay pulse. And who could have imagined that the Champs-Elysées, long given over to chain stores and fast food, would once again be colonised by the smart set?

Paris has always gone through waves of urban planning, be it Charles V putting up a defensive wall in the fourteenth century, Colbert honouring Louis XIV with regal squares in the seventeenth, or Haussmann building new roads in the nineteenth. Planning continues today, as different areas are in their turn developed. Despite its historical aura, Paris is a modern city, with some of the bravest recent architectural interventions in Europe, and a whole wave of new parks, new museums and housing projects that are breathing life into previously neglected corners.

Luckily for the visitor, Paris is easy to get around and its geography easy to comprehend. The city is divided into 20 *arrondissements* which form a snail-shell spiral beginning at Notre-Dame and finishing at Porte de Montreuil, on the eastern edge of the city limits. Public transport is plentiful and it's easy to walk between many of the major sights. The Seine, whose banks are easily bridged, is at the heart of the city's past, and at the forefront of its plans for the future: new footbridges continue to link the two *rives*, the quais may one day be slightly less traffic-laden and a new riverside walk is envisaged.

Ile de Chatou

Renoir painted *Le Déjeuner des Canotiers* at the bucolic Maison Fournaise. The island is liveliest during the spring and autumn ham and antiques fair.

Ile de la Jatte

The Ile de la Jatte was immortalised in Seurat's promenade scene *La Grande Jatte*. Nowadays restaurant Café de la Jatte is a popular media spot and a favourite with families for Sunday lunch.

Levallois Perret

Nanterre

S E I N E

Downstream

After numerous loops, via vast Port de Gennevilliers and barging centre Conflans Ste-Honorine, the river meanders past new towns Poissy and Mantes-la-Jolie and the troglodyte **Château de la Roche-Guyon**, through **Rouen** and past the ruined abbey at Jumièges and on to its estuary between Le Havre and Honfleur, where it enters the Channel.

La Défense

Ile de la Jatte

Ile de Puteaux

P A R I S

Allée des Cygnes

Bois de Boulogne

Ile Séguin

The vast, delapidated relics of the former Renault car factory (founded at **Boulogne-Billancourt** in 1898) are soon to be redeveloped.

Statue of Liberty

Horses' bones and dead Protestants were dumped on this island in the sixteenth century; now it's a quiet place to walk. The scaled-down *Statue of Liberty* at the western end is the original maquette designed by Bartholdi and cast in France as a gift to New York.

'The water of the Seine sometimes purges foreigners slightly. What they see as a bad thing is however a benefit; it is a gentle natural purgation, which calms the nerves and the digestive system affected by partaking in too large quantity of new food'. (**Dr Audin Rovière, seventeenth century**)

The Seine

The Seine is the lifeblood of Paris: not simply of its historic heart, but also of the new Paris fast being built up around Bercy and the new Bibliothèque Nationale. Most of the city's great sights line its banks – one reason why you'll now see more tourist boats than freight barges. Beside the river, the cobbled *berges* make a pleasant breather from the streets above. They were the brainchild of the Comte de Laborde, who envisaged 'the splendours of antiquity combined with the delights of Benares on the banks of the Ganges', soon perhaps to come to fruition in a new Seine-side footpath.

Péniches

The artistic or bohemian enjoy abandoning terra firma for the watery life. Boats, moored at various points along the Seine, range from shabby to sophisticated but are often capable of casting off on trips. If anyone should fall overboard, there is a separate river police to fish them out.

Ile de la Cité

Ile St-Louis

Passerelle de Solférino

Designed by architect engineer Marc Mimram, Paris' newest footbridge opened in autumn 1999 linking the **Tuileries** on the *Rive Droite* to **Musée d'Orsay** on the *Rive Gauche*.

Bridges

37 bridges cross the Seine within Paris (due to be joined by the Bercy footbridge). The oldest surviving bridge is the paradoxically named **Pont Neuf**, opened by Henri IV in 1605, and the first not to have houses atop it. Most romantic is the metal **Pont des Arts** footbridge between the Institut de France and the Louvre. Most ornate is the **Pont Alexandre III**, built for the 1900 *Exposition Universelle*. Most practical is rebuilt **Pont de l'Alma** – the Zouave statue measures the height of the water when the river floods.

Musée de Sculpture en Plein Air

Despite boasting works by Zadkine, Schoffer and César, the outdoor sculpture show on quai St-Bernard often seems more popular with courting couples than art lovers.

Charenton-le-Pont

M A R N E

Upstream

Just outside Fontainebleau, the Yonne meets the Seine. The Yonne is longer than the Seine and therefore should have given its name to the capital's great artery, but tradition has proved stronger than logic; besides, the Seine emerges romantically from the vineyards of Burgundy, whereas the Yonne draws its source from undistinguished hills in the Nièvre.

The Marne

This tributary is famous for popular riverside *guinguette* dance halls, where families go at weekends to be inebriated by the sound of the accordion and the clink of full glasses.

The Islands

At its heart yet distinctly apart from the rest of Paris, Ile de la Cité and Ile St-Louis offer contrasting histories but plenty of island graces.

Ile de la Cité

In the 1st and 4th arrondissements.

The Ile de la Cité was the site of the settlement that grew into Paris, first founded in around 250 BC by the Parisii, and centre of political and religious power under the Romans and in the Middle Ages.

When Victor Hugo wrote *Notre Dame de Paris* in 1831, the Ile de la Cité was a bustling medieval quarter of narrow streets and tall wooden houses: 'the head, heart and very marrow of Paris'. Baron Haussmann put paid to that; he supervised the expulsion of 25,000 people from the island, razing homes, flattening some twenty churches and obliterating most streets. The lines of the old streets in front of Notre Dame are traced into the parvis.

The people were forced to resettle in the east of the city, leaving behind a few large buildings – the **Conciergerie**, the law courts, the Hôtel Dieu hospital, the police headquarters and, of course, **Notre Dame**. The island now plays host to the pillars of officialdom and hordes of tour coaches during the day, but otherwise can seem rather soulless.

The most charming spot is the western tip, where the **Pont Neuf** spans the Seine. Despite its name it is the oldest remaining bridge in Paris, its arches bordered by grimacing faces, supposedly those of Henri IV's courtiers. Go down the steps to a leafy triangular garden known as the square du Vert-Galant. With a wonderful view of the river, it's a great spot for summer picnics, or you can take a boat trip from the quai with the Vedettes du Pont-Neuf. In the centre of the bridge is a statue of Henri IV on his horse, first erected in 1635, destroyed in the Revolution, and then replaced in 1818. On the island-side of the Pont Neuf is the secluded place Dauphine, home to quiet restaurants and wine bars and the belovedly seedy **Hôtel Henri IV**. André Malraux had a Freudian analysis of its appeal – 'the sight of its triangular formation with slightly curved lines, and of the slit which bisects its two wooded spaces. It is, without doubt, the sex of Paris.' Built in 1607, it was, like the place des Vosges, commissioned by Henri IV, who named it in honour of his son, the Dauphin and future King Louis XIII. The red brick and stone houses look out on both *quais* and square, the third, eastern side was demolished in the 1870s.

Lining the Seine on the island's north bank, the view is dominated by the medieval towers of the **Conciergerie**. Along with the Palais de Justice,

it was originally part of the Palais de la Cité, residential and administration complex of the Capetian kings. Long the city's principal fortress, it stands on the probable site of an earlier Merovingian fortress and, before that, the Roman governor's house. In 1358, after Etienne Marcel's uprising caused Charles V to move the royal retinue into the Louvre, it became a prison where people were incarcerated before being executed. The interior is worth visiting for its Gothic vaulted halls, vast kitchens and recreated prison cells, which give a vivid idea of the reality of the French revolution.

Nearby, amid the law courts is the **Sainte-Chapelle**, Pierre de Montreuil's masterpiece of stained glass and slender Gothic columns. It was built as a royal chapel to house relics brought back from the Crusades by France's sainted king, Louis IX. Surrounding it, the Palais de Justice evolved alongside the Conciergerie, enclosing the chapel, and, rebuilt after a serious fire in 1776, entirely

Pont Neuf: *older than it sounds.*

blocking off the chapel's north side. The Neo-Classical entrance courtyard and fine wrought-iron grille date from the 1780s reconstruction by Desmaisons and Antoine. After going through security, you can wander through the marble corridors, visit the Salle des Pas Perdus, busy with plaintiffs and barristers, and sit in on cases in the civil and criminal courts. The Palais is still the centre of the French legal system, but this could change as the government has proposed moving the law courts out to the 13th or 15th *arrondissement*.

Across the boulevard du Palais, behind the tribunal du Commerce, **place Louis Lépine** is now filled by a flower market (9.30am-6.30pm Mon-Sat), and a twittering bird market on Sundays. To the south is the Préfecture de Police, known by its address, quai des Orfèvres, and immortalised in Simenon's *Maigret* detective novels. East of the market sprawls the **Hôtel-Dieu**, founded in the seventh century and rebuilt in the 1860s on the site of a foundling hospital. During the Middle Ages, once inside, your chances of survival were slim. Today it's one of the main hospitals for central Paris, but a much quieter and safer place.

The eastern end of the island is dominated by **Notre Dame** cathedral, with its twin-towered west front, sculpted portals and buttressed east end. Don't miss the ascent to the roof to admire the ghoulish gargoyles and fine view. Look for the bronze marker in front of the cathedral, known as Kilomètre Zéro, the point from which all distances are measured. The **Crypte Archéologique** under the parvis gives a sense of the island's multi-layered past, when it was a tangle of alleys, houses, churches and cabarets.

North-east of the cathedral are a few medieval streets untouched by Haussmann, such as rue Chanoinesse – built to house canons of Notre Dame, rue de la Colombe, rue des Ursins and the narrow rue des Chantres. On the corner of rue des Ursins and rue des Chantres is a pseudo-medieval house restored in the 1950s by architect Fernand Pouillon for the Aga Khan. Steps away from the cathedral at rue du Cloître-Notre-Dame is Le Vieux Bistro, one of the best traditional bistros in Paris. At 9 quai aux Fleurs, commemorated in a stone tablet, was the house where Héloïse lived with her uncle Canon Fulbert, who had her lover Abélard castrated.

In a small garden on the eastern tip of the island is the **Mémorial de la Déportation** (10am-noon, 2-5pm daily), a tribute to the thousands deported to death camps during World War II. Visitors descend a blind staircase to river level, where simple chambers are inscribed with the names of deportees.

Cathédrale Notre Dame de Paris

pl du Parvis-Notre-Dame, 4th (01.42.34.56.10). Mº Cité/RER St-Michel. **Open** 8am-6.45pm daily; *towers* (01.44.32.16.70) 10am-4.30pm daily, entrance at north tower. **Admission** free; *towers* 35F; 25F 12-25s; free under-12s. **No credit cards. Map J7**

Keen to outdo the impressive new abbey at St-Denis, Bishop Maurice de Sully decided to construct a grandiose new edifice for the city. Begun in 1163 the Gothic masterpiece was not completed until 1345, straddling two architectural eras – the great galleried churches of the twelfth century and the buttressed cathedrals which followed – but the overall result is very harmonious. Among its famous features are the three glorious rose windows, and the doorways of the west front, with their sculpted tympanums and rows of saints: the Last Judgement (centre), Life of the Virgin (left), Life of St-Anne (right). In the 1630s Robert de Cotte destroyed the rood screen and choir stalls, making way for the new choir and grille completed only in 1708-25 for Louis XIV. During the Revolution, the cathedral was turned into a temple of reason and a wine warehouse, and the statues of the Kings of Judah higher up the facade were destroyed – those seen today are replicas. Several of the originals were discovered in 1979 and are now on show at the Musée National du Moyen Age. The cathedral was returned to its ceremonial role for Napoléon's coronation as Emperor in 1804, but by the nineteenth century, the structure had fallen into such dilapidation that artists, among them Victor Hugo, petitioned King Louis-Philippe to restore the cathedral, which was masterfully done by Viollet-le-Duc. During the Nazi occupation, the stained-glass windows were removed, numbered and replaced with sandbags to save them from destruction. The cathedral has been undergoing a long-term renovation programme, as sculptures are cleaned or replaced after centuries of pollution and pigeons, but you can once again climb the north bell tower, leading to a gallery adorned with gargoyles.

La Conciergerie

1 quai de l'Horloge, 1st (01.53.73.78.50). Mº Cité/RER Châtelet-Les Halles. **Open** *Apr-Oct* 9.30am-6.30pm daily; *Nov-Mar* 10am-5pm daily. **Admission** 35F; 23F 12-25s, students; free under-12s; 50F with Sainte Chapelle. **No credit cards. Map J6**
The Conciergerie looks like the forbidding medieval fortress and prison it once was. Yet, after damage from fires and revolution much of the pseudo-medieval facade was added in the 1850s; the thirteenth-century Bonbec tower survives from the palace of the Capetian kings. On the corner of boulevard du Palais, the Tour de l'Horloge, built in 1370, was the first public clock in Paris. A visit takes you through the huge medieval kitchens, the Salle des Gardes and the Salle des Gens d'Armes, an impressive vaulted Gothic hall built in 1301-15 for Philippe le Bel. It gradually became a prison under the watch of the Concierge. Inside you can see the cell where Marie-Antoinette was held during the Revolution. Her enemies Danton and Robespierre later ended up here too, following thousands of others who were guillotined under the Terror. The wealthy could pay for the luxury of a private cell with their own furniture; others were crowded together on beds of straw.

La Conciergerie *is where the Concierge took care of Revolutionary prisoners.*

A list of Revolutionary prisoners, including a florist and a hairdresser, shows that far from all were nobles. The Chapelle des Girondins contains Marie-Antoinette's crucifix and a guillotine blade.

La Crypte Archéologique

pl du Parvis-Notre-Dame, 4th (01.43.29.83.51).
M° Cité/RER St-Michel. **Open** *Apr-Oct* 10am-5.30pm; *Nov-Mar* 10am-4.30pm. **Admission** 32F; 21F 12-25s; free under-12s. **No credit cards. Map J7**
The excavations under the parvis span sixteen centuries, from the remains of Gallo-Roman ramparts and a hypocaust, complete with furnace and brick piles, to a nineteenth-century drain. They give a good idea of the city's evolution, with fifteenth-century cellars built into old Roman walls and remains of medieval streets alongside foundations of an eighteenth-century foundling hospital.

Sainte-Chapelle

4 bd du Palais, 1st (01.53.73.78.50). M° Cité/RER Châtelet-Les Halles. **Open** *Apr-Sept* 9.30am-6.30pm daily; *Oct-Mar* 10am-5pm daily. **Admission** 35F; 23F 12-25s, students; free under-12s; 50F with Conciergerie. **Credit** (shop) MC, V. **Map J6**
Inside a courtyard of the Palais de Justice is the exquisite Sainte-Chapelle. Devout King Louis IX (1226-70), later known as St Louis, was a collector of holy relics, often of doubtful authenticity. In the 1240s he ordered Pierre de Montreuil to design a suitable shrine in which to house the Crown of Thorns, which he had just bought. The chapel was built on two levels, the upper one for the monarch, his family and the canons, the lower chapel (repainted under the Second Empire) for palace servants. The chapel is a monument to High Gothic style, its upper level appears to consist almost entirely of stained glass. Bring binoculars to best view the windows, which depict Biblical scenes, and come on a sunny day, when coloured reflections dapple the stone. The chapel is used for concerts by early music ensembles.

Ile St-Louis

In the 4th arrondissement.
The Ile St-Louis is one of the most exclusive residential addresses in the city – discreet and self-contained rather than show-off. Delightfully unspoiled, it has a mix of fine architecture, narrow streets and magnificent views from the tree-lined *quais*.

For hundreds of years the island was a swampy pasture belonging to Notre Dame and a retreat for fishermen, boaters, swimmers and lovers, known as the Ile Notre Dame. In the fourteenth century Charles V built a fortified canal through the middle, thus creating the Ile aux Vaches ('Island of Cows'). Its real-estate potential wasn't realised until 1614, when speculator Christophe Marie persuaded Louis XIII to fill in the canal (now rue Poulletier) and plan streets, bridges and houses. The island was renamed in honour of the King's pious predecessor and, although Marie went bankrupt, the venture proved a huge success. It became highly fashionable as a site for elegant new residences from the 1630s on, thanks to the interest shown by society architect Louis Le Vau, who designed many of the *hôtels* on quai d'Anjou (including his own house at No 3), quai de Bourbon and quai de Béthune, as well as the **Eglise St-Louis-en-l'Ile**. By the 1660s the island was filled, and unlike the Marais, where the smart reception rooms were at the rear of the courtyard, here they were often at the front to allow their residents riverside views.

Running lengthways through the island is the **rue St-Louis-en-l'Ile**, lined with quirky gift shops, quaint tea rooms, lively stone-walled bars and restaurants, as well as fine historic buildings. At the eastern end, the grandiose Hôtel Lambert (2 rue St-Louis-en-l'Ile/1 quai d'Anjou), was built by Le Vau in 1641 for Louis XIII's secretary, with stone lions and palm trees, arranged around *cour d'honneur* and garden, the *hôtel* was famed for its interiors by Le Sueur, Perrier and Le Brun; at 51, the Hôtel Chenizot has a fabulous *rocaille* doorway adorned by a bearded faun and balcony supported by grim-faced dragons. No 54 was once a real tennis court, now the **Hôtel du Jeu de Paume**. At No 31 **Berthillon**, purveyor of the best ice cream in town, often draws a queue down the street, and there are more tempting goodies at L'Epicerie (No 51), Provençal beauty products at **L'Occitane** (No 55) or cheeses at La Ferme St-Aubin (No 76). At the western end, where there are great views of the flying buttresses of Notre Dame and a footbridge across to the Ile de la Cité, are the Flore en l'Ile tea room, and the popular **Brasserie de l'Isle-St-Louis**, which draws Parisians and tourists alike, including many rugby fans.

Among the finest buildings on the island, the 1657 Hôtel de Lauzun (17 quai d'Anjou) with gilded, scaled sea-serpent drainpipes and, even rarer, its original interior with lavish *trompe l'oeils* in the Petit Cabinet and in the bedroom. Here lived La Grande Mademoiselle, cousin of Louis XIV and mistress of the dashing Duc de Lauzun, whose salon was frequented by Racine, Molière and La Fontaine. In the 1840s, it was owned by literary aficionado Jérôme Pichon, who rented out rooms to artists and writers, among them Baudelaire, who wrote part of *Les Fleurs du Mal* here. There are further literary associations at 6 quai d'Orléans, where the Adam Mickiewicz library-museum (01.43.54.35.61/open 2-6pm Thur) is dedicated to the Polish romantic poet who lived in Paris 1832-40.

Eglise St-Louis-en-l'ile

19bis rue St-Louis-en-l'Ile, 4th (01.46.34.11.60).
M° Pont-Marie. **Open** 3-7pm Mon; 9am-noon, 3-7pm Tue-Sun. **Map L7**
Built 1664-1765, following plans by Louis Le Vau and completed by Gabriel Le Duc. The interior follows the classic Baroque model with Corinthian columns and a sunburst over the altar, and is a popular classical concert venue.

Right Bank

From the bucolic to the anarchic, from the industrial to the institutional, the scintillating story of Paris comes to life here.

The Louvre to Concorde

In the 1st arrondissement.

When the monarchs moved from the Ile de la Cité to spacious new quarters on the Right Bank, the Louvre and secondary palaces of the Tuileries and Palais-Royal became the centre of royal power, in an area still full of royal and imperial survivors.

Now a mecca for art-lovers, the **Palais du Louvre** remains the Parisian palace *par excellence*, with huge state rooms, fine courtyards and galleries stretching to the Jardin des Tuileries. Part of Philippe-Auguste's original twelfth-century fortress can be seen within the palace walls, though the Louvre only became the main royal residence in the fourteenth century, and later monarchs divided loyalties between it, the place des Vosges and Versailles. François 1er and his successors replaced the fortress with a more luxurious residence, the Cour Carrée. The Louvre was first opened to the public as a museum by the Revolutionary Convention in 1793, though it continued to be used by governments, royal, imperial or republican. Two hundred years later, the *Grand Louvre* scheme added IM Pei's pyramid in the Cour Napoléon, doubled the exhibition space and constructed the subterranean Carrousel du Louvre shopping mall, auditorium and food halls. Despite initial opposition, the pyramid has become part of the cityscape surprisingly quickly. The steel and glass structure is fascinating for its technical brilliance and the tricks it plays with the fountains. Floodlit by night, it has a mesmerising glow.

Most people now approach the Louvre by the Cour Napoléon from Palais-Royal (*see below*), but it's also worth walking through the peaceful Cour Carrée. The Lescot (western) facade is François 1er's original wing, adorned with writhing Mannerist figures, while through the southern archway you can see over the Pont des Arts footbridge to the Institut de France. An arch in the eastern wing leads through to rue de Louvre, with its grandiose colonnaded facade.

Opposite the palace, standing back from the street on place du Louvre is **St-Germain-l'Auxerrois**, once the French kings' parish church and home to the only original Flamboyant-Gothic porch in Paris. Mirroring it to the left, the other side of a fanciful belfry, is the nineteenth-century Neo-Gothic 1st *arrondissement* town hall, alongside the chic cocktail bar **Le Fumoir**.

The *Grand Louvre* has also rejuvenated the trio of museums run by the Union des Arts Décoratifs, the **Musée des Arts Décoratifs**, **Musée de la Mode et du Costume** and newly opened **Musée de la Publicité**, devoted to advertising, all located in the Galerie Nord. Between the north and south Galeries is the newly restored Arc du Carrousel, a mini-triumphal arch built 1806-09 by Napoléon in polychrome marble and surmounted by the famous Roman bronze horses that he borrowed from St Mark's in Venice. France was obliged to return them in 1815, and they were replaced with replicas in 1828. Through the arch you can now appreciate the extraordinary perspective, known as the *voie royale*, which leads through the restored Jardins du Carrousel and **Jardin des Tuileries** along the Champs-Elysées up to the Arc de Triomphe and beyond to the Grande Arche de la Défense. Originally stretching to the Tuileries palace (burnt down in the Commune), the gardens were laid out in the seventeenth century and remain a living space with cafés, ice-cream stalls and summer funfair. On the flanks of the Tuileries overlooking **place de la Concorde** stand the **Orangerie**, noted for its series of Monet water lilies (currently closed for renovation), and the **Jeu de Paume**, used for exhibitions of contemporary art.

Along the north side of the Louvre, the rue de Rivoli, created by Napoléon for military parades, is remarkable for its uniform, arcaded facades. It runs in a perfect line to place de la Concorde in one direction, to the Marais in the other, where it merges into rue St-Antoine. Though most shops here now sell souvenirs, elegant, old-fashioned hotels still remain, as do gentlemen's tailors, bookshops **WH Smith** and **Galignani**, and the famous tea room **Angelina**. The area formed a little England in the 1830s-40s as aristocracy, writers and artists flooded across the Channel after the Napoleonic Wars. They stayed at the Hôtel Meurice or in rue de la Paix and rue de Castiglione, reading the daily paper published by Galignani and dining in the restaurants of the Palais-Royal; at the time the area was described as 'a true quarter of London transposed to the banks of the Seine'.

At the western end of the Louvre, at the junction of rue de Rivoli and rue des Pyramides, have a look at place des Pyramides. The shiny gilt equestrian statue of Joan of Arc is one of four statues of her in the city – designed, along with Rodin's *Burghers of Calais*, to make Brits feel guilty.

Running parallel to rue de Rivoli, ancient rue St-Honoré features smart shops towards place Vendôme, local cafés and inexpensive bistros towards Les Halles. At No 296, the Baroque church of **St-Roch** is pitted with bullet holes left by Napoléon's troops when they put down a royalist revolt in 1795. Across rue St-Honoré, at 263bis, the 1670-76 Chapelle de l'Assomption has an outsize dome, so disproportionate that contemporaries dubbed it 'dumb dome' (*sot dôme*), a pun on Sodom. Just west of here, much talked-about, pristine-white boutique **Colette** at No 213 has given a shot of adrenaline to the area's rather staid shops. Opposite is rue du Marché St-Honoré, where Le Rubis wine bar hosts the scrum to taste Beaujolais Nouveau every November. It formerly led to the covered Marché St-Honoré (on the site of the Couvent des Jacobins, a famous revolutionary meeting-place), but the market has recently been replaced by the shiny glass and steel offices of the Paribas bank by Spanish architect Ricardo Bofill.

Further west along rue St-Honoré lies wonderful, eight-sided **place Vendôme**, one of Louis XIV's main contributions, with a perspective that now goes from rue de Rivoli up to Opéra.

At the west end of the Tuileries, place de la Concorde, laid out by Jacques Ange Gabriel for Louis XV, is a brilliant exercise in the use of open space. André Malraux called it 'the most beautiful architectural complex on this planet', and it's impossible not to recognise its grandeur, especially at night. The winged Marly horses (copies of the originals by Guillaume Coustou, now in the Louvre) frame the entrance to the Champs-Elysées. There are plans to redo the square and reduce traffic.

Leading to the Madeleine is rue Royale, with stuffy tea room **Ladurée** and the legendary Art Nouveau restaurant **Maxim's** (featured in Lehár's opera *The Merry Widow*). There are more smart shops and fashion-haunt **Buddha Bar** in rue Boissy d'Anglas, while the ultimate sporting luxuries can be found at Hermès on rue du Fbg-St-Honoré, home also to Guy Laroche, Karl Lagerfeld, Lanvin, Gucci and Lolita Lempicka. Fine porcelain, silverware and tea rooms are on the recently revamped Galerie Royale and Passage Royale.

Eglise St-Germain-l'Auxerrois

2 pl du Louvre, 1st (01.42.60.13.96). M° Louvre or Pont-Neuf. **Open** 8am-8pm daily. **Map H6**
This pretty church was for centuries the royal parish church. Its architecture spans several centuries of construction, mostly from the thirteenth to sixteenth. Most striking is the elaborate Flamboyant-Gothic porch dating from 1485. There's a fine doorway on the side built in 1570, which originally led to a cloister. Inside see the thirteenth-century lady chapel and a splendid canopied, carved bench designed by Le Brun. The church achieved notoriety on 24 Aug 1572, when the signal for the St-Bartholomew's Day massacre was rung from here.

Eglise St-Roch

296 rue St-Honoré, 1st (01.42.44.13.20). M° Pyramides or Tuileries. **Open** 8.30am-7.30pm daily. **Map G5**
Curious rather than beautiful, this surprisingly long church begun in the 1650s was designed mainly by Jacques Lemercier, although the lady chapel was designed c1700 by Hardouin-Mansart and the north facade added by Robert de Cotte later. The area was then the heart of Paris, and illustrious parishioners and patrons left notable funerary monuments: Le Nôtre, Mignard, Corneille and Diderot are all here. Look for busts by Coysevaux and Coustou and Falconet's statue *Christ on the Mount of Olives*. Paintings include works by Chassériau, Vignon and Le Sueur. In 1795, a bloody shoot-out occurred in front between royalists and conventionists, led by Napoléon, leaving bullet holes that still pit the facade.

Jardin des Tuileries

rue de Rivoli, 1st. M° Tuileries or Concorde. **Open** *summer* 7am-9pm Apr-Sept; *winter* 7.30am-7.30pm Sept-Mar. **Map G5**
Stretching between the Louvre and place de la Concorde, the gravelled alleyways here have been a fashionable promenade since they opened to the public in the sixteenth century. The gardens were laid out in roughly their present form by André Le Nôtre, who began his illustrious career as royal gardener here in 1664, before going on to such exalted commissions as Versailles and Vaux-le-Vicomte. He created the prototypical *jardin à la française* with its terraces and central vista running through round and octagonal ponds, and continuing along what would become the Champs-Elysées. When the Tuileries palace was burnt down by the Paris Commune in 1871, the park was expanded. As part of the *Grand Louvre* project, the most fragile sculptures, including Coysevox's winged horses, have been transferred to the Louvre and replaced by copies and the Maillol sculptures returned to the Jardins du Carrousel, while replanting has restored parts of Le Nôtre's design and renewed trees damaged by pollution. Several modern sculptures have recently been added to develop a 'living museum', including bronzes by Laurens, Moore, Ernst, Martin and Giacommetti and Dubuffet's *Le Bel Costume*. Gardeners should note the specialist bookshop by place de la Concorde.

Palais du Louvre

entrance through Pyramid, Cour Napoléon, 1st (01.40.20.50.50/recorded information 01.40.20.51.51). M° Palais-Royal. **Open** 9am-6pm Mon, Thur-Sun; 9am-9.45pm Wed. *Temporary exhibitions, Medieval Louvre* 10am-9.45pm Mon, Wed-Sun. **Admission** 45F (until 3pm); 26F Mon, Wed-Sat after 3pm, Sun; free under-18s first Sun of month. **Credit** MC, V. **Map H5**
Arguably the world's greatest art collection, the Louvre's miles of galleries take in antiquities and such icons as the *Mona Lisa* and Delacroix's *Liberty*

*IM Pei's striking pyramid, opened in 1989, is now the main entrance to **the Louvre**.*

Leading the People. The palace was home to generations of French monarchs from the fourteenth century. A section of the massive keep, built in the 1190s by Philippe-Auguste and turned into a royal residence in the mid-fourteenth century by Charles V, is now open to view in the new underground complex. In the 1540s, François 1er asked Pierre Lescot to begin a Renaissance palace (now the western wing of enclosed Cour Carrée). Continued by his successors, the different façades are etched with royal monograms – H interlaced with C and D for Henri II, his queen Catherine de Médicis and favourite Diane de Poitiers. Henri IV and Louis XIII completed the Cour Carrée and built the wing along the Seine. The pedimented façade along rue du Louvre was added by Perrault under Louis XIV, who also brought in Le Vau and Le Brun to refurbish the interior. After the court left for Versailles under Louis XIV, the royals abandoned the palace and the apartments were often occupied by artists and state servants. After the Revolution, Napoléon added the grand stairway by his architects Percier and Fontaine and built the galleries along rue de Rivoli, complete with imperial figures. His nephew Napoléon III added the Cour Napoléon.

The art collection was first opened to the public in 1793, but the Ministry of Finance remained in the palace until the 1980s, when the Louvre's latest great transformation, the *Grand Louvre* project, began, with the 1989 opening of the glass pyramid in the Cour Napoléon, designed by Sino-American architect IM Pei, now the museum's main entrance, and the opening of the Richelieu Wing in 1993, which doubled the exhibition space. *See also chapters* **Museums** *and* **Music: Classical & Opera**.

Place de la Concorde

1st/8th. M° Concorde. **Map F5**
Designed by Jacques Ange Gabriel for Louis XV in 1753 (and then called place Louis XV), this is the largest square in Paris, with open perspectives stretching east-west from the Louvre to the Arc de Triomphe and north-south from the Madeleine to the Assemblée Nationale across the Seine. In 1792, the statue of Louis XV was removed from the centre and a revolutionaries' guillotine set up in its place for the execution of Louis XVI, Marie-Antoinette and many more. Gabriel also designed the two grandiose colonnaded mansions on either side of rue Royale: the one on the west houses the exclusive Crillon hotel and an automobile club, the other is the Navy Ministry. In the 1830s, the square was embellished with the tiered wedding-cake fountains, sturdy lamp-posts and the Luxor obelisk, from the temple of Ramses II in Thebes, a present from the Viceroy of Egypt. Best view is by night, from the terrace by the Jeu de Paume at the end of the Tuileries gardens.

Place Vendôme

1st. M° Tuileries or Opéra. **Map G4**
Elegant place Vendôme got its name from the *hôtel particulier* built by the Duc de Vendôme previously on this site. Inaugurated in 1699 as part of Colbert's grandiose town-planning schemes to glorify Louis XIV, the eight-sided *place* was conceived by Hardouin-Mansart to show off an equestrian statue of the Sun King. The statue was torn down in 1792, and in 1806 the Colonne de la Grande Armée was erected, modelled on Trajan's column in Rome and illustrated with a spiral comic strip illustrating Napoléon's military exploits, made out of 1250 Russian and Austrian cannons captured at the battle of Austerlitz. During the 1871 Commune this symbol of 'brute force and false glory' was pulled down by revolutionaries, at the instigation of painter Courbet, who was subsequently condemned to pay for its restoration. The present column is a replica, retaining most of the original frieze. Hardouin-Mansart only designed the façades; the buildings behind were put up by various nobles and speculators. Today the square is home to Cartier, Boucheron, Van Cleef & Arpels and other prestigious jewellers and fashion names, banks, the Justice Ministry and the Ritz. Chopin died at No 12, in 1849.

Palais-Royal & financial Paris

In the 1st and 2nd arrondissements.
Across the rue de Rivoli from the Louvre, past the **Louvre des Antiquaires** antiques superstore, stands the **Palais-Royal**, once Cardinal Richelieu's private mansion and now home to the Conseil d'Etat and Ministry of Culture; on the south-west corner is the **Comédie Française** theatre. The company created by Louis XIV in 1680 moved here in 1790, a spiritual homecoming, as Molière, who was at the origin of the troupe and remains the backbone of its repertoire, died nearby at 40 rue de Richelieu. (The playwright is commemorated in the Molière fountain on rue de Richelieu, designed by Visconti.) The brass-fronted Café Nemours on place Colette is popular with thespians. George Sand used to buy her tobacco across the square at cigar shop A la Civette.

Now cherished for tranquility, in the 1780s the Palais-Royal was a rumbustious centre of Parisian life, where aristocrats and the grubby inhabitants of the *faubourgs* rubbed shoulders in subversive abandon. The coffeehouses in its arcades attracted radical debate. Here Camille Desmoulins called the city to arms on the eve of Bastille Day. After the Napoleonic Wars, Wellington and Field Marshal von Blücher supposedly lost so much money at the gambling dens that Parisians claimed they had won back their entire dues for war reparations. In Balzac's day the area housed a leprous twilight world of debauched gaming rooms, prostitutes and courtesans, depicted in such novels as *La Peau de chagrin*. Only haute-cuisine restaurant **Le Grand Véfour** (17 rue de Beaujolais) survives from this era, although there are several less sumptuous places to eat *al fresco*. Wander under the arcades to browse in this eccentric world of antiques dealers, philatelists and specialists in tin soldiers and musical boxes, the period housewares and kitsch contemporanea of

*Once a hotbed of gambling and prostitution, the **Palais-Royal** today is far more genteel.*

Galerie Jean de Rohan-Chabot, tablewares of **Muriel Grateau** or vintage clothes specialist **Didier Ludot**. Go through the arcades to rue de Montpensier to the west, and the neo-rococo Théâtre du Palais-Royal. Opposite, next to busy bar L'Entracte, is one of several narrow, stepped passages that run between this road and rue de Richelieu, which with parallel rue Ste-Anne is a focus of Paris' Japanese community, all sushi restaurants and noodle bars.

Squeezed between the elegant calm of the Palais-Royal and the frenzied Grands Boulevards lies Paris' traditional business district, run at a considerably less frantic pace than Wall Street. The Banque de France, France's central bank, has occupied the seventeenth-century Hôtel de Toulouse since 1811. Very little of the original remains, but its long gallery is still hung with old masters. Nearby the pretty **place des Victoires** was designed, like place Vendôme, by Hardouin-Mansart, forming an intimate circle of buildings today dedicated to fashion. The two worlds meet in bistro Chez Georges, where bankers and fashion moguls rub shoulders. West of the *place*, along rue des Petits-Champs, explore the shop-lined covered **Galerie Vivienne** and **Galerie Colbert** and the **Bibliothèque Nationale Richelieu**, the old national library, founded when Colbert moved the royal library to the site in the 1660s; the bulk of the national library has been transferred to the Left Bank. On the corner of Galerie Vivienne and rue de la Banque is luxury *épicerie* and wine merchant **Legrand**. Take a detour along the passage des Petits-Pères to the **Eglise Notre-Dame-des-Victoires,** the remains of an Augustine priory with seven canvases by Carle Van Loo.

Rue de la Banque now leads to **La Bourse** (stock exchange), behind a commanding Neo-Classical colonnade. Otherwise the area has a relaxed feel, at weekends positively sleepy, although its habitual good behaviour was momentarily disturbed in 1999 by the arrival of an art squat across the square, which injected a colourful dose of anarchy until its inhabitants were evicted in the summer. For business lunches and after-work drinks, stockbrokers and journalists converge on the **Vaudeville** brasserie. On rue des Colonnes, you'll find a quiet street of graceful porticos and acanthus motifs dating from the 1790s, a rare example of architecture from the revolutionary period. Across the rue du Quatre-Septembre stands the 70s concrete and glass HQ of Agence France-Presse, France's biggest news agency. This street and its continuation rue Réaumur were built up by the press barons with some striking Art Nouveau buildings. Most newspapers have since left; *Le Figaro* remains in rue du Louvre.

Bibliothèque Nationale Richelieu

58 rue de Richelieu, 2nd (01.47.03.81.26).
M° Bourse. **Open** *Galerie Mansart/Mazarine* 10am-7pm Tue-Sun. *Cabinet des Médailles* 1-5pm Mon-Sat; noon-6pm Sun. **Admission** *Galerie Mansart/Mazarine* 35F; 24F under-26s, over-60s. *Cabinet des Médailles* 22F; 15F students, over-60s, under-26s. **No credit cards. Map H4**
The genesis of the French National Library dates

*Cardinal Richelieu lived at the **Palais-Royal**; now it's home to the Ministry of Culture.*

from the 1660s, when Louis XIV's finance minister Colbert brought together the manuscripts of the royal library in the lavish Louis XIII townhouse which was once Cardinal Mazarin's. First opened to scholars in 1720, by 1724 the institution had received so many new acquisitions that the neighbouring Hôtel de Nevers was added. Libraries confiscated in the Revolution again enlarged the collection. The complex was transformed in the 1860s by the innovative, circular, vaulted reading room designed by Henri Labrouste and the new facade on rue de Richelieu. The library is now curiously empty as the books have moved to the gigantic new Bibliothèque Nationale François Mitterrand on the Left Bank. Some of the original painted decoration by Romanelli and Grimaldi can still be seen in Galerie Mazarine, now used for exhibitions of manuscripts and prints. Coins and royal memorabilia can be seen in the Cabinet des Médailles. *See chapter* **Museums**.

La Bourse

Palais Brongniart, pl de la Bourse, 2nd (01.49.27.55.55). M° Bourse. **Guided tours** Call for details. **Admission** 30F; 15F students. **No credit cards. Map H4**

The stock exchange found its home in 1826 in this building designed by Alexandre Brongniart under Napoléon, testament to First Empire taste for Ancient Greece with Corinthian columns and allegorical statues. It was enlarged in 1906 to create a cruciform interior, where brokers buzzed around a central enclosure, the *corbeille* (or crow's nest). Computers have made it obsolete, but the atmosphere remains frenetic.

Louvre des Antiquaires

2 pl du Palais-Royal, 1st (01.42.97.27.00). M° Palais-Royal. **Open** 11am-7pm Tue-Sun. **Map H5**

This upmarket antiques centre houses 250 dealers. Louis XV furniture, tapestries, Sèvres and Chinese porcelain, silver and jewellery, model ships and tin soldiers can all be found here for a price.

Palais-Royal

main entrance pl du Palais-Royal, 1st. M° Palais-Royal. **Open** *gardens only* dawn-dusk daily. **Admission** free. **Map H5**

Built for Richelieu by Jacques Lemercier, this was first known as the Palais Cardinal. Richelieu left it to Louis XIII, whose widow preferred it to the chilly Louvre and gave it its name. In the 1780s, the Duc d'Orléans enclosed the gardens in a three-storey peristyle. Housing cafés, theatres, shops and apartments, its arcades became a society trysting place. The cafés saw pre-revolutionary plotting, and the Palais-Royal became known as a hotbed of gambling and prostitution. Today the gardens are a tranquil spot in the heart of Paris, while many shops sell prints and antiques. The former palace houses the Conseil d'Etat and the Ministry of Culture. Daniel Buren's sculpture of black-and-white striped columns of different heights graces the main courtyard.

Place des Victoires

1st, 2nd. M° Bourse. **Map H5**

Louis XIV introduced the grand Baroque square with circular place des Victoires, commemorating victories against Holland. It was designed in 1685 by Hardouin-Mansart with decorative closed arcades and pilasters to set off a statue of the king. The original disappeared in the Revolution, replaced in 1822. Today, rather than aristocratic residents, the sweeping facades shelter fashion names Kenzo, Victoire and Thierry Mugler.

Mainly in the 2nd, 8th and 9th arrondissements.

One of Napoléon III's architectural extravaganzas was the wedding cake design of Charles Garnier's **Palais Garnier** opera house. Covered inside and out with a feast of sculpture, the exterior is currently under wraps (until at least mid-2000) for restoration. Evoking opera at its grandest, it's not hard to see why the Phantom of the Opera legend started here. Garnier also decorated the Café de la Paix, with a terrace overlooking place de l'Opéra, part of the Grand Hôtel, built as the *quartier* boomed in the 1860s. Behind, in the Jockey Club (now **Hôtel Scribe**, 14 rue Scribe), the Lumière brothers held the world's first public cinema screening in 1895. On the opposite corner (12 boulevard des Capucines) is the wooden frontage of the delightfully old-fashioned emporium Old England. Inside are Jacobean-style plaster ceilings and equally dated goods and service. The **Olympia** concert hall at No 28, the legendary venue of Piaf and other greats, was recently knocked down and rebuilt a few metres away. Across the road at No 35, pioneering portrait photographer Nadar opened a studio in the 1860s, soon frequented by writers, actors and artists – Dumas *père*, Doré, Offenbach – and in 1874 the setting for the ground-breaking first Impressionist exhibition.

This stretch of boulevard des Capucines and its continuation boulevard de la Madeleine were recently spruced up, attracting a wave of Gap, Zara and other high-street stores. Two elegant rotundas crown the entrance to rue Caumartin, designed in the 1780s by André Aubert as grandiose residences. Take a detour down the rue Edouard VII, a crescent of shops laid out in 1911, leading to an imposing octagonal *place* with an equestrian statue of the monarch by Landowski and the Théâtre Edouard VII. An archway leads through to another square and the *belle époque* Théâtre de l'Athénée-Louis Jouvet.

Like a classical temple at the end of the boulevard stands the **Madeleine**, a vaguely religious monument to Napoléon. Its huge Corinthian columns mirror the Assemblée Nationale across the Seine, while the interior is a riot of marble and altars to saints who look like Roman generals. Most visit the square, though, to ogle **Fauchon**, Paris' most extravagant delicatessen, **Hédiard**, **La Maison de la Truffe**, and the other luxury foodstores, or for haute cuisine restaurant **Lucas Carton**, with Art Nouveau interior by Majorelle.

The *grands magasins* (department stores) **Printemps** and **Galeries Lafayette**, just behind the Opéra, opened in the late nineteenth century. Awash with tourists all year and with Parisians at Christmas and during sales, both are much altered. Printemps still has an imposing domed entrance and Lafayette an impressive stained glass dome. Behind the latter, on rue Caumartin, stands the austere, newly cleaned facade of Lycée Caumartin, designed as a convent in the 1780s by Bourse architect Brongniart to become one of Paris' most prestigious *lycées* under Napoléon. A little further west along Haussmann's boulevard are the small square containing **Chapelle Expiatoire** built by Louis XVIII in memory of Louis XVI and Marie-Antoinette. Beyond, looking over the busy junction, imposing Haussmannian apartment blocks and the Cercle Militaire, the Second Empire **St-Augustin** church is a clever exercise in cast iron by Baltard, architect of the Les Halles market pavilions.

Chapelle Expiatoire

729 rue Pasquier, 8th (01.42.65.35.80).
M° St-Augustin or Havre-Caumartin. **Open** 1-5pm Thur-Sat. **Map F3**
The Neo-Classical chapel was commissioned from Fontaine in 1815 by Louis XVIII in memory of his executed predecessors Louis XVI and Marie-Antoinette. Their remains, along with those of 3000 revolutionary victims, including Philippe-Egalité, Charlotte Corday, Mme du Barry, Camille Desmoulins, Danton, Malesherbes and Lavoisier, were found in 1814 on the exact spot where the altar stands. Two marble statues represent Louis XVI supported by an angel and Marie-Antoinette kneeling at the feet of Religion, represented by the King's sister, Mme Elisabeth. The chapel draws fervent royalists for a memorial service every January.

Eglise St-Augustin

46 bd Malesherbes, 8th (01.45.22.23.12).
M° St-Augustin. **Open** 8.30am-6.45pm Mon-Fri; 8.30am-1pm, 2.30-6.45pm Sat, Sun. **Map F3**
Testimony to nineteenth-century eclecticism, the domed, neo-Renaissance stone exterior of this church, curiously getting wider towards the rear to adapt to the triangular site, is merely a shell. Within, architect Victor Baltard used an iron vault structure as at Les Halles; even the decorative angels are cast in metal. Note the William Bouguereau paintings in the transept.

Eglise de la Madeleine

pl de la Madeleine, 8th (01.44.51.69.00).
M° Madeleine. **Open** 7.30am-7pm Mon-Sat; 9am-1pm, 3.30-7pm Sun. **Map G4**
The building of a giant church on this site began in 1764. In 1806 Napoléon continued the project as a 'Temple of Glory' dedicated to his Grand Army, and commissioned Barthélemy Vignon to transform the design into a semi-Athenian temple. After the Emperor's fall construction slowed, but the building was finally consecrated in 1845. The reliefs on the bronze doors depict the Ten Commandments. Inside are three and a half giant domes and pedimented, pseudo-Grecian side altars amid a sea of multi-coloured marble. The painting by Ziegler in the chancel depicts the history of Christianity, Napoléon prominent in the foreground. The church is a favourite for celebrity weddings and funerals.

Passages through time

The picturesque glass-roofed *galeries* and *passages* that thread their way between Paris' boulevards were built by speculators in the early nineteenth century, when properties confiscated from the church or nobility under the Revolution brought vast tracts of land on to the market. Precursors of the department stores, *galeries* allowed strollers to inspect novelties safe from rain, mud and horses. Astute pedestrians can still make their way entirely undercover from the Grands Boulevards to the Palais-Royal. Over 100 *galeries* existed in 1840; less than 20 remain today, mostly in the 1st, 2nd and 9th, but renovation has brought them back into fashion; they remain a wonderful source of curios. Visit in daytime: most are locked at night and on Sundays.

Galerie Véro-Dodat

2 rue du Bouloi/19 rue Jean-Jacques-Rousseau, 1st. M° Louvre or Palais-Royal. **Map G5**
Véro and Dodat, prosperous *charcutiers*, built this arcade in the Restoration, equipping it with gaslights and charging astronomical rents. The tiled floor and wooden shopfronts, with Corinthian colums and arcaded arched windows, are beautifully preserved along with the *loge du gardien* and little stairways leading up to apartments.

Attractions include vintage **Café de l'Epoque**, antique dolls and teddies at Capia, shops selling architectural salvage, and make-up at By Terry.

Galerie Vivienne & Galerie Colbert

rue 6 Vivienne/4 rue des Petits-Champs and 5 rue de la Banque, 2nd. M° Bourse. **Map G4**
Vivienne, with its stucco bas-reliefs and mosaic pavement, houses Gaultier's couture, second-hand books, **Pylones** gift shop and pretty tea room A Priori Thé. Colbert boasts a huge glass dome.

Passage du Caire & Passage du Ponceau

2 pl du Caire/33 rue d'Alexandrie and 119 bd de Sébastopol/212 rue St-Denis, 2nd. M° Réaumur-Sébastopol. **Map J/K4**
Now taken up by clothing workshops, Passage du Caire is interesting for its Egyptian motifs and Ponceau for its narrow walkway and high ceiling.

Passage de Choiseul

40 rue des Petits-Champs/23 rue St-Augustin, 2nd. M° Pyramides or Quatre-Septembre. **Map G4**
Colourfully depicted in Céline's *Mort à crédit*, this is where the writer grew up. Its charm lies in the ordinariness of its clothing and discount stores.

Passage du Grand Cerf

10 rue Dussoubs/145 rue St-Denis, 2nd. M° Etienne-Marcel. **Map H5**
Notable for its wrought iron and hanging lanterns, this has recently been restored and is undergoing a renaissance with unusual design shops including **As'Art**, PM & Co and La Corbeille.

Passage des Panoramas

10 rue St-Marc/11 bd Montmartre, 2nd. M° Richelieu-Drouot. **Map H4**
The earliest surviving passage is named after the giant illuminated paintings of capital cities, created by Robert Fulton and Pierre Prévost. Take in the superb premises of Stern, engraver since 1830.

Passage Jouffroy & Passage Verdeau

10-12 bd Montmartre/9 rue de la Grange-Batelière, 9th. M° Richelieu-Drouot. **Map H4**
With a grand barrel-vaulted glass and iron roof, Hôtel Mercure straddles the entrance, over Café Zephyr and **Musée Grévin** waxworks. Within are the old-fashioned **Hôtel Chopin**, printsellers, antiquarian booksellers, **Pain d'Epices** dolls-houses and walking stick specialist Mr Segas.

Passage Brady & Passage du Prado

46 rue du Fbg-St-Denis/43 rue du Fbg-St-Martin, 16 rue du Fbg St-Denis/16 bd St-Denis, 10th. M° Château d'Eau. **Map J4**
Brady hums with Indian grocers, barbers and inexpensive curry houses, while the passage Prado boasts Art Deco motifs.

Palais Garnier

pl de l'Opéra, 9th (box office 08.36.69.78.68/tours 01.40.01.22.63). M° Opéra. **Open** *visits* 10am-4.30pm daily; *tours* (in French) 1pm Tue-Sun (60F). **Admission** *museum* 30F; 20F 10-25s, over-60s; free under-10s. **No credit cards. Map G4**

Awash with gilt, satin, red velvet and marble, the opulent Palais Garnier, with its sumptuous grand staircase, sculptures and glittering chandeliers, is a monument to the ostentatious Second Empire French haute bourgeoisie. Designed by Charles Garnier in 1862 and used for performances of both opera and ballet, it has an immense stage and an auditorium for over 2000 people. The exterior is equally opulent, with sculptures of music and dance, a gaudy Apollo topping the copper dome, nymphs holding torches, and a ramp up the side of the building on rue Scribe for the Emperor to drive his carriage to the royal box. Carpeaux's sculpture *La Danse* shocked Parisians with its frank sensuality and, in 1869, someone threw a bottle of ink over its marble thighs; the original is safe in the Musée d'Orsay. Visitors can see the library, museum, Grand Foyer, Grand Staircase and the auditorium with its controversial false ceiling, painted by Chagall in 1964 with scenes from operas and ballets – there's occasional talk of returning to the original, still underneath. *See also chapters* **Museums**, **Dance**, *and* **Music: Classical & Opera**.

Quartier de l'Europe

The area north of Opéra stretching between Gare St-Lazare and the boulevard des Batignolles was built up in the late nineteenth century with streets named after various European capitals. Then known for its prostitutes or *lorettes* (*see below*, **La Nouvelle Athènes**), the Quartier de l'Europe, described in Zola's *La Bête Humaine*, is the Impressionist quarter *par excellence*, if hardly a tourist draw now. The exciting new steam age, a quintessential image of modern life, was depicted by Monet in the 1870s in numerous versions of *La Gare St-Lazare* and in *Pont de l'Europe* – the bridge by place de Europe giving a magnificent view over the railway tracks; Caillebotte and Pissarro painted views of the new boulevards, and Manet had a studio on rue de St-Petersbourg, where he entertained sitters and exhibited works. Rue de Budapest remains a sleazy red-light district, 2 rue de Londres was once a celebrated brothel where the Casque d'Or (depicted by Simone Signoret in Jacques Becker's 1952 film) plied her wares, while rue de Rome has long been home to Paris' stringed-instrument makers – the music conservatoire was formerly nearby in rue de Madrid. Just east of Gare St-Lazare, look out for the imposing **Eglise de la Trinité**.

Eglise de la Trinité

pl Estienne d'Orves, 9th (01.48.74.12.77). M° Trinité. **Open** 7.15am-7.30pm Mon-Sat; 8.30am-1pm, 5-8pm Sun. **Map G3**

Dominated by the tiered wedding-cake belltower, the church was built (1861-67) by Théodore Ballu in a neo-Renaissance style typical of the era's historical eclecticism, and is famous as the church where composer Olivier Messiaen (1908-92) was organist for over 30 years. Guided tours on Sundays.

The Grands Boulevards

Contrary to popular belief, the string of Grands Boulevards between Madeleine and République (de la Madeleine, des Capucines, des Italiens, Montmartre, Poissonnière, Bonne-Nouvelle, St-Denis, St-Martin) were not built by Haussmann but by Louis XIV in 1670, replacing the fortifications of Charles II's city wall. This explains the strange changes of level of the eastern segment, as steps lead up to side streets or down to the road on former traces of the ramparts. The boulevards burgeoned in the early nineteenth century, often built on lands repossessed from aristocrats or the church after the Revolution. The boulevards feel anonymous today, although they still have a gaudy character, with theatres, burger joints and sleazy discount stores. The area is up for renovation on the city's agenda. Towards Opéra, the grandiose domed banking halls of disaster-prone Crédit Lyonnais, being rebuilt after a serious fire in 1996, and the Sociéte Générale reflect the business boom of the late nineteenth century.

Tucked between busy boulevard des Italiens and rue de Richelieu is pretty place Boïeldieu and the **Opéra Comique**. Built 1781-83 as the Comédie Italienne, the theatre was rebuilt in 1894-98 as a Neo-Classical confection with caryatids and ornate lamp-posts. Alexandre Dumas *fils* was born across the square at No 1 in 1824.

The *mairie* (town hall) of the 9th *arrondissement* (6 rue Drouot) occupies the elegant eighteenth-century Hôtel d'Augny. After the Revolution and the fall of Robespierre, the building became home to the famous *bals des victimes*, where every guest had to have had a member of their family decapitated by Mr Guillotine's infamous invention.

In the square stands the modern **Drouot** auction house. Around it are the offices of specialist antiques shops, coin and stamp dealers and Les Caves Drouot brasserie and wine bar, where auction-goers and valuers congregate. There are several grand if a little delapidated *hôtels particuliers* on rue de la Grange-Batelière, which leads on one side down curious Passage Verdeau and on the other back to the boulevards via picturesque **Passage Jouffroy**, with its book and print dealers, quaint **Hôtel Chopin** and the colourful carved entrance of the **Musée Grévin** waxworks museum. Across the boulevard is the **Passage des Panoramas** and next to it the Théâtre des Variétés, now mainly used for low-brow comedies, but where Offenbach premiered many of his operettas in the area's entertainment heyday.

Doorway to Paris: **Porte St-Denis** *is one of the city's gates in the form of a triumphal arch.*

At 7 rue du Fbg-Montmartre is the budget eatery **Chartier**, originally a *bouillon* or cheap working man's soup kitchen, worth a visit for the experience of eating in the clamorous *belle époque* dining hall, rather than for gastronomic finesse, and at No 35, vintage sweetshop **A la Mère de Famille**, founded in 1761. Wander down cobbled Cité Bergère, built in 1825 as desirable residences; though most are now budget hotels; the pretty iron and glass *portes-cochères* remain. The Faubourg area is home to numerous synagogues and kosher restaurants, and livens up with the **Folies-Bergère** (currently offering musicals rather than cabaret). The rue du Faubourg-Poissonnière also merits exploring, with its mix of rag-trade outlets and fine *hôtels*. Look out for the Hôtel Titon at No 58, built in Neo-Classical style by Delafosse, and the Hôtel Cheret at No 30, by Ledoux.

Back on the boulevard, the palatial Art Deco cinema **Le Grand Rex** offers an interesting backstage tour. East of here are Louis XIV's triumphal arches, the Porte St-Martin and Porte St-Denis.

Le Grand Rex

1 bd Poissonnière, 2nd (01.45.08.93.58). M° Bonne-Nouvelle. **Tour** *Les Etoiles du Rex* 10am-7pm Wed-Sun, public holidays, daily in school holidays. **Admission** 45F; 40F 3-12s; free under-3s; 75F tour and film; 70F under-12s. **Credit** MC, V. **Map J4**
Opened in 1932, this huge, 2800-seat Art Deco cinema was designed by Auguste Bluysen with fantasy Hispanic interiors by US designer John Eberson. See behind the scenes in the wacky, 50-minute Les Etoiles du Rex guided tour. Visitors are shown the projection room, taking in newsreel footage of Rex history and an insight into film production tricks with Sensurround effects to jolt the strongest nerves.

Hôtel Drouot

9 rue Drouot, 9th (01.48.00.20.20/recorded information 01.48.00.20.17). M° Richelieu-Drouot. **Open** 11am-6pm Mon-Sat. Closed Aug. **Admission** free. **Map H4**
A spiky aluminium and marble-clad concoction is the setting for the hub of France's secondary art market. Architects Biro and Fernier, who designed it in the early 80s to replace the crumbling former premises, wanted to achieve a 'surrealist interpretation of Haussmann'. Inside, shiny escalators whizz you up to 16 small salerooms, where anything from medieval manuscripts and Rococo furniture to modern paintings or fine wines, plus a considerable amount of junk, might be up for sale. Drouot makes a great free exhibition. Details of forthcoming sales are published in the weekly *Gazette de l'Hôtel Drouot*, sold at newsstands. The French auction system is undergoing radical change. The European Union insisted French barriers be opened, and Sotheby's and Christie's should in theory have been allowed to enter the French market since 1998 but have been prevented by legal technicalities.
Branches: Drouot-Montaigne, 15 av Montaigne, 8th (01.48.00.20.80); Drouot Nord, 64 rue Doudeauville, 18th (01.48.00.20.990).

Porte St-Denis & Porte St-Martin

corner rue St-Denis/bd St-Denis, 2nd/10th; 33 bd St-Martin, 3rd/10th. **Map K4**
These twin triumphal gates were erected in 1672 and 1674 at important entry points as part of Colbert's

strategy for the aggrandisement of Paris to the glory of Louis XIV's victories on the Rhine. Modelled on the triumphal arches of Ancient Rome, the Porte St-Denis by François Blondel is particularly harmonious, based on a perfect square, with a single arch. Porte St-Bernard on the Left Bank has been demolished.

Les Halles & Sentier

In the 1st and 2nd arrondissements.
Few places epitomise the transformation of central Paris more than Les Halles, wholesale fruit and veg market for the city since 1181, when the covered markets were established by King Philippe-Auguste. Zola called it the 'belly of Paris', the nerve centre of life in the capital, a giant covered market graced with Baltard's green iron pavilions. In 1969 the trading market moved to a new site in the suburb of Rungis, leaving a giant hole – long nicknamed *le trou des Halles* (a pun on arsehole) – that was only filled in the early 80s, by the miserably designed **Forum des Halles** shopping mall, after long political dispute. One pavilion was saved and reconstructed in the suburbs at Nogent-sur-Marne (*see chapter* **Beyond the Périphérique**).

After an initial burst of cool, the complex has become seedier by the year. As 'social exclusion' has risen as one of France's major problems, the Forum has become a mecca for the homeless, punks and junkies, the epitome of the Paris of Luc Besson's 1985 movie *Subway*, making surviving market restaurants like L'Escargot Montorgueil at 38 rue Montorgueil increasingly incongruous.

East of the Forum is the place des Innocents, centred on the Renaissance Fontaine des Innocents. The four-sided roofed structure was designed by Pierre Lescot, moved here from the city's main burial ground, nearby Cimetière des Innocents, demolished in 1786 after flesh-eating rats started gnawing into people's living rooms, and the bones transferred to the Catacombes. Rue des Lombards is a centre for nightlife, with bars, restaurants and the **Baiser Salé**, **Sunset** and **Duc des Lombards** jazz clubs. In ancient rue de la Ferronnerie, Henri IV was assassinated in 1610 by Catholic fanatic François Ravaillac (who had followed the royal carriage held up in the traffic). The street has now become an extension of the Marais gay circuit with the thriving **Banana Café** and other gay bars.

The ancient easternmost stretch of the rue St-Honoré (*see above*, **Louvre to Concorde**) runs into the southern edge of Les Halles. The Fontaine du Trahoir designed by Soufflot (better known for having designed the Panthéon) in 1767 with Neo-Renaissance icicles stands at the corner with rue de l'Arbre-Sec. Opposite, the fine Hôtel de Truden (52 rue de l'Arbre-Sec) was built in 1717 for a wine merchant, with wrought-iron balcony and carved armorials.

By the Pont-Neuf is **La Samaritaine** department store. It's chaotically organised inside but has a fantastic Art Nouveau staircase and glass *verrière*. The Toupary restaurant and tea room at the top offers a panoramic view. From here quai de la Mégisserie leads towards Châtelet, lined with horticultural suppliers and pet shops.

West of the Forum, the Jardin des Halles was an attempt to bring greenery to the development, even if the parks often seem inhabited largely by the homeless. Looming over them is the **Eglise St-Eustache**, with Renaissance motifs inside and chunky flying buttresses without. At the western end of the gardens is the circular **Bourse du Commerce**, once the main corn exchange. It was built on the site of a palace belonging to Marie de Médicis, recalled only in the astronomical column outside, once associated with occult practices. Hints of the market past linger in the 24-hour brasserie Au Pied de Cochon and all-night bistro **La Tour Montlhéry**, restaurant supply shops and kitchen equipment emporia A Simon and E Dehillerin.

North and west of Les Halles is packed with clothes shops – **Agnès b**'s empire extends along most of rue du Jour, with **Kabuki, Barbara Bui** and Ron Orb on rue Etienne-Marcel, and more streetwise outlets like **Kiliwatch** on rue Tiquetonne, alongside fashion-world rendezvous **Le Café**. Amid the frippery, the **Tour de Jean Sans Peur**, a strange relic of the medieval fortified townhouse of Jean, Duc de Bourgogne, has recently been opened to the public.

Pedestrianised rue Montorgueil, with its busy shops and cafés, is an irresistible place to while away a few hours, part of a historic *quartier* (look at Rococo No 73 and the painted front of the Rocher de Cancale restaurant at No 78) that is gradually being smartened up as designers and decorators move into the renovated **Passage du Grand-Cerf**.

Bourse du Commerce

2 rue de Viarmes, 1st (01.55.65.78.41). M° Louvre.
Open 9am-5.30pm Mon-Fri. **Tours** groups of up to 30, reserve in advance, 250F. **No credit cards.**
Map H6
Now a commodity market for coffee and sugar, world trade centre and Paris Chamber of Commerce, the city's former main grain market was built in 1767 by Nicolas Le Camus de Mézières on a circular plan. It was later covered with a dome in wood, replaced by an avant-garde iron structure in 1809 (then covered in copper, now in glass).

Eglise St-Eustache

2 rue du Jour, 1st (01.40.26.47.99). M° Les Halles/ RER Châtelet-Les Halles. **Open** *May-Oct* 9am-8pm Mon-Sat; 9am-12.30pm, 2-7pm Sun. *Nov-Apr* 9am-7pm Mon-Sat, 9am-12.30pm, 2-7pm Sun. **Map J5**
This barn-like church (built 1532-1640) dominates

Stroll through the pedestrianised **rue Montorgueil** *to sample Paris street life.*

Les Halles. Its elaborately buttressed and monolithic vaulted structure is essentially Gothic, but the decoration with pedimented entrance and Corinthian capitals down the nave is distinctively Renaissance. Paintings in the side chapels include *Descent from the Cross* by Luca Giordano; works by Thomas Couture adorn the early nineteenth-century lady chapel, and there's a relief of market characters by British artist Raymond Mason. A favourite with music-lovers, it boasts a magnificent 8000-pipe organ (free recitals 5.30pm Sun).

Forum des Halles

1st. Mº/RER Châtelet-Les Halles. **Map J5**
This labyrinthine concrete mall extends three levels underground and includes the Ciné Cité multiplex, the Forum des Images and a swimming pool, as well as mass-market clothing chains, branches of Fnac, Habitat and – a result of empty outlets – the Forum des Créateurs, a section given over to young designers. The first part of the centre was completed in 1979, the second phase added in 1986. Despite some attempts at redecoration, both are now severely shabby, but you're bound to end up here sometime, if only to use the vast Métro and RER interchange which disgorges thousands of commuters and shoppers every day through the Forum's depths.

Tour Jean-Sans-Peur

20 rue Etienne-Marcel, 2nd (01.40.26.20.28).
Mº Etienne Marcel. **Open** *termtime* 1.30-6pm Wed, Sat, Sun; *school holidays* 1.30-6pm Tue-Sun.
Admission 30F; 20F 7-18s, students; free under-7s.
Guided visit 50F. **Credit** MC, V. **Map J5**
This is the remnant of the townhouse of Jean Sans Peur, Duc de Bourgogne, once one of the most exten-

sive medieval edifices in Paris. The original *hôtel* spanned Philippe-Auguste's city wall and the base of a turret is still concealed inside. Jean got his nickname (the fearless) from his exploits in Bulgaria, but has gone down in French history as a nasty piece of work, responsible for the assassination in 1407 of Louis d'Orléans, his rival and cousin of king Charles VI, sparking point for the Hundred Years War. Jean escaped from Paris but returned two years later to add this show-off tower to his mansion, but got his comeuppance when assassinated by a partisan of the Dauphin (future Charles VII) in 1419. Today you can climb the multi-storey tower he commissioned from master mason Robert de Helbuterne. Halfway up the spiral staircase is a remarkable vault carved with naturalistic branches of oak, hawthorn and hops, symbols of Jean Sans Peur and Burgundian power.

Rue St-Denis & Sentier

Away from the crowded malls of Les Halles, Sentier is a Parisian backwater. For years the district was all crumbling houses, run-down shops and downmarket strip-joints. The tackiness is pretty unremitting along the traditional red-light district of rue St-Denis, which snakes north from the Forum. Kerb-crawlers gawp at the neon adverts for *l'amour sur scène*, and size up sorry-looking prostitutes in doorways. In recent years, the prostitutes and peep-shows have been partly pushed back by an energetic pedestrianisation around the Quartier Montorgeuil.

Between rue des Petits-Carreaux and rue St-Denis is the site of what was once known as the

When in Paris… **Eglise St-Vincent de Paul** resembles Rome's Spanish Steps.

Cour des Miracles, where paupers would return after a day's begging to 'miraculously' regain use of their eyes or limbs. An abandoned aristocratic estate, it was a refuge for the underworld for decades until cleared out in 1667 by Louis XIV's chief of police, La Reynie. The surrounding Sentier district is centre of the rag trade, where sweatshops copy the catwalks and the streets fill with porters carrying linen bundles over their shoulders. Streets like rue du Caire, rue d'Aboukir and rue du Nil, testifying to a fit of Egyptomania after Napoléon's Egyptian campaign, are connected by a maze of passages lined with wholesalers. The area attracts illegal and semi-legal foreign workers, who line up for work in place du Caire.

Fbg-St-Denis to Gare du Nord

North of the Porte St-Denis triumphal arch (*see above* **Grands Boulevards**), there's an almost souk-like feel to frenetic rue du Fbg-St-Denis with its food shops, narrow passages and sinister courtyards leading off on either side. The brasserie Julien boasts one of the finest Art Nouveau interiors in Paris, with wood carved by Majorelle, stunning painted panels, and eternally fashionable statues, while up dingy cobbled Cour des Petites-Ecuries, theatre-goers flock to **Brasserie Flo**. Garishly lit Passage Brady is a piece of India, full of restaurants and hairdressers. Rue des Petites-Ecuries ('stables street') was once known for saddlers but now has numerous Turkish shops and cafés as well as top jazz venue the **New Morning**.

Nearby rue de Paradis has long had showrooms for crystal- and porcelain-makers and still glistens with discount glass and china outlets. At No 18 is the extravagant glazed facade of the former Magasin des Faïenceries de Choisy-le-Roi Boulenger. A little further along, the **Musée du Cristal-Baccarat** is a showcase for the excesses – and technical brilliance – of nineteenth-century crystal manufacture. The area is decidedly rundown, but the Hôtel de Bourrienne, hidden away at 58 rue d'Hauteville (open 1-6pm 1-15 July, Sept or by appointment/ 01.47.70.51.14), points to a grander past.

The top of rue d'Hauteville affords one of the most unexpected views in Paris. **Eglise St-Vincent de Paul**, with its twin towers and cascading terraced gardens, is about as close as Paris gets to Rome's Spanish Steps. Just behind on rue de Belzunce are the excellent modern bistro **Chez Michel** and inexpensive offshoot Chez Casimir. On boulevard Magenta, the **Marché St-Quentin** is one of the busiest surviving covered iron markets, built in the 1860s.

Boulevard de Strasbourg was one of Haussmann's new roads, designed to give a grand perspective up to the new Gare de l'Est and soon built up with popular theatres – the mosaiqued neo-Renaissance Théâtre Antoine-Simone Berriau

and the Art Deco Comedia. At No 2, another neo-Renaissance creation houses Paris' last fan makers and fan museum, the **Musée de l'Eventail**. Sandwiched between Gare de l'Est and Canal St-Martin (*see below*, **North-East Paris**) stand the near derelict remains of the **Couvent des Récollets** and its former gardens – now the Square Villemin, a small park.

Couvent des Récollets

bd de Strasbourg, 10th. **Map L3**
This seventeenth-century Franciscan convent served as women's shelter, barracks and hospital after the Revolution, but the last tenant, an architectural school, moved out in 1990. In July 1997, an artists' association held Sunday open events in the gardens. The convent's future is under evaluation, with the artists supporting plans for a Cité Européenne de la Culture.

Eglise St-Vincent de Paul

pl Franz-Liszt, 10th (01.48.78.47.47). M° Gare du Nord. **Open** 8.30am-noon, 2-7pm daily. **Map K2**
Imposingly set at the top of terraced gardens, the church was begun in 1824 by Lepère and completed from 1831-44 by Hittorff, replacing an earlier chapel to cater to the newly populous district. Twin towers, pedimented Greek temple portico and evangelist figures on the parapet are in classical mode. Original enamel paintings by Jules Jollivet were deemed too risqué and removed. The interior has a double-storey arcade of columns, murals by Flandrin, and church furniture by Rude.

Gare du Nord

18 rue de Dunkerque, 10th (01.55.31.10.00). M° Gare du Nord. **Map K2**
The grandest of the great nineteenth-century train stations (and Eurostar terminal since 1994) was built by Haussmann's pet architect Hittorff in 1861-64. A vast, bravura iron-and-glass vault hides behind a much more conventional stone facade, with Ionic capitals and statues representing towns of northern France and Europe served by the station.

Beaubourg & the Marais

In the 3rd and 4th arrondissements.
Between boulevard Sébastopol and the Bastille lies Beaubourg – the historic area in which the Centre Pompidou landed in 1977 – and the Marais, built up between the sixteenth and eighteenth centuries and now a magnet for unusual boutiques, interesting museums and trendy bars.

Beaubourg & Hôtel de Ville

Contemporary Parisian architecture began with the **Centre Pompidou**, opened in 1977 in a formerly rundown area still known by its medieval name Beaubourg ('beautiful village'). Just reopened after extensive renovation, this international benchmark of high-tech was always intended to be as much of an attraction as its contents. Out on the piazza is the **Atelier Brancusi**, the sculptor's reconstructed studio. On the other side of the piazza, peer down rue Quincampoix for its art galleries, bars and curious passage Molière. It was here that Scottish financier John Law ran his speculative venture that crashed when the South Sea Bubble burst in 1720; hounded by the mob, he took refuge in the Palais-Royal. Beside the Centre Pompidou is place Igor Stravinsky, with the red brick **IRCAM** contemporary music institute and the playful Fontaine Stravinsky by Nikki de Saint Phalle and Jean Tinguely. On the south side of the square is the church of St-Merri, with a Flamboyant Gothic facade complete with an androgynous demon over the doorway. Inside are a carved wooden organ loft, the oldest bell in Paris (1331), and sixteenth-century stained glass. There are free chamber music concerts most weekends.

Between Beaubourg and rue de Rivoli is a maze of narrow pedestrianised streets. On the river side of rue de Rivoli stands **Tour St-Jacques**, alive with Gothic gargoyles, and place du Châtelet. Site of a notorious prison in the Middle Ages, the *place* houses twin theatres designed by Davioud in the 1860s: **Châtelet Théâtre Musical de Paris**, a classical and opera venue, and the leading contemporary dance space, **Théâtre de la Ville**, either side of an Egyptian-style fountain.

Beyond Châtelet looms the Hôtel de Ville, of which the Mayor's apartment occupies an entire floor. Centre of municipal rather than royal (or republican) power since 1260, it overlooks a square of the same name, once known as place de Grève, by the original Paris port. Here disgruntled workers gathered – hence the French for 'strike' (*grève*) – but today it's a more light-hearted rendezvous when an outdoor ice rink is set up in winter. Protestant heretics were burnt in the place during the Wars of Religion, and the guillotine first stood here during the Terror, when Danton, Marat and Robespierre made the Hôtel their seat of government. Revolutionaries made it their base in the 1871 Commune, but the building was wrecked in savage fighting. It was rebuilt on a grander scale in fanciful neo-Renaissance style with statues representing French cities along the facade.

In front of the town hall on quai de l'Hôtel de Ville, an equestrian statue of Etienne Marcel recalls the rebellious *prévôt* (precursor of the mayor) who led a rebellion against royal power in 1357. The quai has two very popular inexpensive bistros, Trumilou and Louis-Philippe Café, with excellent views to the Ile de la Cité.

Centre Pompidou

rue St-Martin, 4th (01.44.78.12.33). Mº Hôtel-de-Ville or Rambuteau/RER Châtelet-Les Halles. **Open** 11am-10pm Mon, Wed-Sun. Closed 1 May. **Admission** *Mnam/exhibitions* 30F-50F; 20F-40F students; free under 18s. **Credit** V. **Map K5** Commissioned in 1968 by President Pompidou, the

Centre was designed by Italo-British duo Renzo Piano and Richard Rogers. Their notorious 'inside-out', boilerhouse approach put air-conditioning, lifts and escalators outside, leaving a flexible, freely adaptable space inside.When it opened in 1977, the content was as revolutionary as its architecture: a truly multidisciplinary arts centre, featuring not only the colossal reserves of art of the Musée National d'Art Moderne (Mnam), but also temporary exhibitions and avant-garde music (at affiliated IRCAM), dance, a cinema and huge public library (the BPI), not to mention the stunning views from the escalators. Success exceeded all expectations, leading to inevitable wear and tear, but also to a gradual fossilisation of the institution. Beaubourg (as it is often dubbed) reopened after a major revamp in January 2000 with enlarged museum, renewed performance spaces and way-out new restaurant by Jakob and MacFarlane, along with a mission to get back to the stimulating inter-disciplinary mix of old. *See also chapters* **Museums, Children, Dance, Film** *and* **Music: Classical & Opera**.

Eglise St-Gervais-St-Protais

pl St-Gervais/rue des Barres, 4th (01.48.87.32.02). Mº Hôtel de Ville. **Open** 5am-10pm daily. **Map K6** This church is late Gothic from rue des Barres and classical on place St-Gervais, where the facade added in 1621 was the first in Paris to use the three orders (Doric, Ionic, Corinthian). Inside is an impressive triple nave and series of side chapels, together with a central choir with carved choir stalls. The Couperin dynasty of composers were organists here.

Tour St-Jacques

pl du Châtelet, 4th. Mº Châtelet. **Map J6** Much-loved by the Surrealists, this solitary gargoyle-covered Flamboyant Gothic bell-tower is the remains of the St-Jacques-La-Boucherie church, built for the Butchers' Guild in 1523. Pascal did experiments on the weight of air here in the seventeenth century. A weather station now crowns the 52m-high tower, which can only be admired from outside.

The Marais

East of Roman rue St-Martin and rue du Renard lies the Marais, a magical area of narrow streets dotted with aristocratic *hôtels particuliers* (*see page 68*), narrow cobbled alleyways, art galleries, fashion boutiques, offbeat designers (*see chapter* **Fashion**) and stylish cafés. The big city slows down here, giving you time to notice carved doorways and early street signs carved into the stone.

The Marais, or 'marsh', started life as an uninhabited piece of swampy ground used for market gardening, inhabited only by a few religious foundations. In the sixteenth century the elegant **Hôtel Carnavalet** and **Hôtel de Lamoignan** prefigured its phenomenal rise as an aristocratic residential area after Henri IV began constructing the **place des Vosges** in 1605. Soon nobles began building smart townhouses where famous literary ladies like Mme de Sévigné and Mlle de Scudéry

*Paris' **town hall** has had a tumultuous past.*

and influential courtesan Ninon de l'Enclos held court. The area fell from fashion a century later; happily, many of the narrow streets were essentially unchanged as mansions became industrial workshops, schools, tenements, even a fire station. The current renaissance dates from 1962 and a preservation order from then-Culture Minister André Malraux, which safeguarded many endangered buildings for use as museums. Now it's one of Paris' liveliest, most international areas, and property prices have soared into the luxury bracket.

The rue des Francs-Bourgeois runs through the heart of the Marais. The street soon forgets its Les Halles legacy in the food shops of rue Rambuteau to become packed with elegant mansions and original shops: fashion boutiques such as Et Vous, **Blanc Bleu**, **Plein Sud** and **Abou Dhabi**, flower arrangements, housewares and garden gadgets at **Millefeuilles**, the delectable bathroom accessories of **Bains Plus**, the funky knickknacks of **La Chaise Longue**… The tea room Les Enfants Gâtés ('spoiled children') sums up the mood. For a little culture, seek out the elegant **Hôtel d'Albret** (No 31), with its Rococo facade, and the enormous early eighteenth-century **Hôtel de Soubise** (No 60), the national archives, of which a turreted medieval gateway survives on rue des Archives. Its interiors by Boucher and Lemoine can be seen as part of the **Musée de**

l'Histoire de France. On the corner of rue des Francs-Bourgeois and rue Pavée is the austere, renaissance **Hôtel de Lamoignon**. Built in 1585 for Diane de France, Henri II's illegitimate daughter, it now houses the Bibliothèque Historique de la Ville de Paris.

At its eastern end, the street runs into the place des Vosges, one of the most beautiful and intimate squares in Paris. Perfectly proportioned red brick and stone arcades of townhouses stand around a garden once much used for duels. At one corner is the **Maison de Victor Hugo**, once occupied by the author. Luxurious **Ambroisie** restaurant is for special treats; much simpler is touristy but charming Ma Bourgogne. An archway leads from the southwest corner into the garden court of the elegant **Hôtel de Sully**.

Just behind Hôtel de Soubise, the **Hôtel Guénégaud** (60 rue des Archives) was built in 1654 for Louis XIV's Secretary of State by Mansart, and now houses the **Musée de la Chasse et de la Nature**. Look out for one of the city's few remaining Gothic cloisters adjoining classical Eglise des Billettes, sandwiched at No 22 between the cafés and gay bars, and the curious Gothic turret on the corner of rue des Francs-Bourgeois and rue Vieille-du-Temple – the remains of the Hôtel Hérouët built c1500 for Jean Hérouët, Louis XII's treasurer. Huge Medusa-adorned oak doors at No 47 lead to the **Hôtel des Ambassadeurs de Hollande**, where Beaumarchais wrote *The Marriage of Figaro*.

Even workaday rue du Temple, once the road leading to the Templars' church, is full of surprises. Near rue de Rivoli, the Latina cinema specialises in Latin American films. At No 41 an archway leads into the courtyard of the former Aigle d'Or coaching inn, now the **Café de la Gare** café-théâtre, **Le Studio** Tex-Mex and dance studios. (Further north among bag and accessory wholesalers, this was also Paris' first 'Chinatown' and still celebrates Chinese New Year every year.) The imposing **Hôtel de St-Aignan** at No 71 contains the new Jewish museum. Just beyond it is the newly restored **Hôtel du Montmor** at No 79. Round the corner, **Hôtel de Hallwyl** is a rare domestic building by Ledoux.

The district's two most important museums are also in sumptuous *hôtels*. The **Musée Carnavalet** on rue de Sévigné, dedicated to Paris history, runs across the **Hôtel Carnavalet**, once home to famous letter-writer Mme de Sévigné, and the later Hôtel le Peletier de St-Fargeau. Curiosities include faithful reconstructions of Proust's bedroom and the Fouquet jewellery shop. The **Hôtel Salé** on rue de Thorigny, built and named in 1656 for a salt tax collector, has been finely restored and extended to house the **Musée National Picasso**. Fine *hôtels particuliers* abound: pretty **Hôtel Libéral Bruand** is now a lock museum, on rue du Parc-Royal; houses along the quieter northern

Marais mansions

Many of the finest Marais *hôtels particuliers* can be visited as museums, while the courtyards of others are often visible from the street. For some of the more private buildings, try a walking tour, or join the queues on the Journées du Patrimoine in September (*see chapter* **Paris by Season**).

Hôtel d'Albret
31 rue des Francs-Bourgeois, 4th. Mᵒ St-Paul. **Map L6**
The courtyard facade was built 1635-50, while the streetside facade was reconstructed in pure Rococo style in the 1740s. In the 1650s, Mme de Montespan, mistress of Louis XIV, was introduced here to Françoise d'Aubigné, widow of writer Scarron, who became governess to her eight illegitimate children. Françoise worked her way up via court governess to become the king's new official mistress, Mme de Maintenon. Now used by the cultural affairs department of the Ville de Paris. You can wander into the courtyard during the week.

Hôtel des Ambassadeurs de Hollande
47 rue Vieille-du-Temple, 4th. Mᵒ St-Paul. **Map K6**
Aka Hôtel Amelot de Bisseuil, this house (not open to the public) was built 1650-1660 by Pierre Cottard. Here in 1778 Beaumarchais wrote *The Marriage of Figaro*; seen as a narrowly disguised criticism of the court, it was initially censored. In the Revolution the hôtel became a dance hall. Behind the two massive oak doors decorated with Medusas are two courtyards, the first with sundials and stone figures of Romulus and Remus.

Hôtel Beauvais
68 rue François-Miron, 4th. Mᵒ St-Paul. **Map K6**
Now being restored, this sumptuous mansion was built in the 1650s for Catherine-Henriette Bellier, a chambermaid of Anne of Austria who married ribbon merchant Pierre de Beauvais. From here, Anne watched her son Louis XIV arrive with new bride Marie-Thérèse in 1660. Later the young Mozart performed here. The central balcony is adorned with goats' heads; the most innovative element is the courtyard, with a rotunda over the doorway.

Hôtel Carnavalet
23 rue de Sévigné, 3rd. Mᵒ St-Paul. **Map L6**
Begun c1550 for Jacques de Ligneries by Pierre Lescot, Carnavalet's U-shaped layout set the model for the Paris *hôtel particulier*: main building at the rear of a courtyard, lateral wings with stables and kitchens, entrance doorway closing the court from the street. In the 1660s, Mansart rebuilt the streetside building and added the grand staircase. Famous letter writer Mme de Sévigné (1626-96) spent her last 20 years here. Since 1866, Carnavalet has been the museum of Paris history (*see also chapter* **Museums**).

Hôtel Donon
8 rue Elzévir, 3rd. Mᵒ St-Paul. **Map L6**
Built for the royal buildings inspector, this pretty mansion gives an impression of verticality with its long windows, steep roof and narrow wings. Now housing the Musée Cognacq-Jay, it is one of the best places to see eighteenth-century panelled interiors.

Hôtel Guénégaud
60 rue des Archives, 3rd. Mᵒ Rambuteau. **Map K5**
A spare, almost sombre building from the outside, this has been attributed to François Mansart for its harmonious proportions. The building fell into a state of dereliction but has been beautifully restored.

Hôtel de Hallwyll
28 rue Michel-le-Comte, 3rd. Mᵒ Rambuteau. **Map L6**
A rare example of domestic architecture by Nicolas Ledoux, known for toll gates around the city. In the 1760s Ledoux brought the three-storey building into line with severe, geometrical Neo-Classical style, creating an Antique-inspired colonnade at the rear.

Hôtel Hénault de Cantorbe
5-7 rue de Fourcy, 4th. Mᵒ St-Paul. **Map L6**
Built in the early 1700s for the tax collector Hénault de Cantorbe, this place suffered a typical Marais decline, housing a cheese shop, ice-cream maker

and rundown flats, but has since been rescued to house the **Maison Européenne de la Photographie** with a modern extension by Yves Lion.

Hôtel Lamoignan
24 rue Pavée, 4th. M° St-Paul. **Map L6**
One of the earliest noble Marais mansions, it was built in 1585 for Diane de France, illegitimate daughter of Henri II. Jutting out into the street is a curious square turret. The courtyard has giant Corinthian pilasters and a Greek key frieze. Writer Alphonse Daudet had rooms here in the nineteenth century. The monumental building is now home to the **Bibliothèque Historique de la Ville de Paris;** the reading room still has its original painted beamed ceiling.

Hôtel Libéral Bruand
1 rue de la Perle, 3rd. M° St-Paul. **Map L6**
Built in 1685 by the architect of Les Invalides and the Salpêtrière for himself. The lovely main facade has a pediment decorated with cherubs round an *oeil de boeuf* window. There's a collection of locks and keys inside (*see* **Musée de la Serrure**).

Hôtel de Soubise/Hôtel de Rohan
60 rue des Francs-Bourgeois, 3rd.
M° Hôtel-de-Ville. **Map L6**
This is one of the grandest of *hôtels*. Built for the Prince and Princesse de Soubise, architect Delamair incorporated the turreted medieval gateway of the Hôtel de Clisson into one side of the colonnaded *cour d'honneur*, while the Rococo apartments (visible within the Musée de l'Histoire de France, *see chapter* **Museums**) were decorated by Boucher, Natoire, Restout and Van Loo. The adjoining Hôtel de Rohan (*87 rue Vieille-du-Temple*) also by Delamair, for Soubise's son, Bishop of Strasbourg, later Cardinal de Rohan, has a wonderful relief by Robert Le Lorrain, *The Horses of Apollo*.

Hôtel de St-Aignan
71 rue du Temple, 3rd. M° Rambuteau. **Map K6**
The austere street facade gives few hints of the grandeur within, but once in the courtyard you might think this *hôtel* was built for giants. Though most of the original interiors have been destroyed, frescoes in the vaulted dining room were rediscovered during renovation. In 1998 the hôtel opened as the Musée d'Art et d'Histoire du Judaïsme (*see chapter* **Museums**), which includes a tribute to Jewish families deported from their flats here during World War II.

Hôtel Salé
5 rue de Thorigny, 3rd. M° Chemin-Vert. **Map M6**
This *hôtel* built 1656-59 by architect Jean Boullier soon acquired the name *salé* from the salt tax which made the resident tax collector Fontenay his fortune. A spectacular semi-circular courtyard is overlooked by sphinxes; the grand stairway is carved with garlands and cupids. *See also* **Musée Picasso**.

Hôtel de Sens
1 rue du Figuier (01.42.78.14.60). M° St-Paul or Pont-Marie. **Map L7**
This rare example of Parisian medieval architecture was built 1475-1519 as a pied à terre for the wealthy Archbishops of Sens. Its fanciful turrets owe something to the nineteenth-century restorers' imagination. In the Wars of Religion, the Guise brothers hatched anti-royalist plots within its walls. Queen Margot lived here after she was repudiated by Henri IV, having failed to provide an heir. Today, it is home to the Bibliothèque Forney, devoted to applied and graphic arts. *See also* **Museums**.

Hôtel de Sully
62 rue St-Antoine, 4th (01.44.61.20.00). M° St-Paul or Bastille. **Open** *courtyards* 9am-6.30pm daily. **Map L7**
Designed by Jean Androuet du Cerceau in 1624, this *hôtel* was bought by Henri IV's former minister, the Duc de Sully. Today it houses the Caisse Nationale des Monuments Historiques and the Mission du Patrimoine Photographique. The fine interior is closed to the public, but walk through the two beautifully proportioned courtyards with carved reliefs. At the rear of the second one is a rare orangery.

reach of rue Vieille-du-Temple and rue Debelleyme hide the lofty spaces of some of Paris' most avant-garde art galleries (*see chapter* **Galleries**). Speculator Michel Villedo built several of the *hôtels* on rue de Turenne in the 1630s including Nos 52-54 and the graceful Hôtel d'Equevilly at No 60, subsequently redesigned in Rococo style. Its rear facade looks over a quiet, little-known public garden on pedestrianised rue de Hesse. Just beyond, the 1826-35 Eglise St-Denis-du-St-Sacrement was one of several Roman basilica-style churches built by Hippolyte Godde during the restoration.

The Marais is home to Paris' oldest Jewish community, centred on rue des Rosiers, rue des Ecouffes and rue Pavée (where there's a synagogue designed by Guimard). Originally mainly Eastern European Ashkenazi Jews who arrived last century after the pogroms (many were later deported during World War II), the community expanded in the 1950s and 60s with a wave of Sephardic Jewish immigration following French withdrawal from North Africa. Thus there are now falafel shops alongside the Jewish bakers and delis, such as Finkelstijn and **Chez Marianne**, and Paris' most famous Jewish eatery, Jo Goldenberg, its exterior badly pockmarked after a terrorist attack in the 1980s.

The lower ends of rue des Archives and rue Vieille-du-Temple are the centre of café life and happening bars, like cutesy **Petit Fer à Cheval** and cosmopolitan La Chaise au Plafond and Café du Trésor in the neighbouring impasse du Trésor. Rue des Archives, rue Ste-Croix-de-la-Bretonnerie and rue du Temple are the hub of the Paris gay scene, particularly thriving at happy hour. Charming place du Marché Ste-Cathérine is worth seeking out for the characterful Bar de Jarente and Jewish/East European restaurant Pitchi-Poï.

Place des Vosges
4th. M° St-Paul. **Map L6**
With its harmonious red-brick-and-stone arcaded facades and steeply pitched roofs, the first planned square in Paris feels far more intimate than the pomp of later Bourbon Paris. Laid out for Henri IV in 1605-12 on a perfectly symmetrical plan, the actual plots behind the facades were let out to speculators. Originally the place Royale, the square's name dates from the Napoleonic Wars, when the Vosges was the first region of France to pay its war taxes. Mme de Sévigné was born here in 1626. Then the garden saw duels and romantic trysts; now it attracts *boules* players and children.

The Temple & Arts et Métiers

The northern, less gentrified half of the Marais stretching towards place de la République is home to tiny local bars, costume-jewellery and rag-trade wholesalers and industrial workshops, alongside recently arrived fashion designers. The Quartier du Temple was once a fortified, semi-independent entity under the Knights Templar. The round church, keep and palace have long been replaced by Square du Temple, a romantic garden square full of ponds and curious bits of statuary, and the Carreau du Temple, rag trade and clothes market.

*Vosges in vogue: Henri IV's harmonious housing in the Marais' chic **Place des Vosges**.*

The keep became a prison in the Revolution, where the royal family were held in 1792. On rue de Bretagne are food shops and fashionable couscous restaurant **Chez Omar**; the Marché des Enfants Rouges, a seventeenth-century covered market closed despite vociferous local protest in 1995 – rumour has it it may reopen. The **Web Bar** on rue de Picardie runs exhibitions and concerts.

Back towards Beaubourg is the Arts et Métiers area, originally the powerful Abbey of St-Martin-des-Champs, transformed after 1789 into the **Musée des Arts et Métiers** (due to reopen in October 2000 after archaeological digs and renovation). This area is not as forgotten as it may look, with pricey, shabby-chic bistro **Ami Louis** and trendy Latin American restaurant **Anahi**. No 3 rue Volta was long thought the city's oldest house, but recent analysis puts its half-timbered structure in the sixteenth century. The earliest domestic dwelling in Paris is, however, nearby Auberge Nicolas Flamel (51 rue de Montmorency), now a bistro, built in 1407 for alchemist Nicolas Flamel.

The St-Paul District

In 1559, Henri II was mortally wounded in a jousting tournament on what is now broad, busy rue St-Antoine. He is commemorated in a grieving marble Virgin by Pilon commissioned by his widow Catherine de Médicis, now in the Jesuit church of **St-Paul-St-Louis**. Towards the Bastille, the heavily domed church of the Visitation Ste-Marie was designed in the 1630s by Mansart. South of rue St-Antoine towards the Seine is a more sedate residential area known as St-Paul. There are still plenty of fine houses, but the overall mood is more discreet. The **Village St-Paul**, a colony of antiques sellers between rues St-Paul, Charlemagne and quai des Celestins, is a promising source of 1930s and 50s furniture (open Mon, Thur-Sun). On rue des Jardins-St-Paul is the largest surviving section of the **wall of Philippe-Auguste**. The infamous poisoner Marquise de Brinvilliers lived at Hôtel de Brinvilliers (12 rue Charles V) in the 1630s. She killed father and brothers to get her hands on the family fortune, and was only caught after her lover died… of natural causes.

Two of the Marais' finest mansions are on rue François-Miron, an ancient fork of rue St-Antoine. **Hôtel de Beauvais**, No 68, is still being restored, while **Hôtel Hénault de Cantorbe** has been renovated with a striking modern extension as the **Maison Européenne de la Photographie**. Down rue de Fourcy towards the river, see the formal gardens of the **Hôtel de Sens**, a fanciful ensemble of Gothic turrets decorated with stone wolves and monsters, which houses the **Bibliothèque Forney**. Across from the tip of the Ile St-Louis, the small square Henri-Galli contains a rebuilt fragment of the Bastille prison (*see below*)

*Turrets and timelessness mark the **Marais**.*

and the **Pavillon de l'Arsenal**, built by a rich timber merchant to put on private art shows, is now used for architectural exhibitions.

Eglise St-Paul-St-Louis

99 rue St-Antoine, 4th (01.42.72.30.32). M° Bastille or St-Paul. **Open** 7.30am-8pm Mon-Wed, Sat; 7.30am-10pm Thur; 9am-8pm Sun. **Map L7**
The domed Baroque Counter-Reformation church, completed in 1641, is modelled like all Jesuit churches on the Gesù in Rome, with its three-storey hierarchical facade bearing statues of saints Louis, Anne and Catherine, single nave and side chapels. Its dome was the first important Baroque dome in Paris. The hearts of Louis XIII and XIV were stolen from here in the Revolution. Most of the original paintings were removed too, and the church became a temple of reason. In 1802 it was reconsecrated and now houses Delacroix's *Christ in the Garden of Olives*.

Fortified Wall of Philippe-Auguste

rue des Jardins-St-Paul, 4th. M° Pont Marie or St-Paul. **Map L7**
King Philippe-Auguste (1165-1223) was the first great Parisian builder since Roman times, enclosing the growing city on Left and Right banks within a great defensive wall. The largest surviving section, complete with towers, extends along rue des Jardins-St-Paul. Another chunk can be seen at 3 rue Clovis in the Latin Quarter; remnants of towers are dotted around St-Germain-des-Prés.

Mémorial du Martyr Juif Inconnu

17 rue Geoffroy l'Asnier, 4th (01.42.77.44.72).
M° St-Paul. **Open** 10am-1pm, 2-5.30pm Mon-Fri,
Sun. Closed Sat, Jewish holidays. **Admission** 15F;
free under-12s. **No credit cards. Map K6**
A reminder that many of the Jews rounded up in
World War II were residents of the Marais, this mon-
ument also serves as an archive and exhibition centre.

The Bastille & Eastern Paris

In the 11th and 12th arrondissements.
Traditionally a boundary point between central
Paris and the more proletarian east, **place de la
Bastille** has remained a potent symbol of popular revolt ever since the prison-storming that
inaugurated the Revolution, and is still a favoured spot for demos and gatherings. Since the 1980s,
it has also been a magnet for new cafés, galleries
and bars, transforming the area from one of craft
workshops into a young hotspot.

The site of the prison is now a Banque de France
office and the gap left by the castle ramparts forms
the present-day square, dominated by the massive
Opéra Bastille. Opened in 1989 on the bicentennial of Bastille Day, it remains highly controversial – but productions sell out and, along with the
creation of the Port de l'Arsenal marina to the
south, it has contributed to the area's rejuvenation.

Rue de Lappe typifies the Bastille's tranforma-
tion, as the last remaining furniture workshops,
the 1930s **Balajo** (*Bal à Jo*) dance hall, old
Auvergnat bistro **La Galoche d'Aurillac** and
grocer Chez Teil hold out against a dizzying array
of theme bars, gift shops and pseudo-Cuban cafés.

You can still catch a flavour of the old working-
class district at the Sunday morning market on
boulevard Richard Lenoir or up rue de la Roquette.
Rue du Fbg-St-Antoine still has numerous furniture-makers' *ateliers* and gaudy furniture stores,
but is being colonised by clothes shops and bars:
one can't but help feel a twinge of regret for when
the last neo-Louis XV chair or nubian slave candelabra disappears. Rue de Charonne has trendy
bars and bistros like **La Fontaine** (next to an
eighteenth-century fountain), **Chez Paul** and
Pause Café, as well as art galleries and shops full
of weird 60s furniture. Along with rue Keller, the
patch is a focus for record shops, streetwear and,
increasingly, young fashion designers.

But the main thoroughfares tell only half the
story, for the area developed its own distinctive
style of architecture. Behind narrow street front-
ages are quaintly named cobbled alleys, dating
back to the eighteenth century, lined with craftsmen's workshops or quirky bars and bistros.
Investigate the Cours de l'Ours, du Cheval Blanc,
du Bel Air (with hidden garden), de la Maison
Brûlée or the Passage du Chantier on Fbg-St-
Antoine, where a gaggle of salesmen try to lure
unsuspecting customers into its workshops, the
rustic-looking Passage de l'Etoile d'Or and the
Passage de l'Homme with old wooden shop fronts
on rue de Charonne. This land originally lay outside the city walls on lands belonging to the royal
Convent of St-Antoine where, in the Middle Ages,
skilled furniture-makers were free from the city's
restrictive guilds, beginning a tradition of independence and free-thinking that made this area a
powder keg during the Revolution. Now, however, many of the workshops are the studios of
artists, architects, designers or ad agencies.

East of Métro Ledru-Rollin is the bustling North
African-flavoured market of place d'Aligre and
covered Marché Beauvais, whose cast-iron structure dates from 1843. Nearby are lively wine bar Le
Baron Rouge and modish bistro **Le Square
Trousseau**, whose *belle époque* interior has featured in many ads. The Faubourg runs east to place
de la Nation, a traffic junction and red-light district
interesting for its two square pavilions and Doric
columns, remnants of the tax-collectors' wall built
by Ledoux pre-Revolution. In the centre is Dalou's
grandiose allegorical Triomphe de la République,
commissioned for the Revolution's centenary, 1889.

Boulevard Beaumarchais separates rowdy
Bastille from the elegant Marais. Look out for the
wonderful polygonal **Cirque d'Hiver Bouglione**, designed in 1852 in imitation of antique
polychromy by Hittorrf to house the circus in winter, and still used today. On rue Amelot, the
Clown Bar is where the circus *artistes* traditionally gathered before shows. East on rue de la
Roquette, a small park and playground surrounded by modern housing mark the site of the former
prison de la Roquette. The gateway has been preserved and a plaque remembers the 4000 resistance members imprisoned here in World War II.

Opéra Bastille

*pl de la Bastille, 12th (box office 08.36.69.78.68/
visits 01.40.01.19.70). M° Bastille.* **Tour** phone for
details. **Admission** *visits* 50F; 30F students, under-
16s, over-60s. **No credit cards. Map M7**
The megalithic Opéra Bastille has been a controversial *Grand Projet* for several reasons: the cost of
upkeep, its scale, the quality of the architecture, the
productions. Opened in 1989, some thought it a stroke
of socialist genius to implant a high-culture edifice in
a traditionally working-class district; others thought
it a typical piece of Mitterrand skulduggery. Recent
attention has centred on the building itself: netting
was put up to stop granite slabs falling on people
below, suggesting major repairs are already needed.
It was intended as an 'opera for the people', but that
never really happened; opera and ballet are now
shared with the Palais Garnier. *See also chapters*
Dance *and* **Music: Classical & Opera.**

Place de la Bastille

4th/11th/12th. M° Bastille. **Map M7**
Nothing remains of the prison which, on 14 July

1789, was stormed by the forces of the plebeian revolt. Though only a handful of prisoners remained, the event provided rebels with gunpowder and gave the insurrection momentum. It remains the eternal symbol of the Revolution, celebrated here with a lively street *bal* every 13 July. The prison was quickly torn down, its stones used to build Pont de la Concorde, though supposed chunks could also be bought from local entrepreneurs as souvenirs; vestiges of the foundations can be seen in the Métro; there's part of a reconstructed tower at square Henri-Galli (*see above*, **St-Paul district**). The Colonne de Juillet, topped by a gilded *génie* of Liberty, in the square's centre, remembers the Parisians killed in the revolutions of July 1830 and 1848.

South of the Bastille

A newish attraction here is the **Viaduc des Arts**, a former railway viaduct now containing glass-fronted craft and design boutiques. Atop the viaduct, the **Promenade Plantée** continues through the Jardin de Reuilly and east to the **Bois de Vincennes**. Further along, avenue Daumesnil is fast becoming a silicon valley of computer outlets. The area around the lion-gushing fountain of place Félix-Eboué is largely residential but a couple of oddities merit a visit: the tiny **Cimetière de Picpus**, a moving memorial to the French Revolution, and, at 186, one of the oddest churches in Paris, the **Eglise St-Esprit**, a concrete copy of Istanbul's Hagia Sophia. Just before the Périphérique, at No 293, the **Musée des Arts d'Afrique et d'Océanie** contains fantastic tribal art and an aquarium beloved by children.

It's hard to believe now that as late as the 1980s, wine was still unloaded off barges at Bercy, and the area was riddled with warehouses. This stretch of the Seine is firmly part of redeveloped Paris with the massive Ministère de l'Economie et du Budget – one of Mitterrand's *Grands Projets* – **Palais Omnisports de Paris-Bercy**, a pyramid-shaped sports stadium and concert venue with grass growing up the outside, the dramatic American Center (set to become the new Maison du Cinéma) by American architect Frank Gehry with cascading skyline overlooking the pleasant new **Parc de Bercy** and the Bercy Expo centre. At the eastern edge of the park, in striking contrast to the modern Ciné Cité multiplex, 42 *chais* or brick wine warehouses along the Cour St-Emilion have happily been preserved and will hopefully re-inject some animation into the area as they open as wine bars, crêperies and cafés. A further group has been converted as the Pavillons de Bercy, containing the Musée des Arts Forains fairground collection of mechanical music and Venetian carnival salons (open to groups by appointment 01.43.40.16.22).

Bois de Vincennes
12th. M° Porte-Dorée or Château de Vincennes.
The royal hunting forest of the Valois was made into

Ghost train

In the **Parc des Buttes-Chaumont**, children slide down the embankment and run along an old railway track and into disused tunnels. In the 20th *arrondissement* one can walk through a former station entrance, go past the closed ticket window and have a drink or meal overlooking phantom tracks in what has become a popular meeting place for young Parisians, the **Flèche d'Or** café. Of a Sunday, people stroll along the line.

Running 20 miles around the city boundaries, the small circular railway line known as the Petite Ceinture (small belt) was built under Napoléon III. At first, it was a freight line between mainline stations such as the Gare du Nord and the Gare du Lyon, but later it was converted into an urban railway that was used by millions. It continued to be widely travelled even after the opening of the Métro in 1900. But the line was virtually killed by the automobile boom in the 1920s and 30s and ceased operating in 1934.

First signs of rebirth came when part of the railway was used for the high-speed suburban RER commuter service and, more recently, for the automatic Météor Métro line. City planners have been examining how it might be used in the new millennium. Luckily, it is too narrow for a motorway or ring road. Pascal Payen-Appenzeller, the noted historian of Paris, says it will certainly be preserved and predicts that it will live again as a cycle route and perhaps as a run for Paris' hundreds of thousands of inline skaters.

Paris' biggest park in 1860 by Napoléon III, and owes much to Haussmann's landscape architect Alphand, who added the lake and cascades that are a major part of its charm. Boats can be hired on the lake, and there are cycle paths, a Buddhist temple, a racetrack, baseball pitch and flower gardens. It also contains Paris' main **Zoo** and the **Cartoucherie** theatre complex. The Parc Floral de Paris (01.43.43.92.95) boasts horticultural displays, summer concerts, a picnic area, exhibition space, children's amusements and crazy golf. Next to the park is the imposing **Château de Vincennes**, where England's Henry V died in 1422. *See also chapters* **Beyond the Périphérique, Children** *and* **Music: Rock, Roots & Jazz.**

Cimetière de Picpus

35 rue de Picpus, 12th (01.43.44.18.54). M° Nation. **Open** *15 Apr-14 Oct* 2-6pm Tue-Sun; *15 Oct-14 Apr* 2-6pm Tue-Sat. **Admission** 15F. **No credit cards. Map Q8**
This cemetery is redolent with revolutionary associations, both French and US, and is resting place of more than 1300 victims of the *semaine sanglante*, who were guillotined at place du Trône Renversé (now place de la Nation) between 14 June and 27 July 1794. At the end of a walled garden (complete with beehives and chicken coop) is a cemetery full of aristocratic French families (Noailles, Rochefoucauld, etc) almost everyone seems to be a count or marquess, and many have given their names to Paris streets. In one corner, shaded by stars and stripes reflecting a different revolution, is the tomb of statesman La Fayette, who'd fought in the American War of Independence and had been married to a Noailles. You can see the communal grave where the bodies were deposited and, at the end of the garden, the doorway where the carts carrying the bodies arrived; it was only thanks to a maid who had seen the carts that the site was rediscovered and the cemetery and adjoining convent founded by descendents of the Noailles family. Visit the small chapel, where two tablets on either end of the transept list the names and occupation of those executed: 'domestic', 'farmer', 'employee', figure alongside 'duchess', 'lawyer', 'abbess' and bring potent human sense to the Revolution.

Eglise St-Esprit

186 av Daumesnil, 12th (01.44.75.77.50). M° Daumesnil. **Open** 8am-7pm. **Map Q9**
If you've visited Istanbul, you're sure to feel a sense of *déjà vu* here: architect Paul Tournon was directly inspired by the Hagia Sofia. Behind a red brick exterior cladding, the 1920s concrete church follows a square plan around a central dome, lit by a scalloped ring of windows. Wall paintings are by Maurice Denis and others.

Parc de Bercy

rue de Bercy, 12th. M° Bercy. **Map N9**
On the site of the Bercy warehouses across the river from the new library, Bercy combines French love of geometry with that of food. There's a large lawn crossed by paths with trees and pergolas, and a grid with square rose, herb and vegetable plots, an orchard, and gardens representing the four seasons.

La Promenade Plantée

av Daumesnil, 12th. M° Bastille, Ledru-Rollin, Gare de Lyon or Daumesnil. **Map M8/N8**
There's life above art as the railway tracks atop the Viaduc des Arts have been replaced by a promenade planted with roses, shrubs and rosemary, offering a traffic-free, high-level view into Parisian lives. It continues at ground level through the Jardin de Reuilly and the Jardin Charles Péguy on to the Bois de Vincennes at the Porte Dorée in the east. Rollerbladers are banned, but no one seems to have noticed.

Le Viaduc des Arts

15-121 av Daumesnil, 12th. M° Bastille, Ledru-Rollin or Gare de Lyon. **Map M8**
Under the arches of a disused railway viaduct, chic glass-fronted workshops opened in 1995 now provide a showroom for designers and craftspeople, continuing the long tradition of furniture trades in the Faubourg St-Antoine. Some outlets are rather twee, but the variety is fascinating: from contemporary furniture designers to picture-frame gilders, tapestry restorers, porcelain decorators, architectural salvage and a French hunting horn maker.

The Champs-Elysées

In the 8th, 16th and 17th arrondissements.
Parisians (who don't often go there) can barely mention the avenue des Champs-Elysées without adding: 'the most beautiful avenue in the world'. If, on first, tourist-filled sight, the 'Elysian Fields' can be a disappointment, the avenue remains the symbolic gathering place of a nation – for France's victory in the 1998 football World Cup (the biggest crowd since the Liberation), 14 July, the final stage of the Tour de France, and the hub of Paris' celebrations welcoming in the new millennium.

After many years dominated by burger bars, overpriced cafés, car showrooms and synthetic shopping malls, the Champs-Elysées have been going through something of a renaissance. One of Jacques Chirac's worthier mayoral efforts was a major facelift here, with new underground car parks and smart granite paving. Upmarket shops and hotels have moved back in the past couple of years, including branches of **Louis Vuitton**, **Sephora**, **Fnac**, the **Ladurée** tea room and Marriott hotel, while a flock of stylish new restaurants, such as **Spoon, Food & Wine**, **Man Ray** and Lo Sushi, has arrived in surrounding streets. At night, there's an impressive vista from floodlit place de la Concorde to the Arc de Triomphe, with the crowds lining up for the glitzy **Lido** cabaret, **Queen** nightclub and numerous cinemas.

The great spine of western Paris started life as an extension to the Tuileries gardens, laid out by Le Nôtre in the seventeenth century. By the Revolution, the avenue had been laid along its full

Atop a former railway viaduct on the **Promenade Plantée**, *smell roses rather than traffic fumes.*

stretch, but was more a place for a Sunday stroll than a street. Shortly before the Revolution the local guard worried that its dark corners offered 'to libertines and people of bad intentions a refuge that they can abuse'. During the Second Empire, the avenue of world repute was born as the Champs-Elysées became a focus for fashionable society and theatre, for military parades and royal processions. Bismarck was so impressed when he arrived with the conquering Prussian army in 1871 that he had a replica, the Kurfürstendamm, built in Berlin. Smart residences and hotels sprang up along its upper half (among them Le Claridge, still a hotel residence, and the grandiose Elysée-Palace, now the CCF bank), together with streetlights, pavements, sideshows, concert halls, theatres and exhibition centres. As with the Prussians before, Hitler's troops in 1940 made a point of marching down it, to a silently hostile reception, but loud celebrations accompanied the victory march along the avenue in August 1944 (there are plans to erect a commemorative statue of De Gaulle striding down the avenue).

South of the avenue, the glass-domed **Grand Palais** and **Petit Palais**, both built for the 1900 *Exposition universelle* and still used for major shows, create an impressive vista across elaborate Pont Alexandre III to Les Invalides. The rear wing of the Grand Palais opening on to avenue Franklin D Roosevelt contains the **Palais de la Découverte** science museum.

To the north is a Paris of smart shops and officialdom. On circular place Beauvais a wrought-iron gateway leads to the Ministry of the Interior. At 55-57 rue du Fbg-St-Honoré lurks the eighteenth-century Palais de l'Elysée, the official presidential residence, with gardens extending to the edge of the Champs-Elysées. At No 35-39 are the equally palatial British Embassy (once the Hôtel Borghèse inhabited by the Princesse Borghèse, sister of Napoléon) and adjoining ambassadorial residence, as well as pricey fashon outlets, antiques shops and the exclusive **Hôtel Bristol**.

The lower, landscaped reach of the avenue hides two theatres and haute-cuisine restaurants **Laurent** and **Ledoyen** in fancy Napoléon III pavilions. At the Rond-Point des Champs-Elysées, Nos 7 and 9 give some idea of the splendid mansions that once lined the avenue. From here, the dress code leaps a few notches as avenue Montaigne reels off its array of haute-couture houses: Ungaro, Mugler, Dior and Chanel and more recent ready-to-wear arrivals 51 Montaigne, Prada and Calvin Klein in smart *hôtels particuliers*. Look for the lavish **Plaza Athénée** hotel and Auguste Perret's innovative 1911-13 **Théâtre des Champs-Elysées** concert hall topped by the fashionable Maison Blanche restaurant.

At the western end of the avenue, the **Arc de Triomphe** towers above the crazy traffic junction of place Charles de Gaulle, better known as the Etoile. Begun to glorify Napoléon, the giant triumphal arch was modified after his disgrace to celebrate the armies of the Revolution. The square was commissioned later by Haussmann and most of its harmonious facades, designed by Hittorff, are well preserved. From the top, you can look down on swathes of prize Paris real estate: the swanky mansions along avenue Foch – the city's widest street – or the prestige office buildings of avenues Hoche and Wagram.

Avenue de la Grande-Armée continues the *voie royale* towards the Grande Arche de la Défense via Porte Maillot, where the Palais de Congrès auditorium, hotel, conference and shopping centre put up in 1974 was recently reclad with a new exterior by Christian de Portzamparc.

Arc de Triomphe

pl Charles de Gaulle (access via underground passage), 8th (01.43.80.31.31). Mº Charles de Gaulle-Etoile. **Open** *Apr-Oct* 9.30am-11pm daily. *Nov-Mar* 10am-10.30pm daily. Closed public holidays. **Admission** 40F; 32F 12-25s; free under-12s. **Credit** MC, V. **Map C3**

The Arc de Triomphe forms the centrepiece of Paris' grand east-west axis from the Louvre, through the Arc du Carrousel and the place de la Concorde up to the Grande Arche de la Défense. The Arc is 50m tall, 45m wide and decorated with a giant frieze of battle scenes and sculptures on its flanks, including Rude's *Le Départ des Volontaires*, also known as *La Marseillaise*. Commissioned by Napoléon in 1806 as a tribute to his own military victories, it was completed only in 1836. In 1920 the Tomb of the Unknown Soldier was laid at the arch's base, and an eternal flame burns to commemorate the dead of World Wars I and II. From the top, there's a wonderful view of the twelve avenues radiating out.

Grand Palais

av Winston-Churchill, av du Général-Eisenhower, 8th (01.44.13.17.17/01.44.13.17.30). Mº Champs-Elysées-Clemenceau. **Map E5**

You can't miss the immense glass dome and galloping bronze horses pulling chariots atop the Grand Palais, built for the 1900 *Exposition universelle*. Its three facades were designed by three different architects, which explains the eclectic wealth of decoration. During World War II, it was used to hold German tanks. The wing on avenue du Général-Eisenhower is used for blockbuster art shows; the avenue Franklin D Roosevelt wing contains the **Palais de la Découverte**; the avenue Winston-Churchill wing was hurriedly closed down mid-exhibition in 1993 for structural repairs, when bits of metal started falling off the roof. The huge expense of restoration leaves some doubt whether it will ever reopen. *See chapter* **Museums**.

Petit Palais

av Winston-Churchill, 8th (01.42.65.12.73). Mº Champs-Elysées-Clemenceau. **Open** 10am-5.40pm. Tue-Sun. **Admission** 45F; 35F 7-16s, students; free under-7s. **Map E5**

Also built for the 1900 *Exposition universelle*, only here the style is rather more charmingly Rococo. Look for the grandiose barrel-vaulted entrance hall with painted ceilings and an attractive semi-circular courtyard garden surrounded by a marble-columned arcade. *See chapter* **Museums**.

Monceau & Batignolles

At the far end of avenue Hoche is intimate **Parc Monceau**, with its Antique follies and large lily pond. The park is usually full of neatly dressed children and nannies, and surrounded by some of the dearest apartments in Paris, part of the planned late nineteenth-century expansion of the city over the plaine Monceau. Three worthwhile museums give an idea of the extravagance of the area when newly fashionable, and the treasures amassed by some of its banking fortunes: the **Musée Nissim de Camondo** (a fantastic collection of eighteenth-century decorative art) and **Musée Cernuschi** (Chinese art), both overlooking the park, and the **Musée Jacquemart-André** (Old Masters and decorative art) on boulevard Haussmann. There are some nice exotic touches, such as the unlikely red lacquer Galerie Ching Tsai Too (48 rue des Courcelles, 8th), built in 1926 for a Chinese art dealer near the fancy wrought-iron gates of Parc Monceau, or the onion domes of the Russian Orthodox **Alexander Nevsky Cathedral** on rue Daru. Built in the mid-nineteenth century when a sojourn in Paris was an essential part of the education of every young Russian aristocrat, it is still at the heart of an emigré little Russia. The Fbg-St-Honoré contains the **Salle Pleyel** concert hall. At 11 rue Berryer, on the site of the house where Balzac died, stands the 1870s mansion built for Salomon de Rothschild, now the **Centre National de la Photographie**. The pedimented Neo-Classical church of St Philippe du Roule by Chalgrin, 1774-84, which served as a model for later basilica-style churches, takes one back down rue La Boétie to the Champs-Elysées.

Famed for its stand during the Paris Commune, the Quartier de Batignolles to the northeast of Parc Monceau, far from the clichéd image of the 17th *arrondissement*, is much more working-class, with the rue de Lévis street market and tenements overlooking a deep railway canyon. Overlooking the semi-circular place du Dr-Lobligeois are the pretty church of Ste-Marie des Batignolles and sleek cocktail bar **L'Endroit**. Behind the church, the Square de Batignolles was laid out by Haussmann's emissary Alphand with grotto and lake.

Alexander Nevsky Cathedral

12 rue Daru, 8th (01.42.27.37.34). Mº Courcelles. **Open** 3-5pm Tue, Fri, Sun. **Map D3**

With enough onion domes and gilding, icons and frescoes to make you think you were in Moscow, this Russian Orthodox church was built 1859-61 in the Neo-Byzantine Novgorod-style of the 1600s, on a Greek-cross plan by the Tsar's architect Kouzmine.

Cimetière des Batignolles

rue St-Just, 17th (01.46.27.03.18). Mº Porte de Clichy. **Open** *May-Oct* 8am-6pm daily; *Nov-Apr* 8am-5pm.

Squeezed between the Périphérique and the boulevards des Amiraux lie the graves of poet Paul

And God created Paris...

Notre Dame, la Sainte Chapelle, St-Germain-des-Prés... Paris is full of sumptuous reminders of France's status as a centre of Christianity. But a wander off the well-worn pilgrims' path can be enlightening.

The Jewish tradition favours intimate places of worship, but one notable exception is the lavish, late nineteenth-century **Grande Synagogue de la Victoire** (44 rue de la Victoire, 9th/01.40.82.26.26), the second-biggest synagogue in Europe. The Marais, where many Ukrainian and Polish Jews settled after the pogroms, boasts a number of smaller synagogues. Two fine examples of Art Nouveau architecture can be found at 21bis rue des Tournelles (4th/01.42.74.32.65) and 10 rue Pavée (4th/01.48.87.21.54), where the facade representing the Tablets was commissioned in 1913 from the architect Guimard (of Métro station fame). More recently, a contemporary synagogue opened in 1997 in **Le Perreux** (173 av du Général de Gaulle, 94170 Le-Perreux-sur-Marne/01.48.72.88.65), just outside Paris. Its high ceilings, blond wood interior, generous views and seating for women have earned it the nickname of 'the year 2000 synagogue'.

It's not the Himalayas, but the boating lake in the Bois de Vincennes provides a suitably pastoral setting for the Tibetan Temple in Paris. Housed in the brightly coloured Kagyu-Dong Centre, the temple can be visited by appointment. The centre is part of the **International Buddhist Institute of Paris** (route de la ceinture du Lac Daumesnil, 12th/01.40.04.98.06), a striking group of buildings left from the 1931 Colonial Exhibition. This is the site of festivities (9 Apr, 21 May, 18 June, 16 July, 24 Sept, 15 Oct in 2000), when the grounds fill up with stalls selling food and the smell of spices and incense mingle in the air. There are smaller temples in Chinatown, in the 13th, where Buddha is paraded in the streets during the Chinese New Year.

The **Grande Mosquée de Paris** (pictured, *see chapter* **Left Bank**) was built in the 1920s in honour of the Muslims who fought for France in World War I. It also houses the Institute of Muslim studies and a public complex with Turkish baths and a popular tea room. The elaborate woodwork and mosaics were created by Paris-based Moroccan craftsmen. Paris abounds with smaller mosques, including **Khaled Ib Wallid** (28 rue Myrha, 18th), which is occasionally raided by police looking for Islamic radicals. Its imam, Cheikh Sahr Aoui, was assassinated on the premises in 1995.

Housed in a former cabinetmaker's workshop, the principal Hindu temple in Paris is dedicated to Ganesh, the elephant-headed god of wisdom and families (Sri Manicka Vinayakar Alayam, 72 rue Philippe de Girard, 18th/01.40.34.21.89). Paris' Hindu community is mainly Sri Lankan and Indian but also counts a number of French-speakers from Mauritius, Martinique, Réunion and Guadeloupe. Every September (10th in 2000), amid garlands of flowers and fronds of peacock feathers, the statue of Ganesh is paraded through the streets on an elaborate chariot pulled by bare-chested, barefoot men. The exuberant procession weaves past Indian shops whose owners offer food and drink to participants. The route is sprayed with rose water by municipal lorries commandeered for the occasion.

You don't have to practise a particular religion to sit in Japanese architect Tadao Ando's meditation space, a stark 33m^2 cylinder commissioned by UNESCO to symbolise peace (*see chapter* **Left Bank**). The floor is paved with granite exposed to the atomic bombing of Hiroshima (since decontaminated) – a suitably sombre subject to ponder for people of all religions.

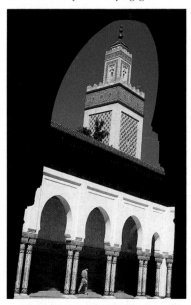

If it's haute couture it's here: **Avenue Montaigne** *in the rejuvenated Champs-Elysées area.*

Verlaine, Surrealist André Breton, and Léon Bakst, costume designer of the Ballets Russes.

Parc Monceau
bd de Courcelles, av Hoche, rue Monceau, 8th.
Mº Monceau. **Map E2**
Surrounded by grand *hôtels particuliers*, Monceau is a favourite with well-dressed *BCBG* children and their nannies. It was laid out in the late eighteenth century for the Duc de Chartres (Philippe-Egalité) in the English style that was then so fashionable, with an oval lake, spacious lawns and a variety of follies: an Egyptian pyramid, a Corinthian colonnade, Venetian bridge and ancient tombs.

The 16th Arrondissement

South of the Arc de Triomphe, avenue Kléber leads to the monumental buildings and terraced gardens of the Trocadéro, an area transformed for the 1937 *Exposition universelle*. The vast symmetrical curved wings of the **Palais de Chaillot** dominate the hill, with spectacular views over the river to the Eiffel Tower (the central parvis is currently closed for structural repairs). It houses maritime and anthropological museums, the Cinémathèque and the Théâtre National de Chaillot. The surrounding Trocadéro gardens, laid out in picturesque meanders and terraces, have become a little dilapidated (there are plans to restore the aquarium), but the impressive central pool with bronze and stone statues showered by powerful fountains forms a spectacular ensemble with the Eiffel Tower and Champ de Mars across the river.

Hidden among the shops on avenue Victor-Hugo, behind conventional-looking apartments, is the Galerie Commerciale Argentine, a brick and cast-iron apartment block and shopping arcade, now mostly empty, designed by ever-experimental Henri Sauvage and Charles Sarazin in 1904.

At place d'Iéna stands the circular Conseil Economique, a striking example of the concrete architecture of Auguste Perret, opposite the rotunda of the **Musée Guimet**, with its collection of Asian art (reopening after renovation autumn 2000). Like the Palais de Chaillot and Conseil Economique, the Palais de Tokyo on avenue du Président-Wilson was built for the 1937 Exposition. Today the left wing is home to the **Musée d'Art Moderne de la Ville de Paris**, which holds excellent exhibitions of modern and contemporary art. The other wing will open as the Centre de la Jeune Création, showing young artists, in autumn 2000. Opposite, the **Musée de la Mode et du Costume** houses temporary fashion-related exhibitions. On avenue Marceau, the 1930s church of St-Pierre de Chaillot is a massive neo-Byzantine structure with reliefs by Bouchard. Paris acquired a de facto new monument at the place de l'Alma after the fatal accident of Princess Diana and Dodi Al-Fayed in the Alma tunnel on 31 August 1997. Proposals have been put forward for an official memorial, but the golden flame (a replica of that on the Statue of Liberty given as a return homage by the city of New York) at the junction with avenue de New-York has been covered in flowers and messages ever since.

Cimetière de Passy

2 rue du Commandant-Schloesing, 16th (01.47.27.51.42). Mº Trocadéro. **Open** *summer* 8am-5.45pm daily; *winter* 8am-5.15pm. **Map B5**
Behind a 30s Modernist portal, tombs include those of composers Debussy and Fauré, Impressionist painters Manet and his sister-in-law Berthe Morisot, Art Deco designer Ruhlmann and writer Giraudoux, amid numerous generals and politicians.

Palais de Chaillot

pl du Trocadéro, 16th. Mº Trocadéro. **Map C5**
Looming across the river from the Eiffel Tower, the immense pseudo-classical Palais de Chaillot was built by Azéma, Boileau and Carlu for the 1937 international exhibition, over the foundations of an earlier complex put up for the 1878 World Fair. The giant colonnaded facade and marble foyers are typical of the monumental official architecture of the time and expression of state prestige, though accusations of totalitarianism are probably an anachronistic reading. It is adorned with inscriptions by Paul Valéry, sculpted bas-reliefs and, at the end of the two central pavilions, giant bronzes of *Apollo* (by Bouchard) and *Hercules* (by Pommier). The Palais is home to the **Musée de la Marine** (marine and naval history) and **Musée de l'Homme** (ethnology, anthropology, human biology) in the western wing, and in the eastern, the former Musée des Monuments Historiques, due to reopen as the Centre pour le Patrimoine Monumental et Urbain in 2001, and **Théâtre National de Chaillot**. The **Cinémathèque** repertory cinema has reopened after a fire, but the Musée du Cinéma, currently closed, is likely to move to Bercy.

Passy & Auteuil

West of here, most of the 16th *arrondissement* is pearls-and-poodle country, dotted with important curios, avant-garde architecture and classy shops.

When Balzac lived at 47 rue Raynouard (now **Maison de Balzac**), Passy was a village noted for its vines and aristocratic residences, where people came to take cures for anaemia at its mineral springs. Many Parisians, however, perversely preferred the dubious delights of drinking the Seine (one theory being a confusion between the words Seine and *saine* – meaning healthy). Perched above the river, imposing 30s apartment blocks now dominate rue Raynouard, including No 55 by the Perret brothers, but the Maison de Balzac still gives a feel of this rural past, even more so if you take a detour along cobbled rue Bertin – used by Balzac to escape from his creditors. Amid the private houses of square Charles-Dickens, the **Musée du Vin** is located in what were the cellars of a wine-producing monastery destroyed in the Revolution.

Passy was absorbed into the city in 1860 and today is full of smart Haussmannian apartment blocks, but readily available building land also meant that behind the bourgeois respectability, Passy and adjoining Auteuil were prime territory

for the experiments of avant-garde architects. Centre of life is rue de Passy, the former village high street, with Franck et Fils department store, upmarket fashion and food shops, the covered Marché de Passy and partially pedestrianised rue de l'Assomption. From place du Costa-Rica, rue Benjamin-Franklin (the US statesman was another Passy resident) leads towards Trocadéro (*see above*). At No 8, the apartment of French statesman Georges Clemenceau can be visited (01.45.20.53.41/Tue, Thur, Sat, Sun 2-7pm/25F, 20F students); Perret's ground-breaking apartment building at 25bis (a concrete structure clad in floral ceramic tiles) now contains clothes store **APC**.

The best things, however, take a bit of searching out: exclusive residential cul-de-sacs or houses and gardens affordable only by those with film star incomes. Explore the Villa Beauséjour, where three Russian wooden *dachas* by craftsmen from St Petersburg were rebuilt after the 1867 *Exposition universelle*, then join local families-plus-dogs for lunch at trendy **La Gare** restaurant in the former Passy-La Muette train station.

The **Jardins du Ranelagh**, laid out as high-society pleasure gardens, modelled on the bawdy eighteenth-century London version, are now a family park with a charming hand-wound, iron merry-go-round. On the western edge, the **Musée Marmottan** (rue Louis-Boilly) features a fabulous collection of Monet's late water lily canvases.

Next to the Pont de Grenelle is the circular drum of **Maison de Radio-France**, the giant Orwellian home to the state broadcasting bureaucracy, opened in 1963. You can attend concerts or take guided tours round its endless corridors and Musée de Radio France (*see chapters* **Museums**, *and* **Music: Classical & Opera**); employees nickname it 'Alphaville' after the Godard film.

From here, in upmarket Auteuil, go up rue La Fontaine, the best place for specimens of Art Nouveau architecture by Hector Guimard. Despite extravagant iron balconies, **Castel Béranger** at No 14 was originally low-rent lodgings; Guimard also designed the whole block that curves fluidly round the corner of 43 rue Gros, 17-19 rue La Fontaine and 8-10 rue Agar, incorporating the adorable **Café Antoine**, the rather gloomy Hôtel Mezzara at 60 rue La Fontaine, as well as a house, office and *atelier* in 1911 at 122 avenue Mozart for himself and his American artist wife Adeline Oppenheim. At 96 rue La Fontaine a plaque marks the house where Marcel Proust was born in 1871.

The area around Métro Jasmin is the place to pay homage to the area's other prominent architect, Le Corbusier. The **Fondation Le Corbusier** is in two of his avant-garde houses in the square du Dr-Blanche. A little further away, rue Mallet-Stevens features six white geometric houses and studios designed 1926-27 by Robert Mallet-Stevens. Most have been rather altered, but one has a fantastic stained glass stairwell. Round the corner, in a studio crammed with sculptures, casts and moulds is the **Musée Henri Bouchard**.

There are plenty of exclusive *villas* in Auteuil, too, like Villa Montmorency, with its little gardens off boulevard de Montmorency and winding Avenue de la Réunion off rue Chardon-Lagache. The *quartier* centres on rue d'Auteuil, with its cafés, pâtisseries, vintage sweetshop Dragées d'Auteuil, and souvenirs of former aristocratic residents: the garden facade of the Hôtel de Verrière, where the father of George Sand was born, and a house where Molière used to live. The Eglise d'Auteuil was designed by Vaudemer in the Romano-Byzantine style popular at the end of the nineteenth century. At the western edge of Auteuil are Parc des Princes sports stadium, home to Paris St-Germain football club; Roland Garros tennis courts, home of the French Open; and **Les Serres d'Auteuil** greenhouses and gardens, once part of Louis XV's nurseries and still the municipal florist.

West of the 16th sprawls the bois de Boulogne, once a royal hunting reserve and made into a park by Napoléon III, full at weekends now with dog-walking Parisians.

Bois de Boulogne

16th. M° Porte-Dauphine or Les Sablons.
Covering 865 hectares, the Bois was the ancient hunting Forêt de Rouvray. A series of gardens within scrubby woodland, cut through by roads, footpaths and tracks for horse riders and cyclists, it was landscaped in the 1860s when grottoes and cascades were created around the Lac Inférieur, where you can hire rowing boats in summer. Within the Bois, the Jardins de Bagatelle (route de Sèvres à Neuilly, 16th/ 01.40.67.97.00/open 9am-5.30pm/8pm summer), surrounding a château that belonged to Richard Wallace, the Marquis of Hertford, are famous for their roses, daffodils and water lilies. The **Jardin d'Acclimatation** is an amusement park for kids. The Bois also has two racecourses (Longchamp and Auteuil), sports clubs, the **Musée des Arts Populaires** and the **Pré Catelan** restaurant. Packed at weekends with dog walkers, picnickers and sports enthusiasts, at night it's more seedy; despite clean-up attempts it is still associated with kerb-crawling.

Castel Béranger

14 rue La Fontaine, 16th. Closed to the public. **Map A7**
Guimard's masterpiece built 1895-98 is the building that epitomises Art Nouveau in Paris. Guimard sought not just a new aesthetic, in rejection of historical eclecticism of the Beaux-Arts style, but also explored new materials. Here you can see his love of brick and wrought-iron, asymmetry, the inspiration of the vegetal and renunciation of harsh angles not found in nature. Along with the whiplash motifs characteristic of Art Nouveau, there are still signs of Guimard's earlier taste for fantasy and the medieval, as a disciple of Gothic revivalist Viollet-le-Duc. Green seahorses climb up the facade, and the faces on the balconies are supposedly a self-portrait of Guimard, inspired by Japanese figures to ward off evil spirits. Guimard had his architecture studio here and neo-Impressionist painter Paul Signac was an early tenant. Guimard designed all the interiors, too, from door handles and keyholes to fireplaces and fitted kitchens.

*In contrast to the fat cats of nearby Monceau, **Batignolles** keeps its working-class flavour.*

Fondation Le Corbusier

Villa La Roche, 10 square du Dr-Blanche, 16th (01.42.88.41.53). M° Jasmin. **Open** 10am-12.30pm, 1.30-6pm Mon-Thur; 10am-12.30pm, 1.30-5pm Fri (library 1.30-6pm). Closed Aug, Christmas. **Admission** 15F; 10F students. **No credit cards.**

This house, designed by Le Corbusier in 1923 for Swiss art collector Raoul La Roche, is where the architect tried out his radical ideas, later enunciated in *Cinq Points d'une architecture nouvelle*. Here are all the typical pilotis (stilts), strip windows, roof terraces, built-in furniture, and play of space and light through split volumes and internal balconies, though no stereotype Modernist white – the interior, hung with Le Corbusier's paintings and furnished with his and Charlotte Perriand's furniture, is painted in muted pinks, greens, browns and blues.

Les Serres d'Auteuil

3 av de la Porte d'Auteuil, 16th (01.40.71.75.23). M° Porte d'Auteuil. **Open** 10am-5pm daily. **Admission** 5F; 2.50F 6-12s, over-60s, under-6s. **No credit cards.**

These wonderfully romantic glasshouses were opened in 1895 to cultivate plants for parks and public spaces across Paris. Today there are seasonal displays of orchids and begonias. Best of all is the steamy tropical central pavilion with palm trees, birds and a pool of Japanese ornamental carp.

Montmartre & Pigalle

Mainly in the 9th and 18th arrondissements.

Montmartre, away to the north of the city centre on the tallest hill in the city, is the most unabashedly romantic district of Paris. Despite the onslaught of tourists who throng Sacré-Coeur and place du Tertre, it's surprisingly easy to get away from the main tourist drag. Climb and descend quiet stairways, peer into little alleys, steep stairways and deserted squares or find the ivy-clad houses with gardens to catch its old village atmosphere.

For centuries, Montmartre was a quiet, windmill-packed village. Then, as Haussmann sliced through the city centre, working-class families began to move out from the old city in search of accommodation and peasant migrants poured into industrialising Paris from across France. The hill was absorbed into Paris in 1860, but remained fiercely independent. In 1871, after the Prussians capitulated, the new right-wing French government sought to disarm the local National Guard by taking away its cannons in Montmartre. An angry crowd led by teacher and radical heroine Louise Michel drove off the government troops, killing two generals and taking over the guns, thus starting the Paris Commune, commemorated by a plaque on rue du Chevalier-de-la-Barre. From the 1880s artists moved in. Toulouse-Lautrec patronised Montmartre's bars and immortalised its cabarets in his posters; later it was frequented by artists of the Ecole de Paris, Utrillo and Modigliani.

The best starting point is the Abbesses Métro,

one of only two in the city (along with Porte Dauphine) to retain its original Art Nouveau glass awning designed by Hector Guimard. Across place des Abbesses is the Art Nouveau church **St-Jean de Montmartre**, with its turquoise mosaics around the door. Along rue des Abbesses and adjoining rue Lepic, which winds its way up the *butte* (hill), are many excellent food shops, wine merchants, busy cafés, including the heaving **Sancerre** and quieter Le Chinon, and offbeat boutiques, such as Bonnie Cox, Omiz, **Futurewear Lab** and crazy hat shop **Têtes en l'Air**. Wander up impasse Marie-Blanche, where there's a strange neo-Gothic house. In rue Tholozé is the famous **Studio 28** cinema, opened in 1928. Buñuel's *L'Age d'Or* had its riotous première here in 1930 and the interior, hung with canvases by Miró, Ernst and Dalí, was sacked; you can still see footprints made by Buñuel and Cocteau in the foyer.

In the other direction from Abbesses, at 11 rue Yvonne-Le-Tac, is the Chapelle du Martyr where, according to legend, St Denis picked up his head after his execution by the Romans in the third century. Montmartre probably means 'hill of the martyr' in his memory, or it may derive from temples to Mars and Mercury in Roman times.

Around the corner, the cafés of rue des Trois Frères are popular for an evening drink. At the lower end the street leads into place Charles-Dullin, with the Atelier Théâtre, at the upper end, into place Emile-Goudeau, whose staircases, wrought-iron streetlights and old houses are particularly evocative, as is the unspoiled bar Chez Camille. At No 13 stood the Bateau Lavoir, named after the medieval washing stands along the Seine. Once a piano factory, it was divided in the 1890s into a warren of studios where artists lived in total penury, among them Braque, Picasso and Juan Gris. Among the ground-breaking works of art created here was Picasso's *Desmoiselles d'Avignon*. The building burned down in 1970, but its replacement still rents out space to artists. Further up the hill on rue Lepic are the village's two surviving windmills. The Moulin de Radet was moved here in the seventeenth century from a hillock in rue des Moulins near the Palais-Royal. The Moulin de la Galette, made famous by Renoir's painting of an evening's revelry, is now a restaurant.

On top of the hill, the seething thoroughfare rue du Mont-Cenis, place du Tertre and adjoining streets express all that's worst about Montmartre today, packed with souvenir shops and touristy restaurants. Dozens of so-called artists compete to sketch your portrait or try to flog lurid sunset views of Paris; there's slightly more illustrious art at the **Espace Dalí** on rue Poulbot. According to legend, it was in the square that one of the best-known French words had its origins, as occupying Russian soldiers in 1814 demanded to be served quickly, or *'bistro'* in their native tongue.

Just off the square is the oldest church in the district, **St-Pierre-de-Montmartre**, whose columns have grown bent with age. Founded by Louis VI in 1133, it is a fine example of early Gothic, and a striking contrast to its extravagant neighbour and Montmartre's most prominent landmark, **Sacré-Coeur**, standing on the highest point in the city. If you're climbing up from square Willette, avoid the main steps and try the less-crowded steps of rue Foyalter or rue Maurice-Utrillo on either side.

Descending the hill northwards in rue des Saules is the **Montmartre vineyard** planted in 1933 in memory of the vineyards that covered the hillside ever since the Gallo-Roman period. The grape-picking each autumn is an annual ritual. As for the wine itself, a local ditty proclaims that for every glass you drink, you pee twice as much out (*see chapters* **Paris by Season** *and* **Food & Drink**). Further along on rue St-Vincent, weeds grow in abundance at the Jardin Sauvage de St-Vincent, intended as a conservation area. Nearby in rue Cortot is the quiet manor housing the **Musée de Montmartre**, devoted to the area and its former inhabitants. Dufy, Renoir, Valadon and Utrillo all had studios in the entrance pavilion.

Further down the hill amid rustic, shuttered houses is the **Lapin Agile** cabaret at 22 rue des Saules, another legendary meeting point for Montmartre artists, which derived its name from André Gill, who painted the inn sign of a rabbit (*lapin à Gill*). Singers of nostalgic ilk still appear here today. A series of pretty squares leads to rue Caulaincourt, towards the **Cimetière de Montmartre**, a curiously romantic place. Winding down the back of the hill, broad avenue Junot is lined with exclusive houses, among them the one built by Adolf Loos for Dadaist poet Tristan Tzara at No 15, a monument of modernist architecture.

Cimetière de Montmartre

20 av Rachel, access by stairs from rue Caulaincourt, 18th (01.43.87.64.24). M° Blanche. **Open** *summer* 9am-5.45pm daily; *winter* 9am-5.15pm. **Map G1**
This small, romantic ravine was once quarries, then a communal burial pit. Here you will find Sacha Guitry, Truffaut, Nijinsky, Berlioz, Degas, Greuze, Offenbach, Feydeau, Dumas *fils*, German poet Heine and many others reflecting the area's artistic past. There's also La Goulue, real name Louise Weber, first great star of the cancan and model for Toulouse-Lautrec, celebrated beauty Mme Récamier, and the consumptive heroine Alphonsine Plessis, inspiration for Dumas' *La Dame aux Camélias* and Verdi's *La Traviata*. Flowers and poems are still left daily for Egyptian diva Dalida, who lived nearby.

Sacré-Coeur

35 rue du Chevalier-de-la-Barre, 18th (01.53.41.89.00). M° Abbesses or Anvers. **Open** *church* 6am-11pm daily; *crypt/dome* 9am-6pm daily. **Admission** *church* free. *Crypt or dome* 15F; 8F

6-16s, students, over 60s; free under-6s. *Crypt and dome* 30F; 16F 6-25s; free under-6s. **No credit cards. Map J1**
The icing sugar-white dome is one of the most visible landmarks in Paris. Begun as an act of penance after the nation's defeat by the Prussians in 1870, it wasn't finished until 1914; consecration finally took place in 1919. A jumble of architects worked on the mock Romano-Byzantine edifice. The interior is lavishly adorned with gaudy Neo-Byzantine mosaics. The view from the dome gallery is fabulous.

Pigalle

Straddling the 9th and 18th *arrondissements* from busy place de Clichy with its multiplex cinema and glitzy Brasserie Wepler along boulevards de Clichy and de Rochechouart, Pigalle has long been the most important sleaze centre of Paris. By the end of last century, of the 58 houses on rue des Martyrs, 25 were cabarets (a few, such as drag shows **Michou** and **Madame Arthur**, remain today); others were dubious hotels used for illicit liaisons. Flashing neon signs still offer live peep shows and erotic videos, and coachloads of tourists file along to inspect the sex shops. The tradition has been given a cultural twist by the erotic art collection at the **Musée de l'Eroticisme**. Marked by its red windmill on place Blanche, the **Moulin Rouge**, once the image of naughty *fin de siècle* Paris, has become a tourist draw. Its befeathered dancers still cancan across the stage but are no substitute for La Goulue and Joseph Pujol – the *pétomane* who could fart melodies – of earlier times. Next door under a curved iron sign, the Cité Véron is a picturesque cobbled alley with a small theatre and cottagey apartments, among them 6bis (01.46.06.73.56 open by appointment), where Boris Vian lived 1953-58, filled with memorabilia.

This brash area has recently become a trendy night spot inhabited by the mediarati. The Moulin Rouge's old restaurant has become the **MCM Café**, **Folies Pigalle** cabaret is a hip club. What was once the Divan Japonais depicted by Toulouse-Lautrec has been transformed into **Le Divan du Monde**, a streetwise nightclub and music venue. Laidback youth pile into **La Fourmi** bar, while the **Elysée Montmartre** *belle époque* music hall puts on an eclectic array of bands.

La Nouvelle Athènes

Just south of Montmartre lies this mysterious, often overlooked *quartier* that was once beloved of artists of the Romantic era. Long-forgotten actresses and *demi-mondaines* had bijoux mansions built there on their money or gold Louis put up by wealthy admirers. Some of the prettiest can be found in tiny rue de la Tour-des-Dames, which refers to one of the many windmills owned by the once-prosperous Couvent des Abbesses.

The beautiful and the bizarre

Sifting through other people's junk is, after the cinema, France's most popular pastime. It is such an integral part of French life that there is a special word for it: *chiner*, 'to hunt for antiques'. And although the days when priceless artefacts could be picked up for a song from naive dealers are long gone, the beautiful and the bizarre can still be had.

Even if you do not plan to buy, the *marché aux puces* (flea market) at the Porte de Clignancourt, actually located in suburban St-Ouen, provides an aesthetic feast for anyone who is interested in history or fashion or is just plain curious about other people's lives. The largest antiques market in the world, it boasts over 2000 stands and is in fact 13 separate markets, each with its own distinctive character. Don't be discouraged by the ramshackle stalls which line the route from the Métro, but continue past the gypsy fortune-teller and the hot-dog stands, pass under the thundering *périphérique* and turn left into the rue des Rosiers, the main drag.

Marché Vernaison

If you have time for only one market, choose this, the oldest and most charming. Small shops spill an intriguing mishmash of objects out into the labyrinth of narrow alleyways. Vernaison is particularly good for china dolls, Steiff teddy bears, elegant Art Deco light fixtures, old train sets, vintage advertising posters and exquisite fabrics. Pascal Evenu (150bis, Allée 7) has an extensive array of French kitsch, including 50s ashtrays advertising Dubonnet or Gauloises. Antik'art (157, Allée 2) stocks Bakelite radios. Francine (stand 121-123, Allée 7), has an excellent collection of bedlinen, old lace and embroidered silks.

Marché Malik

The vintage clothes market has sadly been largely taken over by stands selling cheap modern fashions. However, it is worth visiting for the couple of goldmines which remain. Top designers, including Gaultier and Galliano, regularly scour Malik for inspiration. Go to Violette et Sarah (42 rue Paul Bert) for nineteenth-century silk gowns, 1940s rayon dresses and velvet evening bags. Brigitte (3 rue Jules-Vallès) often has more affordable prices, as does neighbour Monique.

Marché Serpette

The carpeted, heated Serpette is the most luxurious and expensive of the markets and, for sheer comfort, is the place to head on a cold, rainy day. There is a lot of Art Deco, Vuitton luggage, paintings and jewellery. Go to number 13, allée 3, where the extravagantly moustachioed Alain Broussaille repairs and sells old lighters and fountain pens. One of his own paintings forms the background to his Gothic stand. Look out for Olwen Forest's glamorous costume jewellery.

Marché Paul Bert

Prices are lower at the open-air market next to Serpette. Here you might find anything: a stuffed leopard in a glass case, a 50s jukebox or an oversized clock from a Paris street corner. One stall is a treasure trove of high-quality if pricey old French kitchenwares.

Best of the rest

The Marché Biron is the place to find over-the-top Louis XV gilt chairs, an ormolu candelabra, crystal glasses, expensive jewellry. Built in 1989 and 1991, Malassis and Dauphine lack the old-world charm of Vernaison or Paul Bert, but are still worth a visit. For lunch, don't miss Chez Louisette, a kitsch old café tucked away at the end of the Marché Vernaison where you can listen to ageing crooners perform renditions of Piaf or Aznavour.

Making the most of your visit

• Do not underestimate how much there is to see: set aside at least an entire morning or afternoon.
• Always bargain. Most dealers will knock 10 to 15 per cent off the marked price.
• Take cash. Dealers will almost always give a better price if you pay *en liquide*.
• Be wary of pickpockets, especially in the crowded Marché Malik.

M° Porte de Clignancourt. Open 7am-6pm Mon, Sat, Sun.

The windmill stood until 1822, by when superstars such as the legendary Mlle Mars had moved in. She had a splendid place built at No 1, replete with skylight and deliciously lurid fake marble, which can be glimpsed through the glass door. Wander through the adjoining streets and passageways to catch further angles of these miniature palaces and late eighteenth-century *hôtels particuliers*, especially on rue La Rochefoucauld. The area round the Neo-Classical Eglise Notre-Dame-de-Lorette, which includes rue Taitbout, haunt of Balzac's fallen heroine in *Splendeurs et Misères des Courtisanes*, was built up in Louis-Philippe's reign and was famous for its courtesans, known as *lorettes*. From 1844 to 1857, Delacroix had his studio at 58 rue Notre-Dame-de-Lorette (next to the house, at No 56, where Gauguin was born in 1848). The painter later moved to place de Furstenberg in the 6th *arrondissement* (now Musée Delacroix).

Just off rue Taitbout stands square d'Orléans, a remarkable housing estate built in 1829 by English architect Edward Cresy. This ensemble of flats and artists' studios attracted the glitterati of the day, including the divine Taglioni, Pauline Viardot, George Sand and her lover Chopin. The couple each had first-floor flats and could wave at each other from their respective drawing rooms. The **Musée de la Vie Romantique** in nearby rue Chaptal displays the writer's mementoes in a perfect setting. Take in place Gustave-Toudouze, with pleasant tea room Thé Folies, and glorious circular place St-Georges, home to the Bibliothèque Thiers at No 27, a library specialising in French nineteenth-century history, and to the notorious Païva, true Empress of Napoléon III's Paris, who lived in the richly sculpted Neo-Renaissance No 28.

The **Musée Gustave Moreau**, meanwhile, is grounds alone for a visit. Originally the artist's studio, it was actually planned by him to become a museum to house several thousand works which he bequeathed to the nation. Fragments of *la bohème* can still be gleaned in the neighbourhood, though the Café La Roche, where Moreau met Degas for drinks and rows, has been downsized to the utterly forgettable La Jaconde on the corner of rues La Rochefoucault and La Bruyère. Degas painted most of his ballet scenes round the corner in rue Frochot and Renoir hired his first decent studio at 35 rue St-Georges. A couple of streets away in Cité Pigalle, a charming collection of studios, stands Van Gogh's last Paris house (No 5), before he moved to Auvers-sur-Oise. There is a plaque here, but nothing on the building in rue Pigalle where Toulouse-Lautrec drank himself to death in 1903.

La Goutte d'Or

For a very different experience, head for Barbès-Rochechouart Métro station and the area north of it, known as the Goutte d'Or. In Zola's day this was (and it still is) one of the poorest districts in the city. Zola used it as a backdrop for *L'Assommoir*, his novel set among the district's laundries and absinthe bars. Now it's primarily an African and Arab neighbourhood, with plenty of colour to make up for the modest housing. Depending when you come it can seem like a colourful slice of Africa or a state under police siege, with frequent sweeps on *sans-papiers* (illegral immigrants), drug dealers or suspected Islamic terrorists. Off the main boulevards, rue de la Goutte-d'Or itself has been done up, but other parts are still slums. Down rue Doudeauville, you'll find African musical shops, rue Polonceau has African grocers and Senegalese restaurant Chez Aïda, while Square Léon is the focus for la Goutte d'Or en Fête every June which tries to harness some of the cosmopolitan local talent. Some bands, such as Africando and the Orchestre National de Barbès, have become well known across Paris. Plans to develop the area include various projects for young designers and entrepreneurs, headlined by fashion workshops in rue des Gardes, dubbed 'rue de la mode', and fashion and dance studios at 8bis rue Polonceau.

There's a lively street market under the Métro tracks (Mon, Wed, Sat morning), renowned for stalls of exotic vegetables and rolls of African fabrics. From here rue d'Orsel leads back to Montmartre via Marché St-Pierre. The covered market hall is now used for exhibitions of naïve art but, in the street, outlets like Dreyfus and Moline vie with discount fabrics.

On the northern edge of the city at Porte de Clignancourt is Paris' largest flea market, the **Marché aux Puces de St-Ouen** (*see page 83*).

North-East Paris

In the 10th, 11th, 19th and 20th arrondissements.
The old working-class area north and east of République is in transformation, mixing pockets of charm with grotty or even dangerous areas. The main attraction is Père Lachaise cemetery. Ménilmontant, the area around it, and neighbour Belleville, once villages where Parisians escaped at weekends, were absorbed into the city in 1860.

Canal St-Martin to La Villette

Canal St-Martin, built 1805-25, begins at the Seine at Pont Morland, disappears underground at the Bastille, then re-emerges at rue du Fbg-du-Temple east of place de la République. This stretch has the most charm, lined with shady trees and crossed by iron footbridges and locks. Most of the old warehouses have closed, but the area is still semi-industrial and a bit shabby, with the odd barge puttering

Step classes will help: the old village of **Montmartre** *is on the highest hill in Paris.*

into view. Designers have begun snapping up old industrial premises and unusual bars like **La Patache** and **Chez Prune** have multiplied.

You can take a boat up the canal between the Port de l'Arsenal and the Bassin de la Villette. Between the fifth and sixth locks at 101 quai de Jemmapes is the **Hôtel du Nord**, which inspired Marcel Carné's 1938 film, though most locations were recreated in a studio. The hotel has reopened as a lively bar, used for blues and comedy evenings. East of here is the **Hôpital St-Louis** (main entrance rue Bichat), founded in 1607 to house plague victims, and built as a series of isolated pavilions to stop disease spreading. Behind the hospital, the rue de la Grange-aux-Belles housed the infamous Montfaucon gibbet, built in 1233, where victims were hanged and left to the elements. Much of the area has been redeveloped, but today the street contains music cafés **Chez Adel** (No 10) and Apostrophe (No 23), the Squart art squat (No 31), still fighting a long-running battle against eviction. Only the inconspicuous Le Pont Tournant café, on the corner with quai de Jemmapes overlooking the swing bridge, still seems to hark back to canal days of old.

East lies the Parti Communiste Français, place du Colonel-Fabien, a curved glass curtain raised off the ground on a concrete wing, designed in 1968-71 by Brasilia architect Oscar Niemeyer with Paul Chemetov and Jean Deroche. It is the HQ of perhaps the only influential CP left in Europe.

To the north, place de Stalingrad was landscaped in 1989 to expose the Rotonde de la Villette, one of Ledoux's grandiose tollhouses which now houses exhibitions and archaeological finds. Here the canal widens into Bassin de la Villette, built for Napoléon in 1808, bordered by new housing developments and **MK2 sur Seine** cinema, as well as some of the worst of 60s and 70s housing. At the eastern end of the basin is an unusual 1885 hydraulic lifting bridge, the **Pont de Crimée**. East of here, the Canal de l'Ourcq divides: Canal St-Denis runs north through St-Denis towards the Seine, Canal de l'Ourcq runs towards the Marne. The area has been revitalised in the last decade by the **Cité des Sciences et de l'Industrie** science museum, the activity-filled **Parc de la Villette** and **Cité de la Musique** concert hall and music museum.

Parc de la Villette

av Corentin-Cariou, 19th. Mᵒ Porte de la Villette. or av Jean-Jaurès, 19th. Mᵒ Porte de Pantin. **Map inset** A giant arts and science complex, La Villette's programmes range from avant-garde music to avant-garde circus. The site of Paris' main cattle market and abattoir, it was to be replaced by a high-tech slaughterhouse but was instead turned into the **Cité des Sciences et de l'Industrie**, a futuristic, interactive science museum. Outside are the shiny spherical **Géode** cinema and Argonaute submarine. Dotted with the quirky, bright-red pavilions or *folies*

designed by Swiss master planner Bernard Tschumi, the park itself is a postmodern feast (guided tours 08.03.30.63.06/3pm Sun, Mar-Oct from 'La folie information' in front of exit of Mᵒ Porte de Pantin; 35F/30/f, free under-12s). The *folies* serve as glorious climbing frames in addition to such uses as first-aid post, burger bar and children's art centre. Kiddies shoot down a Chinese dragon slide and a meandering suspended path follows the Canal de l'Ourcq. As well as big lawns, there are ten themed gardens with evocative names such as the Garden of Mirrors, of Mists, of Acrobatics and of Childhood Fears. South of the canal are the **Zénith**, used for pop concerts, and the Grande Halle de la Villette, part of the old meat market now used for trade fairs, exhibitions and the **Villette Jazz Festival**. It is winged by the Conservatoire de la Musique on one side and on the other the **Cité de la Musique**, designed by Christian de Portzamparc, with its concert halls, rehearsal rooms and **Musée de la Musique**. *See chapters* **Paris by Season, Museums, Children, Music: Classical & Opera, Music: Rock, Roots & Jazz, Theatre**.

Ménilmontant & Charonne

Once some houses on a hill where vines and fruit trees were cultivated, Mesnil-Montant (uphill farm) expanded with bistros, workers' housing and bordellos. It was incorporated in Paris in 1860 with Belleville and has a similar history: workers' agi-

Pont de Crimée : *relic of the industrial age.*

tation, resistance in the Commune, immigrant population. Today it's a thriving centre of alternative Paris, as artists and young Parisians have moved in. Flanking boulevard du Ménilmontant, the **Cimetière du Père Lachaise** is the most illustrious burial site in Paris.

The area is a curious blend of 1960s and 70s monster housing projects and little dwellings that are the remnants of the Ménilmontant of another age, now a mix of gentrification and near dereliction. Below the appropriately hilly-sounding rue des Pyrénées, poke your nose down the Cité Leroy or Villa l'Ermitage – calm houses with gardens and an old-fashioned carpenter's workshop – not missing the odd, red-brick Neo-Gothic house at 19 rue de l'Ermitage, and the rustic Cité de l'Ermitage.

For a restful glass, try laidback Lou Pascalou (14 rue des Panoyaux), La Buvette (same street) or **Le Soleil** on the boulevard (No 136). While side streets still contain male-only North African cafés, old *parigot* locals and half-bricked up houses, the rue Oberkampf has had a meteoric rise. What only four or five years ago consisted largely of small grocers and 5F stores today draws queues to some of the city's hippest bars: Le Mecano, Mercerie, **Scherkhan**, **Les Comptoirs de Charbon** and **Cithéa**. Offbeat art shows are put on at **Glassbox**, while another cultural concentration is growing on rue Boyer with the **Maroquinerie** literary café and quirky bistro **Chez Jean**.

East of Père-Lachaise is the former village of Charonne, which joined Paris in 1859. The bucolic **Eglise St-Germain de Charonne**, place St-Blaise, is the city's only church, apart from St-Pierre de Montmartre, still to have its own graveyard. Mainly early fifteenth-century Gothic, the church's buttressed square tower is earlier. The rest of Charonne, centred on rue St-Blaise, is a prettified backwater of quiet bars and bistros.

Cross the Périphérique at Porte de Montreuil for the junky **Puces de Montreuil** fleamarket.

Cimetière du Père Lachaise

entrance bd de Ménilmontant, 20th (01.43.70.70.33). M° Père-Lachaise. **Open** 9am-5.30pm daily. **Map P5**
With thousands of tightly packed tombs arranged along cobbled lanes and tree-lined avenues, this is said to be the world's most visited cemetery. Named after the Jesuit Père de la Chaise, Louis XIV's confessor, it was laid out by the architect Brongniart in 1804. The presumed remains of medieval lovers Abélard and Héloïse were moved here in 1817, along with those of Molière and La Fontaine, in a bid to gain popularity for the site. Famous inhabitants multiplied: Sarah Bernhardt, Egyptologist Champollion (appropriately marked by an obelisk), painters Delacroix, Ingres, Géricault, composers Bizet, Chopin, writers Balzac, Proust, Colette and singer Piaf. Jim Morrison, buried here in 1971, still attracts a flow of spaced-out pilgrims; follow the graffiti. Oscar Wilde's headstone is a naked angel which was considered so offensive that it was neutered by the

Mystic Mr Fix-it

TRAVAIL SERIEUX, EFFICACE, RAPIDE, RÉSULTATS IMMÉDIATS
PAIEMENT APRÈS RÉSULTAT - CONTACTEZ .

♥ ☞ **Mr GASSAMA** ☜ ♥

☞ **GRAND MEDIUM, VOYANT, ASTROLOGUE**

RÉSOUD TOUS VOS PROBLÈMES AVEC EFFICACITÉ : AMOUR, AFFECTION RETROUVÉE, FIDÉLITÉ ABSOLUE ENTRE ÉPOUX, RETOUR AU FOYER DE LA PERSONNE AIMÉE, MARIAGE, CHANCE, PROTECTION CONTRE LES DANGERS, EXAMENS, CONCOURS, TRAVAIL, SUCCÈS, SPORTS, SITUATION, AFFAIRE, DÉSENVOÛTEMENT, ETC

Apporter une photo ou un objet

Reçoit tous les jours de 8 h à 21 h

Even in this age of alternative therapy and renewed interest in the occult, a man who claims to solve *all* your problems seems too good to be true. Yet wild and wonderful promises abound on the palm-sized leaflets distributed outside Métro stations or along streets in the Goutte d'Or. In endearingly clunky French, they advertise the services of the (usually) Senegalese or Malian soothsayers and faith-healers known as *marabouts*, who list exorcism, fortune-telling, charms for business success and cures for impotence among their services. Unlucky in love? No problem – the person who ditched you 'will follow you like a dog' (a claim which conjures up images of that heartless ex gambolling behind you in the street, eager-eyed and tongue lolling – a satisfying form of revenge, if nothing else).

Still, do the 'cures' actually work? 'Payment after results' seems like a failsafe clause but, in reality, a consultation itself costs 100F, and that's just the beginning: despite claims of 'immediate results', most *marabouts* will prescribe a course of treatment that could go on indefinitely. Some leaflets give precise directions to their clinics ('Staircase B, 4th floor, end of corridor' – usually in the 18th and 19th), but ringing in advance is a good idea, and a chance to judge whether your man is *bona fide* or bogus. Those who get evasive (not to say shifty) when quizzed about their working methods usually fall into the second category – bear in mind, too, that the standard strong African accent can make comprehension tricky. Some work by correspondence, and a handful are now media savvy: one has a website (http://professeurcisse.com), while Professeur Karamba hosts a twice-weekly radio phone-in (BRFM 106.7 Thur 10.30am; Espace FM 98.8, Sat 10am). Meanwhile the flimsy, coloured leaflets multiply, with their misprints, can-do optimism – and the same outrageous promises.

head keeper, who used the offending member as a paper-weight. The Paris Commune made its last defensive stand here on 27 May 1871, marked by several hours of bloody fighting. The next day, 147 surrendered and were shot against the eastern wall of the cemetery, since known as the Mur des Fédérés.

Puces de Montreuil

Mº Porte de Montreuil. **Open** 7.30am-7pm Mon, Sat, Sun. Very second-hand clothing, contraband videos, broken chairs and miscellaneous rubbish dominate this grungy flea market. It's much more anarchic than Clignancourt and little here is pre-1900, but you may find fun collectables like *pastis* jugs.

Belleville

Incorporated into Paris in 1860, largely agricultural Belleville became a work and leisure place for the lower classes, while many bourgeois still had country houses in the area. Despite attempts to dissipate workers' agitation by splitting the village between 11th, 19th and 20th *arrondissements*, it was the centre of opposition to the Second Empire – and the last *quartier* to surrender during the Commune. Legend has it Piaf was born on the pavement outside 72 rue de Belleville in 1915, commemorated in a stone tablet above the door. In the 30s and 40s, Belleville was the place to dance to the songs of Piaf or Chevalier. The **Java**, now a salsa club, still has its original *bal-musette* décor. Devoted fans maintain a shrine to 'the little sparrow', the **Musée Edith Piaf**, in rue Crespin-le-Gast, off rue Oberkampf (*see chapter* **Museums**).

A walk could begin at the top of the Parc de Belleville, with the panoramic view from rue Piat. Below, on boulevard de Belleville, Chinese and Vietnamese restaurants and supermarkets rub shoulders with Muslim and kosher groceries, couscous and falafel eateries. On market day (Tue, Fri mornings), Belleville seems like a slice of Africa.

On the small streets off the rue de Belleville, old buildings hide courtyards and gardens. Rue Ramponneau mixes new housing and relics of old worker's Belleville. At No 23, down a crumbling alley, an old iron smithy has become La Forge, a squat for artists, many of whom are members of La Bellevilloise Association, which is trying to maintain the community and stop redevelopment.

Up avenue Simon Bolivar is the eccentric **Parc des Buttes-Chaumont**, one of the most attractive landscaping feats of Baron Haussmann's designers. East of the park, between place des Fêtes and place de Rhin et Danube, are a number of tiny, hilly streets in an area known as Mouzaia, lined with small houses and gardens that still look positively provincial.

Parc des Buttes-Chaumont

rue Botzaris, rue Manin, rue de Crimée, 19th. Mº Buttes-Chaumont. **Map N3** This fantasy wonderland is the perfect, picturesque meeting of nature and the artificial, with meandering paths and vertiginous cliffs. It was designed for Haussmann in the 1860s on the site of a gypsum quarry, rubbish tip and public gibbet. Waterfalls cascade out of a man-made cave, complete with fake stalactites, while out of the artificial lake rises a 50m-high rock reached by a suspension bridge.

High suspense: cross at your peril above the cliffs and waterfalls of **les Buttes-Chaumont.**

Left Bank

This is still the heart of Paris' renowned intellectual and artistic life – despite ever-increasing commercialism and redevelopment.

The Latin Quarter

In the 5th arrondissement.
This section of the Left Bank east of boulevard St-Michel is probably so named because students here spoke Latin until the Revolution. Or, the name may allude to the vestiges of Roman Lutétia, of which this area was the heart. The first two Roman streets were on the site of present-day rue St-Jacques (later the pilgrims' route to Compostella) and rue Cujas. The area still boasts many medieval streets, scholarly institutions and the city's most important Roman remains: the Cluny baths, now part of the **Musée National du Moyen Age** and the **Arènes de Lutèce** amphitheatre.

Quartier de la Huchette

The area is full of tourists, who pour down boulevard St-Michel and adjoining streets in summer. The boulevard, symbolic of student rebellion in May 1968, has largely been taken over by fast-food giants and downmarket shoe and clothes chains, though giant book emporium **Gibert Joseph** is over a century old, and the fountain with its statue of St Michael slaying the dragon in place St-Michel is an ever-popular meeting point. Down pedestrianised rue de la Huchette and rue de la Harpe you'll find more Greek restaurants and café tables than evidence of medieval learning. Above the kebabs and taverna signs of rue de la Harpe remain some elegant eighteenth-century wrought-iron balconies and carved masks. Find, too, rue du Chat-Qui-Pêche, supposedly Paris' narrowest street, and rue de la Parcheminerie, named for the parchment sellers and copyists who once lived here. The tiny **Théâtre de la Huchette** on rue de la Huchette has been playing the original production of Ionesco's *The Bald Prima Donna* ever since 1957. Sticking up amid the tourist paraphernalia is Paris' most charming medieval church, the **Eglise St-Séverin**, which has an exuberant Flamboyant Gothic vaulted interior. In its garden are the remains of a Gothic charnel house, where bodies dug up in communal pits were stored before burial in the adjacent cemetery.

Across the ancient rue St-Jacques, where the timewarp bar **Polly Magoo** still accumulates a curious cross-section of night owls, is the ancient **Eglise St-Julien-le-Pauvre**, built as a resting place for pilgrims in the twelfth century. Rue Galande has over-hanging medieval buildings and **Studio Galande** cinema, famed for weekly screenings of *The Rocky Horror Picture Show*.

By the river, back from the *bouquinistes* or booksellers who line the *quais*, second-hand English bookshop **Shakespeare & Co** (37 rue de la Bûcherie) is a port of call for expatriate literati, though no relation to the rue de l'Odéon original.

Across boulevard St-Germain stands the **Musée National du Moyen Age – Thermes de Cluny**, a magnificent collection of medieval art housed in the Gothic mansion of the Abbots of Cluny, itself built over ruined Roman baths, whose imposing remains are visible from boulevard St-Michel. The surrounding square is currently being replanted as a medieval garden (opens September 2000).

East of here place Maubert, now a morning marketplace (Tue, Thur, Sat), was used in the sixteenth century to burn books and hang heretics, particularly Protestants. Just beyond the place the Baroque church of St-Nicolas-du-Chardonnet (30 rue St-Victor), which houses the tomb of the painter Charles Le Brun, is today associated with the far right and the Catholic integrist movement, which continues to practise the Catholic mass in Latin. The little streets between here and the traffic-heavy *quais* are among the city's oldest. The picturesque galleried houses of rue de Bièvre chart the course of the river Bièvre, which flowed into the Seine at this point in the Middle Ages. Religious foundations once abounded; remnants of the Collège des Bernardins can be seen in rue de Poissy. On the quai de la Tournelle, look for the elegant seventeenth-century Hôtel Miramion at No 53, now the **Musée de l'Assistance Publique**, telling the history of Paris hospitals. There's food for all pockets, from the illustrious **Tour d'Argent** (No 15, a restaurant since 1582, though the present building dates from the 1900s) to the Tintin shrine *café-tabac* **Le Rallye** (No 11). Below, moored in this former dock for hay and wood, are numerous houseboats and barges.

Eglise St-Julien-le-Pauvre

rue St-Julien-le-Pauvre, 5th (01.43.54.52.16). M° Cluny-La Sorbonne. **Open** 10am-7.30pm daily. **Map J7**
St-Julien was formerly a sanctuary offering hospitality to pilgrims en route for Compostella. The present church dates from the late twelfth century, on the cusp of Romanesque and Gothic. Originally part of a Cluniac priory, it became the university church when colleges migrated to the Left Bank from Notre-Dame. In the later Middle Ages, it was used for stu-

dent assemblies that became so raucous the church was closed in 1524. Since 1889, it has been used by the Greek Melchite church. The sober outside looks rather bashed up, but inside is well-preserved. The capitals are richly decorated with vine and acanthus leaves; one even has winged female harpies. *Concerts.*

Eglise St-Séverin

1 rue des Prêtres-St-Séverin, 5th (01.42.34.93.50). M° Cluny-La Sorbonne. **Open** *11am-7.45pm Mon-Fri; 8am-9.30pm Sat; 9am-9.30pm Sun.* **Map J7**
Primitive and Flamboyant Gothic styles merge in this complex, composite little church, mostly built between the thirteenth and fifteenth centuries. The double ambulatory is famed for its remarkable 'palm tree' vaulting and unique double spiral column. The windows include modern stained glass by Jean Bazaine.

Musée National du Moyen Age – Thermes de Cluny

6 pl Paul-Painlevé, 5th (01.53.73.78.00). M° Cluny-La Sorbonne. **Open** *9.15am-5.45pm Mon, Wed-Sun.* **Admission** *30F; 20F 18-25s, all Sun; free under-18s, CM.* **Credit** *(shop)* V. **Map J7**
Along with the Hôtel de Sens in the Marais, this crenellated building is Paris' only remaining example of important fifteenth-century secular architecture. It was built – atop an earlier Gallo-Roman baths complex dating from the second and third centuries – by Jacques d'Amboise in 1485-98 at the request of the Abbé de Cluny, for lodging priests. It set new standards for domestic comfort and, with its main building behind a courtyard, was a precursor of the Marais *hôtels particuliers.* Admire the polygonal staircase, Gothic mullioned windows and balustrade lined with gargoyles. The baths are the most important Roman remains in Paris. Three large rooms – the impressive vaulted frigidarium (cold bath), tepidarium (warm bath) and caldarium (hot bath) – and parts of the hypocaust system are visible. A printer, a laundry and cooper set up shop here in 1807, before it became a museum in 1844. The structure remains largely intact, including the Flamboyant Gothic chapel. It houses an exceptional collection of medieval art, notably the Lady and the Unicorn tapestry cycle. *See also chapter* **Museums**. *Bookshop. Concerts. Guided tours.*

The Sorbonne & the Montagne Ste-Geneviève

The Montagne-Ste-Geneviève still contains a remarkable concentration of academic institutions, from the Sorbonne to research centres to *Grandes Ecoles* such as the Ecole Normale Supérieure. In the 30 years since May 68, its warren of narrow streets has attracted the well-heeled, pushing accommodation beyond most students' pockets, but scholarly conversations still fill local bistros and students still throng outside lecture halls. The intellectual tradition persists, too, in countless specialist book stores and the art cinemas of rue Champollion and rue des Ecoles, such as **Action Ecoles, Le Champo** with

its eternal Hitchcock retrospectives, the **Reflet Médicis Logos** and film-themed café **Le Reflet**.

The district began its long association with learning in about 1100, when a number of scholars, including Peter Abélard, began to live and teach on the Montagne, independent of the established Canon school of Nôtre-Dame. This loose association of scholars began to be referred to as a University. The Paris schools soon attracted scholars from all over Europe, and the 'colleges' – really just student residences – multiplied, until the University of Paris was given official recognition with a charter from Pope Innocent III in 1215.

By the sixteenth century, the university – now known as the **Sorbonne**, after the most famous of its colleges – had been co-opted by the Catholic establishment. A century later, Cardinal Richelieu rebuilt the Sorbonne, but the place slowly slid into decay. After the Revolution, when the whole university was forced to close, Napoléon resuscitated the Sorbonne as the cornerstone of his new, centralised education system. The university participated enthusiastically in the uprisings of the nineteenth century, and was also a seedbed of the May 1968 revolt. Nowadays the university is less turbulent, not least because the Sorbonne is now only one of 18 faculties of the University of Paris dotted around city and suburbs. The present buildings are mostly late nineteenth century; only the Baroque Chapelle de la Sorbonne, where Richelieu is buried, survives from his rebuilding. The courtyard is open to the public; you can sometimes sneak into lectures in the main amphitheatre.

Also on rue des Ecoles stand the late eighteenth-century buildings of the eminent, independent **Collège de France**, founded in 1530 with the patronage of François 1er by a group of humanists led by Guillaume Budé. Recent notables have included Claude Lévi-Strauss, Emmanuel Le Roy Ladurie and Georges Duby. Lectures are free and open to the pubic (11 pl Marcelin-Berthelot, 5th/ 01.44.27.12.11). For intellectual fodder, neighbouring **Brasserie Balzar** remains fashionable; regulars here even set up Les Amis du Balzar in protest at its 1998 acquisition by the Groupe Flo.

Climb up rue St-Jacques, winding rue de la Montagne-Ste-Geneviève or take rue des Carmes, with the Baroque chapel of the Syrian church and rue Valette past the brick and stone entrance of the Collège Ste-Barbe, where Ignatius Loyola and later Montgolfier and Eiffel studied, to place du Panthéon. The huge domed **Panthéon**, originally commissioned by Louis XV as a church to honour the city's patron Ste Geneviève, was converted in the Revolution into a secular temple for France's *grands hommes.* In the surrounding square, con-

Highbrow: the intellectual tradition persists in the Latin Quarter, home of the **Sorbonne**.

ceived by the Panthéon's architect Soufflot, is the elegant classical *mairie* (town hall) of the 5th *arrondissement*, mirrored by the law faculty. On the north side, the **Bibliothèque Ste-Geneviève**, built 1844-50 by Labrouste (who later designed the reading room of the Bibliothèque Nationale Richelieu), has medieval manuscripts and a magnificent iron-framed reading room. On the other side is the **Hôtel des Grands-Hommes**, where Surrealist André Breton invented 'automatic writing' in the 1920s.

In the northeast corner of the square stands the more intimate church of **St-Etienne-du-Mont**, with a remarkable Renaissance rood screen. Pascal and Racine are both buried here, as are the remains of Paris' patron saint, Ste Geneviève. Jutting up behind is the Gothic-Romanesque Tour de Clovis, the only remaining part of the once giant abbey of Ste-Geneviève, though parts of a cloister have recently been excavated in the grounds. Further along rue Clovis is a chunk of Philippe-Auguste's twelfth-century city wall. Both rue du Cardinal-Lemoine and rue Descartes were inhabited by Hemingway (plaque at No 74 rue du Cardinal-Lemoine). At 65 rue du Cardinal-Lemoine, the severe seventeenth-century buildings of the former Collège des Ecossais, founded in 1372 to house Scottish students, is the resting place for the brain of James II, who died at St-Germain-en-Laye. At No 75 hides the charming **Hôtel des Grandes-Ecoles**. Cheap eats abound here; **L'Ecurie**, opposite the Ecole-Polytechnique at 2 rue Laplace, is housed in underground medieval stables.

Eglise St-Etienne-du-Mont

pl Ste-Geneviève, 5th (01.43.54.11.79). M° Cardinal-Lemoine/RER Luxembourg. **Open** 8am-noon, 2-7.15pm Tue-Sat; 9am-noon 2.30-6.30pm Sun. **Map J8**
An important pilgrimage site since the Dark Ages for the shrine of Ste-Geneviève, who saved the city from Attila the Hun in 451. The present church was built in an amalgam of Gothic and Renaissance styles between 1492 and 1626, and originally adjoined the abbey church of Ste-Geneviève. The curiously charming facade mixes Gothic rose window with classical columns and pediment. The stunning Renaissance roodscreen staircase is the only one left in Paris, and possibly the work of François 1er's architect Philibert Delorme, with its double spiral staircase and ornate stone strapwork. Admire also Germain Pilon's wooden Baroque pulpit (1651), with massive female figures of the virtues. In the ambulatory are tablets to Racine and Pascal. Ste-Geneviève's elaborate brass-covered shrine is to the right of the choir, surrounded by plaques giving thanks for miracles she has performed.

Le Panthéon

pl du Panthéon, 5th (01.44.32.18.00). RER Luxembourg. **Open** *Apr-Sept* 9.30am-6.30pm daily; *Oct-Mar* 10am-5.30pm daily. **Admission** 35F; 23F 12-25s; free under-12s. **Credit** MC, V. **Map J8**
Soufflot's Neo-Classical megastructure was the

Panthéon: *the good, the great and the scholarly.*

architectural *Grand Projet* of its day. A grateful Louis XV had it built to thank Ste-Geneviève for helping him recover from illness. But events caught up with its completion in 1790, and post-Revolution it was re-dedicated as a 'temple of reason' and the resting-place of the nation's great men. It was definitively secularised in 1885, in a neat reversal of the history of Rome's famed Pantheon, upon which it was modelled, which started as a pagan temple only to be turned into a Catholic church. In the recently restored interior admire the elegant Greek columns and domes, as well as the nineteenth-century murals by Puvis de Chavannes. The crypt of greats includes statesmen, politicians and thinkers: Voltaire, Rousseau, Victor Hugo and Zola. New heroes are added rarely: Pierre and Marie Curie's remains were transferred here in 1995, she being the first woman to be interred here in her own right; André Malraux, De Gaulle's culture minister, arrived in 1996. The steep spiral stairs lead up to the colonnade around the dome giving wonderful views over Paris.

La Sorbonne

17 rue de la Sorbonne, 5th (01.40.46.20.15). M° Cluny-La Sorbonne. **Open** courtyards 9am-4.30pm Mon-Fri. **Map J7**
Founded in 1253 by the cleric Robert de Sorbon as one of several separate theological 'colleges' in the area, the University of the Sorbonne was at the centre of the Latin Quarter's intellectual activity from the Middle Ages until May 1968, when its premises were occupied by students and stormed by the CRS

(riot police). The authorities subsequently splintered the University of Paris into less-threatening suburban outposts, but the Sorbonne remains home to the Faculté des Lettres. Rebuilt by Richelieu and reorganised by Napoléon, the present buildings mostly date from 1885 to 1900 and include a labyrinth of classrooms and quaint lecture theatres, as well as an observatory tower, visible from the rue St-Jacques. The elegant dome of the seventeenth-century chapel dominates place de la Sorbonne; Cardinal Richelieu is buried in an ornate tomb inside.

Mouffetard

At the top of rue du Cardinal-Lemoine is picturesque **place de la Contrescarpe**, a famous rendezvous since the 1530s, when writers Rabelais, Ronsard and Du Bellay frequented the cabaret de la Pomme de Pin at No 1, and still known for its lively cafés. Off to the south winds the **rue Mouffetard**, originally the road leading towards Rome, one of the oldest and most characterful streets in the city. This area was once a mixture of poverty and bohemia. Cheap bistros, Greek restaurants and ethnic knick-knack shops still give it a bohemian air, but it's rather more touristy than when Hemingway described it as 'that wonderful narrow crowded market street'. The lower half, towards the late Gothic church of **St-Médard**, has a busy street market (Tue-Sat and Sun morning) that spills on to the square in front of the

Meander and munch at **Mouffetard** market.

church with its laidback cafés; particularly seething at weekends. There's another busy market at place Monge (Wed, Fri, Sun morning). Among the narrow streets off rue Mouffetard is rue du Pot-de-Fer, where (at No 6) George Orwell stayed in a cheap boarding house in 1928-29 during his time as a *plongeur*, and vividly depicted it in *Down and Out in Paris and London* as 'a ravine of tall, leprous houses'. Take a detour along rue Tournefort, with its elegant, restored houses, no longer the cheap lodgings and gloomy garrets depicted by Balzac in *Père Goriot*.

Beyond rue Soufflot is one of the most picturesque stretches of the rue St-Jacques containing several ancient buildings. Note the elegant *hôtel* at No 151 with elaborate balcony, but also good food shops, vintage bistro Perraudin and Aussie bar **Café Oz**. In the shadow of the Panthéon, the rue d'Ulm houses the elitist intellectual Ecole Normale Supérieure, which was taken hostage in demos by the unemployed in January 1998, when several students joined the occupiers in an echo of 1968. Turn off up hilly rue des Fossés-St-Jacques to discover place de l'Estrapade, tucked behind the Panthéon, much more welcoming now than when it was used for torture by *estrapade*, a wooden tower from which deserters were dropped. To the west, broad rue Gay-Lussac, a hot spot in the May 1968 riots, leads to the **Jardins du Luxembourg**. Further down rue St-Jacques is another eminent landmark, the **Val-de-Grâce**, least-altered and most ornate of all Paris' Baroque churches.

Eglise St Médard
141 rue Mouffetard, 5th (01.44.08.87.00).
Mº Censier-Daubenton. **Open** 9am-noon, 2.30-7pm Tue-Sat; 9am-noon Sun. **Map K9**
The original chapel here was a dependency of the Abbaye de Ste-Geneviève, but rebuilding at the end of the fifteenth century created a much larger, late Gothic structure, with light-filled clerestory and elaborately vaulted ambulatory. Some of the capitals were fluted to suit 1780s Neo-Classical fashion.

Eglise du Val-de-Grâce
pl Alphonse-Laveran, 5th (01.40.51.47.28). RER Port-Royal. **Open** Call to arrange guided visits. **Map J9**
This church and its Benedictine monastery – now a military hospital and the Musée du Service de Santé des Armées devoted to military medecine (*see chapter* **Museums**) – were built by François Mansart and Jacques Lemercier, to fulfil Anne of Austria's vow to erect 'a magnificent temple' if God blessed her with a son. He presented her with two. Extraordinarily expensive and built over decades, the recently restored church is the most luxuriously Baroque of the city's seventeenth-century domed churches, influenced by the Redentore in Venice, with a few Bernini-esque touches like the baldaquin with six barleysugar spiral columns borrowed from St Peter's in Rome. Bernini admired Pierre Mignard's dome fresco, calling it 'the masterpiece of French art'. Its swirling colours and forms are meant to prefigure heaven. *Concerts.*

*Paris' botanical garden, the **Jardin des Plantes**, with its zoo and yew maze, dates from 1626.*

The Jardin des Plantes District

At the eastern end of rue des Ecoles, east of rue Monge, you move into a quieter area that nonetheless contains Roman relics, several major academic institutions, and is a focus for Paris' Muslim community. Old-fashioned bistros on rue des Fossés-St-Bernard contrast with the brutal 1960s-70s slab architecture of Paris university's campuses VI and VII (known as Jussieu), large parts of which are closed for asbestos removal. Nestling between the Seine and Jussieu is the striking modern **Institut du Monde Arabe**, which has a busy programme of concerts and exhibitions while, stretching along the banks of the river, the **Jardin Tino Rossi** contains the dilapidated Musée du Sculpture en Plein Air.

The Paris mosque is not far away up rue Linné, although you may want to stop off on the way at the **Arènes de Lutèce**, the Roman amphitheatre, entered from rue Monge or rue des Arènes. Rediscovered in 1869 during the building of rue Monge, the central arena and many tiers of stone seating remain. The green-roofed **Mosquée de Paris** was built in 1922, partly after Granada's Alhambra, though the popular Moorish tea room within is a very Parisian experience.

The mosque looks out onto the **Jardin des Plantes**, Paris' botanical garden. Established in 1626 as a garden for medicinal plants, it features an eighteenth-century maze, a winter garden brimming with rare plant species and the brilliant renovated Galerie de l'Evolution of the **Museum National d'Histoire Naturelle**. There's also the **Ménagerie**

zoo, an unlikely by-product of the Revolution, when various noble and royal collections of wild animals were impounded. Botanical and zoological hints abound in the area, from street names like Buffon and Linné (botanists) and Daubenton (anatomist) to the charming Fontaine Cuvier on rue Cuvier (pale-ontologist) with a figure of Natural History supported on a smiling lion and grinning crocodile.

Arènes de Lutèce
entrances rue Monge, rue de Navarre, rue des Arènes, 5th. Mº Cardinal-Lemoine or Jussieu. **Open** 10am-dusk daily. **Map K8**
The Roman arena, where roaring beasts and wounded gladiators met their deaths (in alternance with less bloodthirsty theatre performances) once sat 10,000. Now amid a romantically planted garden, the site was discovered in 1869. Today it's used by kids playing ball, skateboarders and *boules*-players.

Institut du Monde Arabe
1 rue des Fossés-St-Bernard, 5th (01.40.51.38.38). Mº Jussieu. **Open** 10am-6pm Tue-Sun. *Library* 1-8pm Tue-Sat. *Café* 2.30-6.30pm Tue-Sat; noon-3pm Sun. **Admission** *roof terrace, library* free. *Museum* 25F; 20F 12-25s, students; free under-12s, CM. *Exhibitions* 45F; 35F students, over-60s. **Map K7**
This wedge-shaped *Grand Projet* was purpose-designed by French architect Jean Nouvel in 1980-87. It's a clever blend of high-tech steel and glass architecture and Arab influences. Nouvel took his inspiration from the screens of Moorish palaces; the design is based on the principle of a camera aperture, using programmed photo-electic cells to adjust automatically to admit constant amounts of daylight,

although these no longer function fully. Inside is a collection of Middle Eastern art, archaeological finds, exhibition spaces, a library and café. There's a performing-arts programme of dance and classical Arab music, and great views from the rooftop.

Jardin des Plantes

pl Valhubert, rue Buffon or rue Cuvier, 5th (01.40.79.30.00). M° Gare d'Austerlitz or Jussieu. **Open** *summer* 7.30am-8pm daily; *winter* 7.30am-5.30pm daily (*Alpine garden* Apr-Sept Mon-Fri 8am-11am, 1.30-5pm; *greenhouses* 1-5pm Mon, Wed-Fri; 10am-5pm Sat, Sun; *ménagerie* winter 9am-5pm/5.30pm daily; summer 9am-6pm/6.30pm). **Admission** free; *greenhouses* 15F; *ménagerie* 30F/20F. **Map L8**

Although small and slightly run-down, the Paris botanical garden contains over 10,000 species, including rose, winter and Alpine gardens and tropical greenhouses. Originally planted by Louis XIII's doctor Guy de la Brosse as the royal medicinal plant garden in 1626, it opened to the public in 1640. It also contains the **Ménagerie**, a small zoo, and the **Muséum National d'Histoire Naturelle**, of which the magnificently revovated 1880s Grande Galerie de l'Evolution sits resplendent like a palace at the end of formal beds. Behind, an eighteenth-century yew maze, designed by botanist Buffon, spirals up a little hill to an iron gazebo. Several ancient trees include a false acacia planted in 1636 and a cedar planted by Bernard de Jussieu in 1734. A tablet on the former laboratory announces that this is where Henri Becquerel discovered radioactivity in 1896. *See also chapters* **Museums** *and* **Children**.

Jardin Tino Rossi (Musée du Sculpture en Plein Air)

quai St-Bernard, 5th. M° Gare d'Austerlitz. **Map K7/L8**
An open-air sculpture museum by the Seine is a fine idea – a pity that this one is so disappointing. The garden could almost be described as a concrete plantation, not helped by the traffic noise from the quais. Look for Etienne Martin's bronze *Demeure I* and the Carrera marble *Fenêtre* by Cuban artist Careras, but most of the works are second rate.

La Mosquée de Paris

1 pl du Puits-de-l'Ermite, 5th (01.45.35.97.33/tea room 01.43.31.38.20/Turkish baths 01.43.31.18.14). M° Censier-Daubenton. **Open** *tours* 9am-noon, 2-6pm Mon-Thur, Sat, Sun (closed Muslim holidays); *tea room* 10am-10pm daily; *baths (women)* 10am-9pm Mon, Wed-Sat; *(men)* 2-9pm Tue; 10am-9pm Sun. **Admission** 15F; *tea room* 7-25s, over-60s; free under-7s; *tea room* free; *baths* 85F. **No credit cards. Map K8**
Built 1922-26, the mosque's green-and-white minaret oversees the centre of the Algerian-dominated Muslim community in France. Built in Hispano-Moresque style, with elements inspired by the Alhambra and Fez' Mosque Bou-Inania, the mosque is a series of buildings and courtyards in three sections: religious (grand patio, prayer room and minaret); scholarly (Islamic school and library); and, entered from rue Geoffrey-St-Hilaire, commercial (domed *hammam* or Turkish baths, shop and relaxing Moorish tea room).

St-Germain & Odéon

Ever chic St-Germain-des-Prés is where the great myths of Paris café society and intellectual life grew up. Here Verlaine and Rimbaud went drinking while, a few generations later, Sartre, Camus and de Beauvoir scribbled their first masterpieces, and musicians congregated around writer, critic and trumpeter Boris Vian in Paris' postwar jazz boom.

But St-Germain has changed. Earnest types still stride along clutching weighty tomes and the literati still gather on café terraces – to give TV interviews – but so expensive has the area become that any writers who inhabit it are either well-established or rich Americans pretending to be Hemingway. Over the past few years, luxury fashion groups have moved in, often replacing venerable bookshops. Armani has taken over the old Drugstore, Dior a bookshop, Cartier a classical record shop and Louis Vuitton has unpacked its bags at place St-Germain, while as the All Jazz Club and La Villa Jazz Club closed in 1999, musicians have crossed the river. In 1997 a band of intellectuals, led by 60s singer Juliette Greco, founded SOS St-Germain to try and save the area's soul. But the literary-fashion split is not always clear: Sonia Rykiel is among the campaigners, Karl Lagerfeld has opened his own photo gallery in rue de Seine and, in spring 2000, 20 contemporary artists are installing works in both fashion and cultural sites in the area. Let's hope that rather than just preserving the area in aspic, they can make it swing again.

From the Boulevard to the Seine

Nerve centre of the district is boulevard St-Germain, cut through by Haussmann in 1855, centred around the medieval church of St-Germain; some fine eighteenth-century *hôtel* facades survive on the southern side. At No 151 is politicians' favourite **Brasserie Lipp**, at 172 the **Café de Flore**, which likes to think of itself as the birthplace of existentialism and, just the other side of late-night bookshop **La Hune**, intellectual rival **Les Deux Magots** (6 pl St-Germain-des-Prés). Look also at Art Nouveau *bouillon* Vagenende (No 140). During World War II, hit by shortages of coal, Sartre descended from the ivory tower of his apartment on rue Bonaparte to save a bundle in heating bills. 'The principal interest of the Café de Flore,' he noted, 'was that it had a stove, a nearby Métro and no Germans'. Although you can now spend more on a few coffees there than you would on a week's central heating, it remains a favourite with the literati. Earlier it was also frequented by Picasso, Apollinaire and the Surrealists. The Deux Magots, named after the two statues of Chinese mandarins inside, now provides an interesting sociological cross-section of tourists, but can no longer really claim to be a hotbed of intellectual life.

Strictly academic

The Academie Française has been guardian of the purity and clarity of the French language since Cardinal Richelieu founded it in 1635 during the reign of Louis XIII. It is the most famous of the various learned academies housed in the magnificent, domed Institut de France. Its 40 (notoriously aged) members are known as 'immortals' from the inscription, 'To Immortality' on the original seal presented to the Academy by Richelieu (1585-1642). What is almost immortal is the Academy itself. It is one of the very oldest of France's great institutions and the 700 members since the seventeenth century have been working on their famous dictionary for three and half centuries, interrupted only by revolution and war from 1793 to 1803. The dictionary, the last word on questions of usage and grammar, has been edited nine times: 1694, 1718, 1740, 1762, 1798, 1835, 1878, 1932-53 with the ninth edition in 1992 (as far as E). This latest massive undertaking comprising 45,000 words is only now becoming generally available, but will soon be on Internet.

The Academy also awards a staggering 80 literary prizes a year. The work of the Academy has become more official, more important in recent years following laws and decrees designed to protect French from the incursion of Anglo-American words. Previously, it was the colourful ceremony for new members which attracted most attention. Academicians dressed in gold braided uniforms with touches of green, dating from the 1799 Consulate, put on capes and cocked hats, strapped on swords and proceeded to the hall under the great Coupole to hear brilliant speeches from members (poets, novelists, critics, philosophers, actors, doctors, scientists, generals, cardinals and a few ex-politicians – Baudelaire is famously among the rare few who have turned membership down).

In 1990, the Academy went modern, dropped some circumflex accents and approved some foreign words (diesel, media). The government, however, opted for new French words: *baladeur* for walkman, *jeu décisif* for tie-break, *logiciel* for software. Laws barred English on television and in advertising and official documents. The Academy's task was to make sense of this backlash, to honour François 1er's injunction 'to be clear so that there's no ambiguity or doubt about the meaning of legal texts'. Interestingly, the socialist government elected in 1997 has itself largely ignored the refusal of the Academy to accept *madame la ministre* in place of *madame le ministre*.

The Academy has moved with the times. It has one of the most informative, colourful and clear Internet sites in France (www.academie-francaise.fr) and has just voted a woman, the former political science professor and noted Sovietologist Hélène Carrère d'Encausse, a dynamic 70-year-old as its first woman 'perpetual secretary', the key person among what the Academy's site calls, rather immodestly, 'the talent, intelligence, culture, literary and scientific imagination that lie behind French genius'.

Across from the terrace of the Deux Magots is the oldest church in the city, **St-Germain-des-Prés**, dating back to the sixth century. By the eighth century it was one of the most important Benedictine monasteries in France and host to an important medieval fair. What you see today is a shadow of its former glory, as the church was severely damaged by a Revolutionary mob in 1792. A remnant of the garden survives in front of a curious glazed tile wall, designed for the 1900 Great Exhibition to show off Sèvres production.

Traces of the cloister and part of the Abbot's palace remain behind the church on rue de l'Abbaye. Built in 1586 in red brick with stone facing, it prefigures the place des Vosges. The charming place Furstenburg (once the stableyard of the Abbot's palace), now shades upmarket furnishing fabric stores and the house and studio where the painter Delacroix lived (*see* **Musée Delacroix**). Rue de l'Echaudé shows a typical St-Germain mix: cutting-edge fashion at **L'Eclaireur** (No 24) and bistro cooking at ancient L'Echaudé-St-Germain (No 21). Rue Jacob is particularly charming with its elegant seventeenth-century *hôtels,* containing specialist book, design and antiques shops, pleasant hotels and bohemian throwbacks like *chansonnier* bistro **Les Assassins**. Illustrious former residents include Ingres, Wagner and Colette.

Further east along the boulevard at Odéon, the rue de Buci contains a top-class market, running into rue de Seine with a lively scene centred around the **Bar du Marché** and Chai de l'Abbaye cafés. Rue Bonaparte (where Manet was born at No 5 in 1832), rue de Seine and the rue des Beaux-Arts are still packed with small art galleries, specialising in twentieth-century abstraction, tribal art and Art Deco furniture (*see chapter* **Galleries**). Oscar Wilde died 'beyond his means' at what was then the inexpensive Hôtel d'Alsace, now the fashionably over-the-top **L'Hôtel** in rue des Beaux-Arts. **La Palette** and **Bistro Mazarin** are good stopping-off points with enviable terraces on rue Jacques-Callot. Rue Mazarine, with interesting shops of lighting, vintage toys and jewellery, is now home to Conran's brasserie **L'Alcazar** (No 62) in a former cabaret. At the northern end of rue Bonaparte is the entrance to the seventeenth-century building, once a monastery, of the **Ecole Nationale Supérieure des Beaux-Arts**, Paris' main fine-arts school. Complementing it on the quai de Conti is the **Institut de France**, recently cleaned to reveal its crisp classical decoration. Built with money bequeathed by Louis XIV's minister Cardinal Mazarin, it now houses eminent institutions including the Académie Française, jealous guardian of the French language (*see p97,* **Strictly academic**). Next door the Neo-Classical Hôtel des Monnaies, formerly the mint (1777-1973), is now the **Musée de la Monnaie**, an engrossing coin museum. Opposite, the iron Pont des Arts footbridge leads across to the Louvre.

On rue de l'Ancienne-Comédie is the famous Café Procope, where coffee was first brought to the Parisian public in 1686. Frequented by Voltaire, Rousseau, Benjamin Franklin, revolutionary Danton and later Verlaine, it is now a disappointing restaurant aimed at tourists, although it does contain some

Will **St-Germain**, *once the hub for intellectuals, artists and jazz lovers, swing again?*

remarkable memorabilia, including Voltaire's desk and a postcard from Marie-Antoinette. The back opens on to the cobbled passage du Commerce St-André, home to toy shops, jewellers and chintzy tea rooms. In the eighteenth century, Dr Joseph-Ignace Guillotin first tested out his notorious execution device – on sheep, supposedly – in the cellars of what's now the Pub St-Germain.

To the east, a web of narrow streets centres on winding rue St-André-des-Arts, once noble but today lined with giftshops, crêperies and an arts cinema. Look up to see grand eighteenth-century doorways and iron balconies, especially at Nos 27, with fine Rococo balcony, 47, 49 and 52; the former home of Jacobin regicide Billaud-Varenne at No 45 became the Lycée Fenelon, the first girls' *lycée* in Paris, in 1883. Quiet sidestreets, like rue des Grands-Augustins, rue de Savoie and rue Séguier, feel far removed from the bustle of the main thoroughfare, with printers, bookshops and dignified seventeenth-century buildings. On the corner of rue and quai des Grands-Augustins, the restaurant Lapérouse still boasts a series of private dining rooms, while **Les Bookinistes** offers contemporary flavours. The turreted Hôtel de Fécamp, at 5 rue de Hautefeuille, was the medieval townhouse of the abbots of Fécamp, begun in 1292. Later lodgers included Godin de Ste-Croix, lover and accomplice of notorious poisoner the Marquise de Brinvilliers. Rue Gît-le-Coeur ('here lies the heart') is so-called, legend has it, because one of Henri IV's mistresses lived here, more probably after a cook, Guy or Gilles-le-Queux. At No 9 is the Hôtel du Vieux Paris, or the 'Beat Hotel', where William Burroughs and pals revised *The Naked Lunch*.

Ecole Nationale Supérieure des Beaux-Arts (Ensb-a)

13 quai Malaquais, 6th (01.47.03.52.15). Mº Odéon or St-Michel. **Open** *courtyard* 8.30am-8pm Mon-Fri. *exhibitions* 1-7pm Tue-Sun. **Admission** *exhibitions* 20F; free under-12s, students. **Credit** V. **Map H6**
Paris' most prestigious fine-arts school is installed in what remains of a seventeenth-century convent, the eighteenth-century Hôtel de Chimay and some later additions. After the Revolution, the buildings were transformed into a museum of French monuments and in 1816 into the Ecole. Today it's often used for exhibitions (*see chapter* **Museums**).

Institut de France

23 quai de Conti, 6th (01.44.41.44.41). Mº St-Germain-des-Prés. **Guided tours** 9am, 2pm Sat, Sun (call ahead). **Admission** 20F. **No credit cards. Map H6**
Designed by Le Vau, the classical Baroque building housing the Institut dates from 1663-84. Overlooking the Seine, the semi-circular domed structure was founded by Mazarin as a school for provincial children. In 1805 the five academies of the Institut (Académie Française, Académie des Inscriptions et Belles-Lettres, Académie des Sciences, Académie des Beaux-Arts, Académie des Sciences Morales et

Politiques), were transferred here. Most prestigious is the Académie Française, whose 40 eminences work steadily on the dictionary of the French language. Inside is Mazarin's ornate tomb by Hardouin-Mansart, and the Bibliothèque Mazarine, which holds 500,000 volumes. Surprisingly, access to the library is open to anyone over 18 who turns up with ID, two photos and 100F for a one-year library card.

Eglise St-Germain-des-Prés

3 pl St-Germain-des-Prés, 6th (01.43.25.41.71). Mº St-Germain-des-Prés. **Open** 8am-6.30pm daily. **Map H7**
On the advice of Germain (later bishop of Paris), Childebert, son of Clovis, had a basilica and monastery built towards 543. The oldest church in Paris, for many years it was known as St-Germain-le-Doré because of its copper roof. The original was pillaged by Normans, and rebuilt around 1000 in Romanesque style. Most of the present structure is twelfth century, albeit heavily altered after the Revolution, when the abbey was burnt and a salt-petre refinery installed in the church. Today, only some ornate carved capitals and the tower remain of the eleventh-century church. The top was altered during clumsy nineteenth-century restoration, when a spire was added, as were the frescoes in the nave by Hippolyte Flandrin. Interesting tombs include that of Jean-Casimir, deposed king of Poland who became abbot of St-Germain in 1669, and Scottish nobleman William Douglas. Under the window in the second chapel is the funeral stone of the philosopher Descartes, whose ashes (bar his skull) have been in the church since 1819.

St-Sulpice & the Luxembourg

South of boulevard St-Germain between Odéon and Luxembourg is a quarter that epitomises civilised Paris, full of historic buildings and interesting shops. Just off the boulevard lies the old covered market of St-Germain, once the site of important St-Germain Fair. Following redevelopment it now houses an underground swimming pool, auditorium, a few surviving food stalls and a rather soulless shopping arcade, although the Irish pub **Coolín** is a pleasant stopping-off point. Rue Guisarde is nicknamed *rue de la soif* (street of thirst) thanks to the merry carousers who swarm its bars and bistros by night. Rue Princesse and rue des Cannettes are a beguiling mix of lively bistros, like **Mâchon d'Henri** and **Brasserie Fernand**, and budget eateries, and some well-hidden late-night haunts including the Birdland bar, Bedford Arms, lively Argentine La Milonga and notoriously elitist **Castel's** nightclub.

Dawdle past the fashion boutiques, antiquarian book and print shops and high-class pâtisseries and you come to **St-Sulpice**, a surprising eighteenth-century exercise in classical form with two uneven turrets and a colonnaded facade. Delacroix painted the frescoes, in the first chapel on the right. The square contains Visconti's imposing, lion-

The Jardins du Luxembourg: *beloved of students, joggers and wandering Lotharios.*

flanked Fontaine des Quatre-Points Cardinaux – its name a pun on the compass points and four clerics who didn't (*ne point*) become cardinal – and is used for an antiques fair and a poetry fair every summer as part of the Foire St-Germain. The innocuous-looking **Café de la Mairie** remains a favourite with intellectuals and students, a classic example of anti-chic, while between shops of religous artefacts, the chic boutiques along place and rue St-Sulpice include Yves Saint Laurent, Christian Lacroix, **Agnès b**, **Vanessa Bruno**, **Muji**, perfumier Annick Goutal, the furnishings of **Catherine Memmi** and milliner **Marie Mercié**. Most of the houses date from the eighteenth century. Look out for the doorway of No 27, the Hôtel de Forgères, adorned with carved garlands of fruit.

To the west, prime shopping territory continues: the clothes shops of rue Bonaparte and rue du Four, leather and accessory shops of rue du Dragon, rue du Cherche-Midi and rue de Grenelle, including fashion-victim essentials like **Prada**, Victoire, Patrick Cox, Joseph and **Stéphane Kélian**, although if you see a queue into the street it's most likely for the bread of **Poilâne**. At busy carrefour de la Croix-Rouge, wine bar **Au Sauvignon** is renowned for people-watching rather than its wine.

South of St-Sulpice on rue de Vaugirard, and now hidden within the Institut Catholique is the early Baroque chapel of St-Joseph de Carmes, once part of a Carmelite convent and the site of a blood-thirsty massacre in 1792, when 115 priests were killed. To the east, wide rue de Tournon, lined by some very grand eighteenth-century residences, such as the elegant Hôtel de Brancas (now the Institut Français de l'Architecture) with allegorical figures of Justice and Prudence over the door, opens up to the Palais du Luxembourg and its adjoining park. Built for Marie de Médicis, the palace now serves as the French Senate. Ever popular with joggers and *dragueurs*, the Jardins du Luxembourg are much beloved of a population starved of greenery, with formal paths, legions of sculptures and a pond for sailing toy boats on.

Returning north towards boulevard St-Germain, you pass the Neo-Classical **Odéon, Théâtre de l'Europe** built in 1779, one of Paris' leading subsidised theatres. Beaumarchais' *Marriage of Figaro* was first performed here in 1784. The semi-circular place in front was home to revolutionary hero Camille Desmoulins, at No 2, now La Mediterranée restaurant, decorated by Jean Cocteau. A more seedy, studenty hangout is **Le Bar Dix** among the antiquarian bookshops on rue de l'Odéon. James Joyce's *Ulysses* was first published in 1922 next door at No 12 by Sylvia Beach at the legendary, original Shakespeare & Co.

Back on the boulevard St-Germain is a statue of Danton, who lived on the site before the construction of the boulevard. Now it's a popular meeting point, thanks to numerous cinemas and cafés. Up the street at 12 rue de l'Ecole-de-Médecine is the colonnaded Neo-Classical Université René Descartes (Paris V) medical school, designed in the late eighteenth century by Jacques Gondoin and home to the **Musée d'Histoire de la Médicine**. Across the street, the Gothic refectory remains

The **Palais du Luxembourg** *was built for Marie de Médicis; today it's the French Senate.*

from the **Couvent des Cordeliers** (No 15), an important Franciscan priory founded by St-Louis in the Middle Ages and later hotbed of Revolutionary plotting by the Club des Cordeliers. Marat, one of the club's leading lights, met his waterloo in the tub at his home in the same street (then called rue des Cordeliers), when he was stabbed in 1793 by Charlotte Corday, but gained eternity through David's celebrated painting of his wet demise. Look out for the magnificent doorway of the neighbouring *hôtel* and the domed building at No 5, once the barbers' and surgeons' guild. Climb up rue André-Dubois to rue Monsieur-le-Prince, which follows the ancient ramparts of Philippe-Auguste's fortifications, for the popular budget eatery **Polidor** at 41, which has been feeding students and tourists since 1845 and, near the junction with boulevard St-Michel, the 3 Luxembourg arts cinema. On rue Racine, the **Bouillon Racine**, once an Art Nouveau, working-class dining hall, has been restored as a Belgian eatery.

Eglise St-Sulpice
pl St-Sulpice, 6th (01.46.33.21.78). Mº St-Sulpice. **Open** 8am-7.30pm daily. **Map H7**

Work on this giant church began in 1646, but it was only completed 120 years and six architects later. The grandiose Italianate facade with its double colonnade is by Jean-Baptiste Servandoni, from 1733-45, although the two towers remained unfinished at his death. The one on the right has never been completed, and is still five metres short of its neighbour. Servandoni had originally planned to construct a semi-circular *place* in front of the church,

but this was never carried out and the present one was designed in the last century by Visconti, who also designed the fountain. The interior is famed for the three murals by Delacroix in the first chapel on the right of the entrance, depicting Jacob's fight with the Angel, Heliodorus chased out of the temple and St Michael killing the Dragon.

Jardins and Palais du Luxembourg
pl Auguste-Comte, pl Edmond-Rostand or rue de Vaugirard, 6th. Mº Odéon/RER Luxembourg. **Open** *summer* 7.30am-9.30pm daily; *winter* 8am-5pm daily. **Map H8**

The Palais du Luxembourg was built in the 1620s for Marie de Médicis, widow of Henri IV, by Salomon de Brosse, on the site of the former mansion of the Duke of Luxembourg. Its Italianate style, with ringed columns and rustication, was intended to resemble the Pitti Palace in her native Florence, although she did not live here for long, as Richelieu had her exiled to Cologne. The palace, reworked by Chalgrin in the eighteenth century, remained in royal hands until the Revolution, when it passed to the state; it now houses the French Senate.

The gardens were also created for Marie de Médicis. Part formal garden with terraces and gravel paths, part 'English garden' of lawns and part amusement centre for gardenless Parisians, it is the quintessential Paris park. Dotted around the park is a veritable gallery of French sculpture, from the looming Cyclops on the 1624 Fontaine de Médicis, to wild animals, queens of France, a mini Statue of Liberty and a monument to Delacroix. There are orchards, with over 300 varieties of apples, and an apiary where you can take courses in beekeeping.

The Musée du Luxembourg in the former Orangerie is used for exhibitions. The Luxembourg is a must for those with an interest in social anthropology. You can watch chessplayers, joggers and martial arts practictioners. Children enjoy pony rides, sand-pits and roundabouts; there are tennis courts, *boules* pitches, a café and bandstand, while the green park chairs are beloved of booklovers and *dragueurs*.

The Monumental 7th & West

Mainly 7th arrondissement, parts of 6th and 15th.
Smart townhouses spread west from St-Germain into the 7th *arrondissement*, as the vibrant street and café life subsides in favour of residential blocks and government offices. The 7th easily divides into two halves. The more intimate Faubourg St-Germain to the east became part of the city in 1704, and was soon colonised by the nobility. It still contains historic mansions and fine shops. West of Les Invalides, built up in the nineteenth century, the windswept expanses of wide avenues number the most famous sight of all, the Eiffel Tower.

The Faubourg St-Germain

Often written off by Proust as a symbol of staid, *haute-bourgeois* and aristocratic society, this area (despite the Revolution) remains home to some of Paris' oldest and grandest families, although most of its eighteenth-century *hôtels particuliers* have now been taken over by embassies and government ministries. You can admire their stone gateways and elegant courtyards, especially on rues de Grenelle, St-Dominique, de l'Université and de Varenne. Among the most beautiful is the Hôtel Matignon (57 rue de Varenne), residence of the Prime Minister; the facade is sometimes visible through the heavily guarded entrance portal. Used by Talleyrand for lavish receptions, it boasts sumptuous interiors and the biggest private garden in Paris. The Cité Varenne at No 51 is a lane of exclusive houses with private gardens. To see the decorative interiors and private gardens of others like the Hôtel de Villeroy (Ministry of Agriculture, 78 rue de Varenne), Hôtel Boisgelin (Italian Embassy, 47 rue de Varenne), Hôtel d'Estrée (residence of the Russian ambassador, 79 rue de Grenelle), Hôtel d'Avaray (residence of the Dutch ambassador, 85 rue de Grenelle) or 1777 Hôtel de Monaco (Polish Embassy, 57 rue St-Dominique), you'll have to wait for the open-house **Journées du Patrimoine**.

Two *hôtels* that can be visited are the Hôtel Biron, (*see below*) and Hôtel Bouchardon (**Musée Maillol**, (59-61 rue de Grenelle), which retains wooden panelling and a magnificent entrance curved around Bouchardon's 1739-45 fountain of the Four Seasons.

South of here, the area boasts the famous **Bon Marché** (or 'good bargain') department store, Paris' first, and the chic food and design shops of

rue du Bac, including a branch of **Hédiard**, the Conran Shop, the colourful tablewares of **Dîners en Ville** and, towards the river, Christian Liagre's sophisticated furniture and the stuffed animal emporium **Deyrolle**. Across the square Boucicaut from the Bon Marché is the upmarket **Lutétia** hotel, built 1907-11 to serve out-of-towners up for a shopping spree. Wander down the rue Récamier, with old-fashioned Burgundian restaurant Le Récamier and the **Espace Electra** exhibition space in a former electricity substation, to discover the tiny, hidden garden of Square Récamier. Along rue du Cherche-Midi are agreeable shops and tea rooms, and the **Musée National Hébert**, of interest for its setting in a mid-eighteenth-century house as much as for the paintings. There are good design shops beneath the smart apartments on boulevard Raspail, along with Paris' most successful *Marché biologique* on Sunday mornings. You may see coaches lined up beside the Bon Marché; these come not to shop but to pay pilgrimage at the **Chapelle de la Médaille Miraculeuse**.

Towards the Seine, high-quality antiques dealers abound in the Carré Rive Gauche, the quadrangle enclosed by the quai Voltaire (often known as *quai des antiquaires*) and rues des Sts-Pères, du Bac and de l'Université (*see chapter **Paris by Season***). Tapestries, Louis XV commodes, chandeliers and statuary make fine window shopping. Rue de Verneuil gets pilgrims of another sort as groupies and would-be poets come to leave graffiti on the former residence of Serge Gainsbourg. Just west of here is one of Paris' most important cultural sights, the **Musée d'Orsay**, a *fin-de-siècle* railway station now home to the national collection of Impressionist and nineteenth-century art. A new footbridge across to the Tuileries by architect-engineer Marc Mimram opened at the end of 1999. Across from the parvis is the **Musée de la Légion d'Honneur**, with a quirky, semi-circular pavilion, devoted to France's honours system.

Continuing westwards along the Seine, facing the Pont de la Concorde and the place de la Concorde across the river, is the **Assemblée Nationale**, the lower house of the French parliament. Originally built for a daughter of Louis XIV, the entrance on elegant place du Palais-Bourbon shows its domestic origins. Take a detour up the rue de Bourgogne to the church of Ste-Clotilde on rue des Las-Cases, an early example of nineteenth-century Gothic Revival.

Beside the Assemblée is the Foreign Ministry, often referred to by its address, the quai d'Orsay. Beyond it stretches the long, grassy esplanade leading up to the golden-domed **Invalides**, the vast military hospital complex which now houses the **Musée de l'Armée**. Cannons line the grand pavilions of the 196-metre-long facade, decorated with allegorical tributes to Louis XIV. The two churches inside – St-Louis-des-Invalides and the Eglise du Dôme – glorify the various French mon-

Rhyme, reason and the rush hour

'*Sous le pont Mirabeau coule la Seine…*' almost a century after Apollinaire penned the much-memorised line, the Seine continues to flow and so does the poetry. Springtime in Paris tends to bring poets out of hibernation and, if the French ministries of Culture and Education have their way, the week-long **Printemps des Poètes** will become as much a part of the cultural year as the Fête de la Musique, on which it is modelled. The fledgling festival will explore relationships between poetry, theatre and public spaces in venues from the Cinémathèque to the Jardin des Plantes. Schools, museums, bookshops and town halls are in on the act: keep an eye on the municipal electronic noticeboards for a poem popping up between the dreary bulletins about air quality and traffic jams.

A star venue for the Printemps des Poètes is the recently restored **Théâtre Molière**, which has superb acoustics especially designed for the spoken voice – performers can whisper and still be heard in the back row. Its current programme includes performances of the work of Cocteau and Mandelstam. The Théâtre Molière is the jewel in the crown of the **Maison de la Poésie**, which also houses an impressive all-poetry library, mounts exhibitions, holds conferences and publishes the review *Poésie 98*.

If all this seems too ethereal, the **Club des Poètes**, a well-established convivial rendezvous, offers *nourritures terrestres* before serving up the more spiritual 'anti-pollutant of mental space, the counterweight and the antidote of an existence which tends to turn us into robots'. Dinner is at 8pm nightly: the anti-pollutant kicks in at 10pm. Eminent poets Pablo Neruda and Octavio Paz have passed by. If you just want the dinner without the spiritual sustenance, **La Maison de Verlaine** offers a substantial, if prosaic, three-course menu for 99F, a price even starving poets can afford. And if your spleen packs it in, you can always visit Baudelaire's grave in that most literary of graveyards, the Cimetière de Montparnasse, and muse about mortality.

So far, so French. But speaking of *le spleen*, how do you translate a poem and still keep its spirit and imagery intact? The **Festival Franco-anglais de poésie**, also in the spring, has been addressing this question for 20 years. It brings English-and French-language poets together and lets them loose on each other's work, with fascinating results. Participants have included Denise Levertov, John Montague and Galway Kinnell. The poems rarely lose anything in translation and, in the right hands, can even be improved.

June brings the warming sight of 450 different publishers putting up their tents for the annual **Marché de la poésie** on place St-Suplice. Over 140 poets and writers from 50 countries attend.

Festivals apart, there's a plethora of poets in pubs: notably at **Scarbo** and **Carr's** which both host local English-language poetry groups. Bookshops such as the **Village Voice** also feature visiting poets. Even the RATP has been in on the act: following the example of London's Poems on the Underground, it not only provides poetry for the punters in the Métro, it holds competitions and then publishes commuter-penned verses. Which goes to show that the muse can strike anywhere, transforming the bowels of Montparnasse station at rush hour into the dizzying heights of Mount Parnassus.

Printemps des Poètes *(01.44.59.65.39). 20-26 Mar 2000.* **Théâtre Molière/Maison de la Poésie** *passage Molière, 157 rue St Martin, 3rd (01.44.54.53.00). M° Rambuteau.* **Festival Franco-Anglais de Poésie** *(01.40.09.94.19). 15-20 May 2000.* **Le Club des Poètes** *30 rue de Bourgogne, 7th (01.47.05.06.03). M° Rue du Bac.* **La Maison de Verlaine** *39 rue Descartes, 5th (01.43.26.39.15). M° Cardinal-Lemoine.* **Marché de la Poésie** *pl St-Sulpice, 6th (01.48.34.73.95). M° St-Sulpice.* **Scarbo** *1bis passage St-Sébastien, 11th (01.47.00.58.59). M° Bastille.* **Carr's** *1 rue du Mont-Thabor, 1st (01.42.60.60.26). M° Tuileries.*

archs. Inside the Eglise du Dôme is Napoléon's tomb. The esplanade gives a perspective across ornate, cherubim-laden **Pont Alexandre III** to the Grand and Petit Palais, all three constructed for the 1900 *Exposition Universelle*.

Just beside Les Invalides, a far cosier place to visit is the **Musée Rodin**, housed in the charming eighteenth-century Hôtel Biron and its huge gardens. Rodin was invited to move here in 1908 on the understanding that he would bequeath his work to the state. As a result, you can now see many of his great sculptures, including *The Thinker* and *The Burghers of Calais*, in a beautiful setting. Not far from here on rue de Babylone, an interesting architectural oddity is La Pagode cinema, a genuine Japanese pagoda constructed in 1895. It is currently closed for renovation, but the exotic structure can be admired from the outside.

Assemblée Nationale

33 quai d'Orsay, 7th (01.40.63.60.00). M° Assemblée Nationale. **Guided tours** 10am, 2pm, 3pm Sat when Chamber not in session; ID required. **Map F5**
The Palais Bourbon has been home to the lower house of the French parliament since 1827, and was the seat of the German military administration during the Occupation. Built in 1722 for Louis XIV's daughter, the Duchesse de Bourbon, the palace was extended by the Prince de Condé, who added the Hôtel de Lassay, now official residence of the Assembly's president. The Greek-style facade facing the Seine was stuck onto the building in 1806 to echo that of the Madeleine across the river. Inside, the library is decorated with Delacroix's *History of Civilisation*. Visitors can attend debates.

Chapelle de la Médaille Miraculeuse

Couvent des Soeurs de St-Vincent-de-Paul, 140 rue du Bac, 7th (01.49.54.78.88). M° Sèvres-Babylone. **Open** 7.45am-1pm, 2.30-7pm daily. **Map F7**
Reliefs to the left of the entrance recount the life of saintly nun Catherine Labouré. In 1830 she had a visit from the Virgin, who gave her a medal which performed many miracles. The kitsch chapel is one of the most visited pilgrimage sites in France, with two million faithful every year. It's an extraordinary concoction of statues, mosaics and murals, where the bodies of Catherine and her mother superior lie embalmed.

Les Invalides

esplanade des Invalides, 7th (01.44.42.54.52/Musée de l'Armée 01.44.42.37.67). M° Invalides. **Open** *Apr-Sept* 10am-6pm daily; *Oct-Mar* 10am-5pm daily. **Admission** *courtyard* free. *Musée de l'Armée & Eglise du Dôme* 37F; 27F 11-18s, students under-26; free under-11s, CM. **Credit** MC, V. **Map E6**
Visible miles away because of the gleaming Eglise du Dôme, the classical-style Hôtel des Invalides, designed by Libéral Bruand (1671-76) for Louis XIV as a military hospital and retirement home for the wounded, at one time housed up to 6000 invalids (hence the name). Part of it is still a hospital but much of it contains the **Musée de l'Armée**, with its staggering display of wartime paraphernalia, and

Musée de l'Ordre de la Libération. The Eglise du Dôme is a highly decorated example of French architecture under Louis XIV. Designed by Hardouin-Mansart, it is one of the grandest Baroque churches in the city. Since 1840 it has been dedicated to the worship of Napoléon, whose body was brought here from St Helena nineteen years after he died. It now lies beneath the coffered dome, in a red porphyry sarcophagus in a hushed circular crypt. The church of St-Louis is also known as the Church of the Soldiers, decorated with captured flags, its crypt filled with the remains of military men. Cannon barrels are littered everywhere but, even if you're not interested in military history, it's worth wandering through the gardens and the principal courtyard with its double-storey arcade to get a feeling of the power of royal patronage. Note the sundial and the elaborate dormer windows.

Musée d'Orsay

1 rue de la Légion d'Honneur, 7th (01.40.49.48.14/ recorded information 01.45.49.11.11). *M° Solférino/RER Musée d'Orsay.* **Open** 10am-6pm Tue, Wed, Fri, Sat; 10am-9.30pm Thur; 9am-6pm Sun. **Admission** 40F; 30F 18-25s, over-60s, Sun; free under-18s. **Credit** (shop) AmEx, MC, V. **Map G6**
The Musée d'Orsay was originally a Beaux-Arts train station, designed by Victor Laloux for the 1900 *Exposition Universelle*. You can still see the names of towns it once served on the Seine-side facade. Trains ceased to run there in the 1950s as its platforms proved too short, and for a long time it was threatened with demolition until, in the late 70s, President Giscard d'Estaing bowed to public pressure and decided instead to turn it into a museum spanning the fertile period 1830-1914, in a boldly redesigned interior by Italian architect Gae Aulenti. Opened in 1986, the main attraction is the skylit Impressionist gallery on the upper floor, filled with masterpieces by Monet, Degas, Renoir, Pissarro and Van Gogh. *See also chapter* **Museums**.

West of Les Invalides

To the west of the Invalides is the massive Ecole Militaire, the military academy built by Louis XV where Napoléon graduated, and which is still in army use today. Designed in 1751 by Jacques Ange Gabriel, this stern, imposing exercise in classicism isn't open to the public. Opposite its south entrance are the Y-shaped **UNESCO** building, built in 1958, and another monumental structure, the 30s Modernist Ministry of Labour. But off the wide avenues of Suffren, Rapp and de la Bourdonnais, there's also a sense of life beyond official-cialdom; on rue St-Dominique, with old-fashioned bistro Thoumieux at No 79, a favourite with local families and, at No 129, the attractive Fontaine de Mars on an arcaded square; or among the smart food shops of rue Cler; the avenue de Saxe offers up one of the most scenic street markets in Paris.

Les Invalides: *military hospital turned museum displays weaponry and Napoléon's tomb.*

Unlikely as it may seem, this des-res area was once far more industrial. On the corner of rue Surcouf and rue de l'Université, the **Musée de la Seita**, tobacco museum and art gallery, stands on the former site of the Manufacture du Gros Caillou. The tobacco factory employed over 1000 workers in the early nineteenth century, was the first factory in France to use steam power, and the place where France's first cigarettes were made in 1845.

From the north-western side of the Ecole Militaire begins the vast Champ de Mars, a former market garden converted into a military drilling ground in the eighteenth century and used after the 1789 Revolution for Bastille Day celebrations. Now it forms a spectacular backdrop to the most famous Parisian monument of them all, the **Eiffel Tower**, tallest building in the world from 1889 until New York's skyscrapers began sprouting in the 30s. It was intended only as a temporary structure, a bravura show of the new-found mastery of iron construction. Maupassant claimed he left Paris because of it; William Morris visited daily to avoid having to see it from afar, yet it is the satisfyingly phallic Eiffel Tower that has become the most potent international symbol of Paris.

Les Egouts de Paris

entrance opposite 93 quai d'Orsay, by Pont de l'Alma, 7th (01.53.68.27.81). M° Alma-Marceau/RER Pont de l'Alma. **Open** *May-Sept* 11am-5pm Mon-Wed, Sat, Sun; *Oct-Apr* 11am-4pm Mon-Wed, Sat, Sun. Closed three weeks in Jan. **Admission** 25F; 20F students, 5-16s, over 60s; free under 5s, CM. **Map D5**

For centuries the main source of drinking water in Paris was the Seine, which was also the main sewer. Construction of the sewers began in 1825, to be taken in hand by Haussmann and his engineers from 1853. Today, the Egouts de Paris have been made into one of the smelliest museums in the world. Each sewer is marked with a replica of the street sign above it, making the 2100km system a real city beneath a city.

Eiffel Tower

Champ de Mars, 7th (01.44.11.23.45/recorded information 01.44.11.23.23). M° Bir-Hakeim/RER Champ-de-Mars. **Open** *Sept-9 June* 9.30am-11pm daily; *10 June-Aug* 9am-midnight. **Admission** *By lift 1st level* 1 22F; 13F 3-12s; *2nd level* 42F; 23F 3-12s; *3rd level* 62F; 32F 3-12s; free under-3s. *By stairs 1st & 2nd levels* 20F. **Credit** AmEx, MC, V. **Map C6**

What for many is the symbol of Paris was the tallest building in the world at 300m when built in 1889 for the *Exposition Universelle* on the centenary of the Revolution. Now, with its aerial, it reaches 321m. The view of it from Trocadéro across the river is monumental, but the distorted aspect from its base most dramatically shows off the graceful ironwork of Gustave Eiffel and brings home its simply massive scale. Be prepared for a long wait to ride in the lifts – in 1998 the tower beat its previous record to receive six million visitors, its present popularity contrasting with the indignation which greeted its construction. The lifts travel 100,000km a year. To

save time and money you can stop at the first or second platform, but those who go on to the top can view Eiffel's cosy salon and enjoy amazing panoramas: over 65km on a good day. The queue is not so long at night, when the city lights against the Seine live up to their romantic image. There's the Altitude 95 bistro on the first level, and the smart Jules Verne restaurant on the second, as well as souvenir shops. *Wheelchair access (1st & 2nd levels only).*

UNESCO

pl de Fontenoy, 7th (01.45.68.10.00). M° Ecole-Militaire. **Open** 9am-6pm Mon-Fri. **Map D7**

The Y-shaped UNESCO headquarters was built in 1958 by a multinational team – an American (Breuer), an Italian (Nervi) and a Frenchman (Zehrfuss). A giant construction in concrete and glass, it's worth visiting for the sculptures by Picasso, Arp, Giacometti and Calder in the lobbies. Inside it buzzes with palpable postwar idealism. Behind there's a Japanese garden, with a concrete contemplation cylinder by Japanese minimalist architect Tadao Ando.

Village Suisse

38-78 av de Suffren/54 av de la Motte-Picquet, 15th. M° La Motte-Picquet-Grenelle. **Open** 10.30am-7pm Mon, Thur-Sun. **Map D7**

The mountains and waterfalls created for the Swiss Village at the 1900 *Exposition Universelle* have long since gone, but the village lives on. Rebuilt as blocks of flats in the 1920s and again in 1960s, the street level has been colonised by some 150 boutiques offering high-quality antiques and collectables. Sundays tend to be busy as the village with its gardens makes a pleasant walk.

Fronts de Seine

Downstream from the Eiffel Tower, the 15th *arrondissement* has few tourist sites. Near the Pont Bir-Hakeim on quai Branly stands the high-tech **Maison de la Culture du Japon**, its frosted pale green glass a reference to Japanese jade. The riverfront has been taken over by 70s tower block developments, some of the most jarring in Paris. Signs of improvement further west are the sophisticated headquarters of the Canal+ TV channel, 2 rue des Cévennes, designed by American Richard Meier, and, surrounded by well-thought out modern housing, the **Parc André Citroën**, opened in 1992 on the site of a former Citroën car factory.

Parc André Citroën/Millennium Balloon

rue Balard, rue St-Charles, quai Citroën, 15th. M° Javel or Balard. **Map A9**

Laid out in 1993, this is the twenty-first-century equivalent of a French formal garden, comprising glasshouses, computerised fountains, waterfalls, a wilderness and gardens planted with different-coloured plants and even sounds. Modern-day Le Nôtres (Gilles Clément and Alain Prévost) have been at play: stepping stones and water jets prove that this is a garden for pleasure as well as philosophy. Until the end of 2000, a huge captive balloon gives spectacular views over the city (33F-66F).

The sky's the limit in the **Millennium balloon**.

Montparnasse & Beyond

Mainly 6th and 14th arrondissements, parts of 13th and 15th.

In the early 1900s artists like Picasso, Léger and Soutine, as well as the poet Apollinaire, came to 'Mount Parnassus' to escape the rising rents of Montmartre, bringing cutting-edge intellectual life to the area. Between the wars they were joined by Chagall, Zadkine and other escapees from the Russian Revolution who set up the lively restaurant **Dominique**, and by Americans Man Ray, Henry Miller, Ezra Pound and Gertrude Stein. The neighbourhood symbolised modernity: jazz, *bal nègre*, Surrealism, and *fureur de vivre*. Mondrian claimed he moved here in 1926 to indulge in the charleston.

To some extent their legacy has lived on, but Montparnasse is a sadder, more disparate place now. The high-rise **Tour Montparnasse**, Paris' failed tribute to Manhattan, is the most visible of several infelicitous projects of the 70s; at least there are good views of the city from the top. The old Montparnasse railway station, where the Germans surrendered Paris on 25 August 1944, has been transformed into a maze of steel and glass corridors, with the new **Jardin de l'Atlantique** suspended over the TGV tracks. This is the main point of arrival from Brittany, as reflected in the numerous *crêperies* scattered around. Fronting the boulevard

is a shopping complex and sports centre. To the west is Ricardo Bofill's circular place de Catalogne, typical of his postmodern version of Classicism.

Nearby rue de la Gaîté, once renowned for its cabarets, has fallen prey to strip joints and sex shops, although boulevard Edgar-Quinet has pleasant cafés and a street market (Wed, Sat mornings). The boulevard du Montparnasse still buzzes at night, thanks to its many cinemas and its legendary brasseries: the famed **Dôme** at No 108, now a luxurious fish restaurant and bar; giant Art Deco brasserie **La Coupole** at No 102, which opened in 1927, is ever busy despite the construction of a block of flats on top; and classic late-night café **Le Select** at No 99. Further east legendary literary café **La Closerie des Lilas**, opened as a dance hall in the 1840s, was a favourite with everyone from Lenin and Trotsky to Picasso and Hemingway and still draws politicians and publishers today. Le Nègre de Toulouse and the Dingo are long gone but there's still a sense of the *louche* at the **Rosebud** in rue Delambre. Boulevard Raspail boasts Rodin's 1898 *Balzac;* his rugged, elemental rendition of the novelist caused such a furore that it wasn't displayed in public for 40 years.

Artists' studios were dispersed over much of the 14th *arrondissement*, as well as parts of the 6th, 13th and 15th. Large windows testify to studios now frequently converted into apartments, such as the strange tiled studio building at 31 rue Campagne-Première (once home to Man Ray and featured in Godard's *A bout de Souffle*), around the courtyard at 126 boulevard du Montparnasse, on boulevard Raspail and rue Notre-Dame-des-Champs, or the old academies of rue de la Grande-Chaumière, where young artists too broke to hire a model went to draw from the nude. One of these academies survives, untouched and poignantly atmospheric, at 14 rue de la Grande Chaumière, where you can still go and sketch by the hour, just next to where Modigliani died at No 8 in less than picturesque misery. Russian artist Marie Vassilieff ran her avant-garde Academie Vassilieff in the row of ivy-hung studios at 21 avenue du Maine (recently saved from redevelopment as the **Le Chemin de Montparnasse**), the scene of lively fêtes with Picasso, Braque and Modigliani. The studios of sculptors Zadkine (100bis rue d'Assas) and Bourdelle (16 rue Bourdelle) are now museums, while Brancusi's studio, originally in the 15th, has been rebuilt outside the Centre Pompidou. A more recent addition is the glass and steel **Fondation Cartier** on boulevard Raspail, an exhibition centre for contemporary art.

Inexpensive clothes and a **Fnac** can be found on rue de Rennes. There are numerous shoe, food and children's shops on rues Vavin and Bréa, which lead to the Jardins du Luxembourg. Stop for a coffee at Café Vavin and look at Henri Sauvage's white tiled apartment building at 6 rue Vavin, built in 1911-12.

While the rest of the neighbourhood has gone a

bit downhill, Montparnasse cemetery has grown in status as a resting place for literary and artistic greats, though it's less crowded than Père-Lachaise.

Le Chemin de Montparnasse
21 av du Maine, 15th (01.42.22.91.96).
M° Montparnasse-Bienvenüe or Falguière. **Open** *during exhibitions* 1-7pm Wed-Sun. **Admission** 20F; 15F 6-16s, students under-26, over-60s; free under-6s. **No credit cards. Map F8**
This row of ivy-hung studios is a relic of the artists' alleyways that once threaded Montparnasse. One resident was Marie Vassilieff, whose avant-garde Académie Vassilieff dispensed with formal teaching for classes given by the pupils. During World War I she ran a canteen for impoverished artists like Braque and Modigliani, and in the 20s was famed for artistic *bals*. Temporary exhibitions are linked to past and present artists working in the area.

Cimetière de Montparnasse
3 bd Edgar-Quinet, 14th (01.44.10.86.50). M° Edgar-Quinet or Raspail. **Open** *16 Mar-5 Nov* 9am-6pm daily; *6 Nov-15 Mar* 9am-5.30pm daily. **Map G9**
Many of those who have marked Left Bank cultural life have ended up in Montparnasse, since the cemetery opened under Napoléon. Pay homage to writers Jean-Paul Sartre and Simone de Beauvoir, Baudelaire, Maupassant, Tzara, Beckett, Ionesco and Duras, composers César Frank and Saint-Saëns, sculptors Dalou, Rude, Bartholdi, Laurens (with his own sculpture *Douleur* on the tomb) and Zadkine, the unfortunate Captain Alfred Dreyfus, André Citroën of car fame, and Mr and Mme Pigeon reposing in their double bed. From cinema and showbiz come Jean Seberg, waiflike star of *A bout de souffle*, directors Jacques Becker and Jacques Demy, beloved comic Coluche and *provocateur* Serge Gainsbourg. In the north-east corner, Brancusi's sculpture *Le Baiser* (The Kiss), adorns one of the tombs.

Jardin de l'Atlantique
entry from Gare Montparnasse or pl des Cinq-Martyrs-du-Lycée-Buffon, 15th. M° Montparnasse-Bienvenüe. **Open** dawn-dusk daily. **Map G9**
Perhaps the hardest of all Paris' new gardens to find, the Jardin de l'Atlantique, opened in 1995, takes the Parisian quest for space airbound with an engineering feat suspended 18 metres over the tracks of Montparnasse station. It is a small oasis of granite paths, trees and bamboo in an urban desert of modern apartment and office blocks. Small openings allow you to peer down on the trains below.

Tour Maine-Montparnasse
33 av du Maine, 15th (01.45.38.52.56). M° Montparnasse-Bienvenüe. **Open** 9.30am-10.30pm daily. **Admission** *exhibition/ terrace* 46F; 38F over-60s; 35F 14-20s, students; 30F 5-14s; free under-5s. **No credit cards. Map F9**
Built in 1974 on the site of the former Gare Montparnasse, this steel-and-glass monster, at 209m high, is lower than the Eiffel Tower, but more central, and offers excellent views. A lift whisks you up to the 56th floor, where you'll find a display of aerial views of Paris, allowing you to see how the city has changed since 1858, and there's a terrace on the 59th floor. There's rarely a queue.

Denfert-Rochereau & Montsouris

A spookier kind of burial ground can be found at place Denfert-Rochereau, entrance to the **Catacombs**, where the bones of six million people were transferred just before the Revolution from over-

An oasis in the urban jungle: the **Jardin de l'Atlantique** *is 18m above a railway station.*

crowded Paris cemeteries to a veritable gruyère cheese of underground tunnels that spreads under much of the 13th and 14th *arrondissements*. The entrance is next to one of the toll gates of the **Mur des Fermiers-généraux** built by Ledoux in the 1780s, marking what was then the boundary of the city. A bronze lion, sculpted by Bartholdi of Statue of Liberty fame, dominates the traffic junction, replica of the Lion de Belfort in eastern France, symbol of resistance against Germany in 1870 under Colonel Denfert-Rochereau, a curious coincidence of name as the gateway was previously known by the much more sinister Porte d'Enfer (gate of hell).

Returning towards Montparnasse along the avenue Denfert-Rochereau you'll come to the Observatoire de Paris (62 av de l'Observatoire), built by Perrault for Louis XIV's minister Colbert in 1668 (open to the public by appointment only, first Sat of the month). This is where the moon was first mapped, where Neptune was discovered and the speed of light first calculated. The French meridian mapped by politician and astronomer François Arago in 1806 (in use before the Greenwich meridian was adopted as an international standard) runs north-south through the building. Both Arago and the meridian have an unusual minimalist memorial by Dutch artist Jan Dibbets in the form of 135 bronze medallions, embedded along the Paris meridian line, on its route through the 18th, 9th, 2nd, 1st, 6th and 14th *arrondissements*, passing through some of the city's most celebrated sites, including Sacré Coeur, Palais-Royal, the Louvre and Jardins du Luxembourg. One is in the square of the l'Ile de Sein (where the meridian crosses boulevard Arago) on the empty base of the original statue to Arago, melted down during World War II. Next door the Maison du Fontainier (42 rue de l'Observatoire), was part of Marie de Médicis' underwater reservoir, designed to feed her fountains just as much as the people. The reservoir is now dry(ish) and can be visited on the **Journées du Patrimoine**. Further down the boulevard, past the Prison de la Santé, built as part of Haussmann's urban redevelopment, Laurens, Picasso and Maillol all had studios at the rustic-looking Cité Fleurie, still occupied by artists today. It's closed to the public, but you can peer through the gate into the gardens.

The 14th *arrondissement* to the south of place Denfert-Rochereau is mainly residential. The small but lively food market and several cafés on **rue Daguerre** are favourite local rendezvous. East of avenue du Général-Leclerc, the area around rue Hallé, formerly part of the village of Montrouge incorporated into the city in 1860, was laid out in little crescents in an early attempt at a garden city. In the 30s, writers Henry Miller and Anaïs Nin and sculptor Chana Orloff lived in villa Seurat, off rue de la Tombe-Issoire, where architect André Lurçat built several of the houses, and where Seurat once

Rue Daguerre *market: a popular rendezvous.*

lived. Foodies make the trek to avenue Jean-Moulin for bistro **La Régalade**. At 4 rue Marie Rose is the Maison de Lénine (01.42.79.99.58/ by appointment), where Lenin lived 1909-12 with Nadejda Krpskaïa. Once a compulsory stop for East European dignitaries, today it's a forlorn place financed by the French Communist party, exhibiting his furniture, some of which looks as if it would be more suitable for the flea market at the **Puces de Vanves** on the southwest edge of the *arrondissement*.

The 14th *arrondissement* also boasts a lovely large park, the **Parc Montsouris**. On the park's opening day in 1878 the man-made lake suddenly and inexplicably emptied and the engineer responsible promptly committed suicide. Many of the artists who gave Montparnasse its reputation actually lived around here. Around the western edge of the park are several small streets such as rue du Parc Montsouris and rue Georges-Braque that were built up in the early 1900s with charming small villas and artists' studios, many by distinguished avant-garde architects, including the Villa Ozenfant (53 av Reille), designed in 1922 by Le Corbusier for painter Amédée Ozenfant, and the elegant Villa Guggenbuhl (14 rue Nansouty) designed in 1926-27 by Lurçat. On the southern edge of Montsouris the **Cité Universitaire**, home to 6000 foreign students, is worth visiting for its themed pavilions, designed by eminent architects.

Les Catacombes

1 pl Denfert-Rochereau, 14th (01.43.22.47.63).
M° Denfert-Rochereau. **Open** 2-4pm Tue-Fri; 9-11am,
2-4pm Sat, Sun. Closed public holidays. **Admission**
33F; 22F 8-25s, over-60s; free under-7s, CM. **No
credit cards. Map G10**
The miles of dank, subterranean passages have existed, originally as stone quarries, since Roman times.
In the 1780s, the contents of the overcrowded Paris
cemeteries were transferred here. Stacks of bones
alternate with tidy rows of skulls, while macabre quo-
tations (Lamartine, Virgil, etc) on stone tablets add
philosophical reflections on the inevitability of death.
There are supposedly bits of six million people down
here, including victims of the Terror. One section was
used by the Résistance during World War II. Avid
'cataphiles' are renowned for finding obscure
entrances for underground parties, but would you
really want to spend a night down here?

Cité Universitaire

bd Jourdan, 14th. RER Cité Universitaire.
The Cité Universitaire was founded on an interwar
ideal of internationalism and a desire to attract foreign
students. Among landscaped gardens, the 40 pavilions,
inspired by Oxbridge and US/UK campuses (although
here purely residential) were designed in supposedly
national style, some by architects of the country like
the De Stijl Collège Néerlandais by Willem Dudok, others in exotic pastiche, like the Asie du Sud-Est pavilion with its Khmer sculptures and bird-beaked roof.
The Swiss pavilion (1935) and Brazilian pavilion (1959)
by Le Corbusier reflect his early and late styles. You
can visit the Swiss pavilion (01.44.16.10.16; 8am-noon,
2-8pm Mon-Fri; 10am-noon, 2pm-8pm Sat, Sun) which
has a tiled Le Corbusier mural on the ground floor.

Marché aux Puces de Vanves

*av Georges Lafenestre (on bridge after Périphérique)
and av Marc-Sangrier, 14th. M° Porte de Vanves.*
Open 7.30am-7pm Sat, Sun.
The smallest and friendliest of Paris' flea markets
seems to have taken a dive in quality recently and
discount clothing stalls have encroached on the
antiques. Worth a look, though, for vintage lace and
small decorative and household items.

Parc Montsouris

bd Jourdan, 14th. RER Cité-Universitaire.
One of Haussmann's parks laid out by Alphand,
with obligatory lake and artificial cascades. Its gently sloping lawns descend towards a lake, with tur-
tles and ducks, and the variety of bushes, trees and
flowerbeds make it the most colourful of the capital's parks. Spot the bed planted with different roses
for French newspapers and magazines.

15th Arrondissement

The 15th is Paris' largest *arrondissement* and the
one that probably has the least for the tourist. Staid
and residential, it is centred on the foodshops of rue
du Commerce and rue Lecourbe. It's worth making
a detour to passage de Dantzig to visit **La Ruche**
('beehive'), designed by Eiffel as a wine pavilion for

the 1900 exhibition. Afterwards it was acquired by
philanthropic sculptor Alfred Boucher, who had it
rebuilt on this site and let it out as studios for 140
artists. Chagall, Soutine, Brancusi and Modigliani
all spent periods here, and the studios are still much
sought after by artists. Nearby on rue des Morillons
the **Parc Georges Brassens** was opened in 1983
on the site of the former Abattoirs de Vaugirard.

Parc Georges Brassens

rue des Morillons, 15th. M° Porte de Vanves. **Map D10**
Built on the site of the former Abbatoirs de
Vaugirard, Parc Georges Brassens prefigured the
industrial recuperation of Parc André Citroën and
La Villette. The gateways crowned by bronze bulls
have been kept, as have a series of iron meat market pavilions, which house a busy antiquarian and
second-hand book market at weekends. The interesting Jardin des Senteurs is planted with aromatic
species, while in one corner, a small vineyard produces 200 bottles of Clos des Morillons every year.

Paris Expo

*Porte de Versailles, 15th (01.43.95.37.00). M° Porte
de Versailles.* **Map B10**
The vast exhibition centre hosts everything from
fashion to medical equipment fairs. Many are open
to the public, such as the Foire de Paris, the Salon
de l'Agriculture or the contemporary art fair FIAC.

The 13th Arrondissement

A working-class area that became one of the most
industrialised parts of Paris in the nineteenth century, the 13th has been one of the most marauded
areas of Paris since World War II, from the tower
blocks of Chinatown to the new national library
and the burgeoning development zone around it.

Gobelins & La Salpêtrière

Although its image may be of tower blocks, the
13th also contains some historic parts of Paris,
expecially where it borders on the 5th (*see above*,
Latin Quarter). The **Manufacture Nationale
des Gobelins** is home to the French state weaving companies. The tapestries and rugs produced
here (usually on government commission) continue a tradition dating back to the fifteenth century,
when Jean Gobelin set up his dyeing works by the
river Bièvre. Followed by tanneries and other
industries, the river became notorious for its pollution until covered over in 1912, while the slums
were depicted in Hugo's *Les Misérables*. The area
was tidied up in the 30s, when the **Square Réné
Le Gall**, a small park, was laid out on former
tapestry-workers' allotments. On rue des Gobelins,
where Gobelin lived, the so-called **Château de la
Reine Blanche** is a curious medieval relic.

On the western edge of the *arrondissement*, next
to the Gare d'Austerlitz, sprawls the huge Hôpital
de la Pitié-Salpêtrière, one of the oldest hospitals

Les Grands Moulins de Paris: *being swallowed up by redevelopment in the eastern 13th.*

in Paris, founded in 1656, and where Princess Diana was brought after her fatal crash. It is also known for the beautiful **Chapelle St-Louis-de-la-Salpêtrière**, designed by Libéral Bruand.

The busy road intersection of place d'Italie has seen more developments with the Centre Commercial Italie, opposite the town hall, a bizarre high-tech confection designed by Japanese architect Kenzo Tange, which contains the Gaumont Grand Ecran Italie cinema. There's a good food market on boulevard Auguste-Blanqui (Tue, Fri, Sun mornings) and the sharply contrasting attractions of Chinatown and the Butte aux Cailles.

Chapelle St-Louis-de-la-Salpêtrière

47 bd de l'Hôpital, 13th (01.42.16.04.24). M° Gare d'Austerlitz. **Open** 8.30am-6.30pm daily. **Map L9**
The austerely beautiful chapel was designed by Libéral Bruand in 1657-77 with an octagonal dome in the centre and eight naves in order to separate the sick from the insane, the destitute from the debauched. Around the chapel are some of the buildings of the Hôpital de la Pitié-Salpêtrière, founded on the site of a gunpowder factory (hence its name from saltpetre) by Louis XIV to round up vagrant and unwanted women, becoming a research centre of the insane in the 1790s. Charcot pioneered neuro-psychology here, receiving a famous visit from Freud. It is now one of Paris' main teaching hospitals, but the chapel is regularly used for contemporary art exhibitions.

Château de la Reine Blanche

17 rue des Gobelins, 13th. M° Gobelins. **Map K10**
Through a gateway you can spot the turret and overhanging first floor of an ancient house. The curious

relic is named after Queen Blanche of Provence who had a château here, but was probably rebuilt in the 1520s for the Gobelin family. Blanche was also associated with the nearby Couvent des Cordeliers, of which a tiny fragment of the Gothic refectory survives on the corner of rue Pascal and rue de Julienne.

Manufacture des Gobelins

42 av des Gobelins, 13th (01.44.08.52.00). M° Gobelins. **Tours** 2-2.45pm Tue-Thur. **Admission** 50F; 40F 7-25s. **No credit cards. Map K10**
Tapestries have been woven on this site almost continuously since 1662 when Colbert, Louis XIV's jack of all trades, set up the Manufacture Royale des Meubles de la Couronne. Also known as the Gobelins after Jean Gobelin, a dyer who previously owned the site, the factory was at its wealthiest during the *ancien régime* when tapestries were produced for royal residences under the direction of artists such as Le Brun and Oudry. Today tapestries are still woven (mostly for the state) and visitors can watch weavers at work. The guided tour (in French) through the 1912 factory gives you a chance to understand the complex weaving process and takes in the eighteenth-century chapel and the Beauvais tapestry workshops. Arrive 30 minutes before the tour.

Chinatown

South of the rue de Tolbiac is Paris' main Chinatown, centred between the 60s tower blocks along avenues d'Ivry and de Choisy, and home to a multi-Asian community. The bleak modern architecture could make it one of the most depressing areas of Paris, yet it's a fascinating piece of

South-East Asia, lined with kitsch restaurants, Vietnamese *pho* noodle bars and Chinese patisseries, as well as the large **Tang Frères** supermarket on avenue d'Ivry. Less easy to find is the Buddhist temple hidden in an underground car park beneath the tallest tower block (Autel de la culte de Bouddha, av d'Ivry, opposite rue Frères d'Astier-de-la-Vigerie, open 9am-6pm daily). Come here for the traditional lion and dragon dances at Chinese New Year (*see* **Paris by Season**).

La Butte aux Cailles

In striking contrast to nearby Chinatown, the villagey Butte aux Cailles is a neighbourhood of old houses, winding cobblestone streets and funky bars and restaurants, just southwest of the Place d'Italie. This workers' neighbourhood, home in the 1800s to many small factories, including a tannery, was one of the first to fight during the 1848 Revolution and the Paris Commune. The Butte has preserved its insurgent character and, in recent years, has resisted the aggressive forces of city planning and construction companies. The steep, cobbled rue de la Butte-aux-Cailles and the rue des Cinq-Diamants are the headquarters of the arty, *soixante-huitard* bohemian forces. For a complete village tour, saunter down the rustic rues Alphand, Buot and Michal. Villa Daviel contains neat little villas, while the cottages built in 1912 in a mock-Alsatian vernacular style at 10 rue Daviel were one of the earliest public housing schemes in Paris. Behind the small garden at the place Paul-Verlaine lies an attractive brick Arts-and-Crafts style swimming pool fed by an artesian well. Further south, explore passage Vandrezanne, the square des Peupliers, and the rue Dieulafoy, and the botanically named streets of the Cité Florale.

To discuss art, music or the most recent workers' strikes, the Butte offers a selection of relaxed, inexpensive bistros: le Temps des Cérises, run as a cooperative, busy **Chez Gladines** and more upmarket **Chez Paul**. Two feisty bars, **La Folie en Tête** and **Le Merle Moqueur,** offer music, cheap beer on tap and youthful crowds spilling out on to the pavement.

The Developing East

Dominique Perrault's controversial **Bibliothèque Nationale de France François Mitterrand,** the last of the *Grands Projets,* forms the centrepiece of a massive redevelopment of a desolate area formerly taken up by railway yards. The ZAC Rive Gauche includes new housing and office developments, the covering-over of some of the remaining railway lines with the grandiosely named avenue de France, and the swallowing-up of existing industrial buildings in the area, such as **Les Frigos** former refrigerated warehouses (now containing artists' studios), whose tenants are at the forefront of the residents' struggle to have a say in the future of the area, and the majestic **Grands Moulins de Paris,** mysteriously partly burnt down in 1996 (*see chapter* **Architecture**). Much of the area resembles a building site and is in a state of constant flux as new tower blocks appear overnight, shops open and roads change names. Happily, a growing flotilla of music bars moored on the Seine, the **Batofar, Péniche Blues Café** and **Péniche Makara,** provides signs of new life in the air. Across the railway tracks, a pioneering art nucleus called **ScèneEst** is burgeoning among the offices and housing developments, with the arrival of six adventurous young galleries on rue Louise-Weiss. Overlooking the boulevards des Amiraux, Le Corbusier's **Armée du Salut** hostel points to an earlier phase of urban planning. Another unlikely monument (despite rumours of its destruction) is the rue Watt. Once used for offbeat happenings, it is famed as the lowest road in Paris.

Bibliothèque Nationale de France François Mitterrand

quai François-Mauriac, 13th (01.53.79.53.79).
M° Bibliothèque or Quai de la Gare. **Open** 10am-7pm Tue-Sat; noon-6pm Sun. Closed two weeks in Sept. **Admission** *day* 20F; *annual* 200F; student 100F. **Credit** MC, V. **Map M10**

Opened in December 1996 by President Chirac, the gigantic new French national library (dubbed 'TGB' or *Très Grande Bibliothèque*) was the last of Mitterrand's *Grands Projets* and also the most expensive and most controversial. Architect Dominique Perrault was criticised for his curiously dated-looking design, which hides readers underground and stores the books in four L-shaped glass towers (intended to resemble open books), necessitating the installation of wooden shutters to protect them from sunlight. In the central void is a garden (open only to researchers) filled with 140 trees, uprooted from Fontainebleau at a cost of 40 million francs. The research section, below the public reading rooms, opened in autumn 1998, whereupon the massive computer system failed to get the right books to the right person and staff promptly went on strike. The library houses over ten million volumes, 420km of shelves and room for 3000 readers. Books, newspapers and periodicals are on public access to anyone over 18. An audio-visual room allows the public to browse through photo archives, film documentaries or sound recordings, and there are regular concerts and exhibitions. *See chapters* **Museums, Directory.**
Concerts. Exhibitions. Wheelchair access.

Cité de Réfuge de l'Armée du Salut

12 rue Cantagrel, 13th (01.53.61.82.00).
M° Bibliothèque.
The Salvation Army hostel was designed by Le Corbusier in 1929-33 to provide accommodation for 1500 homeless men. Its use of reinforced concrete and modular structure were an early attempt to put his theories of mass habitation into practice and a precursor of his influential Unités d'Habitation.

Beyond the Périphérique

To many Parisians, the banlieue just spells trouble, but there are landmarks to discover beyond the city zone.

Boulogne & the West

Paris' most desirable suburbs lie to the west of the city, supposedly the result of prevailing winds which carried industrial grime eastwards. Between the wars, the middle classes began to build expensive properties here, and further out there are large expanses of forest. Decentralisation also means that La Défense, Neuilly, Boulogne, Levallois and Issy-les-Moulineaux have become work places for residents of Paris, especially in the service, advertising and media industries.

Neuilly-sur-Seine is the most sought-after residential suburb, where smart apartment blocks have gradually replaced the extravagant mansions built around the Bois de Boulogne. Expect to see lots of velvet hairbands and Hermès scarves.

Boulogne-Billancourt is the main town in the region outside Paris. In 1320 the Gothic Eglise Notre Dame was begun in tribute to a statue of the Virgin washed up at Boulogne-sur-Mer. By the eighteenth-century, the village of Boulogne was known for its wines and its laundries and, early this century, for its artist residents (Landowski, Lipchitz, Chagall, Gris), while Billancourt was known for its industries (cars, aviation and cinema). The famous film studios where Abel Gance shot *Napoléon* were recently demolished. Between Boulogne and Sèvres across the Seine on the Ile Séguin, the now-disused Renault factory sits in the river like a long ocean liner or, since closure in 1992, rather more of a beached whale. It's due to be redeveloped in a scheme of offices and residential buildings by Bruno Fortier, despite a last-ditch attempt led by architect Jean Nouvel and the AMIS (Association pour la mutation de l'Ile Séguin) to save the former industrial buildings. Near the Bois de Boulogne are elegant villas, and some fine examples of 1920s and 30s architecture by Le Corbusier, Mallet-Stevens, Perret, Lurçat and others, well pinpointed by plaques around the town. In the town centre, the white Modernist town hall was designed by Tony Garnier in 1934. Next door, the **Musée des Années 30** focuses on artists and architects who lived in the town at that time. Just across the Seine is **St-Cloud**, site of a château that burnt down in the Franco-Prussian war. The extensive **Parc de St-Cloud** remains surrounded by streets of often romantic villas. South of St-Cloud is Sèvres, site of the famous porcelain factory, now the **Musée National de Céramique**. Although an avenue of lime trees points to the demolished château of the Ducs de Guise, **Meudon** is often associated with sculptors, including Rodin, whose Villa des Brillants is now a museum, and abstract sculptor Jean Arp, whose house and studio was designed by his wife Sophie Taeuber-Arp.

The **Château de Malmaison** at Rueil-Malmaison was a favourite residence of Napoléon and Josephine, who transformed its interior in Empire style. The eccentric **Château de Monte Cristo** (01.30.61.61.35) at Port Marly was built for Alexandre Dumas with a tiled Moorish room. In the grounds, the strange Château d'If is inscribed with the titles of his numerous works.

The town of **St-Germain-en-Laye** is a smart commuter suburb, dominated by a forbidding château, where Henri II lived with his wife Catherine de Médicis and his mistress Diane de Poitiers. Louis XIV was born here, Mary Queen of Scots grew up here, and the dethroned James II lived here from 1689 until his death in 1701. It was restored by Napoléon III, who turned it into the **Musée des Antiquités Nationales**. The château overlooks the Grande Terrasse, a popular promenade laid out by Le Nôtre, on the edge of a huge forest. The rest of the town is marked by upmarket shops, the **Musée Départemental Maurice Denis**, a superb collection of Nabi and Post-Impressionist art, in the former royal priory where the Nabi painter lived. Behind the tourist office, the Musée Claude Debussy (38 rue au Pain/01.34.51.05.12), the house where the composer was born in 1862, contains his collection of Japanese sculpture, letters, sketches and desk, and is used regularly for concerts.

Further west up the Seine, the former royal town of Poissy was once important for its livestock market. Today dominated by a car factory, it merits the visit for the Gothic Collégiale Notre Dame (8 rue de l'Eglise), much restored by Viollet-le-Duc, and Le Corbusier's avant-garde **Villa Savoye**.

Les Jardins Albert Kahn

14 rue du Port, 92100 Boulogne (01.46.04.52.80).
M° Boulogne-Pont St Cloud. **Open** 11am-6pm Tue-
Sun. **Admission** 22F; 15F 8-21s, students, over-60s;
free under-8s. **No credit cards**.

With red bridges, coloured maples, bamboos, Japanese
shrines, cascading streams and geometric landscaping, the gardens created by financier Albert Kahn
(1860-1940) should be twee, yet somehow never are.
Instead there's an enormous variety of habitats,
species and moods crammed in a small space. The
famed Japanese garden precedes a quadrangle of roses
and fruit trees, then leads via the Blue Forest – where
misty spruces and tall cedars cast an undeniably blue
haze – and marshy Marais to the boulders, ferns and
pines of the Vosgeian forest, like a lump of Alsace
transplanted. Water and evergreens dominate the gardens, making them interesting even in winter.

Parc de St-Cloud

92210 St-Cloud (01.41.12.02.90). M° Pont de Sèvres
and cross river. **Open** *Mar-Oct* 7.30am-10pm; *Nov-*
Feb 7.30am-8pm. **Admission** free; 20F for cars.
Credit V.

You can play football or frisbee, walk or picnic on the
grass, cycle or hire a peddle car here, yet this is another classic French park laid out by Le Nôtre, and all
that remains of a royal château that belonged to
'Monsieur', brother of Louis XIV. It was destroyed by
fire in 1870, three months after the Franco-Prussian
war was declared in the château. There are complex
avenues that meet in stairs, long perspectives,
stepped terraces, stretches of forest, a great view over
Paris from the Rond-Point du Balustrade and a series
of pools and fountains: most spectacular is the Grande

Cascade, a multi-tiered feast of dolphins and sea
beasts, switched on at 4pm on the second and fourth
Sundays of the month from May to September.

Villa Savoye

82 rue de Villiers, 78300 Poissy (01.39.65.01.06).
RER Poissy + 15 min walk. **Open** *Apr-Oct*
9.30am-12.30pm, 1.30-6pm Mon, Wed-Sun; *Nov-Mar*
9.30am-12.30pm, 1.30-4.30pm Mon, Wed-Sun.
Admission 25F; 15F 15-25s; free under-12s.

Built in 1929 for a family of rich industrialists, this
luxury house set in spacious grounds is perhaps Le
Corbusier's most successful work, noted especially
for its sculptural spiral staircase and roof terraces.
It still has much of its original built-in furniture, plus
seminal pieces, such as the famous Le Corbusier and
Perriand chaise-longue.

La Défense

Paris' mini-Manhattan is only a hop, skip and a
jump from central Paris, but as you emerge from
the depths of the RER, its giant skyscrapers and
walkways feel like a different world. Even if somewhat cold and anonymous, it is surprisingly lively: overwhelmingly businessy during the week,
filled with visitors and shoppers on the weekends.

La Défense (named after a stand against the
Prussians in the 1870 Franco-Prusian war) has been
a showcase for French business since the mid-50s,
when the triangular **CNIT** exhibition hall
(01.46.92.11.11/open 7am-11pm daily) was built for
trade shows. It was a landmark in its day, and still
has the largest concrete vault in the world (a 230m
span). Successive governments developed the idea

The main town west of Paris, **Boulogne-Billancourt** *has a rich artistic and industrial history.*

of giving Paris a new, separate district for modern business, and it soon proved popular with big corporations such as Elf, Gan and Fiat.

Today, over 100,000 people work on this reservation, and another 35,000 dwell in the futuristic blocks of flats on the southern edge. None of the skyscrapers display any great architectural distinction, although together they make an impressive sight. Jean Nouvel's plans for La Tour Sans Fin, a never-ending skyscraper destined to merge into the clouds, remain on the drawing board, but a recent wave of development has seen westward growth and includes a new church by Franck Hammoutan.

The **Grande Arche de la Défense**, completed for the bicentenary of the Revolution in 1989, is now a major tourist attraction with a superb view from the top. Outside on the giant forecourt are fountains and sculptures by artists including Miró, Serra, Calder and César's *Thumb*. Even more fun are the kitsch computer-controlled fountains and Takis' flashing light poles. The **Info-Défense** kiosk (01.47.74.84.24/open 9.30am-5.30pm Mon-Fri) in front of CNIT has maps and guides of the area.

La Grande Arche de la Défense

92400 Paris la Défense (01.49.07.27.57). M° La Défense. **Open** 10am-7pm daily (last ride to the rooftop at 6pm). **Admission** 43F; 33F under-18s, students. CM. **Credit** AmEx, MC, V. **Map inset**
Planned to complete the axis of the Champs-Elysées and the Arc de Triomphe – and then skewed at a slight angle – the Grande Arche is simultaneously one of the most pointless and most successful of the *Grands Projets* and catapulted obscure Danish architect Johan Otto von Spreckelsen to fame. Only from close up do you realise how vast the structure is. A stomach-churning ride in high-speed glass lifts soars up through the 'clouds' to the roof where there is a bird's eye view into Paris and out to the city's western reaches.

St-Denis & the North

The suburbs north and east of Paris were the first to be industrialised, from the 1860s onwards, and they remain the grimmest parts of the greater Paris region. In the 1950s, huge estates of tower blocks were built swiftly on cheap industrial land to meet the postwar housing crisis and accommodate newly arrived immigrant labour. Most famous is Sarcelles, long a symbol of urban misery.

Amid the suburban sprawl, at the heart of the old town of **St-Denis**, stands one of the treasures of Gothic architecture: the **Basilique St-Denis**, where most of France's monarchs were buried. St-Denis also boasts the innovative **Musée de l'Art et d'Histoire de St-Denis** in the scrupulously preserved remains of a Carmelite convent founded in 1625, a busy covered market, some fine contemporary buildings, such as Niemeyer's 1989 headquarters for Communist newspaper

Grande Arche de la Défense: what's the point?

L'Humanité and Gaudin's extension to the town hall, and a gleaming new tramway. Across the canal is the elegant **Stade de France**, with flying-saucer-like roof, designed for the 1998 Football World Cup. The *département* of Seine St-Denis also has a lively cultural scene, notably the Théâtre Gérard Philipe at St-Denis and MC93 at Bobigny, and hosts prestigious jazz and classical music festivals, while the Parc de la Corneuve hosts the annual Fête de l'Humanité in September. **Le Bourget**, home to Paris' first airport (still used for VIP and private aircraft) contains the brilliant **Musée de l'Air et de l'Espace**.

North of Sarcelles, **Ecouen**, noted for its Renaissance château, now the **Musée National de la Renaissance**, gives glimpses of a rural past. **Enghien-les-Bains**, set around a large lake where you can hire rowing boats and pedalos, provided a pleasure haven last century with the development of its spa as a cure for ulcers, a casino (still the only one in the Paris region) and a racecourse.

Basilique St-Denis

6 rue de Strasbourg, 93200 St-Denis (01.48.09.83.54). M° St-Denis-Basilique. **Open** *Apr-Sept* 10am-7pm Mon-Sat; noon-7pm Sun. *Oct-Mar* 10am-5pm Mon-Sat; noon-5pm Sun. **Admission** *nave* free. *Royal tombs* 32F; 21F 12-25s, students; free under-12s. **Guided tours** 11.15am, 3pm daily (25F audio guide in English). **No credit cards.**

Legend has it that when St-Denis was beheaded, he picked up his head and, accompanied by a choir of angels, walked to Vicus Catulliacus (now St-Denis), where he wished to be buried. The first church on this site was built over his tomb in around 475. The present edifice is regarded as the first example of true Gothic architecture. The basilica was begun by Abbot Suger in the twelfth century; in the following century master mason Pierre de Montreuil erected the spire and rebuilt the choir, nave and transept, with elaborate rose windows. This was the burial place for all French monarchs (except three) between 996 and the end of the *ancien régime*, so the ambulatory amounts to a veritable museum of French funerary sculpture. The basilica was badly damaged during the Revolution in 1792 when the tombs were desecrated and the royal remains thrown into a communal pit nearby. Part of the fifth-century Merovingian church can be seen in the crypt.

Cimetière des Chiens

4 pont de Clichy, 92600 Asnières (01.40.86.21.11).
M° Mairie de Clichy. **Open** *Apr-Oct* 10am-6pm Mon, Wed-Sun; *Nov-Mar* 10am-5pm, Mon, Wed-Sun.
Admission 17F; 8F 6-12s. **No credit cards.**
Paris has 200,000 dogs and some of them, along with many cats, a horse and a monkey, end up here on a slightly forlorn island in the Seine. A decaying neo-Byzantine entrance points to a grander past: just within lies a grand monument, a small girl draped over a large dog: Barry the St Bernard 'who saved the lives of 40 people. He was killed by the 41st.' Here we are in a poignant otherworld of Trixies, Oscars and much-missed Fidos, redolent of beloved animals and lonely lives. There is even room for 'the errant dog' who, one summer day in 1958, died at the gates of the cemetery and was the 40,000th beast to be buried here.

Eglise Notre Dame du Raincy

av de la Résistance, 93340 Le Raincy
(01.43.81.14.98). SNCF/RER E Raincy-Villemomble.
Open 10am-noon, 2-6pm Mon-Fri; 10am-noon Sat.
Auguste Perret's little-known Modernist masterpiece was built 1922-23 as a low-budget war memorial. Its structure is of brick and concrete, with impressively simple interior traversed by ribbed concrete columns; even the altar is of reinforced concrete. In place of conventional stained glass, the windows by Maurice Denis are coloured glass blocks that create fantastic reflections on the interior.

Stade de France

rue Francis de Pressensé, 93200 St-Denis
(01.55.93.00.00). M° St-Denis Porte de Paris/RER B La Plaine-Stade de France/RER D-Stade de France St-Denis. **Open** 10am-5.30pm daily (except during events). **Admission** 35F; 28F 6-17s, students; free under 6s. *Coulisses du Stade* (10am, 2pm, 4pm) 90F; 65F 6-17s, students; free under-6s (reserve for visits in English). **Credit** MC, V.
The flying-saucer Stade de France landed on the edge of Paris just in time for the 1998 football World Cup. Architects Zubléna, Macary, Regembal and Constantini pipped Jean Nouvel to the post in a con-

troversial competition and the stadium was put up in record time (31 months). It has quickly become a landmark with its spectacular steel and aluminium oval roof suspended from masts, with a great view from the A1 when floodlit by night. The design is such that the Stade can be adapted for various sports and festivities, seating 76,000 for athletics, 80,000 for soccer and rugby and over 100,000 for rock concerts. The 90-minute guided visit takes in the stands and VIP box, changing rooms and entry tunnel – be prepared to climb 200 steps.

Vincennes & the East

The more upmarket residential districts in the east surround the Bois de Vincennes, such as **Vincennes**, dominated by its imposing medieval castle and home to Paris' main zoo. Riverside **Joinville-le-Pont**, once famed for its rowing clubs and for movie studios where Marcel Carné shot *Les Enfants du Paradis*, and neighbour **Champigny-sur-Marne** draw Parisians at weekends along the footpaths along the banks of the Marne and *guinguette* dance halls like **Chez Gégène** or hipper **La Guinguette de l'Ile du Martin-Pêcheur** on its own little island. In Champigny-sur-Marne, the **Musée de la Résistance Nationale** tells the history of the French Résistance. Look out for two architectural curiosities: the surviving Baltard pavilion from Les Halles at **Nogent-sur-Marne**, and Chinagora, a mock pagoda which has recently gone bust but whose green glazed tiles still stand out in Alfortville. Further out, Créteil, a planned new town, was built in the 1960s around a man-made lake.

Château de Vincennes

av de Paris, 94300 Vincennes (01.48.08.31.20).
M° Château de Vincennes. **Open** *Nov-Mar* 10am-5pm daily; *Apr-Oct* 10am-6pm daily.
Admission 32F; 21F 12-25s; 25F, 15F 12-25s (Ste-Chapelle only). **No credit cards.**
An imposing curtain wall punctuated by towers encloses this medieval fortress, still home to a French garrison. Few traces remain of Louis VII's first hunting lodge, or the fortified manor built by Philippe-Auguste. The square keep was begun by Philippe VI and completed by defence-obsessed Charles V, who also added the curtain wall and began rebuilding the pretty Flamboyant-Gothic Ste-Chapelle (open on guided visits). The keep originally housed elaborate royal apartments and is where Henry V of England died in 1422. Louis XIII used the château for a hunting lodge and had the Pavillon du Roi and Pavillon de la Reine built by Louis Le Vau (completed 1658). Both were sumptuously decorated but, along with the rest of the castle, were transformed into barracks in the nineteenth century.

Pavillon Baltard

12 av Victor Hugo, 94130 Nogent-sur-Marne
(01.48.73.45.81). RER Nogent-sur-Marne.
Open during salons/exhibitions only.
In the 1970s when Les Halles was demolished some-

*Sway, swing or boogie at the **guinguette** dance halls along the banks of the Marne river.*

one had the foresight to save one of Baltard's iron and glass market pavilions (No 8: the egg and poultry shed), and resurrect it in 1977 in the Paris suburbs. Since augmented by the grandiose organ built in 1930 for the Gaumont Palace cinema, the pavilion is used for salons, concerts and exhibitions.

Sceaux & the South

Interwar and postwar urbanisation transformed this area as former villages – like Sceaux, Antony and Vanves – and a ring of defensive fortresses – Forts d'Issy, Vanves, Montrouge, Bicêtre and d'Ivry – metamorphosed from a past of vineyards, agriculture and aristocratic residences to areas of workers' housing. Bordering Paris, the 'red' (left wing) suburb of Malakoff is home to numerous artists. Leafy **Sceaux** was formerly the setting for a sumptuous château built in the seventeenth century for Louis XIV's finance minister Colbert. The present building housing the Musée de l'Ile de France (01.46.61.06.71) dates from 1856 but the park with its Grand Canal and waterfalls more or less follows Le Nôtre's original design; the Orangerie by Hardouin-Mansart is used for chamber music in summer. Nearby at **Châtenay-Malabry**, the 1930s Cité de la Butte-Rouge garden-city estate was a model of its time for social housing. Writer Chateaubriand, forced to leave Paris because of his criticism of Napoléon, lived in a pretty villa (**Maison de Chateaubriand**) in the romantically named Vallée-aux-Loups, where the spectacularly landscaped park is

evidence of his passion for gardening.

The south-eastern suburbs boomed during nineteenth-century industrialisation, witness **Ivry-sur-Seine** with its warehouses and the Manufacture des Oeillets, a former rivet factory that is now a theatre and art gallery. The picturesque windmill (place du 8 mai 1845) testifies to an agricultural past – but Ivry is today known for its enlightened social policies, in housing projects like L'Atelier built in the 70s with a multiplicity of levels and roof gardens.

The bleak new town of **Evry,** 30km south of Paris, was created in 1969. It is of note for thenradical housing projects like Les Pyramides and the modern **Cathédrale de la Résurrection**.

Arcueil Aqueduct

Spanning the Bièvre valley through Arcueil and Clamart is the impressive double-decker structure that brings water from Wissous to Paris, along the same route as in Roman times. The first aqueduct, built in the second or third century AD, existed a few metres from this one. In 1609 Henri IV decided to reconstruct the Roman aqueduct, a project continued by his widow Marie de Médicis. By 1628 the aqueduct provided water through 14 fountains on the Left Bank and two on the Right Bank.

Cathédrale de la Résurrection

1 clos de la Cathédrale, 91000 Evry (01.64.97.93.53). SNCF Evry-Couronnes. **Open** 10am-1pm, 2-6pm Mon-Fri; 10am-noon, 2-6pm Sat; 2.30-6.15pm Sun. Completed in 1995, this was the first new cathedral built in France since the war. A new aesthetic of religious architecture is the result of Swiss Mario Botta's rather heavy, truncated, red-brick cylindrical form.

Dalí in Paris

"The phantasmagoric World of Dalí"
The **Espace Montmartre Dalí** presents a collection of original sculptures and graphic works in a single, stunning, permanent exhibition through a spectacular path of sights and sound.

The only one of its kind in France.

Open daily 10am-6.30pm (8.30pm in Summer)
11 rue Poulbot (Montmartre) 18th. M° Anvers/Abbesses
Tel: 01.42.64.40.10 or 01.42.64.44.80
5F discount on presentation of this guide.

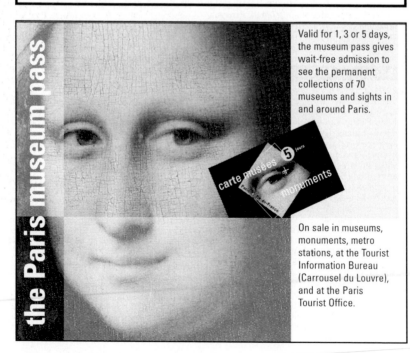

the Paris museum pass

Valid for 1, 3 or 5 days, the museum pass gives wait-free admission to see the permanent collections of 70 museums and sights in and around Paris.

On sale in museums, monuments, metro stations, at the Tourist Information Bureau (Carrousel du Louvre), and at the Paris Tourist Office.

Museums & Galleries

Museums

Medical gore, fashion, perfume, architecture, planes – paintings are not the only things on view in Paris' rich array of museums.

Paris is a museum city par excellence. If you are interested in history of art, the **Musée du Louvre** alone could keep you occupied for weeks, before continuing with subsequent periods at **Musée d'Orsay** and the **Centre Pompidou**. But there are also more intimate collections built up by impassioned amateurs, such as the **Musée Jacquemart-André** and **Musée Cognacq-Jay**, a clutch of museums dealing with the city's artistic and literary greats and less-greats (often in the houses where they lived) and museums for the most demanding specialist, from medical history to collections of fans or locks, and science and transport displays which remind us that France is the birthplace of Ariane as much as of Poussin.

The mammoth Louvre rehang has virtually finished, but the *Grand Louvre* project continues to unfold at the Union des Arts Décoratifs, where the revamped **Musée de la Publicité** finally opened its doors in late 1999, and at the **Orangerie**. The Musée National d'Art Moderne at the Centre Pompidou has reopened, enlarged and rehung, while the **Musée des Arts et Métiers** science and technology collection reopens in spring 2000, and the stupendous Buddhist sculptures from Angkor Wat can again be seen at the **Musée National des Arts Asiatiques – Guimet** in autumn 2000. In the much longer term, Chirac's grand scheme for a Musée des Arts Premiers (the politically correct expression for 'tribal art') has resurfaced, and an architectural contest has been launched for a new museum on the quai Branly, which will house a collection made up in part from the **Musée de l'Homme** and the **Musée des Arts d'Afrique et d'Océanie**.

Note that most museums are closed on Monday or Tuesday. To avoid queues, try to visit major museums and exhibitions on weekdays, especially at lunch time or evening; reduced rates on Sunday often generate big crowds. Guided visits in English tend to be available only in major museums (*see chapter* **Directory** for tours in English that sometimes include museums). Reduced admission charges apply often to pensioners or students, but make sure you have an identity card or a passport proving your status. Most ticket counters close 30-45 minutes before closing time. Prebooking is now often possible – and sometimes essential – for major shows at the **Grand Palais**. It's also possible to prebook for the Louvre. National museums are free on the first Sunday of the month.

Paris Carte Musées et Monuments (CM)

Price one day 80F, three days 160F, five days 240F. This card gives free entry into 70 museums and monuments all around Paris (indicated below by CM), and allows you to jump queues. It's very good value if you're in Paris for a few days and plan on intensive museum visiting, although you have to pay extra for special exhibitions. It can be bought at museums, monuments, tourist offices, branches of Fnac and principal Métro and RER stations.

Fine Art

Centre Pompidou (Musée National d'Art Moderne)

rue St-Martin, 4th (01.44.78.12.33). M° Hôtel-de-Ville or Rambuteau/RER Châtelet-Les Halles. **Open** 11am-9pm Mon, Wed-Sun. Closed Tue, 1 May. **Admission** 30F; 20F 18-26s; free under-18s. *exhibitions* (includes museum) 40F-50F; 30F-40F 18-26s. **Credit** MC, V. **Map K6**

The Musée National d'Art Moderne reopened after major renovation of the Centre Pompidou, with enlarged galleries that now incorporate architecture and design, as well as the unparalleled collection of fine art. The route now starts on level four with the contemporary (post 1960 to today) period. It opens with Tinguely's *Requiem sur une feuille morte*, a work that symbolises the ambiguity and uncertainty in much modern art, going on via Saint-Phalle and Beuys sculpture, Richter paintings, installations by Kienholz, Dubuffet, *Arte Povera*, Boltanski and Calle, before, in a new emphasis on young generation, works from the past decade by Guilleminot, Ruff, Closky and Gordon. Level five deals with the historic period 1905-60, opening with the Douanier Rousseau's premonitory *Le Rêve*, a historic route with Matisse, Kandinsky, lots of Picassos, an extensive section on Dada and Surrealism, including a reconstruction of André Breton's studio and the newly acquired *Le Dresseur d'Animaux* by Picabia, up to Klein, Hantaï, and Pollock and the American Abstract Expressionists in the 50s. In a pluri-disciplinary approach, temporary exhibitions are often linked to performances, concerts and debates. Major shows in 2000 of Brassaï (Apr-June), Picasso's sculpture (June-Sept), 'Les bons génies de la vie domestique', about household appliances (autumn), and 'Sons et Lumières' (Nov-Dec) about art as spectacle, are complemented by smaller shows by young

Take the pyramid route to the buried treasures at the **Musée du Louvre.**

artists, such as Mariko Mori and Pierre Huyghe. Artists featured in 2001 include Hains, Giacommetti, Dubuffet and Nan Goldin. *See also chapters* **Right Bank, Architecture** *and* **Children**. *Shop. Children's workshops. Wheelchair access.*

Musée d'Art Moderne de la Ville de Paris/ARC

11 av du Président-Wilson, 16th (01.53.67.40.00). Mº Iéna or Alma-Marceau. **Open** 10am-6pm Tue-Fri; 10am-7pm Sat, Sun. Closed Mon, some public holidays. **Admission** (includes exhibition) 27F-50F. **Credit** (shop) AmEx, DC, MC, V. **Map D5**

This monumental museum was built as the Electricity Pavilion for the 1937 *Exposition Universelle*, and Dufy's vast mural *La Fée Electricité* can still be seen in a curved room. Today the building holds the municipal collection of modern art, which is strong on the Cubists, Fauves, the Delaunays, Rouault, Soutine, Modigliani and the Ecole de Paris, with some recently discovered panels from an early version of Matisse's *La Danse*, alongside his later reworking (1932-33). Contemporary artists Boltanski, Lavier, Sarkis, Hantai and Buren are also represented. The museum is particularly reputed for its dynamic exhibitions, with major names of modern art (Fauvism and *Die Brücke* to Rothko), plus adventurous, often experimental, contemporary shows put on by ARC (Animation, Recherche, Confrontation), ranging from established names to first museum shows of young artists. *Bookshop. Café. Concerts. Wheelchair access.*

Musée Cognacq-Jay

Hôtel Donon, 8 rue Elzévir, 3rd (01.40.27.07.21). Mº St-Paul. **Open** 10am-5.40pm Tue-Sun. Closed Mon, some public holidays. **Admission** 15F free under-26s, over-60s, CM; *during exhibition* 22F; 9F under-26s, over-60s. **No credit cards. Map L6**

This intimate museum in a carefully restored *hôtel particulier* houses the collection put together in the early 1900s by Ernest Cognacq, founder of La Samaritaine, and his wife Louise Jay. Their tastes stuck mainly to the French eighteenth century, focusing on French Rococo artists such as Watteau, Fragonard, Boucher, Greuze and pastellist Quentin de la Tour, although some English (Reynolds, Lawrence, Romney), Dutch and Flemish (Rembrandt, Ruysdael, Rubens), and a sprinkling of Canalettos and Guardis have slipped in for good measure. Pictures are displayed in period panelled rooms (some original to the *hôtel*, some rescued from other locations), alongside furniture, ceramics, tapestries and sculpture of the same period to give a good impression of the original private house context. *Bookshop. Children's workshops.*

Musée Départemental Maurice Denis, 'Le Prieuré'

2bis rue Maurice Denis, 78100 St-Germain-en-Laye (01.39.73.77.87). RER A St-Germain-en-Laye. **Open** 10am-5.30pm Wed-Fri; 10am-6.30pm Sat, Sun. Closed 1 Jan, 1 May, 25 Dec. **Admission** 25F; 15F 12-25s, students, over-60s; free under-12s, CM (35F and 25F during exhibitions). **No credit cards.**

Out in the elegant commuterland of St-Germain-en-Laye, this former royal hospital became home and

studio to Nabi painter Maurice Denis in 1915. The remarkable collection, housed in ancient wards and attics, comprises paintings, prints and decorative objects by the Nabis, who sought a renewed spirituality in painting (a group that also included Sérusier, Bonnard, Vuillard, Roussel and Valloton). There are also paintings by their forerunners Gauguin and the Pont-Aven school, and by Toulouse-Lautrec. Denis also painted the frescoes and designed the stained glass in the small chapel. *Bookshop.*

Musée Jacquemart-André

158 bd Haussmann, 8th (01.42.89.04.91). Mº Miromesnil or St-Philippe-du-Roule. **Open** 10am-6pm daily. **Admission** 49F; 37F 7-17s, students; free under-7s. **Credit** AmEx, MC, V. **Map E3**

The magnificent collection gathered by Edouard André and his wife Nélie Jacquemart is as worth visiting for its illustration of the life of the nineteenth-century haute bourgeoisie, as for the paintings and other treasures they unearthed in salerooms or on tours through Europe. André had the magnificent Hôtel André constructed in the 1870s in the newly desirable neighbourhood outlined by Baron Haussmann. On the ground floor are the circular Grand Salon, rooms of tapestries and French furniture, Boucher mythological fantasies, and the library with Dutch paintings including Rembrandt's *The Pilgrims of Emmaus*, smoking room with Moorish stools and English portraits and the magnificent polychrome marble winter garden with double spiral staircase. Up on the stairway three newly restored Tiepolo frescoes depict the arrival of Henri III in Venice. Upstairs, what was to have been Nélie's studio (she gave up her brushes on marriage) became their 'Italian museum': a small, exceptional Early Renaissance collection that includes Uccello's exquisite *St George and the Dragon*, Virgins by Perugino, Botticelli and Bellini, Mantegna's *Ecce Homo*, a superb Schiavone portrait, a Carpaccio panel and Della Robbia terracottas. The audioguide (available in English) is extremely informative. *Audio guide. Bookshop. Café (11.30am-5.30pm). Partial wheelchair access.*

Musée Marmottan – Claude Monet

2 rue Louis-Boilly, 16th (01.42.24.07.02). Mº La Muette. **Open** 10am-5.30pm Tue-Sun. Closed Mon, 1 May, 25 Dec. **Admission** 40F; 25F 8-25s, over-60s; free under-8s. **Credit** MC, V.

This museum achieved fame with Michel Monet's bequest of 165 works by his father, including a breathtaking series of late water-lily canvases, displayed in a special basement room. Sit and absorb the intensity of viridian green and electric blue: these exercises in pure colour show Monet at his most daring and closest to abstraction. The collection also contains Monet's *Impression Soleil Levant*, which gave the Impressionist movement its name, and Impressionist canvases by Sisley, Renoir, Pissarro, Caillebotte and Berthe Morisot as well as some by the nineteenth-century Realists. The rest of the collection should not be ignored. There's a room containing the Wildenstein collection of medieval

From one train station to another: Monet's Gare St-Lazare *at the* **Musée d'Orsay**.

illuminated manuscripts, the recently restored ground- and first-floor salons house smaller Monets, early nineteenth-century gouaches, a curious clock and other fine First Empire furnishings in keeping with the house, much of it adorned with pharaohs' busts, eagles and sphinxes, under the influence of Napoléon's Egyptian campaigns.
Shop. Partial wheelchair access.

Musée de l'Orangerie
Jardin des Tuileries, 1st (01.42.97.48.16). M° Concorde.
Open from late 2001, ring for details. **Admission** ring for details. **Credit** ring for details. **Map F5**
Monet's eight, extraordinarily fresh, huge, late Nymphéas (water lilies) (*see also above* **Musée Marmottan**), conceived especially for two oval rooms in the Orangerie, were left by the artist to the nation as a 'spiritual testimony' and first presented to the public in 1927. The museum is closed until the end of 2001 for a major overhaul. On reopening the Jean Walter and Paul Guillaume collection of Impressionism and the Ecole de Paris (Soutine, Renoir, Cézanne, Sisley, Picasso, Derain, Matisse, Rousseau, Modigliani) will go on show again, complemented by furniture and decorative objects.

Musée National d'Orsay
1 rue de la Légion d'Honneur, 7th (01.40.49.48.14/ recorded information 01.45.49.11.11). M° Solférino/ RER Musée d'Orsay. **Open** 10am-6pm Tue, Wed, Fri, Sat; 10am-10pm Thur; 9am-6pm Sun. Closed Mon, some public holidays. **Admission** 40F; 30F 18-25s, all on Sun; free under-18s; CM. **Credit** (shop) AmEx, MC, V. **Map G6**
Opened in 1986, the Musée d'Orsay fills a Beaux-Arts train station built for the 1900 *Exposition Univer-*

selle, saved from demolition to become Paris' museum devoted to the pivotal years 1848-1914. Architect Gae Aulenti remodelled the interior, inserting postmodern partitions and lift shafts, keeping the iron-framed coffered roof and creating galleries off either side of a light-filled central canyon. Fifteen years on, the drawbacks of her conversion are apparent and some of the materials are looking a little shoddy, but the museum still draws long queues. Much of the problem is that the famous Impressionists and Post-Impressionists are knee-deep in tourists upstairs, while too much space and prestige are given downstairs to *art pompier* – the languid nudes of Couture or the grandiose history paintings of Meissonier. The museum follows a chronological route, starting on the ground floor, running up to the upper level and finishing on the mezzanine, thus showing both continuities between the Impressionists and their forerunners, the Realists and Barbizon School, and making apparent their revolutionary use of light and colour.

The right Lille side of the central aisle is dedicated to the Romantics and history painters. Cool portraits by Ingres contrast with the Romantic passion of Delacroix's North African period, and his pupil Chassériau. Further on are examples of early Degas, and melancholy mystical works by the Symbolists Moreau and Puvis de Chavannes.

The first rooms to the Seine side of the central aisle are given over to the Barbizon landscape painters Corot and Daubigny, and Millet's idealised depictions of rural virtue, including *L'Angélus*. Don't miss the set of clay busts by Daumier caricaturing notables of his time. One room is dedicated to Courbet, with *The Artist and his Studio* and his monumental *Burial at Ornans*, which seem to form a bridge with

Learning to love the Louvre

Although the Louvre first opened to the public in 1793, before the Richelieu wing was even built, President Mitterrand's *Grand Louvre* project doubled the exhibition space and transformed this venerable institution into one of the world's most modern museums. The metamorphosis continues with new rooms recently opened in the Objets d'Art and Prints and Drawings departments. The collections are based around the original royal collections, augmented by revolutionary seizures and later acquisitions. It's important to be selective, as the museum is truly huge. It is organised into wings – Richelieu (along rue de Rivoli), Sully (round the Cour Carrée), Denon (along the Seine) – which lead off on three sides from beneath the glass pyramid. Each department is colour coded and labelled, and illustrated signs point to key works, such as the *Mona Lisa* or *Winged Victory of Samothrace*, for those planning a lightning tour. It's almost impossible not to get lost at some point, so be sure to pick up the useful free orientation leaflet at the entrance. Exhibition Apr-Jul 2000: 'l'Empire du temps, mythes et créations'.

French Painting
Richelieu, Sully: second floor; Denon: first floor.
A quick survey of French painting begins in the Richelieu and Sully wings, starting with late medieval and Renaissance work, including the striking *Diana the Huntress* by an unknown artist, thought to be an idealised portrait of Diane de Poitiers. There are landscapes by Claude Lorrain, and Poussin's *The Four Seasons*. Le Nain's peasant scenes and Georges de la Tour's *Les Tricheurs* (card cheats) and *Angel Appearing to St-Joseph* give way to the Rococo frivolity of Watteau, Fragonard and Boucher, and the more sentimental style of Greuze. Smaller nineteenth-century works including Ingres' erotic *The Turkish Bath* are also in the Sully wing, while large-format paintings are in the Denon wing. Neo-Classicists – David's *Sabine Women*, his portraits *Mme Récamier* and *Juliette de Villeneuve*, Ingres' *Grande Odalisque* and Gros' rendition of Napoléon on campaign – are pitted against Romantics – including Géricault's *Raft of the Medusa* and Delacroix's *Liberty Leading the People* – in the battle of the styles.

French Sculpture
Richelieu: ground floor.
The most dramatic feature of the Richelieu wing are its two magnificent sculpture courts covered by a high-tech glazing system. The Cour Marly gives pride of place to Guillaume Coustou's *Chevaux de Marly* of 1745, two giant naturalistic horses being restrained by grooms in a freeze-frame of rearing struggle. In the Cour Puget, admire the four bronze captives that originally adorned a statue in place

des Victoires and Clodion's Rococo frieze. Side rooms are devoted to medieval tomb sculpture, including the remarkable fifteenth-century tomb of Burgundian aristocrat Philippe Pot supported by ominous black-cowled figures, the original Renaissance reliefs by Jean Goujon for the Fontaine des Innocents in Les Halles, as well as pompous Neo-Classical mythological subjects and heroic portraits.

Objets d'Art
Richelieu: first floor; Sully: first floor.
Highlight is the medieval Treasure of St-Denis. There are also Renaissance enamels, furniture and early clocks, and later decorative art. Napoléon III's opulent apartments have been preserved with chandeliers and upholstery intact. Seven new rooms opened in December 1999, with *objets d'art* mainly from the Restoration and July monarchy.

Italian Painting
Denon: first floor.
Two new rooms of Renaissance frescoes by Botticelli, Fra Angelico and Luini open the fantastic Italian collections, leading the way to Florentine Early Renaissance paintings by, among many, Cimabue, Fra Angelico, Filippo Lippi, and Uccello. The Grande Galerie includes Leonardo's *Virgin on the Rocks* and *The Virgin, The Child and St-Anne*, two delectable tiny Raphaels, Mantegna, Perugino and Ghirlandaio, and in a side room of Siennese art, Piero della Francesca. In the Salle des Etats, the *Mona Lisa* in a bulletproof case tends to monopolise attention but in 2001-02 will be given its own small room, leaving space to appreciate Venetian masterpieces, such as Titian's *Man with a Glove* and early *Fête Champêtre*, Tintoretto portraits and Veronese's magisterial *The Marriage at Cana*.

Northern Painting
Richelieu: second floor.
The Dutch, Flemish and German schools have been given new breathing space, although many major works are still tucked away in small rooms or cabinets: Bosch's *Ship of Fools*, a Dürer self-portrait, Holbein's *Anne of Cleves*, Rembrandt self-portraits and Vermeer's *Lacemaker* and *The Astronomer*. Rubens' 24 typically bravura canvases commissioned by Marie de Médicis for the Palais du Luxembourg to celebrate her own virtues are displayed in the Galerie Médicis. During the course of 2000, three new rooms will open, housing the eighteenth- and nineteenth-century collections.

Spanish & English Painting
Denon: first floor.
There is a small collection of English painting (Fusseli, Turner, Lawrence). The Spanish collection (Velasquez, Ribera, Goya) has been moved to six new Spanish galleries, including a Goya room.

The Myth of Endymion *by Trioson.*

Non-French European Sculpture

Denon: ground floor.
Michelangelo's *Dying Slave* and *Rebel Slave*, created for the tomb of Pope Julius II in 1513-15, are the best-known works of post-Classical sculpture, but there are also pieces by Donatello, Cellini, Giambologna, Della Robbia, Neo-Classical, Spanish and northern European works.

Greek, Etruscan & Roman Antiquities

Denon: ground floor; Sully: ground and first floors.
Greek treasures include the *Venus de Milo*, a masterpiece of second-century BC classical sculpture, the magnificent *Winged Victory of Samothrace* on her ship's prow at the top of the grand staircase and over 2000 painted vases. Massive halls of Roman sculpture and sarcophagi are drawn largely from the Borghèse (*Borghèse Vase* and *Borghèse Gladiator*) and Richelieu collections. The charming Etruscan terracotta sarcophagus of a *Married Couple* depicts a couple reclining at a banquet. There are mosaics from Carthage, Pompeii and Antioch.

Egyptian Antiquities

Sully: ground and first floors; Richelieu: ground floor.
The huge Egyptian department had its beginnings in Champollion's voyages in Egypt. He first decyphered the hieroglyphics and created the Egyptian department in 1827. Arranged thematically on the ground floor, chronologically on the first floor, exhibits include the bust of Amenophis IV (all that remains of a colossal statue), the pink granite Giant Sphinx, sarcophagi, statues and a whole room of mummified cats, birds and even fish. The Coptic section, including the church from Baouit, and Roman Egypt section, are in Denon, due to be joined in early 2000 by works from Syria, Palestine, Nubia and Sudan.

Islamic and Oriental Art

Islamic: Richelieu basement. Oriental: Richelieu and Sully ground floors.
The Islamic collections include early glass, Iznik ceramics, Iranian blue and white ware, intricately inlaid metalwork, carpets and funerary stele and pierced screens. Collections of Anatolian, Iranian and Mesopotamian art are displayed in the Richelieu wing around a magnificent reconstruction of the courtyard of Khorsabad, with breathtaking Assyrian winged bulls.

Musée National du Louvre

entrance through Pyramid (Cour Napoléon) or Porte des Lions (from quai des Tuileries or Carrousel gardens), 1st (01.40.20.53.17/recorded information 01.40.20.51.51/advance booking 08.03.80.88.03).
M° Palais-Royal. **Open** 9am-9.45pm Mon,Wed; 9am-6pm Thur-Sun. *Temporary exhibitions, Medieval Louvre, bookshop* 9am-9.45pm Mon, Wed; 9am-6pm Thur-Sun. Closed Tue, some public holidays.
Admission 45F (until 3pm); 26F (after 3pm & Sun); free under-18s, CM, first Sun of the month.
Temporary exhibitions 30F; combined museum exhibition 60F, 40F. **Credit** MC, V. **Map G5**

the Impressionists. His sexually explicit *L'Origine du Monde* still has tremendous power to shock today. This floor also covers pre-1870 works by the Impressionists (Monet, Pissarro, Van Gogh, Manet) and precursor Boudin, several of whom are shown in Fantin-Latour's *Un atelier aux Batignolles*.

Standing out in the scupture aisle is the work of Carpeaux, whose faces have an almost rococo sensibility, including his controversial *La Danse* for the facade of the Palais Garnier, which shocked nineteenth-century moralists with its naked dancers. A model of the opera reveals just how much of the building is taken up by reception rooms and the lavish stairway and how little by the auditorium.

Escalators whisk you upstairs, where you can see masterpieces by Pissarro, Renoir and Caillebotte, Manet's controversial *Déjeuner sur l'Herbe* and wonderful portrait *Berthe Morisot*, several of Monet's paintings of Rouen cathedral, in which he explored the changing qualities of light at different times, and depictions of his garden at Giverny, and paintings, pastels and sculptures by Degas, whose Japanese-influenced backstage ballet scenes broke all previous rules of composition. The riches continue with the Post-Impressionists. Among the boiling colours and frantic brushstrokes of Van Gogh are his *Church at Auvers* and his last painting, *Crows*. There are Cézanne still lifes, Gauguin's Breton and Tahitian periods, including his *Self-Portrait with Yellow Christ*, Toulouse-Lautrec's depictions of Montmartre lowlife and the Moulin Rouge, the Pointillists Seurat and Signac, the mystical works of Redon and the primitivist jungle of the Douanier Rousseau.

On the mezzanine are the Nabis painters – Vallotton, Denis, Roussel, Bonnard and Vuillard – treating religious and domestic scenes in a wonderfully flat, decorative style. Several rooms are given over to the decorative arts with a mouth-watering collection of Art Nouveau and Jugendstil furniture and fine paintings by Munch and Klimt, as well as rooms devoted to architectural drawings and photography. The sculpture terraces include powerful busts and studies by Rodin, heads by Rosso and bronzes by Bourdelle and Maillol.

Temporary exhibitions in 2000 widen the perspective: 'La Dame aux éventails – Nina de Villard, modèle de Manet' (Apr-July); Polish painter Malczewski (until May). Finally, visit the ornate salon of the former station hotel and the museum's Café des Hauteurs. *See also chapter* **Left Bank**. *Audioguide. Bookshop. Café-restaurant. Cinema. Concerts. Guided tours. Library (by appointment). Wheelchair access.*

Musée du Petit Palais

av Winston-Churchill, 8th (01.42.65.12.73). M° Champs-Elysées-Clemenceau. **Open** 10am-5.40pm Tue-Sun. Closed Mon, some public holidays. **Admission** 27F; 14.50F 18-25s, students; free under-18s, over-60s, CM. *Temporary exhibitions* 45F; 35F 7-25s, students, over-60s; free under-7s. **Credit** (shop) MC, V. **Map E5**

Standing across the road from the Grand Palais (*see below* **Exhibition Centres**), and likewise constructed for the 1900 Grand Exposition, the Petit

Palais contains a hotchpotch of collections belonging to the city, including Greek painted vases and Antique sculpture, Chinese porcelain, Beauvais tapestries, French furniture, paintings by Delacroix, Millet, Géricault, Daumier, Courbet, Redon, works by Vuillard and Bonnard, a selection of Impressionists, plus maquettes for public sculpture around Paris. Most visitors come for stylishly presented temporary exhibitions – from April 2000, 'L'Eternel Mexique' charts the country's artistic heritage from the pre-Columbian era to the present. The museum will close for renovations in 2001 for 18 months. *Bookshop. Guided tours. Library. Wheelchair access.*

One-Man Shows

Atelier Brancusi

piazza Beaubourg, 4th (01.44.78.12.33). M° Hôtel-de-Ville or Rambuteau/RER Châtelet-Les Halles. **Open** noon-10pm Mon, Wed-Fri; 10am-10pm Sat, Sun. Closed Tue. **Admission** (included with Centre Pompidou – Musée National d'Art Moderne) 30F; 20F 18-26s; free under-18s. **No credit cards. Map K6**

When Constantin Brancusi died in 1956 he left his studio in the 15th *arrondissement* and all its contents, including sculptures, maquettes, tools, photos, his bed and his wardrobe, to the French state. Rebuilt first within the Palais de Tokyo and then in 1977 outside the Centre Pompidou, the studio has since been completely reconstructed as a faithful reproduction of the artist's living and working spaces. His fragile works in wood and plaster, including his celebrated endless columns and streamlined bird forms, show how Brancusi revolutionised sculpture early this century.

Atelier-Musée Henri Bouchard

25 rue de l'Yvette, 16th (01.46.47.63.46). M° Jasmin. **Open** 2-7pm Wed, Sat. Closed last two weeks of Mar, June, Sept and Dec. **Admission** 25F; 15F students under-26; free under-6s. **No credit cards.**

Prolific sculptor Henri Bouchard moved here from Montparnasse in 1924 and bought the house with vacant plot next door to construct his studio. Today, lovingly tended by the artist's son and daughter-in-law, his dusty studio, crammed top to toe with sculptures, casts and moulds, sketchbooks, tools and the naily wooden board against which he sculpted large works, gives an idea of the official art of the time. Aaround 1907-09 Bouchard moved from realism, in studies of children and peasants, to a more stylised, pared-down, linear modern style, as seen in his reliefs for the Eglise St-Jean de Chaillot and the monumental *Apollo* for the Palais de Chaillot.

Espace Dalí Montmartre

11 rue Poulbot, 18th (01.42.64.40.10). M° Anvers or Abbesses. **Open** 10am-6.30pm daily. **Admission** 40F; 35F over-60s; 25F 8-25s, students; free under-8s. **Credit** (shop) AmEx, DC, MC, V. **Map H1**

The black-walled interior, artistically programmed lighting and specially composed soundtrack make it clear that this is a high-marketing presentation of the artist's work. Don't come expecting to see Dalí's celebrated Surrealist paintings: the museum con-

Colourful clutter at **Musée Gustave Moreau.**

centrates on two less-known facets of his output: sculptures (mainly bronzes) often taking elements in the paintings, from the 70s, at the tacky end of his career; and his book illustrations (La Fontaine's fables, Freud, de Sade, Dante, *Alice in Wonderland*) – lithographs and engravings where he fully exploited his taste for the fantastic and the sexual.
Shop.

Fondation Dubuffet
137 rue de Sèvres, 6th (01.47.34.12.63). Mº Duroc.
Open 2-6pm Mon-Fri. Closed Aug, public holidays.
Admission 25F. **No credit cards. Map E8**
Changing display of drawings and sculptures by the French artist (1901-85), plus maquettes of the monumental architectural sculptures from his *L'Hourloupe* cycle.
Archives (by appointment). Bookshop.

Musée Bourdelle
16-18 rue Antoine-Bourdelle, 15th (01.49.54.73.73). Mº Montparnasse-Bienvenüe or Falguière.
Open 10am-5.40pm Tue-Sun. Closed Mon, public holidays. **Admission** 17F; 9F students, over-60s (30F and 20F during exhibitions); free under-7s, CM. **No credit cards. Map F8**
An interesting museum devoted to Rodin's pupil, sculptor Antoine Bourdelle, who produced monumental works, like the Modernist relief friezes at the Théâtre des Champs-Elysées. Housed around a small garden in a mix of buildings, the museum includes the artist's studio and apartments, a 1950s

extension revealing the evolution of Bourdelle's monument to General Alvear in Buenos Aires, and bronzes and maquettes in a new wing by Christian de Portzamparc. Other artists also had studios here, including, briefly, Chagall.
Bookshop. Children's workshops. Reference library (by appointment). Wheelchair access.

Musée Delacroix
6 pl Furstenberg, 6th (01.44.41.86.50). Mº St-Germain-des-Prés. **Open** 9.30am-5pm Mon, Wed-Sun. Closed Tue, some public holidays.
Admission 23F; 18F 18-25s, over-60s; free under-18s, CM. **No credit cards. Map H6**
Eugène Delacroix moved to the pretty place Furstenberg in 1857 to be nearer to the Eglise St-Sulpice where he was painting murals, and lived here until his death in 1863. The Louvre and the Musée d'Orsay house his major paintings, but the collection displayed in his apartment and the studio he had built in the garden includes small oil paintings (among them a self-portrait as Hamlet and a portrait of his housekeeper), some free pastel studies of skies and sketches for larger works, and still maintains some of the atmosphere of the studio as it must have been. Other displays relate to his friendships with Baudelaire and George Sand. Recent extension has added a documentation room.
Bookshop.

Musée-Jardin Paul Landowski
14 rue Max Blondat, 92100 Boulogne-Billancourt (01.46.05.82.69). Mº Boulogne-Jean Jaurès. **Open** 10am-noon, 2-5pm, Wed, Sat, Sun. **Admission** 15F; 10F 18-25s, over-60s. **No credit cards.**
Landowski (1875-1961) won the Prix de Rome in 1900, and was thereafter kept busy with state commissions throughout his career. Most of his work was on a monumental scale, treating both classical and modern themes, and embued with some of the expressionism he admired in Rodin's work. His most ambitious work was *Temple*: four sculpted walls depicting 'the history of humanity'.

Musée Maillol
59-61 rue de Grenelle, 7th (01.42.22.59.58). Mº Rue du Bac. **Open** 11am-6pm Mon, Wed-Sun. Closed Tue. **Admission** 40F; 30F students, over-60s; under-18s. **Credit** (shop) AmEx, MC, V. **Map G7**
Dina Vierny met sculptor Aristide Maillol (1861-1944) at the age of 15, and for the next ten years was his principal model, idealised in such sculptures as *Spring, Air* and *Harmony*. In 1995 she opened this museum in a carefully restored eighteenth-century *hôtel*, displaying his drawings, pastels, a decorative faïence fountain and wooden cradle, engravings, tapestry panels and his early Nabis-related paintings (a delectable *Jeune Fille au chapeau noir*), as well as numerous sculptures and studies. There are also works by his contemporaries (Vierny also sat for Matisse, Dufy and Bonnard), including Picasso, Rodin, Gauguin, Degas and Cézanne; some rare Surrealist documents and multiples by Marcel Duchamp and Villon; naive painters like Camille Bombois and André Bouchart; and works by the

Russian artists Vierny has championed from Kandinsky and Poliakoff to Ilya Kabakov, whose installation *The Communal Kitchen* recreates the atmosphere and sounds of a shared Soviet kitchen. Interesting temporary exhibitions have included Valloton, the School of London and Boulatov. *Bookshop. Café. Wheelchair access.*

Musée Gustave Moreau

14 rue de la Rochefoucauld, 9th (01.48.74.38.50). M° Trinité. **Open** 11am-5.15pm Mon, Wed; 10am-12.45pm, 2-5.15pm Thur-Sun. Closed Tue, some public holidays. **Admission** 22F; 15F 18-25s, Sun; free under-18s, CM. **Credit** MC, V. **Map G3**

Most eccentric of all the one-man museums, this is not only where Symbolist painter Gustave Moreau (1825-98) lived, worked and taught, but was also designated by the artist to become a museum after his death – the first curator was his former pupil Rouault. The enormous double-height studio, with a further storey above reached by an impressive spiral staircase, is crammed wall to wall with Moreau's paintings and there are thousands more of his drawings and watercolours to pull out from shutters on the walls. Moreau developed a personal mythology, filling his detailed canvases with images of *St John the Baptist, St George* and lascivious *Salomé,* griffins and unicorns, using jewel-like colours that, like those of the Pre-Raphaelites, owed much to the rediscovery of the early Italian masters. Don't miss the small private apartment where he lived with his parents. *Bookshop. Library (by appointment).*

Musée National Hébert

85 rue du Cherche-Midi, 6th (01.42.22.23.82). M° St-Placide or Vaneau. **Open** 12.30-5.30pm Mon, Wed-Fri; 2-5.30pm Sat, Sun and public holidays. Closed Tue, 1 Jan, 1 May, 25 Dec. **Admission** 16F; 12F 18-25s; free under-18s, CM. **No credit cards. Map F7**

Now largely forgotten, Ernest Hébert (1817-1908) was a painter of Italian landscapes and figurative subjects, who bent to the fashion of the time with pious portraits and depictions of sentimental shepherdesses during the mid-century, and brightly coloured, Symbolist-influenced muses, Ophelias and Impressionist-tinged ladies towards the end of his career. The endless watercolours and oils are mostly unremarkable, if an interesting testament to nineteenth-century taste – though the run-down house, built in 1743, is strangely appealing.

Musée National Jean-Jacques Henner

43 av de Villiers, 17th (01.47.63.42.73). M° Monceau or Malesherbes. **Open** 10am-noon, 2-5pm, Tue-Sun. Closed Mon, some public holidays. **Admission** 21F; 17F students under 25; free under-18s, CM. **No credit cards. Map E2**

Henner's nephew bought artist Dubufe's studio in 1920 to house his uncle's work. Very popular in his own day (critic Véron called him 'a nineteenth-century Leonardo'), Henner (1829-1905) today seems less interesting than his Post-Impressionist contemporaries. His sketches, drawings and letters give an insight into his creative process and appeal more than his society portraits, nymphs and naïads.

Musée National Picasso

Hôtel Salé, 5 rue de Thorigny, 3rd (01.42.71.25.21). M° Chemin-Vert or St-Paul. **Open** 9.30am-5.30pm (9.30am-6pm Apr-Oct) Mon, Wed-Sun. Closed Tue, 25 Dec, 1 Jan. **Admission** 30F; 20F 18-25s, all on Sun (38F and 28F during exhibitions); free under-18s, CM. **Credit** (shop) MC, V. **Map L6**

An unparalleled collection of paintings and sculpture by Pablo Picasso (1881-1973), its nucleus acquired by the state in lieu of inheritance tax, is housed in one of the grandest mansions in the Marais. The collection represents all phases of the master's long and varied career, showing Picasso's continual inventiveness and, rare in great art, his sense of humour. Masterpieces include a gaunt, blue-period self-portrait, son *Paolo as Harlequin,* his Cubist and classical phases, the surreal *Nude in an Armchair,* lively beach pictures of the 1920s and 30s, portraits of his favourite models Marie-Thérèse and Dora Maar plus the unabashedly ribald pictures he produced in his later years. The unusual wallpaper collage, *Women at their Toilette,* originally intended as a cartoon for a tapestry, gets its own small room. The drawings for the pivotal *Demoiselles d'Avignon* are here, as well as prints and ceramics that demonstrate his versatility. But it is perhaps the sculpture which stands out above all, from the vast plaster head on the staircase to a girl skipping and a small cat. Look closely at the sculpture of an ape – you'll see that its face is made out of a toy car. Also here is Picasso's collection of tribal art – juxtaposed with 'primitive' wood figures he carved himself – and paintings by Matisse and Douanier Rousseau he had acquired. *Audiovisual room. Bookshop. Outdoor café Apr-Oct. Wheelchair access.*

Musée Rodin

Hôtel Biron, 77 rue de Varenne, 7th (01.44.18.61.10). M° Varenne. **Open** Apr-Sept 9.30am-5.45pm Tue-Sun; Oct-Mar 9.30am-4.45pm Tue-Sun. Closed Mon, public holidays. **Admission** 28F; 18F 18-25s, all on Sun; free under-18s, art students, CM. *Gardens only* 5F. **Credit** MC, V. **Map F6**

The Rodin museum occupies the *hôtel particulier* where Rodin lived and sculpted at the end of his life. The famous *Kiss,* moving *Cathedral,* studies for *Balzac* and other pieces of note are indoors, accompanied by several works by Rodin's mistress and pupil Camille Claudel, and paintings by Van Gogh, Monet, Renoir, Carrière and Rodin himself. In the recently replanted gardens are the moving *Burghers of Calais,* the elaborate *Gates of Hell,* the final proud portrait of *Balzac,* the eternally absorbed – and absorbing – *Thinker, Orpheus* under a shady stretch of trees, several unfinished nymphs seemingly emerging from the marble and 40 restored marbles behind glass including *Victor Hugo.* Fans can also visit the Villa des Brillants at Meudon (01.41.14.35.00; May-Oct, 1-6pm Fri-Sun), where he worked from 1895. *Bookshop. Garden café. Partial wheelchair access. Visits for visually handicapped (by appointment).*

Musée Picasso: *a sculptural setting for the artist's paintings and sculpture.*

Musée Zadkine

100bis rue d'Assas, 6th (01.43.26.91.90).
M° Notre-Dame-des-Champs/RER Port Royal. **Open**
10am-5.30pm Tue-Sun. Closed Mon, public holidays.
Temporary closure Mar-Oct 2000. **Admission**
17.50F; 9F students (30F and 20F during exhibitions);
free under-18s, CM. **No credit cards.** **Map G8**
Arresting works by the Russian-born Cubist sculptor Ossip Zadkine are displayed around the garden
and over the tiny house he inhabited from 1928 until
his death in 1967. Zadkine's compositions include
musical, mythological and religious subjects and his
style varies with his materials: bronzes tend to be
geometrical, wood more sensuous, flowing with the
grain. Sculptures are cleverly displayed on ledges at
eye-level, along with drawings by Zadkine and some
paintings by his wife Valentine Prax. The studio is
used for temporary exhibitions of contemporary art.
*Library (by appointment). Certain works accessible
for the visually handicapped (by appointment).*

Photography

Caisse des Dépôts et Consignations

13 quai Voltaire, 7th (01.40.49.41.66). M° Rue du Bac.
Open noon-6.30pm Tue-Sun. Closed public holidays.
Admission free. **No credit cards.** **Map G6**
This hugely wealthy quango has substantial collections of contemporary photography. Solo shows by
contemporary artists, photographers and videomakers that have included Bill Viola, Claude Closky,
Marie-Ange Guilleminot and Guillaume Paris.
Wheelchair access.

Centre National de la Photographie

*Hôtel Salomon de Rothschild, 11 rue Berryer, 8th
(01.53.76.12.32). M° Charles de Gaulle-Etoile.* **Open**
noon-7pm Mon, Wed-Sun. Closed Tue, 1 May, 25 Dec,
1 Jan. **Admission** 30F; 15F 10-25s, over-60s; free
under-10s. **Credit** MC, V. **Map D3**
Housed in a former Rothschild mansion, the
National Photography Centre takes a largely contemporary line. Major retrospectives have included
Hannah Collins, Sophie Calle, Thomas Struth, Vik
Muniz and Michael Snow, while the Atelier gives
space to young artists exploring new frontiers of photography in installation, video and digital images.
Wheelchair access (telephone beforehand).

Maison Européenne de la Photographie

*5-7 rue de Fourcy, 4th (01.44.78.75.00). M° St-Paul
or Pont-Marie.* **Open** 11am-8pm Wed-Sun. Closed
Mon, Tue, public holidays. **Admission** 30F; 15F
students, over-60s; free under-8s, all 5-8pm Wed.
Credit MC, V. **Map L6**
This new institution in a restored Marais mansion,
with striking minimalist extension by architect Yves
Lion, usually runs several shows at once, including
historic and contemporary, art and documentary
photography. Solo shows have included Cartier-Bresson, Weegee, Pierre et Gilles and Baudrillard;
Bettina Rheims is scheduled until Apr 2000. The cellars are used for more experimental and multimedia
works. Organises the biennial *Mois de la Photo.*
Auditorium. Café. Library. Wheelchair access.

Mission du Patrimoine Photographique

*Hôtel de Sully, 62 rue St-Antoine, 4th
(01.42.74.47.75). M° Bastille or St-Paul.* **Open**
10am-6.30pm Tue-Sun. Closed Mon, some public
holidays. **Admission** 25F; 15F students, under-25s,
over-60s; free under-10s. **Credit** MC, V. **Map L7**
Historic photographic shows – often in association
with bodies like the Royal Photographic Society –
feature figures, such as Cecil Beaton, Jacques-Henri
Lartigue, W Eugene Smith, or varied themes (the
Egyptian pyramids, crime photography).

Renn 14/16 Verneuil

*14/16 rue de Verneuil, 7th (01.42.61.25.71). M° Rue
du Bac.* **Open** (during exhibitions) noon-7pm Tue-Sat. Closed Mon, Sun. **Admission** free. **Map G6**
The gallery owned by film director Claude Berri has
changed address and style – rather than abstract
painting it now concentrates on photography. Bernd
& Hilda Becher start off 2000.

Decorative Arts

Musée des Antiquités Nationales

*Château, pl du Château, 78100 St-Germain-en-Laye
(01.39.10.13.00). RER A St-Germain-en-Laye.* **Open**
9am-5.15pm Mon, Wed-Sun. Closed 25 Dec, 1 Jan.
Admission 25F; 17F students 18-25, all on Sun; free
under-18s. **Credit** (shop) MC, V.
If you've been struck up by millennium fever, a visit to
this museum in the rambling château which dominates St-Germain-en-Laye is a humbling cure.
Thousands of years spin by from one cabinet to the
next, putting our own era in awe-inspiring context.
Some of the early Paleolithic animal sculptures and
stone carvings existed long before the Ancient
Egyptians. The museum includes the Romans in
Gaul, where the artefacts are more familiar but of fine
quality, including an immaculate mosaic floor and
jewellery which since seems only to have been imitated and 'reinvented'. The collection is well presented and not short of amusing curiosities: massive
antlers from a prehistoric Irish deer and a set of eighteenth-century cork models of ancient sites, including the Orange amphitheatre prior to restoration.
Shop.

Musée des Arts Décoratifs

*Palais du Louvre, 107 rue de Rivoli, 1st
(01.44.55.57.50). M° Palais-Royal.* **Open** 11am-6pm
Tue, Thur, Fri; 11am-9pm Wed; 10am-6pm Sat, Sun.
Closed Mon, some public holidays. **Admission** 35F;
25F 18-25s; free under-18s, CM. **Credit** MC, V.
Map H5
This rich collection of decorative arts is currently
undergoing a major facelift as part of the *Grand
Louvre* project. So far only the Renaissance and
Middle Ages galleries are open, with the remaining
departments scheduled to be completed in 2002.
Unlike the Louvre where many works have a royal
origin, here the collection is essentially a representation of bourgeois life. In addition to fine sixteenth-century Venetian glass and Flemish tapestries, there
are two reconstructions of period rooms, one a panelled Gothic Charles VIII bedchamber complete with

tapestries and furniture, the other a Renaissance room in fake marble as existed in Italian and French homes of the fifteenth century. The religious art is dominated by the Gothic collection of architect and decorator Emile Peyre, a gift from the beginning of the century, notable for a wonderful altarpiece of the life of John the Baptist by Luis Borassa.
Library. Shop. Wheelchair access (105 rue de Rivoli).

Musée National de Céramique

pl de la Manufacture, 92310 Sèvres (01.41.14.04.20). M° Pont de Sèvres. **Open** 10am-5pm Mon, Wed-Sun. Closed Tue, public holidays. **Admission** 22F; 15F 18-25s; free under-18s, CM, all on Sun. **Credit** (showroom) MC, V.

Founded in 1738 as a private concern, the porcelain factory moved to Sèvres from Vincennes in 1756 and was soon taken over by the state. Finely painted, delicately modelled pieces that epitomise French Rococo style, together with later Sèvres, adorned with copies of Raphaels and Titians, demonstrate extraordinary technical virtuosity. The collection also includes Delftware, Italian majolica, Meissen, Della Robbia reliefs, Oriental and Hispano-Moorish pieces. Don't miss the outstanding Ottoman plates and tiles from Iznik and the elegantly decorated, eighteenth-century faïence commode.
Shop and showroom. Wheelchair access.

Musée de la Chasse et de la Nature

Hôtel Guénégaud, 60 rue des Archives, 3rd (01.53.01.92.40). M° Rambuteau. **Open** 11am-6pm

Musée des Arts Décoratifs: *virtuoso style.*

Tue-Sun. Closed Mon, public holidays. **Admission** 30F; 15F 16-25s, students under 26, over-60s; 5F 5-16s; free under 5s. **No credit cards. Map K5**

Housed on three floors of a beautifully proportioned mansion built by François Mansart in 1654, this museum brings together a group of objects ranging from Stone Age arrow heads to Persian helmets via Louis XV console tables under the common theme of hunting – nature, unless in the form of an alarming array of stuffed animals, doesn't get much of a look-in. The highlight are the wonderfully ornate weapons: crossbows inlaid with ivory and mother-of-pearl, guns decorated with hunting scenes, swords engraved with arabesques or masks, all reminders that hunting was a luxury sport and its accoutrements important status symbols. There are also hunting pictures by French artists like Chardin, Oudry and Desportes, and a Rembrandt sketch.
Bookshop.

Musée du Cristal Baccarat

30bis rue de Paradis, 10th (01.47.70.64.30). M° Poissonnière. **Open** 10am-6pm Mon-Sat. Closed Sun, public holidays. **Admission** 15F; 10F 12-25s, students; free under-12s. **Credit** (shop) AmEx, DC, MC, V. **Map H5**

The showroom of celebrated glassmaker Baccarat, with a museum attached. The main interest is in seeing which fallen head of state or deposed monarch used to drink out of Baccarat glasses. There are also some kitsch but technically magnificent pieces produced for the great exhibitions of the 1800s. Baccarat moved its workshops here in 1832, and this street remains full of glassware and china outlets.
Shop.

Musée de l'Eventail

2 bd de Strasbourg, 10th (01.42.08.90.20). M° Strasbourg-St-Denis. **Open** 2-6pm Mon-Wed. *Workshop* 9am-12.30pm, 2-6pm Mon-Fri. Closed Aug, public holidays. **Admission** 30F; 15F under 12s. **No credit cards. Map K4**

The fan-making Hoguet family's collection is housed in the atelier's neo-Renaissance showroom complete with its original 1893 walnut fittings. Exhibits go from eighteenth-century fans with mother-of-pearl and ivory sticks to contemporary fans by designers such as Karl Lagerfeld. There's also an interesting display on the techniques and materials used to make these luxury items – which, until the French Revolution, only the nobility were permitted to use.
Shop.

Musée de la Mode et du Costume

Palais Galliéra, 10 av Pierre 1er de Serbie, 16th (01.47.20.85.23). M° Iéna or Alma-Marceau. **Open** during exhibitions 10am-6pm Tue-Sun. Closed Mon, public holidays. **Admission** 45F; 32F over-60s; 23F 8-26s; free under-8s. **Credit** MC, V. **Map C5**

Opposite the Musée d'Art Moderne de la Ville de Paris (*see above* **Fine Art**) this fanciful 1890s mansion opens its doors to the public during exhibitions that go from historical periods or themes to individual dress designers. In 2000: 'Mutations modes' (Mar-July); 'Cotton through the ages' (autumn).

Musée de la Mode et du Textile

Palais du Louvre, 107 rue de Rivoli, 1st
(01.44.55.57.50). M° Palais-Royal. **Open** 11am-6pm
Tue, Thur, Fri; 11am-10pm Wed; 10am-6pm Sat, Sun.
Closed Mon. **Admission** 35F; 25F 18-25s; free under-
18s, CM. **Credit** MC, V. **Map G5**
The fashion museum moved into a much bigger
space as part of the *Grand Louvre* project. An annually rotated display gives a sampling of reserves that
span the seventeenth century to the very newest of
the new, with an emphasis on twentieth-century couture. 'Garde-Robes' (until autumn 2000) exhibits
complete wardrobes (hats, shoes, dresses, *et al*) as
they were donated or bequeathed by their enormously wealthy (and usually) aristocratic owners.
*Research centre (by appointment). Shop. Wheelchair
access (105 rue de Rivoli).*

Musée National du Moyen Age – Thermes de Cluny

*6 pl Paul-Painlevé, 5th (01.53.73.78.00). M° Cluny-
La Sorbonne/RER St-Michel.* **Open** 9.15am-5.45pm
Mon, Wed-Sun. Closed Tue, some public holidays.
Admission 30F; 20F 18-25s, all on Sun; free under-
18s, CM. **No credit cards. Map J7**
Occupying the Paris mansion of the medieval abbots
of Cluny (*see chapter* **Left Bank**), the museum of
medieval art and artefacts retains a domestic scale
suitable for the intimacy of many of its treasures.
Most famous of them is the *Lady and the Unicorn*
tapestry cycle, depicting convoluted allegories of the
five senses, beautifully displayed in a special circular room. The millefiore-style tapestry, filled with
rabbits and flowers, is wrought in exquisite colour
and detail. Elsewhere there are enamel bowls and
caskets from Limoges, carved ivory, gold reliquar-
ies and church plate, medieval books of hours to leaf
through, wooden chests and locks. Precious fabrics
include ancient Coptic weaving from Egypt and
heavily embroidered bishops' copes, while a new
room is devoted to chivalry and everyday life at the
end of the Middle Ages. Amid carved capitals from
churches all over France are the heads of the kings
of Judah from Notre Dame, which had been muti-
lated in the Revolution under the mistaken belief
that they represented the kings of France, and were
rediscovered by chance (minus their noses) in 1979.
Bookshop. Concerts. Guided tours.

Musées des Parfumeries-Fragonard

*9 rue Scribe, 9th (01.47.42.93.40) and 39 bd des
Capucines, 2nd (01.42.60.37.14). M° Opéra.* **Open**
9am-5.30pm Mon-Sat. Closed Sun, 25 Dec. (*Apr-Oct
rue Scribe open daily).* **Admission** free. **Credit**
AmEx, MC, V. **Map G4**
Get on the scent at the two museums showcasing
the collection of perfume house Fragonard. The five
rooms at rue Scribe range from Ancient Egyptian
ointment flasks to eighteenth-century vinaigrettes
and Meissen porcelain scent bottles, while the
second museum contains bottles by Lalique and
Schiaparelli, among others. Both have displays on
scent manufacture and an early twentieth-century
'perfume organ' with rows of the ingredients used
by 'noses' when creating their valuable concoctions.
Shop.

Musée de la Publicité

*Palais du Louvre, 107 rue de Rivoli, 1st
(01.44.55.57.50). M° Palais-Royal.* **Open** 11am-6pm
Tue, Thur, Fri; 11am-9pm Wed; 10am-6pm Sat-Sun.

René Gruau's posters give a graphic dimension to the **Musée de la Publicité**.

Closed Mon, some public holidays. **Admission** 35F; 25F 18-25s; free under-18s, CM. **Credit** MC, V. **Map H5**

Paris' advertising museum opened in 1999. Its stunning, fashionably distressed interior by architect Jean Nouvel was inspired by the city, with brut concrete in the multimedia space, an exposed brick café, a steel-covered internal street, and fragments of ceiling mouldings, wall partitions and peeling wallpaper that are highly contemporary yet respectful of the historic Louvre setting. Only a tiny proportion of its 50,000 posters from the thirteenth century to World War II, 50,000 since 1950, advertising clips, newspaper ads, promotional objects and packaging will ever be on show at one time. Instead, the museum serves for temporary exhibitions, that started with nonagenarian graphic artist René Gruau, while the multimedia space allows you to access historic posters in the reserves by artists like Toulouse-Lautrec, Chevet, Mucha or Savignac. A vital element is collaborations with young French artists, intended to reflect the ad world as a realm of creativity. *Café. Shop. Wheelchair access.*

Musée Nissim de Camondo

63 rue de Monceau, 8th (01.53.89.06.40). M° Villiers or Monceau. **Open** 10am-5pm Wed-Sun. **Admission** 30F; 20F 18-25s; free under-18s, CM. Closed Mon, Tue, some public holidays. **Credit** MC, V. **Map E3**

The Camondos were rich bankers who moved to Paris from Constantinople in 1867. The collection put together by Count Moïse de Camondo exploits to the full a love for fine French furniture and ceramics, as well as loudly patterned Italian marble, and is named after his son Nissim, who died in World War I (the rest of the family died at Auschwitz). Moïse replaced the family's two houses near Parc Monceau with this palatial residence in 1911-14, and lived here in a style quite out of his time. Grand first-floor reception rooms are crammed with furniture by leading craftsmen of the Louis XV and Louis XVI eras, including Oeben, Riesener and Leleu, huge silver services and sets of Sèvres and Meissen porcelain, set off by carpets and tapestries (Gobelins, Aubusson, Beauvais, Savonnerie), in extremely good condition and a surprising riot of colour. Most remarkable is the circular Salon de Huet, overlooking Parc Monceau, adorned by eighteenth-century pastoral scenes. There are also rooms for daily use, including a spectacularly plumbed bathroom on the second floor, and the recently opened kitchens. *Bookshop.*

Musée National de la Renaissance

Château d'Ecouen, 95440 Ecouen (01.34.38.38.50). SNCF from Gare du Nord to Ecouen-Ezanville, then bus 269. **Open** 9.45am-12.30pm, 2-5.15pm Mon, Wed-Sun. Closed Tue, 1 Jan, 1 May, 25 Dec. **Admission** 25F; 17F 18-25s Sun; free under-18s, CM. **No credit cards.**

Overlooking an agricultural plain, yet barely outside the Paris suburbs, the Renaissance château built 1538-55 for Royal Constable Anne de Montmorency and his wife Margaret de Savoie is the authentic setting for a wonderful collection of sixteenth-century decorative arts. The display is low-key but there are some real treasures, arranged over three floors of the château (some parts only open in the morning or afternoon). Best of all are the imposing, original painted chimneypieces, not unlike those at Fontainebleau, only here the caryatids and grotesques as well as the Biblical and mythological scenes are painted. Complementing them are furniture, Limoges enamels, tin-glazed earthenware decorated with Classical and religious scenes, armour, embroideries, rare painted leather wall hangings, and a magnificent tapestry cycle depicting the story of David and Bathsheba. *Bookshop. Wheelchair access (call ahead).*

Musée de la Serrurerie – Musée Bricard

Hôtel Liberal Bruand, 1 rue de la Perle, 3rd (01.42.77.79.62). M° St-Paul. **Open** 2-5pm Mon; 10am-noon, 2-5pm Tue-Fri. Closed Sat, Sun, two weeks in Aug, public holidays. **Admission** 30F; 15F students, over-60s; free under-18s. **No credit cards. Map L6**

This museum is housed in the cellars of the elegant mansion that architect Libéral Bruand built for himself in 1685. The collection focuses on locks and keys from Roman times to the end of the last century, but also takes in window fastenings, hinges, tools and the elaborate, gilded door handles from Versailles complete with Louis XIV's personal sun-burst.

Architecture & Urbanism

Cité de l'Architecture et du Patrimoine

Palais de Chaillot, pl du Trocadéro, 16th (01.44.05.39.10). M° Trocadéro. **Open** 2002. **Map B5**

The former Musée des Monuments Français was founded by Gothic revivalist Viollet-de-Duc to record the architectural heritage of France, with plaster casts of famous monuments, such as Vézelay. It reopens in 2002 with an enlarged collection and brief that brings it up to modernity, amalgamated with the Institut Français d'Architecture (*see below*).

Musée des Années 30

Espace Landowski, 28 av André-Morizet, 92100 Boulogne-Billancourt (01.55.18.46.45). M° Marcel Sembat. **Open** noon-6pm Tue; 10am-6pm Wed, Sat; 2-8pm Thur; 2-6pm Fri; 1-6pm Sun. Closed Mon, 15-31 Aug, public holidays. **Admission** 30F; 20F students, over-60s; free under-16s. **No credit cards.**

In a building that smacks just a little too much of the municipal, the Musée des Années 30 reminds that an awful lot of second-rate painting and sculpture was produced in the 1930s, notably the muscular nudes of the classical revival, alongside curiosities like 'colonial' works depicting France's imperial subjects. There are decent Modernist sculptures by the Martel brothers, graphic designs and Juan Gris still lifes and drawings, but the highlight is the furniture and designs by avant-garde architects including Perret, Le Corbusier, Lurçat and Fischer when this suburb was expanding in the 30s. *Shop. Wheelchair access.*

Institut Français d'Architecture

6 rue de Tournon, 6th (01.46.33.90.36). M° Odéon. **Open** (during exhibitions) 12.30-7pm Tue-Sun.

Admission free. **No credit cards. Map H7**
Exhibitions examining twentieth-century architects
or aspects of the built environment. The emphasis
is on modernist pioneers.
Lectures. Library. Wheelchair access. Workshops.

Pavillon de l'Arsenal
21 bd Morland, 4th (01.42.76.33.97).
M° Sully-Morland. **Open** 10.30am-6.30pm Tue-Sat;
11am-7pm Sun. Closed Mon, 1 Jan. **Admission** free.
Credit (shop) MC, V. **Map L7**
This centre presents imaginative exhibitions on
urban design and architecture, in the form of drawings, plans, photographs and models, often looking
at Paris from unusual perspectives, be it that of theatres, hidden courtyards, the use of glass or the
banks of the Seine. There's a 50-square-metre model
of Paris, and a permanent exhibition 'Paris, la ville
et ses projets' on the historic growth of the city.
Bookshop. Guided tours. Lectures. Wheelchair access.

Ethnology, Folk & Tribal Art

Musée des Arts d'Afrique et d'Océanie
*293 av Daumesnil, 12th (01.44.74.84.80/recorded
information 01.43.46.51.61). M° Porte Dorée.* **Open**
10am-5.20pm Mon, Wed-Sun. Closed Tue, 1 May.
Admission 30F; 20F 18-25s, all on Sun; free under-
18s, CM. **Credit** (shop) MC, V.
This museum has a winning combination of tropical fish and live crocs in the basement, tribal art up
above. The building was designed for the 1931
Exposition Coloniale, with an astonishing bas-relief
on the facade that reeks of colonialism and two Art
Deco rooms by Ruhlmann. On either side of a vast
reception room are Aboriginal and Pacific island art,
including carved totems from Vanuatu, anthropo-
morphic vases from New Caledonia and hook figures from Papua New Guinea. Upstairs, stunning
African masks and statues include Dogon statues
from Mali, pieces from Côte d'Ivoire and Central
Africa, Benin bronzes and other Nigerian art. There
are also fabrics, jewellery and embroidery from the
Maghreb. The second floor is used for temporary
displays, both traditional and contemporary. The
tribal art will eventually become part of the Musée des
Arts Premiers. As for the crocs…
Aquarium. Shop.

Musée National des Arts et Traditions Populaires
6 av du Mahatma-Gandhi, 16th (01.44.17.60.00).
M° Les Sablons. **Open** 9.30am-5.15pm Mon, Wed-
Sun. Closed Tue, some public holidays. **Admission**
22F; 15F 18-25s, over-60s, students; free under-18s,
CM. (Temporary exhibitions 23F and 16F.) **Credit**
(shop) AmEx, MC, V.
In contrast with its 1960s building, this important,
yet under-visited, centre of French folk art, in the
Bois de Boulogne, spotlights the traditions and popular culture of pre-industrial France, depicting rural
life through agricultural tools, household objects,
furniture and costumes. The liveliest sections are
those devoted to customs and beliefs – where you'll
find a crystal ball, tarot cards, thunder stones and

early medicines – and popular entertainment, with
displays on the circus, sport and puppet theatres.
The museum may move to Marseilles.
*Auditorium. Shop. Library/sound archive (by
appointment).*

Musée Dapper
50 av Victor-Hugo, 16th (01.45.00.01.50).
M° Victor-Hugo. **Open** closed until autumn 2001.
Admission ring for details. **Map B4**
The Fondation Dapper organises one or two beautifully displayed, themed exhibitions of African art
every year, but is currently closed for refurbishment.

Musée de l'Homme
*Palais de Chaillot, pl du Trocadéro, 16th
(01.44.05.72.72). M° Trocadéro.* **Open** 9.45am-
5.15pm Mon, Wed-Sun. Closed Tue, public holidays.
Admission 30F; 20F 5s-16s, over-60s; free under-4s.
Credit (shop) MC, V. **Map B5**
Starting off with an exhibition on world population
growth, this compendious museum goes on to consider birth control, death, disease, genetics and racial
distinction before turning to tribal costumes, tools,
idols and ornaments from all over the world.
Displays are arranged by continent, with Africa and
Europe on the first floor and Asia and the Americas
on the second. A section devoted to music provides
curious instruments and recordings of the noises
they make. The displays tend to be dowdy and could
do with some labelling in English, but the variety of
the collections (eventually due to form the core of
Chirac's Musée des Arts Premiers), including a
shrunken head, a stuffed polar bear and a reconstruction of a Mayan temple, makes this an ideal
departure point for exotic escapism on a rainy day.
*Café. Cinema. Lectures. Library. Photo Library.
Wheelchair access.*

Oriental Arts

Musée National des Arts Asiatiques – Guimet
*6 pl d'Iéna, 16th (01.45.05.00.98), closed until 2000.
Galeries du Panthéon Bouddhique, 19 av d'Iéna,
16th (01.40.73.88.11). M° Iéna.* **Open** 9.45am-
5.45pm Mon, Wed-Sun. Closed some public holidays.
Admission 16F; 12F students 18-25, all on Sun; free
under-18s, CM. **Credit** (shop) MC, V. **Map E5**
The stunning national collection of Oriental and
Asian art, notably the Cambodian Khmer Buddhist
sculptures from the civilisation of Angkor Wat, is
due to reopen after renovation in autumn 2000. The
Panthéon Bouddhique remains open in a Neo-
Classical *hôtel*: Emile Guimet's original collection
tracing the religious history of China and Japan from
the fourth to nineteenth centuries.
Shop.

Musée Cernuschi
*7 av Velasquez, 8th (01.45.63.50.75). M° Villiers or
Monceau.* **Open** 10am-5.40pm Tue-Sun. Closed Mon;
public holidays. **Admission** 17.50F; 9F 18-25s; free
under-18s, over-60s, CM (35F and 25F during
exhibitions). **No credit cards. Map E2**

Pavillon de l'Arsenal: *an overview of the development of the city.*

Erudite banker Henri Cernuschi amassed the nucleus of this collection of Chinese art on a long voyage to the Far East in 1871 and housed it in his mansion near the Parc Monceau. It ranges from Neolithic terracottas to Han and Wei dynasty funeral statues – in which Chinese potters displayed their inventiveness by creating entire legions of animated musicians, warriors, dancers, animals and other accessories to take to the next world. Other highlights include refined Tang celadon wares, Sung porcelain, fragile paintings on silk, bronze vessels and jade amulets. Among recent additions is some contemporary Chinese painting.
Wheelchair access (call ahead).

Musée d'Ennery
59 av Foch, 16th (01.45.53.57.96). M° Porte Dauphine. **Open** from 2001 (ring to check); 2-5.45pm Thur, Sun. **Admission** free. **No credit cards. Map A4**
This extraordinary collection of Oriental decorative arts, put together by author Adolphe d'Ennery and his wife, is as interesting for what it says about late nineteenth-century taste as for the objects themselves. The 5000 items are still in the d'Ennerys' lavish Napoléon III *hôtel*, many still in their original rosewood and mother-of-pearl showcases. The collection, dating from the seventeenth to nineteenth centuries, includes lacquer, ceramics, crystal, jade, ivories, bronzes, masks, wood carvings and netsuke.

Musée de l'Institut du Monde Arabe
1 rue des Fossés-St-Bernard, 5th (01.40.51.38.38). M° Jussieu. **Open** 10am-6pm Tue-Sun. Closed Mon, 1 May. **Admission** 25F; 20F 18-25s, students, over-60s (30F and 25F during exhibitions); free under-18s, CM. **Credit** MC, V. **Map K7**

Opened in 1987 as a *Grand Projet*, the institute of the Arab world brings together a library, cultural centre, exhibitions and the 'Museum of the Arab Museums', displaying items on long-term loan from museums in alternating Arab countries (Syria and Tunisia started the ball rolling) alongside its own permanent collection. The objects, covering a huge geographical (India to Spain) and historical (prehistoric to contemporary) span, are set off well in the high-tech space and include examples from almost every branch of the applied arts, calligraphy, metalwork, ceramics, textiles and miniatures. Particularly strong are the collections of early scientific instruments, nineteenth-century Tunisian costume and jewellery and contemporary fine art. Temporary exhibitions have ranged from ancient Syrian sculpture to Matisse's Moroccan paintings. *Bookshop. Cinema. Lectures. Library. Tea Room. Wheelchair access (call ahead).*

History

Mémorial du Maréchal Leclerc de Hauteclocque et de la Libération de Paris & Musée Jean Moulin
23 allée de la 2ᵉ DB, Jardin Atlantique (above Grandes Lignes of Gare Montparnasse), 15th (01.40.64.39.44). M° Montparnasse-Bienvenüe. **Open** 10am-5.40pm Tue-Sun. Closed Mon, public holidays. **Admission** 22F; 15F under-26s (30F and 20F during exhibitions). **No credit cards. Map F9**
A serious, sometimes drily academic approach to the Second World War and the Résistance characterises this double museum, dedicated to Free French Forces commander General Leclerc and left-wing Résistance

Musée des Arts d'Afrique et d'Océanie: *tribal art in a setting redolent of colonialism.*

martyr Jean Moulin. Temporary exhibitions, photographs and extensive documentary material are backed up by film archives; in the first part captions are translated into English, though the translations inexplicably disappear in the Résistance room. An impressive 270° slide show (with soundtrack) relates the liberation of Paris. Memorable documents include a poster exhorting Frenchmen in occupied France to accept compulsory work service in Germany – to act as 'ambassadors of French quality'.
Bookshop. Lectures. Research centre. Wheelchair access (call ahead).

Musée de l'Armée

Hôtel des Invalides, esplanade des Invalides, 7th (01.44.42.37.72). M° Varenne or Latour-Maubourg. **Open** *Apr-Sept* 10am-6pm daily; *Oct-Mar* 10am-5pm daily. Closed 1 Jan, 1 May, 1 Nov, 25 Dec. **Admission** 37F; 27F under-18s, students under 26; free under-12s, CM. **Credit** MC, V. **Map E6**
After checking out Napoléon's tomb under the vast golden dome of Les Invalides, many tourists don't bother to pursue their visit with the army museum, included in the ticket. If you are interested in military history, the museum is a must, but even if sumptuous uniforms and armour are not your thing, the building is in itself a splendour. Besides military memorabilia from antiquity on, the rooms are filled with fine portraiture (don't miss Ingres' masterpiece of Emperor Napoléon on his throne), some well recreated interiors, as well as the newly reopened museum of maquettes of fortifications. The World War I rooms are particularly immediate and moving, the conflict brought vividly to life by documents and photos. A new World War II display opens on 18

June 2000, concentrating on the role of Charles de Gaulle. *See also* **Les Invalides** *in chapter* **Left Bank.** *Café. Films. Concerts. Lectures. Shop.*

Musée d'Art et d'Histoire de St-Denis

22bis rue Gabriel-Péri, 93200 St-Denis (01.42.43.05.10). M° St-Denis Porte de Paris. **Open** 10am-5.30pm Mon, Wed-Sat; 2-6.30pm Sun. Closed Tue, public holidays. **Admission** 20F; 10F students, over-60s; free under-16s. **No credit cards.**
This prizewinning museum in the suburb of St-Denis is housed in the former Carmelite convent that in the eighteenth century numbered Louise de France, daughter of Louis XV, among its incumbents. Although there are displays of local archaeology, prints about the Paris Commune, Modern and post-Impressionist drawings and documents relating to the poet Paul Eluard who was born in the town, the most vivid part is the first floor where the nuns' austere cells have been preserved.

Musée du Cabinet des Médailles

Bibliothèque Nationale Richelieu, 58 rue de Richelieu, 2nd (01.47.03.83.30). M° Bourse. **Open** 1-5.45pm Mon-Fri; 1-4.45pm Sat; noon-6pm Sun. Closed one week in Sept, public holidays. **Admission** 22F; 15F students, over-60s, 13-25s; free under-13s. **Credit** (shop) MC, V. **Map H4**
With attention now focused on the new Bibliothèque François Mitterrand, the original building cuts a rather melancholy figure. On the first floor is the anachronistic Cabinet des Médailles; the extensive collection of coins and medals is for specialists, but efficient sliding magnifying glasses help bring exhibits to life. Probably the most interesting aspect for the general public are the museum's parallel

Greek, Roman and medieval collections, where oddities include the Merovingian King Dagobert's throne and Charlemagne's chess set, nestling among Greek vases and miniature sculptures from all periods. Attendants seem slightly put out by visitors. *Shop. Partial wheelchair access.*

Musée Carnavalet

23 rue de Sévigné, 3rd (01.42.72.21.13). M° St-Paul. **Open** 10am-5.40pm Tue-Sun. Closed Mon, some public holidays. **Admission** 30F; 20F students; free under-26s, over-60s, CM (exhibitions 35F; 30F; free under-7s). **Credit** (shop) AmEx, MC, V. **Map L6**

The museum of Paris history owes its origins to Baron Haussmann who, in 1866, persuaded the city to buy the Hôtel Carnavalet to house some of the interiors from buildings destroyed to make way for his new boulevards. Since then the museum has added a second *hôtel* and built up a huge collection which tells the history of the city from pre-Roman Gaul to the twentieth century, through archeological finds, *objets d'art*, paintings and furnishings.

The Hôtel Carnavalet contains the main collection and retains much of its old atmosphere, with an attractive *cour d'honneur* and a formal garden. Carnavalet's most famous resident was Mme de Sévigné, whose letters to her daughter bring alive aristocratic life under Louis XIV, and portraits of the author and her circle, her Chinese-export, lacquered desk and some of her letters, displayed in the panelled first-floor gallery and salon. All that remains of the adjoining seventeenth-century Hôtel Le Peletier de St-Fargeau, linked since 1989, is the elegant grand staircase and one restored, panelled cabinet.

Displays are chronological. The original sixteenth-century rooms house the Renaissance collections with portraits by Clouet, and furniture and pictures relating to the Wars of Religion that dominated French politics for most of the period. The first floor covers the period up to 1789 with furniture, applied arts and paintings displayed in restored, period interiors. The bold colours, particularly in the oval boudoir from the Hôtel de Breteuil (1782), may come as a shock to those with pre-conceived ideas about subdued eighteenth-century taste; however the use of royal blues and vivid greens is correct as the colours have been copied from original paint samples. Interesting interiors include the Rococo cabinet painted for engraver Demarteau by his friends Fragonard, Boucher and Huet in 1765, chinoiserie rooms and the Louis XIII-style Cabinet Colbert.

The collections from 1789 on are housed in the *hôtel* next door. The Revolutionary items are the best way of getting an understanding of the convoluted politics and bloodshed of the period from the calling of the Estates General through to the Directory. There are portraits of all the major players, prints, objects and memorabilia including a bone model of the guillotine made by French prisoners of war in England, Hubert Robert's gouaches, commemorative china and a small chunk of the Bastille prison. Those of a sentimental bent should look at the pathetic souvenirs from the Temple prison where the royal family were held: among them, the

Dauphin's lead soldiers and Louis XVI's shaving kit.

Highlights of the later collections include items belonging to Napoléon, views of Paris depicting the effects of Haussmann's programme, the ornate cradle given by the city to Napoléon III on the birth of his son, the early twentieth-century ballroom of the Hôtel Wendel and Fouquet, the Art Nouveau boutique designed by Mucha in 1901, with a sea-horse fountain. Rooms devoted to French literature finish the tour with portraits and room settings, including Proust's cork-lined bedroom. From September 2000, the Neolithic dug-out canoes excavated at Bercy will go on display in the renovated Orangery.

Bookshop. Guided tours. Reference section (by appointment). Lectures. Wheelchair access.

Musée Grévin

10 bd Montmartre, 9th (01.47.70.85.05). M° Grands Boulevards. **Open** Apr-Aug: *term-time* 1-7pm daily; *school holidays* 10am-7pm daily. Sep-Mar: *term-time* 1-6.30pm daily; *school holidays* 10am-6.30pm daily. **Admission** 58F; 38F 6-14s; 30F students; free under-6s. **Credit** MC, V. **Map J4**

The French version of Madame Tussaud's is over a century old, but is smaller than its London counterpart. Realism is variable (Depardieu's nose is well done but Gainsbourg's stubble is unconvincing), though the costumes are very good. There are some odd touches: spot the recurring black cats and the collection of famous revolutionaries' death masks. Although there is a fair quota of international film stars and well-known statesmen (Clinton, Kohl), the emphasis is on episodes from French history (the trial of Joan of Arc, the death of Marat) and personalities. New arrivals in 2000 include Lara Croft, Elvis Presley and Albert Einstein. A full list of all the figures is not available until you get to the souvenir stand at the end: it costs 10F.

Bookshop. Wheelchair access, ground floor only.

Musée de l'Histoire de France

Hôtel de Soubise, 60 rue des Francs-Bourgeois, 3rd (01.40.27.62.18). M° Hôtel-de-Ville or Rambuteau. **Open** noon-5.45pm Mon, Wed-Fri; 1.45-5.45pm Sat, Sun. Closed Tue, public holidays. **Admission** 20F; 15F 18-25s; free under-18s. **No credit cards.** **Map K6**

Housed in one of the grandest mansions in the Marais, this museum of French history is part of the National Archives. A display of historical documents covers themes like the Middle Ages, the Revolution and Republican politics; other rooms are used for temporary exhibitions. All slightly dry, but the Hôtel de Soubise also contains the finest Rococo interiors in Paris: the apartments of the Prince and Princesse de Soubise, decorated with superb plasterwork, panelling and paintings by artists of the period including Boucher, Natoire, Restout and Van Loo. *Shop.*

Musée National de la Légion d'Honneur

2 rue de la Légion d'Honneur, 7th (01.40.62.84.25). M° Solférino/RER Musée d'Orsay. **Open** 11am-5pm Tue-Sun; Closed Mon, 1 Jan, 1 May, 1 Nov, 25 Dec. **Admission** 25F; 15F students 18-25; free under-18s, CM. **Credit** (shop) MC, V. **Map G6**

Opposite Musée d'Orsay is the museum devoted to France's honours system, housed in the stables of the suberb Hôtel de Salm, bought by Napoléon in 1804. The museum itself is undergoing a facelift, in time for the bicentenary of the Ordre de la Légion d'Honneur in 2002. The array of official gongs and lookalike mayoral chains is enlivened by some suberb portraiture, including an effective display which combines the cloak of the Ordre du St-Esprit and an eighteenth-century portrait by Van Loo of the creation of the Order, featuring the same costume. A room dedicated to Napoléon includes a dashing representation by Gros and the pistols he presented to Tsar Alexander I. A new gallery evokes World War I through sketches, portraits and medals. *Shop.*

Musée de la Marine

Palais de Chaillot, pl du Trocadéro, 16th (01.53.65.69.69). M° Trocadéro. **Open** 10am-6pm Mon, Wed-Sun. Closed Tue. **Admission** 38F; 25F under-26s, over-60s; free under-5s, CM. **Credit** (shop) AmEx, MC, V. **Map B5**

The ideal place to find your sealegs, the maritime museum concentrates on French naval history via detailed carved models of battleships and Vernet's imposing series of paintings of the ports of France (1754-65) to a model of a nuclear submarine, as well as the Imperial barge, built when Napoléon's delusions of grandeur were reaching their zenith in 1811. There are also carved prows, old maps, antique and modern navigational instruments, ships in bottles, underwater equipment and romantic maritime paintings plus a new area devoted to the modern navy. Part of the museum will close in Sept 2000. *Shop.*

Musée de la Monnaie de Paris

11 quai de Conti, 6th (01.40.46.55.35). M° Odéon or Pont-Neuf. **Open** 11am-5.30pm Tue-Fri; noon-5.30pm Sat, Sun. **Admission** 20F; 15F students 18-25; free under-18s, over-60s, CM, all on Sun. **Credit** (shop) MC, V. **Map H6**

Housed in the handsome Neo-Classical mint built in the 1770s by Jacques-Denis Antoine, this high-tech museum tells the story of France's coinage from pre-Roman origins to the present day through a series of sophisticated displays and audiovisual presentations. The history of the French state is directly linked to its coinage, and the museum is informative about both. If your French is sufficient for the tour, a visit to the still-functioning *ateliers,* taking in foundry, engraving and casting of coins and medals, is fascinating for those interested in how things are made. *Shop. Visit to atelier (2.15pm Wed, Fri reserve ahead).*

Musée de Montmartre

12 rue Cortot, 18th (01.46.06.61.11). M° Lamarck-Caulaincourt. **Open** 11am-6pm Tue-Sun. Closed Mon, 1 Jan, 1 May, 25 Dec. **Admission** 25F; 20F students, over-60s; free under-8s. **Credit** (shop) MC, V. **Map H1**

At the back of a peaceful garden, this seventeenth-century manor is a haven of calm after touristy Montmartre. The museum is administered by the Société d'Histoire et d'Archéologie du Vieux

Montmartre, which since 1886 has aimed to preserve documents and artefacts relating to the historic hilltop. The collection consists of a room devoted to Modigliani, who lived in rue Caulaincourt, the recreated study of composer Gustave Charpentier, some original Toulouse-Lautrec posters, porcelain from the short-lived factory at Clignancourt and a tribute to the local cabaret, the Lapin Agile. The studios above the entrance pavilion were occupied at various times by Renoir, Emile Bernard, Raoul Dufy and Suzanne Valadon with her son Maurice Utrillo. *Archives (by appointment). Bookshop.*

Musée de la Préfecture de Police

1bis rue des Carmes, 5th (01.44.41.52.54). M° Maubert-Mutualité. **Open** 9am-5pm Mon-Fri; 10am-5pm Sat. Closed public holidays. **Admission** free. **No credit cards. Map J7**

Upstairs in a police station, the history of Paris is viewed via crime and its prevention since the founding of the Paris police force in the sixteenth century. Among eclectic treasures are prisoners' expenses from the Bastille, including those of dastardly jewel thief the Comtesse de la Motte, the exploding flowerpot planted by Louis-Armand Matha in 1894 in a restaurant on the rue de Tournon and the gory *Epée de Justice,* a seventeenth-century sword blunted by the quantity of noble heads chopped.

Musée de la Résistance Nationale

Parc Vercors, 88 av Marx Dormoy, 94500 Champigny-sur-Marne (01.48.81.00.80). RER

Royal barge ahoy at the **Musée de la Marine.**

Champigny-St-Maur then bus 208. **Open** 9am-12.30pm, 2-5.30pm Tue-Fri; 2-6pm Sat, Sun. Closed Mon. **Admission** 25F; 12.50F students; free schoolchildren, war veterans. **No credit cards**.

Occupying five floors of a nineteenth-century villa, the Résistance museum starts at the top with the pre-war political background and works down, via defeat in 1940, German occupation and the rise of the *maquis*, to victory. Given the universal appeal of the Résistance movement, it's slightly odd that no effort is made for foreign visitors: hundreds of photos aside, the bulk of the material consists of newspaper archives, both from official and clandestine presses, with no English translations. Three short archive films and a few solid artefacts are more accessible, with a sobering wall of machine guns and pistols, a railway saboteur's kit (cutters to chop through brake pipes, sand to pour into gearboxes and logs to lay across tracks) and a homemade device for scattering tracts. Displays steer clear of wallowing in collaborationist disgrace and of Résistance hero tub-thumping, making for a detailed and fascinating chronicle of some of France's darkest days.

Literary

Maison de Balzac

47 rue Raynouard, 16th (01.55.74.41.80). M° Passy. **Open** 10am-5.40pm Tue-Sun. Closed Mon, public holidays. **Admission** 30F; 20F over-60s; 15F 7-26s; free under-7s, CM. **No credit cards. Map B6**

Honoré de Balzac (1799-1850) rented a flat at this address in 1840 to avoid his creditors and established a password to sift friends from bailiffs. The museum now spread over several floors gives a rather dry presentation of his work and life, but the garden is pretty and gives an idea of the sort of country villa that lined this street when Passy was a fashionable spa. A wide range of memorabilia includes first editions, letters, corrected proofs, prints, portraits of friends and Polish mistress Mme Hanska, plus a 'family tree' of Balzac's characters that covers several walls. The study houses his desk, chair and the monogrammed coffee pot that fuelled all-night work on much of *La Comédie humaine*. *Library (by appointment).*

Maison de Chateaubriand

La Vallée aux Loups, 87 rue de Chateaubriand, 92290 Chatenay-Malabry (01.47.02.08.62). RER B Robinson + 20min walk. **Open** (guided tours only except Sun) *Apr-Sept* 10am-noon, 2-6pm Wed, Fri-Sat, Sun; *Oct-Mar* 2-5pm Tue-Sun. Closed Mon, Jan, 25 Dec. **Admission** 30F; 20F students, over-60s; free under-8s. **No credit cards**.

In 1807, attracted by the quiet Vallée aux Loups, Chateaubriand (1768-1848), author of *Mémoires d'outre tombe*, set about transforming a simple eighteenth-century country house into his own Romantic idyll and planted the park with rare trees as a reminder of his travels. Most interesting are the over-the-top double wooden staircase, based on a maritime design, a reminder of the writer's noble St-Malo birth, and the portico with two white marble

Grecian statues supporting a colonnaded porch. Anyone familiar with David's *Portrait of Mme Récamier* in the Louvre will find the original chaise longue awaiting the sitter, who was one of Chateaubriand's numerous lovers, no doubt to the discomfort of his stern wife, Céleste. After a politically inflammatory work Chateaubriand was ruined and in 1818 had to sell his beloved valley.

Concerts/readings (spring, autumn). Shop. Tea room.

Maison de Victor Hugo

Hôtel de Rohan-Guéménée, 6 pl des Vosges, 4th (01.42.72.10.16). M° Bastille or St-Paul. **Open** 10am-5.40pm Tue-Sun. Closed Mon, public holidays. **Admission** 22F; 15F students; free under-26s, over-65s, CM. **No credit cards. Map L6**

Victor Hugo (1802-85) lived in this historic townhouse from 1832 until he was forced to flee – first elsewhere in Paris and then to Guernsey – after the 1848 Revolution. Here he wrote part of *Les Misérables* and a number of poems and plays. When not writing, Hugo clearly kept himself busy – as well as typical period portraits of the writer and his large family, the collection includes his own drawings, the carved pseudo-Oriental furniture he designed himself, and his and his sons' experiments with the then new middle-class hobby of photography.

Musée de la Vie Romantique

16 rue Chaptal, 9th (01.48.74.95.38). M° Blanche. **Open** 10am-5.45pm Tue-Sun. Closed Mon, public holidays. **Admission** 17.50F; 9F over-60s, students (27F and 19F during exhibitions); free under-18s, CM. **No credit cards. Map G2**

When artist Ary Scheffer lived in this villa, this area south of Pigalle was known as the New Athens because of the concentration of writers, composers and artists living here. Baronne Aurore Dupin, alias George Sand (1804-76), was a frequent guest at Scheffer's *soirées*, and the house is now devoted to the writer, her family and her intellectual circle, which included Chopin, Delacroix (art tutor to her son) and composer Charpentier. Quietly charming, the museum reveals little of her writing or proto-feminist ideas, nor her affairs with Jules Sandeau, Chopin (represented by a marble bust) and Alfred de Musset; rather it presents a typical bourgeois portrait in the watercolours, lockets and jewels she left behind. In the courtyard, Scheffer's studio containing several of his *pompier*-type portraits and history subjects, is used for exhibitions.

Bookshop. Concerts (summer).

Musée Mémorial Ivan Tourguéniev

16 rue Ivan-Tourguéniev, 78380 Bougival (01.45.77.87.12). M° La Défense, plus bus 258. **Open** *Apr-Nov* 10am-6pm Sun. **Admission** 25F; 20F 12-26s; free under-12s. **No credit cards**.

The proverbial Russian soul persists in unexpected places like tranquil, Seine-side Bougival. The sumptuous datcha where novelist Ivan Turgenev lived for several years until his death in 1883 was a gathering spot for composers Saint-Saëns and Fauré, opera divas Pauline Viardot and Maria Malibran, and writers Henry James, Flaubert, Zola and Maupassant.

As well as letters and editions (mainly in Russian), there's the music room where Viardot held court. *Bookshop. Concerts.*

Music & Media

Musée du Cinéma Henri Langlois
rue de Bercy, 12th. **Open** from 2001.
The collection of early cinema paraphernalia, posters, costumes and sets was begun by Henri Langlois, founder of the Cinémathèque. It is in the process of moving to the former American Center.

Musée Edith Piaf
5 rue Crespin-du-Gast, 11th (01.43.55.52.72). Mᵒ Ménilmontant. **Open** by appointment 1-6pm Mon-Thur (call a couple of days ahead). Closed Sept. **Admission** donation. **No credit cards. Map N5**
Les Amis d'Edith Piaf run this tiny two-room museum in a part of Paris familiar to the singer. The memorabilia exudes love for the 'little sparrow', her diminutive stature graphically shown by a lifesize cardboard cut-out. Her little black dress and tiny shoes are particularly moving, and letters, posters and photos provide a personal touch. There's a sculpture of the singer by Suzanne Blistene, wife of Marcel who produced most of Piaf's films, and CDs and books on sale for the devoted fan.
Shop.

Musée de la Musique
Cité de la Musique, 221 av Jean-Jaurès, 19th (01.44.84.45.00). Mᵒ Porte de Pantin. **Open** noon-6pm Tue-Thur; noon-7.30pm Fri, Sat; 10am-6pm Sun. Closed Mon, some public holidays. **Admission** 35F; 25F 18s-25s; 10F 6-18s; free under-6s, over-60s, CM. **Credit** MC, V. **Map insert**
Alongside the concert hall in the striking modern Cité de la Musique, the innovative music museum houses the gleamingly restored collection of instruments from the old Conservatoire, interactive computers and scale models of opera houses and concert halls. On arrival you are supplied with an audioguide in a choice of languages. Don't spurn this offer, for the musical commentary is an essential part of the enjoyment, playing the appropriate music or instrument as you approach the exhibit. The thrill of seeing a superb three-manual Flemish harpsichord and hearing it play is tremendous. Alongside the trumpeting brass, curly woodwind instruments and precious strings are more unusual items, such as the Indonesian gamelan orchestra, which so influenced Debussy and Ravel. The models of concert halls and opera houses appeal to all ages. The Baroque opera at Versailles is particularly evocative. The route ends with a model of IRCAM and some pioneering synthesisers, now showing their age. Simple-to-use computers provide basic information about composers and musical periods (albeit only in French). Some of the concerts in the museum's amphitheatre use historic instruments from the collection. *See also chapters* **Right Bank** *and* **Music: Classical & Opera.**
Audioguide. Shop. Library. Wheelchair access.

Musée de l'Opéra
Palais Garnier, 1 pl de l'Opéra, 9th (01.40.01.24.93). Mᵒ Opéra. **Open** 10am-4.30pm daily. **Admission** 30F; 20F 10-25s, students, over-60s; free under-10s. **No credit cards. Map G4**
The magnificently restored Palais Garnier houses small temporary exhibitions relating to current opera or ballet productions, and a permanent collection of paintings, scores and bijou opera sets in period cases. The picture gallery is a sort of National Portrait Gallery for musicians. The ticket includes a visit to the auditorium (rehearsals permitting). *Bookshop.*

Religion

Musée d'Art et d'Histoire du Judaïsme
Hôtel de St-Aignan, 71 rue du Temple, 3rd (01.53.01.86.53). Mᵒ Rambuteau. **Open** 11am-6pm Mon-Fri; 10am-6pm Sun. Closed Sat, some Jewish holidays. **Admission** 40F; 25F 18-26s, students; free under-18s. **Credit** (shop) MC, V. **Map K5**
Opened in 1998 in an imposing Marais mansion, the new Jewish museum gives Jewish heritage an impressive showcase. Focusing on migrations and communities, exhibits bring out the importance of ceremonies, rites and learning, and show how styles were adapted across the globe. A silver Hannukah lamp made in Frankfurt, finely carved Italian synagogue furniture, embroidered Bar Mitzvah robes, Torah scrolls and North African dresses put the emphasis on fine craftsmanship but also on religious practice, for which a certain familiarity with both Judaism and the decorative arts is helpful. There are also documents relating to the Dreyfus case, from Zola's *J'Accuse* to anti-Semitic cartoons, and an impressive array of paintings by the early twentieth-century avant-garde and the Ecole de Paris (El Lissitsky, Mané-Katz, Modigliani, Soutine and Chagall). The Shoah is side-stepped – with the exception of a work by Christian Boltanski that commemorates the Jews who were living in the Hôtel St-Aignan in 1939, thirteen of whom died in concentration camps, thus bringing the collection back to the district in which it is set.
Auditorium. Café. Library. Shop. Wheelchair access.

Musée de la Franc-Maçonnerie
16 rue Cadet, 9th (01.45.23.20.92). Mᵒ Cadet. **Open** 2-6pm Tue-Sat. Closed Mon, Sun, public holidays, 14 July-15 Aug. **Admission** 10F; free under-12s. **No credit cards. Map H3**
At the back of the Grand Orient de France (French Masonic Great Lodge), a school-hall type room traces the history of freemasonry from medieval stone masons' guilds to the present via prints of famous masons (General Lafayette and 1848 revolutionary leaders Blanc and Barbès), insignia and ceremonial objects, but despite the potentially interesting subject you come out feeling none the wiser.
Bookshop.

In the jet stream at La Villette's **Cité des Sciences et de l'Industrie.**

Science, Medicine & Technology

La Cité des Sciences et de l'Industrie

*La Villette, 30 av Corentin-Cariou, 19th
(01.40.05.80.00/01.40.05.12.12). Mᵒ Porte de la
Villette.* **Open** 10am-6pm Tue-Sun. Closed Mon,
public holidays. **Admission** 50F; 35F 7-16s,
students under 25, over-60s; free under-7s; all on Sat;
Cité/Géode pass (Tue-Fri) 92F; 79F children, students
under 25, over-60s. **Credit** MC, V. **Map insert**
The ultra-modern science museum at La Villette has
been riding high since its opening in 1986 and pulls
in over five million visitors a year. Originally intended as an abattoir, the expensive project was derailed
mid-construction and cleverly transformed into a
gigantic, state-of-the-art science museum. **Explora**,
the permanent show, occupies the upper two floors,
whisking visitors through 30,000 m² of 'space, life,
matter and communication', where scale models of
satellites including the Ariane space shuttle, planes
and robots make for an exciting journey. There's an
impressive array of interactive exhibits on language
and communication enabling you to learn about
sound waves and try out different smells. Put on
your Michael Fish act and pretend to be a weather-
man in the Espace Images, try out the delayed camera and other optical illusions in the Jeux de lumière,
or draw 3D images on computer. The Serre 'garden
of the future' investigates futuristic developments
in agriculture and bio-technology. The **Espace** section, devoted to man's conquest of space, lets you
experience the sensation of weightlessness. Other
sections feature climate, ecology and the environment, health, energy, agriculture, the ocean and vol-
canoes. The Automobile gallery looks at the car both
as myth and technological object, with driving sim-
ulator and displays on safety, pollution and future
designs. The lower floors house temporary exhibitions, a documentation centre and children's sections. The Louis Lumière cinema shows films in 3-D,
and there's a restored submarine moored next to the
Géode. Until Dec 2000, 'The Adventure of Learning'.
See also chapters **Right Bank, Film** *and* **Children**.
*Bookshop. Café. Cinema. Conference centre. Library
(multimedia). Wheelchair access & hire.*

Musée de l'Air et de l'Espace

*Aéroport de Paris-Le Bourget, 93352 Le Bourget
Cedex (01.49.92.71.99/recorded information
01.49.92.71.71). Mᵒ Gare du Nord then bus 350/
Mᵒ La Courneuve then bus 152/RER Le Bourget then
bus 152.* **Open** May-Oct 10am-6pm; Nov-Apr
10am-5pm Tue-Sun. Closed Mon. **Admission** 30F;
22F 8-16s, students; free under-8s. **Credit** MC, V.
The air and space museum is a potent reminder that
France is a technical and military as well as cultural power. Housed in the former passenger terminal
at Le Bourget airport, the collection begins with the
pioneers, including fragile-looking biplanes, the contraption in which Romanian Vivia succeeded in flying twelve metres in 1906, and the strangely nautical
command cabin of a Zeppelin airship. Outside on the
runway are Mirage fighter planes, a Boeing 707, an
American Thunderchief with painted shark-tooth
grimace and Ariane launchers 1 and 5. Within a vast
hangar, walk through the prototype Concorde 001
and view wartime survivors, a Spitfire and German
Heinkel bomber. Further hangars are packed with
military planes, helicopters, commercial jets and
bizarre prototypes like the Leduc, designed to be
launched off the back of another plane, stunt planes,

Bony beasts in the Paleontology gallery at the **Muséum National d'Histoire Naturelle**.

missiles and satellites. A section is devoted to hot air balloons, invented in 1783 by the Montgolfier brothers and swiftly adopted for military reconnaissance. Most captions are summarised in English. *Shop. Wheelchair access.*

Musée des Arts et Métiers

60 rue Réaumur, 3rd (01.40.27.22.20/ 01.53.01.82.20). M° Arts et Métiers. **Open** from Feb 2000. **Admission** ring for details. **Map K5**
Occupying the medieval abbey of St-Martin-les-Champs, this historic science museum has a wealth of machines and models relating to great inventions from 1500 on, including automatons, Pascal's calculating machine, Blériot's plane and the first steam car. After five years of renovations, the museum finally reopens: the new incarnation features seven sections covering different aspects of science and technology, with visits ending in the twelfth-century chapel.

Musée de l'Assistance Publique

Hôtel de Miramion, 47 quai de la Tournelle, 5th (01.46.33.01.43). M° Maubert-Mutualité. **Open** 10am-6pm Tue-Sat. Closed Mon, Aug, public holidays. **Admission** 20F; 10F students, over-60s; free under-13s, CM. **No credit cards. Map K7**
The history of Paris hospitals, from the days when they were receptacles for abandoned babies to the beginnings of modern medicine with anaesthesia, is explained in a surprisingly lively fashion through paintings, prints, various grisly medical devices and a reconstructed ward and pharmacy; texts are unfortunately in French only.

Musée d'Histoire de la Médecine

Université René Descartes, 12 rue de l'Ecole-de-Médecine, 6th (01.40.46.16.93). M° Odéon. **Open** 15 July-Sept 2-5.30pm Mon-Fri; Oct-13 July 2-5.30pm Mon-Wed, Fri, Sat. Closed Sun, public holidays. **Admission** 20F; free under-12s. **No credit cards. Map H7**
The medical faculty collection covers the history of medicine from ancient Egyptian embalming tools through to a 1960s electrocardiograph. There's a gruesome array of serrated-edged saws and curved knives used for amputations, stethoscopes and syringes, the surgical instruments of Dr Antommarchi, who performed the autopsy on Napoléon, and the scalpel of Dr Félix, who operated on Louis XIV.

Muséum National d'Histoire Naturelle

57 rue Cuvier, 5th (01.40.79.30.00). M° Jussieu or Gare d'Austerlitz. **Open** *Grande Galerie* 10am-6pm Mon, Wed, Fri-Sun; 10am-10pm Thur. Closed Tue. **Admission** *Grande Galerie* 40F; 30F 5-16s, students, over-60s; free under-5s. *Other pavilions, each* 30F; 20F students, 4-16s, over-60s; free under-5s. **No credit cards. Map K9**
Within the Jardin des Plantes botanical garden, the brilliantly renovated Grande Galerie de l'Evolution has taken Paris' Natural History Museum out of the dinosaur age. Architect Paul Chemetov successfully integrated modern lifts, stairways and the latest lighting and audio-visual techniques into the nineteenth-century iron-framed structure. As you enter,

Big nose at **Musée de l'Air et de l'Espace.**

you will be confronted with the 13.66m-long skeleton of a whale: the rest of the ground floor is dedicated to other sea creatures. On the first floor are the big mammals, organised by habitat (savannah, jungle, etc) mostly in the open – with the exception of Louis XVI's rhinoceros, stuffed on a wooden chair frame shortly after its demise (and that of monarchy) in 1793. Videos and interactive computers give information on life in the wild. Glass-sided lifts take you up through suspended birds to the second floor, which deals with man's impact on nature and considers demographic problems and pollution. The third floor traces the evolution of species, while a gallery at the side, deliberately retaining old-fashioned glass cases, displays endangered and extinct species. There's a 'discovery' room for the under-12s and laboratories for teenagers. The departments of geology, fossils, skeletons and insects housed in separate pavilions over the park have just had a facelift. Until 30 Apr 2000, 'Les Ages de la Terre'. *See also chapters* **Left Bank**, **Parks** and **Children**. *Auditorium. Bookshop. Café. Library. Wheelchair access (Grande Galerie).*

Musée Pasteur

Institut Pasteur, 25 rue du Dr-Roux, 15th (01.45.68.82.82). M° Pasteur. **Open** 2-5.30pm daily. Closed public holidays, Aug. **Admission** 15F; 8F students. **Credit** V. **Map E9**
The apartment where the famous chemist and his wife lived for the last seven years of his life (1888-95) has hardly been touched since his death; you can

still see their furniture and possessions, family photos and a room of scientific instruments. The highlight is the extravagant, Byzantine-style mausoleum on the ground floor housing Pasteur's tomb, decorated with mosaics of his scientific achievements, including pasteurisation and a rabies vaccine. *Shop.*

Musée de la Poste

34 bd de Vaugirard, 15th (01.42.79.23.45).
M° Montparnasse-Bienvenüe. **Open** from Jan 2000,
10am-18h Mon-Sat. **Admission** 30F; 20F; free under
12s. **Credit** ring for details. **Map E9**
The museum of postal history has finally reopened after refurbishment. The extensive collection includes postmen's uniforms, letterboxes, stamps and their printing methods. Recent developments in telecommunications are also covered. At the time of going to press, few details were available.

Musée de Radio-France

Maison de Radio-France, 116 av du Président-
Kennedy, 16th (01.42.30.21.80). M° Ranelagh/RER
Kennedy-Radio France. **Open** guided tours 10.30am,
11.30am, 2.30pm, 3.30pm, 4.30pm Mon-Sat.
Admission 25F; 20F 8s-25s, students, over-60s. No
under-8s. **No credit cards. Map A7**
When the cylindrical Radio France building was opened by De Gaulle in 1963 it was a technological wonder, and a visit to the museum (unfortunately only available as a guided tour) starts with an appreciation of its now rather-dated architecture. Audiovisual history is clearly presented with an emphasis on French pioneers such as Branly and Charles Cros, including documentary evidence of the first radio message between the Eiffel Tower and the Panthéon. Exhibits, from primitive crystal sets through suberb Art Deco radios to modern TVs, are illustrated by fascinating clips; particularly interesting is the London broadcast of the Free French with its delightfully obscure coded messages. From the museum you can look through glazed panels on to the making of radio programmes.

Musée du Service de Santé des Armées

pl Alphonse-Laveran, 5th (01.40.51.40.00). RER
Port-Royal. **Open** noon-5pm Tue, Wed; 1pm-5pm
Sat; 1:30-5pm Sun. **Admission** 30F; 15F under-12s;
free under-6s. **No credit cards. Map J9**
Don't be put off by the daunting title, for not only is this an exemplary, newly restored collection, but it is also housed in one of the capital's finest Baroque buildings. The museum traces the history of military medicine, via recreations of field hospitals and ambulance trains, and beautifully presented antique medical instruments and pharmacy jars. World War I brings a chilling insight into the horror of the conflict, when many buildings were transformed into hospitals and, ironically, medical science progressed in leaps and bounds. The collection is also rich in moving pictures of battlefield scenes. If you've ever played doctors and nurses you'll be riveted.

Palais de la Découverte

av Franklin D Roosevelt, 8th (01.56.43.20.21).
M° Franklin D Roosevelt. **Open** 9.30am-6pm Tue-Sat;

10am-7pm Sun. Closed Mon, 1 Jan, 1 May, 14 July, 15
Aug, 25 Dec. **Admission** 30F; 20F 5-18s, students
under 26; free under-5s. *Planetarium* 15F. **Credit** MC,
V. **Map E5**
Join hordes of schoolkids at Paris' original science museum, housing designs from Leonardo da Vinci's extraordinary inventions onwards. Replicas, models, audiovisual material and real apparatus are used to bring the displays to life. Permanent displays cover man and his biology, light and the thrills of thermo-dynamism. The Planète Terre space takes account of developments in meteorology and issues such as global warming, while one room is dedicated to all you could ever want to know about the sun. The planetarium uses fibre optics to give a realistic representation of the starscape and planetary movement. There is also a theatre, where on some days demonstrations of electrostatics are presented, with literally hair-raising effects.
Café. Experiments. Shop.

Eccentricities

Musée de la Contrefaçon

16 rue de la Faisanderie, 16th (01.56.26.14.00).
M° Porte-Dauphine. **Open** 2-5pm Tue-Sun. Closed
Mon, and Sat, Sun in Aug, public holidays. **Admission**
15F; free under-12s. **No credit cards. Map A4**
The small museum set up by the Union des Fabricants, the French anti-counterfeiting association, puts a strong emphasis on the penalties involved (even for the buyer) in forgery. Although the oldest known forgery is displayed (vase covers from c200 BC), the focus is on contemporary copies of well-known brands – Reebok, Lacoste, Hermès, Vuitton, Ray Ban – with the real thing displayed next to the fake; even Babie doll, Barbie's illicit clone, gets a look-in.

Musée de la Curiosité

11 rue St-Paul, 4th (01.42.72.13.26). M° St-Paul or
Sully Morland. **Open** 2-7pm Wed, Sat, Sun (longer
during school holidays). Closed Mon, Tue, Thur, Fri.
Admission 45F; 30F 3-12s; free under-3s. **No credit
cards. Map L7**
The museum of magic gives you a show of card tricks, a talk (in French) on the history of magic going back to Ancient Egypt, and tools of the trade, such as wands, a cabinet for cutting people in half, optical illusions and posters. The welcome is enthusiastic and the guides are passionate about their art.

Musée de l'Erotisme

72 bd de Clichy, 18th (01.42.58.28.73). M° Blanche.
Open 10am-2am daily. **Admission** 40F; 30F
students under 25. **Credit** MC, V. **Map H2**
Opened in 1997 by Joseph Khalifa (a collector of erotic art) and his two associates, the erotic museum has been seen as an attempt to clean up the sleazy image of peep-show Pigalle. Diverse erotic *oeuvres*, sacred and profane, include painting, sculpture, graphic art and *objets d'art* from Latin America, Asia and Europe. Pieces run from Hindu representations of lingam and yoni, African ceremonial masks and Japanese prints of courting couples up to modern and contemporary works. Sadly, pieces are organised

The **Palais de la Découverte** *is a gateway to scientific discoveries.*

haphazardly and labelling is minimal, making it difficult to deduce their origin, age and purpose (if any). *Shop. Wheelchair access.*

Musée de la Poupée

impasse Berthaud, 3rd (01.42.72.73.11). *Mº Rambuteau.* **Open** 10am-6pm Tue-Sun. Closed Mon 25 Dec, 1 Jan. **Admission** 35F; 25F students uner 26, over-60s; 20F 3-18s; free under-3s. **Credit** MC, V. **Map K5**

This private collection of French dolls puts the emphasis on the late nineteenth century, with dolls by manufacturers Jumeau, Steiner and Gaultier. Ringlets, large eyes, rosebud lips, arching eyebrows and peaches-and-cream complexions give a good idea of the period's concept of female beauty. The elaborate costumes and dolls' houses, tea-sets and teddies also give an insight into nineteenth-century middle-class life, although recent temporary shows, such as Barbie, have given doll society an update. *Bookshop. Wheelchair access (telephone ahead).*

Musée de la SEITA

12 rue Surcouf, 7th (01.45.56.60.17). Mº Invalides or Latour-Maubourg. **Open** 11am-7pm Tue-Sun. Closed Mon, public holidays. **Admission** free. *Temporary exhibitions* 25F; 15F students; free under-12s. **Credit** (shop) MC, V. **Map E5**

The museum of the French state tobacco company SEITA traces the development of the lowly weed introduced to France in 1561 by Jean Nicot (of nicotine fame). Smoking paraphernalia from around the world includes snuff boxes, tobacco graters, majolica tobacco jars, pipes (among them George Sand's favourite) and the changing designs of Gauloises and Gitanes packs. High-quality temporary art exhibitions (financed by but unrelated to smoking) have included Basquiat, Dix, Schiele and Kokoschka. *Bookshop. Wheelchair access.*

Musée du Vin

rue des Eaux, 5 square Charles-Dickens, 16th (01.45.25.63.26). Mº Passy. **Open** 10am-6pm Tue-Sun. Closed Mon, 23 Dec-4 Jan. **Admission** 35F; 30F over-60s; 29F 4-18s, students; free under-4s. **Credit** (shop/ restaurant) AmEx, DC, MC, V. **Map B6**

The Ile-de-France was a major wine-producing area in the Middle Ages, as nearby rue Vineuse reminds. The main appeal of the museum is the beauty of the building itself: the vaulted cellars of a wine-producing monastery that was destroyed in the Revolution. The ancient bottles, vats, corkscrews and cutouts of medieval peasants making wine are quickly seen, but at the end there is a *dégustation* (tasting). There is some wine on sale, but thankfully no hard sell. *Restaurant (noon-3pm). Shop.*

Exhibition Centres

Most open only during exhibitions. Various cultural centres also mount shows related to the countries they represent. These include: Centre Culturel Calouste Gulbenkian (Portugal – 51 av d'Iéna, 16th/ 01.53.23.93.93); Centre Culturel Suisse (32-38 rue des Francs-Bourgeois, 3rd/01.42.71.38.38); Centre Wallonie-Bruxelles (127 rue St-Martin, 4th/ 01.53.01.96.96); Goëthe Institut (Germany – 17 av d'Iéna/16th/01.44.43.92.30/and Galerie Condé, 31 rue de Condé, 6th/01.40.46.69.60); Institut Finlandais (60 rue des Ecoles, 5th/01.40.51.89.09);

Institut Néerlandais (121 rue de Lille, 7th/ 01.53.59.12.40); Maison de l'Amérique Latine (217 bd St-Germain, 7th/01.49.54.75.00).

Bibliothèque Forney
Hôtel de Sens, 1 rue du Figuier, 4th (01.42.78.14.60). M° Pont-Marie. **Open** 1.30-8pm Tue-Sat. Closed Mon, Sun, public holidays. **Admission** 20F; 10F students under 28, over-60s; free under-12s. **No credit cards. Map L7**
Set in the turrets and Gothic vaulting of this medieval mansion – the oldest in the Marais – the library specialises in the applied and graphic arts, and has a wing given over to temporary displays. *See also chapter* **Right Bank**. *Bookshop.*

Bibliothèque Nationale de France – Richelieu
58 rue de Richelieu, 2nd (01.47.03.81.26). M° Bourse. **Open** 10am-7pm Tue-Sun. Closed Mon, two weeks in Sept, public holidays. **Admission** 35F; 24F 12-26s, students; free under-12s. **Credit** MC, V. **Map H4**
Within the old Bibliothèque Nationale, the Galeries Mansart and Mazarine hold exhibitions ranging from Indian miniatures or medieval manuscripts to contemporary etchings. From Feb 2000, photos from the Magnum agency. *See also chapter* **Right Bank**.

Bibliothèque Nationale de France – François Mitterrand
quai François-Mauriac, 13th (01.53.79.59.59). M° Bibliothèque or Quai de la Gare. **Open** 10am-7pm Tue-Sat; noon-6pm Sun. Closed Mon, two weeks in Sept, public holidays. **Admission** 35F; 24F 12-26s, students; free under-12s. **Credit** MC, V. **Map M10**
The gigantic new library could not be more different from its historic parent, but shares a similarly erudite programme, which includes photography and an ongoing cycle related to writing. Apr 2000, 'Utopia'. *See chapters* **Left Bank** *and* **Directory**. *Café. Wheelchair access.*

Chapelle St-Louis de la Salpêtrière
47 bd de l'Hôpital, 13th (01.42.16.04.24). M° Gare d'Austerlitz. **Open** 8.30am-6.30pm daily. **Admission** free. **No credit cards. Map L9**
Libéral Bruand's austere chapel provides a fantastic setting for contemporary art, notably installations by Viola, Kawamata and Kapoor for various Festivals d'Automne. *See chapter* **Left Bank**. *Wheelchair access.*

Couvent des Cordeliers
15 rue de l'Ecole-de-Médicine, 6th (01.40.46.05.47). M° Odéon. **Open** hours vary, usually 11am-7pm Tue-Sun. Closed Mon. **Admission** 25F; 15F students, over-60s; free under-3s. **No credit cards. Map H7**
Administered by the Ville de Paris and the medical school, the barn-like medieval refectory of a Franciscan convent is used for varied shows, in both style and quality, of contemporary art. Until May 2000 'Arman, un objet par siècle'.

Ensb-a (Ecole Nationale Supérieure des Beaux-Arts)
13 quai Malaquais, 6th (01.47.03.50.00).

M° St-Germain-des-Prés. **Open** 1-7pm Tue-Sun. Closed Mon, public holidays. **Admission** 25F; 15F students; free under-12s. **Credit** MC, V. **Map H6**
Exhibitions at France's central art college vary from the pick of the previous year's graduates to theme shows of contemporary art (May-July 2000: young Russian painters) or from Ensb-a's rich holdings of prints and drawings (nude studies, Géricault, Dutch and Italian drawing). *See also chapter* **Left Bank**. *Bookshop.*

Fondation Cartier pour l'art contemporain
261 bd Raspail, 14th (01.42.18.56.72/recorded information 01.42.18.56.51). M° Raspail. **Open** noon-8pm Tue, Wed, Fri-Sun; noon-10pm Thur. Closed Mon. **Admission** 30F; 20F under-25s, students, over-60s; free under-10s. **Credit** (shop) MC, V. **Map G9**
Jean Nouvel's glass and steel building is as much a work of art as the exhibitions inside, which alternate shows and installations by contemporary artists like Jean-Pierre Raynaud and Panamerenko, and multi-cultural, century-crossing themes as wide-ranging as birds or love. Concerts, dance and video are presented in 'Soirées Nomades' (June-Sept 8pm Thur). *Bookshop. Wheelchair access.*

Fondation Coprim
46 rue de Sévigné, 3rd (01.44.78.60.00). M° St-Paul. **Open** 10am-6pm Mon-Fri; noon-6pm Sat. Closed Sun, two weeks in Aug, public holidays. **Admission** free. **No credit cards. Map L6**
The gallery belonging to property developer Coprim moved recently to a former print workshop in the Marais. The bent is towards contemporary figurative painting – Gérard Garouste, Combas, etc – and there's also an annual prize for young artists. *Bookshop.*

Fondation EDF-Espace Electra
6 rue Récamier, 7th (01.53.63.23.45). M° Sèvres-Babylone. **Open** noon-7pm Tue-Sun. Closed public holidays, Aug. **Admission** 20F; 10F students, over-60s; free under-10s. **No credit cards. Map G7**
This former electricity substation, owned by the French electricity board, is used for varied fine art, graphic and design exhibitions, from garden designer Gilles Clément to Latin American art. Some have an appropriately electric connection, as in the light installations of James Turrell (Apr-July 2000).

Fondation Mona Bismarck
34 av de New-York, 16th (01.47.23.38.88). M° Alma-Marceau. **Open** 10.30am-6.15pm Tue-Sat. Closed Mon, Sun, Aug, public holidays. **Admission** free. **No credit cards. Map C5**
Chic setting for eclectic exhibitions of everything from Etruscan antiquities to North American Indian art, often lent by prestigious foreign collections.

Galéries Nationales du Grand Palais
av du Général-Eisenhower, 8th (01.44.13.17.17). M° Champs-Elysées-Clemenceau. **Open** 10am-8pm Mon, Thur-Sun; 10am-10pm Wed. Pre-booking compulsory before 1pm. Closed Tue, 1 May, 25 Dec. **Admission** 50F; 38F 18-26s, all on Mon (56F and 41F with prebooking); free under-18s. **Credit** MC, V. **Map E5**
Paris' premier venue for blockbuster exhibitions is

a striking leftover from the 1900 *Exposition Universelle*. The glass-domed central hall is closed for restoration, but two other exhibition spaces remain. Exhibitions for 2000 include 'Colombian gold', '1900' – an exploration of artistic movements at the turn of the century – 'Méditerranée' and 'Visions of the Future: A History of the Fears and Hopes of Humanity'. *See also chapter* **Right Bank**.
Audioguides. Shop. Café. Cinema. Wheelchair access.

Halle St-Pierre – Musée d'Art Naïf Max Fourny

2 rue Ronsard, 18th (01.42.58.72.89). Mº Anvers. **Open** 10am-6pm daily. Closed 1 Jan, 1 May, 25 Dec, Aug. **Admission** 40F; 30F students 12-26, 4-12s; free under-4s. **Credit** (shop) AmEx, DC, MC, V. **Map J2**
The former covered market specialises in Art Brut (a term coined by Dubuffet to describe self-taught *singuliers*, from poor backgrounds or in prisons and asylums, who used poor or idiosyncratic materials) and *art-naïf* (self-taught artists who use more traditional techniques) from its own and other specialist collections. Mar-June 2000: Haitian art.
Bookshop. Café/restaurant. Children's workshops.

Jeu de Paume

1 pl de la Concorde, 8th (01.47.03.12.50). Mº Concorde. **Open** noon-9.30pm Tue; noon-7pm Wed-Fri; 10am-7pm Sat, Sun. Closed Mon, some public holidays. **Admission** 38F; 28F students, over-60s; free under-13s. **Credit** MC, V. **Map F5**
When the Impressionist museum moved from here to the Musée d'Orsay, the former real tennis court of the Tuileries Palace was redesigned by Antoine Stinco for contemporary and modern art exhibitions. Recent emphasis has been on the 1950s and 60s, with

French establishment artists (Arman, César, Alechinsky) drawing an audience to match. A basement cinema shows artists' film and video series.
Bookshop. Café. Cinema. Wheelchair access.

Musée-atelier Adzak

3 rue Jonquoy, 14th (01.45.43.06.98). Mº Plaisance. **Open** depends on show.
The eccentric house and studio built by the late Roy Adzak resounds with traces of the conceptual artist's plaster body columns and dehydrations. Now a registered charity, it gives (mainly foreign) artists a first chance to exhibit in Paris.

Passage de Retz

9 rue Charlot, 3rd (01.48.04.37.99). Mº Filles du Calvaire. **Open** 10am-7pm Tue-Sun. **Admission** 35F; 20F students under 26, over-60s; free under-12s. **Credit** (shop) MC, V. **Map L5**
A Marais mansion which became a toy factory and has now been resurrected as a gallery. Varied shows include contemporary design as well as fine art and fun theme offerings such as techno-music-led Global Techno or a valentine show.
Bookshop. Café.

Pavillon des Arts

101 rue Rambuteau, 1st (01.42.33.82.50). Mº Châtelet- Les Halles. **Open** 11.30am-6.30pm Tue-Sun. Closed Mon, public holidays. **Admission** 30-35F; 20-25F 6-25s, students, over-60s; free under-6s. **No credit cards**. **Map K5**
Next to the Forum des Halles, this gallery hosts varied exhibitions from contemporary photography to Turner to the history of Paris.
Wheelchair access.

Pierrick Sorin's moral of modern life on video at **Fondation Cartier** in spring 2000.

Art Galleries

Paris' contemporary galleries seem to be entering the new millennium with renewed optimism.

The Prix Ricard is trying to promote the idea, for what it's worth, of the 'French touch' in art. In fact the Paris art world is impressively international, both in terms of the artists shown and the thousands of artists who live and work in the city. Undoubtedly, there is a sense of rejuvenation, and young artists, such as Sorin, Closky, Sechas, Jouve and Hybert, are beginning to be seen on the world stage, adding to the handful of internationally recognised names (Bustamante, Boltanski, Buren, Calle, etc) who have been around for decades. Varied media continue to rule, but alongside photo, video and installation art, sound pieces and Web experiments, there are plenty of signs that painting is still alive. As in literature, many of the so-called 'me' generation are concerned with autobiography, but others treat wider issues of the body, sexuality and society, or interact with fashion and music, while some, as artists have done for centuries, create art that is essentially about art.

Gwen Ravillous in the bag at **Galerie Zurcher***.*

ART COLLECTIVES

A burgeoning of art collectives is also challenging ways of presenting contemporary art. Often closer to forums for exchange and information networks than the classic artist's group or stylistic movement, some number curators, fashion and graphic designers, critics and musicians as well as artists, others exist only for specific projects or, like Infozone, are an umbrella to disseminate information on the Web. One of the oldest is Glassbox (113bis rue Oberkampf, 11th/01.43.38.02.82), set up by a group of artists in 1997. Its politically oriented group shows have included art, poetry, design and exchanges with similar associations. Public (4 impasse Beaubourg, 3rd) invites fashion designers and DJs as well as (predominantly video) artists for short shows punctuated by debates. Many events are deliberately transient, taking art into unexpected arenas, like B&B Unlimited's 24-hour occupation of posh Hôtel Scribe, Nøn_Facture's intervention in the Centre Commercial Italie 2, Toasting Agency's year-long project at a hairdresser, or hand-delivered conceptual pizza (varieties by 13 artists to be ordered on 01.40.26.13.40/ www.pizzaproject.com until Sept 2000).

THE ART CIRCUIT

Luckily for keeping track of the art scene, like-minded galleries tend to cluster together. For new, innovative work head for the northern Marais.

Galleries around the Bastille mainly present young artists; those around St-Germain-des-Prés, home of the avant-garde in the 1950s and 60s, largely confine themselves to traditional sculpture and painting; those near the Champs-Elysées, the centre before that, present big modern and contemporary names, but are unlikely to risk the untried. If you're interested in the most conceptual side of young creation, keep an eye on rue Louise-Weiss, behind the Bibliothèque Nationale.

Annual international art fair FIAC in October gives a quick fix on the gallery scene, recently joined by the less-prestigious but refreshing Art-Paris at the Carrousel du Louvre. There are numerous chances to visit artists' studios. The Génie de la Bastille, Ménilmontant and 13ème Art (*see chapter* **Paris by Season**) are the best known, but there are also 'portes ouvertes' (often in May or October) in Belleville, St-Germain, the 10th, 14th and 18th *arrondissements* and the suburbs of Montrouge, Montreuil and Ivry-sur-Seine.

INFORMATION & MAGAZINES

Local publications include *Beaux Arts*, *L'Oeil* and the more contemporary, bilingual *Art Press*. Trendy *Blocnotes* and *Purple* take a multi-disciplinary look, embracing design, philosophy, fashion, music and film in a break from white-cube gallery orthodoxy. The *Journal des Arts* is international news and art-market based. Only a selection of the most active and consistent galleries can be listed here. For information on current shows, look for the *Galeries Mode d'Emploi* (Marais/Bastille/rue Louise-Weiss) and *Association des Galleries* foldouts (Left and Right Bank/suburban cultural centres). Virtually all galleries close in August and often in late July and early September.

Beaubourg & the Marais

Galerie Aréa

10 rue de Picardie, 3rd (01.42.72.68.66). M° Temple or Filles du Calvaire. **Open** 2-7pm Wed-Sat; 3-7pm Sun. **Map L5**

A small, two-level gallery bravely committed to French painters, usually with a figurative/expressionist bent. More experimental work is shown at the Réserve (50 rue d'Hauteville, 10th).

Chez Valentin

9 rue St-Gilles, 3rd (01.48.87.42.55). M° Chemin-Vert. **Open** 2.30-7pm Tue-Sat. **Map L6**

Installations, photography, video and a sense of urban angst predominate among the young French artists *chez* Valentin, which moved to Rizzo's old space last year. Notable are the decay and detritus installations of Véronique Boudier, the photos of Nicolas Moulin and videos of François Nouguiès.

Galerie Cent 8

108 rue Vieille-du-Temple, 3rd (01.42.74.53.57). M° St-Sébastien-Froissart. **Open** 10.30am-1pm, 2.30-7pm Tue-Sat. **Map L5**

Consistently interesting since opening in spring 1998 with Christine Borland's anthropological explorations (back in 2000). Noteworthy shows have included Laurent Parriente and Marina Abrimowicz.

Galerie Chantal Crousel

40 rue Quincampoix, 4th (01.42.77.38.87). M° Rambuteau/RER Châtelet-Les Halles. **Open** 11am-1pm, 2-7pm Tue-Sat. **Map J6**

This long-standing Beaubourg gallery founded in 1980 hosts both the internationally known (Polke, Cragg, Calle, Hatoum) and intriguing installations by the hottest of the new generation, like Thomas Hirshhorn, Abigail Lane and Rikrit Tiravanija.

Galerie de France

54 rue de la Verrerie, 4th (01.42.74.38.00). M° Hôtel de Ville. **Open** 11am-7pm Tue-Sat. **Map K6**

One of the rare galleries to span the entire twentieth century, from Brancusi, the melting heads of Rosso, erotic Surrealism of Mattà and Pop of Raysse to contemporary artists Horn and Kirili.

Galerie Marian Goodman

79 rue du Temple, 3rd (01.48.04.70.52). M° Hôtel de Ville. **Open** 11am-7pm Tue-Sat. **Map K6**

After opening a small showcase a couple of years ago, New York gallerist Goodman has moved to beautiful new quarters in the seventeenth-century Hôtel de Montmor. Alongside established names (Baumgarten, Struth, etc), she has also snapped up brilliant young Brit videomaker Steve McQueen and fast-rising South African William Kentridge.

Galerie Karsten Greve

5 rue Debelleyme, 3rd (01.42.77.19.37). M° St-Sébastien-Froissart. **Open** 11am-7pm Tue-Sat. **Map L5**

This historic Marais building is Cologne gallerist Karsten Greve's Parisian outpost and venue for retrospective-style displays of top-ranking artists.

Bernard Vernet, Jannis Kounellis and Louise Bourgeois are all programmed in 2000.

Galerie Ghislaine Hussenot

5bis rue des Haudriettes, 3rd (01.48.87.60.81). M° Rambuteau. **Open** 11am-1pm, 2-7pm Tue-Sat. **Map K5**

High-concept stuff is presented in a two-level loft, from the date paintings of conceptual guru On Kawara and the sculptural forms of Franz West to the much-hyped fashion model performances of young Italian Vanessa Beecroft.

Galerie du Jour Agnès b

44 rue de Quincampoix, 4th (01.44.54.55.90). M° Rambuteau/RER Châtelet-Les Halles. **Open** 11am-7pm Tue-Sat. **Map J5**

Agnès b's gallery fills the modern space previously used by Fournier. Many artists share the designer's interests in Third World and social issues: British photographer Martin Parr, Africa's Félix Brouly Bouabré and Seydou Keïta, filmmaker Jonas Mekas and Claude Lévêque's sound/light environments.

Galerie Laage-Salomon

57 rue du Temple, 4th (01.42.78.11.71). M° Rambuteau. **Open** 2-7pm Tue-Fri; 11am-7pm Sat. **Map K6**

Ranges from land artists/sculptors Roger Ackling and Hamish Fulton to the feminist slogans of Claudia Hart, and photographers Hannah Collins, Fariba Hajamadi, Candida Höfer and Tracey Moffat.

Yvon Lambert

108 rue Vieille-du-Temple, 3rd (01.42.71.09.33). M° Filles du Calvaire. **Open** 10am-1pm, 2.30-7pm Tue-Fri; 10am-7pm Sat. **Map L5**

A succession of major names – Kiefer, Kosuth, André, Schnabel, Boltanski, Goldin, Serrano – makes this skylit warehouse space an essential stop (Lambert's personal collection goes on show in Avignon in 2000). Young artists are shown Côté Rue (2-7pm Tue-Sat).

Galerie Nikki Diana Marquardt

9 pl des Vosges/10 rue de Turenne, 4th (01.42.78.21.00). M° St-Paul or Bastille. **Open** 11am-6pm Mon-Fri; noon-6pm Sat. **Map L6**

Ulster, Algeria, Palestine and, recently, Lebanon have all featured in the human-rights/politics-inspired agenda in this former industrial building off place des Vosges, where group shows are complemented by related film, poetry or music evenings.

Galerie Moussion

110/121 rue Vieille-du-Temple, 3rd (01.48.87.75.91). M° Filles du Calvaire. **Open** 10am-7pm Mon-Sat. **Map L5**

The undoubted star at Moussion is Pierrick Sorin, the funniest video artist around (back Apr 2000), but it also features Chrystel Egal, dealing with gender and sexuality, young US photographer Chris Verene, some older French artists, such as Degottex, and Korean artists concerned with environmental art.

Galerie Nathalie Obadia

5 rue du Grenier-St-Lazare, 3rd (01.42.74.67.68). M° Rambuteau. **Open** 11am-7pm Mon-Sat. **Map K5**

Obadia supports young talents, often women, from intellectually complicated installations by Nathalie Elemento to decorative paintings by Carole Benzaken, plus some more established names like Bustamente.

Galerie Papillon-Fiat

16 rue des Coutures-St-Gervais, 3rd (01.40.29.98.80). M° St-Paul. **Open** 2-7pm Tue-Fri; 11am-7pm Sat. **Map L6**
Expect shows of important European conceptual and minimalist artists (Carter, Craig-Martin, Dietman, Polke, Roth), but little excitement.

Galerie Gilles Peyroulet

80 rue Quincampoix, 3rd (01.42.78.85.11). M° Rambuteau or Etienne-Marcel. **Open** 2-7pm Tue-Fri; 11am-7pm Sat. **Map K5**
Peyroulet shows works in all media but is often stronger with photo- and sculpture-based pieces. Artists include Kasimir, Hartley, Hansen, Tremorin and Sue Fox. A new contemporary design gallery has opened at No 75 (01.42.78.86.72).

Galerie Polaris

8 rue St-Claude, 3rd (01.42.72.21.27). M° St-Sébastien-Froissart. **Open** 1-7.30pm Tue-Fri; 11am-1pm, 2-7.30pm Sat. **Map L5**
Bernard Utudjian works over the long term with a few artists. Look out for photographers Stéphane Couturier and Anthony Hernandez and photo/performance artist Nigel Rolfe.

Galerie Rachlin Lemarié Beaubourg

23 rue du Renard, 4th (01.44.59.27.27). M° Hôtel de Ville. **Open** 10.30am-1pm, 2.30-7pm Tue-Sat. **Map K6**
When Galerie Beaubourg moved south to Vence, Rachlin and Lemarié took over its list including sculptors Arman and César and *nouvelle figuration* painter Combas, and added a few artists of their own, like François Boisrand and Nichola Hicks.

Galerie Thaddaeus Ropac

7 rue Debelleyme, 3rd (01.42.72.99.00). M° St-Sébastien-Froissart. **Open** 10am-7pm Tue-Sat. **Map L5**
The Austrian-owned gallery is particularly strong on American Pop, neo-Pop and neo-Geo (Warhol, Baechler, Sachs), but also features other major artists including Kabakov, Gilbert & George, Balkenhol and Gormley. Occasional theme shows introduce the younger generation.

Daniel Templon

30 rue Beaubourg, 3rd (01.42.72.14.10). M° Rambuteau. **Open** 10am-7pm Mon-Sat. **Map K5**
A favourite with the French art establishment, Templon shows well-known painters. Salle, Alberola, Viallat and Le Gac are understandable, but it seemed a most unlikely spot for shockers Jake and Dinos Chapman's first Paris presentation.

Galerie Anne de Villepoix

11 rue des Tournelles, 4th (01.42.78.32.24). M° Bastille. **Open** 11am-7pm Tue-Sat. **Map L7**
Anne de Villepoix alternates established older figures, such as photographer John Coplans, with younger artists in all media. Look out for photographers Jean-Luc Moulène and Valérie Jouve, the subtle minimalist paintings of Diti Albroog and installations and varied media of Franck Scurti.

Galerie Anton Weller

57 rue de Bretagne, 3rd (01.42.72.05.62). M° Temple. **Open** 2-7pm Tue-Sat. **Map M5**
Weller often takes an experimental approach, using alternative venues, working with artists' groups or with artists in new media or on the internet.

Galerie Xippas

108 rue Vieille-du-Temple, 3rd (01.40.27.05.55). M° Filles du Calvaire. **Open** 10am-1pm, 2-7pm Tue-Fri; 10am-7pm Sat. **Map L6**
This U-shaped gallery (around Yvon Lambert) presents painters and photographers. William Wood monochromes and Vik Muniz food paintings impressed in 1999; Koen Theys, Per Barclay, Joan Hernandez Pijuan and Lucas Samaras show in 2000.

Galerie Zurcher

56 rue Chapon, 3rd (01.42.72.82.20). M° Arts et Métiers. **Open** 11am-7pm Tue-Sat. **Map K5**
Zurcher specialises in young artists with a new take on painting, among them Camille Vivier, Gwen Ravillous, Philippe Hurteau and Dan Hays.

Bastille

Durand-Dessert

28 rue de Lappe, 11th (01.48.06.92.23). M° Bastille. **Open** 11am-7pm Tue-Sat. **Map M7**
A powerhouse of the French art scene, Durand-Dessert has long been committed to artists associated with arte povera (Pistoletto, Mario Merz), major French names (Morellet, Garouste, Lavier) and photographers (Wegman, Tosani, Burckhardt). There's an excellent contemporary art bookshop.

Galerie Alain Gutharc

47 rue de Lappe, 11th (01.47.00.32.10). M° Bastille. **Open** 2-7pm Tue-Sat; 11am-7pm Sat. **Map M7**
Gutharc works mainly with young French artists: intimate photos by Agnès Propeck, quirky text pieces by Antoinette Ohanassian, videos by Joël Bartoloméo, and Delphine Kreuter's powerfully disturbing slice-of-life images.

Galerie Jousse Seguin

34 rue de Charonne, 11th (01.47.00.32.35). M° Bastille or Ledru-Rollin. **Open** 11am-1.30pm, 2.30-7pm Mon-Fri; 11am-7pm Sat. **Map N7**
This dynamic gallery picks up on topical issues like gender and identity (Chuck Nanney, Serge Conte, Thomas Grunfeld), plus a few painters (Peter Hopkins, Karin Kneffel). A hangar-like second space at 5 rue des Taillandiers is devoted to designers of the 1930s to 50s, such as Perriand and Prouvé, plus occasional trendy collaborations with outside curators.

Le Sous-Sol

9 rue de Charonne, 11th (01.47.00.02.75). M° Bastille. **Open** 2.30-7pm Tue-Sat. **Map M7**
A sign of the times, the Sous-Sol is no longer geared

to the installations of its former cavernous basement, but to small exhibitions often in new media, such as photographer Ivan Balogh, Eric Maillet and Dutch duo Drieussens Verstappen. It also organises external site-specific projects.

Champs-Elysées

Galerie Louis Carré et Cie

10 av de Messine, 8th (01.45.62.57.07). M° Miromesnil. **Open** 10am-12.30pm, 2-6.30pm Mon-Sat. **Map E3**
This gallery was founded in 1938 and shows today largely focus on a small stable of contemporary French artists such as *nouvelle figuration* painter Hervé di Rosa and Haïtian-born sculptor Hervé Télémacque, although you'll also find Calder, Dufy, Delaunay and Léger among the artists in stock.

Galerie Lelong

13 rue de Téhéran, 8th (01.45.63.13.19). M° Miromesnil. **Open** 10.30am-6pm Tue-Fri; 2-6.30pm Sat. **Map E3**
Lelong shows major, post-1945, international names. Scully, Chillida, Alechinsky, Miró and Bacon have featured recently. Branches in New York and Zurich.

Galerie Jérôme de Noirmont

38 av Matignon, 8th (01.42.89.89.00). M° Miromesnil. **Open** 10am-1pm, 2.30-7pm Mon-Sat. **Map E4**
Opening in moneyed avenue Matignon could arouse suspicions that Noirmont sells purely business art. But eye-catching shows by A R Penck, Clemente, Jeff Koons and Pierre et Gilles have made this gallery worth the trip, and an exhibition by Shirin Neshat suggests a broadening of scope.

St-Germain-des-Prés

Galerie 1900-2000

8 rue Bonaparte, 6th (01.43.25.84.20). M° Mabillon or St-Germain-des-Prés. **Open** 2-7pm Mon; 10am-12.30pm, 2-7pm Tue-Sat. **Map H7**
Marcel and David Fleiss show a strong predilection for Surrealism, Dada, Pop art and the Fluxus movement. This is a place to find works on paper (drawings, collage) by anyone from Breton, Léger and De Chirico to Lichenstein and Rauschenberg.

Galerie Claude Bernard

7-9 rue des Beaux-Arts, 6th (01.43.26.97.07). M° Mabillon or St-Germain-des-Prés. **Open** 9.30am-12.30pm, 2.30-6.30pm Tue-Sat. **Map H6**
This large gallery shows mostly conservative, figurative paintings and drawings from the 1960s to the present, by the likes of Hockney and Balthus.

Galerie Jeanne Bucher

53 rue de Seine, 6th (01.44.41.69.65). M° Mabillon or Odéon. **Open** 9am-6.30pm Tue-Fri; 10am-12.30pm, 2.30-6pm Sat. **Map H7**
One of the first galleries to set up on the Left Bank, in 1925, Bucher specialises in postwar abstract (De Staël, Da Silva, Rebeyrolle) and Cobra painters, with a few contemporary sculptors.

Galerie Jean Fournier

22 rue du Bac, 7th (01.42.97.44.00). M° Rue du Bac. **Open** 10am-12.30pm, 2-7pm Tue-Sat. **Map G6**
Fournier has changed *quartier* but still specialises in the French 70s Support-Surface painters Viallat and Buraglio, independents Hantaï, Piffaretti and the US West Coast abstractionists.

Alain Bublex and the art of car maintenance at **Georges-Philippe et Nathalie Vallois**.

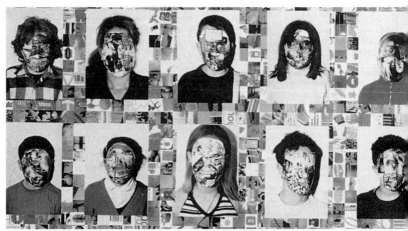

Questions of identity, self-image and portraiture in Portraits d'Image, *Guy Limone's project*

Galerie Maeght

42 rue du Bac, 7th (01.45.48.45.15). Mº Rue du Bac.
Open 10am-6.30pm Tue-Sat. **Map G6**
The world-famous gallery founded by Aimé Maeght in 1946 is now run by his grandchildren, but today's shows pale compared to a past that once included Léger, Braque, Chagall, Giacommetti and Miró. The gallery continues to produce beautiful artists' books.

Galerie Denise René

196 bd St-Germain, 7th (01.42.22.77.57).
Mº St-Germain-des-Prés. **Open** 10am-1pm, 2-7pm Tue-Fri; 11am-1pm, 2-7pm Sat. **Map H7**
Something of an institution, Denise René has remained firmly committed to kinetic art and geometrical abstraction ever since Tinguely first presented his machines here in the 50s.
Branch: 22 rue Charlot, 3rd (01.48.87.73.94).

Galerie Darthea Speyer

6 rue Jacques-Callot, 6th (01.43.54.78.41).
Mº Mabillon or Odéon. **Open** 11am-12.45pm, 2-7pm Tue-Fri; 11am-7pm Sat. **Map H6**
Colourful, representational painting and sculpture and naive artists are the speciality here. It can be kitsch, but at best features the political expressionism of Golub or American dreams of Paschke.

Galerie Laurent Strouk

25 rue Guénégaud, 6th (01.55.42.16.55). Mº Odéon.
Open 10.30am-12.30pm, 2-7pm Mon-Sat. **Map H6**
Strouk specialises in *figuration libre* and *nouvelle figuration* of the 60s and beyond, by artists including Adami, Erro, Combas and Ben.

Georges-Philippe et Nathalie Vallois

36 rue de Seine, 6th (01.46.34.61.07). Mº Mabillon or St-Germain-des-Prés. **Open** 10.30am-1pm, 2-7pm Mon-Sat. **Map H7**
Son of Art Deco furniture and sculpture specialist Galerie Vallois (at No 41), Georges-Philippe takes a

contemporary bent, with sculpture, photo, video and installation from hip young things such as Alain Bublex, Gilles Barbier and Barbier McCarthy.

Galerie Lara Vincy

47 rue de Seine, 6th (01.43.26.72.51). Mº Mabillon or St-Germain-des-Prés. **Open** 2.30-7.30pm Mon; 11am-12.30pm, 2.30-7.30pm Tue-Sat. **Map H7**
Lara Vincy is one of the more eccentric characters of the area and one of the few to retain something of the old St-Germain spirit and sense of 70s Fluxus-style 'happenings' in interesting theme shows and solo shows, including master of the epigram, Ben.

ScèneEst: rue Louise-Weiss

Air de Paris

32 rue Louise-Weiss, 13th (01.44.23.02.77).
Mº Chevaleret. **Open** 2-7pm Tue-Fri; 11am-7pm Sat. **Map M10**
This gallery is named after Duchamp's famous bottle of air and, true to its namesake, shows here tend to be highly experimental, if not chaotic. A young stable includes Paul McCarthy, Philippe Parreno, Liam Gillick, Pierre Joseph and Carsten Höller, who play witty games with the concepts and language behind contemporary art.

Galerie Almine Rech

24 rue Louise-Weiss, 13th (01.45.83.71.90).
Mº Chevaleret. **Open** 11am-7pm Tue-Sat. **Map M10**
Almine Rech has proved one of the more consistent of the ScèneEst, often featuring photography/video or works on paper. Artists have included Americans James Turrell, Alex Bag, Italian Ugo Rondinone and young French discovery Rebecca Bourgnigault.

Galerie Jennifer Flay

20 rue Louise-Weiss, 13th (01.44.06.73.60).
Mº Chevaleret. **Open** 2-7pm Tue-Fri; 11am-7pm Sat.

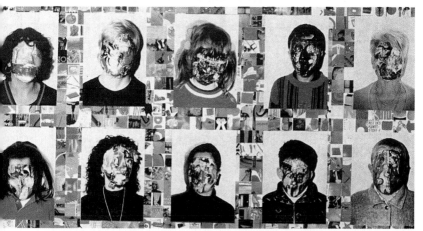

with schoolchildren on his Tapisserie orange *at* **Galerie Emmanuel Perrotin.**

Map M10
New Zealander Jennifer Flay has a talent for picking up on interesting young artists, ensuring that this is a gallery people watch. Come here for a sampling of the French scene from Xavier Veilhan and Claude Closky, European photographers including Richard Billingham and Willie Doherty, and new North American painting from Lisa Milroy and John Currin, plus Cathy de Monchaux and Zoë Leonard.

Galerie Emmanuel Perrotin
30 rue Louise-Weiss, 13th (01.42.16.79.79).
M° Chevaleret. **Open** 2-7pm Tue-Fri; 11am-7pm Sat.
Map M10
Perrotin shows young European artists, many of whom explore portraiture or autobiography, like Maurizio Cattelan, Guy Limone and Alix Lambert, plus cat man Alain Sechas. This is also the place to catch provocative young Japanese artists Noritoshi Hirakawa, Takashi Murakami and glossy cyberpunkette Mariko Mori.

Photography

Photoworks can also be found in many other galleries, while branches of Fnac mount surprisingly erudite photography shows. The biennial Mois de la Photo (next Nov 2000) in public and private galleries across the city features both historic and contemporary photography as does the Paris Photo salon in the Carrousel du Louvre (also Nov).

Galerie 213
213 bd Raspail, 14th (01.43.22.83.23). M° Raspail.
Open 11am-7pm Tue-Sat. **Map G9**
Contemporary photographers, including the fashion world's Elaine Constantine and Peter Fraser, are shown upstairs. Downstairs is a photography bookshop in a listed former Art Nouveau restaurant.

Michèle Chomette
24 rue Beaubourg, 3rd (01.42.78.05.62).
M° Rambuteau. **Open** 2-7pm Tue-Sat. **Map K5**
Classical and experimental photographic work. Alain Fleischer, Lewis Baltz, Felten & Massinger, Bernard Plossu, Holger Trülzsch are regulars.

Agathe Gaillard
3 rue du Pont-Louis-Philippe, 4th (01.42.77.38.24).
M° Pont-Marie. **Open** 1-7pm Tue-Sat. **Map K6**
This long-established gallery specialises in classic masters such as Cartier-Bresson, Kertész and Boubat.

Contemporary Design

See **Galeries Peyroulet** *and* **Jousse Seguin,** *above,* Colette in *chapter* **Specialist Shops.**

Galerie Néotu
25 rue du Renard, 4th (01.42.78.96.97). M° Hôtel de Ville. **Open** 9am-7pm Mon-Sat. **Map K6**
The contemporary furniture, ceramics and carpets shown here are as much art as function, by designers including Kristian Gavoille and Martin Szekely.

de/di/bY
22 rue Bonaparte, 6th (01.40.46.00.20). M° St-Germain-des-Prés. **Open** 11am-7pm Tue-Sat. **Map H6**
Objects and furniture by design gurus include Kuramata, Sottsass, Pesce, Arad and Charpin.

VIA
29-35 av Daumesnil, 12th (01.46.28.11.11).
M° Gare de Lyon. **Open** 9am-7pm Mon-Sat; 11am-6pm Sun. **Map M8**
Installed in three stylish arches in the Viaduc des Arts, VIA (Valorisation de l'Innovation dans l'Ameublement) promotes furniture design by providing information and showcasing talent, from recent graduates to big names, such as Wilmotte or Nouvel.

Evergreen Laurel Hotel

The Evergreen Laurel Hotel is located in a residential and commercial area, 15 minutes from Paris city centre by metro. For your comfort, the hotel offers 338 spacious, elegantly decorated and fully equipped rooms and suites, a gymnasium with sauna, and private parking. The relaxed atmosphere of our piano bar and the refined cuisine of our two restaurants – including a gastronomic Chinese restaurant – will please both tourist and business clients.

Consumer

Accommodation

From budget bohemia to luxury palaces catering to your every caprice, Paris has an abundance of choice.

With almost 1500 hotels in central Paris, visitors have an unrivalled and sometimes bewildering choice. Some establishments recreate the style and charm of a luxurious 19th-century private residence, others are resolutely modern. Even on a limited budget, it's possible to stay in an atmospheric historic building in the heart of the city or to follow in the footsteps of famous former residents.

Official star ratings are not listed here, because the French classification system (from no stars to four) is based on standard factors such as room size, the presence of a lift, services and so on, but not on cleanliness, warmth of welcome or decent décor. In addition, many hotels don't upgrade after renovation, so a two-star hotel may well be better (but not necessarily cheaper) than a three-star one. Justifiably named palace hotels drip with every service you can think of, let alone need, but luxury and often 100 rooms or more can lead to standardisation. If you prefer a more personal approach, the small family-run hotels which abound in Paris may be more your style.

Hotels are often booked solid in high season (May, June, Sept, Oct) and during fashion weeks (Jan and early July for couture, Mar and Oct for *prêt-à-porter*) and trade fairs (spring and autumn). At these times book well ahead. During low season (late July, Aug, Nov-Feb), you may be able to find rooms at less than the prices listed here. Same-day reservations can be made in person at branches of the Office de Tourisme de Paris (*see* chapter **Directory**). A small fee is charged (8F-50F, depending on the hotel category). Prices quoted for a double room are for two people and, unless stated, all rooms have private shower or bath, and telephone. All hotels are also required to charge an additional room tax (*taxe de séjour*) of 1F-7F per person per night, depending on the hotel type, although this is sometimes included in the price.

Palace Hotels

These hotels offer every service you can think of – from minibars to modem links to babysitting – and more, provided you're prepared to pay.

Hôtel Ritz
15 pl Vendôme, 1st (01.43.16.30.30/fax 01.43.16.31.78). *M° Concorde or Opéra.* **Rates** *single* 3000F-3300F; *double* 3600F-4000F; *suite* 4900F-32,900F; *breakfast* 190F-340F. **Credit** AmEx, DC, MC, V. **Map** G4

Coco Chanel, the Duke of Windsor and Proust all stayed at the Ritz, as did Hemingway, who reputedly said he hoped heaven would be as good. Now owned by Mohamed Al Fayed, the Ritz was the setting for Dodi and Di's last supper. The Oriental-carpeted corridors go on for ever and the windows on place Vendôme are sound- and bullet-proof. There are 142 wonderful bedrooms and 45 suites, from the romantic 'Frédéric Chopin' to the glitzy 'Impérial'. There's even a cookery school on the premises.

Le Bristol
112 rue du Fbg-St-Honoré, 8th (01.53.43.43.00/ fax 01.53.43.43.01). *M° Miromesnil.* **Rates** *single* 2600F-3000F; *double* 3250F-4000F; *suite* 4600F-36,000F; *breakfast* 175F-265F. **Credit** AmEx, DC, MC, V. **Map** E4

The Bristol prides itself on discreet class rather than the flashy luxury of some of its rivals, attracting a business rather than pop-star clientele. The 180 rooms are exercises in quiet elegance *à la* Louis XV, with panelling and original prints and paintings. The best suites are larger than most Paris flats and some have terraces. There's an indoor swimming pool on the glass-enclosed rooftop and a first-rate restaurant with highly acclaimed chef Eric Frechon.

Critics'' Choice

Hôtel de Banville Charming and family-run.

Hôtel Beaumarchais Stylish and bright.

Hôtel Costes Chic, opulent and formidably fashionable.

Les Degrés de Notre Dame Delightful staff and excellent value.

Hôtel Delambre Modern touches and colours mixed with the style of Montparnasse's arty heyday.

Hôtel des Grandes Ecoles Serene garden.

L'Hôtel Utterly fab.

Hôtel de Nesle Wacky murals and a hippy past.

Pavillon de la Reine Ivy-covered romance off the Place des Vosges.

Hôtel de Crillon

*10 pl de la Concorde, 8th (01.44.71.15.00/
fax 01.44.71.15.02). M° Concorde.* **Rates** *single*
2950F-3400F; *double* 3500F-4300F; *suite*
4950F-31,000F; *breakfast* 170F-230F. **Credit** AmEx,
DC, MC, V. **Map F4**

If your relationship with AmEx is *très amical*, come
here to live out your Sun King fantasies. This magnificent Neo-Classical palace groans with marble,
mirrors and gilt. The clientele includes film stars,
royalty and heads of state. The Michelin-starred
Ambassadeurs restaurant is sublime, but beware
the tea room, where a straggly black hair recently
accompanied our carpaccio.

Hôtel Plaza Athénée

*25 av Montaigne, 8th (01.53.67.66.65/
fax 01.53.67.66.66). M° Alma-Marceau.* **Rates** *single*
3000F; *double* 3700F-5800F; *suite* 7800F-16,000F;
breakfast 160F-250F. **Credit** AmEx, DC, MC, V. **Map H5**

The Athénée's location allows you to fall straight out
of bed and into the couture shops lining avenue
Montaigne. The look is more flamboyant Versace silk
than discreet chic; chandeliers, gold, elaborate floral
displays. Great toiletries in the bathrooms and hugely covetable dressing gowns add to the attraction. In
summer, the Cour Jardin becomes a six-storey cascade of ivy – a romantic setting for lunch – while Le
Régence restaurant offers creative haute cuisine.

Hôtel Raphaël

*17 av Kléber, 16th (01.44.28.00.28/fax 01.45.01.21.50).
M° Kléber.* **Rates** *single or double* 2340F-5040F; *suite*
up to 18,000F; *extra bed* 450F; *breakfast* 135F-175F.
Credit AmEx, DC, MC, V. **Map C4**

Rich with antiques, sumptuous furnishings and
hand-painted panels, the Raphaël, with just 90
rooms, retains a sense of personal service and privacy. Three unusual suites have recently been
added, including a duplex and a triplex with private
terraces. Numerous celebs have stayed here since
the hotel opened in 1925, including US presidents
Ford and Bush, Serge Gainsbourg – who wrote
songs in his suite here – and singer Lenny Kravitz.
Superb 360° views of Paris can be had from the sev-
enth-floor terrace restaurant.

De Luxe/Expensive

Hôtel Costes

*239 rue St-Honoré, 1st (01.42.44.50.00/
fax 01.45.44.50.01). M° Tuileries.* **Rates** *single*
1750F; *double* 2250F-4500F; *suite* 5250F-10,750F;
breakfast 150F. **Credit** AmEx, DC, MC, V. **Map G5**

This instantly famous hotel, opened in 1995, is the
haunt of top models and film stars. The mood is of
subtly contemporary historicism, from the Italianate
central courtyard overlooked by Roman gods to the
towering conservatory and a restaurant filled nightly with media and film folk ensuring they've been
seen. Bedrooms and bathrooms are firmly in the
opulent spirit of the Second Empire and the Eastern-
inspired pool area is wickedly decadent. Costes provides a frightfully fashionable, incredibly luxurious
bedtime experience at a relatively reasonable price.

Hotel Services *Air con. Bar. Bureau de change.
Lifts. Laundry. Fitness centre/pool. Restaurant.*
Room services *CD player. Fax. Hairdryer. Minibar.
Modem link. Radio. Room service. Safe. TV.*

Hôtel Regina

*2 pl des Pyramides, 1st (01.42.60.31.10/
fax 01.40.15.95.16). M° Tuileries.* **Rates** *single* 1090F-
1690F; *double* 1380F-1980F; *suite* 2300F-4100F;
breakfast 95F-155F. **Credit** AmEx, DC, MC, V. **Map G5**

This hotel, which has been completely refurbished
over the last three years, is an extravagant relic of
another age and retains its Art Nouveau allure. The
old panel clock, which has a face for each of seven
different cities, and the wooden exchange kiosk evoke
the excitement of the first days of transatlantic steam
travel. A pleasant bustle fills the lobby, while upper
rooms offer great views over the Tuileries.

Hotel services *Air con. Babysitting. Bar. Conference
services. Bureau de change. Garden. Laundry. Lift.
Porter. Restaurant.* **Room services** *Hairdryer.
Minibar. Radio. Room service (24-hr). Safe. TV.*

Hôtel Edouard VII

*39 av de l'Opéra, 2nd (01.42.61.56.90/
fax 01.42.61.47.73). M° Opéra.* **Rates** *single*
1000F-1400F; *double* 1400F-1600F; *suite* 2300F;
breakfast 100F. **Credit** AmEx, DC, MC, V. **Map H4**

Two golden lions greet guests at the entrance to this
grandiose eighteenth-century building. Originality
of style is evident throughout, from the animal-print
chairs in the lobby to the individually decorated
floors. Ask for the fifth floor if you want your room
à la Chinoise, or the sixth if Provençal suits better.

Hotel services *Air con. Bar. Lift. Restaurant.* **Room
services** *Hairdryer. Minibar. Room service. Safe. TV*

Pavillon de la Reine

*28 pl des Vosges, 3rd (01.40.29.19.19/
fax 01.40.29.19.20). M° Bastille.* **Rates** *single* 1700F-
1850F; *double* 1900F-2100F; *suite* 2050F-3900F;
breakfast 110F-135F. **Credit** AmEx, DC, MC, V. **Map L6**

Walking through one of the elegant arches of the
romantic Place des Vosges and into the leafy garden
of this ivy-covered mansion is a magical experience.
Inside, lavish furnishings, rustic beams and tapestries contribute to the feeling of tasteful luxury. The
55 rooms, some with romantic four-posters and all
with magnificent antique chests sourced from *brocantes*, overlook flower-filled courtyards.

Hotel services *Air con. Bar. Babysitting. Bureau
de change. Laundry. Lift. Parking. Porter.* **Room
services** *Hairdryer. Minibar. Room service (24-hr).
Safe. TV/VCR. Wheelchair-adapted rooms.*

Hôtel du Jeu de Paume

*54 rue St-Louis-en-l'Ile, 4th (01.43.26.14.18/
fax 01.40.46.02.76). M° Pont Marie.* **Rates** *single or
double* 950F-1625F; *junior suite* 2625F; *breakfast* 80F.
Credit AmEx, DC, MC, V. **Map K7**

This romantic hotel began life as a real tennis court,
ordered by Louis XIII in 1634, when the Ile St-Louis
was being developed with aristocratic homes.

Hôtel Costes: *are you frightfully fashionable
or wickedly decadent enough to stay here?*

Subsequently a warehouse and then a craftsmen's workshop, in 1988 the timber-framed court was converted into a dramatic, airy breakfast room, centrepiece of the 32-room hotel.
Hotel services *Babysitting. Bar. Conference services. Laundry. Lift. Porter. Sauna.* **Room services** *Hairdryer. Minibar. Radio. Room service (24-hr). TV. Whirlpool bath.*

Hôtel de l'Abbaye

10 rue Cassette, 6th (01.45.44.38.11/ fax 01.45.48.07.86). M° St-Sulpice. **Rates** *single or double* 1030F-1600F; *suite* 2100F-2200F; *breakfast included.* **Credit** AmEx, MC, V. **Map G7**
This tranquil hotel was originally part of a convent. Wood panelling, well-stuffed sofas and an open fireplace make for a relaxed atmosphere but, best of all, there's a surprisingly large garden where breakfast is served in warmer months. The 42 rooms are tasteful and luxurious. Suites have roof-top terraces.
Hotel services *Air con. Bar. Babysitting. Bar. Bureau de change. Garden. Laundry. Lift. Porter. Safe.* **Room services** *Hairdryer. Radio. Room service. TV.*

Hôtel Buci Latin

34 rue de Buci, 6th (01.43.29.07.20/ fax 01.43.29.67.44). M° St-Germain-des-Prés. **Rates** *single or double* 970F-1750F; *suite* 1750F; *breakfast included.* **Credit** AmEx, DC, MC, V. **Map H7**
In contrast to mock-ancient St-Germain hotels, the Buci Latin, above lively rue de Buci street market, is proudly postmodern. From papier-mâché lamps to high-backed chairs and colourful sculpture, the emphasis is on humorous elegance – you recognise your room by the painting on the key ring.
Hotel services *Air con. Babysitting. Bar. Bureau de change. Coffee shop. Laundry. Lift. Porter. Restaurant. Safe.* **Room services** *Hairdryer. Minibar. Modem link. Radio. Room service (24-hr). Safe. TV.*

L'Hôtel

13 rue des Beaux-Arts, 6th (01.43.25.27.22/ fax 01.43.25.64.81). M° Mabillon. **Rates** *single or double* 800F-2800F; *suite* 2000F-4000F; *breakfast* 110F. **Credit** AmEx, DC, MC, V. **Map H6**
Camp as a row of pink tents, L'Hôtel is a study in the art of over-the-top. Favourite rooms include the Oscar Wilde, where he 'died beyond his means'. Walls, curtains and bed are swathed in velvet with paintings and battered editions of the writer's work completing the picture. Room 34 is utterly fab, drowning in leopard-print fake fur, and the Chambre Mistinguett is brilliantly music hall. The bar features a horrible fountain, a random tree trunk and lurid green carpet. Popular with the fash-mag pack.
Hotel services *Air con. Bar. Bureau de change. Laundry. Lift. Porter. Restaurant.* **Room services** *Hairdryer. Minibar. Radio. Room service. Safe. TV.*

Hôtel Lutétia

45 bd Raspail, 6th (01.49.54.46.46/fax 01.49.54.46.00). M° Sèvres-Babylone. **Rates** *single or double* 1800F-2300F; *suite* 2800F-15,000F; *extra bed* 450F; *breakfast* 75F-135F. **Credit** AmEx, DC, MC, V. **Map G7**
A masterpiece of Art Nouveau and early Art Deco architecture, the Lutétia opened in 1910 to serve shoppers coming to the Bon Marché. In a less-

glorious interlude, it was used by the Gestapo during the Occupation. Its 250 rooms, revamped in purple, gold and pearl grey, maintain an elegant 30s feel.
Hotel services *Air con. Babysitting. Bar. Bureau de change. Conference services. Laundry. Lift. Parking. Porter. Restaurants.* **Room services** *Hairdryer. Minibar. Modem link. Radio. Room service (24-hr). Safe. TV.*

Relais St-Germain

9 carrefour de l'Odéon, 6th (01.43.29.12.05/ fax 01.46.33.45.30). M° Odéon. **Rates** *single* 1290F; *double* 1600F-1850F; *suite* 2100F; *extra bed* 250F; *breakfast included.* **Credit** AmEx, DC, MC, V. **Map H7**
Near the Odéon theatre, this hotel has preserved the character of its seventeenth-century building. The 22 generous rooms are tasteful, combining antique furnishings, beautiful fabrics and modern fittings; each is named after a French writer, such as the lovely 'Molière' suite. Discreet and accommodating service.
Hotel services *Air con. Bar. Babysitting. Laundry. Lift. Porter. Safe.* **Room services** *Fax. Hairdryer. Minibar. Modem link. Radio. Room service. Safe. TV/VCR.*

La Villa

29 rue Jacob, 6th (01.43.26.60.00/ fax 01.46.34.63.63). M° St-Germain-des-Prés. **Rates** *double/twin* 900F-1800F; *suites* 2000F-3000F. *Breakfast* 80F. **Credit** V, MC, AmEx. **Map H6**
With purple leather everywhere and loud, funky lift music, this is the Keith Richards of Paris hotels. The feel is gaudy, gauche and bloody good fun. The room numbers are projected on to the floor in front of your door (presumably in case it's hard to see straight), and the beds feature sexy leather headboards. The whole place looks like it's spent too long partying too hard, but it's definitely still up for it.
Hotel services *Air con. Babysitting. Bar. Laundry. Lift. Porter.* **Room services** *Hairdryer. Minibar. Room service. Safe. TV.*

Hôtel Duc de Saint-Simon

14 rue de St-Simon, 7th (01.44.39.20.20/ fax 01.45.48.68.25). M° Rue du Bac. **Rates** *single or double* 1350F-1475F; *suite* 1900F-1950F; *breakfast* 70F. **Credit** AmEx, MC, V. **Map F6**
Stepping off the quiet side street into a pretty courtyard gives you a taste of the delights inside. A beautiful living room with the hotel's own-design yellow fabric is as relaxing as the 34 individually decorated bedrooms. Four rooms have terraces above a leafy garden, and the ancient cellars have been neatly converted into a bar, salon and breakfast room.
Hotel services *Babysitting. Bar. Fax. Laundry. Lift. Porter.* **Room services** *Hairdryer. Modem link. Room service. Safe. TV (on request).*

Le Montalembert

3 rue de Montalembert, 7th (01.45.49.68.68/ fax 01.45.49.69.49). M° Rue du Bac. **Rates** *single or double* 1750F-2300F; *suite* 2850F-4400F; *breakfast* 100F. **Credit** AmEx, DC, MC, V. **Map G6**
A successful fusion of traditional and modern lies behind the 1926 Beaux Arts facade of this luxurious hotel. A corner with comfy sofas and open fireplace, a sprinkling of tribal art and a helpful young staff add up to a very stylish sleep. Décor in the 56 rooms ranges from Louis-Philippe to contemporary.

Hotel services *Air con. Babysitting. Bar. Conference facilities. Bureau de change. Laundry. Lift. Porter. Restaurant.* Room services *Fax. Hairdryer. Minibar. Modem link. Radio. Room service (24-hr). Safe. TV/VCR.*

Hôtel Lancaster

7 rue de Berri, 8th (01.40.76.40.76/fax 01.40.76.40.00). M° George V. Rates *single 1650F-1950F; double 2350F-2750F; suite 4500F-10,000F; breakfast 120F.* Credit AmEx, DC, MC, V. Map D4

This elegant townhouse has 60 individually designed rooms, offset by a private collection of *objets d'art.* Going for understated luxury rather then full-blown flash, the Lancaster was a second home to those who wanted to be alone, such as Marlene Dietrich and Greta Garbo.

Hotel services *Air con. Conference services. Health club. Lift. Parking. Porter.* Room services *Double glazing. Hairdryer. Minibar. Safe. TV/VCR.*

Hôtel Sofitel Le Faubourg

15 rue Boissy d'Anglas, 8th (01.44.94.14.00/ fax 01.44.94.14.28). M° Concorde. Rates *single or double 1900-3200F; junior suite 2200F-4000F; suite 4000F-15,000F; breakfast 125F.* Credit AmEx, DC, MC, V. Map F5

The centrepiece of this hotel is the skylit lobby, where sharp suits and slightly-too-wide ties mix with linen dresses and the occasional tracksuit and baseball cap combo. The 174 rooms combine Parisian tradition and contemporary touches with a prevailing sense of calm. The restaurant, Café Faubourg, is an essential lunch address for Fbg-St-Honoré junkies.

Hotel services *Air con. Bar. Health club. Lift. Parking. Porter. Restaurant.* Room services *Triple glazing. Hairdryer. Minibar. Modem. Room service. Safe. TV/VCR.*

Hôtel Scribe

1 rue Scribe, 9th (01.44.71.24.24/fax 01.42.65.39.97). M° Opéra. Rates *single or double 2275F-2700F; suite 3835F-5590F; breakfast 110F-140F.* Credit AmEx, V, MC. Map G4

A few steps from the Opéra Garnier, the Scribe is a study in discreet, intimate comfort: its hallmarks are Haussmannian architecture, Empire furniture, Baccarat chandeliers, rich fabrics and spacious duplex suites. It has a rich artistic history: the Lumière brothers held the world's first public film projection here in 1895. Hemingway and Proust were *habitués* and, more recently, in January '99, the Scribe invited 13 artists to set up installations in the rooms.

Hotel services *Air con. Bar. Lift. Restaurant.* Room services *Air con. Hairdryer. Minibar. Modem link. Safe. TV.*

Hôtel Pergolèse

3 rue Pergolèse, 16th (01.53.64.04.04/ fax 01.53.64.04.40). M° Porte Maillot or Argentine. Rates *single 1000F-1300F; double 1100F-1500F; junior suite 1600F-1800F; breakfast 70F-95F.* Credit AmEx, DC, MC, V. Map B3

This hotel near the Bois de Boulogne boasts a futuristic yet soothing interior. From the lounge's leather sofas and Dalek-like chairs you see a small Japanese-style garden through a curved glass wall. The breakfast room has dynamic Philippe Starck and Hilton

McConnico furniture. The 40 rooms combine grey, pinks and peaches with ash and mahogany furniture.

Hotel services *Air con. Babysitting. Bar. Bureau de change. Laundry. Lift. Porter.* Room services *Hairdryer. Minibar. Modem link. Radio. Room service (24-hr). Safe. TV.*

Hôtel Square

3 rue de Boulainvilliers, 16th (01.44.14.91.90/ fax 01.44.14.91.99). M° Passy/RER Kennedy-Radio France. Rates *single or double 1400F-1800F; suite 2100F-2600F; breakfast 50F-90F.* Credit AmEx, DC, MC, V. Map A7

Though the polished granite curtain wall may look forbidding, the dramatic interior of this courageously modern hotel is welcoming, aided by the personalised service that comes with only 22 rooms. The exotic woods, quality fabrics and paint finishes are striking. The temporary exhibitions in the narrow atrium are by leading artists, such as Ben and Viallat.

Hotel services *Air con. Bar. Babysitting. Conference services. Bureau de change. Laundry. Lift. Porter. Restaurant.* Room services *Fax. Hairdryer. Minibar. Modem. Radio. Room service (24-hr). Safe. TV/VCR.*

Terrass Hôtel

12-14 rue Joseph-de-Maistre, 18th (01.46.06.72.85/ fax 01.42.52.29.11). M° Place de Clichy. Rates *single 1110F-1260F; double 1320F-1470F; suite 1760F; breakfast included.* Credit AmEx, DC, MC, V. Map H1

A stately building near the Montmartre cemetery, with superb views over Paris, the Terrass is owned by the family who built it over 80 years ago. Of 101

L'Hôtel: *a study in the art of over-the-top.*

rooms, 75 are air-conditioned, and an entire floor is non-smoking. A piano bar entertains downstairs, but in good weather go for the roof-terrace restaurant. **Hotel services** *Air con. Bar. Babysitting. Conference services. Bureau de change. Laundry. Lift. Porter. Restaurant.* **Room services** *Hairdryer. Minibar. Radio. Room service. TV.*

Moderate

Hôtel Brighton

218 rue de Rivoli, 1st (01.47.03.61.61/ fax 01.42.60.41.78). Mº Tuileries or Concorde. **Rates** *single* 410F-890F; *double* 650F-890F; *triple* 1025F-1125F; *breakfast* 35F. **Credit** AmEx, DC, MC, V. **Map G5**
The Brighton had been left behind by its luxurious neighbours, offering rue de Rivoli status and Tuileries views at low prices; but a year-long renovation started in March 1999 and prices may rise after completion. Half of the hotel remains open, so the huge rooms, mosaiqued hallway and *faux* marble-columned *salon de thé* can still be enjoyed. **Hotel services** *Bureau de change. Laundry. Lift. Porter. Safe. Tearoom.* **Room services** *Double glazing. Hairdryer. Minibar. TV.*

Le Britannique

20 av Victoria, 1st (01.42.33.74.59/ fax 01.42.33.82.65). Mº Châtelet. **Rates** *single* 725F; *double* 870F-995F; *extra bed* 130F; *breakfast* 60F. **Credit** AmEx, DC, MC, V. **Map J6**
A courteous welcome is offered at this elegant hotel. The English-style sitting room is furnished with burgundy leather chesterfields, model ships and old hat boxes. The 40 recently refurbished rooms have plush vine-pattern curtains and bedcovers. The stand of umbrellas waiting to be borrowed on a rainy day provides an old-fashioned touch of class. **Hotel services** *Laundry. Lift.* **Room services** *Double glazing. Hairdryer. Safe. Minibar. TV.*

Hôtel des Tuileries

10 rue St-Hyacinthe, 1st (01.42.61.04.17/ fax 01.49.27.91.56). Mº Pyramides. **Rates** *single* 790F-1200F; *double* 890F-1200F; *triple* 1400F; *breakfast* 60F. **Credit** AmEx, DC, MC, V. **Map G5**
This is a delightful small hotel on a quiet street near the Tuileries. Ethnic rugs, antique furniture and original pictures decorate the lobby and 26 rooms, and the centrepiece is a listed spiral staircase. The cellar breakfast room gets natural light from an interior greenhouse. The sumptuous yet homely result is popular with the fashion world, so book ahead. **Hotel services** *Air con. Laundry. Lift. Porter. Small meeting room.* **Room services** *Double glazing. Hairdryer. Minibar. Safe. TV.*

Hôtel Baudelaire Opéra

61 rue Ste-Anne, 2nd (01.42.97.50.62/ fax 01.42.86.85.85). Mº Opéra or Pyramides. **Rates** *single* 500F-540F; *double* 640F-700F; *triple* 760F-830F; *breakfast* 42F. **Credit** AmEx, DC, MC, V. **Map H4**
Historical vibes ooze from the walls of this well-situated hotel. Baudelaire lodged here and Céline lived in the passage next door. During the Counter

Reformation, Protestants were forcibly converted to Catholicism in the basement. Thankfully, today's management is more tolerant. The 29 rooms are decorated in bright colours, and five have mezzanines. **Hotel services** *Lift. Safe.* **Room services** *Double glazing. Hairdryer. Minibar. TV.*

Hôtel Caron de Beaumarchais

12 rue Vieille-du-Temple, 4th (01.42.72.34.12/ fax 01.42.72.34.63). Mº St-Paul. **Rates** *single or double* 730F-810F; *breakfast* 54F, *brunch* 78F. **Credit** AmEx, DC, MC, V. **Map K6**
Named after the eighteenth-century playwright who lived just up the street, this charming Marais hotel recreates the refined tastes of Beaumarchais' era, from gilded mirrors to Chinese-style bathroom tiling. The 19 rooms are comfortable if not always spacious. **Hotel services** *Air con. Laundry. Lift. Safe.* **Room services** *Double glazing. Hairdryer. Minibar. TV.*

Hôtel des Deux-Iles

59 rue St-Louis-en-l'Ile, 4th (01.43.26.13.35/ fax 01.43.29.60.25). Mº Pont-Marie. **Rates** *single* 750F; *double* 860F; *breakfast* 52F. **Credit** AmEx, MC, V. **Map K7**
This refined, peaceful hotel in a seventeenth-century townhouse on Ile St-Louis has been done up in faintly colonial style with cane furniture, print curtains and a lovely fireplace in the lobby. The **Hôtel de Lutèce** at No 65 (01.43.26.23.52), under the same management, displays a similar sense of period style. **Hotel services** *Air con. Lift.* **Room services** *Hairdryer. Safe. TV.*

Grand Hôtel Malher

5 rue Malher, 4th (01.42.72.60.92/ fax 01.42.72.25.37). Mº St-Paul. **Rates** *single* 490F-640F; *double* 590F-740F; *suite* 890F-990F; *breakfast* 47F. **Credit** AmEx, MC, V. **Map L6**
The hotel's glossy dark green frontage is impressive and in the airy reception there are large mirrors, a smart marble floor and elegant turquoise window drapes; steep stairs lead down to a seventeenth-century vaulted breakfast room. The 31 cosy rooms have tasteful colour schemes and clean, simple bathrooms. **Hotel services** *Lift. Small conference room. No-smoking rooms. Safe.* **Room services** *Double glazing. Hairdryer. Minibar. TV.*

Hôtel St-Louis Marais

1 rue Charles V, 4th (01.48.87.87.04/ fax 01.48.87.33.26). Mº Sully-Morland or Bastille. **Rates** *single* 400F-550F; *double* 650F-750F; *triple* 950F; *breakfast* 45F. **Credit** MC, V. **Map L7**
At this restful Marais hotel, the reception is reminiscent of a stately home. The 17th-century beams, wooden furnishings and plush carpets give a homely feel to the 16 dark green or deep rose rooms. Look out for a section of arch originally part of an external doorway as you climb the old spiral staircase. **Hotel services** *Laundry. Safe.* **Room services** *Double glazing. Hairdryer. TV.*

Hôtel St-Merri

78 rue de la Verrerie, 4th (01.42.78.14.15/ fax 01.40.29.06.82). Mº Hôtel-de-Ville. **Rates** *single or double* 450F-1100F; *triple* 1300F; *suite* 1800F-2400F;

breakfast 50F. **Credit** AmEx, MC, V. **Map K6**
Nestled against the Gothic church of the same name, the 17th-century St-Merri basks in eccentricity. First the church presbytery, later a brothel, it was bought in 1962 by Christian Crabbe, who has transformed the eleven rooms and one suite by scouring antique salesrooms. A confessional box serves as a phone cubicle and iron candelabras, stone walls and beams add to the charm. The biggest surprise is the flying buttress straddling the bed in No 9. Book in advance. **Hotel services** *Safe.* **Room services** *Double glazing. Hairdryer.*

Les Degrés de Notre Dame
10 rue des Grands-Degrés, 5th (01.55.42.88.88/ fax 01.40.46.95.34). M° Maubert-Mutualité. **Rates** *single* 430F, *double* 600F, *studio* 600F-665F, *breakfast included.* **Credit** MC, V. **Map J7**
Masses of dark wood and lovingly tended rooms make this hotel set back from the Seine a real find. Other assets include Betty, the friendly hostess, and the cunningly concealed studios, some of the best-value places to stay in Paris. The price of a characterless box in most Left Bank hotels gets you one of two studios a few streets away from the hotel, complete with washing machine, power shower and, in one flat, a conservatory filled with fresh flowers. **Room services** *Hairdryer. TV.*

Hôtel des Grands Hommes
17 pl du Panthéon, 5th (01.46.34.19.60/ fax 01.43.26.67.32). RER Luxembourg. **Rates** *single* 700F; *double* 800F; *triple* 900F; *suite* 1200F; *breakfast* 50F. **Credit** AmEx, DC, MC, V. **Map J7**
The Panthéon (resting place of the 'great men' of the name) looms over this eighteenth-century hotel. André Breton invented automatic writing here in 1919. The 32 good-sized rooms have exposed beams, iron bedheads and awesome views from the sixth-floor. **Hotel services** *Air con. Babysitting. Meeting room. Lift. Safe.* **Room services** *Hairdryer. Minibar. TV.*

Hôtel Jardins du Luxembourg
5 impasse Royer-Collard, 5th (01.40.46.08.88/ fax 01.40.46.02.28). RER Luxembourg. **Rates** *single or double* 790F-840F; *breakfast* 50F. **Credit** AmEx, DC, MC, V. **Map H8**
It would be hard to find a quieter location than this cul-de-sac near the Jardins du Luxembourg. Freud stayed here in 1885 so it's probably a good place to come to sort out your ego. Kilim rugs, stripped floorboards and vivid paintwork and floor tiles help keep self-reflective gloom at bay. Even better than Prozac. **Hotel services** *Air con. Laundry. Lift. Sauna.* **Room services** *Hairdryer. Minibar. Safe. TV.*

Hôtel d'Angleterre
44 rue Jacob, 6th (01.42.60.34.72/fax 01.42.60.16.93). M° St-Germain des Prés. **Rates** *single or double* 700F-1200F; *suite* 1500F; *extra bed* 250F; *breakfast* 60F. **Credit** AmEx, DC, MC, V. **Map H6**
Low-key elegance prevails at this former British embassy where the US independence treaty was prepared in 1783. Climb the listed staircase or tinkle away at the grand piano in the salon. Some of the 27 rooms look over the ivy-strewn courtyard which is

the heart of the hotel. Most rooms are a good size. **Hotel services** *Lift (not to all rooms).* **Room services** *Double glazing. Hairdryer. Safe. TV.*

Hôtel Bonaparte
61 rue Bonaparte, 6th (01.43.26.97.37/ fax 01.46.33.57.67). M° St-Sulpice. **Rates** *single* 490F-590F; *double* 620F-745F; *triple* 820F; *breakfast included.* **Credit** MC, V. **Map G7**
Fresh flowers grace this small hotel among the boutiques of St-Sulpice. Behind a Neo-Classical entrance are 29 spacious rooms. The best are on the street side, with decorative fireplaces and gilt mirrors. **Hotel services** *Air con. Lift.* **Room services** *Double glazing. Hairdryer. Safe. TV.*

Hôtel du Danemark
21 rue Vavin, 6th (01.43.26.93.78/ fax 01.46.34.66.06). M° Notre-Dame-des-Champs. **Rates** *single* 620F-690F; *double* 690F-790F; *breakfast* 55F. **Credit** AmEx, DC, MC, V.
The Danemark has a sleek boutique-y look that tones in with the shops along this Montparnasse street near the Jardins du Luxembourg. The décor consists of a modern riot of zigzag rugs and artworks downstairs and new fittings in the 15 rooms. **Hotel services** *Lift. Safe.* **Room services** *Hairdryer. Minibar. Room service. TV.*

Hôtel du Danube
58 rue Jacob, 6th (01.42.60.34.70/ fax 01.42.60.81.18). M° St-Germain des Prés. **Rates** *single or double* 650F-880F; *suite* 1150F; *extra bed* 200F; *breakfast* 50F. **Credit** AmEx, MC, V. **Map H6**
This pretty, family-run hotel spreads over two eighteenth-century buildings around a small courtyard. Styles vary from Chinese to Victorian, with lots of individually chosen furniture. The lounge is overly chintzy, but the breakfast room is charming. **Hotel services** *Lift.* **Room services** *Hairdryer. TV.*

Hôtel Louis II
2 rue St-Sulpice, 6th (01.46.33.13.80/ fax 01.46.33.17.29). M° Odéon. **Rates** *single or double* 555F-820F; *triple* 980F; *breakfast* 52F. **Credit** AmEx, DC, MC, V. **Map H7**
Beams and half-timbered partitions abound in this ancient building in St-Germain. Rooms are small but light, and decorated with amusing, vaguely Gothic fittings and floral wallpaper. The salon has the charming air of a provincial house. **Hotel services** *Lift.* **Room services** *Hairdryer. Minibar. Safe. TV.*

Hôtel des Marronniers
21 rue Jacob, 6th (01.43.25.30.60/ fax 01.40.46.83.56). M° St-Germain des Prés. **Rates** *single* 560F; *double* 755F-905F; *triple* 980F-1080F; *extra bed* 190F; *breakfast* 50F. **Credit** MC, V. **Map H6**
An oasis of calm in lively St-Germain, this hotel has a paved courtyard in front and a lovely conservatory and garden at the back, where you'll find the chestnut trees of the name. The 37 rooms are mostly reasonably sized, with pretty canopies and fabrics. **Hotel services** *Air con. Bar. Conference facilities. Garden. Lift. Safe.* **Room services** *Double glazing. Hairdryer. TV.*

Hôtel Chopin: *for a romantic interlude amid old-fashioned toy shops and printsellers.*

Hôtel Lenox
*9 rue de l'Université, 7th (01.42.96.10.95/
fax 01.42.61.52.63). M° Rue du Bac.* **Rates** *single or
double* 680F-1100F; *duplex* 1500F; *breakfast* 45F.
Credit AmEx, DC, MC, V. **Map G6**
Arty types linger in the bar of this stylish hotel, much
as Hemingway is said to have done. A predominance
of leather, wood and plants add to the air of earnest
artistic endeavour. Handpainted furniture brightens
up some of the 34 tasteful rooms. Also owns the
Hôtel Lenox in Montparnasse (15 rue Delambre,
14th/01.43.35.34.50/ double 560F-690F).
Hotel services *Babysitting. Bar. Laundry. Lift.
Safe.* **Room services** *Hairdryer. Radio. TV.*

Hôtel St-Germain
*88 rue du Bac, 7th (01.49.54.70.00/fax 01.45.48.26.89).
M° Rue du Bac.* **Rates** *double/ twin* 500F-850F;
breakfast 55F. **Credit** AmEx, MC, V. **Map G6**
The flamboyant patron of this hotel is very arts oriented and provides an impressive collection of
coffee-table books and exhibition catalogues. The
place is awash in exposed stone and squishy leather
sofas, and there's a delightful conservatory. The
rooms are slightly disappointing: one is enveloped in
a furious shade of raspberry; another has curtains
that look like imitation Hermès-does-the-Punjab.
Hotel services *Lift .* **Room services** *Safe. TV.*

Hôtel de l'Université
*22 rue de l'Université, 7th (01.42.61.09.39/
fax 01.42.60.40.84). M° Rue du Bac.* **Rates** *single*
500F-700F; *double* 850F-1300F; *triple* 1100F-1500F;
extra bed 200F; *breakfast* 50F. **Credit** AmEx, MC, V.
Map G6
A short walk from the Musée d'Orsay, this spacious

27-room hotel is full of antique wardrobes, warm
colours, velvety carpets and soft furnishings. The elegant vaulted cellar rooms can be hired for functions.
Hotel services *Air con. Lift.* **Room services**
Hairdryer. Safe. TV.

Hôtel Le Lavoisier
*21 rue Lavoisier, 8th (01.53.30.06.06/
fax 01.53.30.23.00). M° St-Augustin.* **Rates** *single or
double* 790F-1190F *(with terrace* 1290F-1490F); *junior
suite* 1690F-1890F; *suite* 1890F-2090F; *extra bed* 100F;
breakfast 70F. **Credit** AmEx, MC, V. **Map F3**
Reopened in March 99 after a complete refit by
designer Jean-Philippe Nuel, the 30-room Le Lavoisier
is a classy affair. Décor is refined and warm, and the
furniture mixes periods and styles to striking effect.
Hotel services *Air con. Lift. Safe.* **Room services**
Hairdryer. Room service. TV.

Hôtel Belle Epoque
*66 rue de Charenton, 12th (01.43.44.06.66/
fax 01.43.44.10.25). M° Bastille.* **Rates** *single*
595F-800F; *double* 650F-820F; *triple* 970F; *breakfast*
55F-75F. **Credit** AmEx, DC, MC, V. **Map M7**
Behind an old façade near the Bastille, this modern
hotel has 31 pleasant rooms decorated with Art Deco-
style furniture based on Printz and Ruhlmann. The
reception, with large club chairs, opens on to a small
courtyard with vines and tables.
Hotel services *Air con. Bar. Laundry. Lift.
Meeting rooms.* **Room services** *Double glazing.
Hairdryer. Minibar. Safe. TV.*

Hôtel Résidence Bouquet de Longchamp
*6 rue du Bouquet de Longchamp, 16th (01.47.04.41.71/
fax 01.47.27.29.09). M° Boissière or Iéna.* **Rates**
single 456F-676F; *double* 512F-752F; *extra bed* 106F;

breakfast 50F. **Credit** AmEx, DC, MC, V. **Map** C5
Hidden down a backstreet near the Palais de Chaillot
is this hotel run by a friendly Austrian who speaks
German, French and English. 17 cosy rooms are nicely decorated in pastel blues or yellows. There's a delicate courtyard with climbing plants.
Room services *Minibar. Room service (24-hr). TV.*

Hôtel de Banville

166 bd Berthier, 17th (01.42.67.70.16/
fax 01.44.40.42.77). M° Porte de Champerret. **Rates**
single 760F; *double* 890F-1050F; *suite* 1450F; *extra bed*
100F; *breakfast* 65F. **Credit** AmEx, DC, MC, V. **Map** C1
Marianne Moreau's mother and grandmother preceded her here and personal touches are proudly maintained. Each of the 38 rooms is individually designed,
with iron or brass beds and warm Italianate colours.
The breakfast room has a *trompe l'oeil*: you can almost
imagine you are among trees and climbing roses.
Hotel services *Air con. Laundry. Lift.* **Room**
services *Safe. TV.*

Hôtel Regent's Garden

6 rue Pierre-Demours, 17th (01.45.74.07.30/
fax 01.40.55.01.42). M° Charles de Gaulle-Etoile or
Ternes. **Rates** *single* 710F-1030F; *double*
780F-1400F; *extra bed* 120F; *breakfast* 50F. **Credit**
AmEx, DC, MC, V. **Map** C3
High ceilings and plush upholstery in the foyer hark
back to the Second Empire, when this house was built
for Napoléon III's physician. The refinement continues in 39 large bedrooms, some with gilt mirrors and
fireplaces. With its walled garden, this is an oasis of
calm ten minutes from the Arc de Triomphe. It is a
Best Western, but doesn't feel at all like a chain.
Hotel services *Air con. Bureau de change. Garden.*
Lift. Laundry. Parking. Safe. **Room services**
Double glazing. Hairdryer. Minibar. Radio. TV.

Inexpensive

Hôtel du Cygne

3 rue du Cygne, 1st (01.42.60.14.16/
fax 01.42.21.37.02). M° Etienne Marcel or Châtelet.
Rates *single* 280F-375F; *double* 420F-490F; *breakfast*
35F. **Credit** MC, V. **Map** J5
The Cygne occupies a renovated seventeenth-century
building in pedestrianised Les Halles. Exposed beams
abound, while furniture bought at *brocantes* by the
two sister-owners adds interest. Rooms are on the
small side, but the 490F 'La Grande' under the eaves
is particularly delightful.
Room services *Hairdryer. Safe. TV.*

Hôtel Vivienne

40 rue Vivienne, 2nd (01.42.33.13.26/
fax 01.40.41.98.19). M° Bourse or Grands
Boulevards. **Rates** *single* 450F; *double* 470F-515F;
triple 650F; *breakfast* 40F. **Credit** MC, V. **Map** H7
Soft yellows and oranges in the reception, wood
floors, chandeliers and wicker add to the charm of
this hotel that seems to have stepped straight out of
a Van Gogh. Barely a stone's throw from the Palais
Garnier and the *grands magasins*.
Hotel services *Lift. Safe.* **Room services**
Hairdryer. TV.

Alhotel Vertus

5 rue des Vertus, 3rd (01.44.61.89.50/
fax 01.48.04.33.72). M° Arts et Métiers. **Rates**
single 450F-480F; *double* 550F-580F; *suite* 680F-710F;
breakfast 38F. **Credit** AmEx, DC, MC, V. **Map** K5
In a renovated seventeenth-century building with
exposed stone walls, this small hotel is decked out in
pale wood and plush green carpets. Its nine rooms
combine original features with modern conveniences.
Hotel services *Laundry. Lift. Safe.* **Room**
services *Double glazing. Hairdryer. TV.*

Grand Hôtel Jeanne d'Arc

3 rue de Jarente, 4th (01.48.87.62.11/
fax 01.48.87.37.31). M° St-Paul. **Rates** *single*
300F-400F; *double* 305F-500F; *triple* 640F; *quad* 600F;
extra bed 75F; *breakfast* 35F. **Credit** MC, V. **Map** L6
The attractive stone-built Jeanne d'Arc is on the corner of a pretty Marais street. Inside are interesting
touches, from 3D door numbers and murals to the
heraldic mosaic mirror in the reception area. The
cheapest of the 36 rooms are small but still good value.
Hotel services *Lift.* **Room services** *TV.*

Hôtel de la Place des Vosges

12 rue de Birague, 4th (01.42.72.60.46/
fax 01.42.72.02.64). M° Bastille or St-Paul. **Rates**
single 365F-485F; *double* 545F-580F; *breakfast* 35F.
Credit AmEx, DC, MC, V. **Map** L6
A few steps from the place des Vosges is this former
muleteer's house, dating from the same period.
There is now an elegant reception, salon and breakfast area. The 16 bedrooms are plainer, but still comfortable. Bathrooms are being refitted in green and
grey marble. There are views over the rooftops from
the top floors, but the lift only goes to the fourth.
Hotel services *Lift. Safe.*
Room services *Hairdryer. TV.*

Hôtel Sansonnet

48 rue de la Verrerie, 4th (01.48.87.96.14/
fax 01.48.87.30.46). M° Hôtel-de-Ville. **Rates** *single*
270F-395F; *double* 400F-440F; *shower* 20F; *breakfast*
33F. **Credit** MC, V. **Map** K6
Behind the listed façade of this Marais building are 25
quiet rooms in a jumble of corridors and wrought- iron
staircases. The rooms are reasonably sized and simply furnished – most singles lack toilet or bathroom,
but all doubles are en suite. The manager of 30 years
gives guests a calm, patient welcome.
Hotel services *Safe.* **Room services** *Double*
glazing. Hairdryer. Room service. TV.

Hôtel du Septième Art

20 rue St-Paul, 4th (01.44.54.85.00/fax
01.42.77.69.10). M° St-Paul. **Rates** *single* 295F-670F;
double 420F-670F; *suite* 620F-670F; *extra bed* 100F;
breakfast 45F. **Credit** AmEx, DC, MC, V. **Map** L7
A movie buff's dream, the Septième Art is stuffed
with film posters and Hollywood memorabilia. The
theme continues with black-and-white checked
floors in reception, while the 23 bedrooms are more
sober in beige and paisley. Popular with media
types, this is a fun, upbeat hotel.
Hotel services *Bar. Washer/dryer (30F/35F).*
Room services *Hairdryer. Safe. TV.*

Familia Hôtel

*11 rue des Ecoles, 5th (01.43.54.55.27/
fax 01.43.29.61.77). Mº Maubert-Mutualité.* **Rates**
single or double 380F-550F; *triple* 620F-680F; *quad*
620F-750F; *breakfast* 30F, 35F in room. **Credit**
AmEx, DC, MC, V. **Map J7**
An enthusiastic welcome awaits at this old-fashioned
hotel whose balconies are hung with plants. Chatty
owner Eric Gaucheron will help you with local lore,
and is immensely proud of the sepia murals and
mahogany furniture in some of the 30 rooms.
Hotel services *Lift. Safe.* **Room services** *Double
glazing. Hairdryer. Minibar. TV.*

Hôtel Esmeralda

*4 rue St-Julien-le-Pauvre, 5th (01.43.54.19.20/
fax 01.40.51.00.68). Mº St-Michel.* **Rates** *single*
160F-420F; *double* 450F-490F; *triple* 550F; *quad* 600F;
breakfast 40F. **No credit cards. Map J7**
This 1640 building looks on to a tree-lined square
and over the Seine to Notre Dame. In the plant-filled
entrance, the resident cat may be curled up in a velvet
chair. Upstairs are 19 floral rooms with antique furnishings and uneven floors. Great location and good
value, the Esmeralda is a cult address so book ahead.
Hotel services *Safe.*

Hôtel des Grandes Ecoles

*75 rue du Cardinal-Lemoine, 5th (01.43.26.79.23/
fax 01.43.25.28.15). Mº Cardinal-Lemoine.* **Rates**
single or double 530F-690F; *triple* 670F-790F;
quad 890F; *extra bed* 100F; *breakfast* 45F.
Credit MC, V. **Map K8**
The Grandes Ecoles stands behind high walls and
you can breakfast in the lovely garden in summer.
There are 51 rustic rooms in three buildings; the
largest also houses the reception area, and an old-
fashioned breakfast room with gilt mirror and piano.
Hotel services *Garden. Lift. Parking (100F). Safe.*
Room services *Double glazing. Hairdryer.*

Hôtel St-Jacques

*35 rue des Ecoles, 5th (01.44.07.45.45/
fax 01.43.25.65.50). Mº Maubert-Mutualité.* **Rates**
single 250F-480F; *double* 420-580F; *triple* 580F-650F;
breakfast 35F. **Credit** AmEx, DC, MC, V. **Map J7**
The new owner has kept the nineteenth-century
atmosphere, while renovating to a high standard. The
35 rooms are spacious, with high ceilings and fresh
fabrics. Original painted ceilings have been uncovered during renovation. Audrey Hepburn and Cary
Grant were filmed here in the 50s comedy *Charade.*
Hotel services *Lift. Safe.* **Room services** *Double
glazing. Hairdryer (in most rooms). TV.*

Les Argonautes

*12 rue de la Huchette, 5th (01.43.54.09.82/
fax 01.44.07.18.84). Mº St-Michel.* **Rates** *single*
255F-355F; *double* 360F-410F; *breakfast included.*
Credit AmEx, MC, V. **MapJ7**
The proprietor has a penchant for leopard-print and
peroxide and the public areas reflect this. Gaudy fabrics, overstuffed sofas and a couple of *louche* felines
decorate the reception. Rooms are clean and simple.
Les Argonautes is in the heart of Paris' 'kebab kingdom'. So if you don't mind dodging touts hassling you

to enjoy three courses for 50F, you're on a roll.
Hotel services *Lift.*

Hôtel des Trois Collèges

*16 rue Cujas, 5th (01.43.54.67.30/fax 01.46.34.02.99).
RER Luxembourg or Mº Cluny-La Sorbonne.* **Rates**
single 400F-610F; *double* 500F-700F; *triple* 800F;
breakfast 42F. **Credit** AmEx, DC, MC, V. **Map J7**
On a quiet street in the Latin Quarter, this contemporary hotel has 44 nicely decorated, if not large
rooms. The breakfast room turns into a pleasant
salon de thé in the afternoons.
Hotel services *Lift. Safe. Tearoom.* **Room
services** *Double glazing. Hairdryer. TV.*

Hôtel du Globe

*15 rue des Quatre-Vents, 6th (01.43.26.35.50/
fax 01.46.33.62.69). Mº Odéon.* **Rates** *single or
double* 390F-565F; *breakfast* 45F. **Credit** AmEx, MC,
V. **Map H7**
The Globe is an eccentric and appealing mix of
styles. Gothic wrought-iron doors lead into florid
corridors, and an unexplained suit of armour super-
vises guests from the tiny salon. A small, winding
staircase may lead to suitcase trouble. Good value.
Room services *Radio. TV.*

Hôtel du Lys

*23 rue Serpente, 6th (01.43.26.97.57/
fax 01.44.07.34.90). Mº Odéon or St-Michel.* **Rates**
single 380F-490F; *double* 520F; *triple* 620F; *breakfast
included.* **Credit** MC, V. **Map H7**
Set back from the traffic fumes of the bd St Michel,

Hôtel du Septième Art: *a film buff's dream.*

this is a haven from the tourist hell outside. With only two tiny singles, it's clear that Bridget Jones types need not apply, but it's the perfect spot for a bargain romantic weekend. The proprietors are charming and take great pride in maintaining the prevailing calm. If you do get round to leaving your room, you'll have St Germain and the Seine on your doorstep.
Room services *Hairdryer. Safe. TV.*

Hôtel St-André-des-Arts

66 rue St-André-des-Arts, 6th (01.43.26.96.16/ fax 01.43.29.73.34). M° Odéon. **Rates** *single 370F; double 470F-510F; triple 580F; quad 640F; breakfast included.* **Credit** MC, V. **Map H7**
In the thick of St-Germain is this sixteenth-century building with an abundance of old beams and stone walls. Once occupied by the king's musketeers, the hotel boasts 33 pleasant rooms and smart bathrooms.
Hotel services *Safe.*

Hôtel de Nevers

83 rue du Bac, 7th (01.45.44.61.30/ fax 01.42.22.29.47). M° Rue du Bac. **Rates** *single 430F; double 480F-540F; extra bed 100F; breakfast 35F.* **No credit cards. Map G6**
This characterful eleven-room hotel was once part of a convent. Everything is scaled down, with mini-wardrobes and neat bathrooms. Rooms are smart, but paintwork on the staircase seems to suffer regular torment as guests carry luggage up. If you can make it to the fourth floor, two rooms have tiny terraces.
Hotel services *Safe.* **Room services** *Minibar. TV.*

Hôtel des Arts

7 cité Bergère, 9th (01.42.46.73.30/ fax 01.48.00.94.42). M° Grands Boulevards. **Rates** *single 360F-380F; double 380F-400F; triple 530F; breakfast 33F.* **Credit** AmEx, DC, MC, V. **Map J4**
In a tiny, tranquil alley of hotels, this is the best, if most unconventional, of the cheapies. Run by the friendly Bernard family, the reception area is bohemian, with Babar the parrot, a bubbling fish tank, and a gaudy grandfather clock. The stairwells are pasted over with theatre and museum posters. The 26 rooms vary in size and species of flowery wallpaper, but all are fresh and clean.
Hotel services *Laundry. Lift. Parking. Safe.* **Room services** *Double glazing. Hairdryer. Radio. TV.*

Hôtel Chopin

46 passage Jouffroy or 10 bd Montmartre, 9th (01.47.70.58.10/fax 01.42.47.00.70). M° Richelieu-Drouot. **Rates** *single 405F-455F; double 450F-490F; triple 565F; breakfast 38F.* **Credit** AmEx, DC, MC, V. **Map J4**
Hidden beyond the Musée Grévin, old-fashioned toy shops and printsellers, you find the delightful 36-room Chopin, built with the passage in 1846. Rooms have been colourfully redone and (except one single) have shower or bath and toilet. Book ahead.
Hotel services *Hairdryer. Lift. Safe.*
Room services *TV.*

Résidence du Pré

15 rue Pierre-Sémard, 9th (01.48.78.26.72/ fax 01.42.80.64.83). M° Cadet. **Rates** *single 425F; double 460F-495F; triple 600F; breakfast*

50F. **Credit** AmEx, DC, MC, V. **Map J3**
On a street of nineteenth-century buildings festooned with ornate iron balconies, the efficient 40-room Résidence du Pré is the least expensive of the Hôtels du Pré. Rooms are spacious with dark wood panelling. Its location by the Gare du Nord makes it a good bet for the early-morning Eurostar dash.
Hotel services *Bar. Lift. Safe. Parking (60F).*
Room services *Double glazing. TV.*

Hôtel Apollo

11 rue de Dunkerque, 10th (01.48.78.04.98/fax 01.42.85.08.78). M° Gare du Nord. **Rates** *single 225F-325F; double 385F-445F; triple 445F-500F; quad 600F; breakfast 30F.* **Credit** AmEx, DC, MC, V. **Map K2**
Opposite the Gare du Nord, the Apollo is a great find in an area full of doubtful budget joints. The 45-room hotel has true rustic charm; rooms are decorated with large wardrobes and florid wallpaper.
Hotel services *Lift.* **Room services** *Double glazing. Minibar. Safe. TV.*

Hôtel Beaumarchais

3 rue Oberkampf, 11th (01.53.36.86.86/ fax 01.43.38.32.86). M° Filles du Calvaire. **Rates** *single 350F-400F; double 450F-500F; suite 700F; breakfast 35F.* **Credit** AmEx, MC, V. **Map L5**
This stylish hotel was redesigned two years ago by its architect owner, with walls, fabrics, wavy headboards and Milan glass bedlamps in bright colours. 33 rooms range from small singles to a good-sized suite; some overlook a pretty courtyard.
Hotel services *Air con. Lift.* **Room services** *Hairdryer. Safe. TV.*

Hôtel Delambre

35 rue Delambre, 14th (01.43.20.66.31/ fax 01.45.38.91.76). M° Edgar-Quinet or Vavin. **Rates** *single 395F; double 460F-550F; mini suite 750F; extra bed 80F; breakfast 42F.* **Credit** AmEx, MC, V. **Map G9**
Elegant cast-iron touches in the 30 rooms give this friendly hotel an individual style, much updated from the 1920s when Surrealist André Breton lived here. Room 7, with private terrace, and the family mini suite in the attic, are particularly pleasing.
Hotel services *Lift. Safe.* **Room services** *Hairdryer. Modem link.Safe. TV. Wheelchair access (one room).*

Hôtel Istria

29 rue Campagne-Première, 14th (01.43.20.91.82/fax 01.43.22.48.45). M° Raspail. **Rates** *single 500F; double 580F-600F; breakfast 45F.* **Credit** AmEx, DC, MC, V. **Map G9**
The Istria has been modernised but has kept the charm which attracted photographer Man Ray and poet Louis Aragon in Montparnasse's heyday. The 26 compact rooms are simply furnished. There's a cosy cellar breakfast room and a comfortable living area. The unusual tiled artists' studios next door featured in Godard's *A Bout de souffle*.
Hotel services *Air con. Fax. Laundry. Lift.* **Room services** *Double glazing. Hairdryer. Safe. TV.*

Hôtel Keppler

12 rue Keppler, 16th (01.47.20.65.05/ fax 01.47.23.02.29). M° Kléber or George V.

Rates *single or double* 430F-480F; *triple* 550F; *breakfast* 35F. **Credit** AmEx, MC, V. **Map C4**
The high ceilings and spacious rooms are typical of this prestigious neighbourhood, but don't often come at these prices. There's a charming spiral staircase and a vintage lift. The reception and breakfast room are businesslike but subtle lighting adds atmosphere.
Hotel services *Bar. Lift.* **Room services** *Hairdryer. Room service (24-hr). Safe. TV.*

Hôtel Ermitage
24 rue Lamarck, 18th (01.42.64.79.22/ fax 01.42.64.10.33). M° Lamarck-Caulaincourt. **Rates** *single* 430F; *double* 500F; *triple* 630F; *quad* 730F; *breakfast included.* **No credit cards. Map H1**
This twelve-room hotel is only five minutes from Sacré-Coeur, but on a peaceful street far from the tourist madness. Rooms are large and endearingly over-decorated; some on upper floors have great views.
Hotel services *Garden.* **Room services** *Double glazing. Hairdryer.*

Prima Lepic
29 rue Lepic, 18th (01.46.06.44.64/fax 01.46.06.66.11). M° Blanche or Abbesses. **Rates** *single* 350F-380F; *double* 380F-440F; *triple* 500F-600F; *quad/quin* 700F; *breakfast* 40F. **Credit** MC, V. **Map H1**
The Prima Lepic, on a lively street near the Moulin Rouge, offers a nostalgic Montmartre experience. From the pretty tiled entrance to the breakfast room with white wrought-iron furniture, it is full of originality. Ribbons and flounces may not be everyone's taste, but the 38 rooms are clean and good-sized.
Hotel services *Lift. Safe.*
Room services *Hairdryer. TV.*

Hôtel Regyn's Montmartre
18 pl des Abbesses, 18th (01.42.54.45.21/ fax 01.42.23.76.69). M° Abbesses. **Rates** *single* 380F-400F; *double* 435F-475F; *triple* 575F-605F; *breakfast* 40F-45F. **Credit** AmEx, MC, V. **Map G1**
This is a great location opposite the Abbesses métro in the heart of Montmartre. There's a pretty breakfast room and six of the 22 rooms have superb views. There are a few shabby edges, but lots of character.
Hotel services *Lift.* **Room services** *Hairdryer. Safe. Radio. TV.*

Budget

Hôtel Henri IV
25 place Dauphine, 1st (01.43.54.44.53). M° Pont Neuf. **Rates** *single* 120F-150F; *double* 155F-285F; *breakfast included.* **No credit cards. Map J6**
This legendary dosshouse is famed for its fab location on the place Dauphine. It's been a hotel for 250 years and can't have been redecorated for at least 100. If you can ignore the smell of pee and damp patches on the walls, you can enjoy the large rooms and beautiful views on to the square. It has a loyal following: old hippy parents recommend it to their European-vacationing offspring – so book a month in advance.

Hôtel de Lille
8 rue du Pélican, 1st (01.42.33.33.42). M° Palais-Royal. **Rates** *single* 210F-290F; *double* 240F-290F;

extra bed 80F; *shower* 30F; *no breakfast.* **No credit cards. Map H5**
None of the glamour of the Palais-Royal, just a few steps away, has rubbed off on this 13-room hotel but, at these prices, who's complaining? The fake flowers and Toulouse-Lautrec prints are unimpressive, but the doubles are a reasonable size. Some rooms have WC and shower, others just a washbasin. No phones.

Hôtel Tiquetonne
6 rue Tiquetonne, 2nd (01.42.36.94.58/ fax 01.42.36.02.94). M° Etienne Marcel. **Rates** *single* 143F-213F; *double* 246F; *shower* 30F; *breakfast* 25F. **Credit** MC, V. **Map H5**
On a paved street near Les Halles, this superb-value hotel has 47 basic but clean rooms. Some are very large for the price, and high ceilings on the lower floors give even more of a sense of space. All doubles have bathrooms; some singles are without.
Hotel services *Lift.*

Hôtel du Séjour
36 rue du Grenier-St-Lazare, 3rd (01.48.87.40.36). M° Etienne Marcel or Rambuteau. **Rates** *single* 180F; *double* 240F-320F; *extra bed* 120F; *shower* 20F. *No breakfast.* **No credit cards. Map K5**
No frills, furbelows or phones here, but this 21-room hotel is a welcoming haven for travellers on a budget. Run by a friendly Portuguese couple for 25 years, most rooms and bathrooms have been smartened up, and the tiny courtyard is freshly painted.
Room services *Double glazing.*

Hôtel Castex
5 rue Castex, 4th (01.42.72.31.52/fax 01.42.72.57.91). M° Bastille. **Rates** *single* 240F-290F; *double* 320F-360F; *triple* 460F; *extra bed* 70F; *breakfast* 25F. **Credit** MC, V. **Map L7**
The Perdigãos have recently taken over this good-value Marais hotel and added a small salon. Neon-lit drinks and snacks machines are incongruous but no doubt handy. The spruced-up kitchen is available to guests. The 27-rooms are plain but pleasant.
Hotel services *Fax. Safe. TV.*

Hôtel de la Herse d'Or
20 rue St-Antoine, 4th (01.48.87.84.09/ fax 01.48.87.94.01). M° Bastille. **Rates** *single* 160F; *double* 200F-295F; *triple* 320F; *shower* 10F; *breakfast* 25F. **Credit** V. **Map L7**
Enter this seventeenth-century building down a stone-walled corridor, and you'll find a cheap and cheerful hotel lacking character but offering good-sized basic rooms in an excellent location. The 35 rooms (many without bathroom) look on to small dark courtyards or the noisy rue St-Antoine.
Hotel services *Safe.*

Hôtel Pratic
9 rue d'Ormesson, 4th (01.48.87.80.47/ fax 01.48.87.40.04). M° St-Paul. **Rates** *single* 200F; *double* 245F-360F; *breakfast* 25F. **Credit** MC, V. **Map L6**
In a great location next to the place du Marché-Ste-Catherine in the Marais, this is a good budget option. Don't expect lavish décor, but the 24 rooms are simple and clean, and some have tiny bathrooms.
Room services *Double glazing. Safe.*

Le Onze

11 rue Maître-Albert, 5th (01.55.42.92.87).
M° Maubert-Mutualité. **Rates** *single* 120F; *double*
190F. **No credit cards.** **Map J7**
A sweet, scruffy but clean hotel, hidden away in the
Latin Quarter, with a genial owner and a fair amount
of guests who, in true Hotel California style, checked
in for a night and ended up staying for years. 13
rooms, all with beams, lead off a rickety staircase.
A brilliant, hidden address and an absolute bargain.

Hôtel de Nesle

7 rue de Nesle, 6th (01.43.54.62.41/fax 01.43.54.31.88).
M° Odéon. **Rates** *single* 275F; *double* 350F-500F; *extra
bed* 75F; *no breakfast.* **No credit cards.** **Map H6**
The eccentric Nesle draws an international back-
packer clientele to be regaled with tales from Madame
of its hippy past; Monsieur is responsible for the
painted figures on the walls of the 20 rooms. No
phones in rooms and no reservations.
Hotel services *Garden.*
Room services *Double glazing.*

Grand Hôtel Lévêque

*29 rue Cler, 7th (01.47.05.49.15/
fax 01.45.50.49.36).* *M° Ecole-Militaire.* **Rates** *single*
270F; *double* 380F-450F; *triple* 550F; *breakfast* 35F.
Credit AmEx, MC, V. **Map D6**
Located on a largely pedestrianised market street
near the Eiffel Tower, the Lévêque is good value for
this chic area. The tiled entrance is charming, while
the 50 newly refurbished rooms are well-equipped,
with sparkling white bathrooms in all the doubles.
Hotel services *Lift.* **Room services** *Double
glazing. Hairdryer. Safe. TV.*

Résidence Hôtel des Trois Poussins

*15 rue Clauzel, 9th (01.53.32.81.81/
fax 01.53.32.81.82).* *M° St-Georges.* **Rates** *single*
380F-520F; *double* 520F-680F; *single studio*
480F-580F; *double studio* 580F-740F; *breakfast* 45F.
Credit AmEx, MC, V. **Map H2**
The Résidence, between the banking centre of Opéra
and picturesque Sacré-Coeur, offers a rare opportunity for self-catering. Of the 40 beamed, floral
rooms, 24 are studios equipped with kitchens.
Hotel services *Bar. Lift.* **Room services** *Double
glazing. Hairdryer. Kitchen. Modem link. Safe. TV.*

Hôtel de Nevers

*53 rue de Malte, 11th (01.47.00.56.18/
fax 01.43.57.77.39).* *M° République.* **Rates** *single*
160F-260F; *double* 180F-275F; *triple* 335F; *quad* 410F;
shower 20F; *breakfast* 25F. **Credit** MC, V. **Map L4**
This is a friendly, good-value base ten minutes from
the Marais. Three languid cats welcome you as one
of the family. The 34 rooms are clean and comfortable. The vintage lift is an experience.
Hotel services *Lift. Porter.*

Hôtel des Sans Culottes

*27 rue de Lappe, 11th (01.48.05.42.92/
fax 01.48.05.08.56).* *M° Bastille.* **Rates** *single* 300F;
double 316F; *breakfast included.* **Credit** AmEx,
MC,V. **Map M7**
Slap bang in the middle of the touristy pub crawl
strip, rue de Lappe, the Sans Culottes is convenient

if a Bastille blow-out is on the agenda. Rooms are
colourful, clean and functional, if a little over-
Airwicked. The hotel is named after a group of revolutionaries and its seedy status has everything to
do with its location and nothing to do with its name.
Room services *Hairdryer. TV.*

Hotel Télémaque

*64 rue Daguerre, 14th (01.43.22.60.08/
fax 01.43.20.72.92).* *M° Denfert-Rochereau.* **Rates**
single 168F-250F; *double* 200F-250F; *breakfast* 15F.
Credit DC, MC. **Map G10**
With large, clean and comfy roooms for under 300F
and a setting on a friendly market street, it's easy to
forgive the Télémarque's youth-hostel feel. Tassled
bedspreads and stucco walls pass for décor but, with
further redecoration planned for this year, things
can only get better for those on a budget.

Hôtel des Batignolles

*26-28 rue des Batignolles, 17th (01.43.87.70.40/
fax 01.44.70.01.04).* *M° Rome.* **Rates** *single* 200F-
320F; *double* 320F-360F; *triple* 430F; *breakfast* 25F.
Credit DC, MC, V. **Map F2**
This still feels a bit like the girls' boarding house it
once was, but provides a good base within reach of
Montmartre. It is simple, quiet and clean, with 33
spacious rooms and a tranquil courtyard.
Hotel services *Safe.* **Room services** *Double
glazing. Hairdryer. TV.*

Hôtel Eldorado

*18 rue des Dames, 17th (01.45.22.35.21/
fax 01.43.87.25.97).* *M° Place de Clichy.* **Rates** *single*
200F; *double* 300F; *triple* 400F; *breakfast* 30F.
Credit AmEx, MC, V. **Map F2**
The Eldorado is hidden behind place de Clichy; from
here you can climb the Butte. The 40 rooms, full of
warm fabrics, are split between the main house and
an annexe in the leafy garden. It is a hip address during the fashion shows when the major agencies use
it as a dormitory for young hopefuls who aren't yet
up to $10,000 a day and palace hotel status.

Youth Accommodation

MIJE

Fourcy *6 rue de Fourcy, 4th (01.42.74.23.45/fax
01.40.27.81.64).* *M° St-Paul.* **Fauconnier** *11 rue du
Fauconnier, 4th (01.42.74.23.45).* *M° St-Paul.*
Maubisson *12 rue des Barres, 4th (01.42.74.23.45).*
M° Hôtel de Ville. **Open** *hostels* 7am-1am daily.
Rates *dormitory* 130F per person (18-30s sharing
rooms); *single* 206F; *double* 316F; *triple* 142F per
person; *membership* 15F; *breakfast included.* **No
credit cards.** **Map L6, L7, K6**
Two 17th-century aristocratic Marais residences
and a former convent are the most attractive budget
sleeps in Paris. Plain but clean rooms sleep up to
eight; all have a shower and basin.

BVJ Paris/Quartier Latin

*44 rue des Bernardins, 5th (01.43.29.34.80/
fax 01.53.00.90.91).* *M° Maubert-Mutualité.* **Open** 24
hours. **Rates** *dormitory* 100F-120F per person; *single*
130F; *breakfast included.* **No credit cards.** **Map K7**

A dilapidated dosshouse on the exclusive Place Dauphine? That's the **Hôtel Henri IV**.

138 beds in bare modern dorms (for up to ten) and singles, a TV lounge and a work room.
Branch: BVJ Paris/Louvre, 20 rue Jean-Jacques Rousseau, 1st (01.53.00.90.90). 200 beds.

Young & Happy Hostel

80 rue Mouffetard, 5th (01.45.35.09.53/ fax 01.47.07.22.24). M° Place Monge. **Rates** *dormitory* 107F per person; *double* 127F per person; *breakfast included.* **Open** 8am-11am, 5pm-2am daily. **Credit** MC, V (300F min). **Map J8**
This friendly hostel on an animated street offers 82 beds in slightly tatty surroundings. The dorms are a bit cramped but the international clientele ensures community atmosphere. There's also a tiny kitchen.

Association des Etudiants Protestants de Paris

46 rue de Vaugirard, 6th (01.46.33.23.30/fax 01.46.34.27.09). M° Mabillon or St-Sulpice. **Open** *office* 8.45am-noon, 3-7pm Mon-Fri; 8.45am-noon, 6-8pm Sat; 10am-noon Sun. *Hostel* 24 hours daily. **Rates** *dormitory* 80F per person; 2100F monthly; *breakfast included.* **No credit cards. Map G7**
In a good location by the Luxembourg gardens, the AEPP offers accommodation for students 18-30 in dormitories of six to eight, plus basic cooking facilities, café and TV lounge. Membership is 10F, to be paid on arrival in addition to a 200F deposit.

Auberge Internationale des Jeunes

10 rue Trousseau, 11th (01.47.00.62.00/ fax 01.47.00.33.16). M° Ledru-Rollin. **Open** 24hrs daily; *rooms closed* 10am-3pm. **Rates** *Nov-Feb* 81F; *Mar-Oct* 91F; *breakfast included.* **Credit** AmEx, MC, V. **Map N7**

Cleanliness is a high priority at this hostel close to the Bastille, where there are rooms for two to six people. Larger ones have their own shower and toilet.

Auberge Jules Ferry

8 bd Jules-Ferry, 11th (01.43.57.55.60/fax 01.43.14.82.09). M° République or Goncourt. **Open** *office* 8am-1am; *hostel* 24 hrs daily, *rooms closed* 11am-2pm. **Rates** *shared* 115F per person; *double* 240F; *breakfast included.* **Credit** MC, V. **Map M4**
Friendly IYHF hostel has rooms for two to six and Internet access. No advance reservations, but they can usually find you a bed here or in another branch.

Résidence Bastille

151 av Ledru-Rollin, 11th (01.43.79.53.86/ fax 01.43.79.35.63). M° Voltaire. **Open** 7am-12.30pm, 2pm-1am daily. **Rates** *shared* 110F-125F per person; *single* 160F-175F; *breakfast included.* **Credit** MC, V. **Map N6**
A renovated hostel with 150 beds for under-35s.

Bed and Breakfast

Alcove & Agapes

Le Bed & Breakfast à Paris, 8bis rue Coysevox, 18th (01.44.85.06.05/fax 01.44.85.06.14).
This B&B service has more than 80 homes, mostly in central Paris (320F-500F for a double). Carefully selected hosts range from artists to grandmothers.

Good Morning Paris

43 rue Lacépède, 5th (01.47.07.28.29/ fax 01.47.07.44.45). **Open** 9am-5.30pm.
Over 50 rooms scattered throughout the city. Prices range from 250F for one person to 490F for three.

Tourisme chez l'Habitant
15 rue des Pas-Perdus, BP 8338, 95804 Cergy St-Christophe Cedex (01.34.25.44.44/fax 01.34.25.44.45). **Open** 9.30am-6.30pm Mon-Fri; 10am-5pm Sat. **Credit** AmEx, MC, V.
Stay a minimum of two nights in one of 80 homes (168F-206F per person, plus 60F booking fee).

Chain Hotels

Holiday Inn
Central reservations across Europe: UK 0800 897121; France 0800 905999. **Rates** prices vary according to hotel and season: *single or double* 665F-1995F; *executive* 1160F-2500F; *breakfast* 45F-125F. **Credit** AmEx, DC, MC, V.
A dependable American-owned chain, with 20 hotels in Paris and suburbs. The grandest is at République.

Hôtel Ibis
Central reservations from the UK 0181.283.4550; from France 01.60.77.52.52/fax 01.69.91.05.63. **Rates** *single or double* 295F-495F; *breakfast* 39F. **Credit** AmEx, DC, MC, V.
This inexpensive French chain has 20 hotels within the Périphérique, and many more in the suburbs.

Libertel
Central reservations in the UK 0990 300200; from France 01.44.74.17.47. **Rates** *single or double* 470F-1700F depending on hotel; *breakfast* 45F-75F. **Credit** AmEx, DC, MC, V.
This chain founded in 1991 has 30 hotels in the city ranging from the delightful 12-room **Prince de Condé** to the 243-room **Terminus Nord**.

Timhôtel
Central reservations 01.44.15.81.15/fax 01.44.15.95.26. **Rates** *single or double* 470F-680F; *triple* 595F-960F; *breakfast* 49F-60F. **Credit** AmEx, DC, MC, V.
A bit different from the hotel chain norm, Timhôtels are individually decorated and well located. Picturesque Timhôtel Montmartre has great views.

Apart-Hotels & Short-Stay Rental

A deposit is usually payable on arrival.

Apparthotel Citadines
Central reservations 01.41.05.79.79/fax 01.47.59.04.70. **Rates** *one-person studio* from 450F; *two* from 530F; *apartment for four* from 760F. **Credit** AmEx, DC, MC, V.
Ten modern complexes (Montparnasse, Montmartre, Opéra, etc) attract a mainly business clientele. Rooms are on the cramped side, but kitchenette and table make them practical for those with children. **Hotel services** *Lift.* **Room services** *Double glazing. Hairdryer. Kitchen. TV.*

Home Plazza Bastille
74 rue Amelot, 11th (01.40.21.20.00/ fax 01.47.00.82.40). M° St-Sébastien-Froissart. **Rates** *single* 787F; *double* 894F; *suite* 1087F-1622F. **Credit** AmEx, DC, MC, V. **Map L5**
Aimed at both business people and tourists, this

Model Montmartre: fashion hangout **Eldorado**.

carefully constructed 'village' of 290 apartments built around a street is reminiscent of a stage set. Rooms are clean and modern with well-equipped kitchenette and spacious bathrooms.
Hotel services *Air con. Bar. Business services. Garden. Parking. Restaurant.* **Room services** *Hairdryer. TV.*

Paris Appartements Services
69 rue d'Argout, 2nd (01.40.28.01.28/ fax 01.40.28.92.01). **Open** 9am-6pm Mon-Fri; 10am-1pm Sat. **Rates** *studio* from 3850F per week; *apartment* from 5250F per week. **Credit** MC, V.
Furnished studios and one-bedroom flats in the 1st to 4th *arrondissements*, with weekly maid service, and a 24-hour helpline. Bilingual staff.

Camping

Camping du Bois de Boulogne
2 allée du Bord de l'Eau, Bois de Boulogne, 16th (01.45.24.30.81/fax 01.42.24.42.95). M° Porte-Maillot (then free shuttle-bus to campsite during summer) or bus 244. **Open** 24 hours daily. **Credit** AmEx, DC, MC, V.
It's unlikely that you'd really come to Paris to camp, but a campsite does exist on the western side of the Bois de Boulogne. A one- to two-person plot with electricity and water for a tent or caravan costs 127F-149F per night; 96F-133F without electricity. Add 24F-31F for each extra person.

Menu Lexicon

An A-Z through the gourmet delights of dégustation *to help you find your way through French menu-speak.*

Abats offal. **Agneau** lamb. **Aiguillettes** (*de canard*) thin slices of duck breast. **Ail** garlic; **aïolï** garlic mayonnaise. **Aligot** mashed potatoes with melted cheese and garlic. **Aloyau** beef loin. **Ananas** pineapple. **Anchoïade** spicy anchovy and olive paste. **Andouillette** chitterling sausage made from pig's offal. **Aneth** dill. **Anguille** eel. **Asperge** asparagus. **Assiette** plate. **Aubergine** aubergine (GB); eggplant (US).

Ballotine meat or fish boned, stuffed and rolled up. **Bar** sea bass. **Barbue** brill. **Bavarois** moulded cream dessert. **Bavette** beef flank steak. **Béarnaise** rich sauce of butter and egg yolk. **Beignet** fritter or doughnut. **Belon** smooth, flat oyster. **Betterave** beetroot. **Beurre** butter. **Biche** venison. **Bifteak** steak. **Bisque** shellfish soup. **Blanc** breast. **Blanquette** a 'white' stew made with eggs and cream. **Blette** Swiss chard. **Boudin noir/blanc** black (blood)/white pudding. **Boeuf** beef; **– bourguignon** beef cooked Burgundy style, with red wine, onions and mushrooms; **– gros sel** boiled beef with vegetables, similar to *pot-au-feu*. **Bouillabaisse** Mediterranean fish soup. **Bourride** a *bouillabaisse*-like soup, without shellfish. **Brebis** sheep's milk cheese. **Brochet** pike. **Brochette** kebab. **Bulot** whelk.

Cabillaud fresh cod. **Caille** quail. **Campagne/campagnard** country-style. **Canard** duck. **Cannelle** cinnamon. **Carbonnade** beef stew with onions and stout or beer. **Carré d'agneau** rack or loin of lamb. **Carrelet** plaice. **Cassis** blackcurrants, also blackcurrant liqueur used in *kir*. **Cassoulet** stew of haricot beans, sausage and preserved duck. **Céleri** celery. **Céleri rave** celeriac. **Cèpe** cep mushroom. **Cerise** cherry. **Cervelle** brains. **Champignon** mushroom; **– de Paris** button mushroom. **Charcuterie** cold cured meats, such as *saucisson* or pâté. **Charlotte** moulded cream dessert with a biscuit edge; also baked versions with fruit. **Chasseur** cooked with mushrooms, shallots and white wine. **Chateaubriand** thick fillet steak, usually served for two with a *béarnaise* sauce. **Chaud** hot. **Chaud-froid** a sauce thickened with gelatine or aspic, used to glaze cold dishes. **Cheval** horse. **à Cheval** with an egg on top. **Chèvre** goat's cheese. **Chevreuil** young roe deer. **Chou** cabbage. **Choucroute** sauerkraut,

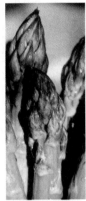

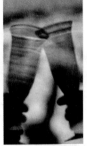

usually served *garnie* with cured ham and sausages. **Chou-fleur** cauliflower. **Ciboulette** chive. **Citron** lemon. **Citron vert** lime. **Citronelle** lemongrass. **Civet** game stew. **Clafoutis** thick batter filled with fruit, usually cherries. **Cochon de lait** suckling pig. **Coco** large white bean. **Colin** hake. **Confit de canard** preserved duck. **Contre-filet** sirloin steak. **Coquelet** baby rooster. **Coquille** shell. **Coquilles St-Jacques** scallops. **Côte** chop; **côte de boeuf** beef rib. **Cornichon** pickled gherkin. **Crème anglaise** custard sauce. **Crème brûlée** creamy custard dessert with caramel glaze. **Crème Chantilly** sweetened whipped cream. **Crème fraîche** thick, slightly soured cream. **Crépinettes** small, flattish sausages, often grilled. **Cresson** watercress. **Crevettes** prawns (GB), shrimps (US). **Croque madame** sandwich of toasted cheese and ham topped with an egg; **croque monsieur** sandwich of toasted cheese and ham. **En croûte** in a pastry case. **Cru** raw. **Crudités** assorted raw vegetables. **Crustacé** shellfish.

Darne (de saumon) salmon steak. **Daube** meat braised slowly in red wine. **Daurade** sea bream. **Dégustation** tasting or sampling. **Désossé** boned. **Dinde** turkey. **Duxelles** chopped sautéed mushrooms.

Echalote shallot. **Eglefin** haddock. **Endive** chicory (GB), Belgian endive (US). **Entrecôte** beef rib steak. **Entremets** cream or milk-based dessert. **Epices** spices. **Epinards** spinach. **Escabèche** sautéed and marinated fish, served cold. **Escargot** snail. **Espadon** swordfish. **Estouffade** meat that has been marinated, fried and braised.

Faisan pheasant. **Farci** stuffed. **Faux-filet** sirloin steak. **Feuilleté** 'leaves' of (puff) pastry. **Fève** broad bean. **Filet mignon** beef tenderloin. **Fines de claire** crinkle-shelled oysters. **Fines herbes** mixed herbs. **Flambé** flamed in alcohol. **Flétan** halibut. **Foie** liver; **foie gras** fattened goose or duck liver. **Forestière** with mushrooms. **au Four** baked. **Fraise** strawberry. **Framboise** raspberry. **Friandises** sweets or petits-fours. **Fricadelle** meat-ball. **Fricassé** meat fried and simmered in stock, usually with creamy sauce. **Frisée** curly endive. **Frites** chips (GB), fries (US). **Froid** cold. **Fromage** cheese; **– blanc** smooth cream cheese. **Fruits de mer** shellfish. **Fumé** smoked.

Galantine boned meat or fish pressed together, usually with a stuffing. **Galette** round flat cake of flaky pastry, potato pancake or buckwheat savoury *crêpe*. **Garni** garnished. **Gâteau** cake. **Gelée** aspic. **Gésiers** gizzards. **Gibier** game. **Gigot d'agneau** leg of lamb. **Gingembre** ginger. **Girolle** prized species of chanterelle mushroom. **Glace** ice cream. **Glacé** frozen or iced. **Goujon** strips of fish, coated breadcrumbs and fried. **Granité** water-ice. **Gras** fat. **Gratin dauphinois** sliced potatoes baked with milk, cheese and garlic. **Gratiné** browned with breadcrumbs or cheese. **à la Grèque** vegetables served cold in the cooking liquid including oil and lemon juice. **cuisses de Grenouille** frogs' legs. **Griotte** morello cherry. **Groseille** redcurrant. **Groseille à maquereau** gooseberry.

Haché minced. **Hachis Parmentier** shepherd's pie. **Hareng** herring. **Haricot** bean; **– vert** green bean. **Homard** lobster. **Huître** oyster.

Ile flottante poached whipped egg white floating in vanilla custard.

Jambon ham; **– cru** cured raw ham. **Jarret de porc** ham shin or knuckle. **Julienne** vegetables cut into matchsticks.

Langoustine Dublin Bay prawns, scampi. **Lait** milk. **Lapin** rabbit. **Lamelle** very thin slice. **Langue** tongue. **Lard** bacon; **lardon** small cube of bacon. **Légume** vegetable. **Lentilles** lentils. **Lièvre** hare. **Lieu** pollack. **Limande** lemon sole. **Lotte** monkfish.

Mâche lamb's lettuce. **Magret** duck breast. **Maison** of the house. **Maquereau** mackerel. **Marcassin** young wild boar. **Mariné** marinated. **Marmite** small cooking pot. **Marquise** light mousse-like cake. **Marron** chestnut. **Merguez** spicy lamb/beef sausage. **Merlan** whiting. **Merlu** hake. **Meunière** fish floured and sautéed in butter. **Miel** honey. **Mignon** small meat fillet. **Mirabelle** tiny yellow plum. **Moëlle** bone marrow; **os à la –** marrow bone. **Morille** morel mushroom. **Moules** mussels; **– à la marinière** cooked with white wine and shallots. **Morue** dried, salted cod; **brandade de –** puréed with potato. **Mousseline** lightened with whipped cream or egg white. **Moutarde** mustard. **Mûre** blackberry. **Muscade** nutmeg. **Myrtille** bilberry/ blueberry.

Nage aromatic poaching liquid. **Navarin** lamb and vegetable stew. **Navet** turnip. **Noisette** hazlenut; small round portion, usually meat. **Noix** walnut. **Noix de coco** coconut. **Nouilles** noodles.

Oeuf egg; **– en cocotte** baked egg; **– en meurette** egg poached in red wine; **– à la neige** see *Ile flottante*. **Oie** goose. **Oignon** onion. **Onglet** cut of beef, similar to *bavette*. **Oseille** sorrel. **Oursin** sea urchin.

Pain bread. **Palourde** type of clam. **Pamplemousse** grapefruit. **Panaché** mixture. **Pané** breaded. **en Papillote** cooked in paper packet. **Parfait** sweet or savoury mousse-like mixture. **Parmentier** with potato.

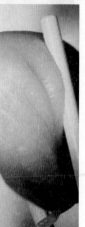

Pâtes pasta or noodles. **Paupiette** slice of meat or fish, stuffed and rolled. **Pavé** thick steak. **Pêcheur** based on fish. **Perdrix** partridge. **Persil** parsley. **Petit salé** salt pork. **Pied** foot (trotter). **Pignon** pine kernel. **Pintade/pintadeau** guinea fowl. **Pipérade** scrambled egg with Bayonne ham, onion and peppers. **Pistou** pesto-like basil and garlic paste. **Plat** dish; main course; **– du jour** daily special. **Pleurotte** oyster mushroom. **Poire** pear. **Poireau** leek. **Poisson** fish. **Poivre** pepper. **Poivron** red or green (bell) pepper. **Pomme** apple. **Pomme de terre** potato; **pommes lyonnaises** potatoes sliced and fried with onions. **Potage** soup. **Pot au feu** boiled beef with vegetables. **Poulet** chicken. **Poulpe** octopus. **Pressé** squeezed. **Prune** plum. **Pruneau** prune.

Quenelle light, poached fish (sometimes poultry) dumpling. **Quetsch** damson. **Queue de boeuf** ox-tail.

Ragoût brown meat stew. **Raie** skate. **Raifort** horseradish. **Râpé** grated. **Rascasse** scorpion fish. **Réglisse** liquorice. **Reine-claude** greengage plum. **Rillettes** potted meat, usually pork and/or goose. **Ris de veau** veal sweetbreads. **Riz** rice. **Rognons** kidneys. **Rôti** roast. **Rouget** red mullet. **Roussette** rock salmon (dogfish).

Sablé shortbread biscuit. **St Pierre** John Dory. **Salé** salted. **Salmis** game or poultry stew. **Sandre** pike-perch, a freshwater fish. **Sanglier** wild boar. **Saucisse** sausage. **Saucisson** small sausage. **Saucisson sec** dried sausage eaten cold. **Saumon** salmon. **Sec/sèche** dry. **Seiche** squid. **Sel** salt. **Suprême** (*de volaille*) fillets (of chicken) in a cream sauce. **Supion** small squid.

Tapenade Provençal black olive and caper paste, often with anchovies. **Tartare** raw minced steak (also tuna or salmon). **Tarte aux pommes** apple tart. **Tarte Tatin** warm, caramelised apple tart cooked upside-down. **Tête** head; **– de veau** calf's head. **Thé** tea. **Thon** tuna. **Timbale** dome-shaped mould, or food cooked in one. **Tisane** herbal tea. **Tournedos** small slices of beef fillet, sautéed or grilled. **Tourte** covered pie or tart, usually savoury. **Travers de porc** pork spare ribs. **Tripes** tripe. **Tripoux** Auvergnat dish of sheep's tripe and feet. **Truffes** truffles. **Truite** trout.

Vacherin cake of layered meringue, cream, fruit and ice cream; a soft, cow's milk cheese. **Vapeur** steam. **Veau** veal. **Velouté** stock-based white sauce; creamy soup. **Viande** meat. **Vichyssoise** cold leek and potato soup. **Volaille** poultry.

Cooking time (La Cuisson)

Cru raw. **Bleu** practically raw. **Saignant** rare. **Rosé** pink (said of lamb, duck, liver, kidneys). **A point** medium rare. **Bien cuit** well done. **Très bien cuit** very well done.

Restaurants

From bustling bistros to designer dining rooms, from Burgundy to Savoie, Paris has an eatery to please every palate.

With a lofty culinary reputation to maintain, Paris restaurants have been suffering something of an identity crisis at the dawn of the 21st century. Torn between preserving the classic techniques that give French cuisine its refinement and opening themselves to 'le world-food', even top chefs can seem confused. Take Alain Ducasse: with three stars each for his restaurants in Monaco and Paris, he has branched out with a modern bistro, **Spoon, Food and Wine**, where BLT sandwiches and Ben & Jerry's ice cream have achieved snob status.

But Spoon and its ilk (**Man Ray**, Lo Sushi) around the Champs-Elysées do not tell the whole story. Whatever the people-watching joys such spots offer, Parisians still take their food extremely seriously. Dining out is not a diversion, but an event which often eats up a full evening. It's also one of the city's more democratic pastimes; an exceptional meal can cost 150F – or 1,500F.

Hence the true change in recent years: many of the city's most talented chefs have opted to run affordable bistros rather than pursue coveted Michelin stars. Pierre Jay at **L'Ardoise**, Philippe Duclos at **Le Buisson Ardent**, and Christian Etchebest at **Le Troquet** now offer some of the best-value meals in Paris. Burgundy's **Bernard Loiseau** has joined the list of haute-cuisine chefs (**Guy Savoy**, **Michel Rostang**) with spin-off baby bistros, opening two 'aunts' including **Chez Tante Louise**. Haute-cuisine restaurants set themselves apart with their lavish décor, more polished service and luxury ingredients.

Chefs who are showing the way forward are those who delve into the riches of France's regions to seek out exceptional products, then treat them with respect. Food health crises in Europe have renewed Parisians' concerns about quality, and this is reflected even in the better budget spots, which proudly name their suppliers and select wines from small producers.

Restaurants are listed by *arrondissement* order within each category. For more detailed listings and a larger selection, see the annual *Time Out Paris Eating & Drinking Guide*.

PRICES & PRIX FIXE

Prices are based on the cost of a starter (*entrée*), main course (*plat*) and dessert chosen *à la carte*, but do not include drinks. It is quite acceptable to order only an *entrée* and *plat*, or *plat* and dessert, rather than all three courses. *Prix fixe* refers to a *menu* or *for-*

mule, which offers a more limited choice at a set price, again usually three courses, and may include wine. By law, all restaurant and café prices include a 12-15 per cent service charge. Tables at haute-cuisine and classic restaurants often need to be booked weeks or, even, months in advance.

Bistros

L'Ardoise
28 rue du Mont-Thabor, 1st (01.42.96.28.18). M° Concorde or Tuileries. **Open** noon-2.15pm, 7.15-11.15pm Tue-Sun. Closed first week Jan, one week May, three weeks Aug. **Prix fixe** 170F. **Credit** MC, V. **Map F9**
Chef Pierre Jay, formerly of La Tour d'Argent, has made this contemporary bistro a worthy word-of-mouth address. Typical of his style are crab 'flan' in a creamy parsley emulsion, and a *fondant de joue de boeuf* (beef cheeks). It's noisy and cramped – we hope success might mean a move to larger quarters.

La Tour de Montlhéry (Chez Denise)
5 rue des Prouvaires, 1st (01.42.36.21.82). RER Châtelet-Les Halles. **Open** 24 hours, 7am Mon-7am Sat. Closed 14 July-15 Aug. **Average** 220F. **Credit** MC, V. **Map J5**
This famous all-night mecca – a relic of Les Halles' market past – sees a cheerful rabble of regulars tucking into huge main courses like piles of lamb chops or hearty rabbit simmered in mustard sauce with *frites*. Just the ticket for ravenous nightbirds. Reserve.

Willi's Wine Bar
13 rue des Petits-Champs, 1st (01.42.61.05.09). M° Pyramides. **Open** noon-2.30pm, 7-11pm Mon-Sat. **Average** 195F. **Prix fixe** 185F (dinner only). **Lunch menu** 148F. **Credit** MC, V. **Map H4**
Run by English duo Mark Williamson and Tim Johnston, Willi's serves some of the best *bistro à vins* food in town and a stunning selection of Côtes du Rhône to a fascinating mingling of fashion types, stockbrokers and foreigners. A meal might begin with a minestrone with *pistou* (Provençal pesto), followed by grilled sea bream with sweet peppers, capers and cumin. Desserts are wonderful. This is a place to savour a leisurely meal.

Le Gavroche
19 rue St-Marc, 2nd (01.42.96.89.70). M° Richelieu-Drouot. **Open** noon-1.30am Mon-Sat. Closed Aug. **Average** 150F. **Credit** MC, V. **Map H4**
This place gives a sense of what the French business lunch once was: disorder reigns and no one is in a rush except the harried waiters. Main dishes revolve around steak that shows cholesterol to be alive and

well in France. Beaujolais rules a well-chosen wine list. Finding room for dessert is a struggle, but the *millefeuille* is sumptuous.

La Fontaine Gourmande
11 rue Charlot, 3rd (01.42.78.72.40). M° Filles du Calvaire. **Open** noon-2pm, 7-10pm Mon-Fri. Closed Aug. **Average** 180F. **Credit** MC, V. **Map L5**
This little lace-curtained bistro has just eight tables, a peaceful atmosphere and lovingly prepared food – though service can be a bit absent-minded. Chunks of dark venison in potent wine-flavoured sauce came with luxuriously fat, long yellow ribbons of home-made pasta, and a potato cake with duck *confit* and *girolles* was subtly sweet with onions and honey.

Le Pamphlet
38 rue Debelleyme, 3rd (01.42.72.39.24). M° Filles du Calvaire. **Open** noon-2.30pm, 7.30-11.30pm Mon-Fri; 7.30-11.30pm Sat. **Prix fixe** 160F. **Credit** MC, V. **Map L5**
Chef Alain Carrère has come up with a delicious contemporary take on Béarn/Basque cuisine for this new bistro. Starters like a creamy lentil soup with prawn tail garnish get the meal off to an impressive start.

Critics' Choice

Gourmet feasts for under 200F

1st L'Ardoise (see Bistros)

2nd Gallopin (see Brasseries)

3rd Le Pamphlet (see Bistros)

4th Café de la Poste (see Budget)

5th Le Coupe-Chou (see Classics)

6th L'Epi Dupin (see Contemporary)

7th Au Bon Accueil (see Bistros)

8th La Fermette Marbeuf 1900 (see Classics)

9th Chez Catherine (see Bistros)

10th Marines (see Fish & Seafood)

11th Le Repaire de Cartouche (see Bistros)

12th L'Encrier (see Budget)

13th La Zygothèque (see Bistros)

14th La Régalade (see Bistros)

15th Le Troquet (see Bistros)

16th A&M le bistrot (see Bistros)

17th Le Graindorge (see Regional)

18th Chez Toinette (see Budget)

19th Lao Siam (see The Far East)

20th La Boulangerie (see Budget)

Perfectly cooked baby sole meunière or scallops with chorizo sausage are good main course choices. *Wheelchair access.*

Baracane – Bistro de l'Oulette
38 rue des Tournelles, 4th (01.42.71.43.33). M° Bastille. **Open** noon-2.30pm, 7pm-midnight Mon-Fri; 7pm-midnight Sat. **Average** 200F. **Prix fixe** (dinner) 135F, 215F. **Lunch menu** 82F. **Credit** MC, V. **Map L6**
Marcel Baudis and Alain Fontaine of l'Oulette have kept these little premises going with aplomb, at a standard of cooking way above bistro norm. Two superb-value, *menus du marché* might be typified by a wild mushroom *velouté* and lambs' kidneys in a madeira sauce, while a pricier *menu-carte* focuses on Southwestern classics like *cassoulet*.

Le Grizzli
7 rue St-Martin, 4th (01.48.87.77.56). M° Hôtel-de-Ville or RER Châtelet-Les-Halles. **Open** noon-2.30pm, 7.30-11pm Mon-Sat. **Average** 220F. **Prix fixe** 160F. **Lunch menu** 120F. **Credit** AmEx, MC, V. **Map K6**
This bistro seems to have it all – a blissfully untouched olde worlde setting, quietly competent waiters and solidly good, traditional food. The *fricot de veau* is a toothsome house speciality, as are all meat and fish dishes cooked *sur l'ardoise*, or on heated pieces of slate, as in the Auvergne.

Les Vins des Pyrénées
25 rue Beautreillis, 4th (01.42.72.64.94). M° Bastille or St-Paul. **Open** noon-2.30pm, 8-11.30pm Mon-Sat; noon-4pm Sun. **Average** 165F. **Credit** MC, V. **Map L6**
Choir stall seats, vintage skates and old wooden skis make up the quirky décor of this agreeable Marais establishment. The cuisine is a balance of fish and meat, tradition and modernity. If the cooking misses the odd beat, the atmosphere is right on key, prices are reasonable and there's a lively, non-posey crowd. *Wheelchair access.*

Le Buisson Ardent
25 rue Jussieu, 5th (01.43.54.93.02). M° Jussieu. **Open** noon-2pm, 7.30-10pm Mon-Fri; 7.30-10pm Sat. Closed Aug, one week at Christmas. **Prix fixe** 160F. **Lunch menu** 90F. **Credit** AmEx, MC, V. **Map K8**
This delightful new bistro is full of little details like fresh flower arrangements that show a sincere desire to please. Hearty main courses include duck breast with peppers and a rib of pork on a bed of lentils garnished with foie gras. There's a nice wine list, too. This place has already developed a relaxed crowd of Latin Quarter regulars, so book in advance.

Les Fontaines
9 rue Soufflot, 5th (01.43.26.42.80). RER Luxembourg. **Open** noon-3pm, 7-11pm Mon-Sat. **Average** 200F. **Credit** MC, V. **Map J8**
Agile waiters here spirit around pots of enormous sautéed potatoes and sizzling steaks and game. A starter of *fricandeau du Cantal*, a rough-hewn pork paté, or sensational duck breast salad would easily satisfy as main courses. If you know someone who says they've never really 'got' French food, take them here and put an end to the disagreement.

Moulin à Vent – Chez Henri: *red meat, red wine and more red meat and red wine.*

Le Moulin à Vent – Chez Henri
20 rue des Fossés-St-Bernard, 5th (01.43.54.99.37).
Mº Jussieu. **Open** 12.30-2pm, 7.30-10.15pm Tue-Sat.
Closed Aug. **Average** 250F. **Credit** MC, V. **Map K7**
Red meat and red wine are the staples of this venerable establishment, favoured by Left Bank intellectuals in search of their roots. All the legends of French cuisine feature: frogs' legs, foie gras, snails, *andouillette* and *chateaubriand* steak.

Au Bon St-Pourçain
10bis rue Servandoni, 6th (01.43.54.93.63).
Mº St-Sulpice. **Open** noon-2pm, 8-10.30pm Mon-Sat.
Average 180F. **No credit cards. Map H7**
The sturdy country fare is at odds with the chic St-Germain diners (including, recently, the daughter of PM Lionel Jospin), but the legendary François manages to cajole just about everyone into ordering ambitiously, then cleaning their plates. Start off with the snails or a rabbit terrine, before attacking savoury *sauté d'agneau* or hearty beef stew with olives.

Les Brézolles
5 rue Mabillon, 6th (01.43.26.73.70). Mº Mabillon.
Open 7.30-10pm Mon; 12.15-2pm, 7.30-10pm
Tue-Sat. Closed three weeks in Aug. **Prix fixe** 195F.
Lunch menu 165F. **Credit** MC, V. **Map H7**
Jean-Paul Duquesnoy, who formerly ran an eponymous restaurant in the 7th, offers more affordable upmarket dining here. Pleasant, if a bit under-seasoned dishes, number inventions like smoked salmon with new potatoes and julienned granny smith.

Le Mâchon d'Henri
8 rue Guisarde, 6th (01.43.29.08.70). Mº Mabillon.
Open noon-2.30pm, 7-11.30pm daily. **Average** 130F

(lunch); 160F (dinner). **No credit cards. Map H7**
This bastion of tradition in the modish district behind place St-Sulpice draws yuppie couples and party-ready French Sloanes for its remarkable food. The menu changes daily, but might be marrow bones with coarse salt, plump anchovies on warm potato salad and juicy *rognons de veau*. Booking a must.

Marie et Fils
34 rue Mazarine, 6th (01.43.26.69.49). Mº Odéon.
Open 8-11pm Mon; noon-2.30pm, 8-11pm Tue-Sat.
Closed three weeks in Aug, Christmas. **Average** 220F.
Prix fixe 120F. **Credit** AmEx, MC, V. **Map H7**
An air of quiet sophistication reigns here, echoed by a fashion-conscious clientele. The menu proudly announces *'cuisine familiale'*, but the cooking is very much in the modern mode: calf's liver with honey and mignon of pork with violet mustard both come served in the fashionable tower style.

Wadja
10 rue de la Grande-Chaumière, 6th (01.46.33.02.02).
Mº Vavin. **Open** 7.30-11pm Mon; noon-2.30pm,
7.30-11pm Tue-Sat. Closed Aug. **Average** 180F.
Prix fixe 89F. **Credit** MC, V. **Map G8**
This friendly Montparnasse bistro has an innovative menu, plus a good-value 89F daily offer inspired by a trip to the market. A stylish crowd of arty locals comes to eat dishes like peppers stuffed with beef and foie gras or red mullet stuffed with garlic. Food is good, service is breakneck and noise levels are high.

L'Affriolé
17 rue Malar, 7th (01.44.18.31.33).
Mº La Tour-Maubourg or Invalides. **Open**
noon-2.30pm, 7.30-10.30pm Mon-Fri; 7.30-10.30pm

Sat. **Average** 260F. **Prix fixe** 190F (dinner only).
Lunch menu 120F. **Credit** MC, V. **Map E6**
An almost exclusively French clientle comes to this
neighbourhood bistro for the inventive cooking of
chef Alain Atibard. Starters like a creamy, smoked
salmon mousse with cucumber, mint, lettuce and
raisins and, as a main course, rabbit stuffed with
mushrooms, artichokes and foie gras, cooked *en
papillotte*, exemplify his approach. Reserve ahead.

Altitude 95
*First level, Eiffel Tower, Champ de Mars, 7th
(01.45.55.20.04). M° Bir-Hakeim/RER Champ de
Mars.* **Open** 11.30am-3pm, 7-9pm daily. **Average**
300F. **Prix fixe** 250F (dinner and Sun lunch). **Lunch
menu** 98F, 127F, 150F. **Child's menu** 46F. **Lift
ticket** 21F. **Credit** AmEx, DC, MC, V. **Map C6**
The interior is all grey and metallic silver, with a
Meccano-beamed ceiling to remind you where you
are (as if you could forget). Recommended are the
delicious *salade aux gésiers de volaille* and a *gigot
d'agneau confit* that melts off the bone.
Wheelchair access.

Au Bon Acceuil
*14 rue de Monttessuy, 7th (01.47.05.46.11).
M° Alma-Marceau/RER Pont de l'Alma.* **Open**
noon-2.30pm, 7.30-10.30pm Mon-Fri. Closed Aug and
one week in Jan. **Average** 300F. **Prix fixe** (dinner)
155F. **Lunch menu** 135F. **Credit** MC, V. **Map D6**
This bistro near the Eiffel Tower fills nightly with
internationals and chic locals for its bargain 155F
cuisine du marché menu. The offer changes twice
daily but might be a superb red pepper mousse with
aubergine caviar, *émincé de boeuf* and comforting
crème brûlée. *A la carte* goes to grander roast turbot with asparagus and Jerusalem artichokes. Booking is essential and, even then, be prepared to wait.

Chez Savy
*23 rue Bayard, 8th (01.47.23.46.98). M° Franklin
D Roosevelt.* **Open** noon-3pm, 7.30-11pm Mon-Fri.
Closed Aug. **Average** 200F. **Prix fixe** 110F, 135F,
168F. **Credit** AmEx, MC, V. **Map E4**
This may be the haunt of solicitors and of stars from
the TV station opposite, but the welcome here is
magnanimous and the rustic Auvergnat cuisine generally faultless. Start with *jambon d'Auvergne* and
then be tempted by beef and lamb from the Cantal
or the gigantic ham hock with lentils.

Chez Catherine
*65 rue de Provence, 9th (01.45.26.72.88).
M° Chaussée d'Antin.* **Open** noon-2pm Mon;
noon-2pm, 7.45-10pm Tue-Fri. **Average** 180F.
Credit MC, V. **Map H3**
Chef Catherine Guerrez offers a delicious take on
Provençal home cooking with dishes like courgette-
flower *beignets*, grilled red peppers, basil-stuffed
ravioli and red mullet cooked with aniseed and
served with fresh pasta. Don't miss the crème brûlée
with pears and pistachios. Very friendly service.

Chez Michel
*10 rue Belzunce, 10th (01.44.53.06.20).
M° Gare du Nord.* **Open** noon-2pm, 7pm-midnight

Tue-Sat. Closed three weeks in Aug, one week at
Christmas. **Prix fixe** 180F. **Credit** MC, V. **Map K3**
Très fake beams and Normandy half-timbering
make a stultifying setting at odds with Thierry
Breton's imaginative, new-wave bistro food. Breton
trained at the Crillon and Tour d'Argent but draws
on his Breton roots with such dishes as succulent
milk-fed pork on a bed of cabbage and bacon, or
juicy roast chicken with morels and crispy ratte
potatoes. A couple of doors down at No 6 is Breton's
cheaper offshoot, Chez Casimir (01.48.78.28.80).

Astier
*44 rue Jean-Pierre-Timbaud, 11th (01.43.57.16.35).
M° Parmentier.* **Open** noon-2pm, 8-11pm Mon-Fri.
Closed Aug, Christmas/New Year. **Prix fixe** 140F.
Lunch menu 115F. **Credit** MC, V. **Map M4**
The wood-panelled walls badly need a makeover and
the service can be frustrating, but no matter – the
140F four-course feast, with a stunning wine list, must
be one of the best-value meals in town. Try classics
like veal kidneys or rabbit in mustard, but be sure to
leave room for the amazing cheese tray and desserts.

Dame Jeanne
*60 rue de Charonne, 11th (01.47.00.37.40).
M° Ledru-Rollin.* **Open** noon-2.15pm, 8-11pm
Mon-Thur; noon-2.15pm, 7.30-11.30pm Fri;
7.30-11.30pm Sat. Closed three weeks in Aug. **Prix
fixe** 110F, 138F, 168F. **Credit** MC, V. **Map N7**
You'll find artistic seasonal cooking at affordable
prices at this bistro run by two alumni of Apicius.
Visiting at lunch, we tried the 110F 'seasonal fruit
and vegetable' *menu*: a rich pumpkin soup, then
chicken rolled around caramelised chicory.
Thoroughly pleasing desserts included a flashy
caramelised poached pear with liquorice ice cream.

Le Repaire de Cartouche
*8 bd des Filles-du-Calvaire, 11th (01.47.00.25.86).
M° St-Sébastien-Froissart.* **Open** 12.30-2.30pm,
7.30-11pm Tue-Sat. Closed Aug. **Average** 180F.
Credit MC, V. **Map L5**
This two-tiered bistro attracts Parisian gourmands
by the truckload. Chef Rodolphe Paquin moulds
memorable dishes from quality ingredients, such as
a superb Madeira-soaked veal chop with brussels
sprouts so fresh and tasty that any school-dinner
traumas vanish. With an excellent wine list and
attentive but comfortably distanced service, Le
Repaire de Cartouche looks set to become a classic.

A Sousceyrac
*35 rue Faidherbe, 11th (01.43.71.65.30). M° Faidherbe-
Chaligny.* **Open** noon-2.15pm, 7.30-10.15pm Mon-Fri;
7.30-10.15pm Sat. Closed Aug. **Average** 260F. **Prix
fixe** 185F. **Credit** AmEx, DC, MC, V. **Map N7**
Luc Asfaux took over this gleaming old bistro (opened
in 1923 by his grandpa) from his dad. Duck and
goose foie gras have pride of place, delivered whole
from the Landes and prepared in Asfaux's kitchens.
Cassoulet, ris de veau and game are also specialities.

St Amarante
4 rue Biscornet, 12th (01.43.43.00.08). M° Bastille.
Open noon-2.30pm, 7.30-10.30pm Tue-Fri;

7.30-10.30pm Sat. Closed mid July-mid Aug.
Average 150F. **Credit** V. **Map I12**
The downside of success is that with only a few blackboard choices every day, this low-key, unobtrusive place runs out of some things if you don't arrive early – but you can always be confident of the freshness. Excellent terrines are a fine prelude to long-simmered braised dishes and *fricassées*.

Le Square Trousseau
1 rue Antoine-Vollon, 12th (01.43.43.06.00).
M° Ledru-Rollin. **Open** noon-2.30pm, 8-11.30pm daily. **Average** 180F. **Lunch menu** 100F, 135F (Mon-Sat). **Credit** AmEx, MC, V. **Map M7**
A popular fashion-world hangout, this picture-perfect *belle époque* bistro has evolved into a gently fashionable, truly relaxed place. The food has also improved, with earthy dishes like *gigot de sept heures* and roast guinea fowl. The proprietor proudly serves wines from his friends' vineyards. Book.

L'Avant-Goût
26 rue Bobillot, 13th (01.53.80.24.00) M° Place d'Italie. **Open** noon-2pm, 8-11pm Tue-Sat. **Average** 170F. **Prix fixe** 145F. **Credit** MC, V. **Map L11**
Chef Christophe Beaufront presides over a big hit here, but it can be deafeningly noisy and there can be strange lapses in the service. Starters are skimpy but appealingly presented; main courses, like veal *onglet* with roast, unpeeled garlic cloves, and *galinette* (a kind of mullet) with fried ginger chips, are accomplished.

Chez Paul
22 rue de la Butte-aux-Cailles, 13th (01.45.89.22.11).
M° Place d'Italie or Corvisart. **Open** noon-2.30pm, 7.30pm-midnight Mon-Sat; noon-3pm, 7.30pm-midnight

Sun. Closed Christmas. **Average** 220F. **Credit** MC, V.
Paul's joviality draws a varied, local crowd. The well-prepared food is big on rediscovered cuts and dishes, supplemented by blackboard offerings and the daily fish catch. Homemade terrines and the frightening-sounding *assiette de cochonnailles* – pig's tail, ears, cheek and snout – feature among the starters. Main courses include *boudin noir* and a fine steak.

La Zygothèque
15bis rue de Tolbiac, 13th (01.45.83.07.48).
M° Bibliothèque. **Open** noon-2.15pm, 8-10.30pm Mon-Fri; 8-10.30pm Sat. **Average** 160F. **Lunch menu** 90F. **Credit** V. **Map N10**
Usefully located near the Bibliothèque Nationale, this new bistro comes from the same team who run Les Zygomates and La Zygotissoire, and serves similar, carefully prepared food. Try the generous *salade Parmentier*, follow with a perfectly cooked calf's liver, or shoulder of lamb stuffed with vegetables.

Natacha
17bis rue Campagne-Première, 14th (01.43.20.79.27).
M° Raspail. **Open** 8.30pm-1am Mon-Sat. Closed three weeks Aug. **Average** 200F. **Credit** AmEx, MC, V.
Map H9
People (Brett Easton Ellis, Mick Jagger) come here late for the buzz of going where others go and for the flattering attentions of hostess Natacha. It has a feeling of almost domestic warmth, a little clubby but not intimidating. Cooking is more than decent, including goat-cheese ravioli and sautéed rabbit.

La Régalade
49 av Jean-Moulin, 14th (01.45.45.68.58). *M° Alésia.*
Open noon-2pm, 7pm-midnight Tue-Fri 7pm-midnight

Wadja: *Noise levels are high at this friendly bistro, but then so are the standards.*

Sat. Closed Aug. **Prix fixe** 175F. **Credit** MC, V.
Yves Camdeborde could easily run an haute-cuisine restaurant – but chooses not to, which is what makes this place exceptional. So popular is his imaginative three-course *menu* that there are three sittings every night, to be booked at least a week ahead. He pulls them in for dishes like duck hearts with oyster mushrooms or sea bass with a 'ravioli' of two celeries.

L'Os à Moëlle
3 rue Vasco-de-Gama, 15th (01.45.57.27.27).
M° Lourmel. **Open** noon-2pm, 7-11.30pm Tue-Sat.
Closed Aug. **Prix fixe** (dinner) 190F. **Lunch menu** 155F. **Credit** MC, V. **Map B9**
This is a lace-curtained haven for young professionals, but don't let that deter you. The daily-changing dinner *menu* offers no choice (except desserts), but the risk is worth it for Thierry Faucher's five-course unveiling of such dishes as coddled eggs with asparagus and red mullet with beetroot chips.

Le Troquet
21 rue François-Bonvin, 15th (01.45.66.89.00).
M° Cambronne or Sèvres-Lecourbe. **Open** noon-2pm, 7.30-10pm Tue-Sat. Closed three weeks in July/Aug.
Average 160F. **Prix fixe** 160F, 175F. **Lunch menu** 130F. **Credit** MC, V. **Map D8**
This new modern bistro has found favour with UNESCO types and local bourgeoisie. Chef Christian Etchebest is an alumnus of Christian Constant's kitchen at the Crillon, and his imaginative cooking reveals his Basque origins: cream of courgette soup with goat-cheese *quenelles*; a pan-roasted *palombe* (wood pigeon); and sheep's cheese served Basque-style with cherry jam.

A&M le bistrot
136 bd Murat, 16th (01.45.27.39.60). M° Porte de St-Cloud. **Open** 12.30-2.30pm, 7.30-10.30pm Mon-Fri; 7.30-10.30pm Sat. Closed two weeks in Aug. **Prix fixe** 170F. **Credit** AmEx, MC, V.
Tucked away in the reaches of bourgeois Auteuil, this bistro from the respected chefs at Apicius (A) and Marius (M) more than warrants the Métro trip. It tends to be filled with business types, munching away while their expense accounts bear the brunt of their appetites. But prices are reasonable, given the quality of ingredients and faultless presentation. **Branch**: 105 rue de Prony, 17th (01.44.40.05.88).

Le Petit Rétro
5 rue Mesnil, 16th (01.44.05.06.05). M° Victor-Hugo.
Open noon-2.30pm, 7.45-10.30pm Mon-Fri; 7.45-10.30pm Sat. Closed two weeks in Aug.
Average 180F. **Lunch menu** 98F.
Credit MC, V. **Map B4**
The beautiful Art Nouveau tiles, warm, yellow-washed walls, bentwood chairs and snug dark wood tables are an ideal setting for the homely classics served here. A blackboard offers daily specials, while the menu parades a list of textbook-perfect favourites, given a few modern twists.

Aux Négociants
27 rue Lambert, 18th (01.46.06.15.11).
M° Château-Rouge. **Open** noon-2.30pm Mon, Fri;

L'Os à Moëlle: *unmissable five-course marvel.*

noon-2.30pm, 8-10.30pm Tue-Thur. Closed Aug.
Average 130F. **Credit** MC, V. **Map J1**
Jean Navier and his wife serve simple, traditional fare – *boeuf bourguignon, blanquette de veau*, huge terrines, happily odiferous cheeses and a rich chocolate mousse – to artsy yuppies, with all the informality that familiarity breeds. They can at times seem grumpy but this is really just a guise.

Patachou
9 pl du Tertre, 18th (01.42.51.06.06). M° Anvers.
Open noon-12.30am (*salon de thé* 8.30am-2am) daily.
Average 240F. **Prix fixe** 180F. **Credit** AmEx, MC, V. **Map H1**
There are three reasons to come here: the view, the view and the view: a panorama of Paris from the heights of Montmartre. Cooking is less spectacular: slightly bland salmon tartare, tasty but tough beef fillet in foie gras sauce. Wines are middle-of-the-French-road and priced about 20 per cent higher than elsewhere. But you'll be happy to be reasonably well fed in such a magical spot.

Chez Jean
38 rue Boyer, 20th (01.47.97.44.58). M° Gambetta.
Open 8-11pm Mon-Fri; noon-2pm, 8-11pm Sat. Closed a week in Aug. **Average** 120F. **Prix fixe** 98F (dinner only). **Lunch menu** 49F, 66F. **Credit** MC, V. **Map P4**
This place has a timeless feel, even if it is part of Ménilmontant's arty renaissance. Loquacious Jean makes new customers feel at home, a mood that is reflected in the cooking and tongue-in-cheek service.

Le Grand Colbert

... a first rate, typically French Brasserie, open until late and affordable for all budgets. Meals vary from simple dishes to the most exquisite cuisine. Whatever takes your fancy, you can savour a relaxful moment in a lovely Parisian atmosphere.

Menu: 160F (including coffee)
Open daily from noon–1am (with last orders taken up until 1am)

2 rue Vivienne, 2nd. Tel: 01.42.86.87.88. M° Bourse

Le Polidor

*In the heart of the Quartier Latin, just a few steps away from
the Panthéon, the Sorbonne and Boulevard St. Michel*

*Enjoy fine French cuisine in a superb historic
surrounding dating back to 1845*

Prix fixe: 110F, à la carte: avg. 130F Lunch menu: 55F

**41 rue Monsieur-le-Prince, 6th, M° Odéon. Tel: 01.43.26.95.34
Open Mon-Sat noon-2.30pm, 7pm-1am, Sun noon-2.30pm, 7pm-11pm**

Main courses such as pork fillet and cod with saffron sauce are satisfying, and the house red is only too drinkable, from a list with unusual regional finds (Jean is a former wine journalist).

Le Zéphyr

1 rue du Jourdain, 20th (01.46.36.65.81). M° Jourdain. **Open** noon-2.30pm, 8-11pm Mon-Fri; 8-11pm Sat. Closed ten days Aug, 23 Dec-2 Jan. **Average** 170F. **Prix fixe** 150F. **Lunch menu** 69F. **Credit** MC, V. **Map P3**

The Zéphyr is worth the trip for the great food, atmosphere and classy 1930s interior complete with a grand piano that is sometimes put to use. Try interesting starters like the langoustine soup with lentils, followed by *confit de canard* or veal in wine sauce. Delicious desserts are a must.

Haute Cuisine

Le Grand Véfour

17 rue de Beaujolais, 1st (01.42.96.56.27). M° Palais- Royal. **Open** 12.30-2.15pm, 7.30-10.15pm Mon-Fri. Closed Aug. **Average** 700F. **Prix fixe** 780F. **Lunch menu** 345F. **Credit** AmEx, DC, MC, V. **Map H5**

Once the scene of Revolutionary fervour, this sumptuous Palais-Royal monument (now in the hands of the Taittinger Group) strives for elegant, special-occasion cooking, as in fabulous Marennes oysters lightly poached in a beetroot sauce, and lamb *noisettes* in an intriguing fennel sauce. The cheese tray is sublime, and piquant desserts include unusual combinations like spinach and cumin pie.

L'Ambroisie

9 pl des Vosges, 4th (01.42.78.51.45). M° Bastille or St-Paul. **Open** noon-1.30pm, 8-9.30pm Tue-Sat. Closed two weeks in Feb, three weeks in Aug. **Average** 1100F. **Credit** AmEx, MC, V. **Map M6**

In a romantic townhouse on the 17th-century place des Vosges, L'Ambroisie's interior drips true chic, with gorgeous tapestries, stone floor and mini-spotlights. Bernard Pacaud's cooking lacks the magic of the setting, though, relying too much on luxury ingredients and too little on imagination. Crisp veal sweetbreads came scattered with tasteless truffles, and turbot was roasted, oddly, in goose fat. Service redefines snooty, and it's hard to spend under 400F on wine. *Wheelchair access.*

La Tour d'Argent

15-17 quai de la Tournelle, 5th (01.43.54.23.31). M° Maubert-Mutualité. **Open** noon-1pm, 7.30-9pm Tue-Sun. **Average** 800F. **Lunch menu** 350F. **Credit** AmEx, DC, MC, V. **Map K7**

Although this renowned dining room with one of the most famous views in Paris, on to Notre Dame, is always fully booked, it still feels very intimate. Old-fashioned kid-glove treatment by the staff is all part of the experience. And the food? The legendary duck preparations are fine, if nowhere near as captivating as the view. However, the rather tame run of stiffly priced but appetising luxury dishes has a time-immemorial quality.

L'Arpège

84 rue de Varenne, 7th (01.45.51.47.33). M° Varenne. **Open** noon-2pm, 7.30-10.30pm Mon-Fri. **Average** 900F. **Prix fixe** 690F. **Lunch menu** 390F. **Credit** AmEx, DC, MC, V. **Map F6**

Rather than picking dishes *à la carte*, it's best to put yourself into cerebral chef Alain Passard's hands. Ask for a *menu surprise* and the daily 390F lunch or 1200F dinner menus turn into a personalised odyssey. Mind-dizzying dishes might include seared scallops with crunchy leeks, a buckwheat pancake studded with pungent truffles and tender, crispy Sarthe duckling with sage and foie gras. Décor is pared-down, to focus your mind on the food.

Le Jules Verne

Tour Eiffel, Champ de Mars, 7th (01.45.55.61.44). M° Bir-Hakeim/RER Champ de Mars. **Open** 12.15-2pm, 7.30-9.30pm daily. **Average** 775F. **Prix fixe** 680F. **Lunch menu** 290F (Mon-Fri). **Credit** AmEx, DC, MC, V. **Map C6**

Despite the mind-blowing views from halfway up the Eiffel Tower, the black walls, halogen lamps and extravagant flower arrangements hint strongly of 1970s disco. The food succeeds in pleasing its international clientele with coquettish doses of luxuries and some daring meat/fish combos, such as swordfish with potato purée and caviar, and marinated salmon and tuna topped by warm foie gras.

Le Bristol

Hôtel Bristol, 112 rue du Fbg-St-Honoré, 8th (01.53.43.43.00). M° Miromesnil. **Open** noon-2pm, 7-10.30pm daily. **Average** 700F. **Prix fixe** 360F, 680F. **Credit** AmEx, MC, V. **Map E4**

Eric Frechon, who made his name with a modern bistro in the 19th, has replaced Michel del Burgo as head chef of Le Bristol. His debut has been auspicious; he has not forsaken trademark dishes like calf's head with salted anchovies now that he has access to one of the grandest pantries in Paris. Ravioli of foie gras in mushroom cream with truffles demonstrate that he knows how to deliver luxury. Desserts are sumptuous, and service is courtly.

Laurent

41 av Gabriel, 8th (01.42.25.00.39). M° Champs-Elysées-Clemenceau. **Open** 12.30-2pm, 7.30-10pm Mon-Fri; 7.30-10pm Sat. **Average** 700F. **Prix fixe** 690F. **Lunch menu** 390F. **Credit** AmEx, DC, MC, V. **Map E4**

Unlike many smart restaurants where the atmosphere is dauntingly hushed, here the mood is cheerily convivial. The semi-circular dining room, very Napoléon III, wavers between class and kitsch. Philippe Braun, a pupil of Joël Robuchon's, has devised a seasonal menu which combines the simple and refined. Starters such as cold salad of cooked spring vegetables with a large chunk of crayfish, or ravioli stuffed with veal and herbs, are masterful. A main course of spring lamb had us in ecstasy. *Wheelchair access.*

Ledoyen

1 av Dutuit, 8th (01.47.42.35.98). M° Champs-Elysées-Clemenceau. **Open** noon-2pm,

7.30-10.15pm Mon-Fri. Closed Aug. **Average** 800F.
Prix fixe 530F, 620F (dinner only). **Lunch menu**
320F. **Credit** AmEx, DC, MC, V. **Map F5**
Jacques Grange's renovation a few years ago of this
magnificent 1842 dining room was a huge success,
as an edge of contemporary chic underlies his rev-
erence for the historic. Young chef Christian Le
Squer, formerly of the Restaurant Opéra, has made
a triumphant entrance with main dishes such as turbot topped with finely chopped truffles and sole
sautéed in sage butter. Cheese is excellent, and
Ledoyen has one of the most extensive, well-
conceived wine lists in town. Service is impeccable.
See also **Cercle Ledoyen, Contemporary.**

Lucas Carton

9 pl de la Madeleine, 8th (01.42.65.22.90) M° Madeleine.
Open 8-10.30pm Mon, Sat; noon-2.30pm, 8-10.30pm
Tue-Fri. Closed three weeks Aug. **Average** 1000F.
Lunch menu 395F. **Credit** AmEx, DC, MC, V. **Map F4**
There are few restaurants where setting alone offers
as much satisfaction as the alluring Art Nouveau
temple directed by Alain Senderens. The 395F lunch
menu is excellent value, offering one of the most metic-
ulous and reliable grand dining experiences in Paris.
The food is audacious, with sweet-savoury combos
a feature. Starters such as ravioli stuffed with tiny
scallops are superb, as are main courses like lamb and
a Moroccan-influenced rabbit *pastilla* with cumin and
foie gras. Service is relaxed, if slightly indifferent.

Pierre Gagnaire

6 rue Balzac, 8th (01.44.35.18.25). M° George V.
Open noon-2pm, 8-10pm Mon-Fri; 8-10pm Sun.
Closed 15 July-15 Aug. **Average** 1000F. **Prix fixe**
480F, 780F, 900F. **Lunch menu** 500F. **Credit**
AmEx, DC, MC, V. **Map D3**
The arrival of legendary chef Pierre Gagnaire was
a great event in Parisian gastronomy. His cooking
is artistic and intellectual; eating one of his dishes is
a mix of unexpected tastes and textures that
engages every sense. The Grand Dessert, a five-
course extravaganza, is not to be missed, but the
wine list is puzzlingly brief. If you are a truly serious eater with a deep curiosity about the frontiers
of taste, you'll find this experience fascinating.

Alain Ducasse

59 av Raymond-Poincaré, 16th (01.47.27.12.27).
M° Victor-Hugo. **Open** noon-2pm, 7.45-10pm
Mon-Fri. Closed mid July-mid Aug; 23 Dec-5 Jan.
Average 1100F. **Prix fixe** 950F, 1490F. **Lunch
menu** 480F. **Credit** AmEx, DC, MC, V. **Map B4**
When, in 1996, Ducasse stepped into retired superchef
Joël Robuchon's outsized shoes at this rather gloomy
belle époque restaurant, we felt he didn't quite fill
them. But over the past few years he has grown bold-
er, and now there are inventive dishes – like *mignon*
of Pyrenean lamb with lemons and capers – alongside traditional luxury fare like frogs' legs and crayfish vol-au-vent. Service is solicitous and suave.
Wheelchair access.

Le Pré Catelan

route de Suresnes, Bois de Boulogne, 16th
(01.44.14.41.14). M° Porte-Maillot, then taxi. **Open**

noon-2.30pm, 8-10.30pm Tue-Sat; noon-2pm Sun. Closed
early Feb. **Average** 600F. **Prix fixe** 550F, 750F.
Lunch menu 295F. **Credit** AmEx, DC, MC, V.
Chef Frédéric Anton has enlivened the kitchen at
this romantic hideaway in the Bois de Boulogne. In
summer you can eat on the flower-bower of a terrace, in winter in the deluxe Second Empire dining
rooms. Anton's prowess is displayed in the 550F
menu, which offers four dishes plus cheese, dessert,
coffee and *petits fours*. We dined on duck foie gras
with beetroot vinaigrette, scallops in cider and a slice
of tender veal flank. Staff are unusually courteous.

Guy Savoy

18 rue Troyon, 17th (01.43.80.40.61).
M° Charles de Gaulle-Etoile. **Open** noon-2pm, 7.30-
10.30pm Mon-Fri; 7.30-10.30pm Sat. **Average** 800F.
Prix fixe 950F. **Credit** AmEx, MC, V. **Map C3**
Although the 80s-style halogen lamps and contemporary art now look a bit dated, there is nothing tired
about the cuisine. Savoy offers uniquely ethereal
meals, without the self-important solemnity of similar establishments: people are actually having a good
time. A winter salad of razor-thin slices of black truffle and dried beetroot on lamb's lettuce; *côte de veau*
with truffled potato purée; then a dessert of a 'rose'
of vanilla custard with petals of dried granny smith
apple in a fresh apple-juice sauce – every bite was
heavenly. The wine list is rather grandiose – the
choice of bottles at 300F-400F should be expanded.
Wheelchair access.

Lucas Carton: *the grandest table in Paris?*

Michel Rostang

20 rue Rennequin, 17th (01.47.63.40.77). M° Ternes or Pereire. **Open** 7.30-10pm Mon, Sat; 12.30-2.30pm, 7.30-10pm Tue-Fri. Closed two/three weeks in Aug. **Average** 700F. **Prix fixe** 640F, 860F. **Lunch menu** 345F. **Credit** AmEx, DC, MC, V. **Map D2**
Dark panelling, pale-yellow linen and Limoges porcelain give this restaurant a seriously sophisticated feel. The food is the same: a frothy Sauternes and lentil soup topped with foie gras, or pumpkin *velouté* with chunks of lobster might be followed by roast guinea fowl with Szechuan peppercorns or a *poule au pot* with truffle juice. Sorbets precede desserts such as pear *sabayon* (egg custard made with wine), decorated with deep-fried mint leaves, and a delicate fennel soufflé with banana and pear compôte.

Contemporary

Restaurant du Palais-Royal

110 Galerie Valois, 1st (01.40.20.00.27). M° Palais-Royal. **Open** 12.30-2.30pm, 7.30-10.30pm Mon-Sat. Closed Christmas/New Year. **Average** 250F. **Credit** AmEx, DC, MC, V. **Map H5**
The tranquil Palais-Royal gardens make this restaurant lovely for sitting out in summer, and a refuge in winter, even if prices do reflect the view. A langoustine salad was skimpy, unlike the juicy duck terrine. Fish, such as John Dory with sautéed red peppers, is beautifully prepared, and desserts are superb.

Macéo

15 rue des Petits-Champs, 1st (01.42.96.98.89). M° Bourse or Palais Royal. **Open** noon-2.30pm, 7-11pm Mon-Sat. **Prix fixe** 220F (dinner only). **Lunch menu** 180F, 195F. **Credit** AmEx, MC, V. **Map H5**
Mark Williamson of Willi's Wine Bar took over the Mercure Galant almost two years ago and has transformed it into a more dressed-up version of Willi's down the street. The modern cuisine includes a vegetarian menu flanking the *prix fixe*, with such dishes as a mushroom and parsley risotto and roast guinea hen with sautéed vegetables. Sample a dessert wine from one of the most varied lists in Paris.

Les Bookinistes

53 quai des Grands-Augustins, 6th (01.43.25.45.94). M° St-Michel. **Open** noon-2.30pm, 7pm-midnight Mon-Fri; 7pm-midnight Sat, Sun. **Average** 250F. **Prix fixe** 140F (vegetarian), 180F (Sun dinner only). **Lunch menu** 160F. **Credit** AmEx, DC, MC, V. **Map J7**
Guy Savoy's Left Bank satellite bistro has become a popular local institution over the past three years. Prices have crept up and the wine list is still pricey for a casual night out – but the quality of the cooking is reliably good. Service can be uneven.

L'Epi Dupin

11 rue Dupin, 6th (01.42.22.64.56). M° Sèvres-Babylone. **Open** noon-2.30pm, 7.30-10.30pm Mon-Fri. Closed three weeks Aug, Christmas. **Prix fixe** 165F. **Lunch menu** 110F. **Credit** AmEx, MC, V. **Map G7**
Prices remain reasonable despite the onslaught of people who have discovered this bistro on a side street near Le Bon Marché. Unfortunately, success

seems to have affected the service, which can be brusque. But the food is delightful: a typical starter might be caramelised chicory filled with goat cheese; a main course, duckling with sweet-and-sour turnips. Desserts are as interesting as the rest of the fare.

Le Maxence

9bis bd du Montparnasse, 6th (01.45.67.24.88). M° Duroc. **Open** noon-2.30pm, 7.30-11pm Mon-Fri; 7.30-11pm Sat. Closed two weeks in Aug. **Average** 350F. **Prix fixe** 190F, 320F. **Credit** AmEx, MC, V. **Map F8**
This sleek restaurant mixes homely dishes like an oxtail *Parmentier* with modern offerings like sole with peppers in a sauce scented with vanilla and lime. Chef David Van Laer's northern French origins come through in starters like scallop *waterzooï* (scallops with leeks and root vegetables in a cream sauce). Desserts are divine, and there is a classy wine list.

Le Buddha Bar

8 rue Boissy d'Anglas, 8th (01.53.05.90.00). M° Concorde. **Open** noon-3pm, 6pm-2am daily. **Average** 275F. **Lunch menu** 190F. **Credit** AmEx, DC, MC, V. **Map F4**
The cavernous, subterranean rendezvous for *le tout Paris* is dominated by a giant Buddha. Cooking spans the Pacific Rim from sashimi, tempura and Chinese chicken salad to a spicy beef fillet, but it's seeing and being seen that count for the clientele of actors, models, designers and wannabes. Reserve.

Café Mosaïc

46 av George V, 8th (01.47.20.18.09). M° George V. **Open** 8am-10.30pm daily. **Average** 250F. **Lunch menu** 180F, 220F. **Credit** AmEx, DC, MC, V. **Map D4**
This Zen-like space a few steps off the Champs-Elysées is the perfect backdrop for tasty, amusingly presented dishes. Snails come stuffed into an upright marrow bone, and scallops, served in their shells, are held shut with clothes pins. Good main courses include a delicious veal chop with a crust of almonds and parmesan, and lacquered herring with a sauce of dill-spiked sheep's cheese. Desserts are unusual, too, and service is pleasant. *Wheelchair access.*

Cercle Ledoyen

1 av Dutuit, 8th (01.47.42.76.02). M° Champs-Elysées-Clemenceau. **Open** 12.30-2pm, 7.30-11pm Mon-Sat. **Average** 240F. **Credit** AmEx, DC, MC, V. **Map F5**
This is one of the rare dressy places in Paris where you can relax while wearing a jacket. An ultra-Parisian crowd of men dining with bored mistresses, slightly lost tourists and small-scale celebrities creates a convivial atmosphere, abetted by attentive service. Chef Christophe Le Squer (also at smarter Ledoyen upstairs, *see* **Haute Cuisine**) produces stylish but satisfying food. Starters include *accras* (deep-fried, Caribbean-style salt cod fritters) and salmon sushi; mains, a lamb fillet stuffed with ricotta and peppers, or fillet of beef with Béarnaise sauce.

Richard Gere wannabes congregate at the cavernous, subterranean **Buddha Bar.**

Au Petit Marguery: *well-sozzled soufflés.*

Man Ray
34 rue Marbeuf, 8th (01.56.88.36.36). M° Franklin D Roosevelt. **Open** noon-2.30pm, 7pm-12.45am daily. **Average** 350F. **Prix fixe** 250F, 350F. **Lunch menu** 120F, 140F. **Credit** AmEx, MC, V. **Map D4**
The sense of déjà vu here is because you've seen it all before at the Buddha Bar – the same vast, sunken space, same mezzanine bar, same deep red pseudo-Orientalism, and same wannabes scanning for famous faces. The food is fashionably pseudo-Oriental, if steeply priced: decoratively presented sushi, flabby *nems* and wok-cooked dishes, like duck with lychees. Desserts head back to Europe. *Wheelchair access.*

Spoon, Food and Wine
14 rue de Marignan, 8th (01.40.76.34.44). M° Franklin D Roosevelt. **Open** noon-2.30pm, 7-11.30pm Mon-Fri. Closed three to four weeks in July or Aug. **Average** 200F. **Credit** AmEx, DC, MC, V. **Map D4**
Gastronomic innovator Alain Ducasse aims here to share foods and techniques he has discovered while globetrotting. Much of it will be familiar to Brits and North Americans – pork and shrimp ravioli, which you eat with Christofle chopsticks, a perilously stacked BLT and grilled fish. Half the wine list is American, with 40 per cent New World and European, and just 10 per cent French. Desserts include doughnuts, cheesecake and Ben & Jerry's ice cream.

Stella Maris
4 rue Arsène-Houssaye, 8th (01.42.89.16.22). M° Charles de Gaulle-Etoile. **Open** noon-2.30pm, 7.45-10.30pm Mon-Fri; 7.45-10.30pm Sat. Closed ten days in Aug. **Average** 350F. **Prix fixe** 460F. **Lunch menu** 250F, 175F. **Credit** AmEx, DC, MC, V. **Map D3**
An expense-account crowd mixes with serious French gourmets in this small vanilla-lacquered restaurant for the very subtle cuisine of Japanese chef Taderu Yoshino. Dishes such as scallops with caramel sauce and sea bass in an olive oil emulsion are delicious and delicate, if restrained.

Contre-Allée
83 av Denfert-Rochereau, 14th (01.43.54.99.86). M° Denfert-Rochereau. **Open** noon-2pm, 8-11pm

Mon-Fri; 8-11pm Sat. **Prix fixe** 155F, 165F, 195F. **Credit** AmEx, MC, V. **Map H10**
This is contemporary cooking that blends Provence and the French classics with international extras. We like the flexible system here: as well as the full three courses or familiar *entrée-plat* or *plat-dessert* options, you can opt for two *entrées* and a dessert. A *pavé* of raw tuna with soya sauce, *tapenade* and sesame seeds is done particularly well, and the shredded *confit de canard* on salad is excellent.

Classic

Le Poquelin
17 rue Molière, 1st (01.42.96.22.19). M° Palais-Royal. **Open** noon-2pm, 7.15-10.30pm Mon-Fri. **Average** 300F. **Prix fixe** 189F. **Lunch menu** 140F. **Credit** AmEx, DC, MC, V. **Map H5**
The kitchen at this impeccably run, jewel-box restaurant offers traditional cooking with inventive touches. The 189F menu features many of the best dishes available *à la carte*, such as chicken with preserved lemon, perfectly cooked lamb chops with a Provençal garnish and ethereal *oeufs à la neige*. Wines are well selected and fairly priced.

L'Ami Louis
32 rue du Vertbois, 3rd (01.48.87.77.48). M° Arts et Métiers. **Open** 12.15-2pm, 8-11pm Wed-Sun. Closed mid July-end Aug. **Average** 500F. **Credit** AmEx, DC, MC, V. **Map K4**
Though it's almost impossible not to fall in love with this stage-set of pre-war Paris – metal pipes venting a coal-burning stove still cross the gaslit dining room – the food is scandalously overpriced and often mediocre. This doesn't seem to bother the wealthy, mainly American clientele (this is where Chirac brought Clinton). The tradition is to start with the foie gras (270F), and then move on to crisp roast chicken and thin *frites* (350F), both cooked in goose fat. There are some excellent wines, and service is friendly. A place for those with money to burn.

Le Coupe-Chou
11 rue de Lanneau, 5th (01.46.33.68.69). M° Maubert-Mutualité. **Open** noon-2pm, 7pm-1am Mon-Sat; 7pm-1am Sun. **Average** 200F. **Prix fixe** 150F, 220F. **Credit** AmEx, MC, V. **Map J8**
In a medieval barbershop (hence the name), this bistro offers a superb 150F *menu: frisée aux lardons*, coddled eggs with cream or duck terrine, followed by a creditable duck *confit* or a generous *boeuf bourguignon*. The Cuvée Coupe-Chou offers no revelations, but will get you through the prissy, often bitchy service. After eating – if you ask nicely – you will be led to a quirky parlour to sip coffee and *digestifs*.

Allard
41 rue St-André-des-Arts, 6th (01.43.26.48.23). M° Odéon. **Open** 12.30-2.30pm, 7.30-11.30pm Mon-Sat. Closed three weeks in Aug. **Average** 250F. **Prix fixe** 200F. **Lunch menu** 150F. **Credit** AmEx, DC, MC, V. **Map H7**
Don't expect any concession to the present or even to the century when you enter the dim rooms of this St-

Germain institution. The food rests on the bedrock of French bourgeois cooking, as seen in family favourites like *canard aux olives* or *pintade aux lentilles*. Gigantic servings leave little room for dessert.

La Fermette Marbeuf 1900

5 rue Marbeuf, 8th (01.53.23.08.00). M° Alma-Marceau. **Open** noon-3pm, 7-11.30pm Sun-Wed; noon-3pm, 7-12.30pm Thur-Sat. **Average** 250F. **Prix fixe** 178F. **Credit** AmEx, DC, MC, V. **Map D4**
This popular Frères Blanc restaurant draws a wealthy, cosmopolitan clientele to its Art Nouveau dining room, rediscovered by accident in 1978. Chef Gilbert Isaac plays it straight, producing light zesty starters, like the thick tomato fondant studded with artichokes, and delicious main courses including sole in Champagne sauce. Finish with the Grand Marnier soufflé. Book.

Maxim's

3 rue Royale, 8th (01.42.65.27.94). M° Concorde. **Open** 12.30-2.15pm, 7.30-10pm Mon-Sat. Closed Mon in July and Aug. **Average** 600F (lunch), 800F (dinner). **Credit** AmEx, DC, MC, V. **Map F4**
Though nostalgia, conspicuous consumption and glamour have long been the main reason to dine at what is probably the most famous restaurant in the world, the surprising news is that new chef Bruno Stril has brought about a quiet culinary renaissance at this citadel of *belle époque* Paris. He offers a dual menu, with a small list of classics, alongside his own gently modern dishes. The waiters remain briskly uninterested in anyone who doesn't have the airs of a free-spending Onassis, but the orchestra is charming, the international crowd out for a special evening communicates a contagious joy and the meticulously restored dining room irresistibly romantic. *Wheelchair access.*

Au Petit Marguery

9 bd du Port-Royal, 13th (01.43.31.58.59). M° Gobelins. **Open** noon-2.15pm, 7.30-10.15pm Tue-Sat. Closed Aug; 24 Dec-2 Jan. **Prix fixe** 210F, 450F (Oct-Dec). **Lunch menu** 165F. **Credit** AmEx, DC, MC, V. **Map J9**
You can eat guinea fowl and steaks here all year round, but in autumn the Cousin brothers' sparkling old bistro comes into its own. Try gamey terrines, tender venison in a wine sauce with raisins and pine kernels, or the house speciality, *lièvre à la royale* (hare's meat in a rich, complex sauce). Desserts go from mildly to wildly alcoholic. Booking advised.

Le Pergolèse

40 rue Pergolèse, 16th (01.45.00.21.40). M° Porte Maillot. **Open** noon-2.30pm, 8-10.30pm Mon-Fri. Closed Aug. **Average** 400F. **Prix fixe** 230F, 290F. **Credit** AmEx, MC, V. **Map B3**
Albert Corre, the handsome, perma-tanned chef-owner of this romantic address, is justifiably proud of his Pergolèse, where *BCBG* locals and business-men enjoy dishes such as an amusing couscous of hot foie gras with tiny vegetables and plump raisins. The roast Bresse pigeon, which arrives majestically in a pastry cage, is a *tour de force*. Don't miss dessert (homemade ice creams, a warm vanilla *mille-feuille*, sensuous chocolate soufflé) – diet tomorrow.

Brasseries

Gallopin

40 rue Notre-Dame-des-Victoires, 2nd (01.42.36.45.38). M° Bourse. **Open** noon-12.30am Mon-Sat. **Average** 200F. **Prix fixe** 156F, 178F. **Credit** AmEx, DC, MC, V. **Map H4**
Standards at this grandiose, historic brasserie remain more stable than the stocks and shares at the Paris Bourse over the road. Trading types gather at lunch to de-stress over foie gras and competent renditions of sole meunière, lamb stew with olives or the unusual *filet de boeuf* flambéed in Champagne. *Wheelchair access.*

Bofinger

5-7 rue de la Bastille, 4th (01.42.72.87.82). M° Bastille. **Open** noon-3pm, 6.30pm-1am Mon-Fri; noon-1am Sat, Sun. **Average** 230F. **Prix fixe** 178F. **Lunch menu** 119F (Mon-Fri). **Credit** AmEx, DC, MC, V. **Map M7**
The only signs of Groupe Flo's 1996 takeover are the cleverly structured *prix fixe* and neat, computerised bills. Otherwise, from the Art Nouveau décor to the uniquely Parisian buzz, things at this beloved brasserie are the same – or better. Happy groups tuck into shellfish, steak tartare, *choucroute*, oxtail *chartreuse* or pan-fried duck foie gras with apples. It would be easy to spend far more for a plainer meal in less lavish surroundings.

Brasserie de l'Isle St-Louis

55 quai de Bourbon, 4th (01.43.54.02.59). M° Pont-Marie. **Open** 11.30am-1am Mon, Tue, Fri-Sun, 5pm-1am Thur. Closed Aug. **Average** 150F. **Credit** MC, V. **Map K7**
The old-fashioned décor and friendly service are as much of a draw as this Alsatian brasserie as the food. Conviviality reigns, attracting a diverse crowd that's perfect for people watching. The food is solid and generous. Start with an onion tart, then try the classic *choucroute garnie*, sausages and pork on a mound of sauerkraut, or the ham hock with lentils.

Le Balzar

49 rue des Ecoles, 5th (01.43.54.13.67). M° Cluny-La Sorbonne. **Open** noon-12.15am daily. **Average** 250F. **Credit** AmEx, MC, V. **Map J7**
Since this Latin Quarter institution passed into the hands of Groupe Flo in 1998, its regulars have been adamant that nothing should change. Well, the place still buzzes with a stylish crowd and the food is better than ever. The famous cheese-capped onion soup is delicious, as are other starters of herring in oil and marinated leeks. Main courses feature perfectly cooked *entrecôte* of salers beef, sole meunière, and *andouillette*. The tarte Tatin remains authentic.

Alcazar

62 rue Mazarine, 6th (01.53.10.19.99). M° Odéon. **Open** noon-3.30pm, 7pm-1am daily. **Average** 250F. **Prix fixe** 100F (bar). **Lunch menu** 140F, 180F. **Credit** AmEx, DC, MC, V. **Map H7**

Group therapy: happy eaters enjoy a uniquely Parisian buzz at beloved **Bofinger**.

Sir Terence Conran calls this modern space in a former St-Germain cabaret his 'brasserie for the 21st century'. There is seating for 300 on red banquettes and aluminium chairs, and a bar with DJs upstairs. The competent but pricey menu includes starters like *pissaladière* (Provençal onion pizza), while main courses range from grilled sea bass with braised fennel to shoulder of lamb with white beans. The wine list, unusually for Paris, spans the world.

Brasserie Lipp

151 bd St-Germain, 6th (01.45.48.53.91).
M° St-Germain-des-Prés. **Open** 11.30am-1am daily.
Average 250F. **Prix fixe** 196F. **Credit** AmEx, DC, MC, V. **Map H7**
Lauren Bacall, Sharon Stone, François Mitterrand and Kosovo peace negotiators have all held court here. Insiders have mapped Lipp's rooms into heaven, hell and purgatory: when you score a table in the right-centre section of the main floor, where Mitterrand often sat, you know you have arrived. This, and the very first words on the menu (the only ones in English) 'NO SALAD AS MEAL', give a foretaste of the welcome you can expect. Traditional fare is reliable and relatively affordable, given the legend.

Brasserie Flo

7 cour des Petites-Ecuries, 10th (01.47.70.13.59).
M° Château d'Eau. **Open** noon-3pm, 7pm-1.30am daily. **Average** 185F. **Prix fixe** 132F (after 10pm), 179F (dinner only). **Lunch menu** 132F. **Credit** AmEx, DC, MC, V. **Map K3**
This may be the definitive Alsatian experience in Paris – the wood-panelled dining hall is fine, the oysters delightfully fresh, although the crowded atmosphere, undeniably part of the experience, can be on the stressful side. Once the food makes its way to your table, however, it soothes frayed nerves. The steaks are tender, the seafood properly sweet and the crêpes and hot profiteroles delicious.

Terminus Nord

23 rue de Dunkerque, 10th (01.42.85.05.15).
M° Gare du Nord. **Open** 11am-1am daily. **Average** 185F. **Prix fixe** 132F (after 10.30pm), 179F. **Lunch menu** 132F. **Child's menu** 62F. **Credit** AmEx, DC, MC, V. **Map K2**
In this surprisingly good brasserie just across the road from the Gare du Nord, luggage piles up against the bar, a buzz of languages swirls round, and amiable waiters bring heaps of seafood and other brasserie fare – onion soup, thick with cheese, bouillabaisse with *rouille* – to packed tables. For dessert, try one of three different crème brûlées.

La Coupole

102 bd du Montparnasse, 14th (01.43.20.14.20).
M° Vavin. **Open** 7.30am-2am daily. **Average** 200F. **Prix fixe** 169F. **Credit** AmEx, DC, MC, V. **Map G9**
This sprawling, legendary Art Deco brasserie was the backdrop of the giddy, artistic life that was 1920s Montparnasse. Rather heavy-handedly restored in 1988 by brasserie-meister Jean-Paul Bucher, it's still a vaguely glamorous place that draws a colourful crowd. Food is reliable: foie gras is fresh and flavourful; *jarret demi-sel* is a tender hunk of salt pork on a

mound of tasty *choucroute,* and the seafood counter is gigantic. Ice cream, a crunchy coffee *parfait* or profiteroles are suitably extravagant.

La Gare

19 chaussée de la Muette, 16th (01.42.15.15.31).
M° La Muette. **Open** noon-3pm; 7pm-midnight daily.
Average 150F. **Credit** AmEx, DC, MC, V. **Map A6**
This cleverly converted railway station is a stylish rendezvous. Tables, complete with carriage seating and luggage racks, are spread over erstwhile tracks and platforms, while a glazed roof over the central canyon lets in sunlight. Fashionable classics include rôtisserie meats, steak tartare and an adventurous *pastilla pintade,* a France-meets-Morocco filo pastry bundle bursting with guinea fowl and coriander. *Wheelchair access.*

La Grande Armée

3 av de la Grande Armée, 16th (01.45.00.24.77).
M° Charles-de-Gaulle-Etoile. **Open** 7am-2am daily.
Average 150F. **Credit** AmEx, DC, MC, V. **Map C3**
This modern brasserie near the Arc de Triomphe has an amusing tongue-in-cheek bordello décor: animal prints meet Napoleonic soldiers. The food is a fine, top-of-the-charts offer of what modish types like best: salmon tartare, carpaccio with rocket and parmesan, oysters, foie gras, steak tartare, grilled steaks, or you can stop off all day for tea or an apéro.

Au Boeuf Couronné

188 av Jean-Jaurès, 19th (01.42.39.54.54). M° Porte de Pantin. **Open** noon, 7.30pm-midnight Mon-Sat; noon-3pm Sun. **Average** 190F. **Prix fixe** 160F, 200F. **Credit** AmEx, DC, MC, V.
This enormous brasserie with its staff of 29 (including one chef who prepares nothing but the excellent soufflé potatoes) boasts irreproachable service. The steak tartare could easily satiate two, and there's a mini seafood *menu* that changes with the seasons – this might include a shellfish platter with mussels, whelks, winkles, shrimps and oysters for 120F.

Regional

Alsace: L'Alsaco

10 rue Condorcet, 9th (01.45.26.44.31).
M° Poissonnière. **Open** noon-2pm, 7.30-11pm Mon-Fri; 7.30-11pm Sat. Closed Aug. **Average** 140F. **Prix fixe** 95F (dinner), 190F. **Lunch menu** 87F. **Credit** AmEx, MC, V. **Map J2**
This clubby little *winstub* goes far beyond the Alsatian stereotype of *choucroute garnie.* Less usual fare includes *pipalakass* (*fromage blanc* with cumin, onion and herbs) and *baeckeoffe* (mutton, beef and potatoes braised in Riesling). Try the munster cheeses and unusual *eaux de vie.* A good selection of regional wines and Météor beer on tap help animate the atmosphere among the crowd of regulars.

Auvergne: La Galoche d'Aurillac

41 rue de Lappe, 11th (01.47.00.77.15). M° Bastille.
Open noon-2.30pm, 7.30-11.30pm Tue-Sat. Closed Aug. **Average** 200F. **Prix fixe** 150F. **Credit** MC, V. **Map M7**

One is tempted to do the clog dance on coming into this quirky Auvergnat stalwart, firmly holding its own against the encroachment of Cuban, Tex-Mex and other upstarts on rue de Lappe. One could easily pig out here on stuffed cabbage, *confit de canard*, *pounti* (meatloaf) or *potée* (meat and veg stew), but the Galoche works a light touch on a salad of *frisée* with duck's gizzards and cured duck breast. To finish, try the *tourtière aux pruneaux*, a refined tart of prunes sandwiched by thin layers of buttery pastry.

Burgundy: Chez Tante Louise

41 rue Boissy d'Anglas, 8th (01.42.65.06.85). *M° Madeleine or Concorde.* **Open** noon-2pm, 7.30-10pm Mon-Fri. **Average** 250F. **Prix fixe** 190F. **Credit** AmEx, MC, V. **Map F4**
Famed chef Bernard Loiseau, based in Burgundy, is behind the resurrection of this endearing 30s-era bistro. His menu features high-brow comfort food like poached eggs in red wine sauce, a mushroom and snail sauté, and rich Tante Louise sole fillets – but the cooking can be inconsistent. There's a nice selection of Burgundies; service is professional.

Corsica: L'Alivi

27 rue du Roi-de-Sicile, 4th (01.48.87.90.20). M° St-Paul. **Open** noon-2.30pm, 7-11.30pm daily. **Average** 180F. **Prix fixe** 112F. **Credit** MC, V. **Map L6**
While you sip a Corsican *apéritif* at this small Marais restaurant, you can peruse the menu's two pages of eulogies from guidebooks and Corsica-linked celebrities like Paris mayor Jean Tiberi. Starters like *u pranzettu*, crisp fried sausage, or soothing *pulenda* (like polenta, but made with chestnut flour) are delectable. Main courses include the challenging *fressure de cabri*, made with goat heart, lung and liver.

Franche-Comté: Chez Maître Paul

12 rue Monsieur-le-Prince, 6th (01.43.54.74.59). M° Odéon. **Open** 12.15-2.30pm, 7.15-10.30pm daily. Closed Sun, Mon lunch in July, Aug. **Average** 220F. **Prix fixe** 165F, 195F. **Credit** AmEx, DC, MC, V. **Map H7**
This venerable restaurant turns out precise, authentic dishes from the rich and consoling cuisine of this eastern French region. Try the Montbéliard sausage to start and then one of the free-range chicken preparations, either served in a sauce made from sherry-like *vin jaune* or roasted and then gratinéed in cream and cheese. Finish with the walnut meringue cake and splurge on an older bottle of Arbois wine.

Normandy: Les Fernandises

19 rue de la Fontaine-au-Roi, 11th (01.48.06.16.96). M° République. **Open** noon-2.30pm, 7.30-10.30pm Tue-Sat. Closed Aug, one week in May. **Average** 190F. **Prix fixe** 130F. **Lunch menu** 100F. **Credit** MC, V. **Map M4**
Boisterous locals fill this informal bistro for honest, Normandy home cooking. The great-value *menu* lets you start with chicken liver terrine or a large crunchy salad, before main dishes like pork ribs with garlic cream sauce and grilled salmon with mashed pumpkin and celeriac. Finish with apple tart or one of the oozing camemberts and succumb to the fine selection of Calvados.

North: Le Graindorge

15 rue de l'Arc de Triomphe, 17th (01.47.54.00.28). M° Charles-de-Gaulle-Etoile. **Open** noon-3pm, 7-11pm Mon-Fri; 7-11pm Sat. Closed three weeks in Aug. **Average** 230F. **Prix fixe** 188F (dinner only). **Lunch menu** 168F. **Credit** AmEx, MC, V. **Map C3**
A down-to-earth clientele with a fair sprinkling of dressed-up Parisians come for chef Bernard Broux's very good Flemish cooking: *waterzooï*, shellfish and fish in broth with vegetables, or delicately grilled scallops in *bière blanche* (wheat beer) sauce, served on a bed of barley. Tempting regional cheeses include aged mimolette and funky maroilles.

Provence: La Bastide Odéon

7 rue Corneille, 6th (01.43.26.03.65). M° Odéon or RER Luxembourg. **Open** 12.30-2pm, 7.30-10.30pm Tue-Sat. Closed three weeks in Aug. **Prix fixe** 150F, 190F. **Credit** AmEx, MC, V. **Map H7**
Tucked beside the Odéon theatre, this elegant bistro, with its cream walls and crisp linen, is host to the inventive, contemporary updated Provençal cooking of young owner-chef Gilles Ajuelos. He's particularly good with fish: recent creations include fried scorpion fish and green asparagus with mashed sweet potato, and a duo of roast cod and cod purée with *tapenade* and leeks.

South-West: Aux Fins Gourmets

213 bd St-Germain, 7th (01.42.22.06.57). M° Rue du Bac. **Open** 7.30-10pm Mon; noon-2.15pm, 7.30-10pm Tue-Sat. Closed Aug. **Average** 200F. **No credit cards. Map G6**
This shabby, no-frills establishment is one of the few on boulevard St-Germain that's oblivious to fashion and *formules*. As it's near the Assemblée Nationale, government officials can be found enjoying marinated herrings, *cassoulet*, *poulet basquaise* and excellent cheeses. There are some interesting regional wines.

Fish & Seafood

L'Ostréa

4 rue Sauval, 1st (01.40.26.08.07). M° Louvre-Rivoli. **Open** noon-2.30pm, 7.30-11pm Mon-Fri; 7.30-11pm Sat. **Average** 150F. **Credit** MC, V. **Map J5**
Nestled in a quiet side street in Les Halles, this is a find for fish-lovers on a budget. A typical starter might be pickled herrings filled with a savoury butter cream. Main courses include thick tuna steak with a carrot, pepper and courgette ratatouille, and steamed sea bass, flavourful but a little soft-fleshed.

Paul Minchelli

54 bd La Tour-Maubourg, 7th (01.47.05.89.86). M° La Tour-Maubourg. **Open** noon-2.30pm, 8-10.30pm Tue-Sat. Closed Aug, 25 Dec-2 Jan. **Average** 600F. **Credit** MC, V. **Map E6**
A drop-dead chic crowd fills this sophisticated restaurant designed by Slavik, who has invested it with the clubbiness of the chef's former kitchen, the exorbitant Le Duc. Minchelli's fashionable minimalism is based on crucial timing – as in the gambas with ground mixed peppers, or the cod steamed over seaweed – with little other adornment.

Marines

70-72 rue du Fbg-Poissonnière, 10th (01.42.46.22.29).
Mᵒ Poissonnière. **Open** noon-2pm, 7.30-10.30pm
Mon-Fri; 7.30-10.30pm Sat. **Average** 160F. **Prix
fixe** 135F. **Credit** AmEx DC MC, V. **Map J4**
The 135F three-course *menu* at this snug, bottle-blue
dining room is a cracking bargain. Good bets are
rich fish soup, salmon with a sweet-and-sour tomato relish or the catch of the day, maybe sea bass or
cod. It's worth paying a supplement for the coffee
soufflé and *crêpes suzette*, prepared tableside.

La Cagouille

10 pl Constantin-Brancusi, 14th (01.43.22.09.01)
Mᵒ Gaîté. **Open** noon-2.30pm, 7.30-10.30pm daily.
Average 200F. **Prix fixe** 150F, 250F. **Credit**
AmEx, MC, V. **Map F10**
If you fancy an *al fresco* seafood feast, the terrace of
this excellent fish house is a first-rate option. A pio-
neer of minimalist fish cookery in Paris, Gérard
Allemandou does dishes like small mussels cooked
on a hot griddle, tuna steak wrapped in bacon and
John Dory with a perfect *beurre blanc*. Consider a
Cognac from one of the best collections in Paris.

Le Dôme

108 bd du Montparnasse, 14th (01.43.35.25.81).
Mᵒ Vavin. **Open** noon-2.45pm, 7pm-12.30am daily.
Average 400F. **Credit** AmEx, DC, MC, V. **Map G9**
This legendary Montparnasse fish house, with slick
chrome and wood décor by Slavik, silly lights and
tobacco-coloured walls, is justly reputed for its
shellfish and sole meunière. Around the corner, the
less-formal Bistrot du Dôme (1 rue Delambre/
01.43.35.32.00) offers the same quality, but with simpler preparations at lower prices.

Budget

Chez Max

47 rue St-Honoré, 1st (01.45.08.80.13. Mᵒ Les Halles.
Open noon-3pm, 7pm-midnight Mon-Fri; 7pm-midnight
Sat. Closed Aug. **Average** 140F. **Prix fixe** 85F, 135F.
Lunch menu 65F, 120F. **Credit** AmEx, MC, V. **Map J5**
Charming host Max Reytet likes to mother his din-
ers and ensure every home-cooked morsel is eaten.
There's a decent choice of adventurous dishes, such
as prawns in *pastis*, alongside traditional
andouillette, roast free-range chicken in tarragon
sauce and *magret de canard* with honey and lime.

Fish and Fun

*55 bd de Sébastopol, 1st (01.42.21.10.10). Mᵒ Etienne-
Marcel.* **Open** noon-4.30pm, 6.30pm-midnight Mon-
Sat. **Average** 50F. **No credit cards. Map K5**
This new place redefines minimalist fish cooking,
serving flash-grilled and steamed fish at ridiculous-
ly low prices. With mashed potato or puréed carrot
on the side, and a choice of sauces, this is probably
the healthiest fast food in Paris. The fresh fish goes
from salmon to swordfish, served in decent portions.

La Potée des Halles

*3 rue Etienne-Marcel, 1st (01.40.41.98.15). Mᵒ
Etienne-Marcel.* **Open** noon-2.30pm, 7pm-midnight
Mon-Fri; 7pm-midnight Sat, Sun. **Prix fixe** 89F.
Lunch menu 69F. **Credit** MC, V. **Map J5**
Enter this timewarp bistro, with its stained glass
and paintings of voluptuous women personifying
wine and coffee, and you can picture the days when
nearby Les Halles was a raucous food market. The
new owner has resurrected the restaurant's original
recipe for *potée* – a hearty, peasant mix of salt pork,

Like a challenge? Go for goat heart, lung and liver at the Corsican restaurant **L'Alivi**.

bacon, sausage, carrots, cabbage, beans and onions in a heavily garlic-infused broth – dating from 1903.

Mimosa
44 rue d'Argout, 2nd (01.40.28.15.75). M° Sentier. **Open** *summer* 11am-10pm Mon-Sat; *winter* 11am-6pm Mon-Sat. **Average** 75F. **Credit** MC, V. **Map J5**
Chef, waiter and wine steward Cédric Ung has created a restaurant that has people queueing in the street. Choose from three platters: the *périgord*, our favourite, is a mix of cured ham, smoked duck, foie gras terrine and assorted veg. Ung offers a small but outstanding selection of wines by the glass. Service is a juggling act, but attention to detail is consistent.

Café de la Poste
13 rue Castex, 4th (01.42.72.95.35). M° Bastille. **Open** noon-3pm, 7-11pm Mon-Fri. **Average** 110F. **Credit** MC, V. **Map L7**
This handkerchief-sized bistro in a sleepy Marais street scores high on artistic presentation. Salads are colourful and fresh, the quality of the steaks is high, and *plats du jour* are honest versions of *coq au vin*, *lapin à la moutarde* and other standards. Regulars arrive late, so make sure you book.

Les Philosophes
28 rue Vieille-du-Temple, 4th (01.48.87.49.64). M° Hôtel-de-Ville. **Open** 9am-2am daily. **Average** 150F. **Prix fixe** 85F, 104F, 136F. **Credit** MC, V. **Map K6**
It's easy to be philosophical about small flaws in the food, given the inventive touches that make this place stand out among budget bistros: spicy *assiette de boudin antillais* with cinnamon rice, or tuna rubbed with subtle tandoori spices. Inexpensive wines come by the bottle or glass.

L'Ecurie
2 rue Laplace, 5th (01.46.33.68.49). M° Maubert-Mutualité. **Open** noon-3pm, 7pm-midnight Mon, Wed-Sat; 7pm-midnight Tue, Sun. **Average** 120F. **Prix fixe** 98F. **Lunch menu** 75F. **No credit cards. Map J8**
A medieval labyrinth of dark vaults and underground archways, 'the stable' combines historic atmosphere and food for hungry carnivores, with abundant charcoal-grilled steaks and roast lamb. The wine list is hardly exhaustive, but then neither are the prices.

L'Escapade
10 rue de la Montagne-Ste-Geneviève, 5th (01.46.33.23.85). M° Maubert-Mutualité. **Open** daily 7pm-1am. **Prix fixe** 105F. **Credit** MC, V. **Map J7**
A 105F *menu* provides three hearty courses and, crucially, a limitless supply of wine. This place is, consequently, a mecca for groups of English revellers. The food is competent – main courses include *boeuf bourguignon* or turkey *brochette*. Wine, which comes on tap, is pretty grim, but no one cares.

Bistrot Mazarin
42 rue Mazarine, 6th (01.43.29.99.03). M° Mabillon. **Open** noon-3.30pm, 7.15pm-midnight daily. **Average** 130F. **Credit** AmEx, MC, V. **Map H7**
Come here for a satisfying feed, drinkable wines and a buzzy terrace full of students and 'creatives'. Salads, charcuterie, veal with lemon and *boeuf bourguignon*

are all fine. Service is a bit slow, but good eavesdropping and the relaxing setting make up for it.

Le Petit St-Benoît
4 rue St-Benoît, 6th (01.42.60.27.92). M° St-Germain des Prés. **Open** noon-2.30pm, 7-10.30pm Mon-Sat. Closed Aug. **Average** 120F. **No credit cards. Map H7**
Open since 1901, Le Petit-St-Benoît prides itself on tradition. The crowd of locals is attracted by authenticity and low prices. Walls feature signed photos of distinguished former customers (Serge Gainsbourg, Paco Rabanne). Food such as country sausage and *gigot d'agneau* is flavourful. Service is friendly, but overworked waitresses may try to speed you along.

Chartier
7 rue du Fbg-Montmartre, 9th (01.47.70.86.29). M° Grands Boulevards. **Open** noon-3pm, 7-10pm daily. **Average** 80F. **Prix fixe** 74F, 110F, 190F. **Credit** MC, V. **Map J4**
Once flagship of a chain of working-class *bouillons* (turn-of-the-century soup kitchens), Chartier is a classic Paris timewarp that relies on its period setting, reputation and atmosphere, rather than quality cuisine. The food is often sadly reminiscent of a school canteen; *plats du jour* are the safest bets.

L'Ebauchoir
45 rue de Cîteaux, 12th (01.43.42.49.31). M° Faidherbe-Chaligny. **Open** noon-2.30pm, 8-10.30pm Mon-Thur; noon-2.30pm, 8-11pm Fri, Sat. **Average** 130F. **Lunch menu** 68F, 85F. **Credit** MC, V. **Map N8**

L'Encrier: *nothing budget about the décor.*

A local crowd packs out this spacious dining hall, enjoying its unpretentious amiability and good value. The lunch menu changes daily, but might run to herrings with potato salad, sautéed lamb or cod fillet in a crab sauce. Sometimes dishes are a little under-seasoned. Traditional desserts are variable.

L'Encrier
55 rue Traversière, 12th (01.44.68.08.16).
Mº Ledru-Rollin. **Open** noon-2.15pm, 7.15-11pm Mon-Fri; 7.15-11pm Sat. Closed one week in Aug, 24 Dec-2 Jan. **Average** 120F. **Prix fixe** 62F. **Credit** MC, V. **Map M7**
With its exposed stone walls, sleek lights and open kitchen, this doesn't look like a budget joint. It doesn't taste like one either. Food is simple, always fresh and never predictable, which makes it quite difficult to get a table at lunch. Roast young rooster comes golden skinned and juicy, and wafer-thin fried potato rounds (house trademark) are crisp and moreish.

Chez Gladines
30 rue des Cinq-Diamants, 13th (01.45.80.70.10).
Mº Corvisart. **Open** noon-3pm, 7pm-midnight daily. Closed Aug. **Average** 100F. **Lunch menu** 60F. **No credit cards.**
This hectic bistro in the villagey Butte-aux-Cailles neighbourhood is a noisy corner of the Pays Basque in Paris. Giant salads served in earthenware bowls are popular, along with South-western duck dishes and a daily 60F lunch *menu*. Try a *pipérade* with *jambon de Bayonne* or fiery red pimentos stuffed with salt cod purée in a spicy tomato sauce.

Ti Jos
30 rue Delambre, 14th (01.43.22.57.69). Mº Vavin.
Open noon-2.30pm, 7pm-12.30am Mon, Wed-Fri; noon-2.30pm Tue. **Average** 70F. **Prix fixe** 55F, 71F. **Credit** V. **Map G9**
Ti Jos is a heavyweight contender for the crêpe quality crown. Traditional Breton style pervades, right down to the cook's handlebar moustache. It's slightly cheaper than your average crêpe joint too, at around 38F-45F an item, but the choice of fillings is basic – variants on ham and cheese. There are also appetising non-crêpe options, such as *moules marinières*. Head-spinning cider is in abundance.

Le Café du Commerce
51 rue du Commerce, 15th (01.45.75.03.27).
Mº Emile-Zola. **Open** noon-midnight daily. **Average** 115F. **Prix fixe** 82F, 117F. **Credit** AmEx, DC, MC, V. **Map C8**
This airy, three-tiered dining hall was once a cheap workers' canteen. Now more upmarket, with an agreeable Mediterranean feel, its prices are still reasonable and the bustle remains. The menu is varied if not stunning: excellent *rillettes aux deux saumons*, passable *confit de canard* and honeyed pork ribs.

Restaurant GR5
19 rue Gustave-Courbet, 16th (01.47.27.09.84).
Mº Trocadéro. **Open** noon-3pm, 7-11pm Mon-Sat. **Average** 150F. **Prix fixe** 118F (dinner only). **Lunch menu** 79F, 90F. **Credit** AmEx, MC, V. **Map B5**
This Alpine-themed, pint-sized restaurant is a haven

of simplicity amid the sleek boutiques of the 16th. The affable service and hearty food evoke the snowy Savoie: *raclette valaisanne* (melted cheese with boiled potatoes), *tartiflette* (a melt of potatoes, cheese and bacon) and *fondue savoyarde* (cheese fondue).

Chez Toinette
20 rue Germain-Pilon, 18th (01.42.54.44.36).
Mº Abbesses. **Open** 8-11pm Tue-Sun. Closed Aug. **Average** 110F. **No credit cards.** **Map H2**
The purely native crowd in this bargain bistro is testimony to a quality of food rare in touristy Pigalle. In its scarlet boudoiresque interior, they demolish dishes like a succulent oyster mushroom *fricassée*, rabbit and tarragon casserole and honeyed duck. A lone waiter means service can be erratic.

Rendez-vous des Chauffeurs
11 rue des Portes-Blanches, 18th (01.42.64.04.17).
Mº Marcadet-Poissoniers. **Open** noon-2.30pm, 7.30-11pm Mon, Tue, Thur-Sun. Closed first two weeks Aug. **Average** 100F. **Prix fixe** 65F (until 8.30pm, Mon-Sat). **Credit** MC, V.
The unimposing exterior and unglamorous location give no hint that this simple restaurant catering to locals is outstanding. The *prix fixe*, offering only four main courses (steak tartare, kidneys, *andouillette* and steak *garni*) but with a *pichet* of wine thrown in, may be the best 65F feed in Paris. Book ahead.

La Boulangerie
15 rue des Panoyaux, 20th (01.43.58.45.45).
Mº Ménilmontant. **Open** noon-2pm, 7.30-11pm Mon-Sat; 11.30-4pm Sun. **Average** 100F. **Prix fixe** 65F (lunch), 78F, 98F (dinner). **Credit** MC,V. **Map P4**
This welcoming new bistro, run by the team of the bar Lou Pascalou nearby, occupies an old bakery decorated with a mosaic floor, bas-reliefs and frescoes. A young, arty crowd comes for the precise cooking and imaginative seasonings to be found in dishes like grilled red mullet and *pot au feu*.

Vegetarian

Galerie 88
88 quai de l'Hôtel de Ville, 4th (01.42.72.17.58).
Mº Hôtel-de-Ville. **Open** noon-2am daily. **Average** 100F. **No credit cards.** **Map K6**
This sly little café hides on the Right Bank waterfront, providing an offbeat breed of cosiness with its funky young clientele, ochre walls, dim lighting and jazz. The food is Mediterranean with the meat taken out – salads, tapas, tagliatelle and soups.
Wheelchair access.

Piccolo Teatro
6 rue des Ecouffes, 4th (01.42.72.17.79). Mº St-Paul.
Open noon-3pm, 7-11pm Tue-Sat; noon-4pm, 7-11pm Sun. **Average** 110F. **Prix fixe** 90F, 115F. **Lunch menu** 63F (Tue-Fri). **Credit** AmEx, MC, V. **Map K6**
This tiny, cellar-like restaurant in the Marais is a gem. Don't be thrown by the purple prose descriptions of the *gratins*: '*appel au soleil*' is a mix of tomatoes, aubergines, cheese and basil, while '*douceur et tendresse*' has spinach, tomatoes and carrots.

Flavours of the Maghreb

Just as curry has come to seem quintessentially English, couscous has surpassed *steak-frites* and even the beloved *pot-au-feu* as the favourite dish of Parisians. Whether in a *boui-boui* (an affectionate term for the humble corner café) or a plush restaurant, the city abounds with places to feast on this fluffy semolina grain from North Africa, most often served with a steaming cauldron of stewed meat and vegetables.

The most obvious explanation for the ever-growing popularity of couscous and *tagines* – fragrant, honey-sweetened stews of meat, vegetables and fruits, named after the conical cooking pot – is immigration. The first wave of 250,000 Maghrebans came during World War I to fight alongside the French and work in factories. The Paris Mosque, built in 1920, honours the 100,000 among them who died on the bat-

tlefields; seven years later, the city's first North African restaurant, Le Hoggar, opened in the Latin Quarter. France again looked to North Africa after World War II, bringing in workers to help rebuild the country.

Immigrants from each of these countries brought their own specialities. Typical starters in Tunisian restaurants, which are numerous in Belleville and around rue du Fbg-Montmartre, are *briks* – layers of paper-thin pastry stuffed with egg, cheese, meat or fish – and a spicy salad of roasted peppers and tomatoes doused in olive oil. Delicate couscous is served with fish, or sometimes tripe. A good place to sample Tunisian specialities is the popular **La Gazelle**,

decorated with rugs, teapots and a kitsch aquarium; such rich *tagines* as the lamb with tomatoes and onions are worth the 20-minute wait.

Algerian cooking is cosmopolitan, having absorbed traditions from Iraq, Turkey and Morocco. Couscous might be served with steamed broad beans, peas or artichokes, or stuffed sheep's stomach (a kind of Algerian haggis). Couscous with grilled meats (*méchoui*) is the signature dish, but you might also find sweet *tagines*, alongside Turkish-inspired *dolmas* (stuffed vine leaves). Paris' best-known Algerian restaurant, **Chez Omar**, attracts fashion and media junkies for its tender grilled meats, and giant platters of fine-quality couscous.

Morocco has the most refined cooking style, blending Bedouin, Berber, Spanish and Jewish influences. Saffron, ginger (powdered, not fresh), cinnamon and orange-flower water impart seductive flavours, as does a blend of 21 spices called *ras el hanout*. One of the best representatives in Paris of this cuisine is Fatéma Hal, who opened her elegant restaurant **Le Mansouria** 15 years ago. Wallowing in orange and purple silk cushions, you might sample her ethereal *tagine* of chicken, rose petals and tomato 'jam', or the *couscous voilé*, a seemingly bottomless dish of tender chicken with sweet onions, raisins and almonds under couscous laced with cinnamon and icing sugar.

Just as inviting is **Le Souk**: past the kilim at the entrance a small spice shop conjures up Marrakesh; the intimate dining room has ochre walls, deep red carpets and round brass trays that serve as tables. A *millefeuille* of roasted peppers and feta is luscious if superfluous before one of the inventive *tagines*, such as plump duckling with figs, apricots and honey.

A place to go less for the food than the festive spirit is **404**, owned by the comedian Smaïn. The likes of Jean-Paul Gaultier and Kate Moss come for the Oriental brunch or the carefully degreased but slightly bland couscous and *tagines*, presented in lovely painted dishes. It's hard not to be drawn in, especially after more than one of the house cocktails of vodka, mint, cane sugar, lemon and fizzy water.

La Gazelle 33 rue Lamartine, 9th (01.48.78.25.69). Mº Cadet. **Chez Omar** 47 rue de Bretagne, 3rd (01.42.72.36.26). Mº Arts et Métiers. **Le Mansouria** 11 rue Faidherbe, 11th (01.43.71.00.16). Mº Faidherbe-Chaligny. **Le Souk** 1 rue Keller, 11th (01.49.29.05.08). Mº Ledru-Rollin. **404** 69 rue des Gravilliers, 3rd (01.42.74.57.81). Mº Arts et Métiers.

Desserts show an English influence, with rhubarb or berry crumble, and delicious fruit tarts. *Wheelchair access.*

Les Quatre et Une Saveurs
72 rue du Cardinal-Lemoine, 5th (01.43.26.88.80). M° Cardinal-Lemoine. **Open** noon-2.30pm, 7-10.30pm Tue-Sun. **Average** 100F. **Prix fixe** 130F. **Credit** MC, V. **Map K8**
An airy setting for fresh, macrobiotic, Japanese-style dishes – no dairy, no eggs, no sugar, 100 per cent organic. Miso and vegetable soups figure among the starters, while *assiettes complètes* often include pasta instead of conventional grains.

Guen Mai
2bis rue de l'Abbaye, 6th (01.43.26.03.24). M° St-Germain des Prés. **Open** 11.45am-3.30pm Mon-Sat. Closed Aug. **Average** 95F. **Credit** MC, V. **Map H7**
This invaluable address pulls a trendy crowd and ladies who lunch. While prices reflect the chic location, salads, quiches and tofu dishes can be uneven.

La Ville de Jagannath
101 rue St-Maur, 11th (01.43.55.80.81). M° St-Maur. **Open** 7.30-11.30pm Mon-Thur, Sun; 7.30pm-12.30am Fri, Sat. Closed one week in Aug. **Prix fixe** 90F, 130F, 160F. **Credit** AmEx, DC, MC, V. **Map N5**
This temple to Indian vegetarian cuisine serves delicately spiced, Buddhist-inspired food. Based on refined *thali*-style dining, it's the contrast between flavours, textures and colours that makes eating here so interesting. Bring your own wine (no surcharge).

You'll be in your element **Chez Marianne.**

Aquarius
40 rue de Gergovie, 14th (01.45.41.36.88). M° Pernéty. **Open** noon-2.15pm, 7-10.30pm Mon-Sat. **Average** 85F. **Lunch menu** 65F. **Credit** MC, V. **Map F10**
This busy Paris institution has the most eclectic vegetarian menu in town. Veggie lasagne, omelettes, ravioli and *tourtes* are on the *carte*, while daily specials may run to polenta with green pepper sauce and ratatouille. Excellent desserts.

International

The Americas

Anahi
49 rue Volta, 3rd (01.48.87.88.24). M° Arts et Métiers. **Open** 8pm-12.30am daily. **Average** 210F. **Credit** MC, V. **Map K4**
Black-clad trendsters and models pile into this South American Marais bistro, run by fiercely elegant Spanish *patronne* Carmen and sister Pilar. Even if dishes, like nicely spiced guacamole and high-quality Argentine *churrasco* steak are a little expensive, it's worth it for the adrenaline buzz and the glitterati.

Le Studio
41 rue du Temple, 4th (01.42.74.10.38). M° Hôtel-de-Ville. **Open** 7.30pm-midnight Mon-Fri; 12.30-3pm, 7.30pm-12.30am Fri-Sun. **Average** 120F. **Credit** AmEx, MC, V. **Map K6**
The historic courtyard of the ancient Aigle d'Or inn is great in summer. The Tex-Mex fare is predictable, but the atmosphere is electric – probably something to do with the fiery Margaritas. Try the *nachos* and the lightly spiced beef *burritos* or chicken tacos.

The Far East

Han Lim
6 rue Blainville, 5th (01.43.54.62.74). M° Place Monge. **Open** noon-2.30pm, 7-10.30pm Tue-Sun. Closed Aug. **Average** 120F. **Lunch menu** 73F. **Credit** MC, V. **Map L6**
Family-run Han Lim is one of Paris' best Korean restaurants. Try the spicy sesame seed and whelk salad, buckwheat noodles in black bean sauce, deep-fried ravioli, and addictive garlic chicken wings. Book.

Khun Akorn
8 av de Taillebourg, 11th (01.43.56.20.03). M° Nation. **Open** noon-2pm, 7.30-11pm Tue-Sun. **Average** 150F. **Prix fixe** 195F, 275F, 325F. **Lunch menu** 125F. **Credit** AmEx, MC, V. **Map Q7**
This Thai restaurant (with branches in Bangkok and London) is calm and spacious. Delectable dishes include chicken and coconut soup tasting of lemon grass, kaffir lime leaves, ginger and tangy fish sauce, and duck chunks bathed in a curry sauce with grapes, lychees and aubergines.

New Nioullaville
32 rue de l'Orillon, 11th (01.40.21.96.18). M° Belleville. **Open** noon-3pm, 7pm-1am daily. **Average** 160F. **Lunch menu** 38F-78F (Mon-Fri only). **Credit** AmEx, MC, V. **Map M4**

Nioulaville: *room for a pan-Asian feast.*

Nioullaville seats 500, but fills up fast, leaving hungry people queueing. The 18-page menu brings on an agony of indecison, but service is kind and amazingly efficient. Specialities include *canard du chef*, which arrives sizzling on an iron plaque with onions, chillies, mushrooms and ginger, or *boeuf sauté au saté*, with green and red peppers and pineapple.

Tricotin

15 av de Choisy, 13th (01.45.84.74.44).
M° Porte de Choisy. **Open** 9.30am-11.30pm daily.
Average 70F. **Credit** MC, V.
Nip into this cheerful storefront at the foot of one of Chinatown's towering apartment blocks for quick and wholesome soups, dumplings or barbecue. Multi-generational family groups congregate at round tables, while phone-toting Asian yuppies sit canteen-style to wolf down a quick *pho*.

Chen

15 rue du Théâtre, 15th (01.45.79.34.34).
M° Charles Michel. **Open** noon-2:30pm, 7.30-10.30pm Tue-Sat. Closed first two weeks in Aug. **Average** 350F. **Prix fixe** 250F (dinner only). **Lunch menu** 190F. **Credit** AmEx, MC, V.
The best Chinese restaurant in Paris? Probably. The menu is ambitious, offering an array of dishes from China's major regional cuisines: steamed prawn and pork dumplings, frogs' legs with garlic, chives, chillies, salt and black pepper, *ma po do fu*, a mix of tofu and minced pork spiced with Szechuan peppercorns, elevated at Chen's into something truly refined.

Lao Siam

49 rue de Belleville, 19th (01.40.40.09.68). M° Belleville.
Open noon-3pm, 6-11.30pm Mon-Fri; noon-11.30pm Sat, Sun. **Average** 120F. **Credit** MC, V. **Map N3**
The freshness and subtlety of the Thai and Laotian cooking have made Lao Siam a favourite of Belleville's multiracial faithfuls. Non-smokers can find a seat in one of the city's few true non-smoking dining rooms. Delicate *salade douce*, with banana flower, grated coconut and prawns, is a typical starter; main courses include crisp-skinned chicken with coriander and *pad thai* (stir-fried noodles).

Italian

Le Fellini

47 rue de l'Arbre-Sec, 1st (01.42.60.90.66).
M° Louvre-Rivoli. **Open** noon-2.30pm, 7-11pm daily.
Average 200F. **Lunch menu** 110F (Mon-Sat).
Credit AmEx, MC, V. **Map J6**
At this warm, popular spot, classic southern Italian dishes predominate, such as a very good *spaghetti alle vongole* (with baby clams) or *tagliolini alla Norma*, with tomato sauce, fresh ricotta cheese and sautéed aubergine. Best bet is the antipasto buffet with its marvellous selection of vegetables, including *girolle* mushrooms, aubergine with capers and sun-dried tomatoes.

Santa Lucia

22 rue des Canettes, 6th (01.43.26.42.68).
M° St-Sulpice. **Open** noon-2.30pm, 7-11.30pm Mon, Wed-Sun. Closed mid July-mid Aug. **Average** 180F.
Credit MC, V. **Map H7**
Italian sources tell us this is the best pizzeria in Paris. The waiters have just enough charm to get away with cheeky innuendo that would be the stuff of sexual harassment suits in Clinton-land. Still, it's not enough to put you off your food: try the pizza mimmo, topped with tomato sauce, mozzarella and aubergine.

Japanese

Laï Laï Ken

7 rue Ste-Anne, 1st (01.40.15.96.90). M° Pyramides.
Open 11.45am-10pm daily. **Average** 90F. **Credit** MC,V. **Map H4/5**
This popular restaurant buzzes with an even mix of Japanese and Western diners, tucking into steaming bowls of *ramen*, soup laden with buttery noodles, bean sprouts and pork. Don't miss the deep-fried *gyoza* (pork and cabbage dumplings), rare in Paris.

Isse

56 rue Ste-Anne, 2nd (01.42.96.67.76). M° Pyramides.
Open noon-2pm, 7-10pm Tue-Fri; 7-10pm Sat. Closed two weeks in Aug. **Average** 300F. **Lunch menu** 150F. **Credit** MC, V. **Map H4/5**
Jetsetting Europeans have been flocking to this slick spot for years. Sushi is very good, although 200F buys a mere nine pieces. The tasty *tamago* omelette is less sickly sweet than elsewhere; the grilled eel and tender cuttlefish are delicious; and the heavenly, hard-to-find green tea ice cream topped with red bean jam makes a worthy conclusion.

Kifuné

44 rue St-Ferdinand, 17th (01.45.72.11.19).
M° Argentine. **Open** noon-2pm, 7-10pm Tue-Sat;
7-10pm Mon. **Average** 350F. **Lunch menus** 125F,
130F, 135F. **Credit** MC, V. **Map C3**
This is the benchmark by which all other Paris sushi
restaurants must be judged. Sushi and sashimi selections are generous and fresh, and service is gracious.
Tekka maki are the best we've had – the tuna is full
of flavour. Kifuné's excellence doesn't come cheap –
but if you're looking for the real thing, this is it.

Jewish

Chez Marianne

2 rue des Hospitalières-St-Gervais, 4th
(01.42.72.18.86). M° St-Paul. **Open** 11am-midnight
daily. **Prix fixe** 55F-75F. **Credit** MC, V. **Map K6**
Students, families and internationals never tire of the
good food and reasonable prices here. The main dining room, with its stone walls and candlelit tables, is
almost always buzzing, so do book. Aubergine
purée, pastrami, *tzatziki*, stuffed vine leaves, felafel,
tabouleh and houmous are freshly prepared.

Other

Armenian: Mayrig Café

116 rue Amelot, 11th (01.48.07.12.04).
M° Filles du Calvaire. **Open** noon-2.30pm, 7-11.30pm
Mon-Sat. **Average** 150F. **Lunch menu** 60F, 64F,
78F. **Credit** AmEx, DC, MC, V. **Map L5**
Fans of this restaurant overlook the gaudy non-décor,
for the fresh Armenian food, served attentively.
Starters like taramasalata and houmous satisfy small
appetites. The ravenous can move on to hearty main
courses such as *manti* – meat dumplings with garlic
yogurt and tomato sauce – or grilled fish and meat.
Wheelchair access.

Belgian: Bouillon Racine

3 rue Racine, 6th (01.44.32.15.60). M° Cluny-
La Sorbonne. **Open** 11am-midnight Mon-Fri;
11am-12.30am Sat; 11am-11pm Sun. **Average** 200F.
Prix fixe 159F. **Lunch menu** 79F, 107F (Mon-Fri).
Credit AmEx, MC, V. **Map H7**
If your idea of Belgian cuisine starts and stops with
mussels and chips, think again. At this stunningly
restored Art Nouveau workers' canteen, main courses include a *waterzooi* (Flemish stew with chicken and
vegetables) and a *carbonnade* of lamb stewed in beer.
For dessert, try the 'véritable' café liégeois – a cup of
frothy warm coffee with ice cream.
Wheelchair access.

British: Bertie's

Hôtel Baltimore, 1 rue Léo-Delibes, 16th
(01.44.34.54.34). M° Boissière. **Open** 12.30-2pm,
7.30-10.30pm Mon-Fri. Closed three weeks in Aug.
Average 250F. **Prix fixe** 220F. **Lunch menu**
190F. **Credit** AmEx, DC, MC, V. **Map B4**
Spotless service contributes to a classy dining experience from London's Roux brothers. Dive into a
quivering rare roast beef with fluffy Yorkshire
pudding or grilled whole Dover sole with whole

boiled potatoes. British farm cheeses are served here
at their peak of ripeness. What else to finish but
rhubarb crumble, smothered in real custard?

Caribbean: Le Marais Cage

8 rue de Beauce, 3rd (01.48.87.31.20). M° Temple.
Open noon-2.15pm, 7-10.30pm Mon-Fri; 7-10.30pm
Sat. Closed Aug. **Average** 170F. **Prix fixe** 99F,
165F, 199F. **Lunch menu** 85F, 135F. **Credit** AmEx,
DC, MC, V. **Map L5**
Le Marais Cage is on a dodgy-looking side street,
but inside it's warm and welcoming. Starters like
crabe farci, boudin créole and *féroce martiniquais* are
a good introduction to the Caribbean. Follow with
mildly curried pork or shark. For dessert, don't miss
the sensational *crêpe Caraïbe*, pineapple pancake
swimming in rum, flambéed by a bow-tied waiter.

Greek: Mavrommatis

42 rue Daubenton, 5th (01.43.31.17.17). M° Censier-
Daubenton. **Open** noon-2.15pm, 7-11pm Tue-Sun.
Average 200F. **Prix fixe** 150F, 165F (for four or
more). **Lunch menu** 120F. **Credit** MC, V. **Map K9**
The food and service here are excellent. *Pikilia*, six
cold appetisers including grape leaves and feta, is
the way to start. Delicious main courses include
squid stuffed with vegetables, and sea bream roasted with tomatoes and black kalamata olives.

Indian: Vishnou

13 rue du Commandant-René-Mouchotte, 14th
(01.45.38.92.93). M° Montparnasse Bienvenüe or
Gaîté. **Open** noon-2pm, 7-11pm Mon-Fri; 7-11pm Sat.
Average 250F. **Prix fixe** 175F, 220F. **Lunch menu**
95F, 150F. **Credit** AmEx, DC, MC, V. **Map F9**
Part museum, part colonial club, Vishnou's attempt
at subdued opulence is camp but charming. And the
sight of real, live Indians eating here can only be a
good sign. The tandoori assortment features tender
salmon, chicken and lamb accompanied by a well-
stocked carousel of sauces. Curries are as they should
be, the spices arresting rather than overwhelming.

Russian: Dominique

19 rue Bréa, 6th (01.43.27.08.80). M° Vavin. **Open**
restaurant 7.30pm-1am Mon-Sat; *bar* noon-1am Tue-
Sat. Closed mid-July to mid Aug. **Average** 180F.
Prix fixe 175F. **Credit** AmEx, DC, MC, V. **Map G8**
Founded in 1928, Dominique was a gathering place
for post-revolution Russian refugees. You'll find the
famed Beluga caviar and *zakuski* (assortment of
chicken liver paté, minced smoked salmon, puréed
aubergine and bulgur wheat *kasha*, etc), best with a
glass of chilled Moscovskaya vodka; salmon
koulebiaka and *kotleti pojarsky* (veal croquettes).

Spanish: Fogon Saint-Julien

10 rue St-Julien-le-Pauvre, 5th (01.43.54.31.33).
M° St-Michel. **Open** noon-3pm, 8pm-1.30am Mon-Sat.
Closed one week in Sept. **Average** 200F. **Prix fixe**
185F. **Lunch menu** 120F. **Credit** MC, V. **Map J7**
At this intimate spot in one of Paris' oldest streets,
you'll find not just one authentic *paella* but several.
The Valencian contains rice, chicken, rabbit, snails
and vegetables, stained ochre with saffron. Splurge
on one of the Riojas, and finish with *crème catalane*.

Cafés & Bars

Looking for a laidback café to while away the hours? Or the most bustling, 'branché' bar? In Paris, you needn't look very far.

More than a question of mere semantics, defining the café is a complicated business. The first place in France to have sold coffee was probably Marseilles, in 1671. The establishment was known as a *maison de café* and, ultimately, simply *café*. The taste soon spread to Paris with the opening of le Procope in 1672 at 6 rue de l'Ancienne-Comédie. Although now mainly a restaurant, it still has a café section. The pioneering cafés served exotic non-alcoholic drinks – coffee, tea, chocolate, sherbet – to an aristocratic clientele. Wine was served in *tavernes* and *cabarets*; beer was sold by *brasseurs*. By the late eighteenth century, the distinction between these different venues was becoming confused and a new word emerged – bistro, ascribed by some to Russian Cossacks in the 1814 occupation of Paris who asked for their food to be brought *bistro* (quickly). By the early nineteenth century, there were some 2,000 cafés in Paris.

Cafés also played a key role in the country's political and artistic life. While the Procope was largely frequented by writers and actors, the Café de Foy at the Palais-Royal was the seat of the *enragés* in the build-up to the 1789 French Revolution. In 1855-56 Courbet, Fantin-Latour, Manet and Degas gathered at the Café Molière after Courbet's exclusion from the Salon. In the early 1900s, Picasso and Braque frequented Les Deux Magots, before heading for Montparnasse, while during the war Café de Flore became home for Sartre and de Beauvoir.

Today's cafés are adapting again, whether for the Internet, live music, comedy or psychology. The hip seek out their hangouts in *branché* areas like Ménilmontant/Oberkampf (**Les Comptoirs de Charbon**), the Marais (**Les Etages**), Abbesses (**La Fourmi**) and the Canal St-Martin (**La Patache**), while the cafés and bars of St-Germain have retained their literary cachet. A major trend is the emergence of the theme bar: while at the start of the 90s, Irish pubs were popping up in every *quartier*, these days you can hardly avoid stumbling into a Latino-themed place.

Classic cafés change function over the course of a day, as customers whizz by for a quick coffee and croissant for breakfast, pile in at noon for a two-hour lunch, relax over a tatty paperback mid-afternoon, or philosophise over a beer by night. Here we've chosen a selection of classic cafés, hip new bars and the best locals, listed by *arrondissement*. Every *arrondissement* has its corner café or neighbourhood bar that is worth discovering.

Prices are lowest standing at the bar, slightly higher seated inside and highest on the terrace. Prices often go up by about 2F after 10pm. As well as beers, most cafés offer wines, spirits, coffee, snacks and meals. Except in various Irish/Anglo bars, beers on tap (*pression*) are usually served as a *demi* (25cl).

Cafés

Café de l'Epoque
2 rue du Bouloi, 1st (01.42.33.40.70). M° Palais-Royal. **Open** *Apr-Nov* 7am-11pm daily; *Dec-Mar* 7am-9pm. Closed two weeks in Aug. **Credit** MC, V. **Map H5**
Opening on to the historic Galerie Véro Dodat, the Epoque's facade is an elegant series of wood-framed arched windows and Corinthian capitals. Inside you'll find all the classic Parisian hallmarks: mirrors, brass, high ceilings, pâtisserie-display cabinets and upholstered banquettes. The reliable food runs to grills and salads; service is calm and leisurely.

Café Marly
93 rue de Rivoli, cour Napoléon du Louvre, 1st (01.49.26.06.60). M° Palais-Royal. **Open** 8am-2am daily. **Credit** AmEx, DC, MC, V. **Map H5**
The glamorous and the curious flock to this elegant Costes bros rendezvous overlooking the Louvre Pyramid. The design is a coolly understated interpretation of historicism, contrasting with the palatial surroundings. Meals add a modish spin to brasserie fare. Come late at night and sip a glass of Champagne – 55F, but worth it for the setting.

10 Top Terraces

Café Marly 1st
Les Caves de Bourgogne 5th
Bar du Marché 6th
Café de Flore 6th
Café de la Mairie 6th
Le Rostand 6th
Les Comptoirs de Charbon 11th
Pause Café 11th
Le Rendez-vous des Quais 19th
Le Soleil 20th

les comptoirs du
CHARBON

'Le plus parisien des cafés parisiens'
Open 7 days a week, 9am-2am Lunch & Dinner every day
Brunch Saturday and Sunday
100 rue Oberkampf, 11th Tel: 01-43-57-55-13

Le Café

*62 rue Tiquetonne, 2nd (01.40.39.08.00). M° Etienne-
Marcel.* **Open** 10am-2am daily. **Credit** MC, V. **Map J5**
The dusky interior of this fashion-pack hangout is
dressed up hotch-potch colonial style and a chaotic
fresco contrasts with the all-black uniform of the
customers. Rocket salads and such make up the suitably trendy fare, served by brisk, unobtrusive staff.

L'Apparemment Café

*18 rue des Coutures-St-Gervais, 3rd (01.48.87.12.22).
M° Filles du Calvaire.* **Open** noon-2am Mon-Fri; 4pm-2am
Sat; 12.30pm-midnight Sun. **Credit** MC, V. **Map L6**
This dimly lit retreat near the Musée Picasso is fur-
nished with armchairs and flea-market finds. A pro-
fessional crowd enhances the sense of a private club.
If bored, whip out a board game or flick through
Paris Match. Design your own salad by ticking
items on the menu chart. Monthly art shows.

Web Bar

*32 rue de Picardie, 3rd (01.42.72.66.55/
webbar@webbar.fr). M° République.*
Open 8.30am-2am Mon-Fri; 11am-2am Sat;
11am-midnight Sun. **Credit** MC, V. **Map L5**
The *net-plus ultra* of Paris cyberspace is more than
just a computer nerd's hangout. In fact, the Web Bar
is a cultural all-rounder; with its poetry nights, concerts, dance displays, films and art shows, it could
be posing as a mini-Beaubourg.

Café Beaubourg

*43 rue St-Merri, 4th (01.48.87.63.96). M° Hôtel-de-Ville/
RER Châtelet-Les Halles.* **Open** 8am-1am Mon-Thur, Sun;
8am-2am Fri, Sat. **Credit** AmEx, DC, MC, V. **Map K6**
Designed by architect Christian de Portzamparc, the
Costes brothers' slick reinvention of the classic café
is a civilised, postmodern affair, drawing members
of the art world from the adjacent Centre Pompidou
and other fashionable types.

Café des Phares

7 pl de la Bastille, 4th (01.42.72.04.70). M° Bastille.
Open 7am-3am Sun-Thur; 7am-4am Fri, Sat.
No credit cards. Map K6
This place started the boom in philosophy cafés in
1992, when Sorbonne lecturer Marc Sautet launched
his Sunday-morning discussions here. Sautet died in
1998, but 200 or so would-be philosophers still pile
in every week, though the clinking of coffee cups and
exchange of money can prevent concentration on
such themes as 'Does the ephemeral have a value?'.

L'Etoile Manquante

*34 rue Vieille-du-Temple, 4th (01.42.72.48.34). M° St-
Paul.* **Open** 8am-2am daily. **Credit** MC, V. **Map L6**
The latest venture in Xavier Denamur's Marais kingdom takes as its theme the threshold between known
and unknown worlds – translating as images of space
discovery and exploration of the body, and very
unique loos where you can watch yourself on video.

Au Petit Fer à Cheval

*30 rue Vieille-du-Temple, 4th (01.42.72.47.47). M° St-
Paul.* **Open** 9am-2am daily. **Credit** MC, V. **Map L6**
Xavier Denamur's quirky, vintage café in the Marais

Café de l'Epoque: *calm, cool and classic.*

is so popular that it's often impossible to squeeze
inside. Almost the entire front room is taken up by
a horseshoe-shaped bar, with a large mirror on either
side and several elaborate electric chandeliers.
Hearty meals in the back room hit the spot.

Le Petit Marcel

*65 rue Rambuteau, 4th (01.48.87.10.20).
M° Rambuteau.* **Open** 7am-1am Mon-Sat; 11am-9pm
Sun. **No credit cards. Map K5**
This tiny, deliciously pretty vintage café near the
Centre Pompidou has a cracked painted ceiling, Art
Nouveau tiles, only eight tables, and simple, sub-
stantial food at eminently reasonable prices.

Les Caves de Bourgogne

*144 rue Mouffetard, 5th (01.47.07.82.80).
M° Censier-Daubenton.* **Open** 6.30am-2am Tue-Sun.
Credit MC, V. **Map J9**
A sleek makeover has transformed this place from
dowdy to decidedly chic, but don't let that deter you
from stopping in for the 62F three-course lunch (not
Sun) after a morning in the Mouffetard market
mêlée. The Latin Quarter crowd includes professor-
ial types, families, students and assorted dogs.

Le Rallye

*11 quai de la Tournelle, 5th (01.43.54.29.65).
M° Jussieu.* **Open** 8am-2am Mon-Fri; 9.30am-2am Sat,
Sun. **No credit cards. Map K7**
This scruffy, family-run *café-tabac* is as close as you
will come to a working-class caff on this exclusive

The Australian Bar

PUBLIC BAR

OPEN EVERY DAY 4PM-2AM

184 RUE ST. JACQUES, 5TH. M° LUXEMBOURG. TEL: 01.43.54.30.48

18 RUE ST. DENIS, 1ST. M° CHATELET. TEL: 01.40.39.00.18

33 PL LOUISE DE BETTIGNIES. 59000 LILLE. TEL: 03.20.55.15.15

Seine-side stretch; it's also a shrine to comic-book hero Tintin. It welcomes a stream of students, workers and locals who gaze at the Ile St-Louis from pavement tables or enjoy cheep beer and simple hot dishes.

Le Reflet

6 rue Champollion, 5th (01.43.29.97.27). M° Cluny-La Sorbonne. **Open** 10am-2am daily. **Credit** MC, V. **Map J7**

Opposite the Reflet Médicis Logos cinema, this relaxed café is full of students and earnest film buffs, here for a chat and cheap, reliable food. The mock movie-studio lighting rig throws light on the conversations. Jazz inevitably plays in the background.

Le Balto

15 rue Mazarine, 6th (01.43.26.02.29). M° Odéon. **Open** 8am-midnight Mon-Fri; 9am-7pm Sat. **Credit** MC, V. **Map H7**

Rugby on the telly, overall-clad workmen at the bar, plus a recently added painting of Zidane, give this café the feel of a friendly local, reinforced by a stream of banter between staff and customers. On Saturdays for lunch St-Germainites of all persuasions pile in for cooking that puts many bistros in the area to shame.

Bar du Marché

75 rue de Seine, 6th (01.43.26.55.15). M° Odéon. **Open** 8am-2am daily. **Credit** MC, V. **Map H9**

The terrace attracts a young crowd of shoppers, students and musicians including rap star MC Solaar. There is lots of atmosphere, thanks to the market-stall holders along adjoining rue de Buci yelling out the virtues of their *moules* and *haricots*. Standards are high, with a rare attention to detail in the menu.

Café de Flore

172 bd St-Germain, 6th (01.45.48.55.26). M° St-Germain-des-Prés. **Open** 7am-1.30am daily. **Credit** AmEx, DC, MC, V. **Map H7**

The existentialist Mecca once frequented by Sartre and de Beauvoir is still abuzz with fervent intellectual prattle in numerous tongues. The 1930s décor hasn't changed, only the prices have risen (astronomically). Karl Lagerfeld, Eric Rohmer and Bernard-Henri Lévy are regulars. Monthly English-language *café philosophique* sessions are held here.

Café de la Mairie

8 pl St-Sulpice, 6th (01.43.26.67.82). M° St-Sulpice. **Open** 7am-2am Mon-Sat; daily in June. **No credit cards. Map H7**

With the summer sun beating down on St-Sulpice church and the magnificent Visconti fountain, it is no wonder the terrace is permanently full. The non-design, anti-chic interior is refreshing. The best time here is evening, when you can enjoy the timeless charm of this spot, emptied of tourists and shoppers.

Les Deux Magots

6 pl St-Germain-des-Prés, 6th (01.45.48.55.25). M° St-Germain-des-Prés. **Open** 7.30am-2am daily. **Credit** AmEx, DC, MC, V. **Map H7**

This famous café, along with the Flore (*see above*), still symbolises so much of the arty myth of St-Germain. Named after the two wise Chinamen inside

the entrance, it has played host to countless writers, artists and thinkers escaping cold garrets: Picasso, Hemingway, Sartre, Mallarmé... But today orange tans and flashy jewellery have replaced the berets and black turtlenecks. Prices, too, are well beyond the reach of hard-up intellectuals; and waiters are stony-faced. Come once to say you've been.

La Palette

43 rue de Seine, 6th (01.43.26.68.15). M° Mabillon. **Open** 8am-2am Mon-Sat. Closed three weeks in Aug. **Credit** V. **Map H7**

This classic turn-of-the-century artists' café, with faded paintings and palettes, is a long-time favourite. The colourful crowd includes local art dealers, students and glam shoppers. Some hot dishes available at lunch, wines and good *tartines* all day.

Le Rostand

6 pl Rostand, 6th (01.43.54.61.58). **Open** 8am-1am daily. **Credit** MC, V. **Map H8**

The terrace facing the Luxembourg gardens has always been the reason to come here, but now swish wicker chairs, golden walls and portraits on the walls have revived the Rostand from its fusty past and mean you might also choose to sit inside.

Le Select

99 bd du Montparnasse, 6th (01.42.22.65.27). M° Vavin. **Open** 7am-3am Mon-Thur, Sun; 7am-4am Fri, Sat. **Credit** MC, V. **Map G9**

Le Select still exudes a genuine whiff of old Montparnasse, with nicotine-stained walls and moulded Deco lights. Would-be bohos and colourful locals pitch up late, a little the worse for wear, and buttonhole you with their story. It serves great cocktails and there are also decent steaks, salads and snacks.

Bar Basile

34 rue de Grenelle, 7th (01.42.22.59.46). M° St-Sulpice. **Open** 7am-9.30pm Mon-Fri; 7.30am-7.30pm Sat. **Credit** MC, V. **Map G7**

Students from the Sciences-Po and intelligentsia with their laptops eat, drink, work and socialise here, drawn by voguish furnishings, sharp service and good, American-influenced food.

Café du Marché

38 rue Cler, 7th (01.47.05.51.27). M° Ecole-Militaire. **Open** 7am-midnight Mon-Sat; 7am-4.30pm Sun. **Credit** MC, V. **Map D6**

The location of this café on the bustling rue Cler is its attraction. People clock up hours here, imbibing the hypnotic sounds and smells. It is always well populated, but the prospect of lunch compiled from fresh market produce is worth braving the rush.

Le Rouquet

188 bd St-Germain, 7th (01.45.48.06.93). M° St-Germain-des-Prés. **Open** 7am-9pm Mon-Sat. **Credit** MC, V. **Map G6**

St-Germain locals prefer to patronise this café, rather than be patronised by the existential waiters of Les Deux Magots. A perfectly preserved 1950s interior, plus a glass-covered terrace, make this an ideal spot for idling away the afternoon.

Bar des Théâtres

6 av Montaigne, 8th (01.47.23.34.63). M° Alma-Marceau.
Open 6am-2am daily. **Credit** AmEx, MC, V. **Map D5**
The unofficial mecca for the collective radius of fashion's happy valley, RTL, France 3 and the Comédie des Champs-Elysées is surprisingly unpretentious. S*teak tartare* is served to famous faces, while a brasserie menu extends into a more formal dining area.

Le Fouquet's

99 av des Champs-Elysées, 8th (01.47.23.70.60).
M° Georges V. **Open** 8am-1am daily. **Credit** AmEx, DC, MC, V. **Map D4**
The venerable hang-out for the flashy film crowd – it is host to the Césars (French Oscars) – has reopened with a new décor by star designer Jacques Garcia and a new chef, Jean-François Lemercier, in the hope of proving there's life in the old dinosaur yet.

Handmade

19 rue Jean-Mermoz, 8th (01.45.62.50.05).
M° Franklin D Roosevelt. **Open** 8am-5pm Mon-Fri.
Credit V. **Map E4**
This temple to chic just off the Champs has limited opening hours and seating for just 16 'lucky few'. Handmade's modish minimalism is proof that small is beautiful. This is the sort of place you expect *Wallpaper** magazine to declare style mecca, whip out a Leica and start shooting everyone in sight.

L'Entracte

1 rue Auber, 9th (01.47.42.26.25). M° Opéra.
Open 7am-12.30am Mon-Sat. **Credit** AmEx, DC, MC, V. **Map G4**
Just steps from the *grands magasins*, this café draws a cosmopolitan mix by day, Gallic lovers by night. Swish wood panelling, velveteen seats and wine memorabilia make up the décor, but aim for a table on the first floor by the huge front window for an unbeatable view across to the Palais Garnier.

Chez Prune

36 rue Beaurepaire, 10th (01.42.41.30.47).
M° Jacques Bonsergent. **Open** 7.30am-1.45am Mon-Sat; 10am-1.45am Sun. **Credit** MC, V. **Map L4**
Overlooking the romantic canal St-Martin with its cast-iron bridges, this happening café-bistro boasts a happy combination of jazzy music, Mediterranean food and teasing staff – hip yet homely.

Bar la Fontaine

1 rue de Charonne, 11th (01.56.98.03.30). M° Bastille.
Open 7.30am-2am Mon-Sat; 10am-2am Sun. **No credit cards. Map M7**
Less chic but no less crucial than other hip tips in the area, this bar attracts a casual crowd and the Radio Nova crew. There are boisterous goings-on and salsa music keeps things swinging. There are good-value salads, *gratins* and *croques* at lunch.

Le Bistrot du Peintre

116 av Ledru-Rollin, 11th (01.47.00.34.39).
M° Ledru-Rollin. **Open** 7am-2am Mon-Sat; 10am-8pm Sun. **Credit** MC, V. **Map N7**
Founded in 1902, this is a fine example of a sophisticated, well-restored Art Nouveau café, with a perfect corner position. The kitchen is reliable with offerings that range from open sandwiches or plates of Auvergnat *charcuterie* to a full three courses.

Pause Café

41 rue de Charonne, 11th (01.48.06.80.33).
M° Ledru-Rollin. **Open** 8.30am-2am Mon-Sat; 8.30am-8.30pm Sun. **Credit** AmEx, MC, V. **Map M7**
A hip, light-hearted Bastille hangout *obligé* for up-and-coming art and film people, the Pause seems to have suffered after renovations that saw it double in size. Go armed with patience as the name aptly describes the slow service. The chrome terrace is well placed for people who need to see and be seen, and featured in the film, *Chacun cherche son chat.*

Café de la Place

23 rue d'Odessa, 14th (01.42.18.01.55).
M° Edgar-Quinet. **Open** 7am-2am Mon-Sat; 9.30am-9.30pm Sun. **Credit** MC, V. **Map G9**
Adorned with *pastis* jugs and old advertising plaques, this lively, revamped vintage café, with a sunny terrace, has become *the* gathering place in the Montparnasse area. There's an excellent choice of French regional wines and a tempting selection of Auvergnat *charcuterie*, salads and hot *plats du jour*.

La Chope Daguerre

17 rue Daguerre, 14th (01.43.22.76.59).
M° Denfert-Rochereau. **Open** 7am-midnight daily.
Credit MC, V. **Map G10**
This is the rendezvous of choice for locals, recently spruced up with dark wood, new chairs and glowering red lamps. Skulk inside over an *apéro* or sun on the terrace and absorb the sights, sounds and smells of the market. Food is fresh and generous.

Au Dernier Métro

70 bd de Grenelle, 15th (01.45.75.01.23). M° Dupleix.
Open 6am-2am daily. **Credit** AmEx, MC, V. **Map G7**
Colourful paintings and old advertising hoardings line the walls of this welcoming establishment peopled by café philosophers , where you're likely to end up talking to the guy next to you about his broken heart or your plans to change the world. Enormous salads and *plats du jour* are always good choices.

Le Roi du Café

59 rue Lecourbe, 15th (01.47.34.48.50).
M° Sèvres-Lecourbe. **Open** 7am-2am Mon-Fri; 7.30am-2am Sat; 9.30am-2am Sun. **Credit** MC, V. **Map G7**
This pretty wood-fronted corner café is where the living congregate in the sleepy 15th. Thirsty hipsters with mobile phones pack out the pavement tables; the authentic bistro, an Art Deco time capsule, serves *frites* to young lovers and single *demoiselles*.

Bar Antoine

17 rue La Fontaine, 16th (01.40.50.14.30).
RER Kennedy-Radio France. **Open** 7.30am-11pm Mon-Sat. **Credit** MC, V. **Map A7**
This tiny café built by Art Nouveau master Hector Guimard has a view over a food market twice a week. Inside is a strawberries and cream idyll – roses on the tiles and a painted glass ceiling. There's excellent Italian espresso and tempting *charcuterie*.

Pause Café: *a hip hangout for those hankering to see and be seen.*

Le Dôme de Villiers

4 av de Villiers, 17th (01.43.87.28.68). M° Villiers.
Open 6am-1am daily. **Credit** AmEx, MC, V. **Map E2**
The buzz here begins at 6am when market stallhold-
ers arrive for 'cockney brunch' – eggs, bacon et al. At
lunch, power business types dine on oysters; locals
come for fresh fish in the evening; and midnight ush-
ers in the film crowd – stars who have been spotted
include Charlotte Gainsbourg and Emmanuelle Béart.

Le Sancerre

35 rue des Abbesses, 18th (01.42.58.08.20). M° Abbesses.
Open 7am-2am daily. **Credit** MC, V. **Map H1**
Big, brash and always packed, this classic yoof
hangout is still more Montmartre café than showy-
bar-doing-coffee-on-the-side *à la* Ménilmontant.
Abundant wines, whiskies and beers, and good food.

Le Rendez-vous des Quais

*MK2 sur Seine, 10-14 quai de la Seine, 19th
(01.40.37.02.81). M° Stalingrad.* **Open** 11.30am-1am
daily. **Credit** AmEx, MC, V. **Map M1**
This bar-restaurant overlooking the Bassin de la Villette
is part of the MK2 multiplex cinema; people come for
the food and the fab heated wooden terrace on the canal.
The 149F *menu ciné* includes a cinema ticket.
Wheelchair access.

Bar aux Folies

8 rue de Belleville, 20th (01.46.36.65.98). M° Belleville.
Open 6am-midnight Mon-Sat; 7am-11pm Sun. **No
credit cards. Map N4**
A mix of Chinese, Jewish, North African, French and
struggling artists crowds in here daily. It is impossible not to enjoy the café's strong sense of neigh-
bourly love. Poetry some Wednesdays.

Le Soleil

*136 bd de Ménilmontant, 20th (01.46.36.47.44).
M° Ménilmontant.* **Open** 8am-2am daily. **No credit
cards. Map P5**
Aptly named, as the *terrasse* catches most of the
afternoon sun, this inexpensive café is a standby for
a relaxed crowd of local artists, musicians and
assorted hipsters. It's totally unexceptional inside,
but you'll want to be outside anyway.
Wheelchair access.

Bars & Pubs

Le Fumoir

*6 rue de l'Amiral-de-Coligny, 1st (01.42.92.00.24).
M° Louvre.* **Open** 11am-2am daily. **Credit** AmEx,
MC, V. **Map H6**
Brought to you by the China Club team, this is one
of the style destinations of the moment. Press
attachés, blazer-wearing wolves and sleep-deprived
artists all stake out their turf in the large, airy space
with a décor that seems inspired by Vienna, Edward
Hopper and Scandinavia. Cocktails are wicked.
Wheelchair access.

Le Café Noir

65 rue Montmartre, 2nd (01.40.39.07.36). M° Sentier.
Open 8am-2am Mon-Fri; 4pm-2am Sat. **No credit
cards. Map J4**
A leopard-skin bicycle above the door, images of
Gainsbourg on the walls: this is an eclectic, unpretentious corner café drawing a good mix of French
and Anglophones. We like its budget prices, light
meals and impressive range of spirits.
Wheelchair access.

The Frog & Rosbif

116 rue St-Denis, 2nd (01.42.36.34.73). Mᵒ Etienne-Marcel. **Open** noon-2am daily. **Credit** MC, V. **Map J5**
With all the trimmings from trad pub grub, real ale and the English papers to punningly named home-brews, this lively spot is the retreat of the Englishman abroad. Live football and rugby broadcasts.
Branch: The Frog & Princess, 9 rue Princesse, 6th (01.40.51.77.38).

Harry's Bar

5 rue Daunou, 2nd (01.42.61.71.14). Mᵒ Opéra. **Open** 10.30am-4am Mon-Sat. **Credit** AmEx, DC, V. **Map G4**
A favourite with sozzled American expats since 1911, this legendary bar is the birthplace of the Bloody Mary and the home of the best dry martini in Paris. Exemplary cocktails are the main attraction, but the atmosphere is fascinating for students of cultural contrasts, a romantic evocation of post-war America – the result more Paris than New York.

Kitty O'Shea's

10 rue des Capucines, 2nd (01.40.15.00.30). Mᵒ Opéra. **Open** noon-1.30am daily. **Credit** AmEx, MC, V. **Map G4**
The décor is imported from Ireland, as are the Guinness and Kilkenny. Packed with bankers early on, the atmosphere becomes more relaxed later, with a civilised mix of Irish, English and French, except on rugby Five Nations Cup days. Irish grub available.
Branch: James Joyce, 71 bd Gouvion-St-Cyr, 17th (01.44.09.70.32).

Le Tambour

41 rue Montmartre, 2nd (01.42.33.06.90). Mᵒ Les Halles. **Open** 24 hrs daily. **Credit** MC, V. **Map J4**
This wacky bar looks like a Swiss chalet outside, a junk shop inside, with turn-of-the-century glass screens, dilapidated statues and bar stools made out of bus stop signs. Men in smart suits mix with students. Drinks are reasonably priced; staff are cheerful.

Chez Richard

37 rue Vieille-du-Temple, 4th (01. 42.74.31.65). Mᵒ St-Paul. **Open** 5pm-2am daily. Closed two weeks in August. **Credit** MC, V. **Map L5**
An abundance of candles and nooks and crannies, a cushioned bar that invites lots of elbows, huge measures and friendly staff ensure that the world looks like a better place once you're ensconced at a table here. There's always a crowd and, at weekends, a fab DJ plays everything from Motown to ambient club.

Les Etages

35 rue Vieille-du-Temple, 4th (01.42.78.72.00). Mᵒ St-Paul. **Open** 5pm-2am Mon-Fri; 11am-2am Sat, Sun. **Credit** MC, V. **Map L5**
Les Etages looks like a funky tapas joint, but rickety stairs behind the bar lead to three floors of intimate rooms full of mismatched sofas for lounging on. Beer doesn't fit the mood so choose from stiffer drinks including a long list of classics and inventive creations.

The Lizard Lounge

18 rue du Bourg-Tibourg, 4th (01.42.72.81.34). Mᵒ Hôtel-de-Ville. **Open** noon-2am daily. **Credit** MC, V. **Map K6**

Le Sancerre: *big, brash and always packed.*

A split-level bar-restaurant with a heavy steel mezzanine, art on the walls and a long bar. Professionals and hip young Anglophones/philes indulge in serious flirting over lethal cocktails, or dine on deli sandwiches and Sunday brunch.

Café Oz

184 rue St-Jacques, 5th (01.43.54.30.48). RER Luxembourg. **Open** 4pm-2am daily. **Credit** MC, V. **Map J8**
A healthy range of draught and bottled beers (Fosters, VA, etc), fabulous if pricey Australian wines, wisecracking staff and an agreeably mixed French/expat crowd make this a popular hideout. Mock aboriginal cave paintings decorate the walls and quaint Aussie mementoes fill the corners.
Branch: 18 rue St-Denis, 1st (01.40.39.00.18). *Wheelchair access.*

Le Pantalon

7 rue Royer-Collard, 5th (01.40.51.85.85). RER Luxembourg. **Open** 8pm-2am Mon-Sat. **Credit** V. **Map J8**
It looks like a teenager's bedroom, with a pair of pants on the wall, a sticker-covered guitar and a graffiti-strewn loo with flashing disco lights. Rosy-cheeked students get happily drunk in this permanently packed neighbourhood bar where the barmen sell single cigarettes and drinks are seriously cheap.

Polly Magoo

11 rue St Jacques, 5th (01.46.33.33.64). Mᵒ Cluny-La Sorbonne. **Open** noon-4am Mon-Thur,

Sun; noon-6am Fri, Sat. **Credit** MC, V. **Map J7**
This friendly if undeniably seedy place has posters for William Klein's eponymous 60s film on its nicotine-stained walls. Expect to share your views on life, your Gitanes and perhaps even your seat with 60s relics, the odd film star or tramp, all of whom drink the night away to an eclectic soundtrack.

Le Bar Dix
10 rue de l'Odéon, 6th (01.43.26.66.83). M° Odéon.
Open 6pm-2am daily. **No credit cards. Map H7**
This bar was a meeting place during the May 1968 riots, and it retains a benignly alternative atmosphere today with its flaking walls and an international crowd of sangria-sipping students.

Chez Georges
11 rue des Cannettes, 6th (01.43.26.79.15).
M° Mabillon. **Open** noon-2am Tue-Sat. Closed Aug.
No credit cards. Map H7
The street-level bar is a perfect locals' haunt – tiled floor, *banquettes*, simple food and good wines. Signed photos pay tribute to Georges' glorious past as a cabaret. The cellar, meanwhile, candlelit and low-slung, caters to a raucous, beer-guzzling, Piaf-listening crowd of students, especially at weekends.

La Closerie des Lilas
171 bd du Montparnasse, 6th (01.40.51.34.50).
M° Vavin/RER Port-Royal. **Open** 11.30am-1am daily.
Credit AmEx, DC, MC, V. **Map G9**
Founded as a lilac-shaded *guinguette* dance hall in

Café Noir: *Anglo-French entente cordiale.*

1847, this bar's famous clients have included Man Ray, Apollinaire, Picasso and Hemingway, as little brass plaques on the tables testify. Now a classy cocktail bar with a piano tinkling in the background, it still attracts the political and cultural establishment. The restaurant has been reinvigorated by a new chef.

La Paillote
45 rue Monsieur-le-Prince, 6th (01.43.26.45.69).
M° Odéon. **Open** 9pm-4am Tue-Sun. **No credit cards. Map H7**
A taste of the South Seas in St-Germain, 'the straw hut' heaves with bamboo and rattan, and serves a jolly decent *punch maison*. The owner plays soothing jazz all night long. Clientele ranges from hapless tourists to *BCBG* youth to fawning couples who seem to believe they really are on a romantic tropical island.

Café Thoumieux
4 rue de la Comète, 7th (01.45.51.50.40). M° La Tour-Maubourg. **Open** noon-2am Mon-Fri; 5pm-2am Sat. Closed 1-15 Aug. **Credit** AmEx, MC, V. **Map E6**
It may be little brother to the long-established bistro Thoumieux around the corner, but the café is a laid-back, sexy destination for cocktails. Décor is pure Moorish luxuriance: rich colours and velour *banquettes*. Stare at the posers over wine and tapas.

Barfly
49-51 av George V, 8th (01.53.67.84.60). M° George V. **Open** noon-3pm, 6pm-2am Mon-Fri; 6pm-2am Sat; noon-4pm, 6pm-2am Sun. **Credit** AmEx, MC, V. **Map D4**
Flashy Eurotrash types sip Champagne and jostle for air-kissing space at this bar where money talks and waiters snarl. Once an 'in' spot for the likes of Naomi Campbell, it has a passé feel now. Beautiful people eat sushi; businessmen and their women sip cocktails. *Wheelchair access.*

Au Général Lafayette
52 rue Lafayette, 9th (01.47.70.59.08). M° Le Peletier. **Open** 8am-4am daily. **Credit** AmEx, MC, V. **Map H9**
Along a bleak stretch of boulevard, it's a relief to find a bar as convivial as this one. Untrendy and unpretentious, it has turn-of-the-century ceilings and a mellow, jazzy atmosphere. Professionals lunch on brasserie fare; come evening, drinkers snack as they sample some of the 130 (mostly Belgian) beers.

La Patache
60 rue de Lancry, 10th (01.42.08.14.35).
M° Jacques Bonsergent. **Open** 7pm-2am daily.
No credit cards. Map L4
This small, cheap, rough-and-ready bar near the Canal St-Martin, with its smoke-stained interior and tins on each table for clients' literary missives, is the real thing. Never having managed to become achingly fashionable, it is rarely too full, and usually features groups of drunken Frenchmen along with some excellent live music and/or drama.

Le Bar Sans Nom
49 rue de Lappe, 11th (01.48.05.59.36). M° Bastille. **Open** 6pm-2am Mon-Sat. **Credit** MC, V. **Map M7**
Junk-shop chic prevails here, via mismatched sofas and a musty smell. The soundtrack ranges from

The literary café rewritten

The Hemingway drinking trail is a well-trod one. **La Coupole**, **La Closerie des Lilas**, the bar at the **Crillon** – any watering hole that still exists from that era will have a Hemingway story to tell. Because he drank. In earnest. The old man's Parisian years were, in fact, one long piss-up punctuated by a few books. The 'Hemingway woz ere' plaques say it all.

You probably know where Sartre used to hang out and can hazard a guess as to where Beckett or Wilde used to knock them back. But Parisian literary activity did not die out with Montparnasse. There is a burgeoning new scene (hanging out at Shakespeare & Co and scribbling 'deep thoughts' on the quais doesn't count) – cafés where you can sip your *crème* surrounded by literary demigods.

Just before his defection to Dublin, media darling and arch miserabilist Michel Houllebecq held court at Les Marronniers (18 rue des Archives, 4th/01.40.27.87.72). So if designer depression is your thing, this is the place to down a *demi*. La Maroquinerie (23 rue Boyer, 20th/01.40.33.64.85) is a good bet for poetry readings and a guaranteed scribbling spot. Hipster Charles Pépin chooses **La Palette** as the setting for a kind of conversion moment from the life of NAP (Neuilly-Auteuil-Passy) parties that the author/character has been leading in his debut novel, *Descente*.

Geoff Dyer's *Paris Trance* charts the dissolution of a generation Xer who's theoretically bashing out a novel but spends rather a lot of time drinking in bars and cafés around the Bastille. Downing *demis* Chez Angèle (5 passage Thiéré, 11th/01.48.07.13.78), a cheap, grungy bar, or looking cool in **Le Pause Café**, the protagonist puzzles the eternal question, 'What makes a great bar?' Dyer's response, 'All great bars are primarily neighbourhood bars', could be seen to apply to many a creative café. It probably has a lot to do with being close to your Mac or your editor, but there are a good crop of places around the corner from Left Bank apartments or publishing houses.

Trumping the newly reopened bar of the Hôtel Pont Royal (5-7 rue Montalembert, 7th/01.42.84.70.00) – once the haunt of Huxley, Miller, Capote, Sagan, TS Eliot and just about anyone ever published by Gallimard – the Hôtel des Sts-Pères (65 rue des Sts-Pères, 6th/01.45.44.50.00) is rapidly becoming a modern equivalent. While the Pont Royal may have the history and lots of books decorating the bar, the

Café de Flore

Sts-Pères, just up the street from Editions Grasset, is the convienient address for a new breed of hip *écrivaines*. Clit-lit queen Lorette Nobécourt, tortured beautiful and Plathesque, angry young woman Claire Legendre, and Virginie Despentes, described by her XCiTés editor as 'the ultimate kick-ass fuck-the-system anarcho-babe', come here to relax after a hard day raging against the machine. This is probably a place to avoid if you're feeling particularly patriarchal.

Whether or not the ghosts of Sartre, de Beauvoir *et al* would approve is debatable, but the **Café de Flore** is perhaps the best postmodern example of the life-imitating-art-imitating-life loop. Jammed up against the smart Germainopratiens and their espressos are the literary types who'd be there anyway – they just happen to write about being there, too. Among this glamourously depraved set cross-referencing is cool: so while Brett Easton Ellis's ultimate antihero, *American Psycho*'s Patrick Bateman, is invited to a Parisian dinner party in Frederick Beigbeder's *Trashed*, Beigbeder hangs out in Flore, which plays an important role in Ellis's latest sex, drugs & name-dropping fest *Glamorama*. Ellis's description of the terrace shortly before his model terrorists bomb the café says it all: 'That outside table where Brad the NYU film student… is sitting with two friends… smoking Malboros… slouching in their seats with perfect hair.' Take an iBook or a Montblanc and you'll blend in perfectly.

MECANO BAR

"cosmopolitan vibe café"

An essential Paris address

As recommended in *Time Out Guides*

Ambiance Music DJ
Open daily 9am-2am
Funky brunches and cuisine all day

99 rue Oberkampf, 11th. M° Parmentier
Tel: 01.40.21.35.28

decent funk to cringe-inducing R Kelly. A good place to pass the time over a beer and some suspect peanuts.

Café Cannibale
93 rue Jean-Pierre-Timbaud, 11th (01.49.29.95.59). M° Couronnes. **Open** 8am-2am Mon-Fri; 9am-2am Sat, Sun. **Credit** MC, V. **Map N4**
This is a casual, spacious establishment where you can perch yourself at the zinc bar for a quick coffee, or settle in at one of the cheerful Formica tables for a light meal. There is a children's area with small tables and chairs, and a copious Sunday brunch.

Les Comptoirs de Charbon
109 rue Oberkampf, 11th (01.43.57.55.13). M° Parmentier. **Open** 9am-2am daily. **Credit** MC, V. **Map N5**
One of the stars of Ménilmontant is this renovated *fin-de-siècle* dancehall. The hip crowd is relaxed by day and lively, though a bit too posey, by night. On Tue-Sat nights, a DJ plays a mix of funk and house. Pity about the insultingly inadequate Turkish loo.

Mégalo
6 rue de Lappe, 11th (01.48.05.05.12). M° Bastille. **Open** daily 6pm-2am. **Credit** MC, V. **Map M7**
Rude murals, 70s disco transfers, retro chandeliers and funk music provide the backdrop for the groovers who pack this place nightly. Grab a barstool, a *demi* and eavesdrop on your neighbours. You're guaranteed to leave with decent stories to tell the next day.

Sanz Sans
49 rue du Fbg-St-Antoine, 11th (01.44.75.78.78). M° Bastille. **Open** 9am-2am daily. **Credit** MC, V. **Map M7**
Here's a destroy-chic-style bar that's packed with sexy party people getting ripped on cocktails and dancing on tables, while bar staff thrash cymbal light fittings in time to the hip-hop hits. Don't bother eating in the mediocre upstairs restaurant.

Le Scherkhan
144 rue Oberkampf, 11th (01.43.57.29.34). M° Ménilmontant. **Open** 5pm-2am daily. **No credit cards. Map N5**
Veering between basement junkshop and Raj-era drawing room, there's a colonial vibe in this comfy bar on the Oberkampf strip, with its rather gloomy lighting and a stuffed tiger. Cocktails are some of the cheapest in the area; service is smooth and sexy.

Barrio Latino
46-48 rue du Fbg-St-Antoine, 12th (01.55.78.84.75). M° Bastille. **Open** 10am-2am daily. **Credit** AmEx, MC, V. **Map M7**
News event of the 1999 *rentrée*, this 900-seater extravaganza is owned by the team which runs the waningly cool Buddha Bar and Barfly. The menu runs to fashion food like salmon tartare and carpaccio. Drinks are sparing, but the neo-Cuban décor, on three dimly lit floors around a central atrium, is rather wonderful.

China Club
50 rue de Charenton, 12th (01.43.43.82.02). M° Ledru-Rollin or Bastille. **Open** 7pm-2am Mon-Thur, Sun; 7pm-3am Fri, Sat. Closed Mon, Sun

July 15-Aug 15. **Credit** AmEx, V. **Map M7**
This sophisticated haven, decorated to resemble a Hong Kong gentleman's club, boasts a speakeasy-style cellar bar (live jazz Fri and Sat), a lacquered *fumoir chinois* and a mile-long main bar. Great cocktails, and good, but pricey, Chinese-inspired food. *Wheelchair access.*

Le Rosebud
11bis rue Delambre, 14th (01.43.20.44.13). M° Vavin or Edgar Quinet. **Open** 7pm-2am daily. Closed Aug. **Credit** MC, V. **Map G9**
A strange relic of Montparnasse's more debauched past, this dimly lit cocktail haunt has become a bit of a middle-aged pick-up joint, where sozzled travellers down martinis at the bar, waiting for strangers-in-the-night encounters. So *ringard*, it's almost chic.

L'Endroit
67 pl du Dr-Félix-Lobligeois, 17th (01.42.29.50.00). M° Rome. **Open** noon-2am daily. **Credit** V. **Map F1**
L'Endroit is *the* place, at least in this sedate area, not renowned for its bar life. Outside it has an enviable terrace; inside a cool soundtrack and well-bred residents. Decent cocktails and salads are served.

Le Bar Jaune
6 rue Germain-Pilon, 18th (01.42.58.03.05). M° Pigalle. **Open** 8pm-2am Tue-Sun. **No credit cards. Map H2**
Artist Gérard Giallella took over a century-old bar in Pigalle, gave it a lick of yellow paint and stirred up a bowl of sangria (15F a glass). The result is a merry mix of artists, thespians, musicians and writers lured by cheap drinks and congenial company.

La Fourmi
74 rue des Martyrs, 18th (01.42.64.70.35). M° Pigalle. **Open** 8.30am-2am Mon-Sat; 10am-2am Sun. **Credit** AmEx, MC, V. **Map H2**
Industrial lighting, a long bar and a Duchampian bottle rack hanging from the ceiling form the décor of this Pigalle bar. Rich Parisian youth and local trendsetters dine on salads, sandwiches and a *plat du jour*.

La Flèche d'Or
102bis rue de Bagnolet, 20th (01.43.72.04.23). M° Alexandre Dumas. **Open** 10am-2am daily. **Credit** V. **Map Q6**
A former train station on the Petite Ceinture railway, this place is popular with music lovers. Live bands vary from funky Caribbean to lame Celtic rock. The bar built from railway sleepers is an inventive touch, but the murals are in very poor teenage taste.

Salons de Thé

Angelina's
226 rue de Rivoli, 1st (01.42.60.82.00). M° Tuileries. **Open** 9am-7pm Mon-Fri; 9am-7.30pm Sat, Sun. **Credit** AmEx, MC, V. **Map G5**
Ladies who lunch have been luxuriating in this neo-rococo setting since the early 1900s. Nowadays the clientele consists of wealthy Parisiennes and Japanese tourists laden with designer goodies. Tea is sipped by those abstemious enough to resist the famously wicked hot chocolate and gooey gâteaux.

L'Ebouillanté

8 rue des Barres, 4th (01.42.71.09.69). M° Hôtel-de-Ville. **Open** *summer* noon-10pm Tue-Sun; *winter* noon-9pm Tue-Sun. **No credit cards. Map K6**
This relaxed retreat on a cobbled street has a comfortably tatty feel, and windows overlooking the Gothic Eglise St-Gervais-St-Protais. Enjoy chilled jazz, excellent *gratins* and salads, and superb cakes.

Le Loir dans la Théière

3 rue des Rosiers, 4th (01.42.72.68.12). M° St-Paul. **Open** 11am-7pm Mon-Fri; 10am-7pm Sat, Sun. **Credit** MC, V. **Map K6**
Packed with arty types, this haphazardly decorated *salon* is a good place to tap into Parisian cultural life while inhaling the scent of varied teas including mint, vanilla and jasmine. Delicious workmanlike cakes.

La Fourmi Aillée

8 rue du Fouarre, 5th (01.43.29.40.99). M° Maubert-Mutualité. **Open** noon-1am daily. **Map J7**
This feminist bookshop-cum-tearoom smacks of the bohemian elegance of Virginia Woolf, the inspiration for its surreal name ('the flying ant'). Tea arrives in copious six-cup pots; *gratins* and quiche are substantial, but the organic bread is flavourless.

La Mosquée de Paris

39 rue Geoffroy-St-Hilaire, 5th (01.43.31.38.20). M° Censier-Daubenton. **Open** 9am-midnight daily. **Credit** MC, V. **Map K9**
You'll find students and intellectuals in the mosque's Moorish mosaic-decorated tea room, imbibing sweet mint tea and honeyed cigar *baklava*. The secluded courtyard is perfect after a stroll in the Jardin des Plantes. *Wheelchair access.*

Ladurée

16 rue Royale, 8th (01.42.60.21.79). M° Madeleine. **Open** 8.30am-7pm Mon-Sat; 10am-7pm Sun. **Credit** AmEx, MC, V. **Map F4**
In this ornate *salon de thé* established in 1862, tea is merely an excuse to taste exquisite pastries. Ask for *une dizaine de petits-fours* so you can sample tarts and biscuits without putting a strain on stomach or purse. **Branch**: 75 av des Champs-Elysées, 8th (01.40.75.08.75).

Wine bars

Juvéniles

47 rue de Richelieu, 1st (01.42.97.46.49). M° Palais-Royal. **Open** noon-11pm Mon-Sat. **Credit** MC, V. **Map H5**
British expats Tim Johnston and Mark Williamson of Willi's Wine Bar attract clients from round the globe to taste their international wines. Food is good standard French or enlightened English pub food.

Le Mauzac

7 rue de l'Abbé de l'Epée, 5th (01.46.33.75.22). RER Luxembourg. **Open** 7.30am-10.30pm Mon-Fri; 7.30am-4pm Sat. Closed three weeks in Aug, one week at Christmas, one week at Easter. **Credit** MC, V. **Map H8**
On a quiet backwater ignored by tourists and traffic, this buzzing bar takes its name from a grape found in the Gaillac region and featured among the well-chosen reds and whites by owner Jean-Michel.

Le Comptoir du Relais

5 carrefour de l'Odéon, 6th (01.43.29.12.05). M° Odéon. **Open** noon-midnight Mon-Thur; noon-2am Fri, Sat; 1-10pm Sun. Closed three weeks in Aug. **No credit cards. Map H7**
This is a fine cinephile refuge with a broad range of modest wines, including rarities like a '93 Bourgogne Irancy and a 1990 Oriu from Corsica. The menu is brief, with toasted *tartines* made of *pain Poilâne* dominating, but the combination of simple savoury food and good wine more than fulfils one's needs.

L'Ecluse

15 quai des Grands-Augustins, 6th (01.46.33.58.74). M° St-Michel. **Open** 11.30am-1.30am. **Credit** AmEx, MC, V. **Map H7**
Once a famous cabaret and now a listed monument, this place is the best of the chain, with a discreet but unstuffy atmosphere. Wine is given pride of place, complemented by carefully wrought dishes.

Au Sauvignon

80 rue des Sts-Pères, 7th (01.45.48.49.02). M° Sèvres-Babylone. **Open** 8.30am-9pm Mon-Sat. Closed Aug. **Credit** MC, V. **Map G6**
Though the waiter at this enduring institution claims the dozen wines are selected personally by the owner, there's no evidence that such purported care breeds success. However, the melting St-Marcellin and a rich, aged Cantal are all you could ask of cheese – and this is a perfect spot to spy on the bourgeoisie at play.

La Cave Drouot

8 rue Drouot, 9th (01.47.70.83.38). M° Richelieu-Drouot. **Open** 6.30am-9.30pm Mon-Fri; 6.30am-7pm Sat. **Credit** MC, V. **Map H4**
At the crack of dawn, the bar is surrounded by workers from the Drouot auction house popping in for coffee or an early glass of white. Drouot specialises in wines from the Southwest. Bar food reflects the owner's Basque roots.

Le Clown Bar

114 rue Amelot, 11th (01.43.55.87.35). M° Filles du Calvaire. **Open** noon-3pm, 7.30pm-1am Mon-Sat; 7pm-1am Sun. Closed a week in Aug. **Credit** MC, V. **Map L5**
This happy, family-run wine bar is next to the historic Cirque d'Hiver, and the listed interior runs amok with clown tiles, posters and memorabilia. Famous French clowns still frequent the bar during runs at the Cirque. M et Mme Vitte and daughter Myriam specialise in Côtes du Rhône. It's advisable to book.

Jacques Mélac

42 rue Léon-Frot, 11th (01.43.70.59.27). M° Charonne. **Open** 9am-5pm Mon; 9am-midnight Tue-Sat. Closed two weeks in Aug. **Credit** MC, V. **Map P7**
Jacques Mélac's philosophy is that wine is all about friendship and should never be drunk on one's own. Consequently you'll find this convivial wine bar crowded with jubilant locals, standing shoulder to shoulder at the bar, quaffing hardy young wines and nibbling on sausage and cheese.

Neo-Cuban news of 'la rentrée' 99: **Barrio Latino** *is a 900-seater extravaganza.*

RECIPROQUE

Nicole Morel

photo: Pascal Faligot

Featured above are clothes from: CHANEL, DIOR, HERMÈS, CHRISTIAN LACROIX, HERVE LEGER, VUITTON, GUCCI, MOSCHINO, PRADA, VERSACE, VIVIENNE WESTWOOD.

photo: Pascal Faligot

Fashion

Haute couture and high street may have gone global but Paris retains its own special cachet, found nowhere else in the world.

Chanel handbags are sold from Dublin to Dubai, but fashion continues to hold a peculiar pre-eminence in Parisian life. It's a magnet for stylists and fashion groupies, and an essential cog in the French economy. You can see a catwalk show anywhere from the traditional grand halls to inside a Métro station. Away from the global names, small shops continue to offer a personal touch, far-sighted explorers like Colette (*see chapter* **Specialist Shopping**), **Absinthe**, **Onward** and **Maria Luisa** are on the trail of the very newest names, while a new breed of designer is emerging, one which has bypassed the media catwalk for the intimacy of presenting their wares direct to the customer (see **Shopping: the third way**, p228).

Designer Directions

Absinthe
74-76 rue Jean-Jacques-Rousseau, 1st (01.42.33.54.44). M° *Les Halles.* **Open** 11am-7.30pm Mon-Sat. Closed Aug. **Credit** DC, MC, V. **Map J5**
In a prettily designed boutique, Marthe Desmoulins nurtures fresh international talent, with an emphasis on the post-grunge Belgian avant-garde. Other designers include Josep Font, Julie Skarland, Christine Palmassio and Gabrielle Hammill.

Barbara Bui
23 rue Etienne-Marcel, 1st (01.40.26.43.65). M° *Etienne-Marcel.* **Open** 1-7.30pm Mon; 10.30am-7.30pm Tue-Sat. **Credit** AmEx, DC, MC, V. **Map J5**
Bui has really caught the mood of today. Long skirts and cropped jackets come in grey, purple and black; T-shirts are packed in space-age plastic packs. Two doors away is the friendly Barbara Bui Café.
Branches: 43 rue des Francs-Bourgeois, 4th (01.53.01.88.05); 35 rue de Grenelle, 7th (01.45.44.05.14); 50 av Montaigne, 8th (01.42.25.05.25).

Cabane de Zucca
8 rue St-Roch, 1st (01.44.58.98.88). M° *Tuileries.* **Open** 10.30am-7pm Mon-Sat. **Credit** AmEx, DC, MC, V. **Map G5**
Akira Onozucca has upped cabin from the Left Bank to the new nucleus around Colette, but goes it alone when it comes to style. Revised workwear in purples and khakis sprout odd details – strange pockets, an extra sleeve – to provoke a little consternation.

Christophe Lemaire
36 rue de Sévigné, 3rd (01.42.74.54.90). M° *St-Paul.* **Open** 10.30am-7pm Tue-Sat; 2-7pm Sun. **Credit** AmEx, DC, MC, V. **Map L6**

Lemaire began with Thierry Mugler and Christian Lacroix, though his style is more street-influenced, espousing a policy of laidback layering. In his beautiful store, tomato-print shirts liven up military slacks, while tops flaunt gaping, slit armholes. Lemaire designs for men, too, and many clothes have a unisex feel.

Comme des Garçons
40, 42 rue Etienne-Marcel, 2nd (women 01.42.33.05.21/men 01.42.36.91.54). M° *Etienne-Marcel.* **Open** 11am-7pm Mon-Sat. **Credit** AmEx, DC, MC, V. **Map J5**
Rei Kawakubo's intellectual designs and geometric silhouettes have been enormously influential in the fashion avant-garde. The *art brut* stores also stock protégé Junya Watanabe.

L'Eclaireur
3ter rue des Rosiers, 4th (01.48.87.10.22). M° *St-Paul.* **Open** 2-7pm Mon, 11am-7pm Tue-Sat. **Credit** AmEx, DC, MC, V. **Map L6**
Leading men's and women's fashions – Dries Van Noten, Ann Demeulemeester, Martin Margiela, Helmut Lang and rising Dutch star Josephus Thimister – are cleverly displayed against iron girders. Miyake's Pleats Please collection has special prominence.
Branches: 24 rue de L'Echaudé, 6th (01.44.27.08.03); 26 av des Champs-Elysées, 8th (01.45.62.12.32) (men only).

Franck et Fils
80 rue de Passy, 16th (01.44.14.38.00). M° *Passy.* **Open** 10am-7pm Mon-Sat. **Credit** AmEx, DC, MC, V. **Map B6**
Opened in 1897, Franck et Fils used to be a fusty department store for dowager duchesses and ladies who lunch. More recently it has reinvented itself, earning a reputation for its *Ab Fab* racks laden with Armani, Chanel, Lacroix, Vivienne Westwood, etc.

Galerie Gaultier
30 rue du Fbg-St-Antoine, 12th (01.44.68.84.84). M° *Bastille.* **Open** 11am-7.30pm Mon, Sat; 10.30am-7.30pm Tue-Fri. **Credit** AmEx, DC, MC, V. **Map M7**
French fashion's oldest *enfant terrible* is renowned for mixing street and ethnic styles with innovative fabrics and sharp tailoring. The new couture line has been hailed a success, but you might prefer JPG, his cheaper cyber/streetwear.
Branch: Boutique Jean-Paul Gaultier, 6 rue Vivienne, 2nd (01.42.86.05.05).

Irié
8 rue du Pré-aux-Clercs, 7th (01.42.61.18.28). M° *Rue du Bac.* **Open** 10.15am-7pm Mon-Sat. Closed first three weeks in Aug. **Credit** MC, V. **Map G6**

Global powerhouses

It's non-stop designer labels along avenue Montaigne and neighbouring streets, where you'll find such worldwide staples as Prada (No 10, 01.53.23.99.40), Christian Dior (designed by John Galliano, No 30/01.40.73.54.44), Céline (designed by Michael Kors, No 36/01.56.89.07.92), Chanel (No 42/01.47.23.74.12), Calvin Klein (No 56/01.56.89.07.92) and nearby Givenchy (designed by Alexander McQueen, 3 av George V/01.44.31.50.23) and Louis Vuitton (designed by Marc Jacobs, 101 av des Champs-Elysées/01.53.57.24.00). Head back towards place Vendôme for Hermès (designed by Martin Margiela, 24 rue du Fbg-St-Honoré, 8th/01.40.17.47.17) and Italian heavyweights Gucci (designed by Tom Ford, 23 rue Royale, 8th/01.40.06.90.12) and Trussardi (8 pl Vendôme, 1st/01.55.35.32.50). Giorgio Armani sowed controversy when he branched out from the Right Bank (25 pl Vendôme, 1st/01.42.61.02.34) with his slick Emporio Armani store and café in a prime position in St-Germain-des-Prés (149 bd St-Germain, 6th/01.45.48.62.15).

For department stores, *see chapter* **Specialist Shopping**.

Fashion editors and chic Parisians make a beeline for this Japanese designer, who gambles on the newest of the new: plastic coatings, stretch wools, chenille, fake fur, sequins and hologram prints are scattered over suits, minidresses and jeans.

Maria Luisa
2 rue Cambon, 1st (01.47.03.96.15). M° Concorde. **Open** 10.30am-7pm Mon-Sat. **Credit** AmEx, DC, MC, V. **Map G5**
Venezuelan Maria Luisa Poumaillou nurtures talented young designers, and was one of Paris' original stockists for Helmut Lang, Ann Demeulemeester, John Galliano and Martine Sitbon. More recent additions to discover here are Fred Sathal, Véronique Leroy and Olivier Theyskens. There are accessories at No 4 (Manolo Blahnik, Lulu Guinness). The men's shop is at 38 rue du Mont-Thabor.

Martine Sitbon
13 rue de Grenelle, 7th (01.44.39.84.44). M° Rue du Bac or Sèvres-Babylone. **Open** 10.30am-7pm Mon-Sat. **Credit** AmEx, MC, V. **Map G7**
The coloured plexiglass entrance nods to a modern art influence in Sitbon's work; within, burnt-out velvet or geometrical abstract dresses bask beneath a huge skylight. Sitbon has recently added menswear.

Onward
147 bd St-Germain, 6th (01.55.42.77.56). M° St-Germain-des-Prés. **Open** 11am-7pm Mon, Sat; 10am-7pm Tue-Fri. **Credit** AmEx, DC, MC, V. **Map G7**
Expect some of the wackiest clothes in the business at this light-filled store spread over three levels. Designers include Jean Colonna, Colette Dinnigan, Peplum, 0.918, Marc Jacobs, Véronique Branquinho, Tom Van Lingen and Matthew Williamson.

Victoire
12 pl des Victoires, 2nd (01.42.61.09.02). M° Bourse or Palais-Royal. **Open** 10am-7pm Mon-Sat. **Credit** AmEx, DC, MC, V. **Map H5**
The well-edited mix here includes capsule collections by Donna Karan, Narciso Rodriguez and hot Brit duo Wilson & Estella. A branch next door carries Victoire's own label at cheaper prices.
Branches: 1 rue Madame, 6th (01.45.44.28.14); 16 rue de Passy, 16th (01.42.88.20.84).

Yohji Yamamoto
3 rue de Grenelle, 6th (01.42.84.28.87). M° Sèvres-Babylone or St-Sulpice. **Open** 10.30am-7pm Mon-Sat. **Credit** AmEx, DC, MC, V. **Map G7**
Yohji Yamamoto's starting point for his asymmetric, destructured clothers is the kimono. Y's is the simpler, slightly less expensive second line.
Branches: 47 rue Etienne-Marcel, 1st (01.45.08.82.45). **Y's:** 25 rue du Louvre, 1st (01.42.21.42.93); 69 rue des Sts-Pères, 6th (01.45.48.22.56).

Affordable Chic

Abou Dhabi
10 rue des Francs-Bourgeois, 3rd (01.42.77.96.98). M° St-Paul **Open** 2-7pm Mon; 10.30am-7pm; 2-7pm Sun. **Credit** AmEx, MC, V. **Map L6**

At **Galerie Gaultier** *France's oldest* enfant terrible *keeps turning out ever-trendy threads.*

A must for all those with mix-and-match wardrobe problems: rails of up-to-the-minute clothes (Ange, Les Petites, Tara Jarmon, Toupy, Paul et Joe, Diabless) from 290F to 890F are meticulously arranged according to fabric and colour.

Agnès b

2, 3, 6, 10, 19 rue du Jour, 1st (women 01.45.08.56.56/ men 01.42.33.04.13). Mº Les Halles.
Open 10am-7pm Mon-Wed, Fri, Sat; 10am-9pm Thur. **Credit** AmEx, MC, V. **Map J5**
Agnès b is shorthand for the French take on basic dressing and there's an Agnès b boutique for everyone on rue du Jour. The emphasis is on neutral colours, natural fabrics and durability. Staple leggings and snap-front cardigans underline the designer's real-life approach, as does the classic men's suit which kitted out the mob in *Reservoir Dogs.* Cotton shirts cost around 500F.
Branches: 83 rue d'Assas (baby/child), 6th (01.43.54.69.21); 13 rue Michelet (women), 6th (01.46.33.70.20); 22 rue St-Sulpice (children), 6th (01.40.51.70.69); 6, 10, 12 rue du Vieux-Colombier (women/beauty/children/men), 6th (01.44.39.02.60); 17, 25 av Pierre 1er de Serbie (women/men), 16th (01.47.20.22.44/01.47.23.36.69).

A.P.C.

3 (women) and 4 (men) rue de Fleurus, 6th (01.42.22.12.77). Mº St-Placide. **Open** 10.30am-7pm Mon-Sat. **Credit** AmEx, MC, V. **Map G8**
Hip Left Bank basics from designer Jean Toitou, long-time *chez* Agnès b. Leather jackets, drainpipe trousers, skinny-rib knits have a *nouvelle vague* film look; nice colours, nice cuts. Prices are reasonable. Magasin Général A.P.C. (45 rue Madame, 6th/

01.45.48.72.42) holds Toitou's pick from his travels: from olive oil to funky notepads.
Branch: 25bis rue Benjamin-Franklin, 16th (01.45.53.28.28).

Diapositive

42 rue du Four, 6th (01.45.48.85.57). Mº Sèvres-Babylone. **Open** 10.30am-7pm Mon-Sat. Closed two weeks in Aug. **Credit** AmEx, MC, V. **Map H7**
A well-priced collection (suits around 2500F) of own-label separates suits a wide range of shapes and sizes, from practical clothes for work to sportier lines.
Branch: 12 rue du Pré-aux-Clercs, 7th (01.45.44.75.02).

Episode

277 rue St-Honoré, 8th (01.49.26.01.48). Mº Concorde. **Open** 10am-7pm Mon-Sat. **Credit** AmEx, MC, V. **Map G4**
Everything in this spacious, well-lit store is so beautifully displayed that the prices – around 1500F for a jacket – come as a surprise. The line emphasises a low-key chic, with a lot of honeyed neutrals offset by black for day, and gold for evening.
Branch: 47 rue Bonaparte, 6th (01.43.29.13.19).

Isabel Marant

16 rue de Charonne, 11th (01.49.29.71.55). Mº Ledru-Rollin. **Open** 2-7pm Mon, 10.30am-7.30pm Tue-Sat. **Credit** AmEx, MC, V. **Map M7**
Shooting out of nowhere, Isabel Marant offers a range characterised by long, long skirts, big knit pullovers, with some ethno-babe brocades. Marant brings in multicultural references to create funky, wearable clothes which are mostly long, sexy and figure-hugging, but never constricting.
Branch: 50 rue de Seine, 6th (01.43.26.04.12).

Junk by Junko Shimada

54 rue Etienne-Marcel, 2nd (01.42.36.36.97).
M° Etienne-Marcel. **Open** noon-7pm Mon; 10am-7pm
Tue-Sat. **Credit** AmEx, MC, V. **Map J5**
Shimada's colourful clothes have a distinctly
Oriental, kitsch take on streetwear, at almost street
prices. Shirtdresses and neat jackets are simply tai-
lored, plasticky fabrics add a cyber touch.

Martin Grant

32 rue des Rosiers, 4th (01.42.71.39.49). M° St-Paul.
Open 1-7.30pm Tue-Sat. **Credit** AmEx, V. **Map L6**
The very first Australian couture outlet in Paris is
on show in an old Marais hairdresser's shop. The
beautiful tiled floors and red velvet chairs provide
the perfect setting for Grant's impeccably cut suits,
low-cut evening wear or strappy summer dresses.

Plein Sud

21 rue des Francs-Bourgeois, 4th (01.42.72.10.60).
M° St-Paul. **Open** 11am-7pm Mon-Sat. **Credit**
AmEx, MC, V. **Map L6**
Fayçal Amor appears to design with a skeletal size
8 in mind, but don't let that put you off if you're
into spiky three-inch heels, extavagantly *décolleté*
evening wear and skirts slit to kingdom come.
Branch: 70bis rue de Bonaparte, 6th (01.43.54.43.06).

Tara Jarmon

18 rue du Four, 6th (01.46.33.26.60). M° Mabillon.
Open 10.30am-7.30pm Mon-Sat. **Credit** AmEx, V.
Map H7
Modern, feminine, uncomplicated and affordable,
this Canadian has scored a big hit. Her sunny, two-
storey boutique in the heart of St-Germain is filled
with beautiful skirts and fabulous winter coats.

Vanessa Bruno

25 rue St-Sulpice, 6th (01.43.54.41.04). M° Odéon.
Open 10.30am-7pm Mon-Sat. **Credit** AmEx, DC,
MC, V. **Map H7**
First Paris store for Parisian Bruno (after four in
Japan), whose young and feminine styles are perfect
for *petites Parisiennes*: gauze and spaghetti straps
in summer, tweeds and the season's lime green in
winter. Prices are reasonable: around 700F a skirt.

Zadig et Voltaire

1 rue du Vieux-Colombier, 6th (01.43.29.18.29).
M° St-Sulpice. **Open** 1-7.30pm Mon; 10.30am-7.30pm
Tue-Sat. **Credit** AmEx, DC, V. **Map G7**
Cool yet comfortable Yoshi Kondo, Helmut Lang
Jeans, All Saints, Jean Colonna and own-label coats
and great jumpers are complemented by fantastic
own-label handbags (from 400F) in clever combina-
tions of leather, suede, nylon, velvet and flannel.
Branches: 9 rue du 29 Juillet, 1st (01.42.92.00.80);
15 rue du Jour, 1st (01.42.21.88.70); 4, 12 rue Ste-
Croix-de-la-Bretonnerie, 4th (01.42.72.09.55/
01.42.72.15.20).

Highstreet, Street & Clubwear

Apart from the following, it's worth taking a look
at the Forum des Créateurs, vacant shops in the
Forum des Halles that have been let out to young
clothes and accessories designers, with an emphasis on the colourful and streetwise.

Antik Batik

18 rue de Turenne, 4th (01.44.78.02.00). M° Bastille.
Open 11am-7pm Tue-Sat; 2-7pm Sun. **Credit** AmEx,
DC, MC, V. **Map L6**
Wafty hippy vibes infuse this popular new Marais
boutique. Ponchos, alpaca and embroidered silk
jackets are all very *tendance*.

Antoine et Lili

90 rue des Martyrs, 18th (01.42.58.10.22).
M° Abbesses. **Open** 11am-8pm Mon-Sat; 2-7.30pm
Sun. **Credit** AmEx, MC, V. **Map H2**
Antoine et Lili's hippie-hippie chic is bursting out in
exuberant fuschia-painted stores all over town – the
latest additions are in the 6th and 10th. Sparkly tops,
floor-sweeping coats, folksy ponchos, ethno jewellery and all sorts of kitsch gifts and oddities.
Branches: Forum des Halles, 1st (01.42.36.89.54);
87 rue de Seine, 6th (01.56.24.35.81); 15 rue Jean-Paul-
Marc, 10th (01.53.28.55.55); 7 rue de l'Alboni, 16th
(01.45.27.95.00).

Kiliwatch

64 rue Tiquetonne, 2nd (01.42.21.17.37).
M° Etienne-Marcel. **Open** 2-7pm Mon; 11am-7pm
Tue-Sat. **Credit** AmEx, MC, V. **Map J5**
The new-look Kiliwatch is a vast hangar filled with
pumping techno sounds and endless clothes-rails.
There is still an extensive selection of 'quality-con-
trolled' second-hand clothes (leather coats 850F,
shirts 160F), but also many new lines: G-star,
Futurware Lab, Pop-arty Miss Sixty, and its own
clubby label. A kiosk is stacked with CDs, vinyl,
with-it magazines and club flyers.

Kookaï

2 rue Gustave-Courbet, 16th (01.47.55.18.00).
M° Trocadéro. **Open** 10.30am-7.30pm Mon-Sat.
Credit AmEx, DC, MC, V. **Map B5**
Kookaï specialises in transferring the latest looks from
catwalk to high street – fast. Stock changes frequently. Look for coats under 1000F, skirts, dresses and
sweaters around 200F. As for the significance of the
man down the plughole ad…
Branches include: Forum des Halles, 1st
(01.40.26.59.11); Kookaï Stock, 82 rue Réaumur, 2nd
(01.45.08.93.69); 155 rue de Rennes, 6th
(01.45.48.26.36); 106 rue du Fbg-St-Antoine, 12th
(01.43.5.83.23).

Marithé et Francois Girbaud Inside

38 rue Etienne-Marcel, 2nd (01.53.40.74.20).
M° Etienne-Marcel. **Open** noon-7pm Mon; 10am-7pm
Tue-Sat. **Credit** AmEx, DC, MC, V. **Map J5**
Creations, displayed in a stylish 450m^2 store by
architect Stefano Carmi, combine the shapes of
streetwear with high-tech fabrics and production
methods, including laser cutting and welding. The
Freedom combat trousers were worn by Denise
Richards in the latest Bond movie.

*Sexy things: **Plein Sud** are the purveyors*
par excellence of spiky heels and slit skirts.

Shopping: the third way

If you're looking for the soul of Paris fashion it's time to explore the city's backstreets, where a new breed of independent designer is springing up. Struggling away on shoestring budgets in tiny workshop/boutiques, these alternative designers – dubbed *les jeunes créateurs* – turn out impeccably crafted and often highly directional collections at surprisingly affordable prices.

The first interesting fact about the *jeunes créateurs* is that many of them are not necessarily *jeune* at all. Junji Tominaga and Alain Camuset, who make up Franco-Japanese duo **Blancs-Manteaux** (42 rue des Blancs-Manteaux, 4th/ 01.42.71.70.00) are both in their 40s. Tominaga honed his razor-sharp tailoring skills as an assistant at Comme des Garçons, while Camuset dropped out of pharmaceutical studies. The Marais-based duo, who go in for minimalist styles with unexpected twists, opened their *atelier-boutique* because of budget constraints.

'We'd love to do a Gucci and have hundreds of boutiques worldwide,' jokes Camuset, 'but being small does have its advantages. There's a really great *ambiance* in the boutique, because customers often call in and chat to us while we work. Customers like meeting the designer behind the clothes and getting a bit of style advice and personal service. Anyway, I'd go off my head if I was stuck behind a drawing-board, doing *essayages* on some anorexic house model. It's much more fun to have women of all shapes and sizes come in and try your clothes on.'

Sitting in her cramped *atelier-boutique* round the corner embroidering glass beads on swathes of organza, **Laure Kczekotowska** (15 rue des Ecouffes, 4th/01.42.77.98.59) agrees that her pattern-cutting is now finely tuned to the morphology of real women. The 33-year-old French designer, who describes her feminine, bias-cut style as 'sophisticated bohemian', has developed a close relationship with her customers. It's not unusual for clients to drop in for coffee and start scrawling dress designs on the back of an envelope. Laure, who trained as an architect, transforms the doodles into precisely cut patterns and, a few days later, a stunning evening dress will begin to take shape at the back of the shop.

This personalised service does not come cheap (6000F for a special creation, 2600F for ready-made), but Laure's dresses – she uses the same fabric suppliers as the big couture houses – are guaranteed to fit like a glove and make you look like a million dollars.

One of Laure's closest friends is fellow *créateur*

Olivier Battino (16 rue Ste-Anastase, 3rd/ 01.42.78.28.13). A graduate of the prestigious Studio Berçot, the 32-year-old has been working out of *ateliers-boutiques* in the Marais for the past four years. He says customers are turning to independent designers 'because they're sick of lookalike fashion from chain stores like Zara and H&M. They can't afford the prices on avenue Montaigne – and anyway, now that LVMH owns just about every major French fashion house, fashion is pretty uniform on that end of the scale too.' Battino, renowned for his understatedly sexy style, points out that independent designers offer customers 'limited edition fashion', truly one-off pieces which can be made to fit sizes 8-18.

Those who enjoy making bold fashion statements should pay a visit to **Iroo**, a Marais boutique (14 rue des Rosiers, 4th/01.40.27.80.90) manned by 30-year-old Korean Il-Kwon Park. Park specialises in witty, innovative touches such as detachable sleeves and pop-off trouser legs and runs his designs up in space-age fabrics including an unusual copper-based one which allows wearers to crumple their garments into different shapes.

'The French are a bit timid about wearing my designs,' admits Park, 'but I get a lot of English, American and Scandinavian customers. I began working at the back of the boutique because I didn't have enough cash to rent a separate workspace. But now I'm really into moving between the *atelier* and the boutique; it's great to meet the people who wear my clothes and chat about the ideas behind the design.'

Just around the corner, **Kyungmee J** (38 rue du Roi-de-Sicile, 4th/01.42.74.33.85) can be found whirring away on the sewing-machine at the back of her store, making full use of precious design time before the first customers of the day arrive. The 33-year-old Korean-American, who moved to Paris from New York five years ago, stage manages an impressive one-woman show. 'I do everything from designing and pattern-cutting to modelling, selling and sweeping the floor,' she says. 'Some days I could do with a bit of help, but the good thing about being small is that you're always 100 per cent in creative control.' Fashion fans have picked up on Kyungmee's easy-to-wear style and her cute hats, bags and jewellery are also beginning to sell well.

In the younger, funkier Bastille neighbourhood, *jeunes créateurs* such as **Anne Willi** and **Gaëlle Barré** weave subtle street influences into their design. Willi's *atelier-boutique* (13 rue Keller,

Heaven, *an independent workshop/boutique,* is a paradise for seekers of the eclectic.

11th/01.48.06.74.06) presents minimalist clothes with an ethnic twist, while Barré's store (17 rue Keller, 11th/01.43.14.63.02) is a treasure trove of original fashion finds. The bustling backstreets around place des Abbesses in the 18th are also a hotbed of independent design. English fashion designer Lea-Anne Wallis has installed her boutique/workshop **Heaven** (83 rue des Martyrs, 18th/01.44.92.92.92) here, sharing a beautifully decorated space with her lamp-designer husband Jean-Christophe Peyrieux. Round the corner, **Patricia Louisor** (16 rue Houdon, 18th/ 01.42.62.10.42) and her sisters dash between their tiny boutiques bearing fresh armfuls of colourful clothes from their communal workshop. Comme des Garçons fans who can't afford Rei Kawakubo's prices should also check out nearby **Futurware Lab** (2 rue Piémontési, 18th/ 01.42.23.66.08). Here, Russian designer Tatiana Lebedev lets her cyber-conceptual streak run riot, creating futuristic streetwear from padded aluminium and neoprene sponge.

Norwegian designer **Julie Skarland** has her shop tucked away in a quieter spot (59 rue Condorcet, 9th/01.49.95.09.85). The 38-year-old, famous for her simple silhouettes and inventive fabric mixes – think boiled wool and lots of fake

fur – came to Paris twelve years ago to study fashion at the Studio Berçot, and opened her *atelier-boutique* only last year because she was 'sick of pottering around trying to work from home. It's great to see people actually wearing your clothes. I used to pack all my collections off to Japan and that's the last I'd ever see of them.'

Skarland's collections are also sold at Absinthe and shown during Paris Fashion Week. But independent designers **Fanche et Flo**, a Franco-Angolan duo based near place des Abbesses (19 rue Durantin, 18th/01.42.51.24.18), have broken free of the constraints of the ready-to-wear calendar. 'We hate having to fit our designs round spring/summer and autumn/winter,' says Fanche, the duo's female half. 'Basically, we let our creative juices flow when they're ready and put the clothes out in the shop when we feel like it.' Fanche et Flo, who started out doing home accessories and textile design, have created an autonomous workshop, doing all their own printing and dyeing on the spot. Funky low-waisted skirts, made from colourful blanket material and cashmere, are strictly limited edition. Flo says: 'People often tell us they get stopped in the street when they're wearing our clothes' – a long way from mass-market fashion routine.

Ron Orb

39 rue Etienne-Marcel, 1st (01.40.28.09.33).
M° Etienne Marcel. **Open** 11am-7pm Mon-Sat.
Credit AmEx, MC, V. **Map J5**
This space-age store has recently hopped up the
street, but its mission statement hasn't altered.
Automatic doors open into a long, tunnel-like shop,
decked out with space-pod seats and mirrors. The
reasonably priced range is unisex and includes
Velcroed chunky shoes and funnel-necked jackets.

Le Shop

3 rue d'Argout, 2nd (01.40.28.95.94). M° Etienne-
Marcel. **Open** 1-7pm Mon; 11am-7pm Tue-Sat.
Credit AmEx, MC, V. **Map J5**
Whether they're into riding waves, concrete or cyber-
space, street-savvy teenagers will enjoy this two-
tiered, market-like collection of individual outlets.
Clothes are awash with pockets and unnecessary zips
from labels including Final Home, Sunn and Freaks.

Tati

4 bd Rochechouart, 18th (01.55.29.50.00).
M° Barbès-Rochechouart. **Open** 10am-7pm Mon-Fri;
9.15am-7pm Sat. **Credit** MC, V. **Map J2**
As much a Paris institution at the bottom end of the
scale as Galeries Lafayette is at the top, Tati is a hectic chaos of crowded racks and cheap goods piled
into boxes. Tati has diversified into jewellery (Tati
Or) and sweets and, although now facing competition from younger chains, the pink Vichy-check carrier bags remain a legend.
Branch: 13 pl de la République, 3rd (01.48.87.72.81).

Mainly Men

Department stores have all revamped their men's
floors (*see chapter* **Specialist Shopping**) and
ever more designers, including **Martine Sitbon**
and **Christophe Lemaire**, do both men's and
women's lines. See also **Agnès b, A.P.C.,**
L'Eclaireur, Maria Luisa, Zadig et Voltaire
and, below, **Jeans & Casual Wear**.

Anthony Peto

56 rue Tiquetonne, 2nd (01.40.26.60.68).
M° Etienne-Marcel. **Open** 11am-7pm Mon-Sat.
Credit AmEx, DC, MC, V. **MapJ5**
The Brit *chapelier* and other half of milliner Marie
Mercié has opened a new outlet in the trendy
Tiquetonne enclave to show off stylish headware
from gentlemanly panamas to rasta crochet berets.

Façonnable

9 rue du Fbg-St-Honoré, 8th (01.47.42.72.60).
M° Concorde. **Open** 10am-7pm Mon-Sat.
Credit AmEx, DC, MC, V. **Map F4**
Façonnable dresses the *BCBG* male from city-slick-
er suits and striped shirts to country-gent cords.
Branch: 174 bd St-Germain, 6th (01.40.49.02.47).

Flower

7 rue Chomel, 7th (01.42.22.11.78). M° Sèvres-
Babylone. **Open** noon-7pm Mon-Sat. Closed Aug.
Credit MC, V. **Map G7**

Ousui Nakamura showcases the latest from Alexander
McQueen, Marc Le Bihan, Raf Simons and Japan's
Nepenthes, and has recently added womenswear.
Unusual accessories by Vava Dudu and Bill Amberg.

Lanvin

15 rue du Fbg-St-Honoré, 8th (01.44.71.33.33).
M° Concorde. **Open** 10am-6.45pm. **Credit** AmEx,
DC, MC, V. **Map F4**
Trad menswear is given a streamlined, contempo-
rary sportswear edge by designer Dominique
Morlotti. The Café Bleu is an elegant business pause.
Branch: 52 rue Bonaparte, 6th (01.53.10.35.00).

Madelios

23 bd de la Madeleine, 1st (01.53.45.00.00).
M° Madeleine. **Open** 10am-8pm Mon-Sat. **Credit**
AmEx, DC, MC, V. **Map G4**
The former Trois Quartiers is now a 4500m² temple
to male fashion from city suits and casuals to
Barbours and Burberrys, along with accessories
(Cartier, Dunhill, Mont-Blanc) and the requisite in-
store café. Status-asserting togs include the latest from
Bikkembergs, Comme des Garçons, YSL, Paul Smith.

Paul Smith

22 bd Raspail, 7th (01.42.84.15.75). M° Rue du Bac.
Open 11am-7pm Mon; 10am-7pm Tue-Sat.
Credit AmEx, DC, MC, V. **Map G7**
Le style anglais in a wood-panelled interior. Smith's
great suits and classic shoes are on the upper floor,
while women and kids get a funkier space below.

Chic on the cheap at the legendary **Tati**.

Victoire Hommes
15 rue du Vieux-Colombier, 6th (01.45.44.28.02).
M° St-Sulpice. **Open** 10am-7pm Mon-Sat. **Credit**
AmEx, MC, V. **Map G7**
The menswear annexe of the famed Victoire
women's boutiques specialises in casual sportswear,
with some suits; shoes by Sam Walker Cheaney.
Branch: 10-12 rue du Colonel-Driant, 1st (01.42.97.44.87).

Jeans & Casual Wear

Autour du Monde
12 rue des Francs-Bourgeois, 3rd (01.42.77.16.18).
M° St-Paul. **Open** 10am-7pm Mon-Sat; 1-7pm Sun.
Credit AmEx, MC, V. **Map L6**
Wholesome, casual classics for both sexes in plain
colours and natural fabrics. 8 rue des Francs-
Bourgeois (01.42.77.06.08) has younger gear and
Shaker-influenced housewares.
Branch: 54 rue de Seine, 6th (01.43.54.64.47).

Blanc Bleu
14 pl des Victoires, 2nd (01.42.96.05.40). M° Bourse.
Open 11am-7pm Mon; 10am-7pm Tue-Sat. **Credit**
AmEx, DC, MC, V. **Map H5**
'Gentleman skipper' chic infuses Patrick Khayat's
line of classic sportswear, often in navy and white.
Branches: 18 rue Royale, 8th (01.42.96.26.10); 5 bd
Malesherbes, 8th (01.47.42.02.18).

Loft Design By
12 rue du Fbg-St-Honoré, 8th (01.42.65.59.65).
M° Concorde or Madeleine. **Open** 10am-7pm Mon-
Sat. **Credit** AmEx, DC, MC, V. **Map F4**
This is where the French came before Gap. Menswear
is generally better than the women's, with lots of navy,
grey and taupe. Prices seem dear for casualwear but
the cut is all French.
Branches: 12 rue de Sévigné, 4th (01.48.87.13.07);
56 rue de Rennes, 6th (01.45.44.88.99); 22 av de la
Grande Armée, 17th (01.45.72.13.53).

Lingerie & Swimwear

Capucine Puerari
63 rue des Sts-Pères, 6th (01.42.22.14.09). M° St-
Germain-des-Prés. **Open** 10am-7pm Mon-Sat. Closed
two weeks in Aug. **Credit** AmEx, MC, V. **Map G7**
Modern, sexy, fashionable lingerie and swimwear,
plus a ready-to-wear collection in the same spirit.

Erès
2 rue Tronchet, 8th (01.47.42.28.82). M°Madeleine.
Open 10am-7pm Mon-Sat. **Credit** AmEx, DC, MC,
V. **Map G4**
Stylish *Parisiennes* from 18-80 will kill to own the latest Erès swimwear, whether it's a demure belted one-
piece or a sexy Bond Girl bikini (you can buy tops and
bottoms in different sizes). Also simple, luxury lingerie.
Branches: 4bis rue du Cherche-Midi, 6th
(01.45.44.95.54); 6 rue Guichard, 16th (01.46.47.45.21).

Laurence Tavernier
7 rue du Pré-aux-Clercs, 7th (01.49.27.03.95).
M° Rue du Bac. **Open** 10am-7pm Mon-Sat. Closed

10-20 Aug. **Credit** MC, V. **Map G6**
Lingerie here looks smart enough to dine out in. Wool
and cashmere bathrobes (1900F) and slippers (900F),
designed by the sister of film director Bertrand.
Branch: 3 rue Benjamin-Franklin, 16th (01.46.47.89.39).

Sabbia Rosa
73 rue des Sts-Pères, 6th. (01.45.48.88.37). M° St-
Germain-des-Prés. **Open** 10am-7pm Mon-Sat. **Credit**
AmEx, MC, V. **Map G7**
Moana Moati has been steering pampered Parisian
wives, execs (50 per cent of the clientele is men) and
models to the right silk undies in varying degrees of
naughtiness for the past 22 years. 800F for a string
bikini; babydoll nighties for 6000F.

Designer Bargains & Vintage

Second-hand can be chic if it has a designer label
attached, but don't expect it to be particularly cheap
(look for the sign *dépôt-vente*). Rue d'Alésia, 14th, is
packed with discount factory outlets (called 'Stock');
trendy club outlet **Kiliwatch** mixes new and old.

Alternatives
18 rue du Roi-de-Sicile, 4th (01.42.78.31.50). M° St-
Paul. **Open** 11am-1pm, 2.30-7pm Tue-Sat. Closed 15
July-15 Aug. **Credit** MC, V. **Map K/L6**
Martine Bergossi accepts only the highest cast-offs in
top condition: Jean-Paul Gaultier, Hermès, Dries Van
Noten and Comme des Garçons. Prices 400F-3000F.

Didier Ludot
19, 20, 23, 24 galerie Montpensier, 1st
(01.42.96.06.56). M°Palais-Royal. **Open** Mon-Sat
10.30am-7pm **Credit** AmEx, DC, V. **Map H5**
A wall-to-wall wardrobe of vintage couture: try on a
Jacques Fath dress, an original 50s Chanel suit, or 70s
beaded Dior. A favourite haunt of supermodels;
Miuccia Prada and Demi Moore have been known to
fly in just to rifle through the impressive collection.

L'Habilleur
44 rue de Poitou, 3rd (01.48.87.77.12).
M° St-Sébastien-Froissart. **Open** 11am-8pm Mon-Sat.
Credit MC, V. **Map L5**
From the smartly attired mannequins in the window,
you wouldn't guess the clothes here are end-of-line
and off-the-catwalk items bought direct from Martine
Sitbon, Patrick Cox, John Richmond, Olivier Strelli,
Plein Sud, Vivienne Westwood etc, sold half price.

Le Mouton à Cinq Pattes
19 rue Grégoire de Tours, 6th (01.43.29.73.56).
M° Odéon. **Open** 10.30am-7.30pm Mon-Fri; 10.30am-
8pm Sat. **Credit** AmEx, MC, V. **Map H7**
Shopping here can be a scrum, but many people
swear by the bargains. Many are *dégriffés* (end of line
clothes) with their label cut out, so you need to know
what you're looking for to recognise the Gaultier,
Lang, Montana and Martine Sitbon pieces.
Branches: 15 rue Vieille-du-Temple, 4th
(01.42.71.86.30); 138 bd St-Germain, 6th
(01.43.26.49.25); 8 (women), 10 (children), 18 (women,
men) and 48 (men) rue St-Placide, 6th (01.45.48.86.26).

Réciproque

88, 89, 92, 95, 97, 101, 123 rue de la Pompe, 16th (01.47.04.82.24/01.47.04.30.28). M° Rue de la Pompe. **Open** 11.15am-7.30pm Tue-Sat. Closed Aug. **Credit** AmEx, MC, V. **Map H7**

The doyenne of Paris' *dépôt-ventes*, Réciproque's side-by-side second-hand boutiques are the answer for those with *couture* taste and limited bank accounts. Prices are not as cheap, however (3000F for a good-condition Dior or Chanel suit, 1300F for a Prada dress), as you might hope. Menswear too.

Shoes & Accessories

Accessoire Diffusion

6 rue du Cherche-Midi, 6th (01.45.48.36.08). M° Sèvres-Babylone or St-Sulpice. **Open** 10am-7pm Mon-Sat. **Credit** AmEx, MC, V. **Map G7**

A French chain selling well-made fashionable styles at reasonable prices, including simple suede pumps and sleek boots. The Détente range is more casual and less expensive.

Branches: 8 rue du Jour, 1st (01.40.26.19.84); 36 rue Vieille-du-Temple, 4th (01.40.29.99.49); 11 rue du Pré-aux-Clercs, 7th (01.42.84.26.85).

Cérize

380 rue St-Honoré, 1st (01.42.60.84.84). M° Concorde. **Open** 10am-7.30pm Mon-Sat. **Credit** AmEx, DC, MC, V. **Map F4**

Women with serious budgets will love this chic, neo-baroque boudoir full of hats, handbags and jewellery. Watch out for designs by French hat queen Marie Mercié and bags by couture embroider François Lesage. Great service, plus you actually get to try everything on in individual changing cabins.

Christian Louboutin

19 rue Jean-Jacques-Rousseau, 1st (01.42.36.05.31). M° Palais-Royal or Louvre. **Open** 10am-7pm Mon-Sat. Closed Aug. **Credit** AmEx, MC, V. **Map J5**

Former assistant to Roger Vivier, maestro of the New Look era, Christian Louboutin draws a gilt-edged clientele for beautiful shoes with such signature details as 18k gold-plated heels, bright red soles or paisley silk. Prices 1400F-3300F.

Branch: 38 rue de Grenelle, 7th (01.42.22.33.07).

Free Lance

30 rue du Four, 6th (01.45.48.14.78). M° St Germain-des-Prés. **Open** 10am-7pm Mon-Sat. **Credit** AmEx, DC, MC, V. **Map H7**

French design duo Guy and Yvon Rautureau let their creative imagination run wild on a multi-trend collection which includes everything from funky men's shoes in rainbow colours to cyberboots and Gucci-style vamp stilettos for girls. Prices are not cheap, but a loud fashion statement is guaranteed.

Jamin Puech

61 rue d'Hauteville, 10th (01.40.22.08.32). M° Bonne-Nouvelle or Poissonnière. **Open** 9.30am-6.30pm Mon-Fri. **Credit** MC, V. **Map K3**

Trendy handbag designers Isabelle Puech and Benoît Jamin recently opened their first store in a former paper-goods shop. Their unpretentious yet wildly inventive handbags and carry-alls use a mad mix of materials from crocheted twine to printed satin plaid canvas. Prices 90F-1800F.

Kabuki

21, 25 rue Etienne-Marcel, 1st (01.42.33.55.65). M° Etienne-Marcel **Open** 1-7.30pm Mon; 10.30am-7.30pm Tue-Sat. **Credit** AmEx, DC, MC, V. **Map J5**

Owner William Halimi has his finger firmly on the fashion pulse at his cutting-edge multi-mark store: shoes and bags downstairs, fashion upstairs (Helmut Lang, Prada, Martine Sitbon). Shoes favour outrageous silhouettes (lots of Miu Miu).

Madeleine Gély

218 bd St-Germain, 7th (01.42.22.63.35). M° Rue du Bac. **Open** 10am-7pm Tue-Sat. Closed Aug. **Credit** MC, V. **Map G6**

This shop probably hasn't changed much since opening in 1834. Short or long, plain or fancy, there's an umbrella or cane here for everyone.

Pallas

21 rue St-Roch, 1st (01.42.61.13.21). M° Tuileries. **Open** 9am-7pm Mon-Fri; 2-7pm Sat. Closed three weeks in Aug. **Credit** AmEx, DC, MC, V. **Map G5**

Elsa Zanetti has been making handbags for the couture houses, including Fath and Balenciaga, for years. Designs range from classic box leather shoulder bags to embroidered evening pouches. All the bags (400F-3000F) are manufactured in an *atelier* at the back, and can be ordered in different colours.

Sequoia

72bis rue Bonaparte, 6th (01.44.07.27.94). M° St-Sulpice. **Open** 10am-7pm Mon-Sat. **Credit** AmEx, DC, MC, V. **Map H6**

This new store showcases Sequoia's well-priced handbags and shoes. Bags in all sizes go from grey flannel to glossy leather. Simply styled mocassins and boots are joined by fun Day-Glo ankle wellies.

Shoe Bizz

42 rue du Dragon, 6th (01.45.44.91.70). M° St-Sulpice. **Open** 2-7.30pm Mon; 10.30am-7.30pm Tue-Sat. **Credit** AmEx, MC, V. **Map G7**

Their bizz is to zero in on the most fashionable shoe shapes of the season, and recreate them at around 30 per cent cheaper than their competitors.

Branch: 48 rue Beaubourg, 3rd (01.48.87.12.73).

Sisso's

20 rue Malher, 4th (01.44.61.99.50). M° St Paul. **Open** Mon-Sat 10am-7pm. **Credit** AmEx, V. **Map L6**

This is a one-stop glamour shop where you can pick up everything from Prada and Hogan shoes to Sequoia clutch bags, jewellery by Kathy Korvin and exciting Franco-Italian design duo Rafia & Bossa.

Stéphane Kélian

13bis rue de Grenelle, 7th (01.42.22.93.03). M° Sèvres-Babylone. **Open** 10am-7pm Mon-Sat. **Credit** AmEx, MC, V. **Map G7**

High-fashion women's shoes and boots from around 1000F, as well as classic woven flats. He also designs for Martine Sitbon.

Dress sense: **L'Habilleur** *sells end-of-line and off-the-catwalk designer clothes at half price.*

Branches: 6 pl des Victoires, 2nd (01.42.61.60.74); 26 av des Champs-Elysées, 8th (01.42.56.42.26); 20 av Victor Hugo, 16th (01.45.00.44.41).

Ursule Beaugeste

15 rue Oberkampf, 11th (01.49.23.02.48). M° Oberkampf. **Open** noon-7pm Mon-Fri. **Credit** MC, V. **Map M5**

Along with its trendy bars, Ménilmontant is now moving on to the fashion map and designer Anne Grand-Clément's plum-coloured boutique is one of the reasons, with her crocheted shopping bags and dressy little tweed handbags.

Hats

Divine

39 rue Daguerre, 14th (01.43.22.28.10). M° Denfert-Rochereau. **Open** 10.30am-1pm, 3-7.30pm Tue-Sat. Closed three weeks in Aug. **Credit** DC, MC, V. **Map G10**

An unexpected treasure trove of new and vintage hats for men and women to suit all sartorial styles, pockets and occasions – including traditional straw boaters, floppy velvet, genuine Basque berets and never-worn 1920s lacy cloches.

Marie Mercié

23 rue St-Sulpice, 6th (01.43.26.45.83). M° Odéon. **Open** 11am-7pm Mon-Sat. **Credit** AmEx, DC, MC, V. **Map H7**

Marie Mercié is the mad hatter who put everyone in big-crowned skypieces, revolutionising the hat industry in our times. There are colourful felt hats in winter, straw and silks in summer, in styles that go from classic to theatrical. One-offs cost from 2500F, the season's lines 1000F-2500F.

Branch: 56 rue Tiquetonne, 2nd (01.40.26.60.68).

Têtes en l'Air

65 rue des Abbesses, 18th (01.46.06.71.19). M° Abbesses. **Open** 2-7pm Mon; 10.30am-7.30pm Tue-Sat. Closed Aug. **No credit cards. Map H1**

This shop features attention-seeking hats, be it a lemon-yellow and lime-green contraption with a caged canary on top, or a Christmas tree. Hats can be made to measure.

Jewellery

Ange

20 rue du Pont-Louis-Phillipe, 4th (01.42.76.02.37). M° Hôtel-de-Ville. **Open** 10.30am-7.30pm Mon-Sat; 12.30-7.30pm Sun. **Credit** AmEx, MC, V. **Map K7**

Paradise for teenage boho wannabes. Trendy necklaces and bracelets are strung up on branches or strips of metal, and a profusion of tacked-on beads creates that sought-after haphazard look. Earrings start at 100F; elaborate necklaces go up to 800F.

Cécile et Jeanne

215 rue St-Honoré, 1st (01.42.61.68.68). M° Tuileries. **Open** 11am-7pm Mon-Sat. **Credit** AmEx, DC, MC, V. **Map G5**

Wire-and-resin creations and modern art-inspired brooches in a colourful baroque setting.

Branches: Carrousel du Louvre, 1st (01.42.61.26.15); 12 rue des Francs-Bourgeois, 3rd (01.44.61.00.99); 4 rue de Sèvres, 6th (01.42.22.82.82); 49 av Daumesnil, 12th (01.43.41.24.24).

Delphine Charlotte Parmentier

26 rue du Bourg-Tibourg, 4th (01.44.54.51.72).
Mº Hôtel de Ville. **Open** 10am-7pm Mon-Fri; 2-7pm
Sat. **Credit** MC, V. **Map K6**
Delphine started out making art-cum-jewellery for
the couture houses before opening her own Marais
boutique in 1997. Dramatic head-dresses, chainmail
bracelets and glass spike chokers are strikingly
sophisticated. Pieces can be made to order.

La Licorne

38 rue de Sévigné, 3rd (01.48.87.84.43). Mº St Paul.
Open 9.30am-7pm daily. **Credit** AmEx, DC, MC, V.
Map L6
A treasure trove of vintage costume jewellery, with
the emphasis on chunky Art Deco bakelite, nine-
teenth-century jet and 50s diamanté. Endless pieces
for fancy dress, or maybe just for raving extroverts.
There's also a repair service.

Marie Streichenberger

23 rue du Cherche-Midi, 6th (01.45.44.93.02).
Mº Sèvres-Babylone. **Open** 10am-7pm Mon-Sat.
Credit AmEx, MC, V. **Map G7**
Marie Streichenberger has designed for Dior, Kenzo
and Montana, as well as bags, belts and jewellery
for Thierry Mugler and Donna Karan. This shop
showcases her own reasonably priced lines, such as
Art Deco lacework silver bracelets (440F-650F).

Les Montres

58 rue Bonaparte, 6th (01.46.34.71.38). Mº Mabillon
or St-Germain-des-Prés. **Open** 10am-7pm Mon-Sat.
Credit AmEx, DC, MC, V. **Map H7**
Status-symbol watches, among them Swiss and
American models. There are also collectors' watch-
es, such as vintage Rolexes from the 1920s.
Branch: 40 rue de Passy, 16th (01.53.92.51.61).

Naïla de Monbrison

6 rue de Bourgogne, 7th (01.47.05.11.15).
Mº Solférino. **Open** 11.30am-1.30pm, 2.30-7pm Tue-
Sat. Closed Aug. **Credit** AmEx, MC, V. **Map F6**
A showcase for contemporary jewellery by world-
famous names: Juliette Polac, Dominique Biard,
Marcial Berro, Giorgio Vigna, Garouste et
Bonnetti… Real works of art – at prices to match.

Perfumes & Cosmetics

L'Artisan Parfumeur

24 bd Raspail, 7th (01.42.22.23.32). Mº Rue du Bac.
Open 10.30am-7pm Mon-Sat. **Credit** AmEx, DC,
MC, V. **Map G7**
Among scented candles, potpourri and lucky
charms, you will find the best vanilla perfume Paris
can offer – Mûres et Musc, a bestseller for more than
20 years. They have recently introduced Dzing!, a
powerful scent for women.

Guerlain

68 av des Champs-Elysées, 8th (01.45.62.52.57).
Mº Franklin D Roosevelt. **Open** 9.45am-7pm
Mon-Sat. **Credit** AmEx, MC, V. **Map E4**
The boutique is one of the last vestiges of the gold-
en age of the Champs-Elysées, but the family concern has recently been sold to LVMH. Many of the
Guerlain fragrances were created with royal or
Proustian inspirations, and even today some of its
scents are sold only in the Guerlain boutiques.
Branches include: 2 pl Vendôme, 1st
(01.42.60.68.61); 47 rue Bonaparte, 6th
(01.43.26.71.19); 29 rue de Sèvres, 6th (01.42.22.46.60);
93 rue de Passy, 16th (01.42.88.41.62).

Lora Lune

22 rue du Bourg-Tibourg, 4th (01.48.04.31.24).
Mº Hôtel-de-Ville. **Open** 2-7.30pm Mon; 11am-7.30pm
Tue-Sat; 1-7pm Sun. **Credit** MC, V. **Map K6**
Practicality is the name of the game in this new boutique. There are huge glass bottles of cream, giant
slabs of soap and baskets of bath salts, and under
expert supervision you can delve in and sample;
price is calculated by weight. Products are based on
natural vegetable oils, and the emphasis is on everyday creams, lotions and perfumes for both sexes.

L'Occitane

55 rue St-Louis-en-l'Ile, 4th (01.40.46.81.71).
Mº Pont-Marie. **Open** 10.30am-8.30pm Mon-Sat.
Credit AmEx, DC, MC, V. **Map K7**
There are now 22 branches of this Provençal chain
around Paris, and it's easy to see why they have
become favourites, for natural products and pretty
packaging. Soap rules the roost, but there's also a
selection of cosmetics, essential oils and perfumes.

Make Up For Ever Professional

5 rue La Boëtie, 8th (01.42.66.01.60).
Mº Miromesnil. **Open** 10am-7pm Mon-Sat. **Credit**
AmEx, DC, MC, V. **Map E3**
Despite the name, this is a French outfit and it deto-
nates an explosion of colour. With loads of glitter, hair
spray, nail varnish, lipstick, fake eyelashes and stick-
on tatoos, you're more likely to emerge as a multi-
ethnic punk than a pristine Parisian.
Branch: 22 rue de Sèvres, 7th (01.45.48.75.97).

Parfums Caron

34 av Montaigne, 8th (01.47.23.40.82). Mº Franklin
D Roosevelt. **Open** 10am-6.30pm Mon-Sat. **Credit**
AmEx, DC, MC, V. **Map E4**
In its elegant Art Deco boutique, Caron sells re-edi-
tions of its classic favourites from 1911-54, includ-
ing the spicy, eastern rose scent Or et Noir.

Les Salons du Palais-Royal Shiseido

142 galerie de Valois, 1st (01.49.27.09.09).
Mº Louvre or Palais-Royal. **Open** 10am-7pm Mon-
Sat. **Credit** AmEx, DC, MC, V. **Map H5**
Tucked under the arcades of the Palais-Royal are the
make-up and perfumes of the Japanese line in a mock
Directoire-period interior, created by Serge Lutens.

Séphora

70 av des Champs-Elysées, 8th (01.53.93.22.50). Mº
Franklin D Roosevelt. **Open** 10am-midnight Mon-Sat;
noon-midnight Sun. **Credit** AmEx, MC, V. **Map E4**
This cosmetic chain flagship carries 12,000 French
and foreign brands of scent and slap. At the 'sampling bar' you can sniff 560 basic scents classified
according to the eight olfactive families.

Techy trendoids and other tribes

In Paris, where fashion forecasters are paid to meticulously track the buying habits of such fashion animalia as 'global surfers' and 'eco-urbanites', each finely honed fashion tribe has claimed its own piece of the city.

St-Germain belongs to the *gauche caviar*, as the fashionable leftists rich enough to reside in the 7th, summer in St-Rémy and sip coffee at the Flore are nicknamed. The cosseted retail zone here runs along the boulevard St-Germain roughly from the western outpost **Bonpoint**, purveyors of pashmina shawls for newborns and herringbone tweed shorts for little boys, to the Left Bank branch of Cartier. In between, shoppers peruse the latest literary prizewinner at **La Hune**, or make their way through the *luxe* lines of the new Left Bank outlets of Vuitton, Dior and Emporio Armani.

Same money, different politics rule over on the Right Bank's avenue Montaigne, where closet royalists and the kind of high-maintenance blondes who get their hair dyed at Carita pose for each other over handbags at Céline, crocodile pumps at Ferragamo, and all the yellow-brick way through Dior's palatial flagship.

Designer devotees, of the kind who buy even their dogs' leather accessories at Gucci, click their stilettoed Manolos together to head for lunch at hyper-trendy **Colette**

(pictured), on the once untrendy (and how short a time ago that was) rue St-Honoré. With all those Spoon-watch and Bless fanatics lingering in Colette's shadows, it's no surprise that a huddle of designer shops, including a new branch of **Zadig et Voltaire**, has sprung up nearby. The Colette shopper can dip into a crop of Italian boutiques for last-minute accessories, buy the latest limited-edition compilation from the DJ at Hôtel Costes or pop into Penny Black for the hippest of Max Mara's many spin-off lines.

Not every shop in Paris has a Japanese fanzine dedicated to it, and that may be the very goal behind Paris' ethno-folklore devotees, whose global vibe takes them, slightly warily, to Barbès, for Senegalese and North African fabrics and trinkets. Parisian streetwear fans – who are currently in a hunkered-down, urban-guerrilla mode, with high-tech protective gear and a metallic sheen to fabrics – find their thing not far away at **Futurware Lab** and the shops around Abbesses, or head to the centre to the hangar-like **Kiliwatch** and **Le Shop**.

A slightly different breed of fashion renegade is harking back to its roots, which in the case of Parisian *mode* nostalgics, seem located somewhere in the summer of 1972. Hippie-chic is strictly something that happened to Tom Ford over at Gucci: retro-fashionistas in Paris are based over at rue Keller, a tiny street behind the Bastille. In between a surprising number of vinyl-record stores and shops devoted to Star Wars collectables are a fistful of retro boutiques selling new and vintage jeans, variegated-colour crochet sweaters (the 70s were a heyday for the home knitter), psychedelic hand-me-downs and orange plastic hi-fi tables.

But the future of fashion, as some Parisian trendoids see it, is not in the slightly queasy, 'didn't-this-used-to-be-hip?' aura of the place des Victoires, but far across town in the lively streets lining the Canal St-Martin in the 10th *arrondissement*. It's a quick deduction to arrive at the fact that all truly avant-garde fashion in Paris (Ann Demeulemeester, Martin Margiela, Véronique Branquino, Viktor & Rolf) comes from those northern European bergs, and hey, doesn't that Canal remind you of Bruges? Sip on a tuberose-coloured cocktail at **Purple** boutique and café (9 rue Pierre-Dupont/01.40.34.14.21) while skimming an issue of *Wallpaper**, or shop for a striped plastic notebook at **Antoine et Lili**, and bask in the prophetic halo of fashion's *fin de siècle*.

Specialist Shops

The best addresses for finding the smartest lamp, the best tablelinen, the wittiest ashtray or the latest French hip hop.

The lifestyle trend just runs and runs in Paris, the department stores are raining men, but beyond the one-stop shop where you can solve your dress dilemmas (but not necessarily budget ones), furnish your flat and buy all your Christmas presents in one fair swoop, Paris still abounds with small specialist stores: fantastic *papeteries*, scholarly bookshops, cavernous kitchen supply shops and eccentric emporia where you can buy nothing but accordions, eco objects or stuffed animals.

In a wildly international market the designer style object competes against ethnic chic from Africa or pottery from Provence, while kitsch and retro are clearly the turn of the century decadence.

ANTIQUES & RETRO

If you're after antiques and retro it helps to know where to go: traditional classy antiques in the Carré des Antiquaires of the 7th, Village Suisse and Fbg-St-Honoré, Art Deco in St-Germain, 1950s-70s retro plastic around rue de Charonne in the 11th, antiquarian books and stamps in the covered passages, in the *bouquinistes* along the quais or at Parc Georges Brassens. Then, of course, there are the Marchés aux Puces at St-Ouen, Montreuil and Vanves and auction house Drouot, due soon to be challenged by the arrival of Sotheby's and Christie's. There are also frequent *brocantes* – antiques and collectors' markets, especially in summer; look for banners in the street and notices in listings magazines.

Books

See also Fnac and Virgin Megastore in **Records, CDs, Cassettes & Hi-Fi** below.

Abbey Bookshop

29 rue de la Parcheminerie, 5th (01.46.33.16.24). M° St-Michel. **Open** 10am-7pm Mon-Sat. **Credit** AmEx, MC, V. **Map J7**
This small Canadian-run bookshop has an extensive section of Canadian writers (including Québecois), as well as English and American titles. Regular author signings and readings.

Brentano's

37 av de l'Opéra, 2nd (01.42.61.52.50). M° Opéra. **Open** 10am-7.30pm Mon-Sat. **Credit** AmEx, MC, V. **Map G4**
A good address for American classics, modern fiction and bestsellers, plus an excellent array of business titles. English-language books are at the front.

The children's section in the basement also offers stories, songs and crafts (Wed afternoon, Sat morning).

La Chambre Claire

14 rue St-Sulpice, 6th (01.46.34.04.31). M° Odéon. **Open** 10am-7pm Mon-Sat. **Credit** MC, V. **Map H7**
Specialises in photography, with plenty of titles in English and a photo gallery downstairs.

Entrée des Artistes

161 rue St-Martin, 3rd (01.48.87.78.58). M° Rambuteau. **Open** 11am-7.30pm Mon-Sat. **Credit** MC, V. **Map K5**
This shrine to celluloid, from the most obscure movies to box-office blockbusters, is packed with film posters, stills and books in French and English.

Galignani

224 rue de Rivoli, 1st (01.42.60.76.07). M° Tuileries. **Open** 10am-7pm Mon-Sat. **Credit** MC, V. **Map G5**
Opened in 1802, Galignani was reputedly the first English-language bookshop in Europe, and at one point even published its own daily newspaper. Today it stocks fine- and decorative arts books and literature in both French and English.

Gibert Joseph

26, 30 bd St-Michel, 6th (01.44.41.88.88). M° St-Michel. **Open** 9.30am-7.30pm Mon-Sat. **Credit** AmEx, MC, V. **Map J7**
Best known as a bookshop serving the Left Bank learning institutions, with some titles in English, as well as a place to flog text books. Also has stationery, office supplies and CDs.

La Hune

170 bd St-Germain, 6th (01.45.48.35.85). M° St-Germain-des-Prés. **Open** 10am-midnight Mon-Sat. **Credit** AmEx, DC, MC, V. **Map G7**
A Left Bank institution, La Hune boasts an international selection of art and design books on the mezzanine and a superb collection of French literature and theory downstairs. Always busy until late with intellectual and arty types.

Institut Géographique National

107 rue La Boétie, 8th (01.43.98.85.00). M° Franklin D Roosevelt. **Open** 9.30am-7pm Mon-Fri; 11am-12.30pm, 2-6.30pm Sat. **Credit** AmEx, MC, V. **Map E4**
Paris' best cartographic shop stocks international maps, as well as detailed walking and cycling maps of France, wine maps and facsimile historic maps of Paris. It also has guides to all of France, and globes.

Librairie Gourmande

4 rue Dante, 5th (01.43.54.37.27). M° St-Michel. **Open** 10am-7pm daily. **Credit** MC, V. **Map J7**

Shakespeare & Co *is still port of call for budding bards.*

Chefs from the world over hunt out Geneviève Baudon's bookstore dedicated to old and newly published books on cooking, gastronomy, wine and table arts. Non-French titles.

La Maison Rustique
26 rue Jacob, 6th (01.42.34.96.60). M° St-Germain-des-Prés. **Open** 10am-7pm Mon-Sat. **Credit** AmEx, DC, MC, V. **Map H6**
Paris' best selection of gardening, botanical and interior design books, with some titles in English.

NQL Librairie Internationale
78 bd St-Michel, 6th (01.43.26.42.70).
RER Luxembourg or Port Royal. **Open** 10am-7pm Mon-Sat. **Credit** AmEx, DC, MC, V. **Map H8**
International bookshop stocks literature, dictionaries and guide books not only in English, but in German, Spanish, Italian and Russian, plus a smallish children's section. Reduced-price books are at No 80, the Comptoir des Soldes (afternoon only).

Shakespeare & Co
37 rue de la Bûcherie, 5th (01.43.26.96.50).
M° Maubert-Mutualité/RER St-Michel. **Open** noon-midnight daily. **No credit cards.** **Map J7**
A Parisian legend still packed with would-be Hemingways, even if no longer on the same site as Sylvia Beach's famous shop. New, used and antique books in English are arranged chaotically, often in heaps on the floor. Service is suitably atmospheric.

Tea & Tattered Pages
24 rue Mayet, 6th (01.40.65.94.35). M° Duroc.
Open 11am-7pm daily; *Aug* noon-6pm Mon-Sat.
No credit cards. **Map F8**
Pick up cheap secondhand paperbacks in English

(most around 30F), sell back your cast-offs and stop for tea and brownies in the American-run tea salon.

Village Voice
6 rue Princesse, 6th (01.46.33.36.47). M° Mabillon.
Open 2-8pm Mon; 10am-8pm Tue-Sat; 2-7pm Sun.
Credit AmEx, DC, MC, V. **Map H7**
The ever-charming Odile Hellier supports alternative literature by stocking the city's best selection of new and hard-to-get fiction and non-fiction in English, plus literary magazines. She also holds literary events and poetry readings.

WH Smith
248 rue de Rivoli, 1st (01.44.77.88.99). M° Concorde. **Open** 9am-7.30pm Mon-Sat; 1-7.30pm Sun. **Credit** AmEx, MC, V. **Map G5**
This long-established branch of the British chain carries over 70,000 titles, including paperback bestsellers, classics, crime, art books, travel guides, cook books and videos. There are good reference, children's and ELT sections and a perpetual mob around the UK and US mag and newspaper racks.

Design & Home Accessories

Avant-Scène
4 pl de l'Odéon, 6th (01.46.33.12.40). M° Odéon.
Open 10.30am-7pm Tue-Sat. Closed 10-20 Aug.
Credit MC, V. **Map H7**
The more baroque side of contemporary furniture and lighting is gathered by Elisabeth Delacarte, who stocks French and European designers, including Mark Brazier Jones, Franck Evennou, Hubert le Gall and Hervé Van der Straeten.

Bô

8 rue St-Merri, 4th (01.42.72.84.64). M° Hôtel de Ville or Rambuteau. **Open** 11am-8pm Mon-Sat; 2-8pm Sun. **Credit** AmEx, DC, MC, V. **Map K6**
Chic, pared-back style. Candlesticks, vases, unusual lights, new agey incense burners and elegant grey Limoges porcelain are all *très bô*.

Catherine Memmi

32-34 rue St-Sulpice, 6th (01.44.07.22.28). M° Mabillon. **Open** 12.30-7.30pm Mon; 10.30am-7.30pm Tue-Sat. **Credit** AmEx, MC, V. **Map H7**
Impeccable and pricey good taste comes in white, cream, grey, chocolate and black only. Tablelinen and sheets are meticulously arranged alongside shirts, dressing gowns, candles, iron lamps, fashionable knitted cushions, vases and furniture.

Cèdre Rouge

25 rue Duphot, 1st (01.42.61.81.81). M° Madeleine. **Open** noon-7pm Mon; 10.30am-7pm Tue-Sat. **Credit** AmEx, MC, V. **Map G4**
The garden-conservatory-interior store offers an undeniably urban interpretation of rusticity. Occasionally twee, often tasteful, china and glass, candles, planters and wrought-iron furniture. **Branches:** 22 av Victoria, 1st (01.45.08.85.61); 116 rue du Bac, 7th (01.42.84.84.00); 1 bd Emile-Augier, 16th (01.45.24.62.62).

CFOC

170 bd Haussmann, 8th (01.53.53.40.80). M° St-Philippe-du-Roule. **Open** 10am-7pm Mon-Sat. **Credit** AmEx, DC, MC, V. **Map E3**
La Compagnie Française de l'Orient et de la Chine is full of eastern promise from Chinese teapots and celadon bowls, lacquerware, Mongolian pottery and Iranian blown glass to slippers and silk jackets. Downstairs is an Art Deco interior by Ruhlmann. **Branches:** 24 rue St-Roch, 1st (01.42.60.65.32); 163, 167 bd St-Germain, 6th (01.45.48.00.18/); 260 bd St-Germain, 7th (01.47.05.92.82); 65 av Victor-Hugo, 16th (01.45.00.55.46); 113 av Mozart, 16th (01.42.88.36.08).

Chimène

25 rue de Charonne, 11th (01.43.55.55.00). M° Bastille. **Open** 11am-7.30pm Tue-Sat; 3-7pm Sun. **Credit** AmEx, MC, V. **Map M7**
Ethnic here appears to mean African and Provence, but the selection is impressive. Patchwork bedspreads and cushions, wrought-iron leafy candlesticks, neo-bamboo coffee cups, Uzes dinner plates and Kenyan soapstone bowls accompany bathtime goodies from Côté Bastide. Larger furniture is in the cellar.

Dîners en Ville

27 rue de Varenne, 7th (01.42.22.78.33). M° Rue du Bac. **Open** 2-7pm Mon; 10.30am-7pm Tue-Sat. Closed two weeks in Aug. **Credit** MC, V. **Map F6**
New and antique tableware gets spectacular window displays full of colourful glasses, Italian earthenware, fancy cutlery and luxurious tablecloths.

DOM

21 rue Ste-Croix-de-la-Bretonnerie, 4th (01.42.71.08.00). **Open** 10.30am-9pm Mon-Thur; 11.30am-11pm Fri, Sat; 2-9pm Sun. **Credit** AmEx,

MC, V. **Map K6**
Assistants dressed in black sell essential items in screaming colours for the home, from Day-glo fish tanks to inflatable sacco armchairs, fluffy lamps and naughty chocs. Chic and kitsch, but not *cher*.

Galerie Van der Straeten

11 rue Ferdinand-Duval, 4th (01.42.78.99.99). M° St-Paul. **Open** 9am-1pm, 2-6pm Mon-Thur; 9am-1pm, 2-5pm Fri; 11am-7pm Sat. **Credit** AmEx, DC, MC, V. **Map K6**
Hervé van der Straeten's own neo-baroque furniture, mirrors, ceramics and jewellery are joined by his one-off collaborations with designers or artisans such as Olivier Gagnère and Thomas Boog, and an array of contemporary jewellery by Eric Halley, Stefano Polleti et al in a lovely skylit gallery.

Maison de Famille

29 rue St-Sulpice, 6th (01.40.46.97.47). M° Odéon. **Open** 10.30am-7pm Mon-Sat. **Credit** AmEx, V. **Map H7**
The busy three-storey boutique is an eclectic bazaar of French finds, from heavy brass garden scissors to rope-soled bedroom slippers, wicker baskets to leather luggage, big wooden vessels, glazed pots and home accessories, to women's and men's clothing. **Branch:** 10 pl de la Madeleine, 8th (01.53.45.82.00).

La Maison Ivre

38 rue Jacob, 6th (01.42.60.01.85). M° St-Germain-des-Prés. **Open** 12-7pm Mon; 10.30am-7pm Tue-Sat. **Credit** MC, V. **Map H6**
Traditional handmade pottery from all over France with an emphasis on yellow and green glazed Provençal wares. Also tablecloths, hand-woven baskets, pretty eggcups and candlesticks.

Muji

27, 30 rue St-Sulpice, 6th (01.46.34.01.10). M°St-Sulpice. **Open** 10am-8pm Mon-Sat. **Credit** AmEx, MC, V. **Map H7**
The famous Japanese 'no brand' brand has taken Paris by storm with its elegantly utilitarian stationery, plastic binders, Japanese kitchenwares, metal storage boxes, nylon shopping bags and bathroom accessories. There are also clothes, including jumpers and socks in rigorous white, black and grey.

Muriel Grateau

130 Galerie de Valois, Jardins du Palais-Royal, 1st (01.40.20.90.30). M° Palais-Royal. **Open** 11am-7pm Mon-Sat. **Credit** AmEx, MC, V. **Map H5**
If your taste is for sobriety, then you'll love Grateau's contemporary minimalist chic. White biscuitware, deep striped linen tablecloths, grey porcelain and glasses, decanters and towels are elegantly displayed. Serious stuff at serious prices. **Branch:** 37 rue de Beaune, 7th (01.40.20.42.82).

N.U

29 rue Mazarine, 6th (01.43.25.04.25). M° Odéon. **Open** 10am-1pm, 2-7pm Mon-Sat. **Credit** AmEx, DC, MC, V. **Map H6**
A zig-zag steel chaise-longue dotted with smartie-coloured cushions sums up the witty approach to furniture, lighting and deco objects of young design-

Reinventing the *Grand Magasin*

Lifestyle stores have put the *Grands Magasins* on their mettle. As stores market furniture, accessories, sporting goods, CDs and clothing all identically as fashion items, Paris' department stores have had to reinvent themselves. Snack bars, photo exhibits, trendy magazines and high-tech gadgets rubbing shoulders with tie and sweater displays are now all part of the retail landscape.

The undoubted story of 1999, though, was men. All the city's department stores have redesigned their men's departments. **Galeries Lafayette** is betting on sheer size: its menswear space due to open in 2000, should, at 10,000m², be the largest menswear store in Europe. Stone floors and dark wood will set off 170 labels, shoppers can send faxes or get shoes shined; trousers are hemmed free within the hour. Its women's store houses the classiest jewellery of any department store in Paris, while fashion departments propose trend boards to direct shoppers to hot items, and a full range of designer labels (Demeulemeester, Comme des Garçons, Jérôme Dreyfuss, Tom Van Lingen). Designer objects for the home on the fifth floor are accompanied by a zone grouping the latest collectibles.

Au Printemps spent two years revising its six-storey Printemps de l'Homme. Lines include Martine Sitbon, Comme des Garçons and Tommy Hilfiger. Gorgeous 25-year-old Frenchmen

cruise gleaming metallic Bobbee backpacks, Armani and Paul Smith, the Institut Nickel proposes hair removal and facials, and the fifth floor boasts the Paul Smith-designed World Bar.

Le Bon Marché has always had a classier image than its competitors. Eiffel helped design its structure and Flaubert wrote *Au Bonheur des Dames* about it. Autumn 1999 saw the debut of 33-1 R.LAX, an in-store boutique showcasing hip magazines, cutting-edge clothing, gadgets and French Touch music. Avant garde and classic collections include Helmut Lang Jeans, Joseph and Marc Jacobs; the beauty department sells aromatherapy along with make-up. An adjoining store houses a gourmet food hall, where *Rive Gauche* careerwomen shop for dinner parties.

BHV has always been famed for phenomenal DIY provisions than for fashion; this is the place to stop by for paint, plumbing supplies and cordless drills or hunt down transformers and adaptors for computers and electrical appliances.

La Samaritaine's four-store complex isn't a mecca of chic, but you can still find almost anything, from DIY Christmas wreaths, to toys (the largest selection in Paris), terrific housewares and linens. Its mens' store is good on young sportswear and offers bespoke suits and shirts and large sizes. Building two has wonderful Art Nouveau balustrades and a view over the Seine from restaurant Le Toupary.

BHV (Bazar de l'Hôtel de Ville)
*52-64 rue de Rivoli, 4th (01.42.74.90.00). M°
Hôtel de Ville.* **Open** 9.30am-7pm Mon-Sat (till
10pm Wed). **Credit** AmEx, MC, V. **Map K6**

Le Bon Marché
*22 rue de Sèvres, 7th (01.44.39.80.00). M° Sèvres-
Babylone.* **Open** 9.30am-7pm Mon-Fri; 9.30am-
8pm Sat. **Credit** AmEx, DC, MC, V. **Map G7**

Galeries Lafayette
*40 bd Haussmann, 9th (01.42.82.34.56/fashion
show 01.42.82.30.25). M° Chaussée d'Antin/ RER
Auber.* **Open** 9.30am-7pm Mon-Sat (till 9pm
Thur). **Credit** AmEx, DC, MC, V. **Map H3**

Au Printemps
*64 bd Haussmann, 9th (01.42.82.50.00). M°
Havre-Caumartin/RER Auber.* **Open** 9.30am-7pm
Mon-Sat (till 10pm Thur). **Credit** AmEx, DC, MC,
V. **Map G3**

La Samaritaine
*19 rue de la Monnaie, 1st (01.40.41.20.20). M°
Pont-Neuf.* **Open** 9.30am-7pm Mon-Sat (till 10pm
Thur). **Credit** AmEx, DC, MC, V. **Map J6**

ers Nathalie Auzepy and Jean-François Leduc, who have just moved from the Marais to St-Germain.

Sentou

26 bd Raspail, 7th (01.45.49.00.05). Mº Sèvres-Babylone. **Open** 2-7pm Mon; 11am-7pm Tue-Sat. Closed mid-Aug. **Credit** DC, MC, V. **Map G7**
Sentou carries modern clasics and contemporary designs, from wood-and-paper lamps by Osamu Noguchi and textiles by Robert Le Héros to the fun candlesticks and tableware of Tsé & Tsé Associés. **Branch**: 18, 24 rue du Pont-Louis-Philippe, 4th (01.42.77.44.79/01.42.71.00.01).

Kitchen & Bathroom

A Simon

36 rue Etienne-Marcel, 2nd (01.42.33.71.65). Mº Etienne-Marcel. **Open** 8.30am-6.30pm Mon-Sat. **Credit** AmEx, MC, V. **Map J5**
This professional kitchen supplier has gigantic tureens and saucepans for feeding two to 200, plus all the plates, wine *pichets*, menu holders and trappings you could possibly want for your own bistro.

Axis

Marché St-Germain, 14 rue Lobineau, 6th (01.43.29.66.23). Mº Mabillon. **Open** 10am-8pm Mon-Sat. **Credit** AmEx, MC, V. **Map H7**
Alessi kettles, Starck lemon squeezers, Pesce resin chairs, flying-saucer lights, fab high-tech trolleys and lots of plastic are a mix of laughable and loveable, designer and gadget. Axis commissions young designers for unusual trays, ceramics and bowls. The branch (13 rue de Charonne, 11th/01.48.06.79.10) concentrates on previous years' items, now collectables.

Bains Plus

51 rue des Francs-Bourgeois, 4th (01.48.87.83.07). Mº Hôtel-de-Ville. **Open** 11am-7.30pm Tue-Sat; 2.30-7pm Sun. **Credit** AmEx, MC, V. **Map K6**
All your bathroom needs are served with the ultimate gentleman's shaving gear, duck-shaped loofahs, seductive dressing gowns, chrome mirrors and stylishly packaged Provençal bath oils and soaps from Côté Bastide. On the pricey side.

La Chaise Longue

20 rue des Francs-Bourgeois, 3rd (01.48.04.36.37). Mº St-Paul. **Open** 11am-7pm Mon-Sat; 2-7pm Sun. **Credit** AmEx, MC, V. **Map L6**
Cheap and cheerful accessories for the kitchen and bath include colourful enamelled toleware, chrome wire soap dishes and saucepan stands fashioned into horses, fish or cats, painted tumblers, kitsch chicken hot water bottles, colourful bathmats and old-fashioned electric fans and kitchen scales. **Branches**: 30 rue Croix-des-Petits-Champs, 1st (01.42.96.32.14); 8 rue Princesse, 6th (01.43.29.62.39).

E Dehillerin

18 rue Coquillière, 1st (01.42.36.53.13). Mº Châtelet-Les Halles. **Open** 8am-12.30pm, 2-6pm Mon; 8am-6pm Tue-Sat. **Credit** MC, V. **Map J5**
Dehillerin has supplied many of the great European chefs since 1820, and the shop is packed with every possible cooking utensil, and huge cooking vessels.

Kitchen Bazaar

11 av du Maine, 15th (01.42.22.91.17). Mº Montparnasse-Bienvenüe. **Open** 10am-7pm Mon-Sat. **Credit** AmEx, MC, V. **Map F8**
High-design and high-tech kitchen equipment and

Marché St-Pierre *offers fabrics for the very wildest of fancy dress.*

accessories, superb chef's knives, spice racks and state-of-the-art chrome storage bins. Bath Bazaar Autrement (6 av du Maine, 15th/01.45.48.89.00), across the street, sells bathroom goodies.

Fabrics & Trimmings

Entrée des Fournisseurs
8 rue des Francs-Bourgeois, 3rd (01.48.87.58.98).
M° St-Paul. **Open** 2.30-7pm Mon, Sun; 10.30am-7pm Tue-Fri; 11am-7pm Sat. Closed two weeks in Aug.
Credit MC, V. **Map L6**
Travaux de dame (needlecraft) heaven: from needles and yarns to mending eggs, ribbons and fancy buttons, as well as 4000 different pearls and beads.
Branch: 9 rue Madame, 6th (01.42.84.13.97).

Maison de la Fausse Fourrure
34 bd Beaumarchais, 11th (01.43.55.24.21).
M° Bastille or Chemin-Vert. **Open** 11am-7pm Mon-Sat. **Credit** AmEx, MC, V. **Map M6**
The 'House of Fake Fur' pays tribute to our furry friends, and everything here is fake and fun. There are synthetic teddy-bear coats, animal print bags and hats in your choice of chic 'leopard' or cheeky 'monkey', as well as bolts of fake fur fabric, lampshades and furniture covered with the stuff.

Marché St-Pierre
Dreyfus *2 rue Charles-Nodier, 18th (01.46.06.92.25);* **Tissus Reine** *5 pl St-Pierre, 18th (01.46.06.02.31);* **Moline** *1 pl St-Pierre, 18th (01.46.06.14.66).* *M° Anvers or Barbès-Rochechourt.* **Open** 1.30-6.30pm Mon; 9.30am-6.30pm Tue-Fri; 9.30am-6.45pm Sat. **Credit** V. **Map J2**
The three shops listed above have the best selections of fabrics, though you'll also find stores all around and off the place St-Pierre. Reine has selections of discounted silks and luxury fabrics. Moline specialises in upholstery fabrics. Dreyfus is a crowded, five-floor warehouse, with linens, silks, woollens, home furnishing fabrics and discounted bolts.

Pierre Frey
2 rue Furstenbourg, 6th (01.46.33.73.00).
M° St-Germain-des-Prés. **Open** 10am-6.30pm Mon-Sat. **Credit** AmEx, DC, MC, V. **Map H6**
This family company's high-quality furnishing fabrics include reproductions of Frey's own historic designs, Jim Thompson's luxuriant Thai silks and subtle African prints. The accessories boutique at 7 rue Jacob sells tasteful lampshades, cushions, tablecloths and quilts and kitsch Tyrol-motif rucksacks.

Florists & Garden Fittings

Christian Tortu
6 carrefour de l'Odéon, 6th (01.43.26.02.56).
M° Odéon. **Open** 9am-8pm Mon-Sat; 11am-7pm Sun. Closed two weeks in Aug. **Credit** AmEx, DC, MC, V. **Map H7**
Paris' most celebrated florist is famous for combining flowers, foliage, twigs, bark and moss into still-lifes. You can also buy his pots, minimalist zinc

Concept Stores

Lifestyle stores are a two-way trend, as fashion designers add their favourite CD or notepad (think Emporio Armani or APC) for the *Wallpaper** pack, and household designers add cocooning-comfy jumpers to match their sofas. Undoubted leader of the pack is **Colette**, where the brilliant global selection puts the Colette seal-of-approval on its choice of what's right in clothing, jewellery, stationery or glassware, all items which may be found elsewhere – but not together, and not with *that* carrier bag. Myriad others are getting in on the game, those who stand out are those who pick the right essentials, the latest trends, the newest design talents.

Bernie x
12 rue de Sévigné, 4th (01.44.59.35.88). M° St-Paul. **Open** 2-7pm Mon; 11am-7pm Tue-Sat; 3-6pm Sun. **Credit** MC, V. **Map L6**
Bernie x is a concept boutique with a difference: walls, furniture, décor and accessories change colour every three months, according to Bernadette's latest whim. Gimmick, perhaps, but great for gifts with an eclectic mix of clothes, jewellery, lamps and work by artist friends.

Castelbajac Concept Store
26 rue Madame, 6th (01.45.48.40.55).
M° St-Sulpice. **Open** 10am-7pm Mon-Sat. **Credit** AmEx, DC, MC, V. **Map G7**
Aristo designer Jean-Charles de Castelbajac has caught on to the lifestyle concept with his sleek new store, where clothes, accessories, furniture and household items come in for a cerebral white-space presentation. Castelbajac's own pieces are displayed alongside prototypes by other designers, from an eco-friendly sofa and Jeremy Scott T-shirts to Pop, the individual bottle of Champagne drunk with a straw.

Colette
213 rue St-Honoré, 1st (01.55.35.33.90).
M° Tuileries. **Open** 10.30am-7.30pm Mon-Sat. **Credit** AmEx, DC, MC, V. **Map G5**
The hyper-trendy 'styledesignartfoodlifestyle' store, which opened in spring 1997,was the success story of the decade, providing a stylish minimalist setting for the latest essentials in fashion and design, plus water bar and exhibition space. Downstairs covetable objects, be it Tom Dixon furniture, a radio, conceptual bar of soap or the perfect teddy, offer affordable present material; upstairs it's fashion and prices are less accessible. Costume National and Alexander McQueen have been joined by Frédérique Hood, Hoa Hoa and Neil Barrett.

vases, concrete planters, glasses and leaf plates, round the corner at 17 rue des Quatre-Vents.

Out of Africa

New Agey vibes have invaded the house in an onslaught of neo-hippy finds from former French colonies in West and North Africa. Significantly many of the new outlets of Afro-chic are in the Marais, for a more authentic edge, head for Barbès and the fabric merchants at the market under the Métro, or for serious tribal art, try the galleries of St-Gemain.

Caravane
6 rue Pavée, 4th (01.44.61.04.20). M° St-Paul.
Open 11am-7pm Tue-Sat. **Credit** V. **Map L6**
In the heart of the style-conscious Marais, Françoise Dorget has created an atmospheric casbah. Moroccan *tagines* and exquisite earthenware jars are displayed alongside contemporary furniture, unusual fabrics and cushions.

As'Art
3 passage du Grand-Cerf, 2nd (01.44.88.90.40). M° Etienne-Marcel. **Open** 11.30am-7.30pm Tue-Sat. **Credit** AmEx, V. **Map J5**
This gallery-boutique scouts out eclectic art and objects from across Africa. Traditional grass skirts from Congo, Nigerian batik fabrics, Masai water pots and masks from Uganda and Mali vie with contemporary jewellery made of bone, coconut and glass paste, crafty bathroom accessories from Kenya and all the plates, pepperpots and candleholders you're ever likely to need. If you're after pure art not utility, then wood or bronze animal sculptures and works by modern African artists complete the picture.

CSAO
1-3 rue Elzévir, 3rd (01.44.54.55.88).
M° St-Paul. **Open** 10.30am-7pm Mon-Sat; noon-7.30pm Sun. **Credit** AmEx, MC, V. **Map L6**
CSAO (Compagnie de Sénégal et de l'Afrique de l'Ouest) is a treasure trove of African arts and crafts. Alongside rag rugs and low wooden chairs, there are briefcases, toy 2CVs and ashtrays made from cheerfully recycled tin cans. *Baba cool* babes can buy beads, ethnic print bags and Xüly Bet's funky fashion creations.

Concept Ethnique
51 rue des Francs-Bourgeois, 3rd (01.42.78.24.09). M° St-Paul. **Open** 10.30am-1.30pm, 2.30-7.30pm Tue-Fri; 10.30am-7.30pm Sat; 2.30-7.30pm Sun. **Credit** AmEx, DC, MC, V. **Map L6**
This beautiful shop is decked out in earthy terracottas; patterned fabrics hang from the roof, while sculptures of tribesmen dot the floor. Throw in rush matting, stone and wood figurines and striking masks and you're well on the way to decorating your home in tribal style.

Despalles
26 rue Boissy d'Anglas, 8th (01.49.24.05 65). M° Concorde. **Open** 10am-7pm Mon-Sat. **Credit** AmEx, MC, V. **Map F4**
This is an inviting jumble of green plants, gardening tools, garden and 'Anglo Indian' wooden furniture, Moroccan tables, cushions and dried flowers.
Branch: 5 rue d'Alésia, 14th (01.45.89.05.31).

Mille Feuilles
2 rue Rambuteau, 3rd (01.42.78.32.93). M° Rambuteau or Hôtel de Ville. **Open** 2-8pm Mon; 10am-7pm Tue-Sat. **Credit** AmEx, MC, V. **Map K6**
Like many shops at the moment, Mille Feuilles mixes the genres, with fresh flowers, garden statuary, ceramics, pots and chandeliers all cluttered together. 2 Mille Feuilles, across the road at 59 rue des Francs-Bourgeois, also has painted wrought-iron garden furniture, glasses and heavy lead planters, made in Holland, according to traditional methods.

Gifts & Oddities

Deyrolle
46 rue du Bac, 7th (01.42.22.30.07). M° Rue du Bac. **Open** 10am-6.45pm Mon-Sat. **Credit** AmEx, MC, V. **Map G6**
A taxidermist's dream, this dusty shop, established 1831, overflows with stuffed animals, ranging from a polar bear to exotic birds. You can also have your own household pets lovingly stuffed here for 3800F (for a cat) upwards or hire a beast for a few days to complete your film set.

Nature et Découvertes
Carrousel du Louvre, 99 rue de Rivoli, 1st (01.47.03.47.43). M° Palais-Royal. **Open** 10am-8pm daily. Closed Aug. **Credit** AmEx, MC, V. **Map H5**
This chain sells useful (and less so) camping and stargazing accessories, musical instruments, art supplies, equipment for windowsill gardeners, candles, divining rods and nature or science games that are also beautiful objects. It has a play space where there are kids' workshops (3.30pm Wed).
Branches include: Forum des Halles, rue Pierre Lescot, 1st (01.40.28.42.16); 61 rue de Passy, 16th (01.42.30.53.87).

Papeterie Moderne
12 rue de la Ferronerie, 1st (01.42.36.21.72). M° Châtelet. **Open** 9am-noon, 1.30-6.30pm Mon-Sat. **No credit cards. Map J5**
Not, as the name suggests, a stationer, but source of those enamel plaques that adorn Paris streets and forbidding gateways. Here you can find that Champs-Elysées sign or the guard-dog with a twist (*attention chien bizarre*) for a mere 40F.

Paris Accordéon
80 rue Daguerre, 14th (01.43.22.13.48). M° Denfert-Rochereau or Gaîté. **Open** 9am-noon, 1-7pm, Tue-Fri; 9am-6pm Sat. Closed Aug. **Credit** MC, V. **Map G10**
'Come share our passion' welcomes this yellow-

*Would-be Yvette Horners get equipped at **Paris Accordéon**.*

painted shop, its shelves lined with the fashionable French national instrument, the accordion, from simple squeeze-box to the most beautiful tortoiseshell, new and second-hand. Sheet music also sold here.

Paris-Musées

29bis rue des Francs-Bourgeois, 4th (01.42.74.13.02). Mº Bastille. **Open** 2-7pm Mon; 11am-7pm Tue-Sun. **Credit** AmEx, MC, V. **Map L6**
Run by the Ville de Paris museums, this shop has a collection of funky lamps and ceramics commissioned from some of Paris' top young designers, and copies of items in city museums, such as a Gallo-Roman carafe from Carnavalet or George Sand's wine glasses from the Musée de la Vie Romantique. **Branch:** Forum des Halles, 1 rue Pierre-Lescot, 1st (01.40.26.56.65).

Des Pieds et des Mains

22 passage Molière, 3rd (01.42.77.53.50). Mº Rambuteau. **Open** 2-6pm Fri, Sat. **No credit cards. Map K5**
The ultimate personal souvenir: Brigitte Massoutier will enshine your hand (adult 1500F), foot or mouth (adult 500F) in plaster. The window is crammed with appendages of past customers from a baby of 57 minutes to a hardy 98-year-old. The process takes seconds – but allow a month for delivery.

Robin des Bois

15 rue Ferdinand-Duval, 4th (01.48.04.09.36). Mº St-Paul. **Open** 10.30am-7.30pm Mon-Sat; 2.30-7.30pm Sun. **Credit** MC, V. **Map L6**
The Robin Hood of the environment is linked to an ecological organisation of the same name. Everything is made with recycled or ecologically sound products, including bottle-top jewellery, natural toiletries and recycled notepaper.

Why!

22 rue du Pont-Neuf, 1st (01.42.33.40.33). Mº Pont-Neuf. **Open** 11am-8pm Mon-Sat. **Credit** AmEx, DC, MC, V. **Map J6**
Alexis Lahellic lawyer-turned-jeweller has been replaced by Lahellic master of kitsch. Furry lamps glow alongside nodding dogs, robot alarm clocks, sushi erasers, tulips to grow in the loo (why not?) and endless other silliness, practical and otherwise. Prize for tackiness goes to the photo booth where for 20F you can be immortalised in a sunsetty postcard. **Branches:** 14-16 rue Jean-Jacques-Rousseau, 1st (01.42.33.36.95); 41 rue des Francs-Bourgeois, 4th (01.44.61.72.75); 14-16 rue Bernard-Palissy, 6th (01.45.48.71.98).

Records, CDs, Cassettes & Hi-Fi

There are clusters of specialist record shops around Les Halles (1st) and rue Keller (11th); second-hand outlets are concentrated in the 5th.

Born Bad

17 rue Keller, 11th (01.48.06.34.17). Mº Bastille or Ledru-Rollin. **Open** noon-8pm Mon-Sat. **Credit** MC, V. **Map N7**
This inspiring shop stocks all manner of punk, ska, hardcore, 60s, surf, rock 'n' roll and exotica, with dozens of tributes and compilations. Vinyl and CD.

Crocodisc

42 rue des Ecoles, 5th (01.43.54.47.95). Mº Maubert-Mutualité. **Open** 11am-7pm Tue-Sat. Closed two weeks in Aug. **Credit** MC, V. **Map J7**

New, second-hand and offbeat pop, rock, funk, Oriental, African and country music and classical. Crocojazz (64 rue de la Montagne-Ste-Geneviève, 5th/ 01.46.34.78.38) specialises in jazz, blues and gospel.

Fnac

74 av des Champs-Elysées, 8th (01.53.53.64.64).
M° George V. **Open** 10am-midnight Mon-Sat.
Credit AmEx, MC, V. **Map D4**
The Fnac emporia are one-stop shops for books, music, computers, stereo, video and photography gear. They also develop film and sell tickets.
Branches: Forum des Halles, 1st (01.40.41.40.00); Fnac Micro, 71 bd St-Germain, 5th (01.44.41.31.50) computers; 136 rue de Rennes, 6th (01.49.54.30.00); 24 bd des Italiens, 9th (01.48.01.02.03); 4 pl de la Bastille, 12th (01.43.42.04.04) music only; 26-30 av des Ternes, 17th (01.44.09.18.00).

Sound Records

6 rue des Prêcheurs, 1st (01.40.13.09.45).
M° Les Halles. **Open** 11am-7.30pm Mon-Sat.
Credit AmEx, DC, MC, V. **Map J5**
Opened in 1987, Sound Records claims to have been the first hip hop outlet in Paris. Rap, R&B, soul, funk, ragga, French rap and breakbeat are stocked along with good mix tapes by aspiring amateurs.

Techno Import

16 rue des Taillandiers, 11th (}1.48.05.71.56).
M° Bastille. **Open** noon-8pm Mon-Sat. **Credit** AmEx, MC, V. **Map N7.**
The biggest and best-stocked techno and dance shop is filled with wannabe DJs frantically track hopping. Staff can be unhelpful with the uninitiated.

Virgin Megastore

52-60 av des Champs-Elysées, 8th (01.49.53.50.00).
M° Franklin D Roosevelt. **Open** 10am-midnight Mon-Sat; noon-midnight Sun. **Credit** AmEx, DC, MC, V.
Map D4
Virgin's huge French flagship seethes at all hours with those trying to listen to the latest CDs. The video department has some non-dubbed English films. There's a café, large bookstore and ticket desk.
Branch: Carrousel du Louvre, 99 rue de Rivoli, 1st (01.49.53.50.00).

Stationery & Art Supplies

Calligrane

4-6 rue du Pont-Louis-Philippe, 4th (01.48.04.31.89).
M° Pont-Marie or St-Paul. **Open** 11am-7pm Tue-Sat. Closed two weeks in Aug. **Credit** MC, V. **Map K6**
Three shops are devoted to handmade paper from all over the world, including encrusted papers, designer office supplies, writing paper and Filofaxes.

Comptoir des Ecritures

35 rue Quincampoix, 4th (01.42.78.95.10).
M° Rambuteau. **Open** 11am-7pm Tue-Sat. Closed Aug. **Credit** MC, V. **Map K5**
This shop specialises in calligraphy, with inks, pens and an incredible range of handmade papers from Asia. It also runs courses and puts on exhibitions.

Graphigro

157-159 rue Lecourbe, 15th (01.42.50.45.49).
M° Vaugirard. **Open** 10am-7pm Mon-Sat. Closed Mon in Aug. **Credit** MC, V. **Map D9**
The largest, cheapest chain of art and graphic supplies, covers all the essential paints and brushes.
Branches: 133 rue Rennes, 6th (01.42.22.51.80); 207 bd Voltaire, 11th (01.43.48.23.57); 120 rue Damrémont, 18th (01.42.58.93.40).

Marie-Papier

26 rue Vavin, 6th (01.43.26.46.44). M° Vavin or Notre-Dame des Champs. **Open** 10am-7pm Mon-Sat.
Credit AmEx, MC, V. **Map G8**
Writing and fancy handmade wrapping paper comes in every imaginable colour.

Papier +

9 rue du Pont-Louis-Philippe, 4th (01.42.77.70.49).
M° St-Paul or Pont-Marie. **Open** noon-7pm Mon-Sat.
Credit MC, V. **Map K6**
Crayons in boxes, notebooks and hand-cut paper.

Sennelier

3 quai Voltaire, 7th (01.42.60.72.15). M° St-Germain-des-Prés. **Open** 2-6.30pm Mon; 9.30am-12.30pm, 2-6.30pm Tue-Sat. **Credit** AmEx, DC, MC, V. **Map H6**
Old-fashioned artists' colour merchant Sennelier has been supplying artists and students since 1887. Oil paints, watercolours and pastels include rare mineral, resin and natural pigments, along with primered boards, varnishes and paper.
Branch: 4bis rue de la Grande-Chaumière, 6th (01.46.33.72.39).

Virgin Megastore: *for late-night listening.*

Food & Drink

If you can consume it or imbibe it, you'll find it in the world's greatest gastronomic centre.

Paris is a gourmand's paradise and a dieter's nightmare. Around every corner, there is something to titillate your tastebuds: humungous hams and pristine pâtés, feathered pheasants, runny-centred cheeses, jewel-like chocolates, glistening pastries and glorious breads. Supermarkets might be making inroads – some Parisians even stock up at suburban *hypermarchés* – but the city remains food-obsessed, as queues outside the better shops attest. Join in to discover one of Paris' great joys.

Bakeries

Au Levain du Marais

32 rue de Turenne, 3rd (01.42.78.07.31). M° St Paul. **Open** 7am-8pm Mon-Sat. **No credit cards. Map L6**
Thierry Rabineau's open-textured baguettes and country *miches*, all produced with organic flour, attract queues that snake out the door. The *millefeuilles* and lemon tarts are also luscious.
Branch: 142 av Parmentier, 11th (01.43.57.36.91).

Maison Kayser

8/14 rue Monge, 5th (01.44.07.01.42/31.61). M° Cardinal Lemoine. **Open** 7.30am-7.30pm Mon-Sat. **Credit** V. **Map K8/KP**
A polished showcase for intensely flavoured, wonderfully textured bread. The moist *baguette au froment* is particularly luscious.

L'Hermeno

114 rue de Patay, 13th (01.45.83.80.13). M° Bibliothèque. **Open** 6.30am-8pm daily; closed Wed. **Credit** AmEx, DC, MC, V. **Map N10**
This bakery specialises in organic bread made with traditional starters rather than yeast. The *tourte au levain* is a springy, slightly tangy loaf; fruit and nut breads are also masterful.

Moulin de la Vierge

166 av de Suffren, 15th (01.47.83.45.55). M° Sèvres-Lecourbe. **Open** 7am-8pm Mon-Sat. **No credit cards. Map E8**
Basile Kamir learned breadmaking after falling in love with an abandoned bakery. His picture-perfect country loaf is thick-crusted, dense and fragrant.
Branches: 82 rue Daguerre, 14th (01.43.22.50.55); 105 rue Vercingétorix, 14th (01.45.43.09.84).

Au Panetier

10 pl des Petits-Pères, 2nd (01.42.60.90.23). M° Bourse. **Open** 8am-7.15pm Mon-Fri. Closed July. **No credit cards. Map H5**
In a turn-of-the-century tiled interior, you'll find superb breads and mouthwatering tarts. The St-

Fiacre, a rustic white bread, has a yeasty flavour and perfect crumb; baguettes are among the best in town.

Poilâne

8 rue du Cherche-Midi, 6th (01.45.48.42.59). M° Sèvres-Babylone or St-Sulpice. **Open** 7.15am-8.15pm Mon-Sat. **No credit cards. Map G7**
Lionel Poilâne makes his legendary *pain* with stone-ground flour and an old-fashioned rising agent. Try the rye bread with raisins or a buttery apple tart.

Max Poilâne

87 rue Brancion, 15th (01.48.28.45.90). M° Porte de Vanves. **Open** 7.30am-8pm Mon-Sat. **No credit cards.**
Using the Poilâne family recipe, the lesser-known Max produces bread that easily rivals his brother Lionel's, in a vintage 1930s setting.

Jean-Luc Poujauran

20 rue Jean-Nicot, 7th (01.47.05.80.88). M° Invalides or Latour-Maubourg. **Open** 8am-8.30pm Tue-Sat. Closed Aug. **No credit cards. Map E6**
This little pink shop bursts with tempting breads studded with nuts, apricots, figs, anchovies, raisins or olives. Baguettes are outstanding.

René-Gérard St-Ouen

111 bd Haussmann, 8th (01.42.65.06.25). M° Miromesnil. **Open** 7.30am-7.30pm Mon-Sat. **No credit cards. Map F3**
Celebrated for his 'bread sculptures' shaped like cats, horses, bicycles and the Eiffel Tower, this baker also makes fine baguettes, *fougasses* (flatbreads made with olive oil) and rye breads.

Pâtisseries

Carton

6 rue de Buci, 6th (01.43.26.04.13). M° Mabillon. **Open** 7am-8pm daily. **Credit** MC, V. **Map H7**
The most mouthwatering stop on this busy market street merits its reputation, with a profusion of glorious cakes, such as the bittersweet *tarte au chocolat*, fluffy *tarte soufflée framboise* and crisp apricot or apple *tartes fines*.

Couderc

6 bd Voltaire, 11th (01.47.00.58.20). M° République. **Open** 8.30am-7.30pm Tue-Sat; 8am-1.30pm, 3-7pm Sun. Closed mid-July to mid-Aug. **Credit** MC, V. **Map L5**
All the cakes are beautiful, but the speciality here is chocolate – the buttery *pains au chocolat* are among the best in town, chocolate pastries are intense and filled chocolates are made on the premises.

Dalloyau

101 rue du Fbg-St-Honoré, 8th (01.42.99.90.00).
M° St-Philippe du Roule. **Open** 8am-9pm daily.
Credit AmEx, DC, MC, V. **Map E4**
This temple to pastry, opened in 1802, has gone modern with a three-level space that includes a vast boutique, a plush tea room and a bar for quick meals.
Branches: 25 bd des Capucines, 2nd (01.47.03.47.00);
2 pl Edmond-Rostand, 6th (01.43.29.31.10); 63 rue de
Grenelle, 7th (01.45.49.95.30); 69 rue de la Convention,
15th (01.45.77.84.27).

Finkelsztajn

27 rue des Rosiers, 4th (01.42.72.78.91). M° St-Paul.
Open 10am-2pm, 3-7pm Mon, Wed-Sun. **No credit cards. Map L6**
For a change from flaky *millefeuilles*, try the dense, satisfying central European pastries filled with poppy seeds, apples or cream cheese at this shop in the heart of the Jewish district.

Jean Millet

103 rue St-Dominique, 7th (01.45.51.49.80).
M° Ecole-Militaire/RER Pont de l'Alma. **Open**
9am-7pm Mon-Sat; 8am-1pm Sun. Closed two-three weeks in Aug. **Credit** MC, V. **Map D6**
Pâtissier Jean Millet displays an abundance of mouth-watering, chocolate-covered meringues with coffee filling, *tuile d'amande* biscuits and apricot *bavarois*.

Gérard Mulot

76 rue de Seine, 6th (01.43.26.85.77). M° Odéon.
Open 6.45am-8pm Mon, Tue, Thur-Sun. Closed mid

Androuet: *odiferous orgy.*

July-mid-Aug. **No credit cards. Map H7**
With its picture-perfect cakes, this shop attracts local celebrities. Try the bitter chocolate tart, fluffy *tarte normande* or the *mabillon*, a combination of caramel mousse and apricot marmalade.

Maison Rollet Pradier

6 rue de Bourgogne, 7th (01.45.51.78.36).
M° Assemblée Nationale. **Open** 8am-8pm Mon-Sat,
8am-7pm Sun. **Credit** MC, V. **Map F6**
Enjoy the sumptuous gâteaux laden with fancy curls of chocolate or crusts of hazelnuts, or the sandwich counter or tea room upstairs. Bread specialities are the *flûte Rollet* and the *boule de levain*.

Cheese

Every *quartier* in Paris has *fromageries*, most offering a superb seasonal selection. The sign *maître fromager affineur* identifies master cheese merchants who buy young cheeses from farmers and then age them on their premises. *Fromage fermier* and *fromage au lait cru* signify farm-produced and raw (unpasteurised) milk cheeses.

Alain Dubois

80 rue de Tocqueville, 17th (01.42.27.11.38).
M° Malesherbes or Villiers. **Open** 8.30am-1pm,
3.45-8pm Tue-Fri; 8am-7.30pm Sat; 9am-1pm Sun.
Credit V. **Map E2**
It's difficult to choose from the bewildering display, including some 70 varieties of goats' cheese. Mr Dubois, who has built a separate cellar to age his prize St-Marcellin and St-Félicien, is the darling of the superchefs. He holds frequent cheese tastings, and happily ships orders.
Branch: 79 rue de Courcelles, 17th (01.43.80.36.42).

Alléosse

13 rue Poncelet, 17th (01.46.22.50.45). M° Ternes.
Open 9am-1pm, 4-7pm Tue-Fri; 9am-1pm, 3.30-7pm
Sat; 9am-1pm Sun. **Credit** V. **Map D2**
People cross town to this large shop for the range of cheeses ripened in its cellars. They include wonderful farmhouse camemberts, delicate St-Marcellins, a very good choice of *chèvres* and several rareties.

Androuët

6 rue Arsène-Houssaye, 8th (01.42.89.95.00).
M° Charles de Gaulle-Etoile. **Open** 10.30am-8pm Tue-
Sat. Closed Aug. **Credit** AmEx, DC, MC, V. **Map D3**
This celebrated *fromagerie* stocks over 200 varieties, and even has an adjoining cheese restaurant. Sample pungent époisses, munsters and maroilles, or go for a *dégustation* of *chèvre*, rolled in pepper, mustard seeds or ash.
Branches: 19 rue Daguerre, 14th (01.43.21.19.09);
83 rue St-Dominique, 7th (01.45.50.45.75).

Barthélémy

51 rue de Grenelle, 7th (01.45.48.56.75).
M° Rue du Bac. **Open** 7am-1pm, 3.30-7.15pm Tue-
Thur; 7am-7.30pm Fri, Sat. **Credit** MC, V. **Map G7**
Roland Barthélémy has a devoted clientele in Paris and Fontainebleau, where he has a second shop. The

Showing patience for the pains *at* **Au Levain du Marais.**

selection is outstanding: creamy Mont d'Or and brie de Malesherbes are particularly tempting.

Laurent Dubois

2 rue de Lourmel (01.45.78.70.58), 15th. M° Dupleix.
Open 9am-1pm, 4pm-7.45pm, Tue-Sat; 9am-1pm
Sun. **Credit** V, MC. **Map I5**
Nephew of the famous cheese specialist Alain Dubois, Laurent Dubois has established himself as a master in his own right. Especially impressive are his aged cheeses, such as the nutty two-year-old comté and the crackly *vieille* mimolette.

Marie-Anne Cantin

12 rue du Champs-de-Mars, 7th (01.45.50.43.94).
M° Ecole-Militaire. **Open** 8.30am-7.30pm Mon-Sat;
8.30-1pm Sun. **Credit** MC, V. **Map D6**
This pristine shop sells cheeses ripened to perfection in its own cellars. Cantin, a vigorous defender of unpasteurised cheese, describes her creamy St-Marcellins, aged *chèvres* and nutty beauforts with obvious – and well-deserved – pride.

Chocolate

A la Mère de Famille

35 rue du Fbg-Montmartre, 9th (01.47.70.83.69).
M° Grands Boulevards. **Open** 8.30am-1.30pm, 3-7pm
Tue-Sat. Closed Aug. **Credit** AmEx, MC, V. **Map J4**
Founded in 1761 and with an interior dating from the early 1900s, the oldest sweetshop in town offers traditional treats such as Tours barley sugar, *pastilles fondantes* from Lyon, *bêtises de Cambrai* and old-fashioned marshmallows. It makes its own chocolates and sells charming tin boxes.

Alliance Chocolat

1 pl Victor Hugo, 16th (01.45.00.89.68).
M° Victor-Hugo. **Open** 9.30am-7.30pm Mon-Sat.
Credit AmEx, DC, MC, V. **Map B4**
The fruit of an alliance between Marquise de Sévigné, Godiva and Salavin, this circular cherry-wood-and-cream space has a workshop devoted to chocolate-making, a display on the history of chocolate, tasting areas and a bookshop.

Cacao et Chocolat

29 rue de Buci, 6th (01.46.33.77.63). M° Mabillon.
Open 10.30am-7.30pm Tue-Sat. **Credit** AmEx,
DC, MC, V. **Map H7**
Opened in 1998, this shop in burnt orange and ochre recalls chocolate's Aztec origins with spicy fillings (honey and chilli pepper, nutmeg, clove and citrus), chocolate masks and pyramids. Bold-tasting chocolates come in lovely wooden boxes.

Christian Constant

37 rue d'Assas, 6th (01.53.63.15.15). M° St-Placide.
Open 8.30am-9pm Mon-Fri; 8am-8.30pm Sat, Sun.
Credit MC, V. **Map G8**
For chocolates, tea or prepared *plats*, Constant is a name among *le tout Paris*. With training in *pâtisserie* and chocolate, he scours the globe for ideas.

Debauve & Gallais

30 rue des Sts-Pères, 7th (01.45.48.54.67).
M° St-Germain-des-Prés. **Open** 9am-7pm Mon-Sat.
Closed Mon in July and Aug. **Credit** MC, V. **Map G6**
This former pharmacy, with a beautiful facade dating from 1800, once sold chocolate for medicinal purposes. Its intense tea, honey or praline-flavoured chocolates do, indeed, heal the soul.

The chocolate treatment heals to perfection at **Debauve & Gallais**.

Branches: 33 rue Vivienne, 2nd (01.40.39.05.50); 107 rue Jouffroy d'Abbans, 17th (01.47.63.15.15).

Jadis et Gourmande

49bis av Franklin D Roosevelt, 8th (01.42.25.06.04).
M° Franklin D Roosevelt or St-Philippe du Roule.
Open 1-7pm Mon; 9.30am-7pm Tue; 9.30am-7.30pm Wed-Fri; 10am-7pm Sat. **Credit** MC, V. **Map H9**
The best place for novelty chocolates. The chocolate Arcs de Triomphe, Santas and letters of the alphabet make fun presents. For inscriptions in white chocolate, order ahead.
Branches: 39 rue des Archives, 4th (01.48.04.08.03); 88 bd du Port-Royal, 5th (01.43.26.17.75).

Jean-Paul Hévin

3 rue Vavin, 6th (01.43.54.09.85). M° Vavin. **Open** 10am-7.30pm Mon-Sat; 10am-2pm, 3-6pm Sun.
Credit MC, V. **Map G8**
Stylish chocolates in a smart window display tempt you inside to test the delicious florentines, *ganaches* and bitter-chocolate orange.
Branches: 231 rue St-Honoré, 1st (01.55.35.35.96); 16 av de La Motte-Picquet, 15th (01.45.51.77.48).

La Maison du Chocolat

89 av Raymond-Poincaré, 16th (01.40.67.77.83).
M° Victor-Hugo. **Open** 9.30am-7.30pm Mon-Sat.
Credit AmEx, MC, V. **Map B4**
This temple to the cocoa bean stocks incredibly rich truffles, wickedly bitter éclairs and chocolate tart. The music-loving owner often gives his creations suitably operatic names.
Branches: 19 rue de Sèvres, 6th (01.45.44.20.40); 225 rue du Fbg-St-Honoré, 8th (01.42.27.39.44); 8 bd de la Madeleine, 9th (01.47.42.86.52).

A la Petite Fabrique

12 rue St-Sabin, 11th (01.48.05.82.02). M° Bastille.
Open 10.30am-7.30pm Tue-Sat. Closed one week in Aug. **Credit** MC, V. **Map M6**
This is truly artisanal chocolate-making – you can see the cauldron being stirred at the back. Hazelnut or almond-studded drops are fresh and inexpensive.

Richart

258 bd St-Germain, 7th (01.45.55.66.00).
M° Solférino. **Open** 10am-7pm Mon-Fri; 10am-7pm Mon-Sat. **Credit** MC, V. **Map F6**
This *chocolatier* has a sophisticated style all his own: each delicate chocolate *ganache* has an intricate design, and no box is complete without a tract on how best to savour chocolate.
Branch: 36 av de Wagram, 8th (01.45.74.94.00).

Treats & Traiteurs

Les Abeilles

21 rue de la Butte-aux-Cailles, 13th (01.45.81.43.48).
M° Place d'Italie. **Open** 11am-7pm Tue-Sat.
Credit MC, V.
In the villagey Butte-aux-Cailles, this shop displays 50 varieties of honey from all over France, including creamy clover, fragrant lavender, chestnut, thyme, rhododendron and holly.

Comptoir de la Gastronomie

34 rue Montmartre, 1st (01.42.33.31.32).
M° Etienne-Marcel. **Open** 6am-1pm, 2.30-7pm Tue-Sat. **Credit** AmEx, MC, V. **Map J5**
This attractive, old-fashioned grocery is laden with *foie gras* from south-west France in all its forms,

along with snails, caviar, *confit de canard,* whole hams, truffles and dried mushrooms.

La Comtesse du Barry

13 bd Haussmann, 9th (01.47.70.21.01).
M° Chaussée-d'Antin. **Open** 9am-7pm Mon-Sat.
Credit AmEx, DC, MC, V. **Map H3**
Staff will package French delicacies, like terrines, pâtés and *foie gras,* in hampers or gift wrap. The lazy can buy high-quality, ready-made tinned stews, soups and sauces.
Branches: 93 rue St-Antoine, 4th (01.40.29.07.14); 1 rue de Sèvres, 6th (01.45.48.32.04); 317 rue de Vaugirard, 15th (01.42.50.90.13); 88bis av Mozart, 16th (01.45.27.74.49).

Davoli – La Maison du Jambon

34 rue Cler, 7th (01.45.51.23.41). M° Ecole-Militaire.
Open 8.30am-1pm, 3.30-7.30pm Tue, Thur-Sat;
8.30am-1pm Wed, Sun. Closed first three weeks in Aug.
Credit MC, V. **Map D6**
French, Spanish and Italian hams hang from hooks and smoked salmon, blinis and *foie gras* jostle for position on the counter. Locals crowd in for anything from a slice of *jambon de Bayonne* to ingredients for a chic dinner party.

L'Epicerie

51 rue St-Louis-en-l'Ile, 4th (01.43.25.20.14).
M° Pont-Marie. **Open** 10.30am-8pm daily. **Credit**
MC, V. **Map K7**
A perfect present shop crammed with pretty bottles of blackcurrant vinegar, five-spice mustard, orange sauce, tiny pots of jam, honey with figs and boxes of chocolate snails.

Fauchon

26-30 pl de la Madeleine, 8th (01.47.42.60.11).
M° Madeleine. **Open** 9.40am-7pm Mon-Sat. **Credit**
AmEx, DC, MC, V. **Map F4**
Paris' most famous food store is like every specialist deli rolled into one, with windows that are as much for tourists as for buyers. There is a museumlike prepared-food section, cheese, fish and exotic fruit counters, an Italian deli, wines in the *cave,* chocolates around the corner, and several cafés.

Flo Prestige

42 pl du Marché-St-Honoré, 1st (01.42.61.45.46).
M° Pyramides. **Open** 8am-11pm daily. **Credit**
AmEx, DC, MC, V. **Map G4**
A pricey but pristine *traiteur,* this has all you need for a luxury picnic – salads, smoked salmon, cold meats, cheeses, cakes and hot dishes of the day.
Branches: 10 rue St-Antoine, 4th (01.53.01.91.91); 36 av de la Motte-Picquet, 7th (01.45.55.71.25); 211 av Daumesnil, 12th (01.43.44.86.36); 352 rue Lecourbe, 15th (01.45.54.76.94); 61 av de la Grande-Armée, 16th (01.45.00.12.10).

La Grande Epicerie de Paris

Le Bon Marché (shop 2), 38 rue de Sèvres, 7th
(01.44.39.81.00). M° Sèvres-Babylone. **Open**
8.30am-9pm Mon-Sat. **Credit** MC, V. **Map G7**
Recently redesigned as a series of islands, this gourmet supermarket carries everything from jars of 'marshmallow fluff' to *foie gras,* plus midget veg-

Pigging out

Parisians have a passion for the pig, as the proliferation of *charcuteries* proves. The word comes from *chaircuitiers,* meaning those responsible for cooking raw flesh. Several specialities, such as *boudin noir* (black pudding), dried sausages and *andouillette* (made with tripe), date back to the Gauls, but the profession of *charcutier* was recognised in Paris only in 1705, when *charcuteries* won the exclusive right to sell pork preparations.

St Antoine is the patron saint of *charcuterie* – in the Middle Ages, when pigs wreaked havoc in the streets of French cities, executioners were authorised to kill all those that did not belong to monks of the St-Antoine order. As many of these semi-wild beasts were riddled with disease, health inspections were imposed from the end of the Middle Ages and tightened in 1907. Today, pork must pass inspections in its raw and cooked form before being sold as *charcuterie,* although these guarantee safety more than quality. Perfectly square slices of ham sold under wrap are most often made of reconstituted, previously frozen meat scraps, high in water content and additives. All the more reason to seek out *charcutiers* who work with the finest raw ingredients, using old-fashioned methods.

No part of the pig is wasted; at one time, even the bladder was dried and used to store tobacco. A few specialities worth trying are:
Jambon de Paris 'au torchon' or *'au bouillon'* – the best-quality ham is made of fresh meat, rump and thigh only, salted by injections into the veins, bathed in a flavoured salt-water solution for three to four days, then wrapped in a towel (*torchon*) and cooked in a *bouillon.*
Jambon supérieur maison – made on the premises, not to be confused with *'jambon supérieur',* which can be industrial. Beware jambon *'surchoix'* and *'premier choix',* made of reconstituted meat scraps.
Saucisson sec – artisanal dried sausage is made with coarsely chopped meat, lard, salt and peppercorns, stuffed by hand into the skin.
Andouillette – Not for the faint of heart, a sausage made of veal or pork tripe precooked in broth or milk. Look for the quality label AAAAA (*Association Amicale des Amateurs d'Andouillette Authentique*).
Rillettes – pork and lard are cooked for five to ten hours to create a preserve. Can also be duck, goose or rabbit cooked in its own fat.

etables, gleaming fresh *charcuterie*, freshly roasted coffee and a well-displayed selection of wines.

Hédiard

21 pl de la Madeleine, 8th (01.43.12.88.88). Mᵒ Madeleine. **Open** *shop* 8am-9pm Mon-Sat; *traiteur* 8am-10pm Mon-Sat. **Credit** AmEx, DC, MC, V. **Map F4**

Paris' second most famous food store has lusciouslooking fruits and veg, a huge variety of jams, beautifully packed spices and oustanding teas and coffees. Cakes and candied fruits look tempting, but prepared savoury foods are unspecacular.
Branches: 126 rue du Bac, 7th (01.45.44.01.98); 70 av Paul-Doumer, 16th (01.45.04.51.92); 106 bd des Courcelles, 17th (01.47.63.32.14).

Lenôtre

61 rue Lecourbe, 15th (01.42.73.20.97). Mᵒ Sèvres-Lecourbe. **Open** 8am-9pm daily. **Credit** AmEx, MC, V. **Map D8**

The Lenôtre shops are known for their prepared dishes, cakes and catering service, but don't miss their intensely flavoured chocolate truffles or Roland Durant's unusual jams.
Branches include: 15 bd de Courcelles, 8th (01.45.63.87.63); 48 av Victor-Hugo, 16th (01.45.02.21.21); 121 av de Wagram, 17th (01.47.63.70.30).

La Maison de l'Escargot

79 rue Fondary, 15th (01.45.75.31.09). Mᵒ Emile-Zola. **Open** 9am-7.30pm Tue-Sat; 9am-1pm Sun. Closed 13 July-1 Sept. **Credit** MC, V. **Map C8**

Two women sit stuffing garlic butter into *petits gris* and Burgundy snails, which you can taste on the premises or heat up at home.

La Maison de la Truffe

19 pl de la Madeleine, 8th (01.42.65.53.22). Mᵒ Madeleine. **Open** 9am-8pm Mon; 9am-9pm Tue-Sat. **Credit** AmEx, DC, MC, V. **Map F4**

Come here for fresh Périgord black truffles (9,980F/kg) – or try the more affordable truffle oils, sauces and vinegars.

Oliviers & Co

28 rue de Buci, 6th (01.44.07.15.43). Mᵒ St-Germain-des-Prés. **Open** Mon 2-7.30pm; Tue-Sun 10am-7.30pm. **Credit** AmEx, MC, V. **Map H7**

Each of the 15 oils from six countries, displayed here in slim glass bottles or beautifully labelled tins, is tested daily to be sure it is at its peak of flavour.
Branches: 34-36 rue Montorgueil, 2nd (01.42.33.89.95); 81 rue St-Louis-en-l'Isle, 4th (01.40.33.89.37); 47 rue Vieille-du-Temple, 4th (01.42.74.38.40).

Regional Specialities

L'Auvergnat

60 rue Oberkampf, 11th (01.48.05.31.83). Mᵒ Parmentier. **Open** 4-7.30pm Mon; 9am-1pm, 4-7.30pm Tue-Sat. Closed two weeks in July. **Credit** MC, V. **Map M5**

Hearty specialities from central France include beautifully displayed cheeses, tempting homemade sausages and hare terrine with prunes.

La Campagne

111 bd de Grenelle, 15th (01.47.34.77.05). Mᵒ La Motte-Piquet. **Open** 8.30am-1pm, 3.30-8pm Tue-Sat; 8am-2pm Sun. Closed Aug. **Credit** MC, V. **Map C7**

Saxe-Breteuil: *pristine produce in a scenic setting.*

Bask in all things Basque: Pyrenean sheep's cheeses, Bayonne ham, fiery Espelette peppers, Irouléguy wines.

Charcuterie Lyonnaise
58 rue des Martyrs, 9th (01.48.78.96.45). M° Notre-Dame de Lorette. **Open** 8.30am-1.30pm, 4-7.30pm Tue-Sat; 8.30am-12.30pm Sun. Closed two weeks in Aug. **Credit** MC, V. **Map H2**
Jean-Jacques Chrétienne prepares Lyonnais delicacies *quenelles de brochet, jambon persillé* and *hure* (pistachio-seasoned tongue).

A la Cigogne
61 rue de l'Arcade, 8th (01.43.87.39.16). M° St-Lazare. **Open** 8am-7pm Mon-Sat. Closed Aug. **No credit cards. Map F4**
Hearty Alsatian fare here includes scrumptious tarts, strüdel and *beravecka* fruit bread plus sausages laced with pistachios.

Le Comptoir Corrézien
8 rue des Volontaires, 15th (01.47.83.52.97). M° Volontaires. **Open** 9.30am-1.30pm, 3-8pm Mon-Sat. Closed Aug. **Credit** MC, V. **Map E9**
Here you'll find fine *foie gras,* fresh and dried mushrooms and an array of duck-based products.

Henri Ceccaldi
21 rue des Mathurins, 9th (01.47.42.66.52). M° Havre-Caumartin/RER Auber. **Open** 8.30am-7.30pm Mon-Fri; 2-6pm Sat (Jan, Feb, Nov, Dec only). Closed Aug. **Credit** MC, V. **Map G3**
Ceccaldi sells freshly imported Corsican specialties: *charcuterie,* goat's and sheep's cheese, chestnut flour, cakes and wines.

Markets

Every *quartier* has its food market, where you can sometimes buy direct from producers. Market streets open 8am-1pm and 4-7pm Tue-Sat; 8am-1pm Sun. Roving markets set up at 8am and vanish in a flurry of street-sweeping trucks at 1pm. Arrive early for the best selection, late for bargains on fresh foods.

Market streets

Rue de Buci
rue de Seine and rue de Buci, 6th. M° Mabillon or Odéon.
Locals and tourists mingle among flower, fruit, wine and cheese shops. Part with your *sous* at *pâtisseries* or the Charcuterie Alsacienne.

Rue Mouffetard
5th. M° Censier-Daubenton.
Wind your way from medieval St-Médard to prod peaches, sample the 'flûte Gana' at Steff le Boulanger (No 123) or succumb to cakes at Le Moule à Gâteau (No 111) and pasta at Italian deli Facchetti (No 134).

Rue Poncelet
rue Poncelet and rue Bayen, 17th. M° Ternes.
Take in the coffee aromas at the Brûlerie des Ternes on this classy street which also boasts cheese shop **Alléosse** and a German deli.

Roving markets

Place Monge
5th. M° Monge. **Open** Wed, Fri, Sun.
Small but high quality. Has a lavish cheese stall and a charming grandma peddling homemade cakes, crêpes and jams.

Marché Biologique
bd Raspail, 6th. M° Sèvres-Babylone. **Open** Sun.
At this *très chic* organic market, much of the produce comes direct from the farm, but at far from rustic prices. Other organic markets are held at boulevard des Batignolles, 17th (Sat) and rue St-Charles, 15th (Tue, Fri).

Saxe-Breteuil
av de Saxe, 7th. M° Ségur. **Open** Thur, Sat.
Probably the most scenic of Paris' markets, with the Eiffel Tower poking up in the background between tree-lined rows of stalls. It caters to well-heeled locals with picture-perfect displays.

Cour de Vincennes
12th. M° Nation. **Open** Wed, Sat.
A classy kilometre-long market reputed for fruit, veg and free-range poultry.

Boulevard de Grenelle
15th. M° La Motte-Picquet-Grenelle or Dupleix. **Open** Wed, Sun.
Cheerful crowds cluster for Provençal oils, free-range chickens and freshly picked salads.

International

Donestia
20 rue de la Grange-aux-Belles, 10th (01.42.08.30.44). M° Colonel-Fabien. **Open** 10am-8.30pm Tue-Sat; 10am-1.30pm Sun. **Credit** AmEx, MC, V. **Map M3**
A small, sunny shop with specialities from the Basque country and Spain, like *paëlla* rice, spiced black pudding and Rioja.

Izraël
30 rue François-Miron, 4th (01.42.72.66.23). M° Hôtel-de-Ville. **Open** 9.30am-1pm, 2.30-7pm Tue-Fri; 9-7pm Sat. Closed Aug. **Credit** MC, V. **Map K6**
Exotic spices and other delights from as far afield as Mexico, Turkey and India – juicy dates, feta cheese, *tapenades* and a huge selection of spirits – will add a kick to your cuisine.

Kioko
46 rue des Petits-Champs, 2nd (01.42.61.33.65). M° Pyramides. **Open** 10am-8pm Mon-Sat. **Credit** MC, V. **Map H4**
Everything you need to make sushi, plus sauces, snacks, sake, Japanese beer, tea and kitchen equipment. On Saturdays, ten per cent off everything.

Mexi & Co
10 rue Dante, 5th (01.46.34.14.12). M° Maubert-Mutualité. **Open** 10.30am-midnight daily. **No credit cards. Map J7**

Everything you need for a fiesta, including marinades for *fajitas,* dried chillis, South American beers, *cachaça* and tequilas.

Le Mille-Pâtes
5 rue des Petits-Champs, 1st (01.42.96.03.04).
M° Bourse. **Open** 9am-8pm Mon-Fri; 9am-7.30pm
Sat. Closed Aug. **Credit** AmEx, DC, MC, V. **Map H4**
A treasure trove of Italian delicacies with tender
amaretti biscuits, Italian *charcuterie,* white truffles
in season, and takeaway panini and hot pastas.

Pickwick's
8 rue Mandar, 2nd (01.40.26.06.58). M° Les Halles.
Open noon-7pm Tue-Sat. **No credit cards. Map J5**
This Liverpudlian wholesaler caters to Brits homesick for baked beans, Ambrosia rice pudding, Hobnobs, Marmite and Crunchie bars. Also stocks
English-language videos.

Sarl Velan Stores
87 passage Brady, 10th (01.42.46.06.06).
M° Château d'Eau. **Open** 9.30am-8.30pm Mon-Sat.
Credit AmEx, MC, V. **Map K4**
Sarl Velan, in an alley of Indian cafés and shops,
stocks spices and vegetables from Kenya and India.

Saveurs d'Irlande
5 cité du Vauxhall, 10th (01.42.00.36.20).
M° République or Jacques-Bonsergent. **Open** 10am-
7pm MonSat (and Mon from Sept-Jan). Closed Aug.
Credit MC, V. **Map L4**
This shop is worth a detour for its real Irish soda
bread, smoked and wild salmon, beers, whiskeys
and Celtic CDs.

Tang Frères
48 av d'Ivry, 13th (01.45.70.80.00). M° Porte d'Ivry.
Open 9am-7.30pm Tue-Sun. **Credit** MC, V.
Chinatown's biggest Asian supermarket is a great
find for flat, wind-dried duck and all sorts of unidentifiable fruit and veg.

Thanksgiving
14 rue Charles V, 4th (01.42.77.68.29). M° St-Paul.
Open 11am-7pm Tue-Sat; 11am-6pm Sun. Closed
three weeks in Aug. **Credit** MC, V. **Map L7**
North American delicacies such as Oreos, canned
pumpkin and Tollhouse chocolate chips comfort the
homesick. The restaurant prepares regional dishes.

Wines, Beers & Spirits

Most *cavistes* are happy to guide their clients, so
don't be afraid to ask for advice if you have a particular wine or dish in mind. To buy direct from
producers, visit the Salon des Caves Particulières
at Espace Champerret in March and December. The
Nicolas and Le Repaire de Bacchus chains have
numerous branches around town.

Bootlegger
82 rue de l'Ouest, 14th (01.43.27.94.02). M° Pernety.
Open Tue-Sat 10.30am-1pm, 4-8.30pm. Closed two
weeks in Aug. **Credit** MC, V. **Map F10**
Around 300 beers on display from 20 countries

include the Hercule and Quitine from Belgium and
Ange Ale, brewed on the premises.

Les Caves Augé
*116 bd Haussmann, 8th (01.45.22.16.97). M° St-
Augustin.* **Open** 1-7.30pm Mon; 9am-7.30pm Tue-Sat.
Closed Mon in Aug. **Credit** AmEx, MC, V. **Map F3**
The oldest wine shop in Paris – Marcel Proust was
a regular customer – is today serious and professional with *sommelier* Marc Sibard advising.

Caves du Marais
64 rue François-Miron, 4th (01.42.78.54.64).
M° St-Paul. **Open** 10.30am-1pm, 4-8pm Tue-Sat.
Closed Aug. **Credit** MC, V. **Map K6**
Wines and cognacs from small producers are displayed like jewels in the window of this small shop.
Jean-Jacques Bailly tastes everything, and offers
some surprising finds.

Les Caves Taillevent
199 rue du Fbg-St-Honoré, 8th (01.45.61.14.09).
M° Charles de Gaulle-Etoile or Ternes. **Open** 2-8pm
Mon; 9am-8pm Tue-Fri; 9am-7.30pm Sat. Closed first
two weeks in Aug. **Credit** AmEx, DC, MC, V.
Map D3
Half a million bottles await you in the Taillevent
empire. On Saturdays, head *sommelier* Michel
Desroche gives tastings of wines starting at 24F a
bottle. Visit the cellars for spiritual temptation by
1914 Hine cognac or 1951 Chartreuse.

Legrand Filles et Fils
1 rue de la Banque, 2nd (01.42.60.07.12).
M° Bourse. **Open** 9am-7.30pm Tue-Fri; 8.30am-1pm,
3-7pm Sat. **Credit** AmEx, MC, V. **Map H4**
This old-fashioned shop is a must for wine lovers,
offering fine wines, brandies, tasting glasses and
gadgets amid chocolates, teas, coffees and *bonbons.*

La Maison du Whisky
20 rue d'Anjou, 8th (01.42.65.03.16). M° Madeleine.
Open 9.30am-7pm Mon; 9.15am-8pm Tue-Fri;
9.30am-7.30pm Sat. **Credit** AmEx, MC, V. **Map F4**
Whisky is taken seriously and Jean-Marc Bellier is
fascinating as he explains which would taste good
with which food or flavours like honey and tobacco.

Tchin Tchin
9 rue Montorgueil, 1st (01.42.33.07.77).
M° Les Halles. **Open** Mon-Sat 10am-9pm; Sun 10am-
7pm. **Credit** MC, V. **Map J5**
Antoine Bénariac opened his cheery shop in
November 1998 and stocks wines from around the
world, as well as French wines from regions such as
Alsace and the Languedoc. A good choice of organic wines starts at around 50F a bottle.

Vignobles Passion
130 bd Haussmann, 8th (01.45.22.25.22).
M° Miromesnil. **Open** 10am-7pm Mon-Sat. **Credit**
AmEx, DC, MC, V. **Map E3**
A young, enthusiastic bilingual team groups together French wine producers to sell and show their
wines. Tastings are offered (possible in English for
groups), as well as deliveries (even to the UK) and
advice on pairing wine with food.

The Montmartre harvest

In a country where wine is revered to a point of idolatry, where practically everyone who can operate a screwpull is an oenophile, where the profession of wine tasting has been elevated to a level just below beatification, it is good to see serious wine people having a bit of fun.

Under tin-grey, rainy skies, the most recent official harvest of the Montmartre Vineyard took place with a show as burlesque as it was traditional. A mix of ordinary residents and local luminaries such as 'Mick' the 'canteen woman of Montmartre', actor Patrick Timsit, the mayor of the 18th Daniel Vaillant, and even a pair of can-can dancers from the Moulin Rouge, rubbed elbows to kick off what must be the world's shortest harvest: 9am to noon (if it's not called off due to bad weather).

This tiny vineyard (one of the smallest in France) covers 1,500 square metres of a northern slope on the rue des Saule in the heart of Montmartre. Looking more like a large garden than a producing vineyard, it is easy to miss given the other attractions of the neighbourhood, the treachery of the cobble-stoned descent and the spectacular rooftop view of Paris the street affords.

Planted during the 1930s, with the encouragement of the artist Poulbot, the township of Montmartre and even the

intervention of the French President, the vineyard's original purpose was to preserve a small patch of land from encroaching developers. Originally dubbed the Square de la Liberté, there were some nasty cracks about its proximity to the Montmartre cemetery, giving rise to the comment that there was probably more of Poulbot in the wine than just his influence in creating the vineyard. It is now owned by the community and cared for by eight City of Paris gardeners, who plant, nurture, screen and also harvest the grapes.

Originally, this practically Alpine tract was planted with pinot and gamay grapes. Since the mid-1990s, however, oeneologist Francis Gourdin has been replacing the gamay with pinot and other varieties in an effort to improve the wine's quality. Currently the *cépage* is 30 per cent pinot, 30 per cent gamay and 30 per cent plantée, but Gourdin says he is aiming for ever higher concentrations of pinot. 'This is a rustic wine,' says Gourdin. 'Low tannin, but full of burned wood, red fruits, blueberry and bayberry. It has a *vin de table* aspect,' he adds, 'Definitely not a Grand Bordeaux.'

Although the wine has been called the 'most expensive bad wine in the world', Gourdin maintains that since his involvement with the vineyard began in 1995, the quality has improved steadily. 1999, he says, will be the best year so far, having benefited from a good combination of temperatures throughout the summer and intense sun in September. He expects a better wine than his 'exceptional' 1998 vintage.

The harvested grapes are taken to the *mairie* (town hall) of the 18th *arrondissement*, surely the only town hall in the world with the distinction of having its own wine press and maturing cellar. There they are sorted, cleaned and the wine made on the premises. Surely this must make the Vin Montmartrois the smallest *cru* in France.

The 1998 vintage wine has a slightly occluded ruby colour. It has a bouquet reminiscent of the Vins Gris of North Africa. If there were any bay or blue berries in the nuances, they were well hidden by the general coarseness and the onslaught of wood as the liquid hit the palate. This is a wine which should definitely see air for a good, long period to soften the initial blow. Overall, the experience could most kindly be described as 'rustic', although 'unfinished' would better describe the wine itself.

The 1998 harvest produced 1065 50cl bottles, or just over 500 litres. 1999 is expected to exceed that total. However, at an average price of 300F per bottle, the wine, and Mr Gourdin, have their work cut out for them.

New Show !

Arts & Entertainment

Cabaret, Circus & Comedy

Avant-garde antics under the big top and visiting stand-ups provide a sharper-edged alternative to befeathered can-can girls.

If the grand cabarets once promised awe-inspiring stunts and risqué glimpses of flesh, they have evolved little in a century, and today play largely to foreign tour groups. The Folies Bergère now serves up musicals, although the **Moulin Rouge** has just introduced a new revue. A more subvesive spirit lives on in Pigalle's alternative drag shows, in crossovers with theatre and dance and in the thriving world of alternative circus, where avant-garde troupes add a hotchpotch of intellectual subtexts to feats of sleight and skill, as circus and cabaret are dosed with dance, rock or video. Young *artistes* show off their skills at the Festival Mondial du Cirque de Demain (usually January or December). Look out also for aquatic extravaganza Crescend'O (recently at Disneyland), Bartabas' equestrian circus Zingaro, which performs occasionally in a fort at Aubervilliers, and the Cirque Tzigane Romanes gypsy circus, so traditional it's modern. More conventional circus abounds, especially at Christmas when the French dynasties Gruss, Bouglione and Pinder are bound to be appearing.

Café-théâtre is less influential than in its post-68 heyday, but a host of little venues, sometimes with bar attached, remain a spawning ground for comic talents. Big-name French stand-ups will even reach the hallowed Olympia (*see chapter* **Rock, Roots & Jazz**) or the Palais des Sports at Paris-Expo.

Café-Théâtre

Au Bec Fin
6 rue Thérèse, 1st (01.42.96.29.35). M° Palais-Royal or Pyramides. **Shows** usually 7pm, 8.15pm, 10pm daily. **Restaurant** noon-2.30pm, 7.30pm-midnight Tue-Sat. **Tickets** 80F; 65F students (except Sat); 50F Mon auditions 9.30pm; *dinner and show* from 178F. **Credit** MC, V. **Map H5**
This 60-seat theatre and the Café de la Gare are the oldest café-théâtres in Paris. Monday-night auditions of untried acts draw a young, irreverent crowd.

Aux Blancs Manteaux
15 rue des Blancs-Manteaux, 4th (01.48.87.15.84). M° Hôtel de Ville. **Shows** 8pm, 9.15pm, 10.30pm daily. **Tickets** 90F; 65F under-25s and Mon; *two shows* 130F. **No credit cards. Map K6**

This popular Marais venue hosts lots of standups and slapstick. Air-conditioned in summer.

Café de la Gare
41 rue du Temple, 4th (01.42.78.52.51). M° Hôtel de Ville. **Shows** 8pm, 10pm Wed-Sat. **Tickets** 100F-120F; 50F-100F students. **Credit** MC, V. **Map K5**
30 years old, and source of inspiration for many others, the largest (seats 300), best reputed and most charming of the café-théâtres, set in a Marais courtyard, spawned such talents as Colouche and Miou-Miou. Shows range from Brecht to one-man stand-up or eleven-strong team Les Voila!

Mélo d'Amelie
4 rue Marie-Stuart, 2nd (01.40.26.11.11). M° Etienne Marcel. **Shows** 8pm, 9.30pm Tue-Sat. **Tickets** 100F; 70F students (Tue-Fri); *two shows* 140F; 100F students (Tue-Fri). **Credit** AmEx, DC, MC, V. **Map J5**
Although it doesn't consider itself a café-théâtre, this cosy venue puts on similar small-scale comedies.

Point Virgule
7 rue Ste-Croix-de-la-Bretonnerie, 4th (01.42.78.67.03). M° Hôtel de Ville. **Shows** 8pm, 9.15pm, 10.15pm daily. **Tickets** 90F; *two shows* 130F; *three shows* 150F; 70F students (Mon-Fri, Sun). **No credit cards. Map K6**
This small Marais theatre is one of the few to stay open in summer. Shows are almost all one- or two-person stand-up, plus a few comic musical acts.

Théâtre et Café Edgar
58 bd Edgar-Quinet, 14th (01.42.79.97.97). M° Edgar-Quinet or Montparnasse-Bienvenüe. **Shows** usually 8.15pm, 9.30pm Mon-Sat. **Tickets** 80F-90F; 65F-70F students, under-25s. **No credit cards. Map G9**
Edgar's two minuscule theatres are easily packed, so you may find yourself sitting on the stage. The one- or two-man shows are designed for this degree of intimacy with the audience. *Les Babas cadres*, the tale of two yuppies who drop out of the city for rural self-sufficiency, has been playing since 1982.

Théâtre Trévise
14 rue Trévise, 9th (01.45.23.35.45/01.41.09.16.69). M° Cadet or Grands Boulevards. **Shows** 8.30pm daily. **Tickets** 100F; 70F under-25s; 50F Sun. **Credit** MC, V. **Map J3**

One-man shows, plus the chaotic FIEALD (Festival International d'Expression Artistique Libre et Désordonnée) open stage every Sunday: a mixed bag of comics, impressionists and improvisation.

Cabaret Glamour

Crazy Horse Saloon
12 av George V, 8th (01.47.23.32.32). M° Alma-Marceau or George V. **Show** 8.30pm, 11pm Mon-Fri, Sun; 7.30pm, 9.45pm, 11.50pm Sat. **Admission** *Champagne* 290F-660F; *dinner* 750F-980F. **Credit** AmEx, DC, MC, V. **Map D4**
Enticingly named (Lumina Neon, Looky Boop, Pussy Duty-Free, etc) 'sculptural dancers' all boast uniformly curvaceous bodies to titillate a high-rolling clientele. The revue *Teasing* is subtitled 'the art of the nude', but the identikit girls are kept at a draconian distance and weighed twice a month.

Le Lido
116bis av des Champs-Elysées, 8th (01.40.76.56.10). M° George V. **Dinner** 8pm. **Show** 10pm, plus *Mar-Dec* midnight. **Admission** *drink* 375F-560F; *dinner* 795F-995F; **Credit** AmEx, DC, MC, V. **Map D4**
The 60 Bluebell Girls shake their endowments in a show entitled *C'est Magique*. Special effects include a fire-breathing dragon, an ice rink and a waterfall. The menu has been redesigned by Paul Bocuse, with less evident uplift than the girls.
Wheelchair access.

Moulin Rouge
82 bd de Clichy, 18th (01.53.09.82.82). M° Blanche. **Dinner** 7pm, **Show** 9pm, 11pm daily. **Admission** *drink* 370F-560F; *dinner* 770F-980F. **Credit** AmEx, DC, MC, V. **Map G2**
The Moulin Rouge finally launched its new revue *Féerie* in time for Christmas 1999, but don't fear too much change. The kitschy Pigalle venue, graced by Piaf, Montand and Sinatra in their day, is the most trad of the glitzy cabarets and still makes its reputation on feathers, breasts and toothpaste smiles as the 60 Dorriss girls can-can across the stage.

La Nouvelle Eve
25 rue Fontaine, 9th (01.48.78.37.96). M° Blanche. **Dinner & Show** 6.30pm, 9.45pm daily. Closed 15 Nov-15 Mar. **Admission** 460F; *dinner* 685F. **Credit** AmEx, MC, V. **Map H2**
Small-fry compared to the big-name cabarets, La Nouvelle Eve offers a more intimate peek at Pigalle traditions. After steak and ice cream, the garish high-kicking show has audiences bellowing for more.

Cabaret Kinks & Turns

Les Assassins
40 rue Jacob, 6th (no telephone). M° St-Germain-des-Prés. **Open** 7pm-midnight Mon-Sat. **Average** 110F. **No credit cards. Map H6**
This St-Germain relic attracts students, hen parties and provincials for double entendres and simple bistro fare. Singer-guitarist Maurice Dulac swings on seaside humour, so you need a decent command

On for laughs

French humour is not easy unless you've got a solid background in Gallic TV, politics and lesser-known pop stars, but at regular intervals the boot is on the other foot, when an almost entirely Anglophone audience crams into the Hôtel du Nord, near the Canal St-Martin, to catch a UK comedy talent hot off the Eurostar. Karel Beer began Laughing Matters in 1995, putting on Eddie Izzard in the suitably sparkly Erotika in Pigalle. 'In such a wonderful city as Paris, the one thing we were seriously lacking was an excellent source of laughter,' explains Beer. Since then visitors have included Alf the Pub Landlord (whose famous xenophobic anti-Europe diatribe hides a mastery of fluent French), Ed Byrne, Dylan Moran and Johnny Vegas. As with all stand-up, there's a certain amount of hit and miss: support acts sometimes sink like a brick and the heckling can be virulent. The cultural divide is not total: Eddie Izzard, after several appearances in perfect schoolboy Franglais – equally comprehensible (or incomprehensible?) to both sides – was back at La Boule Noire in 1999 for a run in French.

Laughing Matters
Information line *01.53.19.98.98.* **Shows** *usually at Hôtel du Nord, 102 quai de Jemmapes, 10th. M° République or Jacques Bonsergent.* **Tickets** 100F; 80F students. **No credit cards.**

of gutter French to keep up. Management boasts 'No reservations, no cheques, no coffee, no telephone.'

Caveau de la République

1 bd St-Martin, 3rd (01.42.78.44.45). M° République. **Show** 9pm Tue-Sat; 3.30pm Sun. Closed July, Aug. **Admission** 145F Tue-Thur; 185F Fri-Sun; 105F over-60s (Tue-Thur); 95F students under-25s (Tue-Thur). **Credit** MC, V. **Map L4**

The *chansonnier* comprises stand-up, verse-monologue and song, with a political-satirical bent. The older performers at this smart basement venue belong to that dinosaur-genre, the 'humourist'; younger acts are exuberantly physical, edgier and naughtier.

Chez Madame Arthur

75 bis rue des Martyrs, 18th (01.42.64.48.27/ 01.42.54.40.21). M° Pigalle. **Dinner** 9.30pm. **Show** 10.30pm daily. **Admission** *drink* 165F; *dinner* 295F-395F. **Credit** AmEx, DC, MC, V. **Map H2**

At the French equivalent of Dame Edna Everage, drag artists and transsexuals mime to female singers or camp-up historic scenes. The make-up is as heavy as the *double entendre*. If you sit at the front, be prepared to be teased, tantalised and kissed.

Chez Michou

80 rue des Martyrs, 18th (01.46.06.16.04). M° Pigalle. **Dinner** daily 8.30pm. **Show** 11pm approx (ring to check). **Admission** *drink* 200F; *dinner* 590F. **Credit** MC, V. **Map H2**

Blue-clad Michou guides proceedings from beside the stage, launching irrepressible salvos of whoops and laughter as larger-than-life incarnations of Josephine Baker, Tina Turner or French torch-song *chanteuse* Barbara. Book ahead if you want to dine.

Au Lapin Agile

22 rue des Saules, 18th (01.46.06.85.87). M° Lamarck-Caulaincourt. **Shows** 9pm Tue-Sun. **Admission** *drink* 130F; 90F students (Tue-Fri, Sun). **No credit cards. Map H1**

This cosy parlour whisks you back to the turn of the century, when it was a fave with Montmartre's bohemians (*see chapter* **Right Bank**). The artists have been replaced by tourists and a team of performers: accordionist Cassita, strident singer-songwriter Arlette Denis and songster Yves Mathieu.

Contemporary Circus Venues

Cirque d'Hiver Bouglione

110 rue Amelot, 11th (01.47.00.12.25). M° Filles du Calvaire. **Shows** times vary. **Tickets** 70F-150F. **Credit** V. **Map L5**

The beautiful winter circus was built in 1852 by Hittorff. It now belongs to the Bouglione circus family and is used by visiting troupes, traditional (Salto back in autumn 2000) and modern.

Espace Chapiteaux

Parc de la Villette, 19th (08.03.07.50.75). M° Porte de Pantin or Porte de la Villette. **Shows** 8.30pm Wed-Sat; 4pm Sun. **Tickets** 110F-150F; 90F-120F 16-25s; 50F-75F 4-15s; free under 4s. **Credit** MC, V. **Map inset**

Daring acrobatics meet intelligent modern circus at La Villette's space for circus tents. Recent tenants include dazzling trapeze troupe Les Arts Sauts, socially aware Cirque Plume, illusionist Cirque Ici, and the highly physical Compagnie Cahin Caha. *Wheelchair access.*

The Centre National des Arts du Cirque bridges genres at the **Espace Chapiteaux**.

Children

Come to Paris with a child and you'll find yourself discovering the city as a true Parisian.

For all its monuments, Paris is a remarkably child-friendly city and, if you're travelling with a young baby, any idea of Parisians as stand-offish will disappear under a barrage of advice and comment. Many of the most famous sights will be on every child's list: the Eiffel Tower, Arc de Triomphe, the glass lifts at the Grande Arche de la Défense, the Centre Pompidou or the pyramid at the Louvre. Parisians start polishing their intellectual credentials at an early age: there are adventurous theatre productions, fledgling cinema seasons and any number of workshops to learn everything from cookery to stained glass. But it doesn't all need to be highbrow. Street markets offer plenty of entertainment, and buying a *baguette* in a bakery or sitting on a café terrace will give the young a feel of the Paris lifestyle.

There are numerous small parks and playgrounds for flat-living Parisians, while the city gets more bicycle- and rollerblade-friendly each year, so that family outings on both are now feasible along the newly created bike lanes, the *promenade plantée* in eastern Paris and by the Seine and Canal St-Martin on Sundays.

A perennial pleasure for children is the funfair. Best-known Parisian fairs include La Fête à Neu-Neu (Bois de Boulogne, autumn) and the carnivalesque Foire du Trône (late Mar-late May, pelouse de Reuilly, Bois de Vincennes). La Fête des Tuileries (Jardin des Tuileries, June-Aug) offers breathtaking views of the city from atop the big wheel.

During the year 2000 it's possible to get a bird's eye view from a hot air balloon in Parc André-Citroën. Seasonal pleasures include fireworks in summer, animated department store windows and free merry-go-rounds all over the city at Christmas; Hallowe'en has recently taken off in a big way, too.

Most kids' events take place on Wednesdays (when primary schools close), weekends and holidays: see the weekly listings in *Pariscope*, *L'Officiel des Spectacles* and *Figaroscope*. The bimonthly freebie *Paris-Mômes* is full of imaginative suggestions; it comes with the daily *Libération* or can be picked up at the Office de Tourisme, Musée d'Orsay, MK2 cinemas and the Louvre's children's bookshop (for more outlets, call 01.49.29.01.21). The *Guide de la Rentrée*, free from the *mairie* (townhall) of each *arrondissement* or at the Kiosque Paris-Jeunes (25 bd Bourdon, 4th/ 01.42.76.22.60), has information about sports facilities and cultural activities for children and teenagers. For more activities, *see* chapter **Sport & Fitness**.

Getting Around

With younger kids, it is best to use public transport between 10am and 5pm to avoid the rush hour. Baby backpacks and quick-folding pushchairs will help you negotiate turnstiles, escalators and automatic doors. The driverless line 14 (Météor) is a must – aim for the front carriage with its head-on views of the tunnel. Line 6 (Nation to Charles-de-Gaulle-Etoile) is mostly overground and crosses the Seine twice, once beside the Eiffel Tower. Scenic bus routes include the 24, 69 and 72, which follow the river and pass the Louvre and Musée d'Orsay. The 29 and 56 have an open deck at the back. Both the Montmartrobus minibus and the Montmartre funicular are part of the RATP public transport system, as is the Balabus (Apr-Sept, Sun and holidays), which takes in most of the sights. Under-4s travel free on public transport, 4-10 year olds are eligible for a *carnet* (ten tickets) at half-price. The annual Carte Imagine-R (1500F) gives 10-26s the freedom of the city – and all of Ile-de-France at weekends and on bank holidays.

Taxi drivers can refuse more than three adults, but will generally take a family of four, as under-10s count as half a passenger. Add 6F for the buggy.

Help & Information

The American Church
65 quai d'Orsay, 7th (01.40.62.05.00).
The noticeboard here is a major source of English-speaking babysitters and au pairs.

Ababa
(01.45.49.46.46). **Open** 8am-8pm Mon-Fri; 11am-7pm Sat. Childminding 34F/hr plus 64F agency fee.
Ababa can provide experienced childminders or babysitters (mainly students) at the last minute.

Inter-Service Parents
(01.44.93.44.93). **Open** 9.30am-12.30pm, 1.30-5pm Mon, Tue, Fri; 9.30am-12.30pm Wed; 1.30-5pm Thur.
Phone service lists babysitting agencies and activities.

Message
(01.48.04.74.61).
English-speaking support group for mothers and mothers-to-be of all nationalities living in Paris. Publishes the useful *ABC of Motherhood in Paris.*

Parks & Playgrounds

Generations of children have grown up amid the sandpits, puppet shows, pony rides and boating ponds of the Luxembourg and Tuileries gardens. Many public gardens offer mini playgrounds and concrete ping-pong tables. Even the posh place des Vosges has small slides and rocking horses. The Bois de Vincennes and Bois de Boulogne provide picnic areas, boating lakes and cycle paths. For adventures there's the artificial cave and waterfall at the Parc des Buttes-Chaumont, while the Jardin du Ranelagh has a hand-cranked iron roundabout. As well as the natural history museum and a small zoo (*see p292*, **Muséum National d'Histoire Naturelle**), the Jardin de Plantes offers a rare endangered species merry-go-round and spiralling yew maze. And at postmodern La Villette, there are themed gardens, a dragon slide, prairies for picnicking and bright red *folies* housing everything from fast food to music workshops. Grass is still out of bounds in the Luxembourg (except for one lawn), Tuileries, Monceau and Palais-Royal parks.

Jardin d'Acclimatation
Bois de Boulogne, 16th (01.40.67.90.82). M° Les Sablons or Porte Maillot + Petit Train (6.50F every 15 mins from L'Orée du Bois restaurant). **Open** *winter* 10am-6pm daily; *summer* 10am-7pm daily. **Admission** 12F; free under-3s. **Credit** MC, V.
Opened in 1860, this amusement park aims to cater for all the family, with zoo and farm animals, a hall of mirrors, *guignol* puppets, mini-golf, table football, billiards, pony club, caterpillar and dragon roller-coasters, trampolines, mini racing circuit and new interactive Exploradome. Some attractions are free, others cost 13F each (book of 16 tickets 150F). There are picnic areas and cafés, activity workshops, and an Easter egg hunt. *See p292*, **Musée en Herbe**.

Jardin des Enfants aux Halles
105 rue Rambuteau, 1st (01.45.08.07.18).
M° Châtelet-Les Halles. **Admission** 2.50F for a one-hour session. **Map J5**
This well-supervised garden with underground tunnels, rope swings, secret dens and pools of coloured ping-pong balls is great for 7-11s, and useful for parents visiting the adjoining Forum des Halles. Parents are allowed in only from 10am-2pm on Saturday, to accompany their under-7s.

Parc Floral de Paris
route de la Pyramide, Bois de Vincennes, 12th (01.43.43.92.95). M° Château de Vincennes. **Open** *summer* 9.30am-8pm; *winter* 9.30am-6pm. **Admission** *summer* 10F; 5F 6-18s, over-60s; free under-6s; *winter* 5F; 2.50F 6-18s, over-60s; free under-6s. **No credit cards.**
A miniature train (6F) chugs around a track between the majestic conifers of this attractive park. The huge adventure playground offers a multitude of slides, swings, climbing frames and giant spider webs. This is also the home of the Maison Paris-Nature, a nature resource centre with exhibitions, books and games, and the Serre des Papillons, where children can wander among the butterflies. In summer there are free concerts and children's shows at the Théâtre Astral (*see p293*, **Entertainment**).

Museums & Galleries

Egyptian mummies at the Louvre, sculptures at Musée Picasso, Dalí's surrealist sense of fun at the Espace Dalí, the intricate Lady and the Unicorn tapestries at the Musée National du Moyen Age, the costumes at the Musée de la Mode et du Textile, the Dégas ballet dancers and the animal statues on the pavement at the Musée d'Orsay, jets and space shuttles at the Musée de l'Air et de l'Espace should all appeal to children, in limited doses – keep the visit short. At many places under-18s get in free. *See chapter* **Museums**. Some museums (Louvre, Petit Palais, Carnavalet) offer guided visits by storytellers. Others (Orsay, Monnaie, Arts et Traditions Populaires, Gustave-Moreau) provide free activity sheets. Many organise Wednesday afternoon workshops (usually in French). The Musée du Moyen Age has both themed visits for 8-12s (medieval beasts, the life of a lord, etc) and *ateliers* for the artistically inclined on the goldsmith's craft, stained glass or medieval architecture (visits 25F, workshops 45F).

Centre Pompidou – Galerie des Enfants
4th (01.44.78.12.33). M° Hôtel-de-Ville/RER Châtelet-Les Halles. **Open** *exhibition* 11am-9pm Mon, Wed-Sun; *workshop* Wed, Sat afternoon. **Workshop & exhibition** 50F. **Map K6**
Beautifully thought-out exhibitions, specially designed by top artists and designers, introduce children to modern art, design and architecture, with related hands-on workshops for 6-12s. Until 31 Aug 2000, in 'En Quête des Objets', seven installations

Making the most of the Mouse

The Mouse has gradually insinuated his way into French affections. Even if Disney is still viewed as an Anglo-Saxon imperialist, the former 'cultural Chernobyl' now gets more visitors than Notre Dame, and a second, film-linked park, Disney Studios, is due to open in April 2002. Once through the sugary pink portals, the phenomenal scale, attention to detail and technical ingenuity of the Magic Kingdom take the breath away and even the most cynical will end up charmed by the Main Street Electric Parade (Sat, Sun; nightly July, Aug), with all the Disney characters and twinkling illuminated floats. At 3pm daily, the new Disney Imagination Parade promises 12m-high floats on the theme of the five continents.

With young children, head to Fantasyland for Dumbo the Flying Elephant and Sleeping Beauty's Castle, where a fire-breathing dragon is chained up in a gloomy dungeon. Even tots will enjoy the Giant Teacup ride and the kitschy Small World, where dolls in national costumes fulfil all sorts of stereotypes. In Frontierland, the Pocahontas Indian village gives kids a chance to let off steam and, in summer, you can take trips on the lake in boats paddled by cast members.

Parents with older children are advised to try the most popular attractions early. White-knuckle thrills include Big Thunder Mountain, the Jules Verne-esque Space Mountain, where you scream around in the dark, and the roller-coaster Indiana Jones et Le Temple de Péril. Only children over 1.4m can go on really fast rides. The whole family will enjoy the Haunted Mansion and Pirates of the Caribbean, a dank boat trip past carousing pirates and cackling parrots. Cinematic experiences include Star Tours, a simulated space ride piloted by a rookie droid, and latest arrival, Honey I Shrunk the Audience, with its gobsmacking hologram effects.

Useful Tips

There are snack bars and souvenir shops spread all over the theme park, as well as more formal, sit-down restaurants – L'Auberge de Cendrillon (French), Blue Lagoon (Caribbean), Walt's American Restaurant – but service can be remarkably show. Optimise time and cash by combining lunch and a show. Café Hyperion in Videopolis has a show based on the latest Disney film (*Mulan* in 2000), while there's often country music at the Cowboy Cookout in Frontierland. The site is exposed to the elements: bring botttled water, straw hats and sunblock in summer; warm hats and gloves in winter. Wear comfortable shoes, too. The park stays open later in summer, but queues are longer; you can do much more out of season, including return visits to favourite attractions. Some of the longest queues are for the train that tours the park but, in fact, all attractions are within easy walking distance. Five minutes from the gates, next to the RER station, the Disney Village complex appeals to teenagers and young adults with bars, restaurants, a multiplex cinema and country music. *Marne-la-Vallée (01.60.30.60.30); from UK 0990 030 303.* **Open** *Apr-June* 9am-8pm daily; *July, Aug* 9am-11pm daily, *Sept-Mar* 10am-6pm Mon-Fri; 9am-8pm Sat, Sun. **Admission** *high season* 220F; 170F 3-11s; free under-3s; *low season* 165F; 135F 3-11s; free under-3s. **Credit** AmEx, DC, MC, V. **Getting there:** RER A or TGV Marne-la-Vallée-Chessy. *By car* 32km by A4 Metz-Nancy exit 14.

put a child's perspective on industrial design; from Aug, contemporary art and performance linked to the exhibition 'Son et Lumière'.

Cité des Enfants/Techno Cité
Level 0, Cité des Sciences et de l'Industrie, 30 av Corentin-Cariou, 19th (01.40.05.12.12). M° Porte de la Villette. **Open** *Cité des Enfants* 10am-6pm Tue-Sun. *Techno Cité* Tue-Sun (times vary).* **Admission** 25F per session. **Credit** MC, V. **Map inset**
The whole of the futuristic Cité des Sciences et de l'Industrie (*see chapter* **Museums**) at Parc de la Villette is a stimulating experience, with plenty of interactive exhibits to help children and adults alike understand light, sound, electricity or space travel, a planetarium, and the Argonaute submarine. The Cité des Enfants (3-12s) and Techno Cité (11-up) are specifically geared to children. Book ahead for 90-minute sessions where 3-5s can build a house using cranes and pulleys, and 5-12s can learn about machines, the body and communication. In Techno Cité, over-11s get hands-on experience of design and technology, from injection moulding to the role of sensors and automation. The Médiathèque multi-media library has a section for under-14s.

Halle St-Pierre
2 rue Ronsard, 18th (01.42.58.72.89). M° Anvers. **Open** 10am-6pm daily. Closed Aug. **Admission** 40F; 30F 4-12s, students under-26; free under-4s. **Credit** (shop) MC, V. **Map J1**
This former covered market specialises in popular and naive art and organises workshops and visits for children linked to its temporary exhibitions, as well as puppet shows (3.30pm, 4.30pm Wed, Sat, Sun). The cosy café serves light meals and is a pleasant place to pass time while the kids explore the exhibits with booklet and pencil in hand.
Café. Shop. Wheelchair access.

Musée de la Curiosité
11 rue St-Paul, 4th (01.42.72.13.26). M° St-Paul or Sully-Morland. **Open** 2-7pm Wed, Sat, Sun; daily during school holidays. **Admission** 45F; 30F 3-12s; free under-3s. **Map L7**
Come here for conjuring shows, optical illusions, psychic phenomena and an exhibition of magic props including boxes for sawing ladies in two. There are English-speaking guides and children's magic courses during the holidays.

Musée en Herbe du Jardin d'Acclimatation
Jardin d'Acclimatation (see above). **Information** *(01.40.67.97.66).* **Open** 10am-6pm Mon-Fri, Sun; 2-6pm Sat. **Admission** 17F; 14F 3-18s, over-60s; free under-3s (plus 13F park entry). **No credit cards.**
Four-12s are introduced to the history of European art from cave paintings to Picasso. There are also themed exhibitions and workshops.
Wheelchair access.

Musée National des Arts d'Afrique et d'Océanie
293 av Daumesnil, 12th (01.44.74.84.80). M° Porte Dorée. **Open** 10am-5.20pm Mon, Wed-Sun. **Admission** 30F (38F with exhibition), 20F (28F with

exhibition) 18-25s; free under-18s. **No credit cards.**
Formerly known as 'the colonial museum', there are ethnic artefacts from all over Africa and the Pacific, including some scary masks. The tropical aquarium downstairs is the real draw: a vast collection of colourful exotic fish placed at just the right height for children. Beware the crocodiles…

Muséum National d'Histoire Naturelle
Jardin des Plantes, 57 rue Cuvier, 5th (01.40.79.30.00). M° Gare d'Austerlitz or Jussieu. **Open** 10am-6pm Mon, Fri-Sun; 10am-10pm Thur. **Admission** 40F; 30F students, 4-16s, over-60s; free under-4s. **Credit** MC, V. *Other pavilions* each 30F; 20F 5-16s, students, over-60s. **No credit cards. Map J9**
The brilliantly refurbished Grande Galerie de l'Evolution borrows cinema techniques to recreate the atmosphere of the savannah. A Noah's Ark of stuffed animals, from elephants to rats, is the centrepiece of the middle floor. Birds in flight are suspended from the upper floors, while the ground floor corresponds to the sea bed. Children love the glass lifts whizzing between the three floors. Under-12s can play interactive games and use microscopes in the small Espace Découverte. The paleontology gallery has a renowned fossil collection, while the mineralogy museum includes some wonderful giant crystals and meteorites.

Palais de la Découverte
av Franklin D Roosevelt, 8th (01.56.43.20.21). M° Franklin D Roosevelt. **Open** 9.30am-6pm Tue-Sat; 10am-7pm Sun. **Admission** 30F; 20F 5-18s, students; free under-5s; *planetarium* add 15F (no under-7s). **No credit cards. Map E5**
This vintage science museum manages to deliver the goods while retaining a historic, wood-panelled feel. Kids can see a colony of ants at work, learn about centrifugal force the hard way and play in an interactive section. A new dinosaur section opens in 2000. Reserve ahead for the planetarium.

Zoos & Theme Parks

Château et Parc Zoölogique de Thoiry
78770 Thoiry-en-Yvelines (01.34.87.52.25). By car A13 direction Dreux until Pont Chartrain, then follow signs. 45km west of Paris. **Open** *winter* 10am-5pm daily; *summer* 10am-6pm daily. **Admission** *park* 105F; 90F over-60s; 79F 3-12s, students under 26; *château* 38F; 30F 9-18s. **Credit** MC, V.
Some 121 species of wild animal roam the château grounds of this safari park just 30 minutes from Paris. Less ferocious beasts can be seen from a little train that tours the gardens. Tea room and picnic area.

France Miniature
25 route du Mesnil, 78990 Elancourt (01.30.62.40.79). Train from Gare Montparnasse to La Verrière, then bus 411. By car A13 direction St-Quentin-en-Yvelines/Dreux, then Elancourt Centre. **Open** *Apr-mid-Nov* 10am-7pm daily (July, Aug 10am-midnight Sat). **Admission** 75F; 50F 4-16s; free under-4s. **Credit** AmEx, MC, V.
The monuments and sights of France rebuilt at

*Feeding time is cuddly at the **Château et Parc Zoölogique de Thoiry**.*

one-thirtieth their original size. Over 200 models include Loire châteaux, the Mont St-Michel, Eiffel Tower, Notre Dame and the Stade de France. *Wheelchair access.*

La Ménagerie

Jardin des Plantes, pl Valhubert, rue Buffon or rue Geoffroy-St-Hilaire, 5th (01.40.79.37.94). M° Gare d'Austerlitz or Jussieu. **Open** *Apr-Sept* 10-6pm daily; *Oct-Mar* 10am-5pm daily. **Admission** 30F; 20F 4-16s, students, over-60s; free under-4s. **No credit cards.** **Map J8**

The Ménagerie, one of the oldest zoos in the world, is on a perfect scale for younger kids. It's a long way from the safari park ideal of modern zoos, but still offers plenty of vultures, monkeys and big cats, and quantities of reptiles.

Musée Vivant du Cheval

60631 Chantilly (03.44.57.13.13). SNCF Chantilly from Gare du Nord. By car 40km from Paris by A1, exit 7. **Open** *Apr-Oct* 10.30am-5.30pm Mon, Wed-Sun (plus 2-5pm Tue *July, Aug*); *Nov-Mar* 2-5pm Mon, Wed, Fri; 10.30am-5.30pm Sat, Sun. **Admission** 50F; 45F over-60s; 35F 4-16s; free under-4s. **Credit** MC, V.

Home to 40 breeds of horse and pony, the historic stables of the Château de Chantilly are a dream for the pony-mad. At 11.30am, 3.30pm, 5.15pm (winter 3.30pm), there are costumed *haute-école* presentations. *See chapter* **Trips Out of Town**.

Parc Astérix

60128 Plailly (03.44.62.34.34). RER B Roissy-Charles de Gaulle 1, then shuttle (9.30am-1.30pm, 4.30pm-closing time). By car A1 exit Parc Astérix.

Open *Apr-mid-Oct* 10am-6pm daily; *10 July-Aug* 9.30am-7pm daily. Closed mid Oct-Mar; ring to check extra closures. **Admission** 175F; 165F over-60s; 125F 3-11s; free under-3s. **No credit cards.**

The French answer to Disneyland is ideal for fans of the cartoon Gaul or students of Latin. Along with Ancient Roman-themed, white-knuckle rides and parades, enjoy the residents of the Dolphinarium and the antics of the Three Musketeers and a giant baby in a self-propelled pram. Look out for artisans working in wood, stone and stained glass in a reconstructed corner of medieval Paris. Shops, restaurant and picnic area on the spot.

Parc Zoölogique de Paris

53 av de St-Maurice, 12th (01.44.75.20.10/00). M° Porte Dorée. **Open** *Apr-Sept* 9am-6pm daily; *Oct-Mar* 9am-5pm daily. **Admission** 40F; 30F 4-16s, students, over-60s; free under-4s. **No credit cards.**

Gibbons leaping around the trees, baboons sliding on their rocks and prowling big cats keep children and parents amused for hours at the Paris zoo; most species wander in relative landscaped freedom, confined on islands rather than behind bars. Don't miss the nocturnal lemurs in their dark habitat or the incomparable smell of hippos and rhinos in their indoor quarters. Check at the entrance for feeding times, especially the seals. A small train tours the zoo. *Wheelchair access.*

Entertainment

Numerous productions for children are put on at theatres and at *café-théâtres*, especially on Wednesdays and at weekends, with two theatres

*The **Croisière Enchantée** boat trip up the Seine has worked magic on Parisian dress sense.*

entirely devoted to young spectators. Over-8s with good French may enjoy Ecla Company's performances of classics (01.40.27.82.05), while Théâtre de la Lune mixes music hall and marionnettes. A profusion of circuses, New Age or otherwise, passes through Paris, especially at Christmas (*see chapter* **Cabaret, Comedy & Circus**). Selected classical concerts at the Maison de Radio France are free for under-12s, accompanied by an adult (brochure on 01.42.20.42.20), as are the **Concerts du Dimanche Matin** (*see below*) workshops.

Apart from the must-see Hollywood/Disney output (usually dubbed), there are children's films at MK2 cinemas (Wednesday and weekend mornings) and at the **Forum des Images**, as well as an annual children's festival at Aubervilliers in November.

Any Parisian park worth its salt has its own *théâtre de Guignol*, named after its principal character, the French equivalent of Mr Punch. There is a lot of frantic audience participation, and the language can be hard to follow. With no Judy, domestic violence is absent from the plot – but the policeman always gets it. Shows (around 20F) are usually hourly on Wednesday afternoon, weekends and school holidays (not July and Aug).

ACT Theatre Company

(01.40.33.64.02). **Tickets** 50F-95F.
This English-language company performs accessible, energetic adaptations of works by British authors (Emily Brontë, Conan Doyle, Oscar Wilde) for mainly school-going audiences at the Théâtre de Ménilmontant and the suburban MJC de Palaiseau.

The American Library

10 rue du Général-Camou, 7th (01.53.59.12.60).
M° Ecole Militaire/RER Pont de l'Alma. **Open** 10am-7pm Tue-Sat (*Aug* noon-6pm Tue-Fri; 10am-2pm Sat).
Map D6
The American Library offers regular storytelling sessions in English: for 3-5s 2.30pm Wed; for 1-3s, 10.30am last Tue of month; for 6-8s, 10.30am, last Sat of month. The library also lends books, magazines, cassettes, CDs and videos.

Concerts du Dimanche Matin

Châtelet, Théâtre Musical de Paris, 1 pl du Châtelet, 1st (01.40.28.28.40/children's programme 01.42.56.90.10). M° Châtelet. **Tickets** 120F; free 4-14s (reservation essential). **Map J6**
Sunday mornings here involve an original package deal for music-loving families. While parents attend the 11am classical concert, 4-9s can explore instruments or composers, thematically linked to the main concert, 8-14s can join DJ Mozart and manipulate sounds by computer. There's also a choir with concert at end of the season.

La Croisière Enchantée

Bateaux Parisiens, Port de la Bourdonnais, 7th (01.44.11.33.44). M° Bir-Hakeim. **Trips** *Oct-June* 2.30pm, 4pm Sat, Sun, public holidays; daily school holidays. **Admission** 55F. **Credit** MC, V. **Map C6**
Two elves take three- to ten-year-olds (and their parents) on a one-hour enchanted boat trip up the Seine, with songs and games laid on (in French).

Forum des Images

2 Grande Galerie, Porte St-Eustache, Nouveau Forum des Halles, 1st (01.44.76.63.44/47).

Mº Châtelet-Les Halles. **Après midi des enfants**
3pm Wed, Sat. **Internet workshop** 2pm Wed (book
ahead). **Admission** 15F (30F adults); *Internet* 10F.
No credit cards. Map J5
The Paris rep cinema and film archive puts on a film,
followed by debate and snack for 5-12s. Check in the
programme to see if it is in VO (original language)
or VF (dubbed into French). If you want to initiate
your toddler into the Seventh Art, look out for the
occasional Babyrama Circus, with film, live music
and clowns for 18-month to five-year-olds.
Wheelchair access (call ahead).

Une Journée au Cirque
*Cirque de Paris, 115 bd Charles de Gaulle, 92390
Villeneuve-La Garenne (01.47.99.40.40). Mº Porte de
Clignancourt, then 137 bus.* **Open** 10am-5pm Wed,
Sun, school holidays. Closed July-Sept. **Tickets**
(reservation essential) 160F-238F; 120F-188F 3-11s;
show only 70F; 45F 3-11s. **Credit** MC, V.
Aficionado Francis Schoeller opens up his circus for
a day-long extravaganza. Children train with circus
artistes in clowning, conjuring, trapeze and tight-
rope skills, lunch with the performers – then watch
the show. Extras include visits with the animals, an
antique merry-go-round and funfair memorabilia.

Théâtre Astral
Parc Floral de Paris (see above). **Information**
(01.43.71.31.10). **Tickets** 29F-34F (+ 5F/10F park
entry). **No credit cards.**
The recently refurbished Astral offers 3-8s epics
about ogres and princesses in a bucolic setting.
Wheelchair access (call ahead).

Théâtre Dunois
*108 rue du Chevaleret, 13th (01.45.84.72.00).
Mº Chevaleret.* **Tickets** 50F; 35F 3-15s. **No credit
cards. Map M10**
Adventurous theatre, contemporary dance and
musical creations by established children's companies will widen expectations of culture for kids with
anything from John Cage or a Fellini tribute to *Les
Mis* with puppets. In June 2000, some performances
by Franco-American duo Blue Palm are in English.
Wheelchair access (call ahead).

Sweet Treats

A la Mère de Famille
*35 rue du Fbg-Montmartre, 9th (01.47.70.83.69).
Mº Grands Boulevards.* **Open** 8.30am-1.30pm, 3-7pm
Tue-Sat. Closed Aug. **Credit** AmEx, MC, V.
The oldest sweetshop in town abounds in tradition-
al regional sweets such as Tours barley sugar,
pastilles fondantes from Lyon, candied violets from
Toulouse and *les bêtises de Cambrai.*

Berthillon
*31 rue St-Louis-en-l'Ile, 4th (01.43.54.31.61).
Mº Sully-Morland.* **Open** 10am-8pm Wed-Sun. Closed
school holidays. **No credit cards. Map K7**
Children get dizzy trying to choose from the array
of homemade ice creams here – from *marrons glâcés*
to honey and nougat.

Jadis et Gourmande
*49bis av Franklin D Roosevelt, 8th (01.42.25.06.04).
Mº St-Philippe-du-Roule.* **Open** 1-7pm Mon; 9.30am-
7pm Tue; 9.30am-7.30pm Wed-Fri; 10-7pm Sat.
Credit MC, V. **Map E4**
This *chocolatier* makes Arcs de Triomphe, Santas,
Champagne bottles and other novelty chocolates.
Letters like giant Scrabble tiles (7F30 each) let you
spell your child's name or other edible message in
chocolate and have the result arranged in a long,
pretty box. Allow 132F for fourteen letters.
Branches: 88 bd Port-Royal, 5th (01.43.26.17 75);
39 rue des Archives, 4th (01.48.04.08.03); 27 rue
Boissy d'Anglas, 8th (01.42.65.23.23).

Toyshops & Bookshops

Small cosy toyshops can be found in every
quartier. The gadgets at Pier Import are a
favourite with pre-teens, while shops like Nature
et Découvertes (branches citywide) blur the distinction between toys for children and desirable
objects for adults. La Samaritaine has a huge toy
department and, if plastic and Gameboys are their
thing, the Grande Recré chain stocks all the main
brands. Browsing is fun in the well-stocked children's sections of the big English-language bookshops WH Smith, Brentano's and Galignani, which
also provide translations of French classics (*see
chapter* **Specialist Shops**). Municipal libraries
(*bibliothèques*) have comfortable children's spaces,
some with a limited selection of books in English.

Au Nain Bleu
*406-410 rue St-Honoré, 8th (01.42.60.39.01).
Mº Concorde.* **Open** 9.45am-6.30pm Mon-Sat. **Credit**
AmEx, MC, V. **Map G4**
Dating from 1836 (as reportedly do some of its staff),
France's most prestigious toy shop is the nearest
you'll get to London's Hamley's only stuffier and
more old-fashioned. Toys from all around the world
range from furry animals to electronic games. No lifts.

La Boîte à Joujoux
*41 passage Jouffroy, 9th (01.48.24.58.37).
Mº Grands Boulevards.* **Open** 10am-7pm Mon-Sat.
Credit MC, V. **Map H4**
This is just the place to find miniatures and mer-
chandising spin-offs of Tintin and other cartoon
characters. It goes in for dressing-up and disguise,
and does a roaring trade at Hallowe'en.

Chantelivre
*13 rue de Sèvres, 6th (01.45.48.87.90). Mº Sèvres-
Babylone.* **Open** 1-7pm Mon; 10am-7pm Tue-Sat.
Credit MC, V. **Map G7**
This well-loved and wide-ranging children's bookshop leads from teenage reading by the door, via
age-related clusters to illustrated books and the
baby section in a bright space under a skylight at
the back. There are publications on children's health
and psychology for parents, a respectable English-
language section for children, plus videos, toys,
posters, stationery and party supplies.

Les Cousines d'Alice

36 rue Daguerre, 14th (01.43.20.24.86). M° Denfert-Rochereau. **Open** 3-7.15pm Mon; 10am-7.15pm Tue-Sat; 11am-1pm Sun. **Credit** MC, V. **Map G10**
Just the sort of neighbourhood toyshop one loves is crammed full with soft toys, wooden Babars and ranches, well-selected books, farm and zoo animals, and plenty of inexpensive pocket money treats from glow-in-the-dark stickers to scary plastic snakes.

Fnac Junior

19 rue Vavin, 6th (01.56.24.03.46). M° Vavin. **Open** 10am-7.30pm Mon-Sat. **Credit** MC, V. **Map G8**
Fnac customers have kids too and the group has adapted its specialities into books, toys, videos and CD-roms for under-12s. The shop lays on story-telling and activities (mainly Wed, Sat) for 3s-up, from make-up, magic and mime to multimedia. **Branches**: Centre Commercial Grand Ciel, 94200 Ivry-sur-Seine (01.46.58.94.86); Centre Commercial Les 4 Temps, La Défense (01.49.07.08.79).

Galerie Bass

9 rue de l'Abbé de l'Epée, 5th (01.56.24.04.54). RER Luxembourg. **Open** 2-7pm Tue-Sat. **Credit** MC, V. **Map J8**
Handcrafted mobiles, winsome wooden 'Pit' and 'Bull' dogs and chunky jigsaw animals all ooze character. There are more toys and books at the neighbouring Un Jour, Un Jouet and Le Petit Bass.

La Maison du Cerf-Volant

7 rue de Prague, 12th (01.44.68.00.75). M° Ledru-Rollin. **Open** 10am-7pm Tue-Sat. **Credit** V. **Map M7**
You can spend anything from 100F to 7000F on brightly coloured kites of every kind: dragons, galleons, geometrical shapes. If it flies, it's here.

L'Ourson en Bois

83 rue de Charenton, 12th (01.40.01.02.40). M° Ledru-Rollin. **Open** 10am-7pm Tue-Sat. **Credit** V. **Map N8**
This toyshop stocks arty-crafty presents, educational toys and musical boxes in wood or fabric, and the excellent German-made Sigiskids soft toys, including the predatory-looking Black Friday Mouse (often given to adults, it seems). A good source of whistles, plastic spiders, balloons and party favours.

Pain d'Epices

29 passage Jouffroy, 9th (01.47.70.08.68). M° Grands Boulevards. **Open** 12.30-7pm Mon; 10am-7pm Tue-Sat. **Credit** MC, V. **Map H4**
This olde-worlde toyshop has everything a self-respecting doll would need in her house, from tiny cutlery to tubes of toothpaste. Plus a selection of traditional teddies, marionettes and wooden toys.

Pylones

57 rue St-Louis-en-l'île, 4th (01.46.34,05.02). M° Pont Marie. **Open** 10.30am-7.30pm daily. **Credit** AmEx, MC, V. **Map K7**
Hilarious gadgets and knick-knacks for kids and kids-at-heart. Furry pencil-cases, animated postcards, Wallace and Gromit toothbrushes, squeaky-toy hair-slides and keyrings, and glasses with toy cars attached so you can send drinks whizzing across the table. Everything you never needed. **Branches:** 52 galerie Vivienne, 2nd (01.42.61.51.60); 7 rue Tardieu, 18th (01.46.06.37.00).

Clothes Shops

Young trendsetters head straight for BabyGap, Gap Kids, Agnès b, Paul Smith and Zara. If you want your child to sport the classic French *BCBG* look, then rush to **Bonpoint**, Jacadi or Tartine et Chocolat. Then again, you might prefer to go the cheap-and-cheerful route at **Du Pareil au Même**, **Dipaki** and Tout Compte Fait, whose solid, brightly coloured clothes are influenced by new fads and fabrics. Natalys caters for mums-to-be as well as children, and also sells cots, car seats and other equipment. Monoprix's and Prisunic's good-value children's sections are worth a look too.

Bonpoint

65-67, 86 rue de l'Université, 7th (01.45.55.63.70). M° Solférino. **Open** 10am-7pm Mon-Sat. Closed Mon in Aug. **Credit** AmEx, DC, MC, V. **Map E5**
For classic, conservative, *BCBG* clothes from babies to teenage, if you like that kind of thing. Budding fashion victims can sport the baby pashmina. Plus furniture and nursery accessories at 7 rue Solférino and last season's clothing at 82 rue de Grenelle. **Branches**: 15 rue Royale, 8th (01.47.42.52.63); 64 av Raymond-Poincaré, 16th (01.47.27.60.81); 184 rue des Courcelles, 17th (01.47.63.87.49).

Dipaki

18 rue Vignon, 9th (01.42.66.24.74). M° Madeleine. **Open** 10am-7pm Mon-Sat. **Credit** MC, V. **Map G4**
One of Paris' best shops for reasonably priced, traditionally styled baby and kids' clothing in bold, primary colours. Sister chain Jacadi is more upmarket and also stocks baby equipment. **Branches include**: 20 rue du Pont-Neuf, 1st (01.40.26.21.00); 22 rue Cler, 7th (01.47.05.47.62); 17 av du Général-Leclerc, 14th (01.43.21.08.86).

Du Pareil au Même

15-17 rue des Mathurins (Maison at 23), 8th (01.42.66.93.80). M° Havre-Caumartin/RER Auber. **Open** 10am-7pm Mon-Sat. **Credit** MC, V. **Map G3**
Colourful streetwise basics (3mths to 14 years) at remarkably low prices; sizing tends to be small. 18 basic shops have been joined by DPAM Maison or DPAM bébé baby shops, which are great for gifts. **Branches include**: 122 rue du Fbg-St-Antoine (Maison at 120), 12th (01.43.44.67.46); 6 rue de l'Ouest (Maison at 15), 14th (01.43.20.59.51).

Petits Petons

135 rue du Fbg-St-Antoine, 11th (01.40.19.07.19). M° Ledru-Rollin. **Open** 10am-7pm Mon-Sat. **Credit** MC, V. **Map N7**
This children's shoe shop prices by size: all size 25-27 cost 259F, for example. Strong, sassy styles. **Branches**: 20 rue St-Placide, 6th (01.42.84.00.05); 23 rue Tronchet, 8th (01.47.42.75.69); 115 rue d'Alésia, 14th (01.45.42.80.52).

Educating the *petite* palate

Eating out is a vital part of French culture and even if the reverentially silent haute-cuisine temple or latest fashion restaurant is out of the question, it's perfectly possible to have an authentic French restaurant experience with the kids in tow. Most places will happily accept children as long as they are kept (relatively) under control.

Informality, speedy service, *croque monsieur*, salads, quiche, baguette sandwiches and chocolate mousse – not to mention the intrigue of expresso machines, beer pumps and lurid drinks – make cafés a good bet with small children. The **Pause Café** (41 rue de Charonne, 11th/ 01.48.06.80.33) seethes with arty Bastille types during the week; at weekends they bring their kids for savoury tarts and hot dishes. Up in Ménilmontant, young trendsetters can head for the copious Sunday brunch at **Café Cannibale** (93 rue Jean-Pierre-Timbaud, 11th/ 01.49.29.95.59) where a special area boasts small chairs and toys. *Crêperies* are another favourite for family outings, and are scattered all over town with a cluster in the Breton heartland of Montparnasse.

When it comes to special menus, most restaurants are sadly unadventurous and stick to the chicken/burger/frankfurter and chips formula. You may do better picking something from the main menu – why not try *boeuf aux carrottes*, roast lamb or *hachis Parmentier* (shepherd's pie)?

For an insight into native mores, try some of the city's old favourites, especially for weekend lunch when the French are most likely to dine out *en famille*. At **Thoumieux** (79 rue St-Dominique, 7th/01.47.05.46.44), you can watch locals from toddler to grannie dining out on traditional *blanquette de veau* or simple roast chicken. At the *belle époque* budget eatery **Chartier** (7 rue du Fbg-Montmartre, 9th/01.47.70.86.29) watching the bustling waiters is full-on entertainment, as at the **Brasserie de l'Isle St-Louis** (55 quai du Bourbon, 4th/01.43.54.02.59) where their well-seasoned repartee suits all ages and nationalities. Kids might try frankfurters and ham with *choucroute*, or there are omelettes and Berthillon ice cream. Toddlers and teenagers alike love the glamorous Art Deco brasserie **La Coupole** (102 bd du Montparnasse, 14th/01.43.20.14.20). It's a classic for steaks and oysters or you can sit in the café section at the front and watch the crowds on the boulevard. Perfect for combining food and sightseeing, **Altitude 95** (1st floor, Eiffel Tower, 7th/ 01.45.55.20.04) has a 46F child's *menu* and hard-to-beat location.

If you're hoping to introduce your offspring to fine French cuisine, top chef Guy Savoy's brasserie offshoot **Cap Vernet** (82 av Marceau, 8th/01.47.20.20.40) makes a rare effort to introduce young palates to gastronomy. The 79F Sunday child's lunch might feature ravioli de Royans, cod with polenta and wild mushrooms, and *clafoutis*.

If you're after organised fun, try ubiquitous steak house **Hippopotamus** (child's *menu* 47F) or the Yankee places, which offer special menus (burgers, nuggets, squidgy chocolate desserts, etc) amid colouring books, balloons, high chairs and decibels: **Chicago Meatpackers** (8 rue Coquillière, 1st/01.40.28.02.33/ child's *menu* 59F); or **Hard Rock Café** (14 bd Montmartre, 9th/01.53.24.60.00/child's *menu* 39F).

For kitsch exotica, **Le Président** (1st floor, 120-124 rue du Fbg-du-Temple, 11th/ 01.47.00.17.18) in Belleville has a vast choice of Chinese and Thai dishes, and on Saturday night you're sure to get the added spectacle of a Chinese wedding party. Nearby **New Nioullaville** (32 rue de l'Orillon, 11th/01.40.21.96.18) amuses with *dim sum* trolleys and fish tanks. There's more chopstick action at **Korean Barbecue** (1 rue du Dragon, 6th/01.42.22.26.63; 22 rue Delambre, 14th/01.43.35.44.32) where you barbecue your own strips of beef over a grill on the table. Finally, if you're hungry after a trawl round the Louvre, **Universelle Resto**, an international food court at the Carrousel du Louvre (01.47.03.96.58), lets you choose from different self-service outlets (pizza, Tex Mex, Lebanese *mezze*, tapas, ice cream, etc) and still sit at the same table.

Clubs

Style and snobbery still count more than the music, but there's a more laidback free party rebellion sweeping Parisian nightlife.

Club culture is more conservative in Paris than in London or Berlin. Musical trends take longer to infiltrate nightclubs, and the preferred clubbing drug of the masses remains alcohol. Numerous little clubs do fill up on weekends but stick strictly to chart music and *chanson française* – with tracks seemingly played in the same order (punters have been known to complain if they're not) every night by a resident DJ. Even in the trendiest clubs there is always at least one couple who dance rock 'n' roll to any type of music. Style and money count, and prime tables are reserved for those who buy drinks by the bottle, even in the hippest places.

A handful of clubs, however, have an up-to-date music policy (**Rex Club, Queen, Le Gibus**). Filtered French- and Chicago-style house dominate, with the odd techno, drum 'n' bass and hardcore night getting a look-in during the week. These clubs often rely on big-name DJs to pull in the crowds rather than a faithful clientele who have made the club their home. Crowd-pulling French DJs such as Laurent Garnier, Daft Punk and Dimitri from Paris, who have gained international fame, remain a select few; other DJs seem to fall in and out of fashion as often as hemlines. The names to look out for in 2000 are DJ Deep (who plays deep house at the Rex Club every Thursday), Charles Schilling, Dan Ghenacia, Rork, with Manu le Malin and Jack de Marseille for harder sounds. Drum 'n' bass DJs worth seeking out are Willyman, (tek step) Volta, Anakyme and Science.

Many Parisians venture out for huge monthly events organised by well-known promoters who make sure that their spot is the place to be for those susceptible to the fashion business hype, even if the DJs are mediocre and unknown. Well-reputed nights to look out for include TGV (Thanx God I'm a VIP), created by Silvie Chateigner and usually held at the Salle Wagram; David Guetta (of Les Bains)'s Scream and King$ at the **Elysée Montmartre**; BMK and Bitchy José, who organise events in big venues such as Salle Gaveau and the Bataclan; Black Label's drum 'n' bass nights at the Concorde Atlantique; and the ravey events put on by Magic Garden. After Mix Move and the Techno Parade (*for both see chapter* **Paris by Season**), numerous parties are held all over Paris.

FREE PARTY SPIRIT

There is an underground rebellion against the snobbery associated with clubbing, as more and more new-generation ravers turn to hardcore techno and drum 'n' bass, gabber and experimental hardcore with a 'free party' spirit more geared to everyday people than VIPs. Until recently this was quite a closed scene, with 'frees' being held in squats or on the outskirts of Paris, but now organisers, like DJ-booking agency Krysalid and Art 226, are holding parties within Paris, combining up to date DJs with free or affordable entrance and drinks, and established clubs, such as the Rex and Gibus, are cashing in with free hardcore events.

CLUB LORE

Getting into a club can be daunting. The door is often guarded by a posse of bulldog-type bouncers, euphemistically known as 'physiognomists', and the odd bitchy drag queen. The golden rule is, walk in like you own the place. In the trendy clubs trainers are acceptable but, if in doubt, wear shoes. A model hanging on your arm guarantees success. Clubs fill up quite late; the coolest people turn up at about 2am, although when big-name DJs play it is best to arrive early. After-hours parties are very popular and are often much more fun than club nights – they attract the real party animals who let loose. The most popular are 'Push' at the **Folies Pigalle** and 'Kwality' at the **Batofar**.

Paris is small enough for clubbers to do a circuit in one evening, often moving on every hour or so – during the week, many clubs offer free entry. There is a rich selection of world music and Latino clubs where punters dance non-stop well into the early hours. The unpretentious *bals* and *guinguettes* are a sure way to really let your hair down, as a mix of young and old gather for a good old knees-up and forget about style and image.

For on-the-ground info, look in *Time Out Paris* at the back of *Pariscope*, or for flyers. Having a flyer helps admission chances and free passes are often hidden among them. Check record shops (try rue Keller/11th), the Marais and hip bars, or tune in to Radio Nova (101.5FM) daily 5-8pm, and Radio FG (98.2FM) Mon-Fri 6.30pm and 7.30pm. Tekno Sphère has a pricey infoline, 08.36.68.01.09. Useful Minitel services are 3615 Party News, 3615 FG and 3615 Rave. For Internet users, www.FG.com is the most useful address.

Note that admission prices often include one free drink (*consommation*) and that credit cards are often accepted at the bar but not at the door. Many clubs close for all or part of August.

Well-behaved BCBGs get a buzz at the **Bus Palladium**.

Gilded Youth

These *clubs privés* (private clubs) make up the door policy as they go along. Prices and entry depend on the size of your wallet or length of your skirt. Dress: Bond, black, sharp and shiny.

Le Cabaret

68 rue Pierre-Charron, 8th (01.42.89.44.14).
M° Franklin D. Roosevelt. **Open** 11pm-4am Mon-Sat.
Admission free. **Drinks** 80F-100F.
Credit AmEx, DC, MC, V. **Map C4**
Eurobabes and wealthy young expats gather at this former cabaret for its trad red-velvet atmosphere. Fussy door staff have been known to allow in regulars but refuse entry to their friends.

Club Castel

15 rue Princesse, 6th (01.40.51.52.80). M° Mabillon.
Open 9pm-dawn Tue-Sat. **Admission** free
(members and guests only). **Drinks** 100F. **Credit**
AmEx, DC, MC, V. **Map H7**
Classy Castel reeks of wallet. Elitist door policy dictates that you must be nominated by two members to join, but it seems that if dressed like a yacht-owner you can breeze inside. Inside, the plush four-floor joint has relaxed its black-tie dress code since octogenarian Castel passed away, though many of his flush cronies still patronise the place. The saprophytic girls are all stunning; only the sour-faced, *liftée* wives don't seem to be enjoying themselves.

Duplex

2bis av Foch, 16th (01.45.00.45.00). M° Charles-de-
Gaulle-Etoile. **Open** 11pm-dawn Tue-Sun.

Admission 100F Tue-Thur, Sun (girls free before midnight); 120F with drink Fri, Sat. **Drinks** 60F.
Credit AmEx, MC, V. **Map C3**
The Duplex caters for young wannabes and marrigeable children of 'Untel' (youth relying on their parent's name and money) often adorned in clothing more suited to their aristocratic grannies. At weekends, there's a queue down the street. A sultry restaurant upstairs serving modern cuisine (spicy prawns, monkfish) from 9pm transforms into a chillout room (or green out when Champagne has flowed too freely for unaccustomed palates).

Cool Clubs

Door policy at these clubs can be incomprehensible – bouncers are given free reign. Club babes and *lookés* are often given priority. A foreign accent helps but if they don't know your face they may just bar your way. Dress: hip but smart (first-timers should avoid trainers).

Les Bains

7 rue du Bourg-l'Abbé, 3rd (01.48.87.01.80).
M° Etienne-Marcel. **Open** 11.30pm-5am daily.
Restaurant 8.30pm-1am. **Admission** 100F Mon-
Thur; 120F Fri-Sun. **Drinks** 70F. **Credit** AmEx, MC,
V. **Map K5**
Les Bains remains the venue for star spotting and home to the beautiful people (free Champagne for models ensures that the chairs are always draped with six-foot beauties), but under Cathy and David Guetta's management, the music is right, too. It is packed every night, but tourists with money to

spend often strike lucky on the door. A surefire method is to book a table at the restaurant, where the real VIPs hang out. Downstairs, the music policy is surprisingly modern with quality DJs spinning house, garage and hip hop on Wednesday and a successful gay night on Monday.

Bus Palladium

6 rue Fontaine, 9th (01.53.21.07.33). Mº Pigalle.
Open 11pm-dawn Tue-Sat. **Admission** 100F (girls free Tue). **Drinks** 50F-80F, Tue free drinks for women. **Credit** AmEx, MC, V. **Map H2**
The odd star pops in here for a drink but the tone is set by French *BCBGs* (Sloanes) who just want to party. It seems that even they want to dance to more up-to-date music as 80s rock and disco are being replaced by commercial house at the weekends.

Hammam Club

94 rue d'Amsterdam, 9th (01.55.07.80.00). Mº Place de Clichy. **Open** 8.30pm-dawn Tue-Sun. **Admission** free Tue-Thur, Sun; 100F Fri-Sat . **Drinks** 50F-70F. **Credit** AmEx, MC, V. **Map G2**
This luxurious restaurant with an Oriental-style dance floor looks like a North African Bains Douches. At weekends, regulars follow their couscous by a boogie to the commercial house played by the resident DJ. Often hired out for private functions or one-offs, it is difficult to know what really goes on here.

Le Divan du Monde

75 rue des Martyrs, 18th (01.44.92.77.66). Mº Pigalle. **Open** 8.30pm/midnight-dawn daily. **Admission** free-120F. **Drinks** 25F-40F. **Credit** MC, V. **Map H2**
Although essentially a concert venue, le Divan sees an eclectic mix of alternative club nights at weekends. There are regular jungle, raï, ragga, R&B, Brazilian and trance events. As the programme is so diverse there is a good mix of people who may take a while to warm – but once defrosted they really go for it. *See chapter* **Music: Rock, Roots & Jazz**.

Elysée Montmartre

72 bd Rochechouart, 18th (01.44.92.45.38). Mº Anvers. **Open** varies. **Admission** 80F-250F. **Drinks** 25F-40F. **Credit** AmEx, DC, MC, V. **Map J2**
The enormous sprung dancefloor makes this one of the leading concert venues in Paris, despite atrocious air conditioning. Clubbers get a look-in too, for the gay Scream and King$, a straight techno/house event, both organised by David Guetta, Midas of the club circuit. Latin lovers head for the monthly Brazilian party put on by the Favela Chic. Second and fourth Saturdays each month welcome the popular Le Bal, where an eclectic set of all ages dances and *yéyés* to a live big band – but girls should come with partners if they want to relax, as it's fiercely predatory.

Folies Pigalle

11 pl Pigalle, 9th (01.48.78.25.26). Mº Pigalle. **Open** midnight-dawn Tue-Sat; 6pm-midnight Sun'. **Admission** free Mon-Thur, 100F Fri-Sat, 40F Sun. **Drinks** 30F-50F. **Credit** V. **Map G2**
This shady ex-strip joint depends on a hardcore of dedicated regulars. Friday and Saturday sees residents spin house and techno, shoving into next

morning's seedy Push. House and garage played by resident DJs rule, and they sometimes don't bother charging entrance during the week. Busy Black Blanc Beur on Sunday (*see chapter* **Gay & Lesbian**).

Le Gibus

18 rue du Fbg-du-Temple, 11th (01.47.00.78.88). Mº République. **Open** Tue 9pm-dawn, Wed-Sat midnight-dawn. **Admission** 50F Tue; free Wed-Thur; 100F Fri-Sun. **Drinks** 40F-50F. **Credit** AmEx, DC, MC, V. **Map L4**
The Gibus has moved a long way from the rock concerts and metal nights it was renowned for. The promoters seem to change every two years, resulting in regular revamps and a transitory clientele, although since recent incumbent Bitchy José, the emphasis has been gay. A VIP area has remained empty, as this grotto-like club has hedonism engrained in its walls, and remains the place to let loose and get wasted. The Gaia-concept trance night on Wednesday has a faithful following. Big-name DJs from the UK and US often bring in the crowds at weekends.

Planet Rock

The Club, 8 rue des Bernardins, 5th (01.43.36.21.66). Mº Maubert-Mutualité. **Open** 11.30pm-dawn Sat. **Admission** 70F; 50F with flyer. **Drinks** 20F-30F. **Credit** MC, V. **Map H2**
DJ G Grebo hosts Paris' virtually only indie night, spinning all manner of pop, alternative rock and big beat. The outfit has been losing out to dance culture, but it's a solid night out, and not overpriced. Be aware that Planet Rock is the night, not the club, and it has a habit of changing venue.

Le Queen

102 av des Champs-Elysées, 8th (01.53.89.08.90). Mº George V. **Open** midnight-dawn daily. **Admission** 50F Mon, Sun; free Tue, Thur; 30F Wed; 100F Fri, Sat. **Drinks** from 50F. **Credit** AmEx, DC, MC, V. **Map D4**
The Queen has become so popular it has launched its own magazine, featuring interviews with DJs and personalities alongside the pumped-up pecs. Wednesday's Respect, the only truly mixed night, has moved on to greater things and is currently doing a world tour. It has been replaced by Secret (the same thing, but 30F and more housey) with resident DJs Dimitri from Paris, Ivan Smagghe and Romain. It still gets so packed that buying a drink is a rigmarole. Thursday and Saturday are both theoretically exclusively gay, when full-on erotic podium dancers and drag queens rule the roost, and girls find it hard to get in unless accompanied by cute males. If you're super-duper camp, don't miss Monday's Disco Inferno and Sunday's Over Kitsch. *See chapter* **Gay & Lesbian**.

Rex Club

5 bd Poissonnière, 2nd (01.42.36.28.83). Mº Bonne-Nouvelle. **Open** 11pm-dawn Wed, Thur, Fri; 11.30pm-dawn Sat. **Admission** 60F Wed; 70F Thur-Fri; 80F Sat. **Drinks** 30F-50F.

The **Divan du Monde** *takes a while to warm up, but then it sizzles.*

Credit AmEx, MC, V. **Map J4**

The Rex prides itself on having quality DJs and refuses to join the VIP fashion hype surrounding Parisian clubs. Entry is refused only if the club is simply too full, which happens quite often (so it is best to arrive early when big name guests play), and the emphasis is on dancing rather than posing, as there are very few tables. The sound system is ear-blasting, and Automatik on Friday night, featuring the best of techno, makes you wish there was a chill-out room to cool down in.

Mainstream

A more mixed crowd at these clubs doesn't guarantee you'll get in with holes in your jeans. Dress: casual but clean.

L'Atlantis

32 quai d'Austerlitz, 13th (01.44.23.24.00). M° Quai de la Gare. **Open** 11pm-dawn Fri-Sat, public holidays. **Admission** 110F. **Drinks** 70F. **Credit** MC, V. **Map M9**

One of the many French Caribbean clubs which relies on a loyal clientele who dress up to the nines and never fail to show up every weekend. Women wear the tightest dresses possible and men wear suits. Once inside, punters wind down to the latest zouk and soukous but, before asking anyone to dance, check there are no jealous partners lurking.

La Locomotive

90 bd de Clichy, 18th (01.53.41.88.88). M° Blanche. **Open** 11pm-dawn daily. **Admission** 60F Mon-Thur, Sun; 100F Fri-Sat (80F before midnight). **Drinks** 40F-50F. **Credit** AmEx, MC, V. **Map G2**

Situated next to the Moulin Rouge, the cavernous three-floor Locomotive has a chronically untrendy reputation, but always packs out with grungy teenagers. In the past half-hearted attempts at techno nights have never proved popular, but that could change, with the arrival of successful jungle/hard techno night Alien Factory from the Gibus in January 2000. The odd hardcore metal concert and one-off event with quality DJs can also surprise.

Le Saint

7 rue St-Séverin, 5th (01.43.25.50.04). M° St-Michel. **Open** 11pm-dawn Tue-Sun. **Admission** free Tue-Wed; 60F Thur, Sun; 90F Fri. **Drinks** 30F. **Credit** DC, MC, V. **Map J7**

Relaxed and unpretentious, Le Saint is patronised mainly by students, au pairs and backpackers. However, it's cheerful and intimate, with a cute dancefloor in a cellar dating in parts to the thirteenth century, and the drinks won't break the bank. Music is a mix of French pop, disco, house and salsa.

Latino, Jazz & World

Latino clubs are one thing Parisians do especially well, and even if the *merengue* doesn't float your boat at home, it's worth having a look-in here. Dress: think Havana.

Le Balajo

9 rue de Lappe, 11th (01.47.00.07.87). M° Bastille. **Open** 9pm-2am Wed; 2.30-6.30pm, 10pm-5am Thur; 11.30pm-5.30am Fri, Sat; 2.30-6.30pm, 9pm-1am Sun. **Admission** 80F Wed (40F women); 100F Thur-Sat; 50F Thur afternoon, Sun. **Drinks** 50F-60F. **Credit** AmEx, DC, MC, V. **Map M7**

The ever-so-kitsch 'bal-à-Jo' (Jo's bal) has been going for over 60 years. Wednesday's rock 'n' roll, boogie and swing session attracts some colourful customers, but it's starting to look a bit washed out. Those in the know have jumped ship long ago, leaving the dance-floor to ditzy tourists, although redecoration is planned. Average age at the weekend tea dance is 70.

Caveau de la Huchette

5 rue de la Huchette, 5th (01.43.26.65.05). M° St-Michel. **Open** 9.30pm-2.30am Mon-Thur, Sun; 9.30pm-3.30am Fri, Sat. **Admission** 60F Mon-Thur, Sun; 55F students; 70F Fri, Sat. **Drinks** from 30F. **Credit** MC, V. **Map J7**

Unpretentious and hospitable, the Caveau has been a jazz hall since 1946 and is still high rollin'. During the week the dancefloor hosts ageing divorcées and wannabe Stones; come the weekend it packs out with a mixed age range of soulful jazz lovers enjoying a bopping rock'n'roll or jazz live act. One of the only places you can catch staff dancing with the clientele. *See chapter* **Music: Rock, Roots & Jazz.**

La Chapelle des Lombards

19 rue de Lappe, 11th (01.43.57.24.24). M° Bastille. **Open** 10.30pm-dawn Thur-Sat; concert Thur 8.30pm (60F-80F). **Admission** 100F Thur (women free before midnight); 120F Fri-Sat. **Drinks** 30F-75F. **Credit** AmEx, MC, V. **Map M7**

A mixed crowd of tourists and Latino and African residents sweats it out in this cramped venue. DJ Natalia La Tropikal mixes salsa, merengue, zouk and tango on weekends. Live concert on Thursdays before the tango begins.

Dancing de la Coupole

102 bd du Montparnasse, 14th (01.43.20.14.20). M° Vavin. **Open** 10pm-4am Tue; 9.30pm-4am Fri, Sat, 3-9pm Sun. **Admission** 40F-100F. **Drinks** 55F-70F. **Credit** AmEx, DC, MC, V. **Map G9**

The basement '*dancing*' of the Art Deco brasserie was one of the first in Paris to risk the tango in the 20s. It still plays Latino tunes, but to a more touristy crowd. A place to flirt and mingle, like most salsa clubs, but more relaxed than predatory.

Les Etoiles

61 rue du Château d'Eau, 10th (01.47.70.60.56). M° Château d'Eau. **Open** 9pm-3.30am Thur; 9pm-4.30am Fri-Sat; 6.30pm. **Admission** 120F with meal; 60F/100F without/with drink from 11pm. **Drinks** 20F-40F. **No credit cards. Map K3**

Formerly a cinema, Les Etoiles has got class. Top-notch musicians electrify a soulful crowd of Latino lovers. There's not much space, but that doesn't stop night-owl groovers giving it loads. Women are not liable to stand around for more than a couple of minutes, and veterans dish out footwork advice on the go as the evening unfolds.

La Java

105 rue du Fbg-du-Temple, 10th (01.42.02.20.52).
M° Belleville. **Open** 11pm-6am Thur-Sat; Sun 2-7pm.
Admission 60F-80F Thur; 100F Fri-Sat; 30F
Sun. **Drinks** 35F-50F. **Credit** AmEx, DC, MC, V.
Map M4

La Java oozes style as a subterranean salsa venue
with a lacquered dancefloor that hosted Piaf. Today
the glamour is still brought alive by the Cuban heels
of hundreds of Latino devotees. The broad spectrum
of talent reflects the extraordinary clientele. Look
out for the *bal* on Sundays, which attracts all ages.

Bar Clubs

These laid-back clubs are some of the better places
to watch live bands and hear the latest music. Some
fashionable restaurants, such as Alcazar and Man
Ray *(see chapter* **Restaurants***)*, are also holding DJ
nights attracting a young yuppie clientele.

Batofar

facing 11 quai François-Mauriac, 13th
(01.56.29.10.00). M° Bibliothèque. **Open** Tue-Sun
8pm-2am. **Admission** free-60F. **Drinks** 15F-45F.
Credit MC, V. **Map N10**

A combination of bar, club and concert venue, this
lighthouse boat from the Irish Sea has become the
most interesting nighttime venue in Paris.
Alternative and often electronic music concerts are
followed by quality DJs, who pack out the dancefloor. Every season the art and music scene of a
European city is represented by means of a festival
with Vienna and London in the pipeline. *See chapter* **Music: Rock, Roots & Jazz**.

Fabled labels

These are the hottest new labels and hippest DJs
in the booming French recording industry.

F Comm

In five years, this has become the major French
house and techno label. Started by veteran DJ
Laurent Garnier.
Artists: Laurent Garnier, Juan Trip, Frédéric
Galliano, Chaotik Ramses, Scan X, Nova Nova,
M Oizo.
Genre: Better known for techno and house but
has also signed pop/rock and retro jazz artists.
Where to find it: Laurent makes an occasional
appearance at the Rex, and F Comm has a special
link with the Batofar.
Philosophy: 'Paris isn't the centre of the universe
as there are interesting music scenes developing in
the rest of France which shouldn't be ignored.'

Yellow

Its first record *Indian Vibes* has been
re-released twice since 1994's original release.
Since then the acid jazz trend has moved on to
house and trip hop – and so has Yellow with a mix
of Latino influences and up-to-date beats.
Artists: Kid Loco, Bob Sinclar, Dimitri from Paris,
Bossa Trés.
Genre: Trip hop, house, Latino, acid jazz.
Where: No regular nights for Yellow; most of its
artists only play huge promotional events,
although Dimitri can be spotted at Secret every
Wednesday at the Queen. A promotional Yellow
night is organised every six months and DJ Yellow
makes an appearance if a crowd is guaranteed.
Philosophy: 'We make coffee-table records rather
than throw-away floor fillers.'

Prozak

Prozak got off to a good start in 1994 with Alëem's
'Félix Yo' and, although Alëem no longer exist its
recent baby Kojak is putting the funk into French

house. Prozak's forte is self promotion with a gift
for eye-catching logos.
Artists: Kojak, Seven Dub, Grant Fabio, Whash.
Genre: Techno, funky house, dub.
Where: A Prozak night is held every first
Saturday at the Gibus. Kojak plays regular sets at
the Rex and Les Bains.
Philosophy: 'We produce music that we like, if
others are into it then *tant mieux.*'

Euterpe and Vitamine

Started in 1998, Euterpe is already showing
potential. Sister label Vitamine specialises in house.
Artists: Olivier Le Castor, Thésee, Scratch
Massive, Oxymore, Demon Richie.
Genre: Techno, electronica, house.
Where: As they haven't been around for very
long it is hard to say but promotional sets have
been performed at the Queen and Batofar. They
have also created a gallery (41 rue de Poitou, 4th)
to promote urban artists.
Philosophy: 'There is more to Paris than French
filtered house.'

Comet Records

Specialising in compilations mixing world music
with modern influences, Comet was started by the
founders of the jazzy concert venue/club Cithéa.
Artists: Tony Allen, Toy Sun, Smadj.
Genre: Jazzy vibes, African rhythms, modern beats.
Where: Although Comet runs Cithéa, its bands
rarely play there as it isn't the right crowd. It
prefers the more avant-garde Batofar.
Philosophy: 'To pioneer and help launch the Afro
beat revival.'

Cithéa

114 rue Oberkampf, 11th (01.40.21.70.95).
Mº Parmentier. **Open** 9.30pm-5am daily.
Admission free Mon, Tue, Sun; 30F Wed, Thur; 60F
Fri, Sat. **Drinks** 35F-60F. **Credit** MC, V. **Map M5**
A quality concert venue for jazz, funk and world
music early on in the evening – but the late licence
attracts all the dregs of the surrounding bars, making weekends a sweaty, uncomfortable nightmare.
Women can't stand alone for more than 30 seconds
without an arm slithered around their waist or a
beery chat-up attempt. Disco and funk reign. *See
chapter* **Music: Rock, Roots & Jazz**.

Factory Café

20 rue du Fbg-St-Antoine, 12th (01.43.45.32.51).
Mº Bastille. **Open** 9pm-6am daily. **Admission** 50F.
Drinks 30F-40F. **Credit** AmEx, DC, MC, V. **Map M7**
Owned by the same team as the Folies Pigalle, the
stark futuristic décor has never quite attracted the
clientele desired. Once a place for fly hip hop boys
and chic R&B lovers to sway in, it is trying to steer
towards the house clientele but relies on a Bastille
location rather than the music to fill the place.
Wheelchair access.

Satellit' Café

44 rue de la Folie-Méricourt, 11th (01.47.00.48.87).
Mº Oberkampf. **Open** 8pm-3am Tue-Thur; 8pm-6am
Fri Sat. **Admission** 50F. **Drinks** 34F-50F. **Credit**
V. **Map M5**
With the rise of the Oberkampf area, this world-music
bar has come into its own, drawing all styles, ages
and races for laidback fun and eclectic sounds. Live
sets (Tue-Thur) showcase talents from Kurdistan to
Rajasthan. Afterwards and at weekends, DJ Philippe
gets the floor moving to French gypsy bands,
Moroccan folk and vintage US funk. Great sound-sys-
tem and attitude kept to a minimum.

Popin

*105 rue Amelot, 11th (01.48.05.56.11). Mº Filles du
Calvaire.* **Open** 6.30pm-1.30am Tue-Sun. **Admission**
free. **Drinks** 14F-35F. **Credit** AmEx, MC, V. **Map L5**
Three small floors pack out with a relaxed overspill
from nearby rue Oberkampf. Predominantly French,
with more than a smattering of students, it also
attracts savvy young internationals looking for a pint
(35F for Kilkenny or Guinness, pitchers at 90F).
Downstairs, the tiny dancefloor heaves at weekends
after midnight as local DJs spin whatever they
fancy, from big beat and hip hop to indie classics.

Underworld Café

25 rue Oberkampf, 11th (01.48.06.35.36)
Mº Oberkampf. **Open** 6pm-2am Mon-Sat.
Admission free-30F. **Drinks** 20F-40F.
Credit AmEx, MC, V. **Map M5**
Weeknights offer an eclectic selection of music from
drum 'n' bass, trip hop, big beat and experimental
electronic to Latin house and UK garage. Weekends
are reserved for quality house and techno and the
occasionally sweaty drum 'n' bass event. When
things really hot up the tables get pushed back and
everyone goes for it. Mondays give unknown DJs a
chance to spin their sounds.

Guinguettes

If you want a taste of authentic dancefloor style,
head to the old-fashioned *guinguette* dancehalls
along the river Marne. Age: 7-70. Dress: floral
frocks for her, *matelot* shirts for him.

Chez Gégène

*162bis quai de Polangis, 94340 Joinville-le-Pont
(01.48.83.29.43). RER Joinville-le-Pont.* **Open** *Apr-
Oct* 9pm-2am Fri, Sat (live band); 7pm-midnight Sun
(recorded). **Admission** 90F (drink); 210F (dinner).
Credit AmEx, MC, V.
This is the classic *guinguette*, unaltered for years.
Elderly French dance fiends, dapper *galants*, multi-
generational families and young Parisians pack the
place. Eat at the front and move to the dance area
later, or dine near the dancefloor and get up for a
quick foxtrot, tango, classic *musette* or rock'n'roll
number between courses.

Guinguette du Martin-Pêcheur

*41 quai Victor-Hugo, 94500 Champigny-sur-Marne
(01.49.83.03.02). RER Champigny-sur-Marne.* **Open**
1 Apr-15 Nov 8pm-2am Tue-Sat; noon-8pm Sun; *10
Nov-23 Dec* Fri-Sat 8pm-2am. **Admission** free Tue-Sat,
40F Sunday. **Drinks** 15F-20F. **No credit cards.**
The youngest (built in the 1980s) and hippest of the
dancehalls is on a tiny, tree-shaded island reached
by raft. The music is great (live orchestra Sat and
Sun afternoon), and it's fun to watch the cute young
trendies trying to look like Gabin and Piaf.

DJ M-Boo on board the **Batofar**.

Dance

A century after the city saw the birth of modern dance, Paris offers the lot from traditional tutus to the virtual dancer.

It's hard to believe that modern dance was born 100 years ago in an inconspicuous Paris flat on avenue de Villiers thanks to an unknown but determined 22-year-old Californian. Isadora Duncan still fascinates people the world over and her grave at Père Lachaise rivals Jim Morrison for visitors. Duncan's revolutionary, even scandalous, ideas (still promoted by the International Isadora Duncan Center/01.43.67.31.92) opened a galaxy of new possibilities in dance: improvising barefoot to classical masterpieces in comfortable unrestricted garments, and promoting dance as a part of children's education. Every dancer-choreographer in France since has found inspiration in her life and art from the Ballets Russes in the 1910s to Maurice Béjart today.

The past century has witnessed more movement experimentation and melting-pot styles in Paris than anywhere else on the continent. But in 2000 it sometimes seems as if everything has already been said and done. Choreographers Boris Charmatz, Christine Bastin and Jean-Michel Agius have resorted to nudity or simulated sex on stage to secure the attention of the 'boys' at the Culture Ministry. Brilliant José Montalvo dabbles in *branché* high-tech. Jean-Christophe Maillot of the Ballets de Monte-Carlo and Maryse Delente of the Ballets du Nord remain more marginal, happily defending their own refreshing aesthetic. The **Ballet de l'Opéra National** remains the pillar of good dance, with a versatile young *corps de ballet* capable of handling any style choreographed for it.

Danse contemporaine had its peak in the 1980s and early 90s fostered by the **Théâtre de la Ville**, but the violent, dismal or overly mellow mood of one-to-many productions have made a fun-seeking public weary, if not cynical. Smaller venues, like **Théâtre de la Bastille** and the **Regard du Cygne**, have gone 'dance light', programming more lucrative music and theatre. As the dance scene becomes increasingly institutionalised, and supply is greater than demand, promising smaller companies never get a break, while countless dancers without the right diplomas or contacts have to reconvert their careers.

Paradoxically, a century after the barefoot revolution, shoes seem to be back on – these days, Nikes and Reeboks in place of Repetto – since it's the less intellectual, more physical, hip hop-related urban dance forms that are drawing a generation of young people who've turned to dance to vent their fears, their anger and their expectations.

Major Dance Venues

Ballet de l'Opéra National de Paris

Palais Garnier *pl de l'Opéra, 9th (08.36.69.78.68).* *M° Opéra.* **Box office** 11am-6.30pm Mon-Sat. **Tickets** 30F-420F. **Credit** AmEx, MC, V. **Map F4**
Opéra de Paris Bastille *pl de la Bastille, 12th (08.36.69.78.68).* *M° Bastille.* **Box office** 11am-6.30pm Mon-Sat. **Tickets** 65F-420F. **Credit** AmEx, MC, V. **Map L7**
After a marvellous renovation of the interior, Palais Garnier now has its exterior wrapped in a wooden box. However, the show goes on. The 1999-2000 season has modern works on an equal footing with the Romantic classics. Revivals include Angelin Preljocaj's controversial ballet about sexuality *Casanova*. There are contemporary creations by Mats Ek, Ohad Naharin of the Batsheva Dance Company, and the guest Nederlands Dans Theatre Jiří Kylián. Romantic ballet fans can indulge in *Cinderella* and *Giselle*. Bastille focuses more on opera; exceptions include a revival of Carolyn Carlson's colourful *Signes* and Nureyev's *Raymonda*.
Wheelchair access (reserve ahead on 01.40.01.18.08).

Centre Pompidou/IRCAM

4th (01.44.78.48.16). *M° Hôtel de Ville/ RER Châtelet-Les Halles.* **Box office** 10am-6pm Mon-Sat. **Tickets** 90F; 60F under-26s. **Credit** AmEx, MC, V. **Map K6**
Dance, sometimes linked to the exhibitions, is on the agenda at the reopened Centre Pompidou, while affiliated IRCAM inaugurated a dance lab in 1998 under François Raffinot. Guests in 2000 include Mark Tompkins and Meg Stuart, and in June the Festival Agora mixes contemporary music and dance.
Wheelchair access.

Châtelet – Théâtre Musical de Paris

1 pl du Châtelet, 1st (01.40.28.28.40). *M° Châtelet.* **Box office** 11am-7pm daily. **Tickets** 30F-345F. **Credit** AmEx , MC, V. **Map H6**
The TMP is essentially a lyric theatre, but the occasional ballet company is hosted, especially when accompanied by a live orchestra. Maurice Béjart's rather kitsch *Nutcracker* led the way in December 1999; 2000 includes two programmes by the excellent Lyon Opéra Ballet and, in May, a not-to-be-missed original music and dance collaboration between soprano Jessye Norman and New York modern jazz choreographer Bill T Jones.
Wheelchair access.

Théâtre de la Bastille

76 rue de la Roquette, 11th (01.43.57.42.14). *M° Bastille.* **Box office** 10am-6.30pm Mon-Fri;

2-6.30pm Sat. **Tickets** 120F; 80F students under-26; over 60s. **Credit** AmEx, MC, V. **Map L6**

Rivalled only by the Théâtre de la Ville in promoting avant-garde movement, the Théâtre de la Bastille has emerged from a difficult period with an international menu that is more diverse than ever. Y2K dance includes *Extra Dry* by Emio Greco, and a double bill by outrageous Hungarian Josef Nadj.

Théâtre des Champs-Elysées

15 av Montaigne, 8th (01.49.52.50.50). M° Alma-Marceau. **Box office** 1-7pm Mon-Sat.; *phone* 10am-noon, 2-6pm Mon-Fri. **Tickets** 60F-390F. **Credit** AmEx, MC, V. **Map C5**

This elegant 1900-seat concert hall, was made famous by Isadora Duncan and Nijinsky. Alongside concerts attracting a tie-and-tails crowd, there are regular dance programmes, like Tango Pasión and the bienniel Paris International Dance Festival, which features world-renowned companies. *Wheelchair access.*

Théâtre de la Ville

2 pl du Châtelet, 4th (01.42.74.22.77). M° Châtelet. **Box office** 11am-7pm Mon; 11am-8pm Tue-Sat. **Tickets** 95F-190F; 70F-90F under-27s on day. **Credit** DC, MC, V. **Map H6**

Paris' leading contemporary dance forum for the *branché* artsy crowd also offers ethnic dance (Indian and flamenco primarily) at the Théâtre des Abbesses (31 rue des Abbesses, 18th). The 1000-seat Châtelet auditorium has excellent sight lines, a strong policy of co-productions and popular prices. The same famous names return frequently: Régine Chopinot, Susanne Linke, Lucinda Childs, Anne Teresa de Keersmaeker and the diva Pina Bausch. Book way in advance, since a successful subscription system leaves only a scattering of seats for the best shows. *Wheelchair access.*

Independent Dance Spaces

Centre Mandapa

6 rue Wurtz, 13th (01.45.89.01.60). M° Glacière. **Box office** 30min ahead or reserve by phone. **Tickets** 80F-120F; 60F-70F students, over-60s; 40F under 5s. **No credit cards. Map H1**

This traditional Indian dance and music centre runs classes and invites companies from India, China, the Middle East, North Africa and Eastern Europe.

Danse Théâtre & Musique (DTM)

6 rue de la Folie-Méricourt, 11th (01.47.00.19.60). M° St.-Ambroise. **Box office** 10am-7pm Mon-Sat. **Tickets** 80F; 60F students, over 60s. **No credit cards. Map L5**

A pioneer contemporary dance space located in a former convent, the friendly 70-seat DTM offers original dance, dance-theatre and music at weekends by lesser-known, but innovative independent companies, including affiliated company Tendanse.

L'Etoile du Nord

16 rue Georgette-Agutte, 18th (01.42.26.47.47). M° Guy-Môquet. **Box office** 10am-6pm Mon-Fri. **Tickets** 50F-120F; 80F students, over 60s; 50F under-26s. **Credit** MC, V.

The ex-Théâtre Dix-Huit has become a serious platform for the more off-beat multimedia contemporary dance scene. 2000 includes *Faits d'Hivers* and short pieces by young dancemakers in *Les Jaloux*.

Charles Cré-ange paints the town red in Movies *at the* **Théâtre de la Ville.**

Le Regard du Cygne

210 rue de Belleville, 20th (01.43.58.55.93).
M° Place des Fêtes or Télégraphe. **Ticket** prices
vary. **No credit cards.**
This historic barn has played an important role over
the past 15 years in promoting new choreographic
talent through its eclectic Worksweeks. New series
Le Regard Kiss-Signe focuses on either male or
female choreographers and *Spectacles Sauvages* is a
fun free-for-all, during which anybody (or nearly)
who wants to dance for a few minutes can...

Théâtre de la Cité Internationale

21 bd Jourdan, 14th (01.43.13.50.50).
RER Cité Universitaire. **Box office** 2-7pm Mon-Sat.
Tickets 110F; 80F over-60s; 55F under-26s, Mon.
No credit cards.
The Cité Universitaire theatre has grown from a
modest student space to a mature professional dance
and theatre venue, thanks to its affiliation with the
Festival d'Automne and the annual Iles de Danses.
Wheelchair access (call ahead).

Information & Classes

Centre National de la Danse

1 rue Victor Hugo, 93507 Pantin (01.41.83.27.27).
M° Hoche. **Open** 9.30am-7pm Mon-Fri.
A former administrative complex has become the
headquarters of the state-funded dance centre. The
Théâtre Contemporain de la Danse (9 rue Geoffroy-
l'Asnier, 4th/01.42.74.44.22), rebaptised Maison des
Compagnies et des Spectacles, is now an annex with
documentation centre, rehearsal space and studio-the-
atre. Classes are also held at the Ménagerie de Verre.

Dance Classes

Académie des Arts Chorégraphiques *4bis Cité
Véron, 18th (01.42.52.07.29).* *M° Blanche.* **Map G2**
Ateliers de Paris-Carolyn Carlson *Cartoucherie
de Vincennes, 12th (01.41.74.17.07).* *M° Château de
Vincennes, then bus 112.*
Centre de Danse du Marais *41 rue du Temple,
4th (01.42.72.15.42).* *M° Hôtel de Ville.* **Map K6**
Centre International Danse Jazz *54bis rue de
Clichy, 9th (01.53.32.75.00).* *M° Place de Clichy or
Liège.* **Map G2**
Centre Chorégraphique Blanca Li *7 rue des
Petites-Ecuries, 10th (01.53.34.04.05).* *M° Château
d'Eau.* **Map K3**
Salle Pleyel *252 rue du Fbg-St-Honoré, 8th
(01.45.61.53.00)* *M° Ternes.* **Map D3**
Most studios offer a variety of classes in contemporary,
ballet, jazz and ethnic dance forms. Pleyel is home to
several ballet-oriented schools. Carolyn Carlson's new
centre offers professional training and workshops in
dance, improvisation, theatre and music.

International Dance Council (UNESCO)

1 rue Miollis, 15th (01.45.68.25.54). *M° Ségur.*
Open hours vary, call for appointment. **Map E8**
Greek dance activist Alkis Raftis aims to make the
Council a hub of international exchange, through
publications, CD-roms and a website. Conferences,
seminars and lecture-demos are planned for 2000.

Virtual steps

Choreography is taking a techno and technological turn as dancemakers are dabbling
more and more with computer effects and
seeking ingenious ways to bring online and
on-screen dance on stage.

It all started with 80-year-old US veteran
Merce Cunningham, who back in the prehistoric days of computer technology, was
already creating productions set to random
electronic music improvised by John Cage.
Back in Paris recently with a revolutionary
new work *Biped*, Cunningham mesmerised
audiences at the Théâtre de la Ville, as three-
dimensional Jurassic Park-sized dancing figures emerged magically from every corner of
the theatre to engage in *pas de deux* and hide-
and-seek sequences with comparatively
Liliputian flesh-and-blood dancers.

European choreographers have been taking up the model. For years William
Forsythe's productions have included computers, but in a more conventional way. Pina
Bausch and Anne Teresa de Keersmaeker
regularly incorporate video, as did Maurice
Béjart in his recent *Nutcracker*. But a couple
of new talents have come to the fore, especially José Montalvo, whose *Dans le Jardin Io
Io Ito Ito* at the Théâtre de la Ville (*pictured*)
created a sensation with projected imaginary
half-human creatures who blended with the
troupe in hilarious dance sequences. The
Paris Opéra grabbed him to create a work for
its repertoire, *Rire de la Lyre,* the first high-
tech work of this kind to be shown at Palais
Garnier, a humorously surreal transposition
of La Fontaine's fairytales.

There will always be propless purists and
costumeless minimalists who believe the only
artistic marriage possible with dance is
music, but the new choreographic generation
is inventing all the time. Perhaps in a few
years, real dancers may not be needed at all.

Film

French cinema still stirs polemic but Europe's leading cinema industry is struggling to make good its promises.

As the last reel of 1999 unwound, the state of French cinema hit the headlines once again. The spark was a letter from director Patrice Leconte to fellow French directors, deploring the perceived 'disloyal' anti-French stance of French critics, that was sent by mistake to the newspapers. Twelve un-named directors including Leconte promptly drafted a manifesto that was distributed to film-goers outside cinemas, complaining about apparently systematically hostile criticism to French films in weeklies *Télérama* and *Les Inrockuptibles* and dailies *Libération* and *Le Monde* (but, interestingly, none of the specialist film magazines). If such abuses were allowed to continue, the manifesto went on, French cinema was in danger of dying out. By way of remedy, it was suggested that negative reviews of French films should not be published until a week after the film's release – although positive reviews could be printed at any time, and foreign product could be slammed at any time. Cinema critics responded in suitably robust terms, and Claude Miller (director of *Garde à vue* and *La Classe de neige*), president of ARP (associ-ation of directors, producers and screenwriters) resigned, unable to put up with the bickering.

There's little the French media love as much as a good row, but the spat was at least a salutary reminder of how seriously the French take the seventh art, and – perhaps more significantly – how woefully out of touch with public tastes French filmmakers have become. Laying the blame on the critics betrays sloppy thinking, but the resulting discussion could only be healthy.

All this might seem a strange state of affairs in a country where cinema attendance in 1999 was nearly twice as high as in 1998, when French feature releases numbered 127 and *Astérix contre César* broke French box office records, and with France still leading the European league for the number of first films. It's only when the box office figures are split up that the worries of Leconte and co become easier to understand. Overall, attendance for French films is in steady decline, and yet the homegrown films keep coming.

Certainly for the time being, there's a shortage of challenging fare. More often than not French

A heavy burden for French cinema: Astérix et Obélix contre César.

films are dialogue-driven (note the respect which surrounds the Jean-Pierre Bacri-Agnès Jaoui partnership, authors of such charming gems as *Un Air de famille* and *On connaît la chanson*), rather than cinematic: the results too often feel like filmed theatre or TV movies (which, to all intents and purposes, many TV-funded films are). Diane Kurys' *Les Enfants du siècle*, focusing on the literary love affair between Alfred de Musset and George Sand, was in many ways typical, blending star-crossed love with literature and sweeping costumes. Love in crisis is stock cinematic subject matter in the country that claims to have invented romance, but how much longer can France go on churning out tales of (usually Paris-based) marriages or affairs gone or going wrong, featuring middle-aged, middle-class urban professionals? What became of the talk two or three years back of 'multicultural revolution' and the 'new direction' suggested by *La Haine*? Why is there nothing in cinema to equal the current boom of immigrant novelists? Where are the films for children, or adequate successors to the popular crime movies of the 50s and 60s? Where are the scriptwriters of the calibre of Michel Audiard (whose razor-edged dialogues find some echoes in Bacri-Jaoui scripts)? Above all, where is the willingness to explore new ways of telling a story in film? Answers to these questions provide a gloomy picture. Yesterday's media darling Matthieu Kassovitz now looks like an oddity: his gritty approach came unstuck with *Assassin(s)*, and his next film is a more traditional thriller adapted from best-selling novel *Les rivières pourpres*, due out in summer 2000. Could it point to a revival of the genre movie?

There are factors to offset the gloom. Women directors are more common in France than in the US, and despite the Paris-heavy setting of many movies, films are being made elsewhere, with Rohmer, Robert Guédigian and Bruno Dumont (writer-director of *L'Humanité*, showered with prizes at Cannes in 1999). A rare piece of experimentation came in *Sombre*, Philippe Grandrieux' daringly disorienting portrait of a serial killer.

And then there's the amazing availability of foreign films in Paris itself, which may, given time, inspire filmmakers to strike out in new directions, and the sheer variety and number of films screened in the capital in any given week, combined with cinema tickets significantly cheaper than in, say, London. The reasons for this variety: cinema has a strong place in French culture, underpinned by an intelligent press willing to give space to obscure films or newcomers, with the result that the public is better informed and in turn willing to try something new. The hostility of the critics is less dangerous to the health of French cinema than the complacency of the filmmakers. As digital technology steadily rewrites the rules of movie-making, French filmmakers have much to chew over.

Aladdin's flicks

The Left Bank ciné village may be shabby, but don't be fooled – its programming is state of the arthouse with timely, thoughtful retrospectives alongside an eclectic pick of current releases. A week's programming might throw up a new print of the *Wizard of Oz*, a John Malkovich season and a 'Panorama des Western'. Moreover you can always catch up on classics like *The Rocky Horror Picture Show* or *Ai No Corrida*. 'I came to France having grown up in LA where the studios dictated what we saw,' says Bob Swaim, Francophile American director of Paris homage *Le Balance*. 'I came to a wealth and diversity of cinema which I found extraordinary. I don't know any other city in the world which has this.' But this diversity is under threat from market forces, the multiplex and the French majors. 'It's more and more difficult because there are fewer and fewer independents, many have been taken over by the big boys. Small cinemas are disappearing because it is difficult to get the films,' says Jean-Marie Rodon of the Action group which moved here from the 9th in the early 80s. 'The next few years are crucial. These cinemas are rightly regarded as national heritage. Even if *Astérix* was pipped at the box office in 1999 by US blockbuster *Star Wars*, France still has its unique Left Bank ciné village. **Action Ecoles** *23 rue des Ecoles, 5th (01.43.29.79.89).* **Le Champo** *51 rue des Ecoles, 5th (01.43.54.51.60).* **Europa Panthéon** *13 rue Victor-Cousin, 5th (01.43.54.15.04).* **Grand Action** *5 rue des Ecoles, 5th (01.43.29.44.40).* **Racine Odéon** *6 rue de l'Ecole-de-Médecine, 6th (01.43.26.19.68).* **Reflet Médicis Logos** *3 rue Champollion, 5th (01.43.54.42.34).* **St-André-des-Arts** *30 rue St-André-des-Arts, 6th (01.43.26.48.18).* **Studio Galande** *42 rue Galande, 5th (08.36.68.06.24).* **Studio des Ursulines** *10 rue des Ursulines, 5th (01.43.26.19.09).*

Ciné Showcases

Le Cinéma des Cinéastes
7 av de Clichy, 17th (01.53.42.40.20). M° Place Clichy. **Map G2**
This three-screen showcase of world cinema (with France at the forefront) was the brainchild of Jean-Jacques *Betty Blue* Beneix and Claude Miller, now ex-president of ARP, the association of French cinema directors and producers. As well as meet-the-director sessions, it has held festivals of Israeli, gay and documentary films. Short films on Fridays.
Air conditioning. Wheelchair access.

Dôme IMAX
1 pl du Dôme, 92095 Paris La Défense (01.46.92.45.50/ 08.36.67.06.06). M° La Défense. **Tickets** 57F; 44F students, over-60s. **Map inset**
This 1114m^2 OMNIMAX screen is the ideal locale for experiencing startling cinema-in-the-round, such as *Les Mystères de l'Egypte* or *Fantasia 2000*.
Wheelchair access.

Gaumont Grand Ecran Italie
30 pl d'Italie, 13th (08.36.68.75.13). M° Place d'Italie. **Map J10**
The huge complex by Japanese architect Kenzo Tange boasts the biggest screen (24m x 10m) in Paris.
Air conditioning. Wheelchair access.

La Géode
26 av Corentin-Cariou, 19th (01.40.05.12.12). M° Porte de la Villette. **Tickets** 57F; 44F students, disabled; *two films* 60F. **Credit** MC, V. **Map inset**
An OMNIMAX cinema housed in a glorious, shiny geodesic dome at La Villette. Most films feature dizzying 3D plunges through dramatic natural scenery. Booking is advisable.
Wheelchair access (reserve ahead).

Le Grand Rex
1 bd Poissonnière, 2nd (08.36.68.05.96). M° Bonne Nouvelle. **Map J4**
The huge Art Deco cinema has blockbuster programming that matches the vast setting, although most foreign fare is dubbed into French.
Air conditioning. Wheelchair access.

Max Linder Panorama
24 bd Poissonnière, 9th (01.48.24.88.88/ 08.36.68.00.31). M° Grands Boulevards. **Map J9**
A state-of-the-art screening facility in a house founded in 1919 by comic Linder. Look out for all-nighters.
Air conditioning. Wheelchair access.

MK2 sur Seine
14 quai de la Seine, 19th (08.36.68.47.07). M° Stalingrad or Jaurès. **Map M2**
Flagship of the ever-expanding MK2 group, this stylish six-screen, canalside complex, complete with restaurant and exhibition space, offers an all-in-one night out. The MK2 chain is a paradigm of imaginative programming, with a policy of screening short films before each feature. The recently opened MK2 Gambetta shows artists videos, and an MK2 multiplex is planned next to the new national library.
Air conditioning. Café-restaurant. Wheelchair access.

UGC Ciné Cité Les Halles
pl de la Rotonde, Nouveau Forum des Halles, 1st (08.36.68.68.58). M° Les Halles. **Map J5**
This ambitious 16-screen development was Paris' first multiplex and screens art movies as well as mainstream stuff. Internet café. UGC has since gone two screens better at the Ciné Cité Bercy (2 cour St-Emilion, 12th/08.36.68.68.58/M° Cour St-Emilion).

Other Art Cinemas

Le Balzac
1 rue Balzac, 8th (01.45.61.10.60/08.36.68.31.23). M° George V. **Map D4**
Built in 1935 with a mock ocean-liner foyer, Le Balzac scores high for design and programming.

Denfert
24 pl Denfert-Rochereau, 14th (01.43.21.41.01). M° Denfert-Rochereau. **Map H10**
A valiant, friendly little spot with an eclectic repertory selection ranging from Kitano to kids' films and new animation.
Air conditioning. Wheelchair access.

Elysées Lincoln
14 rue Lincoln, 8th (01.43.59.36.14/08.36.68.81.07). M° George V or Franklin D Roosevelt. **Map D4**
Arthouse showing smaller-scale and independent films. Frequent meet-the-director screenings.

L'Entrepôt
7-9 rue Francis de Pressensé, 14th (01.45.40.78.38/01.45.39.60.09/08.36.68.05.87). M° Pernéty. **Map F10**
This converted warehouse offers three screens, a restaurant, bar and garden. New and Third World directors, shorts and gay cinema all get a look-in, including theme series that mix films with relevant food, music and exhibitions. For the fortnightly Ciné-Philo a film is followed by a philosophy debate.
Air conditioning. Bar. Wheelchair access to Salle 1.

Le Latina
20 rue du Temple, 4th (01.42.78.47.86). M° Hôtel de Ville or Rambuteau. **Map K6**
Le Latina (established 1913) screens films from Italy, Spain, Portugal and Latin America. There are also Latino dances, a gallery and a restaurant.

Studio 28
10 rue Tholozé, 18th (01.46.06.36.07). M° Abbesses or Blanche. **Map H1**
Historic, family-run Studio 28 offers a repertory mix of classics and recent movies. Decorated with souvenirs and posters, the entrance is pock-marked with footprints of the great.

Public Repertory Institutions

Auditorium du Louvre
entrance through Pyramid, Cour Napoléon, 1st (01.40.20.51.86). M° Palais Royal. **Tickets** 25F; 17F under-18s; membership available. **Map H5**
Like the Louvre pyramid, this 420-seat auditorium

On location

Paris continues to be one of cinema's favourite cities, as recent releases from either side of the puddle confirm.

Alice et Martin

(*André Téchiné, 1998*) Violinist Juliette Binoche offers refuge to provincial runaway Alexis Loret who blossoms into a successful male model. Their courtship (*pictured*) takes them strolling down boulevard Haussmann and to the Fnac and the Quick burger bar in the Forum des Halles.

Jeanne et le garçon formidable

(*Olivier Ducastel/Jacques Martineau, 1998*) One of the sweetest, most Gallic and modern recent French films stars Virginie Ledoyen in an AIDS musical, which manages to be sweet and touching rather than mawkish. Bits of the city featured include the quai de la Seine in front of the MK2 cinema and rue Lacepède in the Latin Quarter.

Everyone Says I Love You

(*Woody Allen, 1996*) While everyone's favourite neurotic New Yorker usually obsesses about women, here the City of Light runs the ladies a close second. Goldie Hawn cavorts around Notre Dame and on the Left Bank *quais* opposite Ile St-Louis.

Ridicule

(*Patrice Leconte, 1996*) This sumptuous costume intrigue starred Charles Berling and Fanny Ardant in the glittering galleries of the Palais de Versailles. The sumptuous setting truly made this a unique and certainly one of the most authentic dramas – the Sun King would have loved it.

Place Vendôme

(*Nicole Garcia, 1999*) The allure of the ultra-prestigious *place* helped the film scoop 11 nominations at the 1999 César awards, clearly capturing the imagination if not statuettes. Director Nicole Garcia and Catherine Deneuve teamed up to bring the luxury and closed world of high-class jewellery to the screen. Seeing this eye-opener makes windowshopping a great deal more satisfying.

Sabrina

(*Sidney Pollack, 1995*) For this stylish remake of the 50s Billy Wilder classic, Pollack took cameras across Paris. One of the most romantic scenes was shot on the wooden Pont des Arts linking the Louvre with the Institut de France. Like lovers past and present, Harrison Ford and Julia Ormond trysted against a Paris skyline shown off to its best at this central point of the river.

Pigalle

(*Karim Dridi, 1994*) Dridi shot *Taxi Driver*-style on the sloping streets of the world-famous centre for girlie shows and sex shops around boulevard de Clichy. Gritty contemporary drama with a high ethnic and violence quotient.

French Kiss

(*Lawrence Kasdan, 1995*) Dizzy Meg Ryan falls for Kevin Kline, playing a devil-may-care Frenchman. They meet at the pre-renovation Hôtel George V, and their adventures take them round the back streets of Paris. One night shoot is on rue des Rosiers where Meg hails a cab – her good luck in tracking one down was part of the film's charm. In neighbouring rue des Ecouffes Kline blasts down the street on a motorbike, a vital tool to showing his French machismo versus his uptight East Coast rival.

Ninth Gate

(*Roman Polanski, 1999*) Paris resident Polanski shot much of this occult thriller in central Paris. One notable address visited by Johnny Depp was on the quai d'Anjou on the Ile St-Louis, as a magnificent waterfront *hôtel particulier* was used as the office of an aristocratic book expert. A few doors down, set builders erected a café where Johnny holed up as he tried to dodge the villains.

Forget Paris

(*Billy Crystal, 1995*) Crystal loves Paris, and this film must have been a real treat, taking him all across town from the quais of Ile St-Louis to the swanky boulevard St-Germain, where American comic enjoyed the shops and bars of the *Rive Gauche*. A somewhat less-glamorous, romantic location was Roissy airport.

Peut-être

(*Cédric Klapisch, 1999*) Klapisch's vision of a Paris that's not so much globally warmed as sandblasted, starring a time-ravaged Belmondo visited by his young father in 2070. The starting point, though, is a raucous booze-and-drug-fuelled soirée to bring in the new millennium. The wild party, which included much noise and trashing, took place in the very respectable rue de Penthièvre in the 8th *arrondissement*.

was designed by IM Pei. Film screenings are sometimes related to the exhibitions, but can be as delightfully unintellectual as 50s 3-D sci-fi. A regular feature are silent movies with live musical accompaniment, often specially composed, which benefit from the excellent acoustics. *Wheelchair access.*

Centre Pompidou
rue St-Martin, 4th (01.44.78.12.33). M° Hôtel de Ville/RER Châtelet-les Halles. **Map K6**
Beaubourg's reopening means the return of some of Paris' most eclectic programming. 2000 includes a winter season of classic British films, the complete Buñuel and experimental and artists' films by Len Lye and Derek Jarman, as well as a weekly documentary session, the annual Cinéma du Réel festival of rare and restored films (this year on the theme of love), and the pick of Annecy's animation festival. *Wheelchair access.*

La Cinémathèque Française
Palais de Chaillot, 7 av Albert-de-Mun, 16th (01.56.26.01.01). M° Trocadéro. **Map C5**
Grands Boulevards, 42 bd Bonne-Nouvelle, 10th (01.56.26.01.01). M° Bonne Nouvelle. **Admission** 29F. **Map J4**
Founded in 1936 by film fanatics Georges Franju and Henri Langlois, the Cinémathèque played a seminal role in shaping the New Wave directors at the end of the 1950s, and subsequently as meeting point for devoted cinephiles. The Palais de Chaillot screen

Plenty for Gabin fans at the **Cinémathèque.**

recently reopened after the 1997 fire, but like the still-closed film museum will probably ultimately move to the new Maison du Cinéma at Bercy. 2000 sees a retrospective of 90s cinema (already!), a John Stahl retrospective and a season of American silent movies.

Forum des Images
2 Grande Galerie, Porte St-Eustache, Forum des Halles, 1st (01.44.76.62.00). M° Les Halles. **Open** 1-9pm Tue, Wed, Fri-Sun; 1-10pm Thur. Closed 2-17 Aug. **Admission** 30F per day; 25F under-30s, over-60s; membership available. **Map J5**
Enlarged and renamed from the Vidéothèque (presumably to take in the wider multimedia definition of images), the Forum des Images is an addictive public archive dedicated to Paris on celluloid from 1895 to the present. No matter how brief the clip – from the Eiffel Tower scene in *Superman II* to the letter of introduction scene in *Babette's Feast* – if Paris is on film, it's here, along with ads, trailers, Pathé news reels, short films, animation and documentaries. An addictive Star Trek-like consultation room has 40 video consoles with Minitel-style keyboards where you can access computerised data by theme, year or author. The auditoria show wide-ranging series of films and videos. 2000 topics include 'Alcohol' and 'Correspondances' (love letters, diaries and telegrams in film). The Forum also screens the Rencontres Internationales du Cinéma (*see below*), the trash treats of L'Etrange Festival and films from the critics' selection at Cannes. *Wheelchair access.*

Festivals & Special Events

Here are some regular, easily accessible events. Also of note are the lesbian film festival (*see chapter* **Gay & Lesbian**), Festival de Film de Paris and Cinéma en Plein Air (*see chapter* **Paris by Season**).

Côté Court
Ciné 104, 104 av Jean Lolive, 93500 Pantin/ 01.48.46.95.08). M° Eglise de Pantin. **Dates** June.
New and old short films.

Festival International de Films de Femmes
Maison des Arts, pl Salvador-Allende, 94000 Créteil (01.49.80.38.98). M° Créteil-Préfecture. **Dates** Mar.
An impressive selection of retrospectives and new international films by female directors. *Wheelchair access (reserve ahead).*

Rencontres Internationales du Cinéma
Forum des Images (see above). **Dates** Oct-Nov.
A truly global choice of new independent feature, documentary and short films in competition for a Grand Prix du Public, plus a workshop series.

CinéMémoire
La Cinémathèque Française (see above) and other venues. **Dates** late Nov-Dec.
This remarkable festival shows rare, restored and rediscovered films as they were intended, at the right speed, often with orchestral accompaniment.

Gay & Lesbian

Gay hair salons, estate agents, portable phone shops and, especially, new legal status have further cemented the Paris community.

PACS, the Pacte Civile de Solidarité, is now law and France moves one step nearer same-sex marriages, as Francis and Dominique from Lille became the first couple to '*pacser*'. Significantly, *Gay Friendly France*, a magazine aimed at American trippers, has been published by the government tourist office. As well as enhancing their legal status, homosexuals in France are fuelling a booming service industry. Now trading are the first 'out' estate agents and portable telephone shop. Both are in the Marais, also home to the first gay beauty parlour. Business is booming at the bright blue hair salon **Space Hair**, and the **Sun Café**, which has taken the place of the Skeud, offers sun beds in the basement. With the increasing muscle of the pink franc comes a very frank approach to socialising. Expect to be handed a condom and gel with your change, for use on the premises, at certain mainstream bars like long-standing **Quetzal** which has added a back room.

Girls, too, are stepping out loud and proud. **Les Scandaleuses**, the highest profile lesbian bar, celebrates its third year, and top tennis player Amélie Mauresmo has become mainstream France's first famous lesbian.

In the Gallic gay club scene, ze accent is on dance and fashion and the trendy crowd. Apart from the gay clubs listed, many clubs have a large gay contingent or specific gay nights. Scream at Elyéee Montmartre is worth a visit if you can stomach priapic go-go dancers in the altogether. The bar-restaurant Man Ray hosts a groovy mixed night called Ceyla, and the perennially trendy Bains has established a thriving gay Monday, Paradisius. Long-running melting-pot Blanc Beur Black packs them in at **Folies Pigalle**. The Maghreb has found its own voice with Algerian hip-hop nights at the Gibus. Happily, something of camp old yesteryear remains. Vast, no-nonsense sex club **Le Dépôt** has quickly become an institution; it even hosted drinks for a gay film season at the Forum des Images. *See also chapter* **Clubs**.

MEDIA

Glossy *Têtu* is the market leader and agenda setter: for World Aids Day they produced a major HIV/Aids supplement. Other principal magazines are *Illico* (newsy), *Double Face* (lifestyle), *Ex Aequo* (politics), *Idol* (young lifestyle), *Projet X* (fetish) and *Lesbia* (women). Radio FG 98.2FM is the source of house music, news, info, club notices and contacts.

In with the proud crowd: the **Pride** *parade.*

Associations

Centre Gai et Lesbien

3 rue Keller, 11th (01.43.57.21.47). Mº Ledru-Rollin. **Open** 2-8pm Mon-Sat. **Map L7**
The Lesbian and Gay Centre has become a valued community resource providing information and a meeting space, a library (2-6pm Fri, Sat), legal and other advice services, and bulletin boards for flat and job hunting. The Association des Médecins Gais (gay doctors) mans a phone line (6-8pm Wed; 2-4pm Sat/01.48.05.81.71). The café is a pleasant place to digest the magazines and flyers on offer.

Act Up Paris

45 rue Sedaine, 11th (answerphone 01.48.06.13.89). Mº Bréguet-Sabin. **Map L6**
The very active branch of the worldwide anti-Aids group, whose zaps have included a flourescent pink condom over the obelisk on place de la Concorde, has just elected an HIV-negative woman president.

Weekly meetings are held Tuesday at 7pm in amphitheatre 1 of the Ecole des Beaux-Arts (14 rue Bonaparte, 6th/M° St-Germain-des-Prés). Publishes free monthly mag *Action*: health, news and hits.

SNEG (Syndicat National des Entreprises Gaies)

44 rue du Temple, 4th (01.44.59.81.01).
M° Rambuteau. **Open** 10am-7pm Mon-Fri. **Map J6**
The gay and lesbian business group unites some 950 companies across France. Organises HIV and safe-sex awareness training and courses on drug abuse for staff, and hands out free condoms.

Gay Bars & Cafés

Amnesia

42 rue Vieille-du-Temple, 4th (01.42.72.16.94).
M° Hôtel de Ville. **Open** 10am-2am daily. **Credit** MC, V. **Map K6**
Amnesia is now a warm meeting place with comfy sofas and easy-going clientele, known to hold Nana Mouskouri soirées in the basement. Though calm in the afternoon, action hots up at night when a critical mass congregates. The popular brunch (noon-4.30pm daily) draws a mixed crowd.

Banana Café

13 rue de la Ferronnerie, 1st (01.42.33.35.31).
M° Châtelet. **Open** 4pm-dawn daily. **Credit** AmEx, MC, V. **Map J5**
Pumping nightly with hedonistic thirtysomethings,

Le Central: *one of Gay Paree's oldest bars.*

gay and straight, the theme nights here are legendary: camp, decadent and often downright silly. The terrace is great for poser-watching in summer; in the cellar bar singers belt out showtunes. *Wheelchair access.*

Le Bar du Palmier

16 rue des Lombards, 4th (01.42.78.53.53).
M° Hôtel de Ville. **Open** 5pm-5am daily. **Credit** AmEx, MC, V. **Map J6**
Gets busy late, but also good during happy hour (6-8pm) when beer and copious nibbles are served. With bizarre pseudo-tropical décor and a nice terrace, this is one of the few places where women are welcome and numerous.

Le Central

33 rue Vieille-du-Temple, 4th (01.48.87.99.33).
M° Hôtel de Ville. **Open** 4pm-2am Mon-Fri; 2pm-2am Sat, Sun. **Credit** MC, V. **Map K6**
Popular with tourists, one of the city's oldest gay hangouts (Paris' only strictly gay hotel is upstairs) still passes muster 20 years on against its sprightly neighbours, but can be a welcome respite after bar-hopping in the area. Older crowd, no attitude.

Coffee Shop

3 rue Ste-Croix-de-la-Bretonnerie, 4th (01.42.74.24.21). M° Hôtel de Ville. **Open** 9am-2am daily. **No credit cards. Map K6**
The laidback Coffee Shop is a popular rendezvous and pick-up joint. MTV plays in a corner, decent bistro food is served until late, but people really come here for the gossip and boxer dog, Margo.

Le Cox

15 rue des Archives, 4th (01.42.72.08.00). M° Hôtel de Ville. **Open** 1pm-2am daily. **No credit cards. Map K6**
This is one of the hottest and most militant Marais gay bars. Afternoons are calm, but evenings hot up with loud music, dishy barmen and a good mix of body-conscious punters.

Le Duplex

25 rue Michel-le-Comte, 3rd (01.42.72.80.86).
M° Rambuteau. **Open** 8pm-2am daily. **Credit** AmEx, MC, V. **Map K5**
Monthly exhibitions and an eclectic music policy attract all sorts to this smoky bar; but don't be fooled, cruising here is down to a fine art.

Okawa

40 rue Vieille-du-Temple, 4th (01.48.04.30.69).
M° Hôtel de Ville. **Open** 11am-2am daily.
Credit AmEx, MC, V. **Map K6**
This French-Canadian bar/coffee shop excels in world play. Okawa means peace pipe in native Indian and *pipe* is French slang for blow job. In addition, the word is Arab slang for coffee, and is also a proud nod to Canada's capital city, Ottawa. In a word: very Queerbécois.

Onik

9 rue Nicolas-Flamel, 3rd (01.42.72.37.72). M° Arts et Métiers. **Open** 3pm-2am daily. **Credit** V. **Map K5**
This recently opened, glossy, primrose and terra-

*Mingle and meet at the **Open Bar**, a pre-party pitstop that's perpetually packed.*

cotta bar with arty fittings is plum centre on the pink route linking the Marais to Les Halles. Crowded with the smart set, it is the jumping-off point for clubbers.

Open Bar

17 rue des Archives, 4th (01.42.72.26.18).
Mᵒ Hôtel de Ville. **Open** 10am-2am daily. **Credit** MC, V. **Map K6**
Thanks to the strategic location on the crossroads with Ste-Croix-de-la-Bretonnerie, the Open Bar has become a Mecca for gay boys meeting up before heading off into the night. A facelift, clearly intended to appeal to the well-heeled, has only increased its popularity, and crowds spill out on to the streets. Now also runs Open Bar Coffee Shop at No 15.

Quetzal

10 rue de la Verrerie, 4th (01.48.87.99.07).
Mᵒ Hôtel de Ville. **Open** 5pm-5am daily.
Credit MC, V. **Map K6**
The cruisiest bar in the Marais with a strategically placed terrace, Quetzal attracts a beefy crowd looking for a drink and company, and has now added a backroom. It's at the end of rue des Mauvais-Garçons (bad boys street), so you know what to expect.

Sun Café

35 rue Ste-Croix-de-la-Bretonnerie, 4th
(01.40.29.44.40). Mᵒ Hôtel de Ville. **Open** 8am-2am daily. **Credit** V. **Map K6**
Upstairs has been transformed from designer den Skeud, now boasting cosy nests of low stools, a food bar and a noticeboard full of snaps from theme nights. But the big difference is the installation downstairs of state-of-the-art sunbeds. Morning tanning is accompanied by a free breakfast.

Le Tropic Café

66 rue des Lombards, 1st (01.40.13.92.62).
Mᵒ Châtelet. **Open** noon-dawn daily. **Credit** AmEx, DC, MC, V. **Map G6**
This bright, upbeat bar is going through a renaissance with some groovy parties that draw a loyal band. Grab a table on the terrace for the people-watching. Now also serves light lunches and tapas. *Wheelchair access.*

Gay Restaurants

Amadéo

19 rue François-Miron, 4th (01.48.87.01.02). Mᵒ St-Paul. **Open** 8-11pm Mon; noon-2pm, 8-11pm Tue-Thur; noon-2pm, 8-11.30pm Fri, Sat. Closed two weeks in Aug. **Average** 165F. **Prix fixe** 110F (Tue), 175F. **Lunch** *menu* 75F, 95F. **Credit** MC, V. **Map K6**
Well-informed Parisians consider this a secret gem. The music is strictly classical and the ochre and petrol-blue colour scheme is typical Marais chic. Inventive *plats du jour* are typified by the foie gras salad, goat cheese ravioli or roast duck slivers with barley. Live opera singer twice a month.

L'Amazonial

3 rue Ste-Opportune, 1st (01.42.33.53.13).
Mᵒ Châtelet. **Open** noon-3pm, 7pm-1am Mon-Fri; noon-5pm, 7pm-1am Sat, Sun. **Prix fixe** 85F, 129F (dinner). **Lunch** *menu* 65F, 85F (Mon-Fri). **Credit** AmEx, DC, MC, V. **Map J5**
Rebuilt a couple of years ago after a fire, Paris' largest gay restaurant has now expanded its terrace with a lot of fake stone and tack. Decent French cuisine with an exotic twist and tight T-shirted waiters.

L'Eclèche et Cie

*10 rue St-Merri, 4th (01.42.74.62.62). M° Hôtel de
Ville.* **Open** 9am-1am daily. **Average** 130F. **Prix
fixe** 100F (dinner); **Lunch** *menu* 55F. **Credit**
AmEx, MC, V. **Map K6**
This popular gay restaurant offers bistro fare like
gigot d'agneau and steak tartare. Relaxed by day, a
great hubbub prevails by mid-evening.

Krokodil

20 rue de La Reynie, 4th (01.48.87.55.67). M° Châtelet.
Open 7pm-2am daily (bar 5pm-2am). **Average**
165F. **Credit** AmEx, MC, V. **Map J6**
This open-plan restaurant-bar, with its sheltered terrace, manages to avoid many fancy pratfalls of disco
dinners. *Brochettes* are the house speciality, while
for exotica, there's ostrich but, alas, no crocodile.

Au Rendezvous des Camionneurs

*72 quai des Orfèvres, 1st (01.43.54.88.74). M° Pont-
Neuf.* **Open** noon-11pm Mon-Sat; noon-5pm Sun.
Average 180F. **Prix fixe** 138F. **Lunch** *menu* 88F.
Credit AmEx, MC, V. **Map J6**
Classic French favourites and a charming location
by Pont Neuf make this restaurant a consistent suc-
cess for those with lorry-driver fantasies.

Le Rude

*23 rue du Temple, 4th (01.42.74.05.15). M° Hôtel de
Ville.* **Open** noon-2am daily. **Average** 100F. **Lunch**
menu 79F, 89F. **Credit** MC, V. **Map K6**
This minimalist spot feeds a mostly gay clientele,
although everyone is welcome. They do good burgers, salads and duck à l'orange; the cheap drinks
spur conviviality, as does chatty Jeff.
Wheelchair access.

Aux Trois Petits Cochons

*31 rue Tiquetonne, 2nd (01.42.33.39.69).
M° Etienne-Marcel.* **Open** 8.30pm-1am Tue-Sun. **Prix
fixe** 135F, 159F. **Credit** AmEx, MC, V. **Map J5**
Three Little Pigs eschews the gimmickry of international boystown cuisine in favour of a tasty, daily-
changing *menu* (perhaps salmon tartare and goose
carpaccio, garlicky tuna, pear and rhubarb dessert).

Gay Clubs & Discos

Check press and flyers for one-nighters and
remember that not much gets going before 1am.
Admission prices often include one drink.

Club 18

*18 rue de Beaujolais, 1st (01.42.97.52.13).
M° Palais-Royal.* **Open** 11pm-dawn Thur-Sat;
5pm-dawn Sun. **Admission** free Thur, Sun; 70F Fri,
Sat. **Credit** AmEx, MC, V. **Map H5**
Time travel is made real in this soopa-doopa camp
club. Friendly, but don't expect unadventurous music.

Le Dépôt

*10 rue aux Ours, 3rd (01.44.54.96.96).
M° Rambuteau.* **Open** noon-7am daily. **Admission**
45F Mon-Thur; 55F Fri-Sun. **Credit** MC, V. **Map K5**
Since opening in October 1998, this colossal disco
sin-bin has been draining the hordes from the
Marais bars. Rainbow flags flutter frivolously outside but inside it is hard business. Décor is block-
house chic with jungle netting and exposed air
ducts. The first floor is devoted to 'cultural events'.
Gay Tea Dance on Sun (5-11pm, 40F-60F); Ladies
Room every Wed.

A return to its dancehall roots for **Le Tango***: waltzes, musettes, slows and yes, tango.*

Folies Pigalle
11 pl Pigalle, 9th (01.48.78.25.26). M° Pigalle.
Open midnight-dawn Tue-Sat; 6pm-midnight Sun'.
Admission free Mon-Thur, Sun; 40F Fri-Sat, 40F Sun.
Drinks 30F-50F. **Credit** V. **Map G2**
Come here for Paris' most popular gay tea dance, the Black Blanc Beur (BBB) party (6pm-midnight Sun; 40F). Instead of Europop or hard techno, you'll find an invigorating mix of Middle Eastern music, salsa, techno-raï and hip hop. There are sometimes live performers, too – 1999 saw Natacha Atlas and Chaba Fadela. *See also chapter* **Clubs**.

L'Insolite
33 rue des Petits-Champs, 2nd (01.40.20.98.59). M° Pyramides. **Open** 11pm-5am daily. **Admission** free Mon-Thur, Sun; 50F Fri, Sat. **Credit** MC, V. **Map H4**
Bright and brassy, this time tunnel takes you back to the 70s, save for the 90s disco glitter ball. Cosy and friendly, with a guarantee to fall into conversation (or more) with someone.

Le Queen
102 av des Champs-Elysees, 8th (01.53.89.08.90). M° George V. **Open** 11.30pm-dawn daily.
Admission 50F Mon; free Tue-Thur, Sun; 80F Fri, Sat. **Credit** AmEx, DC, MC, V. **Map D4**
Still the pick of the crop, even if going to Le Queen takes courage – the door staff are rude and ruthless, especially with women. Top DJs, extravagant (un)dress, drag queens and go-gos galore. House music and hedonism, or don your gaudiest shirt for Monday's Disco Inferno. *See also chapter* **Clubs**.

Scorp
25 bd Poissonnière, 9th (01.40.26.28.30). M° Grands Boulevards. **Open** midnight-6.30am daily.
Admission free Mon-Thur, Sun; 70F Fri, Sat.
Credit AmEx, MC, V. **Map J4**
Shortened in name and sharpened in style, the former Scorpion proves that long relationships are possible in gay Paree. House and dance hits reign. Much less cool than Le Queen, but also much less attitude.

Le Tango
13 rue au Maire, 3rd (01.42.72.17.78). M° Arts et Métiers. **Open** Thur 8pm-2am, Fri, Sat 10.30pm-5am; 6pm-2am Sun. **Admission** 60F Thur (with concert), 30F after 10.30pm; 40F Fri, Sat. **No credit cards**.
Map K5
Le Tango has returned to its dancehall roots for dancing *à deux*, with a clientele that is roughly 50 per cent gay or lesbian, and their friends. Accordion concert on Thur before the *bal* takes over with *musette*, waltzes, tangos and slows.

Men-Only Clubs: The Dark Side

Banque Club
23 rue de Penthièvre, 8th (01.42.56.49.26). M° Miromesnil. **Open** noon-2am Mon-Sat; 2pm-2am Sun. **Admission** 30F 4-6pm, 45F 6-10pm Mon-Fri; 30F Sat; 45F Sun. **Credit** MC, V. **Map E3**
Cruise club with three cellars, videos and cabins.

Key West
141 rue Lafayette, 10th (01.45.26.31.74). M° Gare du Nord. **Open** noon-1am Mon-Thur, Sun; noon-2am Fri, Sat. **Admission** 110F; 60F under-26s; 70F after 10pm. **No credit cards. Map K2**
'Europe's most beautiful sauna', as it modestly describes itself, has a small pool, gym and large steam room. Upstairs are cubicles with TV screens playing saucy videos.

QG
12 rue Simon-le-Franc, 4th (01.48.87.74.18). M° Rambuteau. **Open** 5pm-6am Mon-Thur; 5pm-8am Fri, Sat; 2pm-6am Sun. **Credit** AmEx, MC, V. **Map K6**
No entrance fee, cheap beer, late opening and a sense of humour guarantee success. Things get tough downstairs, and don't even ask what the bath is for.

Le Tranfert
3 rue de la Sourdière, 1st (01.42.60.48.42). M° Tuileries. **Open** midnight-dawn daily.
Credit MC, V. **Map G5**
Tiny but entertaining leather/SM bar.

Le Trap
10 rue Jacob, 6th (unlisted telephone). M° St-Germain- des-Prés. **Open** 11pm-4am daily.
Admission free Mon-Thur, Sun; 50F Fri, Sat. **No credit cards.** **Map H6**
Le Trap has been packing them in for nearly 20 years and has become hip with the fashion crowd. Expect naked dancing (and more! apparently) on Mondays and Wednesdays.

Gay Shops & Services

Boy'z Bazaar
5, 38 rue Ste-Croix-de-la-Bretonnerie, 4th (01.42.71.94.00). M° Hôtel de Ville. **Open** noon-midnight Mon-Sat; 2-9pm Sun. **Credit** AmEx, DC, MC, V. **Map K6**
No 5 caters for that boyz essential tight T-shirt, sportswear and classics, while No 38 serves up titilating videos.

Body Men Village
25 rue du Temple, 4th (01.42.72.17.16). M° Hôtel de Ville. **Open** 11am-9pm Mon-Fri; 10am-8pm Sat. Closed two weeks in Aug. **Credit** AmEx, MC, V. **Map K6**
Boys come here to buff their body shrine. Have a hand massage and facial, or the full (beauty) works.

Eurogays
23 rue du Bourg-Tibourg, 4th (01.48.87.37.77). M° Hôtel de Ville. **Open** Oct-Mar 10am-1.30pm, 2.30-7pm Mon-Fri. *Apr-Sept* 10am-1.30pm, 2.30-7pm Mon-Fri; 11am-5pm Sat. **Credit** MC, V. **Map K6**
From train tickets to world tours, this gay travel agent can book it all, and proposes 80 gay destinations around the globe.

Hôtel Central Marais
33 rue Vieille-du-Temple, 4th (01.48.87.56.08/fax 01.42.77.06.27). M° Hôtel de Ville. **Rates** *single* 450F; *double* 535F; *breakfast* 35F. **Credit** MC, V. **Map K6**

Paris's only strictly gay hotel (above Le Central) has seven rooms (no private bathrooms), plus an apartment (650F-795F). Book in advance. English spoken. **Room services** *Double glazing. Telephone.*

Hôtel Saintonge
16 rue de Saintonge, 3rd (01.42.77.91.13/fax 01.48.87.76.41). M° Filles du Calvaire. **Rates** *single* 490F-520F; *double* 560F-650F; *suite* 720F-790F. **Credit** AmEx, DC, MC, V. **Map L5**
Although this hotel is open to everyone, its owners cultivate a gay clientele. All rooms have a shower. **Room services** *Hairdryer. Minibar. Safe. Telephone. TV.*

IEM
208 rue St-Maur, 10th (01.42.41.21.41). M° Goncourt. **Open** 10am-7.30pm Mon-Sat. **Credit** AmEx, MC, V. **Map M4**
This store has scores of videos, clothes, books and condoms. Upstairs houses all things leather and rubber.
Branches: 43 rue de l'Arbre-Sec, 1st (01.42.96.05.74); 33 rue de Liège, 9th (01.45.22.69.01).

Lionel Joubin
10 rue des Filles-du-Calvaire, 3rd (01.42.74.37.51). M° Filles du Calvaire. **Open** 11am-8pm Mon-Sat. Closed Aug. **Credit** V. Map **L5**
Famous for its extravagant window displays, florist Joubin decorates entire floats for Gay Pride.

Les Mots à la Bouche
6 rue Ste-Croix-de-la-Bretonnerie, 4th (01.42.78.88.30). M° Hôtel de Ville. **Open** 11am-11pm Mon-Sat; 2-8pm Sun. **Credit** MC, V. **Map K6**
Stocks gay-interest literature from around the world, including an English-language section, plus travel guides and magazines. Interesting community meeting board, a good meeting place and there are changing art exhibitions in the basement.

Pharmacie du Village
26 rue du Temple, 4th (01.42.72.60.71). M° Hôtel de Ville. **Open** 8.30am-9.30pm Mon-Sat; 10am-8pm Sun. **Credit** AmEx, DC, MC, V. **Map K6**
If the thought of having to explain intimate problems to aged men in white coats fills you with fear, this gay-staffed chemist is the answer.

Space Hair
10 rue Rambuteau, 3rd (01.48.87.28.51). M° Rambuteau. **Open** noon-10pm Mon; 9am-11pm Tue-Fri; 9am-10pm Sat. **Credit** DC, MC, V. **Map K5**
Always full and always full on, this barber has become an institution on the Paris gay scene. It's so successful that it has expanded next door to Space Hair Classic, where the music is a notch lower.

Lesbian Paris

Lesbians share the Centre Gai & Lesbien with gay men (see above), holding lectures, debates and drinks on Fridays (8-10pm); several militant groups are based at the Maison des Femmes (*see* chapter **Directory**). Look out also for the club nights run by Ladies Room at Le Dépôt.

Les Archives, Recherches, Cultures Lesbiennes (ARCL)
Maison des Femmes, 163 rue de Charenton, 12th (01.43.43.41.13/01.43.43.42.13). M° Reuilly-Diderot. **Open** 7-9.30pm Tue. Closed Aug. **Map N8**
ARCL produces audiovisual documentation and bulletins on lesbian and women's activities, and runs an archive of lesbian and feminist documents.

La Champmesle
4 rue Chabanais, 2nd (01.42.96.85.20). M° Pyramides. **Open** 5pm-dawn Mon-Sat. **Credit** AmEx, MC, V. **Map H4**
This pillar of the lesbian bar community is busiest at weekends and on Thursdays, when there's cabaret. Changing art shows, too.
Wheelchair access.

Pulp
25 bd Poissonnière, 2nd (01.40.26.01.93). M° Grands Boulevards. **Open** midnight-dawn Wed-Sat. **Admission** 50F Fri, Sat. **Credit** AmEx, MC, V. **Map J4**
Pulp has become the happening club: small and intimate, with friendly staff. The musical mix takes in soul, funk, reggae, house, techno and Latin; regulars include DJ Sex Toy. Men admitted if accompanied. Publishes witty fanzine *Housewife*.

Quand les Lesbiennes se font du cinéma
Information Cineffable 01.48.70.77.11. **Dates** late Oct-early Nov.
Women-only film festival screens never-seen-before films, from documentaries and experimental videos to lesbian features, plus debates, exhibitions, bar.

Les Scandaleuses
8 rue des Ecouffes, 4th (01.48.87.39.26). M° St-Paul. **Open** 6pm-2am daily. **Credit** MC, V. **Map K6**
Les Scandaleuses has led the way among the new lesbian bars in the Marais. Chrome bar stools and high tables maximise the space, and the cellar rooms extend the mixing potential. Video monitors and changing exhibits by women artists adorn the walls. Accompanied men welcome.

Unity Bar
176-178 rue St-Martin, 3rd (01.42.72.70.59). M° Rambuteau. **Open** daily 4pm-2am. Closed one week in Dec. **No credit cards. Map K5**
A studenty clientele wears demin, plays pool and sings along to Queen and Suzanne Vega at this refreshingly visible new *bar féminin* by the Centre Pompidou. Cards and board games available at the bar. Men are welcome if accompanied.

Utopia
15 rue Michel-le-Comte, 3rd (01.42.71.63.43). M° Rambuteau. **Open** 5pm-2am Mon-Sat. **No credit cards. Map K5**
Opened by Antoinette and Anne in June 1998, the Utopia has quickly gained a reputation with house beat, billiards tournaments, pinball, Internet, music and café-theatre showcases, and fancy dress parties. The bar is used for art shows, while the lower level resembles a subterranean garden grotto.
Wheelchair access.

Music: Classical & Opera

The millennium finds the Parisian classical music scene pulsing with new ideas – and, as usual, plenty of controversy.

The reopening of the newly restored **Châtelet** means that the capital's opera scene is now firing on all cylinders. The Châtelet is financed by the right-wing Ville de Paris, whereas the **Opéra National de Paris** benefits from centralised funding, and the **Théâtre des Champs-Elysées** is independent. Depending on your point of view, this is either healthy competition or a fatally fragmented arts policy. The new director of the Châtelet, Jean-Pierre Brossmann, earned his credentials at Strasbourg and a scandal-ridden but artistically fruitful period at the Opéra de Lyon. His brief at Châtelet is to popularise the repertoire which, some felt, was on the verge of esoteric overplay. His initial pronouncements on the creation of a permanent festival skate around this mission. His choice of a new opera by John Adams to open the century was brave and interesting, but not exactly lollipop programming.

Operetta makes a welcome reappearance at the Châtelet this year, the sort of repertoire that used to be performed at the **Opéra Comique**, whose future is once again up for grabs, the 1999/2000 season having been cancelled. This charming but dusty institution will have as its new director the colourful theatre producer Jérôme Savary. Previously rumours had suggested that the post would be offered to a leading figure from the Early Music movement, maybe as a richly deserved permanent home for William Christie and the **Arts Florissants**. The thirst for Baroque continues unabated and René Jacobs, Christophe Rousset et al can be sure of an enthusiastic reception from a public who now know their gambas from their viols.

Meanwhile the Opéra National, under the direction of Hugues Gall, continues to provide the expected international casting, but there is a seeming malaise when it comes to the choice of interesting productions. Too often the vast spaces of the Bastille are filled with deconstructionalist stagings, popular with a certain element in the press but deeply unpopular with opera buffs.

Pierre Boulez, who once suggested blowing up all opera houses, remains the intellectual force behind contemporary creation in France. To his credit, the new conservatoire at La Villette has a formidable energy and may yet provide an eminent successor to the modernist master. In terms of orchestral playing the **Ensemble InterContemporain**, now under the direction of David Robertson, shows the virtue of Boulez's disciplined approach to music making. In a recent interview the composer/conductor suggested that French orchestras were undermined by a lack of common purpose between administration, players and conductors. The selling off by the government at a bargain price of the **Salle Pleyel** to a private owner is an example of the sort of destabilising political actions to which he refers. Hire fees are soaring – bad news for smaller orchestras – and practical constraints are making life difficult for the **Orchestre de Paris** and its newly appointed musical director Christoph Eschenbach. There is a feeling abroad that he has sinister extra-musical plans for what is the city's only large concert hall alongside the **Maison de Radio France**'s Salle Messiaen and the new conservatoire.

MUSIC IN CHURCHES

The Festival d'Art Sacré (01.44.70.64.10) highlights religious music in the weeks before Christmas (01.44.70.64.10). Les Grands Concerts Sacrés (01.48.24.16.97) and Musique et Patrimoine (01.42.50.96.18) offer concerts at various churches including Eglise St-Roch, Eglise des Billettes, Eglise St-Julien-le-Pauvre, Eglise St-Séverin, the Madeleine and the Val de Grâce. The emphasis tends to be on Baroque and choral music. Music in Notre-Dame is taken care of by Musique Sacrée à Notre-Dame (01.44.41.49.99),

There is little music from late July until mid-September, except for the Paris, Quartier d'Eté festival, which put on concerts in gardens across the city (*see also chapter* **Paris by Season**). The Carrousel du Louvre also runs quality chamber-music events in summer; there are romantic candlelit concerts in the Orangerie of the Bagatelle gardens, and mainstream, often Baroque, programming in various city churches.

INFORMATION AND RESOURCES

For listings, see *Pariscope* and *l'Officiel des Spectacles*. The monthly *Le Monde de la Musique* and *Diapason* also list classical concerts, while *Opéra International* provides the best coverage of all things vocal. *Cadences* and *La Terrasse*, two free monthlies, are distributed outside concerts. The artists performing largely govern ticket prices and availability. If Giulini is visiting the Orchestre de Paris then it's likely tickets will be booked up ahead and be fairly pricey. Many venues offer cut-rate tickets to students (under 26) an hour before curtain. Beware of ticket touts around the Opéra and big-name concerts. For **La Fête de la Musique**, on 21 June, events are free, as are some concerts at the **Maison de Radio France**, the **Conservatoire de Paris** and churches.

For both instruments and scores, the long-established La Flûte de Pan (49, 53, 59 rue de Rome, 9th (01.42.93.65.05/01.43.87.01.81)/M° St-Lazare), on the traditional *rue des Luthiers*, has the most comprehensive selection.

Orchestras & Ensembles

Les Arts Florissants
William Christie's 'Arts Flo' is France's most highly regarded Early Music group. 1999 saw an exhibition celebrating 20 years of achievement at the Palais Garnier, where the ensemble is frequently invited. Christie, an American, has become a fêted French citizen and his intimate performances of Lully and Rameau have introduced their music to a generation that had consigned it to history.

La Chapelle Royale
Philippe Herreweghe, one of the most celebrated Early Music conductors is, like Frans Brüggen, starting to conduct music of all periods with an eye for authenticity. The choral standards remain consistently high.

Concerts Pasdeloup
This modestly accomplished orchestra (director Jean-Pierre Wallez) offers programmes of orchestral pops with only a very occasional interesting soloist.

Ensemble InterContemporain
Based at the Cité de la Musique, the world-famous, avant-garde ensemble is led by American David Robertson, successor to Pierre Boulez, who still regularly conducts. The standard of playing is high and the modernist programming more varied than in the past, even including a performance of a work by the previously proscribed Steve Reich.

Ensemble Orchestral de Paris
Based at Salle Pleyel. John Nelson presides over this chamber orchestra, whose repertoire ranges from Baroque music to nineteenth-century operetta. This year sees the completion of a mammoth Beethoven cycle as well as an interesting rarity, Messager's *L'Amour masqué* in June.

Orchestre Colonne
Based at Salle Pleyel. This orchestra often fails to live up to its past but recently, under its principal conductor Didier Benetti, it has introduced a series of interesting educational concerts ('*Éveil*') of light music, aimed at encouraging young listeners.

Orchestre d'Ile de France
Based at Salle Pleyel and the Eglise St-Eustache. This orchestra's profile has risen in the last season, during celebrations of its 25th anniversary under longstanding musical director Jacques Mercier. The themed programming, based around the great masters, has been coherent and challenging.

Orchestre Lamoureux
Absent from the Salle Pleyel in 1999/2000, this long-established orchestra seems to find the tough world of soaring fees and competition an ongoing crisis. It would be a shame if this led to its extinction, because standards have been rising in recent seasons.

Orchestre National de France
Based at the Maison de Radio France and Théâtre des Champs-Elysées. Under Canadian Charles Dutoit, an expert in the French Romantic repertoire, the orchestra can now claim to be the finest in the land. Dutoit has proved a popular choice, with nineteenth-century French music dominating the programming.

Orchestre de Paris
Based at Salle Pleyel and Châtelet. The Dohnanyi and Brüggen joint leadership turned out to be a very temporary affair and, with a flourish of press conferences, the Orchestre announced that its new musical director would be Christoph Eschenbach. It remains to be seen if he can survive the notorious level of political problems which currently dog the orchestra. However the roster of visiting *maestri* remains impressive, this season featuring Sawallisch, Maazel and Sir Roger Norrington.

Orchestre Philharmonique de Radio France
Based at the Maison de Radio France and Salle Pleyel. Marek Janowski conducts his final season for the orchestra. In a changing music scene his performances of the Romantic repertoire have been pillars of quality; the search for a suitable replacement will be a tough task for the administration.

Les Talens Lyriques
Christophe Rousset's spin-off from Les Arts Florissants has established its own personality and a soaring reputation. Mostly young singers perform Baroque opera in authentic stagings.

Concert Halls

Théâtre des Bouffes du Nord
37bis bd de la Chapelle, 10th (01.46.07.34.50). M° La Chapelle. **Box office** 11am-6pm Mon-Sat. **Tickets** 70F-160F. **Credit** AmEx, MC, V. **Map L2**
Peter Brook and Stéphane Lissner have reinstated a musical dimension into the programming of the theatre. 1999/2000 saw a magnificent series of chamber music concerts by leading clarinettist Michel Portal, as well as concerts of contemporary music and visits from leading ensembles.

Philippe Fénelon's Salammbô, *based on Flaubert's work, at the* **Opéra Bastille**.

Châtelet – Théâtre Musical de Paris

1 pl du Châtelet, 1st (01.40.28.28.40). M° Châtelet.
Box office 11am-7pm daily; *telephone* 10am-7pm
Mon-Sat. **Tickets** phone for details. **Credit** AmEx,
MC, V. **Map J6**
Jean-Pierre Brossmann's reign at the newly renovated Châtelet continues with a standard of performance that rivals the Opéra National. After Gluck
in 1999/2000, 2000/2001 opens with *La Belle Hélène*,
conducted by Marc Minkowski, a welcome return of
operetta. But Brossmann casts his net wide and
future plans include the world première of an opera
by Eötvös. Whether all this will achieve his aim of
popularising the repertoire is open to question, but
his good relationship with Sir John Elliot Gardiner
looks sure to be artistically profitable. The popular
Sunday morning chamber music concerts at the
Théâtre des Champs-Elysées have now moved here.
Wheelchair access.

Cité de la Musique

*221 av Jean-Jaurès, 19th (recorded information
01.44.84.45.45/reservations 01.44.84.44.84).
M° Porte de Pantin.* **Box office** noon-6pm
Tue-Sun/*telephone* 11am-7pm Mon-Sat, 11am-6pm
Sun. **Tickets** 60F-200F; reduced prices under 26s,
over-60s. **Credit** MC, V. **Map insert**
The complex at **La Villette** contains the new
Conservatoire de Paris (01.40.40.45.45) and Cité de
la Musique concert hall and museum designed by
Christian de Portzamparc. Initially the focus was on
early and contemporary works, but last season saw
an impressive range of music from all periods,
including excursions into jazz and world music.
Summer 2000 features Monteverdi's *Coronation of*

Poppea conducted by Marc Minkowski. Ticket holders can occasionally see rehearsals for free. The
museum has a smaller concert space (*see chapter*
Museums). The Conservatoire, home to 1250 students, is host to world-class performers and profes-
sors, with free concerts given by the student
orchestra or soloists.
Wheelchair access.

IRCAM

*1 pl Igor-Stravinsky, 4th (01.44.78.48.16). M° Hôtel
de Ville.* **Open** phone for details. **Tickets** 90F; 60F
students. **Credit** AmEx, MC, V. **Map K6**
The underground bunker designed to create a new
music for a new century, as part of the Centre
Pompidou, has finally begun to participate in the
musical mainstream. The Agora festival, held from
5-25 June, encourages a diversity of approaches,
including dance and film music. At last, the massive
investment is bearing some fruit.

Maison de Radio France

*116 av du Président-Kennedy, 16th (01.42.30.22.22/
concert information 01.42.30.15.16). M° Passy/RER
Kennedy Radio France.* **Box office** 11am-6pm Mon-
Sat. **Tickets** free-120F. **Credit** MC, V. **Map A7**
Radio station France Musiques has programmed an
impressive range of classical concerts, operas and
ethnic music here. The main venue is the rather
charmless Salle Olivier Messiaen, but the quality of
music compensates. The Orchestre National de
France and Orchestre Philharmonique de Radio
France are based here. Under-26s can buy a bargain
'Passe Musique', 120F, for admission to four con-
certs. Watch out for free events.
Wheelchair access.

Opéra Comique/Salle Favart

*pl Boïeldieu, 2nd (01.42.44.45.40/reservations
01.42.44.45.46). M° Richelieu-Drouot.* **Box office** 14
rue Favart 11am-7pm Mon-Sat; *telephone*
11am-6pm Mon-Sat. **Tickets** 50F-500F.
Credit AmEx, DC, MC, V. **Map H4**
Many French operas have premièred in this century-
old jewel box, including Bizet's *Carmen*, Delibes'
Lakmé, Massenet's *Manon* and Ravel's *l'Heure
Espagnole.* The cancelling of the 1999/2000 season
closes another chapter of underachievement in recent
years. The choice of Jérôme Savary as new director
does not guarantee success. His flamboyant, gag-
based productions sit ill at ease with the simple,
chamber-style ones that the building suggests.
However, he is a popular figure and may breathe life
into what has become a rather dingy institution.
Wheelchair access.

Opéra National de Paris Bastille

pl de la Bastille, 12th (08.36.69.78.68). M° Bastille.
Box office 130 rue de Lyon 11am-6.30pm Mon-Sat/
telephone 9am-7pm. **Tickets** 60F-670F; *concerts*
45F-255F. **Credit** AmEx, MC, V. **Map M7**
There now seems to be a consensus that the Opéra
Bastille is a poorly designed building – even the
director, Hugues Gall, complains of the 32 kilome-
tres of corridors, the unfinished *salle modulable* and
the poor facilities in the public areas. However, he is
a true professional and the house has now attained
an international standard comparable to those the
world over. This relative stability is much to his
credit: having to deal with over 50 announced strikes
last season would sap the morale of a lesser man.
Uniquely in Europe, he has not ignored contemporary creation, with commissions from composers
Philippe Manoury, Pascal Dusapin and Matthias
Pintscher in the pipeline. June and July 2000 see a
well-cast new production of Wagner's *Flying
Dutchman. See chapters* **Right Bank** *and* **Dance.**
*Guided visits (01.40.01.19.70). Wheelchair access
(01.40.01.18.08).*

Opéra National de Paris Garnier

pl de l'Opéra, 9th (08.36.69.78.68). M° Opéra. **Box
Office** 11am-6.30pm Mon-Sat/*telephone* 9am-7pm.
Tickets 60F-670F; *concerts* 45F-255F. **Credit**
AmEx, MC, V. **Map G4.**
Restored to something like its glittering original, the
Palais Garnier is now performing its original func-
tion as an opera house, sharing the task with the
Bastille. The perfect acoustics and undeniable glam-
our make an evening here a privilege, but the build-
ing's tiara shape means some seats have poor
visibility. Summer 2000 sees the opening of Bob
Wilson's production of *Pélleas and Mélisande*, with
a fine cast including José Van Dam. *See chapters*
Right Bank, **Museums** *and* **Dance.**
*Visits 10am-4.30pm daily; guided visits
(01.40.01.22.63). Wheelchair access (01.40.01.18.08).*

Péniche Opéra

*facing 200 quai des Jemmapes, 10th (01.53.35.07.76).
M° Jaurès.* **Box office** 10am-7pm Mon-Fri/
telephone 01.53.35.07.77. **Tickets** 60F-150F.
Credit MC, V. **Map L3**

An enterprising boat-based opera company producing a programme of chamber-scale rarities, often
comic. In previous seasons productions had come
ashore to the Opéra Comique: the precarious future
of the latter could mean choppy waters ahead.

Salle Cortot

*78 rue Cardinet, 17th (01.47.63.85.72).
M° Malesherbes.* **No box office. Tickets** 80F-150F.
Map D2
This intimate panelled concert hall in the Ecole
Normale Supérieure de Musique has an excellent
acoustic for chamber music. This year sees the cul-
mination of the complete Beethoven piano sonatas
played by Marie-Pierre Soma.

Salle Gaveau

45 rue La Boétie, 8th (01.49.53.05.07). M° Miromesnil.
Box office 11am-6pm Mon-Fri. **Tickets** 85F-240F.
Credit AmEx, MC, V. **Map E3**
The charmingly antiquated Salle Gaveau has had
its promised facelift reduced to the status of a project. It may be that a surge of millennium energy will
get things underway. The plan is to improve the
acoustics to allow larger Baroque performances. In
the meantime it continues to be used for recitals and
chamber music; it's also the favoured venue for
senior prima donnas giving farewell recitals.

Salle Pleyel

*252 rue du Fbg-St-Honoré, 8th (01.45.61.53.01).
M° Ternes.* **Box office** 1pm-9pm Mon-Sat; *telephone*
(08.25.00.02.52) 9am-9pm Mon-Fri. **Tickets** 120F-
410F. **Credit** MC, V. **Map D3**
The Salle Pleyel is vast and unatmospheric, but
home to many orchestras and ensembles. The recent
sale by the government to an individual buyer
augurs badly for the future. Hire has become hugely expensive and several smaller orchestras are
being squeezed out. Despite an announcement that
it will continue as a major symphony venue, last season's reduced programme and rumblings of discontent from the Orchestre de Paris are discouraging.
Wheelchair access.

Théâtre des Champs-Elysées

*15 av Montaigne, 8th (01.49.52.50.50). M° Alma-
Marceau.* **Box office** 1pm-7pm Mon-Sat; *telephone*
10am-noon, 2-6pm Mon-Fri. **Tickets** 50F-690F.
Credit AmEx, MC, V. **Map D5**
This beautiful theatre, designed by Auguste Perret
with bas-reliefs by Bourdelle, witnessed the première of Stravinsky's *Le Sacre du Printemps* in May
1913, and the riot that followed. The new director,
Dominique Meyer, is rightly proud of the theatre's
independent status and his opening season has been
of high quality with visits from the New York
Philharmonic, Boston Symphony, London
Symphony and Vienna Philharmonic. Opera has
been well served also with a Haitink *Pélleas and
Mélisande* and a René Jacobs Baroque discovery,
Cesti's *L'Argia.* Recitals by top pianists and a chamber music series to celebrate the 50th birthday of the
festival at Prades, set up by Pablo Casals, complete
the programming.
Wheelchair access.

Théâtre du Tambour-Royal

94 rue du Fbg-du-Temple, 11th (01.48.06.72.34).
M° Belleville or Goncourt. **Box office** 6.30-8pm
Tue-Sat; *telephone* 10am-8pm Mon-Sat. **Tickets**
80F-130F. **Credit** MC, V.
A programme of recitals and chamber opera has made
this a popular venue for talent-spotting young singers.

Théâtre de la Ville

2 pl du Châtelet, 4th (01.42.74.22.77). M° Châtelet.
Box office 11am-7pm Mon; 11am-8pm Tue-Sat;
telephone 11am-7pm Mon-Sat. **Tickets** 95F.
Credit MC, V. **Map J6**
The occasional concerts in this vertiginously raked
concrete amphitheatre feature hip classical outfits like
the avant-garde Kronos Quartet. *See chapters* **Dance,**
Music: Rock, Roots & Jazz *and* **Theatre.**
Wheelchair access.

Music in Museums

For musical memorabilia, *see chapter* **Museums.**

Auditorium du Louvre

Entrance through Pyramid, Cour Napoléon, 1st
(01.40.20.51.86/reservations 01.40.20.84.00).
M° Palais-Royal. **Box office** 9am-7.30pm Mon,
Wed-Fri. **Tickets** 40F-135F. **Credit** MC, V. **Map H5**
Chamber music in imaginative series, as well as music
on film and silent films with live accompaniment.
Wheelchair access.

Bibliothèque Nationale de France

quai François-Mauriac, 13th (01.53.79.40.45/
reservations 01.53.79.49.49). M° Bibliothèque or
Quai de la Gare. **Box office** 10am-7pm Tue-Sat;
noon-7pm Sun. **Tickets** 100F; 65F students.
Credit MC, V. **Map M10**
The new library is building a good public for its
song recitals by top international artists, this year
based around the songs of Gabriel Fauré.
Wheelchair access.

Musée National du Moyen Age (Cluny)

6 pl Paul-Painlevé, 5th (01.53.73.78.00). M° Cluny-
La Sorbonne. **Tickets** (some include
museum entry). **No credit cards. Map J7**
The museum presents medieval concerts that are in
keeping with the collection.

Musée d'Orsay

62 rue de Lille, 7th (01.40.49.47.50). M° Solférino/
RER Musée d'Orsay. **Tickets** 80F-130F; 100F under
26s. **No credit cards. Map G6**
Musical programmes here focus, like the collection,
on the nineteenth century.
Wheelchair access.

Théâtre Grévin

10 bd Montmartre, 9th (01.48.24.16.97). M° Grands
Boulevards. **Tickets** 90F-200F, 75F students;
telephone 11am-7pm Mon-Fri or 1 hour before
concert. **Credit** MC, V. **Map J4**
Small-scale vocal and chamber music.

Incomprehensible? *Moi?*

Molière's play *Les Précieuses ridicules* satirises
the intellectual approach to the arts, which has
characterised Paris from the court to the salons
right up to today's interminable *conférences.*
The positive side of this approach is a musical
culture open to new ideas and sounds; the downside is the risk of Emperor's New Clothes
Syndrome. From Gluck to Berlioz through
Debussy and the scandalous première of
Stravinsky's *Sacre du Printemps*, right up to
Messiaen and Boulez at the end of the century,
the French musical scene has been stimulated
by argument over the avant-garde. Today
IRCAM and La Villette are international centres
for experimental music. Leading composers in
recent years include Dusapin, Grisey, Manoury,
Murail, and the conductor/composer Eötvös.

Complexity and seeming incomprehensibility
have always intrigued an important part of the
intelligentsia. This form of cultural elitism has
perversely led to a creative energy absent from
neighbouring countries with the exception of the
old rival and intellectually respected Germany.
In the nineteenth century the French whole-
heartedly embraced the Wagnerian school; the
high seriousness of the whole enterprise was at
once attractive and in sharp contrast with the
perception of their own music as frivolous and
unworthy. Later, the Second Viennese school
was taken up with equal enthusiasm, which led
to the Stockhausen/Boulez axe of atonality. Only
the group Les Six, including Poulenc and
Honegger, was slightly off message, producing
music that was free from Teutonic rigour and
intellectual baggage.

At the dawn of a new millennium, the future
for contemporary creation has never been more
open. At last, the IRCAM and the conservatoires
seem to have tacitly admitted that microtonality
and serial compositions may not be the only
path for young composers to follow. In summer
2000 watch out for premières of works by Jean-
Luc Hervé, Frédéric Verrières and Jean-Marc
Singier. You can be certain that the judgement
of the public will be based on a rigorous assess-
ment of the position of the music in a historical
perspective rather than a simple emotional
response to the experience.

If you're visiting a city, take a city guide.

Music: Rock, Roots & Jazz

Recent years have seen French rock become as globally credible as English cuisine. Isn't it about time we stopped laughing at it?

The French rock and pop scene has always caused mirth in the Anglo-Saxon world, especially when it came to taunting French exchange students. But these may now visit our shores with their heads held high thanks to the likes of Air, Mr Oizo and a burgeoning indie scene. The French have long championed esoteric British bands such as Tindersticks and Divine Comedy. Now the best Francophone acts are fighting back, combining the language of Molière with hybrids of rock, *chanson*, house, African and Arab beats and a healthy scorn for Johnny Hallyday. French-Algerian rockers Zebda met in a Toulouse housing estate and are now doing sell-out tours of France, poking fun at the right-wing. Their live appearances are legendary – they've even played Glastonbury. In the music of wry, retro Katerine you can hear everything from swing to easy-listening. Dionysus delve into poetry for inspiration, and deliver imaginative melodies that veer from indie sweetness-and-light to ponderous guitar rock, with lyrics of a Brel-like intensity. Les Nubians – French-Cameroonian sisters Celia and Hélène Faussart – weave soul-jazz, hip-hop and R&B into a languid groove that has seen their début album riding high in the *Billboard* charts for months. America loves them.

There are still, of course, some travesties. Old stars do not die in France, they just go on playing the Olympia or Stade de France, releasing albums and appearing on the cover of *Paris Match*. Yet you'll never hear a bad word said about them – the likes of Eddy Mitchell command respect from even the most sullen teenager. Then there's the cheesy pop from the likes of Larusso and Mylène Farmer, who make the Spice Girls look like Pierre Boulez.

With an average of 60 concerts every night and around 200 venues, there's something for everyone's taste and budget, from Senegalese hip-hop to didgeridoo. Parisian audiences are open minded and eclectic. Bear in mind that concerts rarely start at the advertised time and, as if by magic, the audience turns up just as the first few bars are being played. Many venues dispense with a dancefloor in favour of tables and chairs – pogo-ing in the moshpit is clearly not a priority for the French. For ticket agencies, *see chapter* **Directory**.

Stadium Venues

Palais Omnisports de Paris-Bercy
8 bd de Bercy, 12th (08.03.03.00.31). M° Bercy.
Box office 10am-6pm Mon-Fri. **Admission** from 150F. **Credit** MC, V. **Map N9**
With grass on the outside and 20,000 echoing seats inside, Bercy hosts sporting events and music crowdpullers from the three raï giants Khaled, Rachid Taha and Faudel to Whitney Houston. *Wheelchair access (call 01.55.93.00.56).*

Zénith
211 av Jean-Jaurès, 19th. M° Porte de Pantin. **No box office. Admission** from 100F. **Map inset**
A large, warehousey venue that hosts big touring bands from Eric Clapton to Fun Lovin Criminals and Marilyn Manson or French crooner Pascal Obispo.

Rock Venues

La Bataclan
50 bd Voltaire, 11th (01.43.14.35.35). M° Oberkampf.
Box office 11am-7pm Mon-Sat. **Concerts** 8pm.
Admission 100F-200F. **Map M5**
This ornate former theatre has a large dance area and a bar. It hosts quality bands – Les Nubians, Morcheeba and Placebo – plus world and *chanson* artists. *Wheelchair access.*

Café de la Danse
5 passage Louis-Philippe, 11th (01.47.00.57.59).
M° Bastille. **Concerts** 8.30pm. **Admission** 80F-120F. **No credit cards. Map M7**
This spacious, stone-walled former dance theatre is one of the best mid-size venues. Beth Orton, Bis, Ben & Jason and Gomez have graced its stage recently. *Wheelchair access.*

La Cigale/La Boule Noire
120 bd Rochechouart, 18th (01.49.25.89.99).
M° Pigalle. **Box office** noon-7pm Mon-Sat.
Admission 120F-200F. **Credit** MC, V (box office only, not on door). **Map H2**
An old horseshoe-shaped vaudeville house, La Cigale holds 1900 people. It hosts international bands and French groups, from The Frank and Walters, to Stomp and Dolly as well as the odd jazz star. **La Boule Noire**, in the basement, hosts up-and-coming bands.

Ode to Olympia

Olympia is the grand old lady of the French music venue – ancient, snooty and, despite a recent facelift, not what she used to be. She has entertained Parisians for over a century. But it was when Bruno Coquatrix (whose name is still emblazoned everywhere, on carpets, posters, in neon lights at the entrance) took it over in 1954 that it became legendary.

Clinging to his legacy, his family have run the place with a Corleone-like rod of iron since he died in 1979. They even have living quarters there. In 1997, when the place started falling apart, they decided to renovate. The original auditorium was demolished and an exact replica rebuilt a few yards away. The seats are even the exact same shade of red.

The Coquatrix boast that no one has ever turned down an invitation to play at Olympia. The alumni of performers from Bruno's day are indeed enough to make any Francophile drool – Piaf, Brel, Brassens, Ferré, Trenet and Aznavour all trod its boards, as did, later on, The Beatles, Rolling Stones, Sinatra and Dylan. Today, appearances by the fashionable likes of MC Solaar and Laurent Garnier prove that, for a French artist, playing the Olympia is still a defining moment in one's career.

But will Olympia ever recapture the glory of her heyday again? Or rather – where are the Piafs and Brels of today? Apart from the odd international pop act, you can look forward to shows by Johnny Hallyday, Johnny Hallyday's son, Johnny Hallyday's ex-wife, and… well, you get the picture. A visit to grandma, anyone?
28 bd des Capucines, 9th (01.55.27.10.00/ telephone bookings 01.47.42.25.49). M° Opéra.

Véronique Sanson

Le Divan du Monde
75 rue des Martyrs, 18th (01.44.92.77.66). M° Pigalle.
Concerts 7.30pm Mon-Sat; 4pm Sun. **Admission** free Mon; 50F-120F Tue-Sat. **No credit cards. Map H2**
Since it opened in 1995, this former cabaret has established itself as Paris' best medium-small venue. It hosts diverse acts from world music – raï, salsa, Afro-Cuban – to rock and Britpop, with club events later in the evening. *See also chapter* **Clubs.**

Elysée Montmartre
72 bd Rochechouart, 18th (01.55.07.06.00). M° Anvers.
Concerts 7.30pm most nights. Closed Aug.
Admission 90F-160F. **No credit cards. Map J2**
The veteran of musical action in Pigalle has retained its music-hall character. Latin/salsa dance nights are held here as well as vintage reggae names, and international acts both established and up-and-coming (David Bowie, Brand New Heavies, Basement Jaxx, Terry Callier and Everything But The Girl).

Rock in Bars

Chesterfield Café
124 rue La Boétie, 8th (01.42.25.18.06). M° Franklin D Roosevelt. **Restaurant/bar** 10am-5am daily.
Concerts 11.30pm Tue-Sat. **Admission** free.
Credit AmEx, MC, V. **Map E4**
You'll hear narry a French voice in this cavernous, Yankee hangout, but the free concerts give you a chance to catch new American bands before they make it to a bigger venue, as well as oldies making a comeback and some rocking curiosities (John McEnroe, Rolan Bolan). Gospel at 2pm on Sunday.

Le Falstaff
15 rue de Dunkerque, 10th (01 42 85 12 93).
M° Gare du Nord. **Bar** 7am-2am Mon-Wed; 7am-5am Thur-Sun. **Concerts** 9.30pm Mon-Thur; 11pm Fri-Sat. **Admission** free. **Credit** MC, V. **Map K2**
Over 100 different beers and bands doing everything from Oasis covers to thrash in this blokeish pub – if you're killing time before getting the last Eurostar home you could do a lot worse than kill it here.

La Flèche d'Or
102bis rue de Bagnolet, 20th (01.43.72.04.23).
M° Alexandre-Dumas or Gambetta. **Bar** 6pm-2am Mon; 10am-2am Tue-Sun. **Concerts** 9pm Wed-Sat.
Admission 25F-30F. **Credit** MC, V.
Full marks to this boisterous, uninhibited, converted railway station comprising restaurant, large S-shaped bar, stage, dancefloor (hooray!) and decent toilets. Music tends towards Afro-beats, ska, reggae, rock, folk, occasional drum'n'bass. Tuesday night sees jugglers, jesters and minstrels.

Le Gambetta
104 rue de Bagnolet, 20th (01 43 70 52 01).
M° Alexandre-Dumas or Gambetta. **Bar** 9am-2am daily. **Concerts** 8pm most nights. **Admission** free-50F. **Credit** AmEx, DC, MC, V.
The humble next-door-neighbour of La Flèche d'Or is the kind of place you'd go to hide. Locals with mullets haunt this dark, grubby yet oddly appealing little venue and its peace'n'love murals belie the

The DJ Goldie works his magic on the crowds at the **Palais Omnisports de Paris-Bercy**.

feeling that a fight could break out at any minute. It's not unlike a student union. Look out for hardcore punk rock from the likes of Spack and Chain, or anarchic *chansonniers* Mardi Grâve. *Wheelchair access.*

Horse's Mouth
120 rue Montmartre, 2nd (01.40.39.93.66). M° Sentier. **Bar** 10am-2am Mon-Sat. **Concerts** 9.30pm Wed, Thur. **Admission** free. **Credit** MC, V. **Map J4**
Big, comfortable pub that manages to feel reassuringly like London without resorting to tacky stereotypes. Happy hour is held from 4-8pm with regular folk, *chanson*, rock and world acts.

MCM Café
92 bd de Clichy, 18th (01.42.64.39.22). M° Blanche. **Bar** 9am-5am daily. **Concerts** 11pm Mon, Tue, Thur; 1.30, 4.30pm Sun. **Admission** free-50F. **Credit** AmEx, MC, V.
Since its opening in 1998 this flashy spot has been attracting city boys, stag and hen nights and tourists with strip-club fatigue. Cavernous, unfriendly, Americanised and pretentious, it is to be avoided unless you enjoy being ignored by black-clad staff whose dream is to work at the Hard Rock Café. Funk and rock dominate, and there are many DJ evenings. *Wheelchair access.*

Le Réservoir
16 rue de la Forge-Royale, 11th (01.43.56.39.60). M° Faidherbe-Chaligny. **Bar** 8pm-2am Mon-Sat. **Concerts** 11.30pm Tue-Sat; 1pm, 5.30pm Sun. **Admission** free. **Credit** MC, V. **Map N7**
An impressive glam-rustic hotspot, buzzing with good-looking trendies. The huge restaurant area dominates, frustratingly for those with dancing feet. Cocktails burn a hole in your wallet but the music is excellent – soul, groove, reggae and trip hop from the likes of Acid Groove, Backchisha and Dood. *Wheelchair access.*

French Chanson

L'Attirail
9 rue au Maire, 3rd (01.42.72.44.42). M° Arts et Métiers. **Concerts** from 8.30pm most nights. **Admission** free. **Credit** MC, V. **Map K5**
This friendly, unprepossessing, Algerian-run bar tucked away in a Marais alley offers *chanson* every night from the likes of Valse à Risque and Rick et les Affranchis. Some rap, jazz and theatre, too.

Café Concert Ailleurs
13 rue Jean-Beausire, 4th (01.44.59.82.82). M° Bastille. **Bar** 6.pm-1.15am Tue-Sun. **Concerts** 6pm, 9pm Tue-Sun. Closed Aug. **Admission** 30-80F. **Credit** (bar only) MC, V. **Map L7**
Here is an atmospheric, bohemian grotto where young, optimistic yet iffy *chanteurs* deliver songs or poems before a crowd of friends and fellow performers. It's so much like a modern-day *La Bohème* you half expect to see someone coughing to death in the corner.

Casino de Paris
16 rue de Clichy, 9th (01.49.95.22.22/box office 01.49.95.99.99). M° Trinité. **Concerts** 8.30pm Tue-Sat; 4pm Sat, Sun. **Admission** 120F-280F. **Credit** MC, V. **Map G3**
An old-fashioned red velvet theatre welcomes the trad, easy-listening end of French *variété*.

Chez Adel

10 rue de la Grange-aux-Belles, 10th (01.42.08.24.61).
M° Gare de l'Est. **Bar** 10am-2am Mon-Fri, Sun; 5pm-
2am Sat. **Concerts** 8pm Mon-Sat. Closed Aug.
Admission free. **Credit** MC, V. **Map L3**
Adel, from Syria, hosts this cosy, wooden café and
serves up home cooking and a mixture of traditional *chanson*, gypsy songs and world music including
young male trio Monsieur Monsieur.

La Folie en Tête

33 rue de la Butte-aux-Cailles, 13th (01.45.80.65.99).
M° Place d'Italie. **Bar** 5pm-2am Mon-Sat. **Concerts**
mostly 9pm Thur, check for details. **Admission** 40F
(incl 1st drink). **Credit** MC, V.
You'll fall in love with this little café in the crook of
a villagey cobbled street. But don't come with more
than two friends – it's tiny. Sometimes *chanson*,
sometimes world, but always adorable.

Glaz'Art

*7-15 av de la Porte de la Villette, 19th
(01.40.36.55.65). M° Porte de la Villette.* **Concerts**
8.30pm Wed, Thur, Fri; 10pm Sat. **Admission** 50F-
100F. **Credit** AmEx, MC, V. **Map inset**
Don't be put off by the insalubrious location or the
austere exterior (it used to be the Eurolines coach
station) – this is one of the best joints in town and
it's closing down in October 2000. There's a laidback crowd, art on the walls and a covered terrace
for barbecues. Young Francophone artists predominate, but there are also established acts. Daara J,
Baobab and Fantomas have played recently.
Wheelchair access.

Au Limonaire

*18 cité Bergère, 9th (01.45.23.33.33). M° Grands
Boulevards.* **Bar** 6pm-2am Tue-Sun. **Concerts**
8.30pm or 10pm Tue-Sat; 6pm Sun. **Admission** free.
Credit MC, V. **Map J4**
Welcoming, traditional *chanson* venue is a favourite
for Paris' clutch of young *chanson* singers such as
Laurent Madiot, Jean-Louis Blaire and France Léa.

Pari's Aller-Retour

*25 rue de Turenne, 4th (01.40.27.03.82). M° St-Paul or
Bastille.* **Concerts** 8.30pm Mon-Sat. **Admission** 50F
(incl 1st drink). **Credit** MC, V. **Map L6**
For genuine fans of *chanson*, this small venue takes
itself very seriously, despite looking like a cross
between an upmarket strip club and the set of *'Allo
'Allo*. Performers, often grave young women in
black, deliver both old and their own material.

Le Sentier des Halles

50 rue d'Aboukir, 2nd (01.42.36.37.27). M° Sentier.
Concerts 8pm or 10pm Mon-Sat. **Admission** 50F-
100F. **No credit cards. Map J4**
Created as a café-théâtre 18 years ago, this 120-seat
cellar has in the past been considered the headquarters of everything that is most inventive and
vital in French popular music. Magali Dieux, Les
Portugaises Ensablées and Ducky Smokton have
appeared recently but these days the bands are
increasingly being booted off stage to make way for
(more lucrative?) club nights.

Barges

La Balle au Bond

*(01.40.51.87.06). Oct-Mar: facing 35 quai de la
Tournelle, 5th. M° Maubert-Mutualité. Apr-Sept:
quai Malaquais, 6th. M° Pont Neuf.* **Bar** 6pm-2am
Mon-Sat; 6-10pm Sun. **Concerts** 10pm. **Admission**
20F-40F. **Credit** AmEx, MC, V. **Map winter K7;
summer H6**
A mainstream party-boat, La Balle is moored in the
shadow of Notre-Dame in summer; it offers theatre
and club nights as well as concerts featuring the likes
of Racine Blues, Corto, the ubiquitous rockers Molok
& Meleon'K, and Split. It can get touristy.

Batofar

*opposite 11 quai François-Mauriac, 13th
(01.56.29.10.00). M° Bibliothèque or Quai de la
Gare.* **Concerts** from 8pm Tue-Sun. **Admission**
20F-60F. **Credit** MC, V (bar only). **Map M9**
This huge, red, industrial-looking barge is the
acknowledged queen of the Seine and has been haul-
ing 'em in since opening in spring 1999. It has sloping metal floors, a cheap bar and great music, from
live big beat and drum'n'bass to rock from Djins and
jazz from Bugge Wesseltoft. Parisians want to hog
it for themselves, but don't let them.

La Guinguette Pirate

*quai François-Mauriac, 13th (01.56.29.10.20).
M° Bibliothèque.* **Concerts** 3pm/5pm Sun.
Admission free-40F. **Credit** (bar) MC, V. **Map N10**
This wooden Chinese junk with good-time atmosphere boasts an eclectic mix of music, performance
and customers. Regulars have included the soon-to-
be-huge Paris Combo and Les Ogres de Barback.

Péniche Blues Café

*quai de la Gare, 13th (01.45.84.53.53). M° Quai
de la Gare.* **Concerts** 9pm Mon-Thur, Sun.
Admission 40F-70F. **Credit** MC, V. **Map M9**
Spacious and airy, this barge attracts an older,
better-behaved and smaller crowd than its neighbours. Expect to hear soul, jazz, rock and reggae.

Péniche Déclic

7 quai St-Bernard, 5th (01.45.79.08.42). M° Jussieu.
Concerts 9pm Thur-Sat; 7pm Sun. **Admission** 40F.
No credit cards. Map L8
Keep your eyes peeled for this unassuming white
barge that hosts a young, chilled-out crowd. It's by
far the most relaxed barge on the strip. Don't miss the
amazing didgeridoo from Boomerang on Saturdays,
or the salsa parties from Sonando on Sundays.

Péniche Makara

*quai François-Mauriac, 13th (01.44.24.09.00).
M° Quai de la Gare.* **Bar** 7pm-2am Tue-Sun.
Concerts 9pm Tue-Sun. **Admission** 30F-50F.
Credit (bar only) MC, V. **Map M9**
No, you haven't gatecrashed someone's private
party, it's just the most intimate music barge on the
Seine. Small bar, packed dancefloor and an outside
deck to escape to when it all gets too sweaty.
Solarium, Soul Finger, Choukouloujews and funky
Wadjabak are all worth checking out.

Purple light and streaky rain

The romance of jazz in Paris still resonates. Take a walk up, say, the rue Mouffetard or around the little knit of Left Bank streets near St-Germain and you keep bumping into little fragments of it. The postcard photos of Miles and Charlie Parker evoke that post-war period when the Paris of Sartre, cafés and long cigarettes jumped off from reality into myth. It's the Paris of purple light and streaky rain, of literary 'genius' and archly leftist politics. Culturally, things surged during those years and jazz provided the soundtrack, for existentialism and, later, cinema's *nouvelle vague*.

Perhaps the centrality of jazz at such a defining moment for Paris helps to explain its elevated position in the cultural reckoning now. Like cinema, it is taken mightily seriously by both the arts-going public and the self-professed guardians of French culture. Press coverage of jazz rivals that of classical music, theatre and painting, which are mostly still considered more serious fare in the Anglo-Saxon world. Paris is home to no less than three jazz monthies and perhaps only here could you hear a radio programme (the weekly *Black and Blue* on France Culture) featuring a 90-minute discussion on the merits of a particular period of pianist Bill Evans' music, recorded live before a studio audience.

Peel back the mythology and the reality, even in the clubs, is still pretty formidable. The closure since our last edition of All Jazz Club and La Villa has definitively ended Left Bank dominance, moving it – though more by chance than design – to a little clutch of clubs near Métro Châtelet on the Right Bank (*see below* **Le Sunset**, **Le Baiser Salé**, **Petit Opportun** and **Duc des Lombards**). Here you'll find major artists, theme nights and week-long runs that give performers the chance to settle in and explore their own music, before surprisingly young audiences. At Le Sunset, or even at little **Studio des Islettes**, hidden away at the end of a dark courtyard in the Goutte d'Or, Parisians don't tend to talk through sets. This led one visiting Anglo musician to remark recently that he felt like he was playing in a cathedral.

Most Parisian clubs are still smoke-filled, sunken cellars with low ceilings – which only helps to keep the reverie of the jazz dive alive. You're sure to see at least one pacing, hunched club-owner, black guys with blondes on their arm and waitresses in little skirts. Who was it who said that the existentialists were fundamentally sexist?

Another feature of the local scene is that the famous French 'nanny state' subsidises many clubs as a buffer to the market, ensuring a diversity of programming. Stylistically, it may well be that Paris lags behind London as well as New York: fusion took hold here later and it is only in the last few years that it has receded well into the background. The late Coltrane-inspired avant-garde is in evidence and, if you know where to go, you can hear excellent good-time traditional jazz in settings that would soften the heart of even the most ardent new-waver. Top local musicians such as Emmanuel Bex love to play at the **Caveau de la Huchette** because, well, time seems to stand still at a venue that looks much as it did during the New Orleans revival of 40 years ago.

Generally, though, it's a modernist brand of hard bop that dominates at jazz clubs here. Paris is home to a pool of excellent modern players, and there are many others from Italy, Germany and Brussels who come regularly. Visiting American musicians get adulatory treatment. If their predecessors came escaping the rough times and racism of the US in the 50s, the likes of Ahmad Jamal, Jack DeJohnette, Mike Stern, Kenny Garrett and Al Foster come now to bask in the kind of attention reserved elsewhere for rock stars. At Parc Floral (*see* **Saturday afternoon fever,** *p301*), three encores are not uncommon.

Jazz

L'Arbuci Jazz Club

25 rue de Buci, 6th (01.44.32.16.00). M° Mabillon or Odéon. **Concerts** 10.30pm Wed-Sat. **Admission** free (drinks start at 70F). **Credit** AmEx, MC, V. **Map G7**
Classic jazz in the basement of a brasserie stretching back to dixie (catch sax regular Richard Raux) through to swing and R&B.

L'Atmosphère

49 rue Lucien-Sampaix, 10th (01.40.38.09.21). M° Gare de l'Est. **Bar** 11am-2am Tue-Sat; 2pm-9pm Sun. **Concerts** 8pm Tue-Sat; 5pm Sun. **Admission** free. **No credit cards. Map L3**
There's not a jot of pretence about this cosy, smoky little café by the Canal St-Martin despite a rather adventurous programme of experimental music, especially jazz-oriented groups and jazz-folk mixes.

Le Baiser Salé

58 rue des Lombards, 1st (01.42.33.37.71). M° Châtelet. **Concerts** 10pm Mon-Sat; 9.30pm Sun. **Admission** 30F-80F. **Credit** AmEx, DC, MC, V. **Map J6**
Right next to Le Sunset, this little club focuses on a bumptious mix of Latin and Afro-jazz.

Le Bilboquet

13 rue St-Benoît, 6th (01.45.48.81.84). M° St-Germain des Prés. **Concerts** 10pm daily. **Admission** 120F (incl 1st drink). **Credit** AmEx, MC, V. **Map H6**
Launched way back in 1947, this St-Germain *boîte de jazz* has received giants like Billie Holiday and Miles Davis. The club still takes care of its own, but now it's likely to be Black Jacks or Bruce Johnson redoing standards.

La Cave du Franc Pinot

1 quai Bourbon, 4th (01.46.33.60.64). M° Pont-Marie. **Bistro/bar** 6.30pm-2am Tue-Sat. **Concerts** 8.30pm Tue-Thur; 10pm-2am Fri, Sat; noon Sun. **Admission** 80F-120F (incl 1st drink). **Credit** MC, V. **Map K7**
A relative newcomer, this vaulted cellar has given Ile St-Louis the club it deserves. Bob Demeo, from New York's Blue Note club, plays jazz that swings.

Caveau de la Huchette

5 rue de la Huchette, 5th (01.43.26.65.05). M° St-Michel. **Open** 9.30pm-2.30am Mon-Thur, Sun; 9.30pm-3.30am Fri; 9.30-4am Sat. **Admission** 60F Mon-Thur, Sun; 55F students; 75F Fri, Sat. **Credit** MC, V. **Map J7**
You won't find the future of jazz here but you'll dance till you drop in a medieval cellar to a lively mix of swing, trad, boogie and rock'n'roll.

Cithéa

112-114 rue Oberkampf, 11th (01.40.21.70.95). M° Parmentier. **Open** 10pm-5am daily. **Concerts** 11pm Wed-Sat. **Admission** free Mon,Tue, Sun; 30F Wed, Thur; 60F Fri, Sat. **Credit** MC, V. **Map M5**
A winning formula of concerts followed by hip DJ mix, this is the No 1 meeting place for the new fusion with hip-hop, trip-hop, jungle, acid and techno. *See also chapter* **Clubs**.
Wheelchair access.

Duc des Lombards

42 rue des Lombards, 1st (01.42.33.22.88). M° Châtelet. **Concerts** 9pm-3am daily (Fri, Sat in Aug). **Admission** 80F-100F. **Credit** MC, V. **Map J5**
The most *New Yorkais* of the Paris clubs, 'Le Grand Duc' features leading French, and international artists including Henri Texier and Emmanuel Bex.

Le Baiser Salé: *The club isn't big, but the sound is – a bumptious mix of Latin and Afro-jazz.*

Houdon Jazz Club

5 rue des Abbesses, 18th (01.46.06.35.91).
Mº Abbesses. **Concerts** 10pm-2am Fri, Sat.
Admission free. **Credit** MC, V. **Map H2**
A cosmopolitan neighbourhood bistro where a receptive weekend audience enjoys be-bop and free jazz.

Les Instants Chavirés

7 rue Richard-Lenoir, 93100 Montreuil
(01.42.87.25.91). Mº Robespierre. **Concerts** times
vary Tue-Sun. **Admission** 80F; 60F students, over-60s; free under-16s. **No credit cards**.
A magnet for leading contemporary acts worldwide, the accent is on the young and adventurous.
Wheelchair access.

Les 7 Lézards

10 rue des Rosiers, 4th (01 48 87 08 97). Mº St Paul.
Concerts 10pm-1am Wed-Sat. **Admission** 50F-70F.
No credit cards. Map K6
The first year of the capital's newest jazz club featured a several-week residency by Steve Lacy alumni Steve Potts alongside an eclectic mix of musicians.

Lionel Hampton Jazz Club

Hôtel Le Méridien-Etoile, 81 bd Gouvion-St-Cyr, 17th
(01.40.68.34.34). Mº Porte Maillot. **Concerts**
10.30pm/12.30am Mon-Sat. **Admission** 130F-200F
(incl 1st drink). **Credit** AmEx, DC, MC, V.
This leading venue attracts major North American artists – including Oscar Peterson – but its predilection is for blues, gospel soul and big female vocalists.
Wheelchair access.

New Morning

7-9 rue des Petites-Ecuries, 10th (01.45.23.51.41).
Mº Château-d'Eau. **Box office** 4.30-7.30pm Mon-Fri.
Concerts 9pm daily. **Admission** 100F-130F.
Credit AmEx, MC, V. **Map K3**
Since the New Morning (named after a Dylan song) opened in 1981, virtually all the leading exponents of jazz, blues, funk, bebop and Latin have played here, as well as renowned African musicians. It is warm and user-friendly: people come to really listen.

Petit Journal Montparnasse

13 rue du Commandant-Mouchotte, 14th
(01.43.21.56.70). Mº Gaîté. **Admission** 10pm
Mon-Sat. **Admission** 100F-120F (incl 1st drink);
280F-340F (incl dinner). **Credit** MC, V. **Map F9**
The fare in both cuisine and music is classic French, though Archie Shepp and Manu Dibango played recently. The menu is classic jazz, big band and dixieland, with some Latin and R&B. The more rickety Latin Quarter branch goes for New Orleans dixie.
Branch: 71 bd St-Michel, 5th (01.43.26.28.59).

Petit Opportun

15 rue des Lavandières-Ste-Opportune, 1st
(01.42.36.01.36). Mº Châtelet. **Bar** 9pm-5am.
Concerts 10.30pm-3am Tue-Sat. **Admission** 50F
students; 80F. **No credit cards. Map J6**
Little brass nameplates on the bar upstairs show the calibre of musicans to have played here, including Kenny Clarke and Johnny Griffin. Tuesday is *Nuit Blanche* (all-nighter), when up to twelve musicians squeeze on to the floor.

Saturday afternoon fever

Over the past two years, the Paris Jazz Festival in beautiful Parc Floral has featured such associates of the late Miles Davis as Joe Zawinul, Kenny Garrett (pictured), Bob Berg, Mike Stern and Al Foster. To that list, add scions Ahmad Jamal, Milt Jackson and Elvin Jones, singers Dianne Reeves and Dee Dee Bridgewater, not to mention first-order French musicians like Michel Portal and Eddy Louiss. What began in 1994 as an extension of the club scene has branched out to offer some of the best-known jazzers in the world, every Saturday in the late afternoon, over four or five months, for just 10F (to get into the park). The festival features big-name Americans you might not otherwise see, either because they're too expensive in the clubs, or they don't play the clubs, or are elsewhere in Europe for the summer festivals.

There is seating for about 1600 with standing room for a few hundred more. The venue has been remodelled so that now it effectively broadcasts to the park. You can sit well back from the stage, still hear the music and, among the jazz buffs, teenagers, pram-pushers and tourists, stretch yourself out by the water or the flowerbeds.

The recent Miles fetish reveals a broad stylistic reach covering all but the extremes; in other words, no tradies or free-formers. The tilt is mass market, which in jazz looks horribly like an oxymoron, even in Paris. Suffice it to say that the keynote at Parc Floral is accessibility, in the best sense of the term.

Every Saturday from May to September
starting at 4.30pm. Mº Château de Vincennes.
(01.43.43.92.95).

Kenny Garrett

Le Slow Club
130 rue de Rivoli, 1st (01.42.33.84.30). M° Châtelet.
Concerts 10pm Tue-Sat. **Admission** 60F-75F (55F students under 25). **Credit** MC, V. **Map J6**
This little cellar, sister to the Caveau de la Huchette (*see above*), is a great place to dance to classic jazz.

Le Sunset
60 rue des Lombards, 1st (01.40.26.46.60).
M° Châtelet- Les Halles. **Concerts** 9pm Mon-Sun.
Admission 60F-100F. **Credit** V. **Map K5**
When jazz-rock was 'in', it was here – but diverse modern styles now prevail. It's a groovy, serious club with a restaurant offering an 89F *menu* and a long jazz cellar downstairs. Look out for energetic French trio Prysm and American in Paris Steve Lacy.

Studio des Islettes
10 rue des Islettes, 18th (01.42.58.63.33).
M° Barbès-Rochechouart. **Jam sessions** 9pm Mon, Tue, Thur. **Concerts** 9pm Wed, Fri, Sat.
Admission 50F. **No credit cards. Map J2**
This club is iconoclastic and they do next to no publicity. You'll find Real Book sheet music for wallpaper, second-hand furniture and a friendly atmosphere for gigs and jam sessions.

Blues Bars

See also above **Lionel Hampton Jazz Club** *and* **New Morning.**

Maxwell Café
17 bd Vital-Bouhot, 92200 Neuilly-sur-Seine (01.46.24.22.00). M° Pont de Levallois. **Concerts** 10.30pm Thur-Sat. **Admission** 100F; 80F under-25s (Thur). **Credit** AmEx, V.
This miraculously transformed garage attracts African-American musicians like Eddie King and Screamin' Jay Hawkins. Dinner-concert formula.

St-Louis Blues
33 rue Blomet, 15th (01.47.34.30.97). M° Volontaires.
Concerts 9pm-2am Thur-Sat. **Admission** 60F. **No credit cards. Map D9**
Round the corner from UNESCO, this mythical den of iniquity openly contravenes all international conventions on pleasure limitation in what used to be Josephine Baker's Bal Nègre Theatre.

Utopia
79 rue de l'Ouest, 14th (01.43.22.79.66). M° Pernéty.
Concerts 9.30pm, 10.30pm Mon-Sat; Sun jam session.
Admission 50F-70F. **Credit** MC, V. **Map F10**
At the capital's oldest blues haunt, local incarnates of such legends as Memphis Slim and Champion Jack Dupree lean into 12-bar patterns.

World & Traditional Music

Centre Mandapa
6 rue Wurtz, 13th (01.45.89.01.60). M° Glacière.
Box office *telephone* 11am-7pm Mon-Sat. **Concerts** 8.30pm. **Admission** 80F-100F. **No credit cards.**
This intimate 100-seat hall is best-known for Indian

music though you'll see other traditional forms, including from Iran and the Arab world. It's a venue that lets the audience get close to the artists.
Wheelchair access (call ahead).

Cité de la Musique
221 av Jean-Jaurès, 19th (01.44.84.45.00). M° Porte de Pantin. **Concerts** 8pm Tue-Sun plus 4.30pm Sat, 3pm Sun. **Admission** 40F-200F. **Credit** MC, V.
Map F1 (inset La Villette)
La Cité de la Musique's vast, inspiring, year-round world music programme is thematic and broad-ranging, from traditional Moroccan to jazz.

Cabaret Sauvage
bord du Canal, Parc de la Villette, 19th (01.40.03.75.15). M° Porte de la Villette. **Concerts** times vary. **Admission** 50F-120F. **Credit** (bar only) MC, V. **Map inset.**
'Wild Cabaret' rather clunks in translation but successfully evokes the whooping quasi-circus atmosphere that predominates here. Food is on offer with music from the Maghreb in a party atmosphere.

Institut du Monde Arabe
1 rue des Fossés-St-Bernard, 5th (01.40.51.38.14). M° Jussieu. **Box office** 10am-5pm Tue-Sun. **Admission** 100F; 80F students, over-60s. **Credit** MC, V. **Map K7**
The basement auditorium takes airport lounge seating to new heights, but nothing can detract from the riches of the classical Arab music on offer.
Wheelchair access.

Maison de la Culture du Japon
101bis quai Branly, 15th (01.44.37.95.00).
M° Bir-Hakeim. **Concerts** 8.30pm various days.
Admission 60F-100F. **No credit cards. Map C6**
Increasingly active in bringing Japanese artists to Paris, the programme includes dance and theatre.
Wheelchair access.

Maison des Cultures du Monde
101 bd Raspail, 6th (01.45.44.41.42). M° Notre-Dame-des-Champs. **Concerts** 8.30pm Mon-Sat; 5pm Sun. **Admission** 50F-150F; 50F under-26s. **Credit** MC, V. **Map G8**
An excellent cultural venue. Links to the state mean 'diplomatic programming' ties in with art exhibitions: for example, a series of concerts in '99 coincided with a major citywide Moroccan season.

Maroquinerie
23 rue Boyer, 20th (01.40.33.35.05). M° Gambetta.
Concerts 8.30pm Mon-Sun. **Admission** 60F-100F.
No credit cards.
Music here is mostly traditional, though ace saxophonist Rick Margitza and the world-meets-*chanson* ensemble, Paris Combo, have played recently.

Théâtre de la Ville
2 pl du Châtelet, 4th (01.42.74.22.77). M° Châtelet.
Box office (from 9am by telephone) 11am-7pm Mon; 11am-8pm Tue-Sat. **Admission** 95F; 70F under-27s (day of concert). **Credit** MC, V. **Map J6**
World music principally via an excellent 5pm concert series. Programming is often by country.
Wheelchair access (call ahead).

La vie en rose, raï, rap or reggae

Hybridity rocks the Paris music scene. It is the European city most welcoming to all those grooves bundled under the tenuous 'world' label. Contemporary Paris pop finds its inspiration not only in Gainsbourg and Piaf, but also in African, Middle Eastern, Latino and Asian music. Boosted by government quotas for French-language music, rappers like MC Solaar and Menelik and African acts like Youssou N'Dour enjoyed high airplay through the 90s. Maghreban musicians are now on a similar route. Local acts are generating high sales, holding big-venue concerts and producing music that revisits and reinterprets various heritages.

Arab music has moved from the margins to the mainstream of French pop culture. A sign of the times is the marketing of Khaled, Rachid Taha and Faudel as '1, 2, 3 *soleils*', the raï equivalent of the Three Tenors. No longer relegated to a corner of the world beat section, their records now sit alongside those of Vanessa Paradis and Mylène Farmer (with whom Khaled duets) and often occupy slots near the top of the pop charts. Khaled reached beyond his legions of fans to the mass market when he turned to French rather than Arabic on hit album *Aicha*. After ten years on the road, the Toulousan group Zebda, whose tuneful raï-ragga blend has a strong Occitan lilt, made the big time in 1999 with the catchy hit single 'Tomber la Chemise'. When the Anglo-Egyptian diva Natacha Atlas scored a top ten smash with her reinterpretation of the classic 'La Vie en Rose' in 1999, record stores didn't quite know what to make of her fusion of French-language and Egyptian-Electronica. Her disc could be found in the French, English, international, world, hip-hop or electronic sections, depending on the store.

The Gnawas of Marrakesh are another example of the clear affinities Middle Eastern and North African music can have with today's sounds, notably trance and ambient. It's just the

sort of thing that goes down well at the Divan du Monde's fortnightly Maghreban soirée, 'New Bled Vibrations', where DJ Awal spins an 'urbano-oriental' mix (gnawa-fusion, raï and rap) and 'mix nouba' (raï, chaabi, Oriental, Kabyle).

North African immigrants brought traditional Arab music to Paris, but it's second-generation artists like Faudel who are creating the interesting work. Caught between oppositional cultures and often feeling at home in neither, they are sculpting unique sounds that speak about their experiences but also earn mass appreciation. Raï music, for example, was born in rural Algeria as social and political commentaries staged at weddings and *hammams*. An alternative to the official classical Arab-language music permitted on Algerian radio, typified by Egyptian diva Oum Kalsoum, raï is 'music for the people'. Women were considered the most suitable singers, better able to express pain and sorrow as they faced the double burdens of French colonialism and local patriarchy.

The modern Made-in-France raï of Cheb Mami and Rachid Taha remains political but also integrates rap, reggae and French lyrics, and has undergone a little gender-bending as the better-known acts are male. (Notably, however, the hottest raï act in Paris is a woman, the under-promoted Cheikha Rabia – ask local *beurs* for her regular underground club performances.)

Samia Farah (pictured) probably best epitomises this celebration of hybridity. Born in France in 1971 to Tunisian parents, Farah's raspy vocals make her another Billie Holiday heir-apparent. Finding a place for her music, like Atlas' or Zebda's, will be challenging – Farah's autumn 1999 début album *Reggae (té de vivre)* fuses reggae, blues and jazz to create effortlessly seductive rhythms. The best thing about it – and about the entire new wave of Paris pop – is that it dives head-on into all kinds of different worlds to create music that defies classification.

Sport

Can a city of smokers and pleasure-seekers also be sportsmen? Parisians have a panoply of facilities at their disposal.

The best and, very often, the cheapest way to get yourself active in Paris is to make use of the plentiful sports facilities run by the municipal authorities. Here you'll find the standards surprisingly good. The best source of information is the comprehensive *Guide du Sport à Paris*, which is published annually by the Mairie de Paris and available from the *mairie* (townhall) of each *arrondissement*. The booklet covers everything from swimming pools to climbing walls, as well as details of national and local sporting federations and top-level clubs. There's also an information line, **Allô-Sports** (01.42.76.54.54/10.30am-5pm Mon-Thur, 10.30am-4.30pm Fri) which can answer queries about Parisian facilities (in French).

To use certain sports centres, you will need a *carte* for which you must show an identity card or passport (take a photo too) and, for sports perceived as risky such as inline skating or rock climbing, you often need proof of insurance, which you can sometimes buy in specialist shops or else may be included when you join a club.

For equipment, the chains Go Sport and Décathlon have branches in and around the city,

and the sports sections in department stores such as Samaritaine are also worth a look. **Au Vieux Campeur** (*see below*) has different shops specialising in individual pursuits: skiing, climbing, mountain walking and other outdoor sports.

Gyms & Fitness

Despite the Parisian obsession with looking good, there are actually rather fewer *clubs de forme* than you might expect. However, existing ones are well used and well equipped, with staff on hand to advise. Some clubs may pressure you to take out a long *abonnement* (membership) but try to negotiate, and go for a trial visit to make sure it's what you want. Also look out for promotions when membership can be half the price of official rates. For details of dance classes, *see chapter* **Dance**.

Club Quartier Latin
19 rue de Pontoise, 5th (01.55.42.77.88).
Mº Maubert-Mutualité. **Open** 9am-midnight 9.30am-7pm daily. **Membership**: Fitness section *annual* 3300F, 2600F student; *one month* 650F, student 520F; *day pass* 85F, student 70F.

Good sports: *Parisians are appearance-conscious, so they find the time to get physical.*

Credit AmEx, DC, MC, V.
The gym has plenty of well-maintained machines, together with a range of stretch, cardio and other classes. There's also a squash membership (annual 2350F, 1900F students) which grants you access to the centre's four squash courts (in varying states of repair). Both memberships include access to the Piscine Pontoise (*see box* **Testing the waters**).

Espace Vit'Halles

48 rue Rambuteau, 3rd (01.42.77.21.71).
M° Rambuteau. **Open** 8am-10pm Mon, Wed, Fri; 8am-11pm Tue, Thur; 10am-7pm Sat; 10am-4pm Sun. **Membership** *annual* 4450F/student 3560F; *one month* 900F/student 720F; *one visit* 100F.
Credit AmEx, MC, V.
The gym here is good if a little cluttered, but the instructors are knowledgeable and the crowd is non-posey. A bewildering range of classes from Tai Chi to Pump are run by enthusiastic and tolerant instructors. Changing rooms are surgically clean.

Gymnase Club

20 locations in and around Paris, contact
01.44.37.24.24 for full list. The most central are:
Palais Royal 147bis rue St-Honoré, 1st
(01.40.20.03.03), M° Palais-Royal; Champs-Elysées
26 rue de Berri, 8th (01.43.59.04.58), M° George V;
Grenelle (with pool) 8 rue Frémicourt, 15th
(01.45.75.34.00), M° Avenue Emile Zola.
Membership *annual* 4720F-5220F (reductions for some organisations, and for students); *three months* 1950F; *ten visits* 1000F. **Credit** AmEx, MC, V.
The clubs are well-equipped and instruction standards are generally good, offering the usual gamut of classes plus martial arts and weight loss. There are ladies who lunch, muscle-bound men in tight shorts, and everything in between. Check if your company or organisation has an agreement with Gymnase Club – you may be able to get a hefty discount.

Gymnasium

25 locations in and around Paris. Branches include:
62 bd Sébastopol, 3rd (01.42.74.14.56), M° Etienne-
Marcel; 129 bd Haussmann, 8th (01.42.89.89.14),
M° Miromesnil; 226 bd Raspail, 14th (01.43.21.14.40),
M° Vavin; 32 bd des Batignolles, 17th
(01.42.93.77.00), M° Place de Clichy; 60 rue Ordener,
18th (01.42.51.15.15), M° Jules-Joffrin. **Membership**
approx per month 500F. **Credit** AmEx, MC, V.
Less-geared to bulging muscles than Gymnase Club and more concerned with health aspects (weight loss as well as fitness), the Gymnasium franchise offers rowing and cycling machines and cardio-training equipment, and some branches have pools. Courses include aerobics, step, stretching and water-based workouts. Exact membership fees aren't revealed until you go for a look around.

Ken Club

100 av du Président-Kennedy, 16th (01.46.47.41.41).
M° Passy/RER Kennedy-Radio France. **Open** 8am-10pm Mon-Thur; 9.30am-6pm Fri-Sun. **Membership** *annual* 7900F (+ joining fee), *three months* 3700F, *one month* 1900F, *one day* 400F. **Credit** AmEx, MC, V.
This is a favourite hangout for media types and

Rock and stroll

Ancient boulders rise up from deep sand; occasionally, a lizard darts across your path. This is no desert landscape, but the Fontainebleau forest 60km from Paris – an illusory wilderness that attracts 10 million visitors a year.

The rock formations are the remains of lakes that formed 35 million years ago. But the trees were almost all planted by man. Fontainebleau began as a shrubby forest called Bière, a tenth the size of today's expanse. Generations of kings adopted it as their hunting ground; their country home, the Fontainebleau château, was began in the 11th century for Louis VII. With much of the forest destroyed from overuse, replanting began in the 18th century. Today the emphasis has shifted to preserving its unique wildlife, which includes 5600 plant species and 6600 animals.

With hunting restricted, the forest has become a playground for sportsmen. Climbers come from all over the world to pit their skills against the technically challenging sandstone boulders. There are 235 colour-coded circuits: white is for children, yellow and orange for adults, blue for strong climbers, red and black for super-humans.

Hiking is a classic Fontainebleau pastime; blue marks indicate the eleven romantically convoluted *sentiers bleus*. Easier to follow are the GRs (*grandes randonnées*, or 'big hikes') and PRs (*petites randonnées*). The 65km-long Tour du Massif de Fontainebleau (TMF) cuts a path all the way around the forest, and takes three days to complete. Scrambling over boulders gives Fontainebleau hikes a mountain feel, even if altitude reaches only 147m.

To limit environmental damage and accidents, mountain biking is restricted to paths at least 2.5m wide. In the Essonne region, several circuits are marked with two circles topped by a triangle. The forest's long hunting tradition means there is also plenty of opportunity for horse riding.

Never walk in the forest without a map – should you get stranded at night you might just find yourself staring into the beady red eyes of a wild boar.
Further details: L'Association des amis de la forêt de Fontainebleau (AAFF), 26 rue de la Cloche, Fontainebleau (01.64.23.46.45); Mountain Bike Folies, 246 rue Grande, Fontainebleau (01.64.23.43.70/near the train station, bike rentals and information; Club Alpin Français (01.42.02.75.94); Comité départemental du tourisme équestre (01.64.98.42.00).

celebs because of its location next to the Maison de la Radio. Expect lots of Barbies. As well as weights, there's a pool, whirlpool bath and sauna.

Vitatop

Vitatop Plein Ciel *Hôtel Sofitel, 8 rue Louis-Armand, 15th (01.45.54.79.00), Mº Balard.* **Open** 8am-10pm Mon, Wed-Fri; 8am-midnight Tue; 9am-7pm Sat; 9am-5pm Sun. **Vitatop Porte Maillot** *Hôtel Concorde Lafayette, 1 pl du Général-Koenig, 17th (01.40.68.00.21), Mº Porte-Maillot.* **Open** 8am-8pm Mon-Fri; 9am-7pm Sat; 9am-5pm Sun. **Membership** *one year 7200F; couple 13,200F.* These posh, executive gyms are located in two modern, clean hotels. The Porte Maillot branch also has a swimming pool and golf-driving range.

Activities & Team Sports

All-round Sports Clubs

The Standard Athletic Club (Route Forestière du Pavé de Meudon, 92360 Meudon-la-Forêt/ 01.46.26.16.09) is a private, non-profit-making club aimed at Anglo-Saxons living in Paris. Full membership is 3800F per year plus an initial joining fee; there are also cheaper, seasonal memberships for specific sports (such as 1150F for cricket), and student rates (2600F annual). It fields a cricket side (May-Sept), men's and women's hockey and football teams. There are eight tennis courts, two squash courts, a heated outdoor pool, billiards table and an inexpensive bar in the clubhouse. Several top-level French clubs also run teams in numerous sports (athletics, basketball, football, rugby, badminton, hockey, etc), such as **Racing Club de France** (01.45.67.55.86), **Paris Université Club** (01.44.16.62.62) and **Le Stade Français** (01.40.71.33.33).

American Football

American football does happen in the Paris area, and there are six clubs to prove it. **Les Mollosses** (01.39.76.17.05; the answer machine is for a furniture business, but it's correct) has a large squad and trains at Stade Jacques Anquetil (rue Pierre Boudou, Asnières, Mº Asnières-Gennevilliers/RER Les Grésillons). You'll find plenty of hut-huts and high-fives – not to mention a top-class playing field.

Athletics & Running

Paris bristles with tracks. The municipal sites are pretty good; find your local one in the *Guide du Sport* booklet. To give an idea of the scale, Paris has eight indoor running tracks and Britain has two. For an open-air run the Bois de Boulogne and the Bois de Vincennes are beautiful, though some parts of the Bois de Boulogne are frequented by men cruising even in daylight hours – so take note if this does not form part of your training schedule. The Paris marathon in April and the Paris to Versailles 16km run in September are the two main events.

Baseball

Baseball clubs are predictably Americanised and many of the players are English speakers. The **Patriots Baseball Club de Paris** (*recorded*

In Paris you get a good run for your money.

information 01.40.18.05.55) has competitive and recreational sections. Annual membership will set you back 500F and kit can be borrowed for a fee for competitions. Training takes place on Saturdays (6.30-8.30pm) at Gymnase Croix Nivert (107 rue de la Croix-Nivert, 15th/Mº Commerce).

Basketball

Basketball is hugely popular in Paris – and France as a whole – and almost every municipal centre has at least one court and clubs that play there. For something less structured, French teenagers frequent two courts under the Métro tracks near the Glacière stop in the 13th *arrondissement*, at Mº Stalingrad in the 19th, and there's a hoop in the Jardins du Luxembourg in the 6th. This isn't the Bronx, but it's advisable to respect the court hierarchy none the less. The **Comité Parisien de Basketball** (01.53.94.27.90) can supply a list of clubs, including Racing Club de France (01.45.67.55.86) and Paris Université Club (01.44.16.62.62).

Bowling

The Paris region has more than 25 tenpin bowling centres. The two we list below are among the most pleasant; both rent out shoes and have restaurants, games rooms and late hours. There are eight lanes at the very lively **Bowling-Mouffetard** (13 rue Gracieuse, 5th/01.43.31.09.35/Mº Place Monge/ open 3pm-2am Mon-Fri, 10am-2am Sat, Sun). The **Bowling de Paris** (Jardin d'Acclimatation, Bois de Boulogne, 16th/01.53.64.93.00/Mº Les Sablons/open 9am-3am Sun-Thur; 9am-5am Fri, Sat) has 24 lanes plus pool, billiards and video games. You have to pay 13F to get into the Jardin d'Acclimatation before you get to the centre.

The Sporting Year

France's victory in the 1998 World Cup reawakened interest in 'le foot'. Paris' only premier division team is Paris St-Germain, based at **Parc des Princes** (24 rue du Commandant-Guilbaud, 16th/01.42.30.03.60/ M° Porte d'Auteuil). Season tickets (01.40.71.10.73) cost 620F-6800F at the stadium, or get single tickets at Fnac, Virgin or in Samaritaine's sports section (100F-400F). Internationals and the rugby Six Nations Cup take place at the **Stade de France**, (rue Francis de Pressensé, 93210 St-Denis/*switchboard* 01.55.93.00.00, *reservations* 01.44.68.44.44). Southwest France is the heart of rugby union, but Paris' Racing Club de France has been snapping up top players and can be seen at **Stade Yves du Manoir** (12 rue François Faber, 92700 Colombes/01.45.67.55.86). Tickets 60F.

For more esoteric events check out the futuristic stadium and music venue, **Palais Omnisports de Paris-Bercy** (8 bd de Bercy, 12th/*switchboard* 01.40.02.60.60; *reservations* 01.44.68.44.68), which hosts everything from figure skating to indoor mountain biking.

There are seven racecourses in the Paris area. *France Galop* publishes a full race list (01.49.10.20.30) in its Calendrier des Courses. **Auteuil** *Bois de Boulogne, 16th (01.40.71.47.47). M° Porte d'Auteuil.* Steeplechasing. **Chantilly** *41km from Paris (03.44.62.41.00). Train from Gare du Nord.* Flat racing. **Enghien** *18km from Paris (01.34.17.87.00). Train from Gare du Nord.* Steeplechasing and trotting. **Longchamp** *Bois de Boulogne, 16th (01.44.30.75.00). M° Porte d'Auteuil, then free bus.* Flat racing. **Maisons-Laffitte** *1 av de La Pelouse, 78600 Maisons-Laffitte. RER A Maisons-Laffitte and then bus (01.39.62.90.95).* Flat racing. **St Cloud** *1 rue du Camp Canadien, 92210 St-Cloud. RER A Rueil-Malmaison (01.47.71.69.26).* Flat racing. **Paris-Vincennes** *Bois de Vincennes, 12th (01.49.77.17.17). M° Vincennes/RER Joinville le Pont.* Trotting.

January

Horse-racing: Prix d'Amérique Hippodrome de Paris-Vincennes. France's glitzy trotting race.

February

Rugby: Six Nations Cup matches are held at the Stade de France in February, March and April.
Tennis: Open Gaz de France at the Stade Pierre de Coubertin (82 av Georges-Lafont, 16th/01.44.31.44.31/M° Porte de St-Cloud). Big-name women players compete at this WTA indoor event.

March

Cycling: The first stage of the week-long Paris-Nice race starts outside Paris and finishes in the 16th (Valérie Larose on 01.40.93.42.43 for details).
Gymnastics: Internationaux de France at the Palais Omnisports de Paris-Bercy.
Showjumping: Jumping International de Paris, on the World Cup circuit, at Bercy.

April

Athletics: Paris Marathon Starts 9am at av des Champs-Elysées, usually first Sun in April, finishing av Foch. Information or entry forms on 01.41.33.15.68.
Horse-racing: Prix du Président de la République, a top steeplechase race, at Auteuil, third Sun of April.

May

Football: Two top matches for French football teams, the **Coupe de France** final and the **Coupe de la Ligue** final, both at the Stade de France.
Rugby: The **French Championship Final** takes place at the Stade de France.
Tennis: The **French Grand Slam** at the Stade Roland-Garros (01.47.43.48.00) (*see chapter* **Paris by Season**) is at the end of May/early June.

June

Horse-racing: The **Prix de Diane Hermès**, French equivalent of the Derby, at Chantilly.

July

Athletics: FFA Humanité meeting Top athletes gather at the Stade de France.
Athletics: IAAF Grand Prix meeting at the Stade Charléty, bd Kellerman (01.44.16.60.60).
Cycling: The **Tour de France** arrives in Paris for a grand finale on the Champs-Elysées at end of July or early Aug (information 01.41.33.15.00).
Golf: The **French Women's Open** at the Paris International Golf Club, 18 route du Golf, 95160 Baillet-en-France (01.34.69.90.00) in mid-July.

September

Golf: The **Lancôme Trophy**, at Golf de St-Nom-la-Brétèche, 78860 St-Nom-la-Brétèche (01.30.80.04.40).

October

Horse-racing: Flat race and society event **Prix de l'Arc de Triomphe** at Longchamp.

November

Tennis: The Paris Open, a top-ranking international men's indoor tournament, at Bercy.
Skating: Lalique Skating Trophy at Bercy. International ice champions and contenders.

December

Showjumping: Concours hippique international at Paris-Expo, Porte de Versailles, 15th, in association with the annual Salon du Cheval, du Poney et de l'Ane.

Climbing

The French are big on sport climbing and on bolt-ing climbs, so if you come from the UK tradition, there may be a culture gap to overcome. In Paris, there are five municipal *murs d'escalade*, three outdoor and two indoor. They are often reserved for schools and climbing clubs, but facilities are also open to individuals on a one-month membership (20F, with photo, proof of insurance and passport) if you have your own gear. The wall at the **Centre Sportif Poissonnier** (2 rue Jean-Cocteau, 18th/ 01.42.51.24.68/M° Porte de Clignancourt) is the largest municipal facility and has a little 'real rock' section as well as a 21m-high unlit outside wall.

For more of a workout, there is the privately run **Mur Mur** (55 rue Cartier Bresson, 93500 Pantin/ 01.48.46.11.00/ M° Aubervilliers-Pantin Quatre Chemins), said to be the best climbing wall in Europe if not the world, with 1500 square metres of wall and 10,000 holds. It costs 33F-65F for adults, 15F-30F for under-12s per session. There's kit for hire and tuition offered. Newly added is a section to practise ice-climbing (or 'dry-tooling', as they call it).

If you prefer real rock, you can train on the huge, slightly surreal boulders strewn around the Forêt de Fontainebleau (*see box*, **Rock and stroll**).

Cycling

Paris isn't a particularly cycle-friendly city, due to the pushy traffic, but bike lanes have been ambitiously expanded, and increasing numbers of cyclists are taking to the streets. Away from the urban snarl, the Bois de Boulogne and the Bois de Vincennes offer good cycling. The quais of the Seine and the Canal St-Martin, closed to traffic Sundays (10am-4pm) in summer, are probably the nicest stretches of all for cyclists, rollers and pedestrians. (*See chapter* **Directory** for information on cycle lanes.)

Paris has many cycling clubs, both in the competition-based and more leisurely categories. You can find your nearest club by phoning the **Fédération Française de Cyclotourisme** (01.44.16.88.88). Mountain biking (VTT, *vélo tout terrain* in French) is limited in Paris: Parisian MTBers head for the forests of Fontainebleau, Meudon and Montmorency. VTT Evasion guides to bike routes in various forests are produced by the Office National des Forêts and can be bought at good bookshops for 35F each. The **Stade Vélodrome Jacques-Anquetil** (Bois de Vincennes, 12th/01.43.68.01.27) is a functional racing track open to cyclists on a regular basis, if you are a licenced member of a club. For general bike needs, branches of **GoSport** should suffice. For specialist MTB, try **VTT Center** (1 pl Rungis, 13th/01.45.65.49.89), while the **Maison du Vélo** (11 rue Fénélon, 10th/01.42.81.24.72) sells, hires and repairs all types of bikes. There are also a number of companies offering bike tours in and around Paris (*see chapter* **Directory** for details).

Diving

If you are in Paris for some time it's worth joining a club as it works out cheaper. If time is limited, a pricier, commercial outfit will get you your certificate. For a diving shop, try **Plongespace** (80 rue Balard, 15th/01.45.57.01.01).

The **Club de Plongée du 5ème Arrondissement** (01.43.36.07.67) is a friendly club where you can train for the French licence. It organises trips to the Med and meets at the Piscine Jean-Taris (*see box* **Testing the waters**), although there may be a waiting list to join. There are well-qualified, experienced instructors at **Surplouf** (06.14.10.26.11/ 01.42.21.18.14), which offers courses in English. Courses for beginners, including textbooks, insurance and gear rental, cost 1680F for the French licence or 1850F for the PADI certificate.

Football

To find an amateur team to play for, call the **Ligue Ile de France de Football** (01.42.44.12.12) and ask for a contact number in your *arrondissement*.

Golf

Golf has become the French status-seeker's sport of choice now that tennis is more or less democratised. There are no courses in Paris, but scores in the Paris region, many open to non-members. For a full list, contact the **French Golf Federation** (68 rue Anatole France, 92309 Levallois Perret/01.41.49.77.00). The **Golf Clément Ader** (Domaine du Château Péreire, 77220 Gretz Armainvilliers/01.64.07.34.10/ SNCF Gretz Armainvilliers) is a challenging, Japanese-designed course with plenty of water hazards. The **Golf Disneyland Paris Marne-la-Vallée** (77777 Marne-la-Vallée/01.60.45.68.04/ RER Marne-la-Vallée-Chessy then taxi) has everything you'll need: 27 holes, a great clubhouse, American professionals, buggies and equipment for hire, not to mention (Mickey) mouse-shaped bunkers. The **Golf du Réveillon** (Ferme des Hyverneaux, 77150 Lesigny/ 01.60.02.17.33/RER Boissy-St-Léger then taxi) is an attractive, 36-hole public course.

Closer to central Paris is the **Académie de Golf de Paris** at the Paris Country Club, Hippodrome de Saint-Cloud (1 rue du Camp Canadien, 92210 Saint-Cloud/ 01.47.71.39.22/SNCF Suresnes Longchamp), which has a nine-hole course within the Hippodrome horse-racing track, plus pitch and putt facilities. There are also some golf driving ranges, including the one at **Aquaboulevard** (*see box* **Testing the waters**).

Horse Riding

Both the Bois de Boulogne and the Bois de Vincennes are beautiful places to ride but it must be done under the auspices of a riding club. You can join one of the following clubs: La Société d'Equitation de Paris (01.45.01.20.06), the Centre Hippique du Touring (01.45.01.20.88) or the Cercle Hippique du Bois de Vincennes (01.48.73.01.28). Complete beginners can learn to ride in the unpretentious **Club Bayard Equitation** (Bois de Vincennes, Centre Bayard/ UCPA de Vincennes, av de Polygone, 12th/

The Champs-Elysées is not just posh and posey: it gets sweaty during the **Marathon**.

01.43.65.46.87). Membership runs for three months (1252F) or you can do a five-day course in July or August (1615F). The **Haras de Jardy** (bd de Jardy, 92430 Marnes-la-Coquette/01.47.01.35.30) is a lovely equestrian centre near Versailles, which organises accompanied group rides (212F for two hours); or you can take out a three-month membership for 1440F, plus 240F insurance for a year.

Ice Skating

In winter (mid Dec-early Mar) the pretty **place de l'Hôtel de Ville** is transformed into an open-air ice rink. Skate hire is 30F and use of the rink is free. If temperatures drop extremely low, there is skating on Lac Supérieur in the **Bois de Boulogne**. Indoor all-year round rinks include the **Patinoire de Boulogne** (1 rue Victor Griffuelhes, Boulogne-Billancourt/01.46.94.99.74/M° Marcel Sembat) and the **Patinoire d'Asnières-sur-Seine** (bd Pierre de Coubertin, 92600 Asnières/ 01.47.99.96.06/M° Gabriel Péri/Asnières-Gennevilliers), although public opening hours are restricted due to school use.

Rowing & Watersports

In France one learns to scull before doing sweep-oar and you will be marginalised if you can't scull. Children and adults can row, canoe and kayak (Wed, Sat; equipment is provided) in the 600m x 65m basin at the **Base Nautique de la Villette** (15-17 quai de la Loire, 19th/01.42.40.29.90/M° Jaurès). La Défense-based **Société Nautique de la Basse Seine** (26 quai du Président Paul Doumer, 92400 Courbevoie/01.43.33.03.47) has both competitive and recreational sections, good equipment and a strong history. If you're just after some relaxing recreational rowing, you can hire boats by the hour on **Lac Daumesnil** and **Lac des Minimes** in the **Bois de Vincennes** or on **Lac Supérieur** in the **Bois de Boulogne**.

Rugby

If you want to play on a French-speaking team, call the **Comité Ile de France de Rugby** (01.43.42.51.51). Top-level rugby goes on at **Racing Club de France** (5 rue Eblé, 7th/01.45.67.55.86. Ground: Terrain Yves-du-Manoir, 12 rue François Faber, 92700 Colombes). Part of a huge multi-sport club, the top team is professional. For a good club standard try the **Athletic Club de Boulogne** (Saut du Loup, route des Tribunes, 16th/ 01.41.10.25.30), which fields two teams (training 7.30pm Tue-Thur; matches on Sun). The **British Rugby Club of Paris** run by Guy Grundy (01.40.55.15.15) describes itself as convivial rather than fanatical. It runs two Saturday sides and trains Wed 8pm at the Standard Athletic Club (*see above*).

Snooker/Billiards

The French have their own brand of (pocketless) billiards, and many halls and bars here have only French or American pool tables. The rare snooker facilities include the **Bowling de Paris** (*see above* **Bowling**), which has one table among its French ones. A beer-and-Gitanes establishment, the **Académie de Billard Clichy-Montmartre** (84 rue de Clichy, 9th/01.48.78.32.85/M° Place de Clichy) has a full-size snooker table along with a room of French ones, tile floors, high ceilings and tall mirrors. There are French and American tables, a relaxing atmosphere and a bar at the **Blue-Billard** (111-113 rue St-Maur, 11th/01.43.55.87.21/ M° Parmentier), and you can play for free between

Breaking the ice: **the place de l'Hôtel de Ville** *is a friendly, free, open-air rink in winter.*

Testing the waters

Paris has 34 public swimming pools. They have restricted weekday opening hours due to school use. In term time most open early mornings (7-8am) and at lunchtimes (11.30am-1pm) on weekdays, plus Wed afternoons and all day at weekends (longer hours in the holidays). They cost 16F (adults) and 9F (children). Private pools cost more.

Piscine Suzanne-Berlioux
Forum des Halles, 10 pl de la Rotonde, 1st (01.42.36.98.44). Mᵒ Les Halles. **Admission** 25F, 20F children. This 50m private pool with tropical greenhouse in the Forum des Halles is clean, crowded and attracts a young, hip clientele.

Piscine Saint-Merri
16 rue du Renard, 4th (01.42.72.29.45). Mᵒ Hôtel-de-Ville or Rambuteau. 25m pool with greenery.

Piscine Jean-Taris
16 rue Thouin, 5th (01.43.25.54.03). Mᵒ Cardinal Lemoine. Look out on to the Panthéon from this lovely if sometimes cramped 25m pool.

Piscine Pontoise
19 rue de Pontoise, 5th (01.55.42.77.88). Mᵒ Maubert-Mutualité. **Admission** 25F, 19F under-16s, 22F students; 44F at night incl gym access. Art Deco 33m pool has music and underwater lighting by night. See above **Club Quartier Latin.**

Piscine St-Germain
12 rue Lobineau, 6th (01.43.29.08.15). Mᵒ Mabillon. Underground 25m pool in St-Germain.

Piscine Cour-des-Lions
11 rue Alphonse-Baudin, 11th (01.43.55.09.23). Mᵒ Richard-Lenoir. A 25m pool near the Marais.

Piscine Roger-LeGall
34 bd Carnot, 12th (01.44.73.81.12). Mᵒ Porte de Vincennes. **Admission** *winter* 25F, 17.5F children, 17F students; *summer* 36F, 18F children, 26F students, less after 5.30pm. With sauna 50F. This is a private, calm, outdoor pool, covered in winter.

Piscine Butte-aux-Cailles
5 pl Paul-Verlaine, 13th (01.45.89.60.05). Mᵒ Place d'Italie. 33m main pool and two outdoor pools built in the 1920s with Italian tiles.

Piscine Didot
22 av Georges-Lafenestre, 14th (01.42.76.78.14). Mᵒ Porte de Vanves. This 25m pool welcomes diving clubs and aquagym as well as swimmers.

Aquaboulevard
4 rue Louis-Armand, 15th (01.40.60.15.15). Mᵒ Balard. **Admission** *four hours in peak periods* 77F, 3-11s 58F; couple + child 149F (30F for each additional child). An extravagant indoor-outdoor

complex with tropical lagoon, waves, flumes and sun terrace. Great for kids. *See* **Club Forest Hill.**

Piscine Armand-Massard
66 bd du Montparnasse, 15th (01.45.38.65.19). Mᵒ Montparnasse-Bienvenüe. An underground sports centre with three pools.

Piscine Emile-Anthoine
9 rue Jean-Rey, 15th (01.53.69.61.59/ 01.42.76.78.18). Mᵒ Bir-Hakeim. Busy, ultramodern 25m municipal pool with a great view of the Eiffel Tower from the deep end.

Piscine Henry-de-Montherlant
32 bd Lannes, 16th (01.40.72.28.30). Mᵒ Porte-Dauphine. Popular, modern 25m pool (plus beginners' pool) with chic clientele.

Piscine Hébert
2 rue des Fillettes, 18th (01.46.07.60.01). Mᵒ Marx-Dormoy. Crowded 25m pool with retractable roof.

Piscine Georges-Hermant
6-10 rue David d'Angers, 19th (01.42.02.45.10). Mᵒ Danube. **Admission** 22F, 19F under-16s. Privately run, this is Paris' biggest pool (50m x 20m).

Piscine Georges-Vallerey
148 av Gambetta, 20th (01.40.31.15.20). Mᵒ Porte des Lilas. **Admission** 26F, 21F 4-16s. The pool where Johnny Weissmuller (Tarzan) swam to gold in the 1924 Olympics, now split in two.

Piscine en Plein Air du Parc de Sceaux
148 av du Général de Gaulle, 92160 Antony (01.46.60.75.30). RER Croix de Berny. **Admission** 19F-28F. Three outdoor pools with public lawn. Open 9am-9pm, May to September.

noon and 2pm if you have lunch. The velveteen atmosphere and the scent of cigars and cognac makes the **Hôtel Concorde St-Lazare** (108 rue St-Lazare, 8th/01.40.08.44.44/Mº St-Lazare) the most elegant setting for playing French billiards. **Les Mousquetaires** (77 av du Maine, 14th/01.43.22.50.46/Mº Gaîté), a popular young bar with an eleven-table pool room in the back, is a good place to shoot French or American pool.

Inline skating

They're everywhere, weaving through traffic and taking over parks and quays. If a fast night-time glide around Paris appeals, the free Friday Night Fever trip by **Paris Roller** (01.43.36.89.81) leaves at 10pm each Friday from the Place d'Italie and travels up to 30km in three hours with a police escort. With a crowd of participants and a fast pace, you need to be experienced to keep up. The **Roller Squad Institut** (01.45.88.23.75) has free beginners' trips (3pm Sat from Les Invalides), and activities for more advanced bladers. **Roller Nomades** (01.44.54.07.44) also do *balades*, leaving 2.15pm each Sun from their Bastille shop. To skate out on your own, try the Bois de Vincennes (12th), Promenade Plantée (12th) or the Seine quays on Sundays. For stunts, there's a ramp at **Skatepark** (15th/01.40.60.77.18).

Skating shops sell a range of kit, and you can hire blades and protective pads for 50F-80F a day. Specialists include **Parking Bld Roller Station** (01.47.00.99.00), **Vertical Line** (01.47.27.21.21) and **Bike 'n' Roller** (01.44.07.35.89). Most do lessons by

Blades in spades on the streets of Paris.

the hour. Generalist sports shops including **Go Sport** (01.40.26.40.52) and **Au Vieux Campeur** (01.53.10.48.48) also have good skate sections.

Squash

You can play at Club Quartier Latin and the Standard Athletic Club (*see above*), or try **Squash Montmartre** (14 rue Achille-Martinet, 18th/01.42.55.38.30/Mº Lamarck-Caulaincourt) which has four glazed squash courts, and offers lessons. Membership is 3400F per year or 900F for three months, plus reservation and lights each time, or you can pay each visit (80F per person per hour).

Tennis: Public Courts

If you want to make the most of any of the some 170 city-operated courts in Paris, you can either show up and hope for the best or, if you are a resident, you can use Minitel 3615 Paris (*see chapter Directory*) to book a court in advance. To register, pick up an application form from one of the city's 43 tennis centres (or in the *Guide du Sport*) and post it with a copy of your identity card and two passport-size photos; you'll have to wait over a month to get your Carte Paris-Tennis and a reservation number. Whether you use Minitel or just show up, the price is the same: 37F per hour, 53F per hour with lights.

The six asphalt courts in the **Jardins du Luxembourg** (6th/01.43.25.79.18/ Mº Notre-Dame-des-Champs or RER Luxembourg) are a great place to play – and be seen playing. The **Centre Sportif La Falguère** (Route de la Pyramide, Bois de Vincennes, 12th/01.43.74.40.93/Mº Château de Vincennes) is a symmetrical complex, with 21 acrylic and asphalt courts. With seven hard courts, the **Centre Sportif Henry-de-Montherlant** (30-32 bd Lannes, 16th/01.40.72.28.33/Mº Porte-Dauphine) gets a lot of use from students and clubs. There's a free hitting wall for those without a partner.

You can also join a club and play on municipal courts. The cost depends on how long you're staying in Paris. Some clubs cost only 500F in membership fees, plus the 22F court rental fee. Compared to a private club, this is a bargain.

Tennis: Private Clubs

There are some lovely private clubs in and around Paris, but most are expensive and have long waiting lists. Courts are generally in superb condition and you don't have to figure out the Minitel to get a reservation. There are 20 red clay courts (10 indoors) at the **Stade Jean Bouin** (26 av du Général-Sarrail, 16th/01.46.51.55.40/Mº Porte d'Auteuil), the site of the men's qualifying tournament for the French Open. The **Tennis de Longchamp** (19 bd Anatole-France, 92100 Boulogne/01.46.03.84.49/Mº Boulogne-Jean Jaurès) has 20 well-maintained hard courts. **Club Forest Hill** (4 rue Louis-Armand, 15th/01.40.60.10.00/Mº Balard or RER Boulevard Victor) has 14 branches in the Paris region and is an affordable alternative, even if most of its locations are beyond the *périphérique*: annual membership is around 4000F; non-members can play for 150F-250F per visit.

Theatre

Whether you're after a reassuring dose of Molière or the latest avant-garde experiment, it's somewhere on the Paris stage.

The key to finding theatre you enjoy is knowing where to look. Most theatres put on something in the way of Corneille, Racine, Molière and Marivaux. But while playwrights such as **Yasmina Reza** have had huge success overseas as well as in Paris, they are seen as 'commercial', and are almost never staged in the prestigious, subsidised venues, where an evening's theatre is likely to be a classic given a new intellectual twist or a cerebral experimentation in philosophy.

As far as contemporary playwrights are concerned, most will be unfamiliar even to many French people. This is due mostly to the postwar dominance of director-led theatre. In the last few years, though, text has been making a comeback as directors have returned to plays for inspiration, instead of devised works, adaptations of non-theatrical texts and physical theatre. If your French is up to it, Paris continues to live up to its reputation as a hotbed of avant-garde experimentation, replacing the notion that plays need such basics as plot or characters, with theme, poetic language and experiments with structure. For a more visual approach (good if your French isn't as fluent as it could be), try the **Théâtre de la Bastille** or **Théâtre de la Villette**, which experiment with mixing media. If farce, comedy and traditional theatre-as-entertainment is your style, try the theatres of the Grands Boulevards and Montparnasse.

BEYOND THE PERIPHERIQUE

Paris' suburbs are home to some interesting productions, which can be explained as much by the subsidies they enjoy as by a variety intended to please both Parisian intelligentsia and the local working classes. Well-known suburban theatres include: Théâtre de la Commune (2 rue Edouard Poisson, 93300 Aubervilliers/01.48.33.93.93); MC93 (1 bd Lénine, 93000 Bobigny/01.41.60.72.72); Théâtre de Gennevilliers (41 av des Grésillons, 92230 Gennevilliers/01.41.32.26.10); Théâtre des Amandiers (7 av Pablo Picasso, 92022 Nanterre/ 01.46.14.70.00); Théâtre des Quartiers d'Ivry-La Balance (1 rue Simon Dereure, 94200 Ivry-sur-Seine/01.46.72.37.43); and Théâtre Gérard Philipe (59 bd Jules Guesde, 93200 St-Denis/01.48.13.70.00).

PLAYING IN ENGLISH

English-language theatre is booming. As well as the prestigious visiting companies occasionally hosted by the Odéon, MC93 Bobigny and Bouffes du Nord, an ever-growing number of resident theatre companies is performing an increasingly adventurous repertoire, alongside staples Wilde, Pinter and Mamet. Dear Conjunction, On Stage Theatre Co, Walk & Talk Productions and Glasshouse Theatre Co perform new and established plays, as does Bravo Productions which also gives free play readings every Monday at the Café de Flore. Regular venues are the **Petit Hébertot**, Théâtre de Nesle (8 rue de Nesle, 6th/ 01.46.34.61.04) and Théâtre des Déchargeurs (3 rue des Déchargeurs, 1st/01.42.36.00.02). Long-established, educational theatre company ACT (01.40.33.64.02) performs modern classics geared to the French school syllabus. For less highbrow entertainment, the amateur International Players (01.34.62.02.19) stages a musical or comedy every spring in St-Germain-en-Laye.

Booking Tips

For details of current programmes see the *Time Out Paris* section of *Pariscope*. Tickets can be bought direct from theatres, at ticket agencies (*see chapter* **Directory**) and at the following specialist agencies: Minitel, on 3615 THEA; Agence Chèque Théâtre (33 rue Le Peletier, 9th/01.42.46.72.40; open 10am-7pm Mon-Sat) and Kiosque Théâtre (opposite 15 pl de la Madeleine, 9th, and in front of Gare Montparnasse, 15th; open noon-8pm Tue-Sun) which sells same-day tickets at half-price, plus 16F commission per seat. Many private theatres offer 50 per cent reductions on previews and students can also benefit from good same-day deals. A new discount for under-26s gives access to the best seats in 46 theatres for 70F (0800 800 750). Another new initiative: on Thursdays all seats at the four national theatres cost 50F.

National Theatres

Comédie Française

Salle Richelieu *2 rue de Richelieu, 1st (01.44.58.15.15). M° Palais-Royal.* **Box office** 11am-6pm daily. **Tickets** 30F-190F; 65F under-27s (1hr before play). **Credit** AmEx, MC, V. **Map H5**
Théâtre du Vieux-Colombier *21 rue du Vieux-Colombier, 6th (01.44.39.87.00). M° St-Sulpice.* **Box office** 1-6pm Mon, Sun; 11am-7pm Tue-Sat. **Tickets** 160F; 110F over-60s; 85F under-27s; 65F under-27s (45mins before play). **Credit** MC, V. **Map G7**
Studio Théâtre *pl de la Pyramide inversée, Galerie du Carrousel (99 rue de Rivoli), 1st (01.44.58.98.58). M° Palais-Royal.* **Box office** 5.30pm on day. **Tickets** 80F; 45F under-27s. **Credit** MC, V. **Map H5**

Founded in 1680 by Louis XIV, France's oldest company moved to its building adjoining the Palais-Royal just after the French Revolution. This is the only national theatre to have its own permanent troupe, the *pensionnaires*, whose repertoire ranges from Molière and Racine to modern classics (Genet, Anouilh, Stoppard). The Théâtre du Vieux-Colombier offers small-scale classics and contemporary works, and Studio Théâtre is used for short plays, *salons* and a *théâtrothèque* of plays on video (Sat afternoon). *Wheelchair access (call ahead).*

Odéon, Théâtre de l'Europe
1 pl de l'Odéon, 6th (01.44.41.36.36). Mᵒ Odéon/RER Luxembourg. **Box office** 11am-6.30pm Mon-Sat; *telephone* 11am-7pm Mon-Sat (Sun if play on). **Tickets** 30F-180F; 50F student on day. **Credit** MC, V. **Map H7**
Based in a beautiful Neo-Classical theatre, the Odéon, under director Georges Lavaudant, stages a contrasting mix of French and international productions, classic and contemporary. Famous visiting directors have included Deborah Warner, Luc Bondy, Luca Ronconi and Krystian Lupa. *Wheelchair access (call ahead).*

Théâtre National de Chaillot
Palais de Chaillot, 1 pl du Trocadéro, 16th (01.53.65.30.00). Mᵒ Trocadéro. **Box office** 11am-7pm Mon-Sat; 11am-5pm Sun; *telephone* 9am-7pm Mon-Sat; 11am-7pm Sun. **Tickets** 160F; 120F over-60s; 80F under-25s. **Credit** MC, V. **Map B5**
Flamboyant entertainment-value productions are staged here in a monumental 2800-seat, 1930s theatre. Laptop subtitling system for some performances. *Wheelchair access (call ahead).*

Théâtre National de la Colline
15 rue Malte-Brun, 20th (01.44.62.52.52). *Mᵒ Gambetta.* **Box office** 11am-7pm Mon, Wed-Sat; 11am-6pm Tue; 2-5pm Sun if play on; *telephone* Mon-Sat only. **Tickets** 160F; 130F over-60s; 80F under-30s; 110F Tue. **Credit** MC, V. **Map Q5**
This modern theatre directed by Alain Franchon has a remit for twentieth-century drama, with a repertoire mixing French and international bigwigs, like Vinaver, Müller and Bond. Look out for lesser-known names in the Petit Théâtre upstairs. *Wheelchair access.*

Right Bank

Théâtre de la Ville/Les Abbesses
2 pl du Châtelet, 4th (01.42.74.22.77). Mᵒ Châtelet. **Box office** 11am-7pm Mon; 11am-8pm Tue-Sat; *telephone* 11am-7pm Mon-Sat. **Tickets** 95F-140F; half-price on day under-27s. **Credit** MC, V. **Map J6**
Funded by the City of Paris, this major dance venue presents some plays, varying from first-rate to controversial. Les Abbesses (31 rue des Abbesses, 18th/01.42.74.22.77) is its second, Montmartre-based space. *See also chapters* **Dance**, **Music: Classical & Opera** *and* **Music: Rock, Roots & Jazz**. *Wheelchair access.*

Théâtre Essaïon de Paris
6 rue Pierre-au-Lard, 4th (01.42.78.46.42). *Mᵒ Rambuteau.* **Box office** 30mins before, *telephone* 2-10pm daily. **Tickets** 100F-150F; 70F under-25s; 90F-100F over-60s. **Credit** MC, V. **Map K6**
Two ancient cellars converted into smallish theatre spaces host a proudly contemporary repertoire.

Family relationships are explored in Olivier Py's Théâtres, *above, at* **Les Abbesses** *in 2000.*

The playwright's the thing

Who you should know about in French theatre.

Playwrights

Jean-Marie Besset
Master of the well-made, terribly middle-class play, including *Un coeur français*, about political cover-ups, and *Grande École*. Gritty realism it is not. Adaptor of British and US plays into French, including Tom Stoppard and Tennessee Williams.

Hélène Cixous
Playwright and novelist, Cixous works in collaboration with **Mnouchkine**'s Théâtre du Soleil to produce its playscripts, including the recent *Soudain, les nuits d'éveil* and *Tambours sur la digue*.

Xavier Durringer
Writer and director of film as well as theatre, his works have a strong, urban voice combined with a non-realism that lends a poetic rhythm to the dialogue. *Surfeurs* was staged at La Colline in 1999. He also directed Jane Birkin in *Oh Pardon! Tu dormais* at the Gaîté-Montparnasse.

Jean-Claude Grumberg
Writer of accessible, popular plays, including *L'Atelier* (1979 but revived to acclaim in 1998 at the Hébertot), *Adam et Eve* (Chaillot, 1997) and *Rêver, peut-être* (Vieux Colombier, 1999).

Bernard-Marie Koltès
Koltès, who died in 1989, was championed by director **Patrice Chéreau**. His plays are both poetic and black, dealing with the limits of the human condition, as in the animalistic sparring in *Dans la solitude des champs de coton*.

Philippe Minyana
One of the new vanguard of playwrights who has turned from traditional structure to experiment with plot, character and form in recent plays such as *Drames brefs (1)* and *La Maison des morts*.

Valère Novarina
Poet and playwright, Novarina is a master of anarchic, graphic pictures with words. Works include *Le Repas* (Centre Pompidou, 1996), *L'Opérette imaginaire* (Bastille, 1998), *Le Jardin de reconnaissance* (L'Athénée, 1997).

Yasmina Reza
Much fêted author of Paris, West-End and Broadway hit *Art*, her plays are slightly more challenging than the average boulevard comedy.

Eric-Emmanuel Schmitt
A box-office favourite, his hits include *Le Visiteur* (an encounter between Freud and God), *Variations énigmatiques*, marking Alain Delon's theatrical comeback, and *Hôtel des deux mondes*, his latest philosophical foray (into life after death). Slick, witty, with an accessible bent on philosophy.

Michel Vinaver
The patriarch of French contemporary playwrights has been writing since the 1950s, at the same time maintaining a successful career with Gillette. Works (often staged in the UK at the Orange Tree) experiment with multiple viewpoints and explore life from the *quotidien*. His latest, *King*, was staged at La Colline in 1999 alongside the earlier *Les Huissiers*.

Directors

Philippe Adrien
Based at the Cartoucherie's Théâtre de la Tempête and elsewhere, Adrien is well-respected for work with contemporary writers, from Tom Stoppard to Molière prizewinner Arnaud Bédouet.

Stéphane Braunschweig
Colourful, flamboyant director of opera and theatre, based at Gennevilliers. *Peer Gynt* and *Franziska* by Wedekind were particularly memorable.

Patrice Chéreau
Swashbuckling director of stage and screen, responsible for pioneering the work of Koltès, but currently more active in cinema than theatre.

Alain Franchon
Director of the Théâtre national de la Colline, and the champion of Edward Bond in France.

Patrice Kerbrat
Director of popular playwrights including Jean-Marie Besset, Yasmina Reza and, most recently, Marguerite Duras.

Ariane Mnouchkine
Legendary director of the Théâtre du Soleil, where she continues her internationally influenced, ritualistic theatre explorations with Hélène Cixous. In 1999, *Tambours sur la digue* explored traditional Oriental theatre through the invention of an 'ancient' tale using puppets played by actors.

Bernard Murat
Boulevard director extraordinaire, Murat's productions include Eric-Emmanuel Schmitt's big successes and David Hare's *The Blue Room*.

Olivier Py
This writer-director combines a sense of mystery and myth with a lively narrative voice and a terrific sense of humour. His works include *Le Visage d'Orphée* as well as the mammoth, 24-hour-long *La Servante* series.

Bouffes du Nord

37bis bd de la Chapelle, 10th (01.46.07.34.50).
M° La Chapelle. **Box office** 11am-6pm Mon-Sat.
Tickets 80F-140F. **Credit** MC, V. **Map L2**
This famously unrenovated theatre is home to Peter
Brook's experimental company the CICT; Stéphane
Lissner's co-direction has added classical and opera.
Sometimes hosts visiting productions in English.
Wheelchair access (call ahead).

Théâtre de la Bastille

76 rue de la Roquette, 11th (01.43.57.42.14).
M° Bastille or Voltaire. **Box office** 10am-6pm
Mon-Fri; 2-6.30pm Sat, Sun. **Tickets** 120F; 80F
under-26s, over-60s. **Credit** AmEx, MC, V. **Map M6**
Experimental theatre, music and dance by playwrights
like Deutsch or Novarina. *See also chapter* **Dance.**
Wheelchair access ('salle de bas' only).

Cartoucherie de Vincennes

route du Champ de Manoeuvre, bois de Vincennes,
12th. M° Château de Vincennes, then shuttle bus or
bus 112. Each theatre operates independently.
An old cartridge factory houses a complex that includes Mnouchkine's Théâtre du Soleil (01.43.74.24.08),
Théâtre de l'Epée de Bois (01.48.08.39.74), Théâtre de
la Tempête (01.43.28.36.36), Théâtre de l'Aquarium
(01.43.74.99.61), Théâtre du Chaudron (01.43.28.97.04).

Théâtre Paris-Villette

211 av Jean-Jaurès, 19th (01.42.02.02.68). M° Porte
de Pantin. **Box office** from 3pm Mon-Fri; *telephone*
10.30am-6pm Mon-Fri. **Tickets** 135F; 95F Wed, over-
60s; 65F under-26s. **No credit cards. Map insert.**
This stylish, popular venue hosts a varied contemporary programme offering the chance to discover
unknown writers and directors.
Wheelchair access (call ahead).

Boulevard Theatres

Comédie des Champs-Elysées

15 av Montaigne, 8th (01.53.23.99.19).
M° Alma-Marceau. **Box office** 11am-6pm Mon;
11am-7pm Tue-Sat. **Tickets** 110F-250F.
Credit AmEx, MC, V. **Map D5**
Baby brother of the Théâtre des Champs-Elysées
(*see chapter* **Music: Classical & Opera**) offers
mainstream modern and contemporary works.
Wheelchair access (call ahead).

Théâtre de l'Athénée-Louis Jouvet

7 rue Boudreau, sq de l'Opéra-Louis-Jouvet, 9th
(01.53.05.19.19). M° Havre-Caumartin/RER Auber.
Box office 11am-7pm Mon-Fri; 1-7pm Sat. **Tickets**
35F-160F. **Credit** MC, V. **Map G4**
Beautiful old theatre does French and foreign classics.
Wheelchair access (call ahead).

La Bruyère

5 rue La Bruyère, 9th (01.48.74.76.99).
M° St-Georges. **Box office** 11am-7pm Mon-Sat.
Tickets 120F-210F; 70F under-26s (Mon-Thur);
150F over-60s (Mon-Thur). **Credit** MC, V. **Map H2**
This archetypal boulevard theatre is home to count-
less big box-office hits from home and abroad.
Wheelchair access (call ahead).

Théâtre Hébertot/Petit Hébertot

78bis bd des Batignolles, 17th (01.43.87.23.23/Petit
Hébertot 01.44.70.06.69). M° Villiers or Rome. **Box**
office 11am-5.30pm Mon; 11am-7pm Tue-Sat; 11am-
2pm Sun. **Tickets** 105F-265F; *Petit Hébertot* Mon-Wed,
Sun 50F; Thur-Sat 100F. **Credit** MC, V. **Map F2**
This historic venue hosts popular contemporary writ-
ers such as Reza, Besset and Grumberg, alongside
Pirandello and Sartre, plus regular English stagings.
Wheelchair access (call ahead).

Left Bank

Théâtre de la Huchette

23 rue de la Huchette, 5th (01.43.26.38.99). M° St-
Michel. **Box office** 5-9pm Mon-Sat. **Tickets** 100F;
80F students under 25. **No credit cards. Map J7**
Home to Nicolas Bataille's original production of
Ionesco's *The Bald Primadonna* since 1957, in dou-
ble bill with other works by Ionesco and others.
Wheelchair access (call ahead).

Théâtre de la Cité Internationale

21 bd Jourdan, 14th (01.43.13.50.50). RER Cité
Universitaire. **Box office** 2-7pm Mon-Sat. **Tickets** 110F;
80F over-60s; 55F under-26s, Mon. **No credit cards.**
A well-equipped modern theatre offering interna-
tional and French plays and dance.
Wheelchair access (call ahead).

Guichet-Montparnasse

15 rue du Maine, 14th (01.43.27.88.61).
M° Montparnasse-Bienvenüe. **Box office** *telephone*
2-6pm Mon-Sat. **Tickets** 100F; 80F students,
over-60s, Mon. **No credit cards. Map F9**
In a tiny 50-seat auditorium, this lively fringe venue
features new writing, directing and acting talent.

Class act: the beautiful old **Athénée** *theatre.*

Trips out of Town

Trips out of Town

You don't have to venture far from Paris to experience some of France's most phenomenal treasures and fantastical follies.

Stately Châteaux

Versailles

(01.30.83.78.00). 20km from Paris by A13 or D10. RER C Versailles-Rive Gauche. **Open** *Château May-Sept* 9am-6.30pm Tue-Sun; *Oct-Apr* 9am-5.30pm Tue-Sun. *Grand Trianon/Petit Trianon May-Sept* noon-6.30pm daily; *Oct-Apr* noon-5.30pm daily. *Gardens* dawn-dusk daily. **Admission** *Château* 45F; free under-18s; 35F for all after 3.30pm. *Grand Trianon/Petit Trianon* 30F; free under-18s. *Gardens* free *(Grandes Eaux* 30F; free under 10s). **No credit cards.**

Until 1661 Versailles was a simple hunting lodge and boyhood refuge of Louis XIV. In a fit of envy after seeing Vaux-le-Vicomte, he decided on a building to match his ego and dreams of absolute power over the aristocracy. Louis Le Vau and painter Charles Le Brun began transforming the château, while André Le Nôtre set about the gardens, turning marshland into terraces, pools and paths.

In 1678 Jules Hardouin-Mansart took over as principal architect and dedicated the last 30 years of his life to adding the two main wings, the Cour des Ministres and Chapelle Royale. In 1682 Louis moved in and thereafter rarely set foot in Paris. The palace could house 20,000 people, including all the courtiers and royal ministers. With the king holding all the strings of power, nobles had no choice but to leave their provincial châteaux or Paris mansions and pass years in service at court, at great personal expense. In the 1770s, Louis XV chose his favourite architect Jacques Ange Gabriel to add the sumptuous Opéra Royal, sometimes used for concerts by the Centre de Musique Baroque (01.39.20.78.10). With the fall of the monarchy in 1792, most of the furniture was dispersed and after the 1830 Revolution Louis-Philippe saved the château from demolition.

Voltaire described Versailles as 'a masterpiece of bad taste and magnificence', yet you can't help but be impressed at the architectural purity of the vast classical facades, before being bowled over by the 73m-long Hall of Mirrors, where 17 windows echo the 17 mirrors in a brilliant play of light; the King's Bedroom, where the King rose in the presence of the court; the Apollo Salon, the Sun King's appropriately named throne room; and the Queen's bedroom, where queens gave birth in full view of courtiers, there to confirm the sex of the child and to ensure no substitutes were slipped in.

Outside, the park stretches over 815 hectares comprising formal gardens, ponds, wooded parkland and sheep-filled pastures, dominated by the grand perspectives laid out by Le Nôtre. Statues of the seasons, elements and continents, many commissioned by Colbert in 1674, are scattered throughout the gardens, and the spectacular series of fountains is served by an ingenious hydraulic system. Near the château is Hardouin-Mansart's Orangerie, whose vaulted gallery could house over 2000 orange trees. The Potager du Roi, the King's vegetable garden, has been recently restored (01.39.24.62.62/open Apr-Oct, Sat, Sun, tour times vary, 40F).

The main palace being a little unhomely, in 1687 Louis XIV had Hardouin-Mansart build the Grand Trianon, on the north of the park, a pretty, but still hardly cosy palace of stone and pink marble, where Louis stayed with Mme de Maintenon. Napoléon also stayed there with his second empress, Marie-Louise, and had it redecorated in Empire style.

The Petit Trianon is a perfect example of Neo-Classicism, and was built for Louis XV's mistress Mme de Pompadour, although she died before its completion. Marie-Antoinette, however, managed to take advantage of the nearby Hameau de la Reine, the mock farm arranged around a lake, where she could play at being a lowly milkmaid.

Each Sunday afternoon from April to October (plus Sat July, Aug, Sept) the great fountains in the gardens are set in action, to music, in the Grandes Eaux Musicales, while seven times a year extravagant Grandes Fêtes de Nuit capture something of the splendour of the celebrations of the Sun King.

Chantilly

Château (Musée Condé) (03.44.62.62.62/ 03.44.62.62.60). 41km from Paris by A1, exit Chantilly or N16 direct. By train to SNCF Chantilly from Gare du Nord, then 30 min walk or short taxi ride. **Open** *Mar-Oct* 10am-6pm Mon, Wed-Sun; *Nov-Feb* 10.30am-12.45pm, 2-5pm Mon, Wed-Sun. *Montgolfière balloon (03.44.57.29.14) Mar-Nov* 10am-7pm daily (weather permitting). **Admission** 42F; 37F 12-18s; 15F 3-11s; free under 3s; *park only* 17F; 10F 3-11s; *balloon* 49F; 43F 12-17s; 10F 3-11s (plus park entrance). **Credit** MC, V.

In the middle of a lake, cream-coloured Chantilly with its domes and turrets looks like the archetypal French Renaissance château. In fact, the over-the-top main wing is a largely nineteenth-century reconstruction, as much of the original was destroyed during the Revolution. But Chantilly is notable for its artistic treasures – three paintings by Raphael; Filippino Lippi's *Esther and Assuarus*; a cabinet of portraits by Clouet; several mythological scenes by Poussin; and the medieval miniatures from the *Très*

Voltaire described **Versailles** *as 'a masterpiece of bad taste and magnificence'.*

Houses to write home about

The Ile de France has a wealth of lesser châteaux, ranging from medieval to nineteenth-century. Opening times vary, so ring first. Smaller châteaux have guided tours, usually in French. No credit cards, unless otherwise stated.

East along the Marne

Château de Champs-sur-Marne
(01.60.05.24.43). 20km from Paris. **Open** *Apr-Sept* 10am-noon, 1.30pm-4.30pm Mon, Wed-Fri; 10am-noon, 1.30pm-6pm Sat-Sun; *Oct-Mar* 10am-noon, 1.30pm-4.30pm Mon, Wed-Sat; 10am-noon, 1.30pm-5pm Sun. **Admission** 32F; free under-18s.
The richly furnished, early eighteenth-century château was built for wealthy financiers. The Salon Chinois (featured in the film *Ridicule*) is furnished with chairs covered in Beauvais tapestries illustrating La Fontaine's fables. The oval Salon de Musique (chamber music concerts Sundays) offers a magical view over the formal gardens.

Château de Ferrières
(01.64.66.31.25). 24km from Paris. **Guided visits** *May-Sept* 2-7pm Wed-Sun; *Oct-Apr* 2-5pm Wed, Sat-Sun. **Admission** 35F; 25F over-60s, 12-16s; free under-12s. *Park only* 16F; free under-12s.
The largest 'English' country house in France, designed by Joseph Paxton of Crystal Palace fame, for banker James de Rothschild in a Victorian, Gothic revisiting of the Italian Renaissance. Guy and Marie-Hélène de Rothschild took over in 1959 and donated it to the University of Paris.

Château de Guermantes
(01.64.30.00.94). 27km from Paris. **Guided tours** *Apr-Oct* 2-6pm Sat, Sun, bank holidays. **Admission** 30F; free under-12s.
The romantic name inspired Marcel Proust, a friend of the family, to use it for one of the heroines in *A la recherche…* The early seventeenth-century château has souvenirs of the writer, as well as remarkable, unrestored Louis XIII painted rooms. The most spectacular room is a 31m-long gallery, called *La Belle inutile* because of its (highly telegenic) beauty and lack of practical purpose.

South towards Fontainebleau

Courances
(01.40.62.07.62). 50 km from Paris. **Open** *Apr-Oct* 2-6pm Sat, Sun, public holidays. **Admission** 40F; free under-13s; park only 26F.
Courances' famous Le Nôtre water gardens are fed by 16 different springs. The view of the sixteenth-century château mirrored in the lake and canals is exceptional. The highlight is the Galerie des Singes (monkey hall), named for the tapestries which decorate it.

Rambouillet: *a home fit for a queen, but Marie-Antoinette called it 'Toad Hall'.*

Grosbois

Boissy-St-Léger (01.4510.24.24). RER A to Boissy-St-Léger then 5km by taxi. (11km from Créteil).
Guided tours *15 Mar-Nov* 2-5pm Sun, bank holidays. **Admission** 30F; 25F 5-12s; free under-5s.
After being redesigned for one of Napoléon's stalwarts, Maréchal Berthier, only the frescoed dining room by Abraham Bosse has retained its original Louis XIII decoration. The rest is a splendid collection of Napoleonic furniture, works by Winterhalter, Canova and Gérard, and period war memorabilia. Park closed to the public.

West along the Chevreuse

Le Marais

St-Chéron (01.64.58.96.01). 40km from Paris.
Open *15 Mar-15 Nov* 2-6.30pm Sun, bank holidays. **Admission** 25F; free under-14s.
The grandiose château, designed by Barre in the 1770s in Neo-Classical style, is closed to the public, as it is still inhabited by the Talleyrands, owners since 1899. But the adjacent museum is filled with family portraits and souvenirs. The staff are mostly family retainers, anxious to share news of Madame in the big house; all this gives the place an unusually authentic, lived-in atmosphere. A walk round the lake completes the idyll.

Breteuil

Choisiel (01.30.52.05.02). 35km from Paris.
Open 2.30-5.30pm Mon-Sat; 11am-5.30pm Sun, bank holidays; *park* 10am-dusk. **Admission** 58F; 48F 6-18s, students, over-60s; free under-6s; *park only* 30F. **Credit** MC, V.
The park's plunging view over the Chevreuse valley is worth the trip, as are its 175 acres of gardens with splendid alleys leading to two lakes. The Louis XIII period château is fine enough but, in their zeal to bring the place to life, the family have let in a troupe of unimpressive wax figures. Prize possesion (apart from Louis XVIII's wheelchair) is the jewelled Teschen table, given to the Breteuils for mediation in the Treaty of Teschen in 1779.

Dampierre

(01.30.52.53.24). 40km from Paris. **Guided tours** *Apr-15 Oct* 2-6pm Mon-Sat; 11am-noon, 2-6.30pm Sun, public holidays; *park only* 11am-6.30pm daily. **Admission** 50F (park 34F); 38F (park 24F) students, over-60s; 10F under-10s. **No credit cards.**
Against a lush backdrop of parkland, the château was designed 1675-83 by Jules Hardouin-Mansart. The interior boasts ornate salons, panelled dining room and royal suite, where Louis XIV, XV and XVI stayed. In the pseudo-Roman Salle de Minerve, a kitsch 3m copy of Phidias' *Minerva* is the centrepiece to Ingres' vast allegorical fresco *L'Age d'Or.*

Rambouillet

(01.34.83.00.25). 50km from Paris. **Open** *château Apr-Sept* 10-11.30am, 2-5.25pm; *Oct-Mar* 10-11.30am, 2-4.30pm. **Admission** 32F; 21F 12-25s; free under-12s. **No credit cards.**
Marie-Antoinette called it *'La Crapaudière'* (loosely, Toad Hall). Louis XVI, who hunted in the surrounding forest, tried to win her over with a milking parlour: the resulting Neo-Classical temple is the last word in upmarket bovine architecture. The park also contains the national sheep farm, set up by Louis XVI to produce Merino wool. The château, a mix of medieval towers and eighteenth-century additions, is still an official residence. From here De Gaulle ordered the final march on Paris in 1944.

North-West along the Seine

Maisons-Laffitte

(01.39.62.01.49). RER A Maisons-Laffitte. **Open** *Apr-Oct* 10am-noon, 1.30-6pm Mon, Wed-Sun. *Nov-Mar* 10am-noon; 1.30-5pm Mon, Wed-Sun. **Admission** 32F; free under-18s. **Credit** MC, V.
Maisons-Laffitte is now synonymous with the racecourse, but François Mansart's design is a model of French classical architecture. If the interior appears austere, its proportions are magnificent and sculptures, particularly by Jacques Sarrazin, outstanding. In 1818 Laffitte, a banker, bought the château and gave it his name. Later he had to sell everything; the park became a luxury housing estate.

Malmaison

av du Château, Rueil-Malmaison (01.41.29.05.55). M° La Défense, then bus 258. **Open** *Apr-Sept* 10am-noon, 1.30-5pm Mon, Wed-Fri; 10am-5.30pm Sat-Sun. *Oct-Mar* 10am-5pm Sat-Sun. **Admission** 30F; 20F 18-25s; free under-18s.
Empress Joséphine spent a fortune decorating this place and turning the entrance into a military tent to make Napoléon feel he was on a campaign. After their divorce in 1809, she lived here until her death in 1814. After his defeat at Waterloo Napoléon paid a wistful last visit on his way to exile.

La Roche Guyon

1 rue de l'Audience, 95780 La Roche-Guyon (01.34.79.74.42). 50km from Paris. **Open** 10am-6pm Mon-Fri; 10am-7pm Sat, Sun. **Admission** 40F; 25F 6-25s, students; free under-6s. **Credit** AmEx, MC, V.
Built spectacularly into the cliffs where the Seine cuts its way through the chalk landscape, this is a fascinating mix, from medieval keep to eighteenth-century salons. It's largely empty, but the presentation is superb and the secret troglodyte aspect delightful. During World War II, Rommel set up HQ in the tunnels, digging blockhouses which remain eerily atmospheric.

Riches Heures du Duc de Berry (facsimiles only are usually on show).

Today, Le Nôtre's park is rather dilapidated, but still contains an extensive canal system and an artificial 'hamlet' predating that of Versailles. To one side is a nineteenth-century 'English garden'. In summer, a ten-minute ride in a hot-air balloon gives an aerial view of the château, park and forest.

Chantilly's other claim to fame is as the home of French racing: this is where the most important trainers have their stables, and the town has a major racetrack. The eighteenth-century Great Stables once housed 240 horses, 500 dogs and almost 100 palfreys and hunting birds, and today contain the Musée Vivant du Cheval et du Poney horse and pony collection (*see chapter* **Children**).

South of the château stetches the Forêt de Chantilly, which has numerous footpaths and is besieged by picnickers in summer. A pleasant walk (approx 7km) circles the four Etangs de Commelles (small lakes) and passes the 'Château de la Reine Blanche', a mill converted in the 1820s into a pseudo-medieval hunting lodge.

Senlis, 9km east of Chantilly, has been bypassed since its glory days as the royal town where Hugh Capet was elected king in 987. Its historical centre contains several old streets, some handsome mansions, a fine, predominantly Gothic cathedral, some chunks of Gallo-Roman city ramparts and the remains of a Roman amphitheatre.

Compiègne & Pierrefonds

Château de Compiègne *5 pl du Général-de-Gaulle, 60200 Compiègne (03.44.38.47.00).* 80km from Paris by A1. *By train* from Gare du Nord. **Open** *10am-6pm* Mon, Wed-Sun. **Admission** 35F; 23F 18-25s; free under 18s. **No credit cards. Clairière de l'Armistice** *route de Soissons (03.44.85.14.18).* **Open** (museum) *Apr-15 Oct* 9am-12.15pm, 2-6pm; *16 Oct-Mar* 9-11.45am, 2-5pm Mon, Wed-Sun. **Admission** 10F; 6F 7-14s; free under 7s. **No credit cards. Château de Pierrefonds** *60350 Pierrefonds (03.44.42.72.72).* 14km from Compiègne by D973. *Nov-Apr* 10am-12.30pm, 2-5pm Mon-Sat; 10am-5.30pm Sun; *May-Oct* 10am-6pm daily. **Admission** 32F; 21F students, 12-25s; free under 12s. **No credit cards.**

North of Paris on either side of the substantial hunting forest of Compiègne stand two very different châteaux with an Imperial stamp. On the edge of the old town of Compiègne, the **Château de Compiègne** looks out over a huge park and surrounding forest, and is a monument to the French royal family's obsession with hunting. Although there had been a royal residence at Compiègne since the Capetians, it was Louis XV who was responsible for the present look of the château, as in 1751 he entrusted its reconstruction to architect Jacques Ange Gabriel. In the process Gabriel created an austere, classical pleasure palace.

Although some of the decoration dates from the eighteenth century (in particular an elegant, circular bathroom), most of the interior was ruthlessly remodelled by Napoléon for his second wife Marie-Louise and is stuffed with Imperial eagles, bees, palms and busts of the great self-publicist. The Empress' state apartments include fully furnished boudoirs, the ballroom (used as a military hospital in World War I) and her bedroom with its wonderfully over-the-top gilded bed and crimson damask furnishings. The only eighteenth-century piece is a commode, which belonged to Marie-Antoinette, put there as Marie-Louise wanted a souvenir of her unfortunate aunt.

Napoléon III also left his mark at Compiègne, where he and Empress Eugénie hosted lavish house parties every autumn. His most popular legacy was the highly efficient heating system he installed which still works today and makes a visit to the château bearable even in the depths of winter.

In one wing of the château, the Musée de la Voiture is devoted to early transport. You can see Napoléon I's state coach, Napoléon III's railway car and early motorcars, including an 1899 Renault and the Jamais Contente electric car of 1899.

In a clearing in the forest 6km from Compiègne is the **Clairière de l'Armistice** (take the N31 towards Soissons, then follow signs), a memorial to the site where the Germans surrendered to Maréchal Foch, ending World War I, on 11 November, 1918 (it is also where in 1940 the French surrendered to the Germans). There's the mark where the two railway lines met, a statue of Foch, and a reconstruction of his railway-carriage office.

At the other edge of the forest, a sudden dip in the land gives a view of strange turrets. At first sight, the neo-medieval castle of **Pierrefonds** is so clearly fake it's almost grotesque. Yet it well merits a pause. Napoléon bought the ruins of a fourteenth-century castle for 2950F. In 1857, Napoléon III, staying nearby at Compiègne, asked Viollet-le-Duc to restore one of the towers as a romantic hunting lodge. But the project grew and the fervent medievalist ended up reconstructing the whole massive edifice, in part using the remaining foundations, in part borrowing elements from other castles, or simply creating medieval as he felt it should be, converting his Gothic fantasies into reality. Admire the wonderful crocodile waterspouts in the courtyard; the grand baronial halls harbour elaborate chimneypieces carved with beasts, dragons and figures. The magnificent Salle des Preuses was designed as a ballroom for Napoléon III, with a minstrels' gallery; the fireplace is sculpted with figures of nine ladies (one a likeness of the Empress Eugénie). One wing has a permanent exhibition about Viollet-le-Duc. Another fantasist, Michael Jackson, once expressed interest in buying the château, but it was not for sale.

Fontainebleau

77300 Fontainebleau (01.60.71.50.70). 60km from Paris by A6, then N7. By train Gare de Lyon to Fontainebleau-Avon (50 mins), then bus marked Château. **Open** *Nov-Apr* 9.30am-12.30pm, 2-5pm Mon, Wed-Sun; *May, June, Sept, Oct* 9.30am-5pm Mon, Wed-Sun; *July, Aug* 9.30am-6pm Mon, Wed-Sun. **Admission** 35F; 23F 18-25s, all on Sun; free under-18s. **Credit** V.

Fontainebleau would be just another sleepy provin-

*Mind your Mannerists: the Italian style of the day was taken to the limit at **Fontainebleau**.*

cial French town were it not for the sumptuous palace dominating it. In 1528 François 1er brought in Italian artists and craftsmen – including Rosso and Primaticcio – to help architect Gilles le Breton transform it from a neglected royal lodge into the finest Italian Mannerist palace in France. This style is noted for its grotesqueries, contorted figures and crazy fireplaces, which gave sculptors an ideal chance to show off their virtuosity, still visible in the Ballroom and Long Gallery.

Other monarchs added their own touches, so that much of the palace's charm comes from its very disunity. Henri IV added a tennis court, Louis XIII added the celebrated double-horseshoe staircase that dominates the principal 'farewell' courtyard, Louis XIV and XV added further classical trimmings, while Napoléon redecorated in Empire Style.

With its ravines, rocky outcrops and mix of forest and sandy heath, the Fontainebleau Forest, where François 1er liked to hunt, is the wildest slice of nature near to Paris and now popular with Parisian weekenders for walking, cycling, riding and rock climbing (*see chapter* **Sport & Fitness**).

Vaux-Le-Vicomte

77950 Maincy (01.64.14.41.90). 60km from Paris by A6 to Fontainebleau exit; follow signs to Melun, then N36 and D215. By coach **Paris-Vision** *run half-day and day trips from Paris (see chapter* **Directory***).* **Open** *11 Mar-12 Nov* 10am-1pm, 2-6pm Mon-Fri; 10am-6pm Sat, Sun. **Admission** 63F; 49F 6-16s, students, over-60s; free under-6s. *Candlelit visits May-mid Oct* 8pm-midnight Thur, Sat. **Price** 82F; 70F 6-16s; students, over-60s. **Credit** MC V.
This château has a story almost as interesting as the

building itself. Nicholas Fouquet (1615-1680), protégé of the ultra-powerful Cardinal Mazarin, bought the site in 1641. In 1653 he was named Surintendant des Finances, and set about building himself an abode to match his position. He assembled three of France's most talented men for the job: painter Charles Lebrun, architect Louis Le Vau and landscape gardener André Le Nôtre.

In 1661 Fouquet held a huge soirée to inaugurate his château and invited the King. They were entertained by jewel-encrusted elephants and spectacular imported Chinese fireworks. Lully wrote music for the occasion, and Molière a comedy. The King, who was 23 and ruling de facto for the first time, was outraged by the way in which Fouquet's grandeur seemed to overshadow his own. Shortly afterwards Fouquet was arrested, and his embezzlement of state funds exposed in a show trial. His personal effects were taken by the crown and the court sentenced him to exile; Louis XIV changed the sentence to solitary confinement.

As you round the moat, the square, sober frontage doesn't prepare you for the Baroque rear aspect. The most telling symbol of the fallen magnate is the unfinished, domed ceiling in the vast, elliptical Grand Salon, where Lebrun only had time to paint the cloudy sky and one solitary eagle. Fouquet's *grand projet* did live on in one way, however, as it inspired Louis XIV to build Versailles – using Fouquet's architect and workmen to do it.

Watch out for the fountains, which spout from 3pm to 6pm on the second and last Saturday of the month, Apr-Oct. The biggest draw, though, are the candlelit evenings, which transform the château into a palatial jack-o-lantern.

The Châteaux of the Loire

Getting there *By car* By far the best way to explore the region. Take the A10 to Blois (182km), or leave at Mer for Chambord. An attractive route follows the Loire from Blois to Amboise and Tours, along the D761. *By train* local trains run to Amboise (approx 2hrs) from Gare d'Austerlitz; to Tours, slow train from Gare d'Austerlitz (2 1/2hrs) or TGV from Gare Montparnasse (70 mins). **Where to Stay & Eat** The small town of Amboise is a pleasant, centrally placed stopping-off point with several hotels. Within the town, try the *Lion d'Or* (17 quai Charles Guinot/02.47.57.00.23/double 305F-325F) or the grander **Le Choiseul** (36 quai Charles Guinot/02.47.30.45.45/double 950F-1450F), both of which have restaurants. For an experience of château life, try the *Château de Pray* (02.47.57.23.67) at Chargé, 3km outside town (double 550F-720F). *L'Epicerie* (46 pl Michel Debré /02.47.57.08.94/*menus* 110F-220F) is a pleasant restaurant. There are more hotels and restaurants at Tours.

Seat of power of the Valois kings, who preferred to rule from Amboise and Blois rather than Paris, the Loire valley became the wellspring of the French Renaissance. François 1er was the main instigator, bringing architects, artists and craftsmen from Italy to build his palaces, and musicians and poets to keep him amused. Royal courtiers followed suit with their own elaborate residences. The valley is now an easy weekend trip from Paris.

The enormous **Château de Chambord** (02.54.50.40.00/02.54.50.40.28) is François 1er's masterpiece, and was probably designed in part by Leonardo da Vinci. It's a magnificent, but also rather playful place, from the ingenious double staircase in the centre – it was possible to go up or down without crossing someone coming the other way – to the wealth of decoration and the 400 draughty rooms. Built in the local white stone, with decorative diamonds applied in black slate, it is an extraordinary forest of turrets, domes and crazy chimneys .

In total contrast of scale is the charming **Château de Beauregard** (02.54.70.40.05) nearby at Cellettes. Its main feature is the unusual panelled portrait gallery, depicting in naive style 327 famous men and women. The precious character of the room is accentuated by its fragile, blue and white Dutch Delft tiled floor. The château also boasts the tiny Cabinet des Grelots (bells). Outside, the park contains a modern colour-themed garden designed by Gilles Clément.

From here the road to Amboise follows an attractive stretch of the Loire valley, under the looming turrets of the **Château de Chaumont** (02.54.51.26.26) and past roadside wine cellars dug into the tufa cliffs (with equally numerous opportunities to indulge). Chaumont is worth visiting for its innovative garden festival (02.54.20.99.22; mid-June-mid-Oct) when international garden designers, artists and architects create gardens on a set theme.

The lively town of Amboise, not far from Tours, grew up at a strategic crossing point on the Loire. The **Château Royal d'Amboise** (02.47.57.00.98) was built within the walls of a medieval stronghold, although today only a (still considerable) fraction of

Louis XI's and Charles VIII's complex remains. The château's interiors span several styles from vaulted Gothic to Empire. Across the gardens from the main wing, the exquisite Gothic chapel has a richly carved portal, fine vaulted interior and, supposedly, the tomb of Leonardo da Vinci.

It's a short walk up the hill, past several cave dwellings, to reach the fascinating **Clos Luce** (02.47.57.62.88), the Renaissance manor house where Leonardo lived at the invitation of François 1er for the three years before his death in 1519. There's an enduring myth of a – so far undiscovered – tunnel linking it with the château. The museum concentrates on Leonardo as Renaissance Man: artist, engineer and inventor. It is part furnished as a period manor, part filled with models derived from Leonardo's drawings of inventions. An oddity just outside town is the pagoda of Chanteloup, an eccentric eighteenth-century edifice built when chinoiserie was the rage.

South of Amboise, the **Château de Chenonceau** (02.47.23.90.07) occupies a unique site on a bridge spanning the river Cher. Henri II gave the château to his beautiful mistress Diane de Poitiers, until she was forced to give it up to a jealous Catherine de Médicis, who commissioned Philibert Delorme to add the three-storey gallery that extends across the river. Chenonceau is packed with tourists in summer, but its watery views, original ceilings, fireplaces, tapestries and paintings (including Diane de Poitiers by Primaticcio) are well worth seeing.

Seeming to rise out of the water, **Azay-le-Rideau** (02.47.45.42.04), built on an island in the river Indre west of Tours, must be everyone's idea of a fairytale castle. Built 1518-27 by Gilles Berthelot, the king's treasurer, it combines the turrets of a medieval fortress with the new Italian Renaissance style.

At **Villandry** (02.47.50.02.09), it's not the château but the Renaissance gardens that are of interest. One part is a typical formal garden of geometrical shapes made with neatly cut hedges and flowers; more unusual is the *jardin potager*, where the patterns are done with artichokes, cabbages and other vegetables in what has to be the ultimate kitchen garden.

Artists' Haunts

Van Gogh at Auvers-sur-Oise

95430 Auvers-sur-Oise. 35km north of Paris by A15, exit 7 take N184 towards Chantilly, exit Méry-sur-Oise for Auvers. *By train* Gare du Nord or Gare St-Lazare direction Pontoise, change at Persan-Beaumont or Creil, *or* RER A Cergy-Préfecture, then bus for Butry, stopping at Auvers-sur-Oise. Paris Vision (*see chapter* **Directory**) runs coach tours from Paris. **Office de Tourisme** *Manoir des Colombières, rue de la Sansonne (01.30.36.10.06).* **Open** 9.30am-12.30pm, 2-5pm (*Apr-Oct* until 6pm) daily. **Atelier de Daubigny** *61 rue Daubigny (01.34.48.03.03).* **Open** Easter-1 Nov 2-6.30pm Thur-Sun. **Admission** 28F; free under-12s. **Château d'Auvers** *rue de Léry (01.34.48.48.50).* **Open** *May-Oct* 10.30am-6.30pm Tue-Sun; *Nov-Apr* 10.30am-4.30pm Tue-Sun. **Admission** 55F-60F;

45-50F over-60s; 40F 6-25s; free under-6s. **Credit** AmEx, MC, V. **Musée de l'Absinthe** *44 rue Callé (01.30.36.83.26).* **Open** *June-Sept* 11am-6pm Wed-Sun; *Oct-May* 11am-6pm Sat, Sun. **Admission** 25F; 20F students; 10F 7-15s; free under-7s. **Musée Daubigny** *Manoir des Colombières, rue de la Sansonne (01.30.36.80.20).* **Open** 2-6pm Wed-Sun. **Admission** 20F; free under-12s. **Maison de Van Gogh** *Auberge Ravoux, pl de la Mairie (01.30.36.60.60).* **Open** 10am-6pm daily (closed 25 Dec-7 Jan). **Admission** 30F; free under-18s.

Auvers-sur-Oise has become synonymous with the name of Van Gogh, who rented a room here at the **Auberge Ravoux** on 20 May 1890, to escape the noise of Paris. During his stay, he executed over 60 paintings and sketches. On 27 July, he fired a bullet into his chest, and died two days later. He is buried in the cemetery, alongside his brother, Theo. The visit is an evocation of the village as it was during the artist's stay, although there is also a well-prepared video. Downstairs is a pleasant rustic bistro (*menus* 145F, 185F). Upstairs, in perfectly preserved decrepitude, is the tiny attic room where he stayed (the cheapest at 3.50F a day).

Van Gogh was not the only painter to be attracted by Auvers. Equally worth visiting is the **Atelier de Daubigny**, built by the successful Barbizon school artist in 1861. The house and studio are decorated with murals painted by Daubigny, his son and daughter and his friends Corot and Daumier.

Despite being so near to Paris, Auvers retains a surprising degree of rustic charm. Illustrated panels around town let you compare paintings to their locations today. The cornfields, where Van Gogh executed his famous last painting *Crows*, the town hall,

which he painted on Bastille day, and the medieval church, have barely changed. Cézanne also stayed here for 18 months between 1872 and 1874, not far from the house of Doctor Gachet, local doctor, art collector and amateur painter, who was the subject of portraits by both him and Van Gogh. Currently being restored, the doctor's house is due to open to the public in spring 2000.

The seventeenth-century **Château d'Auvers** offers an audiovisual display about the Impressionists, while the **Musée de l'Absinthe** is devoted to the Impressionists' favourite (now banned) drink, depicted by Monet, Van Gogh and many others.

Monet at Giverny

27620 Giverny. 80km west of Paris by A13 to Bonnières and D201 to Giverny. By train from Gare St-Lazare to Vernon 45 mins; then 5km taxi or bus. **Fondation Claude Monet** *(02.32.51.28.21).* **Open** *Apr-Oct* 10am-6pm Tue-Sun. Open Easter and Whit Monday. **Admission** 35F; 25F students; 20F 7-12s; free under-7s. **Credit** (shop only) AmEx, MC, V. **Wheelchair access. Musée Américain Giverny** *99 rue Claude Monet (02.32.51.94.65).* **Open** *Apr-Oct* 10am-6pm Tue-Sun. **Admission** 35F; 20F students, over 60s; 15F 7-12s; free under-7s. **Credit** AmEx, MC, V. **Wheelchair access**.

In 1883, Claude Monet moved his large personal entourage (one mistress, eight children) to Giverny, a rural retreat north-west of Paris. He died in 1926, having immortalised both his flower garden and the water lilies beneath his Japanese bridge. In 1966, Michel Monet donated his father's property to the Académie des Beaux-Arts, which transformed the modest estate into the major tourist site it is today. Don't be put off by the tour buses in the car park or

*Vincent Van Gogh killed himself in the rustic town of **Auvers-sur-Oise**, just outside Paris.*

by the outrageously enormous gift shop – the natural charm of the pink-brick house, with its cornflower-blue and yellow kitchen, and the rare glory of the gardens survive intact. A little tunnel leads (under the road) between the flower-filled Clos Normand garden in front of the house to the Japanese water garden, with all the pools, canals, little green bridges, the punt, willows and water lilies familiar from the paintings. Up the road, the modern **Musée Americain Giverny** is devoted to the often sugary work of American artists who came to France, inspired by the Impressionists.

Rousseau & Millet at Barbizon

77630 Barbizon. 57km from Paris by A6, then N7 and D64; 10km from Fontainebleau. **Office du Tourisme** *55 Grande rue (01.60.66.41.87).* **Open** 1-5pm Wed-Fri; 11am-12.30pm, 2-5pm Sat, Sun. **Maison et Atelier Jean-François Millet** *27 Grande rue (01.60.66.21.55).* **Open** 9.30am-12.30pm, 2-5.30pm Mon, Wed-Sun. **Admission** free. **Musée de l'Auberge du Père Ganne** *92 Grande rue, (01.60.66.22.27).* **Open** *Apr-Oct* 10am-12.30pm, 2-6pm Mon, Wed-Sun; *Nov-Mar* 10am-12.30pm, 2-5pm Mon, Wed-Sun. **Admission** 25F, 13F 12-25s, students; free under 12s. **Credit** MC, V. **Le Cyclope** *2km outside Milly-la-Forêt.* **Open** *May-Oct* 10.15am-4.15pm Fri (book ahead on 01.64.98.83.17)*;* 11am-5pm Sat; 11am-5.45pm Sun (*Oct* last visit Sat, Sun 4.30pm).

A rural hamlet straggling along a single country lane into the forest of **Fontainebleau**, Barbizon was an ideal sanctuary for pioneers Corot, Théodore Rousseau, Daubigny (*see above* **Auvers-sur-Oise**) and Millet. From the 1830s onwards, these artists – the Barbizon school – demonstrated a new concern in painting peasant life and landscape as they really were, and paved the way for the Impressionists. The three main sights at Barbizon are all on the Grande rue and, although it's enormously touristy, some of the atmosphere remains. Commemorative plaques point out who lived where.

Other artists soon followed them to Barbizon. Many stayed at the **Auberge du Père Ganne** inn, painting on the walls and furniture of the long-suffering (or perhaps far-sighted) Ganne, in lieu of rent. The Auberge also contains the municipal art collection. The **Office du Tourisme** is in the former house of Théodore Rousseau. Prints and drawings by Millet and others can be seen in the **Maison et atelier Jean-François Millet**. Millet moved here in 1849 to escape cholera in Paris and remained, living very simply, for the rest of his life, painting the locals and their work in the fields, to which he ascribed an almost saintly value. Millet and Rousseau are both buried in the churchyard at nearby Chailly.

Not far from Barbizon, but coming from a quite different art perspective, is an extraordinary twentieth-century monster. The **Cyclope**, a vast, shimmering, clanking confection of mirrors and iron cogs, lurks down a forest track, rumbling and spitting out balls. The creature was the life work of Swiss artist Jean Tinguely, who began it in 1969, in a rare collaboration with several fellow artists including Nikki de Saint Phalle (with whom he also created the Stravinsky Fountain in Paris), although

Monet's glorious garden at **Giverny**.

it was only finished after his death and opened to the public in 1994. Inside it's as if a DIY addict had gone mad, as machines carry aluminium balls up through the body before ejecting them down the tongue, and a narrow passage leads you past various art works including Spoerri's *Chambre de Bonne* and Eva Aeppli's Holocaust memorial. The exterior can be viewed from behind a fence; reserve with the Office du Tourisme to visit the interior.

Heading for the Coast

Should you long for the sea, the **Baie de la Somme** offers bird reserves and quiet villages, while the busy beaches of **Dieppe** and the 'Alabaster Coast' of northern Normandy, an easy weekend trip, can be combined with a visit to the Norman capital of Rouen (*see below*).

Dieppe & Varengeville

Getting there *By car* (170km north-west) take the A13 to Rouen and then the N27. *By train* from Gare St-Lazare (2 1/2 hours). **Office du Tourisme de Dieppe** *Pont Jehan Ango, 76204 Dieppe (02.32.14.40.60).* **Open** *Apr-Sept* 9am-1pm, 2-8pm daily; *Oct-Mar* 9am-noon, 2-6pm Mon-Sat.

An important port since the Middle Ages, **Dieppe** is also the nearest seaside town to Paris, ideal for a dip and a fish meal. The charming area around the harbour along **quai Henri IV** is lined with little fish

Getting a feel for Lille

Lille, one of the great wool towns of medieval Flanders, became part of France only in 1667. Its culture remains Flemish – mussels, chips, beer, gabled houses. While the region has been hit by industrial decline, Lille is a dynamic capital, a crossroads between the Netherlands, France, Belgium, Germany and Britain – especially with the new TGV and Channel Tunnel. It is home to futuristic Eurolille, the showcase business city by Dutch architect Rem Koolhaas, a lively mix of popular and high culture, from crowded karaoke bars to opera. This is one of the rare provincial cities that does not close at 9pm. Come for La Braderie on the first weekend in September and it doesn't close at all. The 'great clear-out', attracting two million visitors annually, sees 100km of streets lined with jumble and antiques stalls, while mussel shells mount up outside cafés. The fair has existed since the Middle Ages, when townspeople were permitted to clear out their attics, and is still wonderfully anarchic.

Vieux Lille is booming: ornate red-brick and carved-stone Renaissance houses have been renovated, including the lovely 1652-53 Vieille Bourse (old stock exchange) on the Grand' Place at the historic heart of the city. The adjoining place du Théâtre has the nineteenth-century Nouvelle Bourse, a pretty opera house and the *rang de* Beauregard, a row of late seventeenth-century houses. A pedestrianised street leads from the Grand' Place to place Rihour with its café scene; the tourist office is in the Gothic Palais Rihour started in 1454 by Philippe Le Bel, Duc de Bourgogne. Near here is Lille's finest church, the late Gothic Eglise St-Maurice. Upmarket shops have moved into rue de la Grande-Chaussée, rue des Chats-Bossus and the renovated place aux Oignons.

The Musée de l'Hospice Comtesse (32 rue de la Monnaie/03.20.49.50.90) contains displays of Flemish art, furniture and ceramics. Nearby on place de la Treille is Lille's cathedral; begun 150 years ago after a public subscription, it was finally completed in December 1999. Visit the modest brick house where De Gaulle was born (9 rue Princesse/03.28.38.12.05/closing for renovation May-Aug 2000). Across the river Deûle, the Bois de Boulogne has a zoo and the ramparts of the citadel built by Louis XIV.

The palatial Musée des Beaux-Arts (pl de la République/03.20.06.78.00) has one of the best art collections in France – works by Rubens, Jordaens, El Greco, Goya, David, Delacroix and Courbet. East of here, the Porte de Paris was put up by Louis XIV after his conquest of the city, while the Quartier de St-Saveur, notorious for its slums last century, has been rehabilitated since the 1950s. On the edge of town, the Musée d'Art Moderne (1 allée du Musée, Villeneuve-d'Ascq/03.20.19.68.68) houses works by Picasso, Braque, Derain and Modigliani.

Further information

59002 Lille. 220km from Paris by A1 or 1hr by TGV from Gare du Nord. 104km from Calais or 2hr by Eurostar from London. **Office du Tourisme** *Palais Rihour, pl Rihour (03.20.21.94.21).* Open 9.30am-6.30pm Mon-Sat; 10am-noon, 2-5pm Sun. **Hotels** Hôtel de la Treille (7-9 pl Louise de Bettignies/03.20.55.45.46), a pleasant modern hotel (double 410F-450F); the simple Hôtel de la Paix (46bis rue de Paris/ 03.20.54.63.93/double 410F-450F). **Eating** Bistros line Rue de Gand. Try chic L'Huîtrière (3 rue des Chats-Bossus/03.20.55.43.41), or brasserie Alcide (5 rue des Debris-St-Etienne/03.20.12.06.95). Stop for tea at the pâtisserie Méert (27 rue Esquermoise/03.20.57.07.44).

Lille has a dynamic, mainly Flemish culture.

restaurants (endless variations on mussels, skate and sole, plus cider), and prettier than ever now that ferries from Britain go to a new container port and the old railway terminal has been demolished. At one end the **Tour des Crabes** is the last remnant of fortified wall. The interesting maze of old streets between the harbour and the newer quarters fronting the promenade contains numerous sailors' houses built in brick with wrought-iron balconies, many being renovated, and the fine Gothic churches of **St-Jacques**, once a starting point for pilgrimage to Compostella (note the pilgrims' shell motifs) and **St-Rémi**. The beach is shingle except at low tide, but the seafront offers plenty of activities for kids, with mini golf, pony rides, a children's beach and lawns filled with kite flyers. The beach is overlooked from the clifftop by the gloomy **Château de Dieppe** (02.35.84.19.76), now the municipal museum, known for its collection of alabasters and paintings by Pissarro and Braque.

Leave town by the coast road for a twisting, scenic drive along the cliff. Just along the coast to the west is chic **Varengeville-sur-Mer**, celebrated for its clifftop churchyard where Cubist painter Georges Braque (who also designed one of the stained-glass windows in the church) and composer Albert Roussel are buried, for the **Parc du Bois des Moustiers** (02.35.85.10.02), planted by Lutyens and Gertrude Jekyll, famed for its rhododendrons and views, as well as for the unusual sixteenth-century Renaissance **Manoir d'Ango** (02.35.85.14.80/open Apr-Oct daily) which has a galleried courtyard and unusual dovecote. A steep, narrow lane leads down to a sandy cove. On the headland, the **Phare d'Ailly** lighthouse is open for visits (02.35.85.11.19).

Also just outside Dieppe (8km south) is the decorative early seventeenth-century **Château de Miromesnil** (02.35.85.02.80; open 2-6pm May-18 Oct; 20F-30F) where the writer Guy de Maupassant was born in 1850, and which has a historic kitchen garden. Nearby, dominating a little hill at **Arques la Bataille**, are the ruins of a tenth-century castle.

Baie de Somme

Getting There Le Crotoy is 190km from Paris by the A16 new motorway (exit Abbeville Nord). The closest train station is Noyelles-sur-Mer, just after Abbeville, about 2 hours from Gare du Nord. Local buses serve the villages on the bay but are few and far between. Bikes can be hired at St-Valéry-sur-Somme (03.22.26.96.80). Tourist Information **Le Crotoy** *1 rue Carnot (03.22.27.05.25).* **Open** 10am-noon, 3-6pm Mon, Wed-Sat; 10am-noon Sun; July, Aug 10am-7pm daily. **St-Valery-sur-Somme** *2 pl Guillaume Le Conquérant (03.22.60.93.50).* **Open** 10am-noon, 2.30-5pm Tue-Sun; July, Aug 10am-noon, 2.30-7pm Tue-Sun.

The Baie de la Somme is ideal for a quick getaway. Although the somme is now synonymous with World War I battlefields, its coastal area boasts a rich variety of wildlife and has a gentle, ever-changing light that has attracted artists and writers alike. There are many picturesque villages and a coastline that changes from long beaches and rolling sand dunes to pebbles and cliffs within a few miles. A

very popular tourist steam train, the **Chemin de fer de la Baie de Somme** (03.22.26.96.96), tours the bay in summer along 27km of tracks between Le Crotoy, Noyelles, St Valéry and Cayeux (*Apr-June* Wed, Sat, Sun in Sept; 43F-81F; under-18s 35F-65F).

One of the largest towns, **Le Crotoy** is a traditional fishing port, with a fifteenth-century church and a panorama over the bay that inspired Jules Verne to write *20,000 Leagues Under the Sea* and drew Colette, Toulouse-Lautrec and Arthur Rimbaud. It boasts the only sandy beach in northern France that is south facing and as such is a busy resort, with numerous restaurants and brasseries serving excellent fresh fish, as well as hotels, guest houses and camp sites, and opportunities for watersports (03.22.27.04.39), hunting, fishing and tennis.

Across the bay, **St-Valery-sur-Somme** still retains its historic character, with a well-preserved medieval upper town and a domineering position over the bay. William the Conqueror set sail from here in 1066 to conquer England, and Joan of Arc passed through as a prisoner in 1430. The upper town contains a Gothic church, while a second gateway leads to a château that was once part of an abbey, and beyond here to a small chapel overlooking the bay, which houses the tomb of St-Valéry. In the lower town, the Ecomusée Picarvie (5 quai du Romeral/ 03.22.26.94.90/Mar-Sept) recreates aspects of traditional village life. The beachfront has been restored and, strolling from the port to the bay, you can see impressive villas from the turn of the century. Consult tide times: at low tide the sea goes out nearly 14km; and it comes back in in less than five hours.

At the tip of the bay, **Le Hourdel** consists of a few fishermen's houses and a dock where the fishing boats sell their catch of the day. Here you have your best chance to see seals from the largest colony in France. Three miles south from Le Hourdel, is the town of **Cayeux**, which lies below sea-level. A chic resort in the early 1900s, it has beautiful sand beaches at low tide, often almost deserted. From spring to the end of the summer, the seafront is dressed with wooden cabins and planks in a 2km promenade. The open-air market on Tuesday, Friday and Sunday mornings sells everything from comestibles to puppies and sportswear that has fallen off the back of a lorry. Continue southwest along the coast to explore Ault Onival, Le Bois de Cise, Eu and Le Tréport.

The bay has an astounding 2,000 hectares of nature reserves and France's first maritime reserve was created here in 1968. The area is a haven for wildlife with some 200 bird species, notably winter migrants, recorded at the **Parc Naturel du Marquenterre** (03.22.25.03.26; open 15 Mar-11 Nov 9.30am-7pm daily; 12 Nov-10 Mar guided tours only 4pm Sat; 10am, 4pm Sun. Admission 60F; 45F students).

Medieval Cities

Beauvais

Getting there *By car* 75km from Paris by A16 or N1. *By train* from Gare du Nord. **Office du Tourisme** 1 rue Beauregard, 60000 Beauvais (03.44.15.30.30). **Open** *Apr-Oct* 10am-1pm, 2-6pm

*Georges Braque is buried in this churchyard in the seaside town of **Varengeville-sur-Mer**.*

Mon, Sun; 9.30am-7pm. Tue-Sat. *Nov-Mar* 10am-1pm, 2-6pm Mon, 9.30am-6.30pm Tue-Sat; 10am-1.20pm Sun. **Where to eat** Two reliable addresses are restaurant-bar Le Marignan (1 rue Malherbe/ 03.44.48.15.15), and Alsatian brasserie Taverne du Maître Kanter (16 rue Pierre Jacoby/ 03.44.06.32.72).

Beauvais cathedral is both one of the strangest and most impressive of French cathedrals. It has the tallest Gothic vault in the world and a spectacular crown of flying buttresses. The feat entailed numerous construction problems, as first the choir had to be rebuilt – you can still see where an extra column was added between the arches – and then the spire collapsed. The nave was never built at all; the church suddenly stops in a wall at the transept, which only accentuates the impression of verticality.

Left of the choir is a curious astrological clock, made in the 1860s by a local watchmaker, Lucien-Auguste Vérité, and a typically nineteenth-century extravagance of turned wood, gilt, dials and automata; around the corner is a clock dating from the fourteenth century.

Next to the cathedral, a medieval gateway leads into the sixteenth-century bishop's palace, now the **Musée Départemental de l'Oise** (03.44.11.43.83), tracing the region's illustrious heritage in wood and stone sculptures from destroyed houses and churches, Nabis paintings and Art Nouveau furniture and the tapestries for which Beauvais was famed. The tapestry industry reached its peak in the eighteenth century and then stopped when the factory was evacuated to Aubusson in 1939, but has recently been revived at the **Manufacture Nationale de la Tapisserie** (24 rue Henri Brispot/03.44.05.14.28), where you can

watch weavers making tapestries under natural light (2-4pm Tue-Thur). Most of Beauvais was flattened by bombing in World War II, but the centre was rebuilt not unpleasantly in the 50s in a series of low-rise squares and shopping streets. One other impressive medieval survivor remains, the **Eglise St-Etienne**, a mix of Romanesque and Gothic styles, with elaborate gargoyles sticking out in the centre of a traffic island.

Chartres

28005 Chartres. 88km from Paris by A11 direction Le Mans, exit Chartres. *By train* from Gare Montparnasse to Chartres. **Office du Tourisme** *pl de la Cathédrale (02.37.18.26.26).* **Open** *Apr-Sept* 9am-7pm Mon-Sat; 9.30am-5.30pm Sun; *Oct-Mar* 10am-6pm Mon-Sat; 10am-1pm, 2.30-4.30pm Sun. **Where to eat** *La Vieille Maison* (5 rue au Lait/ 02.37.34.10.67) has good classical cooking in an ancient building, and a good-value 168F *menu.* Simpler, but with an attractive setting facing the cathedral, the *Café Serpente* (2 Cloître Notre Dame/ 02.37.21.68.81) triples as a café, a tea room and a restaurant.

Looming over a flat agricultural plain, **Chartres Cathedral** was described by Rodin as the 'French Acropolis'. Certainly, with its two uneven spires – the stubbier from the twelfth century, the taller one completed only in the sixteenth century – and doorways bristling with sculpture, the cathedral has an enormous amount of slightly wonky charm and is a pristine example of Early Gothic art.

Chartres was a pilgrimage site long before the present cathedral was built, ever since the Sacra Camisia (said to be the Virgin Mary's lying-in garment and now displayed in the Cathedral Treasury) was donated to the city in 876 by the Carolingian King Charles I, 'the Bald'. When the church caught fire in 1194, local burghers clubbed together to reconstruct it, taking St-Denis as the model for the new west front, 'the royal portal' with its three richly sculpted doorways. On the cusp between Romanesque and Gothic, the stylised, elongated figure columns above geometric patterns still form part of the door structure. Be sure to walk all round the cathedral as there are two other interesting portals which were added slightly later: the north transept door is a curious, faintly top-heavy concoction of lively figures and slight columns, and there's also an unusual clock.

Inside yet another era of sculpture is represented in the lively, sixteenth-century scenes of the life of Christ that surround the choir. Note also the circular labyrinth of black and white stones in the floor; such mazes used to exist in most cathedrals but have now mostly been destroyed. Chartres is above all famed for its stained-glass windows depicting Biblical scenes, saints and medieval trades in brilliant 'Chartres blue', punctuated by rich reds. To learn all about them, take one of the erudite and entertaining tours given in English by Malcolm Miller, who specialises in deciphering the medieval picture codes. Between Easter and mid-Nov, Mr Miller's tours are at noon and 2.45pm Mon-Sat (40F adults, 20F students). At all other times telephone him on 02.37.28.15.58.

The cathedral may dominate the town from a distance, but once in the town centre's narrow medieval streets, with their overhanging gables, glimpses of it are only occasional. Wander past the iron-framed market hall, down to the river Eure, crossed by a string of attractive old bridges, past the partly Romanesque Eglise St-André and down the rue des Tanneries, which runs along the banks. There's more fine stained glass in the thirteenth-century Eglise St-Pierre.

There's a good view from the Jardin de l'Evêché, located at the back of the cathedral and adjoining the **Musée des Beaux-Arts** (02.37.36.41.39/ 29 Cloître Notre-Dame). Housed in the former Bishop's palace, the collection includes some fine eighteenth-century French paintings by Boucher and Watteau, as well as a large array of medieval sculpture.

The other main tourist attraction is very much of this century and a reminder that Chartres towers over the Beauce region, known as the 'bread basket of France' for its prairie-like expanses of wheat. The **COMPA** agricultural museum (pont de Maenvilliers/02.37.36.11.30) in a converted engine shed near the station has a small but lively presentation of the history of agriculture and food (and consequently, society) from 50,000BC to today, with the emphasis on machinery, from vintage tractors and threshing machines to old fridges.

For curiosity value, you can also visit (Apr-Oct) the **Maison Picassiette** (22 rue de Repos/ 02.37.34.10.78) just outside the centre, a colourful naïve mosaic house constructed with broken pottery by a former civil servant.

Reims

51100 Reims. 150km by A4. *By train* from Gare de l'Est about 1/2 hour. **Office du Tourisme** *2 rue Guillaume-de-Machault, (03.26.77.45.25).* **Open** *mid-Apr-mid-Oct* 9am-7pm Mon-Sat; 10am-6pm Sun; *mid-Oct-mid-Apr* 9am-6pm Mon-Sat; 10am-5pm Sun. **Where to eat** Haute-cuisine mecca is Gérard Boyer's *Château des Crayères* (64 bd Henri-Vanier/03.26.82.80.80) in a Second Empire château to the south-east of town. Boyer no longer owns the lively bistro *Au Petit Comptoir* (17 rue de Mars/ 03.26.40.58.58), but the chef has stayed on. Within town there are numerous brasseries, restaurants and cafés around pl Drouet d'Erlon.

Begun in the thirteenth century, the **Cathédrale Notre-Dame** is of dual importance to the French, as the coronation church of most monarchs since Clovis in 496 and for the richness of its Gothic decoration. Thousands of figures on the portals and the Kings of Judea high above the rose window show how sculptural style developed over the century. Heavy shelling in World War I, together with erosion, means that many of the carvings have been replaced by copies; the originals are on show next door in the **Palais de Tau**, the Bishop's palace. It is possible that some of the masons from Chartres also worked on Reims, but the figures generally show more classical influence in their drapery and increasing expressivity. Look out in particular for the winsome 'smiling angel' sculpture and St-Joseph on the facade, while inside take a look at the capitals decorated with elaborate, naturalistic foliage with birds hiding among the leaves.

A few streets south of the cathedral, the **Musée des Beaux-Arts** (8 rue Chanzy/03.26.47.28.44) has some wonderful portraits of German princes by Cranach, 26 canvases by Corot, and the famous *Death of Marat* by Jean-Louis David. From the museum, head down rue Gambetta to the Basilique de St-Rémi, which honours the saint who baptised Clovis. The church, built 1007-49, is a fascinating complement to the cathedral. Subsequent alterations allow you to see just how the Romanesque style evolved into the Gothic. Don't miss the remarkable cycle of ten sixteenth-century tapestries depicting the life of St Rémi in the **Musée St-Rémi** (53 rue Simon/ 03.26.85.23.36) in the restored monastic buildings next door.

Reims is also, of course, at the heart of the Champagne region. Many leading producers of the famous bubbly are based in the town and offer visits of their caves, an informative insight into the laborious and skilful champagne-making process. The **Champagne Pommery** cellars (03.26.61.62.56) occupy Gallo-Roman chalk mines 30m below ground and are decorated with Art Nouveau bas-reliefs by Emile Gallé. **Taittinger** (03.26.85.84.33) doesn't look like much until you descend into the cellars: on the first level are the vaulted Gothic cellars of a former monastery; below are the strangely beautiful, Gallo-Roman chalk quarries.

Chartres: *Sculptor Rodin called the Gothic cathedral 'the French Acropolis'.*

Rouen

76000 Rouen. 137km west of Paris by A13. *By train* from Gare St-Lazare. **Office du Tourisme** *25 pl de la Cathédrale (02.32.08.32.40).* **Open** *May-Sept* 9am-7pm Mon-Sat; 9.30am-12.30pm, 2.30-6.30pm Sun; *Oct-Apr* 9am-6.30pm Mon-Sat; 10am-1pm Sun. **Eating** Best-known gourmet restaurant is fish specialist *Gill* (9 quai de la Bourse/02.35.71.16.14); there are several cheaper bistros, especially on pl du Vieux-Marché, or the quietly formal *L'Orangerie* (2 rue Thomas-Corneille/02.35.88.43.97).

The capital of Normandy is a cathedral town of contrasts. The centre retains lots of drunken half-timbered buildings and narrow streets, while the port areas by the Seine were almost totally destroyed by bombing during the war. Begun at the start of the thirteenth century, the **Cathédrale Notre-Dame**, depicted at all times of the day by Monet in a famous series of paintings, spans the Gothic periods. The north tower dates from the early period while the more Flamboyant Tour de Beurre is from the late fifteenth century. Nearby, the famous Gros-Horloge gateway, with its ornamental clock over the busy medieval rue du Gros Horloge, leads to picturesque streets of half-timbered houses.

Two more Gothic churches are worth a visit, the Eglise St-Ouen and the Eglise St-Maclou, as well as an enormously fanciful Flamboyant Gothic Palais de Justice. The striking, contemporary Eglise Ste-Jeanne d'Arc, adjoining a funky modern market hall on place du Vieux-Marché, is a boat-shaped structure with a swooping wooden roof and stained glass windows that were recuperated from a bombed city church. The recently renovated **Musée des Beaux Arts** (1 pl Restout/02.35.71.28.40) numbers works by Gérard David, Velázquez, Perugino and Caravaggio, some wonderful oil studies by Géricault (who was a native of Rouen) and Impressionist paintings by Monet and Sisley.

Troyes

10014 Troyes. 150km southeast of Paris by A6 and A5. *By train* from Gare de l'Est (1 hr 15 mins). **Office du Tourisme** *16 bd Carnot, (03.25.82.62.70).* **Open** 9am-12.30pm; 2-6.30pm Mon-Sat. **Branch:** rue Mignard (03.25.73.36.88) **Open** 9am-12.30pm, 2-6.30pm Mon-Sat; 10am-12.30pm, 2-5pm Sun. **Eating** Many consider *Le Clos Juillet* (22 bd du 14-Juillet/03.25.73.31.32) to be the best table in town; its young chef specialises in modernised regional dishes.

Although better known today for its ring of clothes factory discount shops, Troyes still delights with its remarkably preserved half-timbered houses and Gothic churches. Begin your visit with a stroll along the rue Champeaux at the heart of the old city, and don't miss the ruelle des Chats, a narrow lane full of medieval atmosphere which leads to the **Eglise Ste-Madeleine**, the oldest church in the city. Entering the church, you'll be struck by the Flamboyant Gothic rood screen, but the real draw is the superb fifteenth-century stained glass.

Nearby, the **Basilique St-Urbain** was built in 1262-86 on the orders of Pope Urbain IV, a native of Troyes. This church represents an early apogee of Gothic architecture and its ambitions of replacing the heavy masonry of the Romanesque period with lacy stone work and glass. Inside, the *Virgin with the Grapes* is a fine example of local sixteenth-century sculpture.

Heading down rue Champeaux, pass through café-lined place du Maréchal-Foch, with the handsome seventeenth-century Hôtel de Ville, and cross a canal into the oldest part of the city around the **Cathédrale St-Pierre St-Paul**. Part of the impressive facade was done by Martin Chambiges, who also worked on the cathedrals at Sens and Beauvais. The triforium of the choir was one of the first in France to be built with windows instead of blind arcading. The stained glass is a catalogue of styles from the thirteenth to sixteenth centuries; particularly impressive are the richly coloured thirteenth-century scenes from the Virgin's life and the portraits of popes in the choir.

Next door to the cathedral, in the former bishop's palace, the **Musée d'Art Moderne** (pl St-Pierre/03.25.76.26.80) contains numerous canvases by Derain, in both his Fauvist and later styles, in addition to several works by Braque, Courbet, Degas, Seurat and Vuillard, and modern sculpture and drawings. The **Maison de l'Outil** (7 rue de la Trinité/03.25.73.28.26) has a fascinating array of craftsmen's tools on display. The **Musée des Beaux-Arts et d'Archéologie** in the Abbaye St-Loup (4 rue Chrétien de Troyes/03.25.76.21.68) next to the cathedral, has fine Gallo-Roman bronzes and a fantastic treasure of arms and jewellery that was found in a fifth-century Merovingian tomb.

Provins

Getting there *By car* 80km from Paris by A4, exit 13. *By train* from Gare de l'Est. **Office du Tourisme** *rue de Villeran (01.64.60.26.26).* **Open** 9am-6pm daily.

An easy stopping point on the way to Reims, Provins was, like Troyes, a seat of the medieval Counts of Champagne, owing its wealth to two important annual fairs, but its later eclipse meant that its Ville Haute (upper town) still retains its original fortifications and rustic air. Enter the Ville Haute by the picturesque Porte St-Jean. You can walk most of the way round the twelfth-century ramparts, which are punctuated by small, fortified towers and formed part of the impressive medieval defence system.

Within the walls, it's worth wandering along rue de Jouy and rue St-Thibault, both lined with ancient stone houses, some with external stone staircases. Place du Châtel contains grander half-timbered houses and the remains of the twelfth-century church of St-Thibault. Lower down the hill is the curious Eglise St-Quiriace; its nave was never completed and a cupola was added following a fire in 1662. The emblem of the town, however, is the keep, the Tour de César, with its distinctive pyramidal roof. The 'skirt' enclosing its base was added by the English during the Hundred Years War to house artillery. Regular displays of falconry and jousting and summer pageants keep up the medieval illusion.

Directory

Directory

Getting Around

Arriving in Paris

By Eurostar Train
The Eurostar train between London
and Paris takes three hours. You
must check in 20 minutes in advance.
On arrival you are close to the centre
of each city. Eurostar trains from
London Waterloo (01233 617575)
arrive at Gare du Nord (08.36.35.35.39,
2.23F/min; Minitel 3615 SNCF), with
easy access to public transport.

**Roissy-Charles-de-Gaulle
Airport**
Most international flights arrive at
Roissy-Charles-de-Gaulle airport,
30km north-east of Paris. Its two
main terminals are some way apart,
so it's important to check which is
the right one for your flight if you are
flying out. 24-hour information
service in English: 01.48.62.22.80.
The **RER B** is the quickest and most
reliable way to central Paris (about
45 minutes to St-Michel; 49F single).
A new station gives direct access
from Terminal 2 (Air France flights);
from Terminal 1 you take the free
shuttle bus. RER trains run every 15-
20 minutes, 5.24am-12.09am daily.
SNCF information: 01.53.90.20.20.
Air France buses (60F) leave
every 12-20 minutes, 6am-11pm
daily, from both terminals, and stop
at Porte Maillot and pl Charles-de-
Gaulle (35-50 min trip). Air France
buses also run to Gare Montparnasse
and Gare de Lyon (70F) every 30
minutes (45-60 minute trip), 7am-
9.30pm daily. There is also a bus
between Roissy and Orly (70F) every
20-30 minutes, 5.40am-11pm daily.
Information: 01.41.56.89.00. The
RATP **Roissybus** (45F) runs every
15 minutes, 5.45am-11pm daily,
between the airport and the corner of
rue Scribe/rue Auber, near pl de
l'Opéra (at least 45 minutes); tickets
are sold on the bus. Information:
08.36.68.77.14.
The **Airport Shuttle** is a door-to-
door minibus service between the
airports and your hotel, running
6am-6pm daily at 120F per person;
89F each for two or more (reserve
ahead 01.45.38.55.72). **Airport
Connection** (01.44.18.36.02) runs a
similar service at 150F per person,
85F for two or more.
Taxis are the least reliable and most
expensive means of transport. A taxi

to central Paris can take 30-60 mins
depending on traffic and your point
of arrival. Expect to pay 170F-300F,
plus 6F per piece of luggage.

Orly Airport
French domestic and several
international flights use Orly airport,
18km south of the city. It also has
two terminals: Orly-Sud (mainly
international flights) and Orly-Ouest
(mainly domestic flights). English-
speaking information service on
01.49.75.15.15, 6am-11.30pm daily.
Air France buses (01.41.56.89.00;
45F) leave both terminals every 12
minutes, 5.50am-11pm daily, and
stop at Invalides and Montparnasse
(30-45 minutes). The RATP **Orlybus**
to Denfert-Rochereau leaves every 15
minutes, 5.35am-11pm daily (30-
minute trip); tickets (30F) are
available on the bus.
A **taxi** into town takes 20-40 minutes
and costs 100F-170F, plus 6F per
piece of luggage.
The high-speed **Orlyval** shuttle
train runs every 7 minutes (6am-
10.12pm Mon-Fri; 7am-11pm Sat,
Sun) to RER B station Antony
(Orlyval and RER together cost 57F);
getting to central Paris takes about
40 minutes. Alternatively, catch the
courtesy bus to RER C station Pont
de Rungis, where you can get the
Orlyrail to central Paris (30F).
Trains run every 12 minutes, 5.45am-
11.10pm daily; 50-minute trip.

Beauvais Tillé Airport
Ryan Air (03.44.11.41.41) flies from
Dublin and Glasgow to Beauvais,
70km from Paris. A 60-90 minute
bus link (50F) to Porte Maillot.

By Coach
International coach services arrive at
the Gare Routière International Paris-
Galliéni at Bagnolet, 20th (M° Galliéni).
For reservations (in English) call
Eurolines on 08.36.69.52.52 (2.23F/
min), or in the UK 01582 404511.

By Car
For travelling between France and
the UK by car, options include **Le
Shuttle** (Folkestone-Calais c25mins)
(01.43.18.62.22/08.01.63.03.04); seacat/
hovercraft **Hoverspeed**
(08.20.00.35.55/ 03.21.46.14.00); ferry
Brittany Ferries (08.03.828.828),
P&O Stena Line (01.53.43.40.00)
and **Sealink** (08.01.63.63.01).

Public Transport

The public transport system (**RATP**)
consists of **bus** routes, the **Métro**
(underground), the **RER** suburban
express railway which interconnects
with the Métro inside Paris and two
suburban tramways. Pick up a free
map at any Métro station. Paris and
its suburbs are divided into five
travel zones; zones 1 and 2 cover the
city centre. Information 6am-9pm
daily, 08.36.68.77.14/in English
08.36.68.41.14 (2.23F/min). SNCF,
the state railway system, serves the
French regions and international
(*Grandes Lignes*) and the suburbs
(*Banlieue*). *See also below,* **Batobus**,
in **Armchair & Guided Tours.**

Tickets & Travel Passes
RATP **tickets** and passes are valid
on the Métro, bus and RER. Tickets
and *carnets* can be bought at Métro
stations, tourist offices and *tabacs*
(tobacconists). Keep your ticket in
case of spot checks and to exit from
RER stations. Individual tickets cost
8F; it's more economical to buy a
carnet of ten tickets for 55F. *Carte
Orange* travel passes (passport photo
needed) offer unlimited travel in the
relevant zones for a week or month.
A *Coupon Mensuel* (valid from the
first day of the month) zones 1-2
costs 279F. A weekly *Coupon
Hebdomadaire* (valid Mon-Sun
inclusive) zones 1-2 costs 82F and is
better value than *Paris Visite* passes
– a three-day pass for zones 1-3 is
120F; a five-day pass is 175F, with
discounts on some tourist attractions.
A one-day *Mobilis* pass goes from 32F
for zones 1-2 to 110F for zones 1-8 (not
including airports). *Ticket Jeunes*
allows student card holders under 26
to travel in zones 1-3 for 20F (zones 1-
5 40F) , but only at weekends and
holidays. Fares usually go up a little
in July or August.

Métro & RER
The Paris **Métro** is at most times the
quickest and cheapest means of
travelling around the city. Trains run
daily 5.30am-12.30am. Individual
lines are numbered, with each
direction named after the last stop.
So Line 4 northbound is indicated
Porte de Clignancourt, while
southbound is designated Porte
d'Orléans. Follow the orange
correspondance signs to change lines.

Some interchanges, notably Châtelet-Les Halles, Montparnasse-Bienvenüe and République involve a long walk. The exit (*sortie*) is indicated in blue. The high-speed Line 14, **Météor**, opened in 1998 links the new Bibliothèque Nationale to Madeleine. Beware pickpockets, especially on much-touristed Line 1.

The five **RER** lines (A, B, C, D and the new Eole) run 5.30am-1am across Paris and into the Ile-de-France commuter land. Within Paris, the RER is useful for making faster journeys – for example, Châtelet-Les Halles to Charles de Gaulle-Etoile is only two stops on the RER compared with eight on Métro Line 1.

Buses

Buses run from 6.30am until 8.30pm, with some routes continuing until 12.30am, Mon-Sat, with a more limited service on selected lines on Sundays and public holidays. You can use a Métro ticket, a ticket bought from the driver (8F) or a travel pass. Tickets should be punched in the machine next to the driver; passes should be shown to the driver. When you want to get off, press the red request button, and the *arrêt demandé* (stop requested) sign above the driver will light up.

Nightbuses

After the Métro and normal buses stop, the only public transport – apart from taxis – are the 18 **Noctambus** lines, between place du Châtelet and the suburbs (hourly 1.30am-5.30am Mon-Thur; half-hourly 1am-5.30am Fri, Sat). Routes A to H, P, T and V serve the Right Bank and northern suburbs; I to M, R and S serve the Left Bank and southern suburbs. Look out for the owl logo on bus stops. A ticket costs 15F and allows one change; travel passes are valid.

Useful Bus Routes

The following pass interesting places and, unless stated, run daily.

29 Gare St-Lazare, past Palais Garnier and Centre Pompidou, through the Marais, Bastille to Gare de Lyon (Mon-Sat).
38 From Gare de l'Est , past the Centre Pompidou and place du Châtelet, then via the Sainte-Chapelle one direction, Notre Dame the other, then St-Michel, the Sorbonne, Jardins du Luxembourg to the Catacombes.
42 From Gare du Nord, via Opéra, Madeleine, Concorde, Champs-Elysées, over the river, past the Eiffel Tower to Quai André Citroën (Mon-Sat).
48 Literature and art: Montparnasse, St-Germain, the Louvre, Palais-Royal to Gare du Nord (Mon-Sat).
67 From sleazy Pigalle via the Louvre, Ile St-Louis, Latin Quarter and place d'Italie to Porte de Gentilly.
68 From place de Clichy via Opéra,

Palais-Royal, the Louvre and Musée d'Orsay, bd Raspail to Montparnasse, the Catacombes and Porte d'Orléans.
69 From Père Lachaise, via Bastille, Hôtel de Ville and Châtelet along the quais to the monuments of the 7th, the Musée d'Orsay, the Invalides and the Champ de Mars (Mon-Sat).
72 From the 16th to Hôtel de Ville, along the Seine one direction and down arcaded rue de Rivoli the other.
73 From La Défense past the Arc de Triomphe, along the Champs-Elysées to Concorde and over the river to the Musée d'Orsay (Mon-Sat).
82 From smart residential Neuilly to the Jardins du Luxembourg via the Eiffel Tower and Invalides.
84 From Parc Monceau in the 17th via the Grands Boulevards, the Madeleine, St-Germain-des-Prés and St-Sulpice to the Panthéon (Mon-Sat).
86 From Zoo de Paris via Nation, the Bastille and Institut du Monde Arabe to St-Germain-des-Prés (Mon-Sat).
87 From Gare de Lyon to the Bastille, over the Ile-St-Louis, through the Latin Quarter via the Collège de France, Odéon, St-Sulpice and on to UNESCO, ending at the Champ de Mars (Mon-Sat).
95 One hill to another: from Montparnasse to Montmartre.
Montmartrobus Special small bus circulates around Montmartre.
PC Petite Ceinture (the 'small belt') covers the outer boulevards, just within the Périphérique.
Balabus Runs 1-8pm on Sundays Apr-Sept. It links Gare de Lyon with the Grande Arche de la Défense.

Trams

Two modern tramlines operate in the suburbs, connecting at either end with the Métro or RER. Fares are the same as for buses.

Pedestrian Tips

Exploring by foot is the very best way to discover Paris, just remember that to anything on wheels (and this includes cyclists and rollerbladers), pedestrians are the lowest form of life. Crossing Paris' multi-lane boulevards can be lethal to the uninitiated. By law drivers are only fully obliged to stop when there is a red light. Where there is a crossing, whether or not it has a flashing amber light or a sign saying *Priorité aux Piétons*, most drivers will ignore pedestrians and keep going.

Cycle Routes

Since 1996, the Mairie de Paris has been energetically introducing cycle lanes and, in the first two years of the programme, bike traffic increased fivefold. The quais along the Seine

and the Canal St-Martin are usually closed to cars on Sundays (10am-4pm), providing the nicest stretches for cyclists and rollerbladers, along with the bike path by the Canal de l'Ourcq. The Bois de Boulogne and Bois de Vincennes offer paths away from traffic although they are still criss-crossed by roads.

Cycle lanes (*pistes cyclables*) run mostly N-S and E-W; you could be fined (from 230F) if you don't use them. N-S routes include rue de Rennes, bd St-Germain, bd de Sébastopol and av Marceau. E-W routes take in the Champs-Elysées, bd St-Germain, the rue de Rivoli, bd St-Jacques, bd Vincent-Auriol and av Daumesnil. Lanes are at the edge of the road or down *contre-allées*, only a small percentage are separated from motorised traffic, so you may encounter delivery vans, scooters and pedestrians blocking your way; the 900F fine for obstructing a cycle lane is barely enforced. There were 100km of cycle lanes at the end of 1997, and the aim is 150km by the end of 2000. There are even plans for a bicycle 'Périphérique' circling Paris.

You can get a free map of Paris' cycle routes (*Paris à Vélo*) with advice and addresses, at any Mairie or from bike shops. *See also p340,* **Car & Bike Hire**, **Armchair & Guided Tours**, *and chapter* **Sport & Fitness**.

Car & Bike Hire

To hire a car you must normally be 25 or over and have held a licence for at least a year. Some agencies accept drivers aged 21-24, but a supplement of 50F-100F per day is usual (Valem is an exception). Take your licence and passport with you. It is easiest to pay by credit card.

Hire Companies

Ada 01.45.54.63.63/08.36.68.40.02. **Avis** 01.55.38.68.60. **Budget** 08.00.10.00.01. **Europcar** 01.30.43.82.82. **Hertz** 01.39.38.38.38. **Rent-a-Car** 01.45.22.28.28/ 08.36.69.46.95. **Valem** 01.43.14.79.79. There are often good weekend offers (Fri evening to Mon morning). Week-long deals are better at the bigger hire companies – with Avis or Budget, for example, it's around 1600F a week for a small car with insurance and 1700km included. The more expensive hire companies allow the return of a car in other French cities and abroad. Be warned that supposedly bargain companies, such as Ada, may have an extremely high excess charge for dents or damage.

Chauffeur-driven Cars

Les Berlines de Paris *(01.45.33.14.14).* **Open** 8am-7pm daily. **Prices** from 800F airport

Taxi tips

Paris taxi drivers (with some agreeable exceptions) are not known for their charm, nor for infallible knowledge of the Paris street plan – if there's a route you would prefer, say so. Taxi ranks are found on numerous major roads and at stations. The white light on the roof indicates the cab is free. A glowing orange light means the cab is busy. Taxi charges are based on area and time: A (7am-7pm Mon-Sat; 3.53F/km); B (7pm-7am Mon-Sat, all day Sun; 7am-7pm Mon-Sat suburbs and airports; 5.83F/km); C (7pm-7am daily suburbs and airports; 7.16F/km). Most journeys in central Paris average 40F-80F; there's a minimum charge of 13F, plus 6F for each piece of luggage over 5kg or bulky objects, and a 5F surcharge from mainline stations. Most drivers will not take more than three people, although they should take a couple and two children. Don't feel obliged to tip, although rounding up by 2F-5F is polite. Taxis are not allowed to refuse rides because they are too short and can only refuse to take you in a particular direction during their last half-hour of service. If you want a receipt, ask for *un reçu* or *une fiche* (compulsory for journeys of 100F or more). Complaints should be made in writing to the Bureau de la réglementation publique de Paris, 36 rue des Morillons, 75732 Paris Cedex 15.

Taxi companies

The following accept telephone bookings 24 hours daily. However, you also pay for the radioed taxi to get to where you are. If you wish to pay by credit card, mention this when you order. **Accept credit cards over 50F: Alpha** 01.45.85.85.85; **G7** 01.47.39.47.39; **accept credit cards over 100F: Artaxi** 01.42.03.50.50; **Taxis Bleus** 01.49.36.10.10.

transfer; 1100F for four hours. **Credit** AmEx, DC, MC, V. Chauffeur-driven car service and multi-lingual guided tours. **International Limousines** *(01.53.81.14.14).* **Open** 24 hours daily. **Prices** From 848F airport transfer; from 1100F four-hour hire. **Credit** AmEx, DC, MC, V. Limos with English-speaking drivers.

Cycles, Scooters & Motorbikes

Note that bike insurance may not cover theft: be sure to check. **Atelier de la Compagnie** *57 bd de Grenelle, 15th (01.45.79.77.24).* **Open** 10am-7pm Mon-Fri; 10am-6pm Sat. **Credit** V. A scooter for 250F/day or 950F/week; motorbike from 340F/day or 1500F/week. A 14,000F deposit is required, plus passport. **Bicloune** *93 bd Beaumarchais, 3rd (01.42.77.58.06). Mº St-Sébastien-Froissart.* **Open** 10am-1pm, 2-7pm Tue-Sat. **Credit** AmEx, MC, V. **Branch:** *7 rue Froment, 11th (01.48.05.47.75).* Cycles from 90F/day, cycles for sale, repairs. **Maison du Vélo** *11 rue Fénélon, 10th (01.42.81.24.72). Mº Gare du Nord or Poissonnière.* **Open** 10am-

7pm Tue-Sat. **Credit** MC, V. Bikes for hire, new and used cycles on sale, as well as repairs and accessories. **Paris-Vélo** *2 rue du Fer-à-Moulin, 5th (01.43.37.59.22). Mº Censier-Daubenton.* **Open** 10am-12.30pm, 2-6pm daily. **Credit** MC, V. Mountain bikes and 21-speed models for hire.

Driving in Paris

If you bring your car to France, you will need to bring the registration and insurance documents – an insurance green card, available from insurance companies and the AA and RAC in the UK, is not compulsory but is advisable.

As you come into Paris you will inevitably meet the *Périphérique,* the giant ring road that carries traffic in, out and around the city. Intersections, which lead onto other main roads, are called *portes* (gates). Driving on the *Périphérique* is not as hair-raising as it might look, even though it's often congested, especially during rush hour and at peak holiday times. If you've come to Paris by car, it can be a good idea to park at the edge of the city and use public transport.

A few hotels have parking spaces. You can get traffic information for the Ile-de-France on 01.48.99.33.33. In peak holiday periods, the organisation Bison Futé hands out brochures at the motorway *péages* (toll stations), suggesting less-crowded routes. Travelling by car is still the best way to explore France. French roads are divided into *Autoroutes* (motorways, with an 'A' in front of the number), *Routes Nationales* (national 'N' roads), *Routes Départementales* (local, 'D' roads) and tiny, rural *Routes Communales* ('C' roads). *Autoroutes* are toll roads (*péages*), although some sections, including most of the area immediately around Paris, are free. Motorways have a speed limit of 130km/h (80mph). On most *Routes Nationales* the limit is 90km/h (56mph); within urban areas the limit is 50km/h (30mph), 30km/h (20mph) in selected residential zones.

Breakdown Services

The AA or RAC do not have reciprocal arrangements with an equivalent organisation in France, so it is advisable to take out additional breakdown insurance cover, for example with **Europ Assistance** (in the UK 01444 442211). If you don't have insurance, you can use its service (01.41.85.85.85) but it will charge you the full cost. Other 24-hour breakdown services in Paris include **SOS Dépannage** (01.47.07.99.99); **Action Auto Assistance** (01.45.58.49.58); **Adan Dépann Auto** (01.42.66.67.58).

Driving Tips

• At intersections where no signposts indicate the right of way, the car coming from the right has priority. Many roundabouts now give priority to those on the roundabout. If this is not indicated (by road markings or *vous n'avez pas la priorité*), priority is for those coming from the right.
• Drivers and all passengers must wear seat belts.
• Children under ten are not allowed to travel in the front of a car, except in special babyseats facing backwards.
• You should not stop on an open road; pull off to the side.
• When drivers flash their lights at you, this means that they will not slow down and are warning you to keep out of the way. Friendly drivers also flash their lights to warn you when there are gendarmes lurking on the other side of the hill.
• Carry change, as it's quicker to head for the exact-money line on *péages*; but cashiers do give change and *péages* accept credit cards.

Parking

There are still a few free on-street parking areas left in Paris, but they are often full. If you park illegally, you risk getting your car clamped or towed away (*see below*). It is forbidden to park in zones marked for *livraisons* (deliveries) or taxis. Parking meters have now generally been replaced by *horodateurs*, pay-and-display machines, which either take coins or cards (100F or 200F available from *tabacs*). Parking is often free at weekends and after 7pm, and in August. There are numerous underground car parks in central Paris. Most cost 12F-15F per hour; 80F-130F for 24 hours; some offer lower rates after 6pm.

Clamps & Car Pounds

If you've had the misfortune to have your car clamped, contact the local police station. There are eight car pounds (*préfourrières*) in Paris. You'll have to pay a 600F removal fee plus 30F storage charge per day, and a parking fine of 230F for parking in a no-parking zone. Be sure to bring your driving licence and insurance papers. If your car is confiscated at night, it goes first to *préfourrière* Bercy for southern Paris or Europe for the north; and will be sent to the car pound for the relevant *arrondissement* after 48 hours. For details call 08.36.67.22.22 (2.23F/min). **Les Halles** 1st, 2nd, 3rd, 4th (01.40.39.12.20). **Bercy** 5th, 12th, 13th (01.53.46.69.20). **Montparnasse** 6th, 7th, 14th (01.40.47.42.00). **Europe** 8th, 9th (01.42.93.51.30). **Pantin** 10th, 11th, 19th, 20th (01.44.52.52.10). **Balard** 15th/16th (south) (01.45.58.70.30). **Foch** 8th, 16th (north), 17th (01.53.64.11.80). **Pouchet** 17th, 18th (01.53.06.67.68).

Leaving Town

Travelling by Train

Several attractions in the suburbs, notably Versailles and Disneyland Paris, are served by the RER. Most locations farther from the city are served by the SNCF state railway; there are few long-distance bus

services. The TGV (*Train à Grande Vitesse*) high-speed train has revolutionised journey times and is gradually being extended to all the main regions. On the downside, travel by TGV requires a price supplement and reservation, and there are now fewer trains to lesser towns.

SNCF Reservations/Tickets

SNCF national reservations and information: 08.36.35.35.35 (2.23F/min). **Open** 7am-10pm daily. SNCF information (no reservations) in the Ile de France: 01.53.90.20.20. You can buy tickets at counters and machines and at travel agents. If you reserve on Minitel 3615 SNCF or by phone, you must pick up and pay for the ticket within 48 hours. Regular trains have both full-rate White and cheaper Blue periods. You can save on TGV fares by purchasing special cards. *Carte 12/25* gives under-26s a 50 per cent reduction; without it, under-26s are entitled to 25 per cent off. Pensioners benefit from similar terms with a *Carte Vermeil*. Before you board any train, validate your ticket in the orange *composteur* machines located by the platforms, or you might have to pay a hefty fine.

Paris Mainline Stations

Gare d'Austerlitz: Central and SW France and western Spain.
Gare de l'Est: Alsace, Champagne and southern Germany.
Gare de Lyon: Burgundy, the Alps, Provence, Italy.
Gare Montparnasse: West France, Brittany, Bordeaux, the Southwest.
Gare du Nord: Northeast France, Channel ports, Eurostar, Belgium and the Netherlands.
Gare St-Lazare: Normandy.

Major Airlines

Aer Lingus 01.47.42.12.50.
Air France 08.02.80.28.02.
American Airlines 01.69.32.73.07.
British Airways 08.02.80.29.02.
British Midland 01.48.62.55.65.
Continental 01.42.99.09.09.
KLM & NorthWest 01.44.56.18.25.

Tower Air 01.55.04.80.80.
USAir 01.49.10.29.00.

Travel Agencies

Cash & Go *34 av des Champs-Elysées, 8th (01.53.93.63.63). Mº Champs-Elysées-Clemenceau.* **Open** 9am-7pm Mon-Fri; 10am-6pm Sat. **Credit** AmEx, MC, V. Broker with well-priced flights around the world.
Council Travel *1 pl de l'Odéon, 6th (01.44.41.89.80). Mº Odéon.* **Open** 9.30am-6.30pm Mon-Fri; 10am-5pm Sat. **Credit** AmEx, MC, V. Specialises in student tickets.
Havas Voyages *26 av de l'Opéra, 1st (01.53.29.40.00). Mº Opéra.* **Open** 10am-7pm Mon-Sat. **Credit** AmEx, V. General travel agent with more than 15 branches in Paris.
Maison de la Grande Bretagne *19 rue des Mathurins, 9th (01.44.51.56.20). Mº Havre-Caumartin/RER Auber.* **Open** 9.30am-6pm Mon-Fri; 10am-5pm Sat. **Credit** MC, V. All under one roof, the British Tourist Office and other services for travelling to or in the UK including ferry companies, Le Shuttle, British Rail (01.44.51.06.00) and Global Tickets (01.42.65.39.21), a theatre ticket agency for the UK.
Nouvelles Frontières *13 av de l'Opéra, 1st (08.03.333.333/ 01.41.41.58.58). Mº Pyramides.* **Open** 9am-7pm Mon-Sat. **Credit** DC, MC, V. Agent with 18 branches in Paris.
USIT *6 rue de Vaugirard, 6th (01.42.34.56.90/telephone bookings 01.42.44.14.00). Mº Odéon.* **Open** 10am-7pm Mon-Fri; 10am-1pm, 2-6pm Sat. **Credit** MC, V. Coach, air and train tickets for under-26s and for general customers.

Hitch-hiking

Allô-Stop *8 rue Rochambeau, 9th (01.53.20.42.42).* **Open** 9am-7.30pm Mon-Fri; 9am-1pm, 2-6pm Sat. **Credit** MC, V. Call several days ahead to be put in touch with drivers. There's a fee (30F under 200km; up to 70F over 500km), plus 22 centimes/km to the driver. Routes most travelled: Lyon, Toulouse, Rennes, Nantes, Cologne.

Directory

Directory A-Z

Banks & Money

Since 1 Jan 1999 there have been two currencies in France: the franc and the Euro. The French franc is usually abbreviated to F or sometimes FF after the amount. One franc is made up of 100 centimes and the smallest coin in circulation is five centimes. There are coins for five, ten, 20 and 50 centimes, one, two and five francs, and the heavier ten and 20 francs, silver-centred coins with a copper rim.

There are banknotes of 20F, 50F, 100F, 200F and 500F.

The Euro

1 Jan 1999 saw the start of the transition to the Euro, when it became the official currency in France (and ten other nations of the European Union) and the official exchange rate was set at 6.55957F. Shops and businesses are increasingly indicating prices in both currencies. You can open Euro accounts, and some places will accept

payment in Euros by cheque or credit card, although Euro coins and notes will not be circulated until 2002. Beware high bank charges for cashing cheques for Euros from other countries. Travellers' cheques are also available in Euros.

Bureaux de Change

If you arrive in Paris early or late, you can change money at the **Travelex** bureaux de change in the terminals at Roissy (01.48.64.37.26) and at Orly (01.49.75.89.25) airports,

which are open 6.30am to 10.30pm or 11pm daily. **Thomas Cook** has bureaux de change at the main train stations. Hours can vary.
Gare d'Austerlitz 01.53.60.12.97. **Open** 7.15am-8.45pm Mon-Fri; 7.15am-11am, 5-8.45pm Sat, Sun.
Gare Montparnasse 01.42.79.03.88. **Open** 8am-6.55pm daily (until 8pm in summer).
Gare St-Lazare 01.43.87.72.51. **Open** 8am-7pm Mon-Sat; 9am-4.50pm Sun.
Gare du Nord 01.42.80.11.50. **Open** 6.15am-11.25pm daily.
Gare de l'Est 01.42.09.51.97. **Open** Mon-Sat 6.45am-9.50pm, 6.45am-7pm Sun.
Gare de Lyon 01.43.41.52.70. 6.30am-11pm daily.
Some banks have cash exchange machines that accept notes of major currencies in good condition and convert them into francs. **Crédit Commercial de France (CCF)** has automatic change machines at 28 rue de Rivoli, 4th, and at 103 av des Champs-Elysées, 8th.

Banks & Banking Hours
French banks usually open 9am-5pm Mon-Fri (some close at lunch 12.30-2.30pm); some banks also open on Sat. All are closed on public holidays, and from noon on the previous day. Note that not all banks have foreign exchange counters. Commission rates vary between banks. The state Banque de France usually offers good rates. Most banks accept travellers cheques, but may be reluctant to accept personal cheques with the Eurocheque guarantee card, which is not widely used in France.

Bank Accounts
To open an account (*ouvrir un compte*), French banks require proof of identity, address and your income (if any). You'll probably have to show your passport, *Carte de Séjour*, an electricity/gas or phone bill in your name and a payslip/letter from your employer. Students need a student card and may need a letter from their parents. Of the major banks (BNP, Crédit Lyonnais, Société Générale, Banque Populaire, Crédit Agricole), Société Générale tends to be the most foreigner- and student-friendly. Most banks don't hand out a Carte Bleue/Visa until several weeks after you've opened an account. A chequebook (*chéquier*) is usually issued in about a week. Carte Bleue is debited directly from your current account, but you can choose for purchases to be debited at the end of every month. French banks are tough on overdrafts, so try to anticipate any cash crisis in advance and work out a deal for an authorised overdraft (*découvert autorisé*) or you risk being blacklisted as '*interdit bancaire*' –

forbidden from having a current account – for up to ten years. Depositing foreign-currency cheques is slow, so use wire transfer or a bank draft in francs to receive funds from abroad.

Credit Cards & Cash Machines
Major international credit cards are widely used in France; Visa (in French *Carte Bleue*) is the most readily accepted. French-issued credit cards have a special security microchip (*puce*) in each card. The card is slotted into a card reader, and the holder keys in a PIN number to authorise the transaction. Non-French cards should be read in the conventional way. In case of credit card loss or theft, call the following 24-hour services which have English-speaking staff: **American Express** 01.47.77.72.00; **Diners Club** 01.49.06.17.17; **MasterCard** 01.45.67.84.84; **Visa** 08.36.69.08.80. Withdrawals in francs can be made from bank and post office automatic cash machines. The specific cards accepted are marked on each machine, and most give instructions in English. Credit card companies charge a fee for cash advances, but rates are often better than bank rates.

Foreign Affairs
American Express *11 rue Scribe, 9th* (01.47.14.50.00). *M° Opéra.* **Open** 9am-4.30pm Mon-Fri. *Bureau de change* (01.47.77.79.50). **Open** 9am-6pm Mon-Fri; 9am-5pm Sat; 10am-4pm Sun. Bureau de change, poste restante, card replacement, travellers cheque refund service, international money transfers and a cash machine for AmEx cardholders.
Barclays *6 rond point des Champs-Elysées, 8th* (01.44.95.13.80). *M° Franklin D Roosevelt.* **Open** 9.15am-4.30pm Mon-Fri. As well as regular services, Barclays' international Expat Service handles direct debits, international transfer of funds, etc.
Chequepoint *150 av des Champs-Elysées, 8th* (01.49.53.02.51). *M° Charles de Gaulle-Etoile.* **Open** 24 hours daily. Other branches have variable hours; some are closed on Sun. No commission.
Thomas Cook *52 av des Champs-Elysées, 8th* (01.42.89.80.32). *M° Franklin D Roosevelt.* **Open** 9am-10pm daily. Hours of other branches (over 20 in Paris) vary. They issue travellers' cheques and deal with bank drafts and bank transfers.
Western Union Money Transfer *CCF Change, 4 rue du Cloître-Notre-Dame, 4th* (01.43.54.46.12). *M° Cité.* **Open** 9am-6pm daily. CCF is an agent for Western Union in Paris, with several branches in the city. 48 post offices now provide Western Union services (call 01.43.35.60.60 for

details). Money transfers from abroad should arrive within 10-15 minutes. Charges paid by the sender.
Citibank *125 av des Champs-Elysées, 8th* (01.53.23.33.60). *M° Charles de Gaulle-Etoile.* **Open** 10am-6pm Mon-Fri. Existing clients get good rates for transferring money from country to country, preferential exchange rates and no commision on on travellers cheques. European clients can make immediate on-line transfers from account to account on ATM with a Cirrus cashcard.

Beauty Spas
Women's beauty is an obsessive cult in Paris, with local cosmetic shops, beauty parlours and hairdressers around every corner, and numerous branches of affordable chains like Jean-Claude Biguine and Jean-Louis David. Look for cheap promotions on tanning or leg waxing and for cheap cuts at hairdressers if you volunteer to be a guinea pig for student stylists.
Les Bains du Marais *31-33 rue des Blancs-Manteaux, 4th* (01.44.61.02.02). *M° Rambuteau.* **Open** *women* 11am-8pm Mon; 11am-11pm Tue; 10am-7pm Wed; *men* 11am-11pm Thur; 10am-8pm Fri, Sat; *mixed* 7pm-midnight Wed; 11am-11pm Sun. **Credit** AmEx, MC, V. Morrocan décor provides a suitable setting for a steam bath or massage (180F).
Carita *11 rue du Fbg-St-Honoré, 8th* (01.44.94.11.11). *M° Concorde.* **Open** 10am-6.30pm Mon-Fri. **Credit** AmEx, DC, MC, V. A sybaritic heaven of spacious pink and black booths, reclining chairs and wafting music and scents. Treatments range from 'Prolifting' facials (700F-850F) to a special massaging chair.
Charlie en Particulier *1 rue Goethe, 16th* (01.47.20.94.01). *M° Alma-Marceau.* **Open** 9.30am-6pm Mon-Fri. **Credit** AmEx, DC, MC, V. A hair appointment with Charlie is for that special occasion when looking great is a must and money no object (cut 2000F).
Christophe Robin *7 rue du Mont-Thabor, 1st* (01.42.60.99.15). *M° Tuileries.* **Open** 11am-7pm Mon-Fri. **No credit cards.** The young genius of hair colouring is responsible for Catherine Deneuve's and many lesser-known Parisians' blondeness (800F-2000F). To guard your secret, he never takes more than two clients at a time.
Guerlain Institut de Beauté *68 av des Champs-Elysées, 8th* (01.45.62.11.21). *M° Franklin D Roosevelt.* **Open** 9am-6.30pm Mon-Sat. **Credit** AmEx, MC, V. Art Deco touches by Cocteau and Giacometti surround the cabins where miracles occur: try a facial (from 620F), a manicure (210F) or an Acti-Lift (720F).

Directory

Hammam de la Mosquée de Paris *39 rue Geoffroy-St-Hilaire, 5th (01.43.31.18.14).* M° Censier-Daubenton. **Open** *women* 10am-9pm Mon, Wed-Sat. *men* 2-9pm Tue, 10am-9pm Sun. **Admission** 85F. **Credit** MC, V. The Turkish bath at the Mosque is a perfect place to unwind and get the pollution out of your pores. Languish in steam rooms, take an invigorating massage, or lounge on mattresses. It's a favourite girls' treat; on men's days, the atmosphere can get a little steamy.
Institut Lancôme *29 rue du Fbg-St-Honoré, 8th (01.42.65.30.74).* M° Concorde. **Open** 10am-8pm Mon-Fri; 10am-7pm Sat. **Credit** AmEx, DC, MC, V. Art Deco elegance plus efficient and up-to-date skincare. The 90-minute 'Soin Relaxant Douceur' includes a facial, a mask and a 20-minute massage of face, shoulders, hands and feet (600F).
Institut Orlane *163 av Victor-Hugo, 16th (01.47.04.65.00).* M° Victor-Hugo. **Open** 9am-6.30pm Mon-Fri; 9am-1pm Sat. **Credit** AmEx, V. Apart from quality products and treatments, Orlane has a small salon to repair damaged hair.
Villa Thalgo *218-220 rue du Fbg-St-Honoré, 8th (01.45.62.00.20).* M° Ternes. **Open** 8.30am-8.30pm Mon-Thur; 8.30am-7pm Fri; 9am-7pm Sat. **Credit** AmEx, DC, MC, V. Thalassotherapy without the sea. Half a day of 'anti-stress and beauty' treatment, with an Aquagym class, skin exfoliating treatment, toning seaweed wrap and facial costs 980F, including lunch by the pool.

Bureaucracy

Anyone from abroad coming to live in Paris should be prepared for the sheer weight of bureaucracy to which French officialdom is devoted, whether it's for acquiring a *Carte de Séjour* (resident's permit), opening a bank account, reclaiming medical expenses or getting married. Among documents regularly required are a *Fiche d'Etat Civil* (essential details translated from your passport by the embassy/consulate) and a legally approved translation of your birth certificate (embassies will provide lists of approved legal translators; for general translators, *see p320*, **Business Resources**). You need to be able to prove your identity to the police at all times, so keep your passport/*Carte de Séjour* with you.

Cartes de Séjour

Officially, all foreigners, both EU citizens and non-Europeans in France for more than three months, must apply for a *Carte de Séjour*, valid for one year. Those who have had a *Carte de Séjour* for at least three years, have been paying French income tax, can show proof of income and/or are married to a French national can apply for a *Carte de Résident*, valid for ten years.
CIRA (Centre interministeriel de renseignements administratifs) *(01.40.01.11.01).* **Open** 9am-12.30pm, 2-5.30pm Mon-Fri. Advice on French administrative procedures.
Préfecture de Police de Paris *1 rue de Lutèce, 7 bd du Palais, 1st (01.53.71.51.68).* M° Cité. **Open** 8.30am-4pm Mon-Fri. Information on residency and work permits.
Cosmopolitan Services Unlimited *113 bd Pereire, 17th (01.55.65.11.65/fax 01.55.65.11.69).* M° or RER Pereire. **Office hours** 9am-6pm Mon-Thur; 9am-5pm Fri. A good but pricey relocation service. Services include getting work permits and *Cartes de Séjour* approved (*see p313*, **Removals & Relocation**).

Customs

There are no limits on the quantity of goods you can take into France from another EU country for personal use, provided tax has been paid on them in the country of origin. However, customs still has the right to question visitors. Quantities accepted as being for personal use are:
• up to 800 cigarettes, 400 small cigars, 200 cigars or 1kg loose tobacco.
• 10 litres of spirits (over 22% alcohol), 90 litres of wine (under 22% alcohol) or 110 litres of beer.
For goods from outside the EU:
• 200 cigarettes or 100 small cigars, 50 cigars or 250g loose tobacco
• 1 litre of spirits (over 22% alcohol) and 2 litres of wine and beer (under 22% alcohol)
• 50g perfume
Visitors can carry up to 50,000F in currency.

Détaxe

Non-EU residents can claim a refund (average 13 per cent) on VAT if they spend over 1200F in any one shop, and if they've been in the country less than three months. At the shop ask for a *détaxe* form, and when you leave France have it stamped by customs. Then send a stamped copy back to the shop, who will refund the tax, either by bank transfer or by crediting your credit card. *Détaxe* does not cover food, drink, antiques or works of art.

Disabled Travellers

Disabled visitors to Paris are advised to buy **Access in Paris**, an excellent English-language guide by Gordon Couch and Ben Roberts, published by Quiller Press. It can be ordered from RADAR, Unit 12, City Forum, 250 City Rd, London EC1V 8AF/020-1250 3222 (£6.95, incl UK postage, add £2 for Europe, £7 for rest of world). The **Office de Tourisme de Paris** produces *Tourisme pour tout le monde* (60F). Freephone 08.00.03.37.48 gives advice (in French) to disabled persons living in or visiting Paris. We've put wheelchair access in the listings where applicable, but it's always wise to check beforehand. Many additional places are accessible to wheelchair users but do not have accessible or specialised toilets.
Comité national de liaison pour la réadaptation des handicapés (CNRH) *236bis rue de Tolbiac, 13th (01.53.80.66.63).* Publishes *Paris Ile-de-France Pour Tous*, an all-purpose tourist guide for the disabled (60F in Paris; 80F from abroad).
Association des paralysés de France *22 rue du Père-Guérain, 13th (01.44.16.83.83).* M° Place d'Italie. **Open** 9am-12.30pm, 2-6pm Mon-Thur (until 5pm Fri). Publishes *Où ferons-nous étape?* (85F), listing French hotels and motels accessible to those with limited mobility.

Getting Around

Neither the Métro nor buses are wheelchair-accessible, except bus line 20, some No 91 buses and the PC. Forward seats on buses are intended for people with poor mobility. RER lines A and B and some SNCF trains are wheelchair-accessible in parts. All Paris taxis are obliged by law to take passengers in wheelchairs. The following offer adapted transport for the disabled. Book 48hrs in advance.
Aihrop *(01.41.29.01.29).* **Open** 8am-noon, 1.30-6pm Mon-Fri. Transport to and from the airports.
GiHP *24 av Henri Barbusse, 93000 Bobigny (01.41.83.15.15).* **Open** 7.30am-8pm Mon-Fri.

Electricity & Gas

Electricity in France runs on 220V. Visitors with British 240V appliances can simply change the plug or use a converter (*adaptateur*), available at better hardware shops. For US 110V appliances, you will need to use a transformer (*transformateur*) available at the Fnac and Darty chains or in the basement of the BHV store. Gas and electricity are supplied by the state-owned EDF-GDF (Electricité de France-Gaz de France). Contact them about supply, bills, or in case of power failures or gas leaks (*see p308*, **Emergencies**).

Embassies

Before going to an embassy or consulate, phone and check opening

Armchair & guided tours

Boat Trips & Riverbuses

Bateaux-Mouches *pont de l'Alma, Rive Droite, 8th (01.42.25.96.10/recorded info 01.40.76.99.99). M° Alma-Marceau.* **Departs** *summer* every 30min 10am-11pm daily; *winter* approx every hour from 11am-9pm daily; lasts one hour. **Tickets** 40F; 20F under-15s; free under-5s. Lunch 330F; 150F; dinner (smart dress) 500F-700F **Credit** AmEx, MC, V (meal cruises only).

Bateaux Parisiens Tour Eiffel *port de la Bourdonnais, 7th (01.44.11.33.55). RER Pont de l'Alma or M° Trocadéro.* **Departs** *summer & winter weekends* every 30 min 10am-10pm daily; *winter weekdays* every hour 10am-9pm daily. **Tickets** 50F; 25F under-12s. Lunch 300F, 150F under-12s; dinner 560F-750F. **Credit** AmEx, MC, V (meals only).

Bateaux Vedettes de Paris *port de Suffren, 7th (01.47.05.71.29). M° Bir-Hakeim or RER Champ de Mars.* **Departs** every 30 min; *summer* 10am-11pm; *winter* 11am-6pm daily. **Tickets** 50F; 20F 5-12s; free under-4s. **Credit** AmEx, MC, V.

Batobus *(01.44.11.33.99). Apr-Nov.* **Tickets** *one day* 60F; *two days* 90F (reductions with Carte Orange); *season ticket* (Paris residents) 250F. The Seine riverbus has six stops (Eiffel Tower, Musée d'Orsay, St-Germain, Notre Dame, Hôtel de Ville, Louvre).

Les Vedettes du Pont Neuf *square du Vert-Galant, 1st (01.46.33.98.38). M° Pont-Neuf.* **Departs** summer every 30min: 10am-noon, 1.30-6.30pm daily; floodlit evening trips 9-10.30pm daily; winter times depend on demand. **Tickets** 50F; 25F 4-11s; free under-4s. Lunch 290F; 200F under-10s; dinner 350F-470F. **Credit** AmEx, MC, V (meals only).

Canal Trips

Canauxrama *(01.42.39.15.00).* **Departs** *Bassin de la Villette, 13 quai de la Loire, 19th. M° Jaurès.* 9.45am, 2.45pm daily. **Departs** *Port de l'Arsenal, opposite 50 bd de la Bastille, 12th. M° Bastille.* 9.45am, 2.30pm daily. Fewer trips in winter. **Tickets** 75F daily; 60F students, over-65s Mon-Fri; 45F 6-12s; free under-6s. No reductions holidays or weekend afternoons. Trips last 2-3hrs, live commentary in French; in English if enough foreigners.

Navettes de la Villette *(01.42.39.15.00). Shuttle between Parc de la Villette (M° Porte de Pantin) and la Rotonde de Ledoux (5bis quai de la Loire. M° Jaurès).* **Departs** every 30 mins 11am-6pm Sat, Sun and holidays. **Tickets** 10F single; 15F return.

Paris Canal *(Reserve on 01.42.40.96.97). Musée d'Orsay (M° Solférino) to Parc de la Villette (M° Porte de Pantin) or reverse.* **Departs** *Apr-mid-Nov* Musée d'Orsay 9.30am daily; Parc de la Villette 2.30pm daily. *mid-Nov-Mar* Sun only. **Tickets** 100F; 75F 12-25s, over-60s (except Sun pm and holidays); 60F 4-11s; free under-4s. Three-hour trip with commentary in French (and English if enough demand).

Coach Tours

Cityrama *4 pl des Pyramides, 1st (01.44.55.61.00). M° Palais Royal.* **Departs** *summer* hourly 9.30am-4.30pm daily; *winter* 9.30am, 10.30am, 1.30pm, 2.30pm daily. **Tickets** 150F; free under-12s. **Credit** AmEx, DC, MC, V. Two-hour tour with recorded commentary.

Les Cars Rouges *(01.42.30.55.50).* **Departs** every

30 min. *Easter-July* 10am-5pm; *Aug-mid-Oct* 9.45am-4.50pm; *mid-Oct-Easter* 9.55am-2.55pm daily. **Tickets** 125F; 100F students; 60F under-12s; free under-4s. **Credit** AmEx, DC. Red London doubledeckers with recorded commentary in English. You can get off and on at will at any of nine stops; tickets are valid two days. Stops include Eiffel Tower, Notre Dame, Louvre, Opéra, Arc de Triomphe and the Grand Palais.

Paris L'Open Tour *(01.43.46.52.06).* **Departs** every 15-20 mins *Apr-Oct* 10am-6.30pm; every 25-30 mins *Nov-Mar* 10am-6pm, **Tickets** 150F; 110F with Paris Visite pass, 70F children. A similar hop on hop off scheme.

Paris Vision *214 rue de Rivoli, 1st (01.42.60.30.01). M° Tuileries.* **Trips** hourly 9.30am-3.30pm daily (lasts 2 hours). **Tickets** first one 150F, then 100F; 75F 4-11s; free under-4s. **Credit** AmEx, DC, MC, V. Tickets from departure point. Recorded multilingual commentaries.

Cycle Tours

Escapade Nature *(reserve on 01.53.17.03.18).* **Price** *incl bike hire* 100F-160F; 50F-80F 4-12s; less with own bike. Guided rides (90 mins/three hours) take in main sites or themes such as Medieval and Renaissance Paris, plus full-day rides (200F-300F) to Versailles and Fontainebleau. Guides speak English.

Maison Roue Libre *95bis rue Rambuteau, Forum des Halles, 1st (01.53.46.43.77). M° Les Halles.* **Price** *incl bike hire* 105F-165F; 55F-85F 4-12s. Guided rides (90 mins/three hours) from RATP-linked bike shop include Paris Mystérieux and Paris Vert.

Paris à vélo, c'est sympa! *37 bd Bourdon, 4th (01.48.87.60.01). M° Bastille.* **Open** 9am-6pm daily. **Price** *incl bike hire* 150F half-day; 170F night tour; 130F, 150F under-26s; plus 20F membership. Multilingual guided tours, usually leave 10am, 3pm, 8.30pm. Reservation required. Also bike rental.

Walking Tours

Many individual guides organise walks (in French), and details are published weekly in *Pariscope* under Promenades. The **Caisse Nationale des Monuments Historiques et des Sites** (Hôtel de Sully, 62 rue St-Antoine, 4th/ 01.44.61.20.00), does tours of monuments, museums and historic districts (in French).

The tours below have English-speaking guides; their walks are usually listed in the *Time Out Paris* section in *Pariscope*, but most also organise group walks on request. Prices exclude entrance fees for sights.

Paris Contact *Jill Daneels (01.42.51.08.40).* **Tickets** 60F; 50F students, over-60s. Guided weekly walks and customised cultural tours, including Parks and Gardens of Paris and In Jefferson's Footsteps.

Paris Walking Tours *Oriel and Peter Caine (01.48.09.21.40).* **Tours** last 90 minutes, usually daily. **Tickets** 60F; 40F students; free under-10s (except sewers). Regular tours include the Louvre, the Marais, Montmartre and Latin Quarter.

Paristoric

11bis rue Scribe, 9th (01.42.66.62.06). M° Opéra. **Shows** *Apr-Oct* hourly 9am-8pm daily; *Nov-Mar* hourly 9am-6pm daily. **Admission** 50F; 40F over-60s; 30F under-18s, students. A 45-minute, audiovisual ride which flashes through 2000 years of Paris history. Headset commentary in English and other languages.

hours. You may need to make an appointment. Otherwise, the answer-phone will usually give an emergency contact number. There's a full list of embassies and consulates in the *Pages Jaunes* under *Ambassades et Consulats*. For general enquiries or problems with passports or visas, it is usually the consulate you need.

Australian Embassy *4 rue Jean-Rey, 15th (01.40.59.33.00). M° Bir-Hakeim.* **Open** 9am-6pm Mon-Fri; Visas 9.15am-12.15pm Mon-Fri.

British Embassy *35 rue du Fbg-St-Honoré, 8th (01.44.51.31.00). M° Concorde.* **Open** 9.30am-1pm, 2.30-6pm Mon-Fri. Consulate *16 rue d'Anjou, 8th (01.44.51.33.01/ 01.44.51.33.03). M° Concorde.* **Open** 2.30-5.30pm Mon-Fri.

Canadian Embassy *35 av Montaigne, 8th (01.44.43.29.00). M° Franklin D Roosevelt.* **Open** 9am-noon, 2-5pm Mon-Fri. Visas *37 av Montaigne (01.44.43.29.16).* **Open** 8.30-11am Mon-Fri.

Irish Embassy *12 av Foch, 16th.* Consulate *4 rue Rude, 16th (01.44.17.67.00).* **Open** *for visits* 9.30am-noon Mon-Fri; *by phone* 9.30am-1pm, 2.30-5.30pm Mon-Fri.

New Zealand Embassy *7ter rue Léonard de Vinci, 16th (01.45.00.24.11). M° Victor-Hugo.* **Open** Visas 9am-1pm Mon-Fri.

South African Embassy *59 quai d'Orsay, 7th (01.53.59.23.23). M° Invalides.* **Open** 8.30am-5.15pm Mon-Fri, by appointment. Consulate 9am-noon.

US Embassy *2 av Gabriel, 8th (01.43.12.22.22). M° Concorde.* **Open** 9am-6pm Mon-Fri, by appointment. Consulate/Visas *2 rue St-Florentin, 1st (01.43.12.22.22). M° Concorde.* **Open** 8.45-11am Mon-Fri. Passport service 9am-3pm.

English Media

The Paris-based **International Herald Tribune** is on sale throughout the city; British dailies, Sundays and **USA Today** are widely available on the day of issue at larger kiosks in the city centre. On the local front, **Time Out Paris** is a six-page supplement inside the weekly listings magazine *Pariscope*, available at all news stands, covering selected Paris events, exhibitions, films, concerts and restaurants. The quarterly **Time Out Paris Free Guide** is distributed in bars, hotels and tourist centres and **Time Out Paris Eating & Drinking Guide** is available in newsagents across the city. **FUSAC** (France-USA Contacts) is a fortnightly small-ads free-sheet with flat rentals, job ads and appliances for sale. The monthly **Paris Free Voice** is community

oriented with reasonable arts coverage. Both are available at US and English-language bookshops, bars and the American Church. You can receive the **BBC World Service** (648 KHz AM) for its English-language international news, current events, pop and drama. Also on 198KHz LW, from midnight to 5.30am daily. At other times this frequency carries **BBC Radio 4** (198 KHz LW), for British news, talk and *The Archers* directed at the home audience. **RFI** (738 KHz AM) has an English-language programme of news and music from 3-4pm daily.

Flower Delivery

Interflora *(freephone 08.00.20.32.04).* **Open** 8am-8pm Mon-Sat. **Credit** AmEx, DC, MC, V. Prices start at 280F for a standard bouquet delivered in Paris.

Lachaume *10 rue Royale, 8th (01.42.60.57.26). M° Concorde or Madeleine.* **Open** 9am-7pm Mon-Fri; 9am-6pm Sat. **Credit** AmEx, MC, V. Paris' most regal flower shop. Call before noon for same-day delivery.

Health & Hospitals

All EU nationals staying in France are entitled to use of the French Social Security system, which refunds up to 70 per cent of medical expenses (but sometimes much less, eg. for dental treatment). To get a refund, British nationals should obtain form E111 before leaving the UK (or E112 for those already in treatment). Nationals of non-EU countries should take out insurance before leaving home. Consultations and prescriptions have to be paid for in full, and are reimbursed, in part, on receipt of a completed *fiche*. If you undergo treatment while in France the doctor will give you a prescription and a *feuille de soins* (statement of treatment). The medication will carry *vignettes* (little stickers) which you must stick onto your *feuille de soins*. Send this, the prescription and form E111, to the local *Caisse Primaire d'Assurance Maladie* (in the phone book under *Sécurité Sociale*). Refunds can take over a month to come through.

Doctors & Dentists

A complete list of practitioners is in the *Pages Jaunes* under *Médecins Qualifiés*. To get a Social Security refund, choose a doctor or dentist registered with the state system; look for *Médecin Conventionné* after the name. Consultations cost 115F upwards, of which a proportion can be reimbursed. To see a specialist rather than a generalist costs more.

Centre Médical Europe *44 rue d'Amsterdam, 9th (01.42.81.93.33/ dentists 01.42.81.80.00). M° St-Lazare.* **Open** 8am-7pm Mon-Fri; 8am-6pm Sat. Practitioners in all fields under one roof, charging minimal consultation fees (115F for foreigners). Appointments advisable.

Help Lines & House Calls

See also p342, **Emergencies.**

SOS Infirmiers (Nurses) *(01.43.57.01.26/06.08.34.08.92/ 08.36.60.50.50 beeper).* House calls 8pm-midnight; daytime Sat-Sun; generally around 150F.

SOS Dépression *(01.45.22.44.44).* People listen and/or give advice, and can send a counsellor or psychiatrist to your home in case of a crisis.

SOS Help *(01.47.23.80.80).* English-language helpline 3-11pm daily.

SOS Médecins *(01.47.07.77.77/ 01.43.37.77.77).* Doctors make house calls. A home visit starts at 250F if you don't have French Social Security, 145F if you do, before 7pm; from 310F thereafter.

Urgences Médicales de Paris *(01.48.28.40.04).* Doctors make house calls. Some speak English.

Urgences Dentaires de Paris *(01.47.07.44.44).* **Open** 8am-10pm. Will offer advice by phone or refer you to nearby dentists; after 10pm all are sent to the Hôpital Salpêtrière.

SOS Dentaire *87 bd Port-Royal, 5th (01.43.37.51.00). RER Port-Royal.* **Open** 8-11.45pm. Emergency dental care.

Alcoholics Anonymous in English *(01.46.34.59.65).* 24-hour recorded message gives details of AA meetings at the American Church or Cathedral (*see p346,* **Religion**) and members' phone numbers for more information.

Narcotics Anonymous *(01.48.78.77.00).* Meetings in English three times a week

The Counselling Center (01.47.23.61.13) English-language counselling service, based at the American Cathedral.

Hospital Specialities

For a complete list of hospitals consult the *Pages Blanches* under *Hôpital Assistance Publique*, or ring 01.40.27.30.00.

Burns: Hôpital Cochin, *27 rue du Fbg-St-Jacques, 14th (01.42.34.17.58). M° St-Jacques/RER Port-Royal.* **Open** 24 hours daily. Hôpital St-Antoine, *184 rue du Fbg-St-Antoine, 12th (01.49.28.26.09). M° Faidherbe-Chaligny or Reuilly-Diderot.*

Children: Hôpital St Vincent de Paul, *74 av Denfert Rochereau (01.40.48.81.11). M° Denfert-Rochereau.* **Open** 24 hours daily. Hôpital Necker, *149 rue de Sèvres, 15th (01.44.49.40.00). M° Duroc.*

Children's Burns: Hôpital

Emergencies

Most of the following services operate 24-hours daily. In a real medical emergency, call the Sapeurs-Pompiers, who are trained paramedics, rather than the SAMU.

Police	17
Fire (Sapeurs-Pompiers)	18
Ambulance (SAMU)	15
Emergency (from a mobile phone)	112

GDF (gas leaks) (01.47.54.20.20). **Open** 8am-4.30pm daily.
EDF (electricity) (01.40.42.22.22) **Open** 8am-4.30pm daily.
After-hours look in the *Pages Blanches* (heading *Urgence-Dépannage Gaz et Electricité*) for your *arrondissement*.

Armand-Trousseau, *26 av du Dr-Arnold-Netter, 12th (01.44.73.74.75). M° Bel-Air.*
Drugs: Centre Hospitalier Ste-Anne, *1 rue Cabanis, 14th (01.45.65.80.64). M° Glacière.* Hôpital Marmottan, *19 rue d'Armaillé, 17th (01.45.74.00.04). M° Argentine.*
Poisons: Hôpital Fernand Widal, *200 rue du Fbg-St-Denis, 10th (01.40.05.48.48). M° Gare du Nord.* **Open** 24 hours.
American Hospital in Paris *63 bd Victor-Hugo, 92202 Neuilly (01.46.41.25.25). M° Porte Maillot, then bus 82.* **Open** 24 hours daily. A private hospital. French Social Security will refund only a small percentage of treatment costs. All staff speak English.
Hertford British Hospital (Hôpital Franco-Britannique) *3 rue Barbès, 92300 Levallois-Perret (01.46.39.22.22). M° Anatole-France.* **Open** 24 hours daily. Most doctors are English-speaking. Accepts BUPA.

Pharmacies

Pharmacies sport a green neon cross. They have a monopoly on issuing medication, and also sell sanitary products. Most open 9am/10am-7pm/8pm. Staff can provide basic medical services like disinfecting and bandaging wounds (for a small fee) and will indicate the nearest doctor on duty. French pharmacists are highly trained; you can often avoid visiting a doctor by describing your symptoms and seeing what they suggest. Paris has a rota system of *pharmacies de garde* at night and on Sunday. A closed pharmacy will have a sign indicating the nearest open pharmacy. Toiletries and cosmetics are often cheaper in supermarkets

Night Chemists

Pharma Presto (01.42.42.42.50). **Open** 24 hours daily. Delivery charge 150F from 8am-6pm; 250F 6pm-8am. Delivers prescription medication

(non-prescription exceptions can be made), in association with **Dérhy.**
Pharmacie des Halles *10 bd de Sébastopol, 4th (01.42.72.03.23). M° Châtelet.* **Open** 9am-midnight Mon-Sat; noon-midnight Sun.
Dérhy/Pharmacie des Champs *84 av des Champs-Elysées, 8th (01.45.62.02.41). M° George V.* **Open** 24 hours daily.
Matignon *2 rue Jean-Mermoz, 8th (01.43.59.86.55). M° Franklin D Roosevelt.* **Open** 8.30am-2am daily.
Capucines *6 bd des Capucines, 9th (01.42.65.88.29). M° Opéra.* **Open** 8am-12.30am Mon-Fri; 9am-12.30am Sat; 10am-12.30am Sun.
Pharmacie Européenne de la Place de Clichy *6 pl de Clichy, 9th (01.48.74.65.18). M° Place de Clichy.* **Open** 24 hours daily.
Lagarce *13 pl de la Nation, 11th (01.43.73.24.03). M° Nation.* **Open** 8am-midnight daily.
Pharmacie d'Italie *61 av d'Italie, 13th (01.44.24.19.72). M° Tolbiac.* **Open** 8am-midnight Mon-Sat; 9am-midnight Sun.

Opticians

Branches of **Alain Afflelou** and **Lissac** are abundant. They stock hundreds of frames and can make prescription glasses within the hour.
SOS Optique *(01.48.07.22.00).* 24-hour repair service. Glasses repaired at your home by a certified optician.

Complementary Medicine

Most pharmacies also sell homeopathic medicines.
Académie d'Homéopathie et des Médecines Douces *2 rue d'Isly, 8th (01.43.87.60.33). M° St-Lazare.* **Open** 10am-6pm Mon-Thur; 10am-7pm Fri. Health services include acupuncture, aromatherapy and homeopathy.
Association Française d'Acuponcture *3 rue de l'Arrivée, 15th (01.43.20.26.26). M° Montparnasse-Bienvenüe.* **Open**

9am-12.30pm, 2-5.30pm Mon-Fri. Lists professional acupuncturists.
Centre d'Homéopathie de Paris *48 av Gabriel, 8th (01.45.55.12.15). M° Franklin D Roosevelt.* **Open** 8am-7pm Mon-Sat.

AIDS, HIV & Sexually Transmitted Diseases

AIDES *247 rue de Belleville, 19th (01.44.52.00.00). M° Télégraphe.* **Open** 2-6pm Mon-Fri. Volunteers provide support for AIDS patients.
AJCS (Action jeunes conseils santé) *6 rue Dante, 5th (01.46.33.71.83/01.44.78.00.00). M° Maubert-Mutualité.* **Open** Tue-Fri 10am-12.30pm, 2-6pm. Youth association offering info on AIDS, youth and health.
Centre Médico-Social *3 rue Ridder, 14th (01.45.43.83.78). M° Plaisance.* **Open** 8.30am-6.30pm Mon-Fri; 9.30am-noon Sat. Free, anonymous HIV tests noon-6.30pm Mon-Fri; 9.30am-noon Sat. Other services include heart and lung diagnoses, as well as endocrinology and gynaecological exams.
Dispensaire de la Croix Rouge *43 rue de Valois, 1st (01.42.61.30.04). M° Palais-Royal.* Centre specialising in sexually transmitted diseases offers safe, anonymous HIV tests *(dépistages).*
FACTS *(01.44.93.16.69).* **Open** 6-10pm Mon, Wed, Fri. English-speaking crisis line gives information and support for those touched by HIV/AIDS and runs support groups for friends and relatives.
SIDA Info Service *(08.00.84.08.00).* **Open** 24 hours daily. Confidential AIDS-information in French (some bilingual counsellors).

Internet Providers

After a slow start, Internet use has skyrocketed, although there are still complaints about high phone charges. It is also now possible get access via cable in most of Paris.
America Online (freephone 08.00.903.910) or www.aol.fr
Club-Internet (01.55.45.46.47) or www.club-internet.fr
CompuServe (08.03.00.60.00) or www.compuserve.fr
Imaginet (01.43.38.10.24) or www.imaginet.fr
Microsoft Network (01.69.86.47.47) or www.fr.msn.com
Wanadoo (France Télécom) (08.01.63.34.34) or www.wanadoo.fr

Cybercafés

Clickside *14 rue Domat, 5th (01.56.81.03.00). M° Maubert-Mutualité.* **Open** 10am-midnight Mon-Sat; 11am-11pm Sun. Exposed stone, beams and a sexy new iMac: the chic way to do chatrooms.

Cyber Cube *12 rue Daval, 11th* *(01.49.29.67.67). Mº Bastille.* **Open** 10am-10pm Mon-Sat. No nonsense, friendly staff and a high turnover of punters. **Branch:** *5 rue Mignon, 6th.*
Cyber Café Latino *13 rue de l'École-Polytechnique, 5th (01.40.51.86.94). Mº Maubert-Mutualité.* **Open** 11am-2am Mon-Sat; 4-9pm Sun. Bar/cybercafé. Rogelio the host with the most (especially with the laydeez) provides a hyper friendly way to check your mail.

Late Night Shops

Most areas have a local grocer that stays open until around 10pm, as do some branches of Monoprix. At other times, 24-hour garages and the shops listed provide supermarket essentials and help placate midnight munchies.

24-Hour Newsagents

include *33 av des Champs-Elysées, 8th. Mº Franklin D Roosevelt; 2 bd Montmartre, 9th. Mº Grands Boulevards.*

Shops

See also bookshops and record shops in chapter **Specialist Shops**.
L'An 2000 *82 bd des Batignolles, 17th (01.43.87.24.67). Mº Rome or Villiers.* **Open** 5-11 pm Mon-Fri, Sun. **Credit** MC, V. A *traiteur* offering paella, cheese and *charcuterie*.
Boulangerie de l'Ancienne Comédie *10 rue de l'Ancienne-Comédie, 6th (01.43.26.89.72). Mº Odéon.* **Open** 24 hours daily. **Credit** AmEx, MC, V. Bread, *pâtisseries* and sandwiches, plus hot and cold snacks.
Boulangerie Pigalle *28 bd de Clichy, 18th (01.46.06.39.37). Mº Pigalle.* **Open** 24 hours Mon, Tue, Thur-Sun. **No credit cards.** Basic groceries and North African goods.
Elyfleur *82 av de Wagram, 17th (01.47.66.87.19). Mº Charles de Gaulle-Etoile.* **Open** 24 hours daily. Say it with flowers, any time.
Noura *27 av Marceau, 16th (01.47.23.02.20). Mº Iéna or Alma-Marceau.* **Open** 8am-midnight daily. **Credit** AmEx, DC, MC, V. Upmarket Lebanese *traiteur* stocks *meze*, bread, cheese, *charcuterie*, *baklava*, wines.
Prisunic *109 rue La Boétie, 8th (01.53.77.65.65). Mº Franklin D Roosevelt.* **Open** 9am-midnight Mon-Sat. **Credit** AmEx, MC, V. Full-scale

Paris on the Web

Myriad sites cover all aspects of the city and French culture in both English and French. Most major magazines and newspapers have web equivalents of their paper formats. To find out about hot new sites, listen to RTL (104.3 FM) 8pm-midnight Mon-Fri.

News & Media

www.liberation.com *Libé*'s web site provides the current affairs stories covered in its daily paper, plus features on cinema, multimedia and the arts. One section has excerpts from 250 recent books and *BD*s.
www.lemonde.fr France's respected heavyweight daily newspaper, online. Stock exchange information, arts, cinema and literary features. In French only.
www.telerama.fr Online version of the weekly TV, radio and cultural listings magazine, with features, personalised programming and new film releases.

Entertainment & Culture

www.timeout.com *Time Out*'s web site contains information about 29 cities, including Paris, with a weekly updated list of current events and an extensive guide to hotels, restaurants, monuments and the arts.
www.pariscope.fr The weekly online version of the *Pariscope* entertainment guide. Mostly French.
www.parissi.com great graphics, club listings and reviews of art exhibitions. Links to offbeat sites.
www.goodmorningparis.com Paris news, events and restaurants in English.
www.louvre.fr Multilingual visit of the building, its exhibitions and permanent collections. Lots of images.
www.musee-orsay.fr The museum, its collections and key works; reproductions are very small.
www.bnf.fr The real Bibliothèque Nationale may be beset by strikes, but the web site should be immune. Come here for illuminated manuscripts and page-by-page scans from first editions of literary classics.
www.chateauversailles.fr Bilingual visit to the home of the Sun King, includes a 360º view of the Hall of Mirrors, and the King's hot chocolate recipe.
www.tour-eiffel.fr The official Eiffel Tower site, in English and French. Cut-away diagrams of the tower, archive photos, tales from its history and a nifty 360º rotating view across Paris from the summit.

www.ucad.fr the museums of decorative arts, fashion and advertising, not forgetting the warder.
www.jazzfrance.com Jazz information site with clubs, concerts, festivals and reviews. Bilingual.
www.johnny-hallyday.tm.fr The official fan site of the legendary, leathery rocker; discography, audio files, and a shot of Johnny astride his beloved Harley.
www.worldmedia.fr Online magazine covers tourism and the Paris fashion shows, live.

Officialdom

www.elysee.fr Tour the President's official residence, keep up with his recent engagements and speeches, or browse his family album. Multilingual.
www.premier-ministre.gouv.fr Pop in to the Prime Minister's official web site for a similar virtual tour of Hôtel Matignon, plus links to other ministries.
www.mairie-paris.fr Visit Hôtel de Ville, check out the 2000 projects, Paris statistics and municipal info.

Useful

www.iti.fr Plan the best road routes through Europe.
www.meteo.fr/temps The latest satellite pics and forecasts from the French meteorological office.
www.pagesjaune.com France Telecom's online version of the phone book has a useful search engine for Paris streets giving details of every shop, florist or café, plus maps and photos from different angles.
www.paris-anglo.com guide to expat life from second-hand car dealers to translators and small ads.
www.paris.org Exhaustive coverage from the state tourist office about Paris and France. Bilingual.
www.paris-touristoffice.com Official site has info on expos, monuments, parks, events, hotels, etc.

Weird & Wonderful

www.pwa-prod.com Paris With Attitude gives its view of events from clubbing to rollerblading.
altern.org/tidji Street art on the walls of Paris by Mesnager, Miss-Tic, Néné. Good links.
www.multimania.cim/lafouine/kata Images and info on graffiti in the Paris catacombes by cataphiles.
www.multimania.com The *Journal Intime Collectif*, a multi-author open-ended journal of Paris *quartiers*.

supermarket for clothes, make-up, deli, grocery and liquid needs. Packed nightly with foreigners stocking up on French staples.
Select *Shell Garage, 6 bd Raspail, 7th (01.45.48.43.12). M° Rue du Bac.* **Open** 24 hours daily. **Credit** AmEx, MC, V. Shop at the Shell Garage has a large if pricey array of supermarket standards from the Casino chain. No alcohol sold 10pm-6am.

Tobacconists

La Brazza *86 bd du Montparnasse, 14th (01.43.35.42.65). M° Montparnasse-Bienvenüe.* **Open** 6.30am-2am daily.
La Favorite *3 bd St-Michel, 5th (01.43.54.08.02). M° St-Michel.* **Open** 7am-2am Mon-Fri; 8am-2am Sat, Sun.
La Havane *4 pl de Clichy, 17th (01.48.74.67.56). M° Place de Clichy.* **Open** 6.30am-5am daily.

Legal Advice

Mairies also answer legal enquiries. Phone for details and times of free *consultations juridiques.*
Avocat Assistance et Recours du Consommateur *11 pl Dauphine, 1st (01.43.54.32.04). M° Pont Neuf.* **Open** 2-6pm Mon-Fri. Lawyers here deal with consumer-related cases. 200F for a consultation.
Direction Départementale de la Concurrence, de la Consommation, et de la Répression des Fraudes *8 rue Froissart, 3rd (01.40.27.16.00). M° St-Sébastien-Froissart.* **Open** 9-11.30am, 2-5.30pm Mon-Fri. This subdivision of the Ministry of Finance deals with consumer complaints.
Palais de Justice *Galerie de Harlay, escalier S, 4 bd du Palais, 4th (01.44.32.48.48). M° Cité.* **Open** 9.30am-noon Mon-Fri. Free legal consultation. Arrive early.
SOS Avocats *(08.03.39.63.00).* **Open** 7-11.30pm Mon-Fri. Free legal advice by phone.
SOS Racisme *28 rue des Petites Ecuries, 10th (01.42.05.44.44). M° Château d'Eau.* **Open** 9.30am-1pm, 2-6pm Mon-Fri. A non-profit association defending the rights of ethnic minorities.

Libraries

All *arrondissements* have free public libraries. For a library card, you need ID and two documents proving residency, such as a phone bill or tenancy agreement. Book and magazine loan are free; there are charges for CD and video loans. The University of Paris has library facilities for enrolled students.
American Library

10 rue du Général-Camou, 7th (01.53.59.12.60). M° Ecole-Militaire/RER Pont de l'Alma. **Open** 10am-7pm Tue-Sat (shorter hours in Aug). **Admission** *day pass* 70F; *annual* 570F. Claims to be the largest English-language lending library in mainland Europe, and also organises talks and readings. Receives 350 periodicals, plus popular magazines and newspapers (mainly American).
Bibliothèque Historique de la Ville de Paris *Hôtel Lamoignon, 24 rue Pavée, 4th (01.44.59.29.40). M° St-Paul.* **Open** 9.30am-6pm Mon-Sat. Reference books and documents on Paris history in a Marais mansion.
Bibliothèque Marguerite Durand *79 rue Nationale, 13th (01.45.70.80.30). M° Tolbiac or Place d'Italie.* **Open** 2-6pm Tue-Sat. 30,000 books and 120 periodicals, some in English, on women's history and feminism, many of which were assembled by feminist pioneer Durand. The collection includes letters of Colette and Louise Michel.
Bibliothèque Nationale de France François Mitterrand *quai François-Mauriac, 13th (01.53.79.55.01). M° Bibliothèque.* **Open** 10am-7pm Tue-Sat; noon-6pm Sun. **Admission** *day pass* 20F; *annual* 200F. Books, newspapers and periodicals, plus titles in English, are on access to anyone over 18. An audio-visual room lets you browse photo, film and sound archives.
Bibliothèque Publique d'Information (BPI) *Centre Pompidou, 4th (01.44.78.12.33). M° Hôtel de Ville/RER Châtelet-Les Halles.* **Open** 11am-10pm Mon, Wed-Fri; 10am-10pm Sat, Sun. Now on three levels, the Centre Pompidou's vast reference library has a huge international press section, reference books and language-learning facilities.
Bibliothèque Ste-Geneviève *10 pl du Panthéon, 5th (01.44.41.97.97). RER Luxembourg.* **Open** 10am-10pm Mon-Sat. This reference library, with a spectacular, iron-framed reading room, is open to students over 18. Bring ID and photo to register (by 6pm).
BIFI (Bibliothèque du Film) *100 rue du Fbg-St-Antoine, 12th (01.53.02.22.30). M° Ledru-Rollin.* **Open** 10am-7pm Mon-Fri. Film buffs' library offers books, magazines film stills and posters, as well as films on video and CD-Rom.
BILIPO (Bibliothèque des Littératures Policières) *48-50 rue du Cardinal-Lemoine, 5th (01.42.34.93.00). M° Cardinal-Lemoine.* **Open** 2-6pm Tue-Fri; 10am-5pm Sat. Non-lending library of crime, spy and detective fiction.
British Council Library *9-11 rue Constantine, 7th (01.49.55.73.00). M° Invalides.* **Open** 11am-6pm Mon-Fri (until

7pm Wed). **Admission** *day pass* 30F; *annual* 250F; 200F students. Reference and lending library stocks British press and offers an Internet and CD-rom service.
Documentation Française *29 quai Voltaire, 7th (01.40.15.70.00). M° Rue du Bac.* **Open** 10am-6pm Mon-Wed, Fri; 10am-1pm Thur. **Admission** free. The official government archive and central reference library has information on contemporary French politics and economy since 1945.

Maps

Free maps of the Métro, bus and RER systems are available at airports and Métro stations. Other brochures from Métro stations are *Paris Visite – Le Guide*, with details of transport tickets and a small map, and the *Grand Plan de Paris*, a fold-out map that also indicates Noctambus night bus lines (*see p325*). Métro, bus, RER and street maps are also included at the back of this Guide.
If you're staying more than a few days it's worth buying a detailed map book. The Michelin *Paris-Plan, Paris par Arrondissement* (Editions l'Indispensable), the small paperback *Plan de Paris* (Editions Leconte) and the slightly larger *Collection Plan Net* (Ponchet Plan Net) are all available from kiosks and bookshops.

Opening Times

Standard opening hours for shops are 9am/10am-7pm/8pm Mon-Sat. Some shops also close on Mon. Shops and businesses often close at lunch, usually 12.30-2pm. Many shops are closed for all or part of August.

Photo Labs

Photo developing is often more expensive than in the UK or USA. **Photo Station** and **Fnac Service** both have numerous branches and are reasonably priced.

Police/Lost Property

If you are robbed or attacked, you should report the incident as soon as possible. You will need to make a statement (*procès verbal*) at the *commissariat* in the *arrondissement* in which it was committed. To find the appropriate *commissariat*, phone the Préfecture Centrale (01.53.71.53.71) day or night, or look in the phone book. Stolen goods are unlikely to be recovered, but you will need the police statement for insurance purposes.

Bureau des Objets Trouvés
*36 rue des Morillons, 15th
(01.55.76.20.20). M° Convention.*
Open 8.30am-7pm Mon, Wed, Fri;
8.30am-8pm Tue, Thur. Visit in
person to fill in a form specifying
date, time and place you lost the item.

Post

If you're simply sending a letter or
postcard, it is quicker to buy stamps
at a tobacconist (*tabac*) than at a post
office. Post offices (*bureaux de poste*)
are open 8am-7pm Mon-Fri; 9am-
noon Sat. All are listed in the phone
book: under *Administration des PTT*
in the *Pages Jaunes*; under *Poste* in
the *Pages Blanches*. Most post offices
have automatic machines (in French
and English) that weigh your letter,
print out a stamp and give change.
Main Post Office *52 rue du
Louvre, 1st (01.40.28.20.00). M° Les
Halles or Louvre-Rivoli.* **Open** 24
hours daily for *Poste Restante*,
telephones, telegrams, stamps and
fax. This is the best place to get your
mail sent if you haven't got a fixed
address in Paris. Mail should be
addressed to you in block capitals,
followed by *Poste Restante*, then the
post office's address. There is a
charge of 3F for each letter received.
Letters will arrive sooner if they
bear the correct five-digit postcode.
Within Paris: postcodes always
begin with '75'; if your address is in
the 1st *arrondissement*, the postcode
is 75001; in the 15th, the code is
75015. The 16th *arrondissement* is
subdivided into two sectors, 75016
and 75116. Some business addresses
have a more detailed postcode,
followed by a Cedex number which
indicates the *arrondissement*.

Press

Newspapers

The main daily papers are
characterised by high prices and
relatively low circulation. Only 20
per cent of the population reads a
national paper; regional dailies hold
the sway outside Paris.
Serious, centre-left daily **Le Monde**
is essential reading for businessmen,
politicians and intellectuals, who
often also publish articles in it.
Despite its highbrow reputation,
subject matter is surprisingly
eclectic, although international
coverage is selective. Publishes
Aden, a weekly Paris-listings
supplement. Founded post-68 by a
group that included Sartre and de
Beauvoir, trendy **Libération** is now
centre-left, but still the read of the
gauche caviar, worth reading for
wide-ranging news and arts coverage

and guest columnists, such as
Baudrillard. The conservative middle
classes go for **Le Figaro**, a daily
broadsheet with a devotion to
politics, shopping, food and sport.
Sales are boosted by lots of property
and job ads and the Wednesday
Figaroscope Paris listings. Saturday's
edition contains three magazines
which rockets the price from 7F to
25F. Tabloid in format, the easy-read
Le Parisien is strong on consumer
affairs, social issues, local news and
events and vox pops, and has
recently introduced a Sunday edition.
Downmarket **France Soir** has
recently gone tabloid to suit its spirit.
La Croix is a Catholic, right-wing
daily. The Communist Party
L'Humanité has kept going despite
the collapse of the Party's colleagues
outside France. **Le Journal du
Dimanche** is a thin Sunday
broadsheet, which comes with free
Fémina mag. **L'Equipe** is a big-
selling sports daily, with a bias
towards football while **Paris-Turf**
caters just for horse-racing fans. *See
also p342,* **Business Resources.**

Satirical Papers

Le Canard Enchaîné is the Gallic
Private Eye, a satirical weekly
broadsheet that's full of in-jokes and
breaks political and economic
scandals. **Charlie Hebdo** is mainly
bought for its cartoons.

News Magazines

Weekly news magazines are an
important sector in France, taking
the place of weighty Sunday tomes.
Titles range from solidly serious
L'Express and **Le Point** to the
traditionally left-wing **Le Nouvel
Observateur** and sardonic,
chaotically arranged **Marianne**
(**L'Evénement** has been relaunched
as a weekly news-based arts mag).
Similarities tend to be stronger than
political differences. All summarise
the main events of the week, with
more limited cultural sections, but
are of greatest interest for the varied
in-depth reports. **Courrier
International** reprints articles from
newspapers all over the world,
giving perspectives from elsewhere.

Arts & Listings Magazines

Two pocket-sized publications rival
for basic Wednesday-to-Tuesday
listings information: **Pariscope** (3F),
the Parisian cinema-goer's bible,
which includes **Time Out Paris** in
English; and the thinner **Officiel
des Spectacles** (2.80F). Linked to
Radio Nova, monthly **Nova** gives
rigorously multi-ethnic information
on where to drink, dance or hang out.
Technikart tries to mix clubbing
with the arts. Highbrow TV guide
Télérama has good arts and
entertainment features and a Paris

listings insert. *See also above* **Le
Monde** *and* **Le Figaro.**
There are specialist arts magazines
to meet every interest (*see also
chapters* **Art Galleries** *and* **Music:
Rock, Roots & Jazz**). Film titles
include intellectual **Les Cahiers du
Cinéma**, glossy **Studio** and
younger, celebrity-geared **Première.**

Gossip Magazines

Despite strict privacy laws, the
French appear to have an almost
insatiable appetite for gossip. 1998
saw confusingly similar sounding
(and looking) arrivals: **Oh La!** from
Spain's *Hola!* (and UK's *Hello!*) group
and **Allo!** from German-owned
Prisma Presse, already responsible
for France's juiciest scandal sheet
Voici, and **Gala**, which tells the
same stories without the sleaze.
Paris Match is a French institution
founded in 1948, packed with society
gossip and celebrity interviews, but
still regularly scoops the rest with
photo shoots of international affairs.
Point de Vue specialises in royalty
and disdains showbiz fluff. Monthly
Entrevue tends toward features on
bizarre sexual practices, but still
somehow clinches regular exclusives.
Perso presents the stars as they
would like to be seen.

Women, Men & Fashion Magazines

Elle was a pioneer among liberated
women's mags and has editions
across the globe. In France it is
weekly and spot-on for interviews
and fashion. Monthly **Marie-Claire**
takes a more feminist, campaigning
line. Both have design spin offs (**Elle
Décoration**, **Marie-Claire Maison**)
and *Elle* has spawned foodie **Elle à
Table.** **DS** aims at the intelligent
reader, with lots to read and coverage
of social issues. **Biba** treats fashion,
sex and career topics with a younger,
more upbeat approach. **Vogue**, read
both for its fashion coverage and big-
name guests, is rivalled when it
comes to fashion week by **L'Officiel
de la Mode** and **Dépêche Mode.**
The underground go for more radical
Purple (six-monthly art, literature
and fashion tome); newcomers
Tribeca and **WAD** (We Are
Different) consider themselves so hip
it hurts. Men's mags include French
versions of lad bible **FHM**, **Men's
Health** (pronounced menz elth), with
articles on improving abs, and the
disturbing **L'Echo des Savanes**,
which features porny cartoons and
articles about lesbian sex.

Radio

A quota requiring a minimum of 40
per cent French music has led to
overplay of gallic pop oldies and to

the creation of dubious hybrids by local groups that mix some words in French with a refrain in English. Trash-talking phone-in shows also proliferate. Wavelengths are in MHz.

87.8 France Inter State- run, MOR music, international news and Pollen – concerts by rock newcomers.

90.4 Nostalgie As it sounds.

90.9 Chante France 100 per cent French *chanson*.

91.3 Cherie FM Lots of oldies.

91.7/92.1 MHz France Musiques State classical music channel has added an s and brought in more *variété* and slush to its highbrow mix of concerts, contemporary bleeps and top jazz (*see also* Maison de la Radio *in* **Music: Classical & Opera**).

93.1 Aligre From local Paris news to highbrow literary chat.

93.5/93.9 France Culture Verbose state culture station: literature, history, cinema and music.

94.8 RCJ/Radio J/Judaïque FM/ Radio Shalom Shared wavelength for Paris' Jewish stations.

95.2 Paris FM Municipal radio: music, traffic and what's on.

96 Skyrock Pop station with loudmouth presenters. Lots of rap.

96.4 BFM Business and economics. Wall Street in English every evening.

96.9 Voltage FM Dance music.

97.4 Rire et Chansons A non-stop diet of jokes – racist, sexist or just plain lousy – and pop oldies.

97.8 Ado Local music station for ado(lescents).

98.2 Radio FG Gay station. Techno music, rave announcements and very explicit lonely hearts.

99 Radio Latina Great Latin and salsa music, increasingly adding raï, Spanish and Italian pop.

100.3 NRJ Energy: national leader with the under-30s.

101.1 Radio Classique More classical pops than France Musique, but also less pedagogical.

101.5 Radio Nova Hip hop, trip hop, world, jazz and whatever is hip.

101.9 Fun Radio Now embracing techno alongside Anglo pop hits.

102.3 Ouï FM Ouï rock you.

103.9 RFM Easy listening.

104.3 RTL The most popular French station nationwide mixes music and talk programmes. Grand Jury on Sunday is a debate between journalists and a top politician.

104.7 Europe 1 News, press reviews, sports, business, gardening, entertainment, music. Much the best weekday breakfast news broadcast, with politicians interviewed live.

105.1 FIP Traffic bulletins, what's on in Paris and a mix of jazz, classical, world and pop, known for the seductive-voiced *Fipettes*, its female programme announcers.

105.5 France Info 24-hour news, economic updates and sports bulletins. As everything gets

repeated every 15 minutes, it's guaranteed to drive you mad – good though if you're learning French.

106.7 Beur FM Aimed at Paris' North African community.

Recycling & Rubbish

Large, green hive-shaped bottle banks can be found on many street corners. If your building has recycling bins they will fall into two categories: blue lids for newspapers and magazines, white for glass. Green bins are for general household refuse. For getting rid of furniture and non-dangerous rubbish, look for green skips on street corners.

Allô Propreté *(01.43.64.91.91).* **Open** 7.30am-7.30pm Mon-Fri. Recycling information and collection of cumbersome objects.

Mini-déchetteries Small recycling centres which accept household packaging, paper and disposable batteries are at: *132 bd Vincent-Auriol, 13th (01.45.83.06.15). M° Nationale.* **Open** 9am-5.45pm Mon-Fri; 9.30am-5.30pm Sat-Sun. *1 rue Fabert, 7th (01.47.53.90.52). M° Invalides.* **Open** 6am-1.30pm Mon; 6am-7.30pm Tue-Fri; 7am-7.30pm Sat.

Déchetteries

Poterne des Peupliers, 8 rue Jacques-Destrée, 13th (01.46.63.38.59). M° Porte d'Italie. **Open** 9.30am-7pm daily.

quai d'Issy-les-Moulineaux, 15th (01.45.57.27.35). RER Issy. **Open** 9.30am-7pm daily.

17-25 av de la Porte de la Chapelle, 18th (01.40.35.07.90). M° Porte de la Chapelle. **Open** 9.30am-7pm daily.

52 rue de Frères-Flavien, 20th (01.43.64.91.91). M° Porte des Lilas. **Open** 8.30am-noon, 2-7.30pm Mon-Thur; 8.30am-noon Fri, Sat.

These four recycling centres accept all kinds of household packaging, including cans, glass and plastic bottles, aerosols and magazines, as well as motor oil, fridges, car batteries, furniture and wood scraps.

Religion

Churches and religious centres are listed in the phone book (*Pages Jaunes*) under *Eglises* and *Culte*. Paris has several English-speaking churches. The *International Herald Tribune*'s Saturday edition lists Sunday church services in English.

American Cathedral *23 av George V, 8th (01.53.23.84.00). M° George V.*

American Church in Paris *65 quai d'Orsay, 7th (01.40.62.05.00). M° Invalides.*

Church of Scotland *17 rue Bayard, 8th (01.48.78.47.94). M° Franklin D Roosevelt.*

St George's Anglican Church *7 rue Auguste-Vacquerie, 16th (01.47.20.22.51). M° Charles de Gaulle-Etoile.* The YWCA-Cardew club for under-28s meets here.

St Joseph's Roman Catholic Church *50 av Hoche, 8th (01.42.27.28.56). M° Charles de Gaulle-Etoile.*

St Michael's Church of England *5 rue d'Aguesseau, 8th (01.47.42.70.88). M° Madeleine.*

Kehilat Geisher *(01.39.21.97.19).* The Liberal English-speaking Jewish community has rotating services in Paris and the western suburbs.

Removals/Relocation

Grospiron, Arthur Pierre, Interdean, Desbordes and Transpaq International are the big five of removals: see *Déménagements* in the *Pages Jaunes*. Companies targeted at UK/US removals also advertise in the free magazine FUSAC. Relocation services will also help with work papers, flat hunting and opening bank accounts.

Grospiron *15 rue Danielle Casanova, 93300 Aubervilliers (01.48.11.71.71/fax 01.48.11.71.70). M° Fort d'Aubervilliers.* **Open** 9am-6pm Mon-Fri. Corporate-oriented packing, loading and transport service moves people and businesses all over the world. Contact Nancy Cruse for English-speaking service.

Packing & Shipping

Hedley's Humpers *6 bd de la Libération, 93284 St-Denis (01.48.13.01.02). M° Carrefour-Pleyel.* **Open** 8am-6pm Mon-Fri. *102 rue des Rosiers, 93400 St-Ouen (01.40.10.94.00). M° Porte de Clignancourt.* **Open** 9am-1pm Mon; 9am-6pm Sat, Sun. English company specialised in transporting furniture and antiques. **In UK:** *3 Leonards Rd, London NW10 6SX, UK (0181-965 8733).* **In USA:** *21-41 45th Road, Long Island City, New York NY 11101, USA (1.718.433.4005).*

Logistic Air/Sea France *C-O ACM BP 10232 95703 Roissy CDG (01.48.62.13.25).* **Open** 9am-6.30pm Mon-Fri. **Credit** MC, V. Air shipping worldwide for roughly 12F/kg (45kg minimum), up to 100kg. Pick-up charge 500F. Lower rates for shipping by boat.

Renting a Flat

The best flats often go by word of mouth. Northern, eastern and southeastern Paris are generally cheaper than the western, southwestern and central parts of the city. Expect to pay roughly 100F per month/m² (3500F/month for a 35m² flat, and so on). Studio and one-bedroom flats fetch the highest prices proportionally; lifts and central heating will also boost the rent.

Rental Laws

The legal minimum rental lease (*bail de location*) on an unfurnished apartment is three years; one year for a furnished flat. During this period the landlord can only raise the rent by the official construction inflation index. At the end of the lease, the rent can be adjusted, but tenants can object before a rent board if it seems exorbitant. Tenants can be evicted for non-payment, or if the landlord wishes to sell the property or use it as his own residence. It is nearly impossible to evict non-payers Oct-Mar, as it's illegal to throw people out in winter.

Before accepting you as a tenant, agencies or landlords will probably require you to present a *dossier* with pay slips (*fiches de paie*/*bulletins de salaire*) showing three to four times the amount of the monthly rent, and for foreigners, in particular, to furnish a financial guarantee. When taking out a lease, payments usually include the first month's rent, a deposit (*une caution*) equal to two month's rent, and an agency fee, if applicable. It is customary for an inspection of the premises (*état des lieux*) at the start and end of the rental, the cost of which (around 1000F) is shared by landlord and tenant.

Landlords may try to rent their flats *non-declaré* – without a written lease and get rent in cash. This can make it difficult for the tenant to establish his or her rights – which, in addition to avoiding tax, is why landlords do it.

Flat Hunting

The largest lists of furnished (*meublé*) and unfurnished (*vide*) flats for rent are in Tuesday's *Le Figaro*. Most ads are placed by agencies. There are also assorted free ad brochures that can be picked up from agencies. Flats offered to foreigners are advertised in the *International Herald Tribune* and English-language fortnightly *FUSAC*; rents tend to be higher than in the French press. Short-term flat agencies can simplify things, but are not cheap either. Local bakeries often post notices of flats for rent direct from the owner. Non-agency listings are also available in the weekly *Particulier à Particulier*, published on Thursdays, and via Minitel 3615 PAP. There's also a commercial Minitel flat rental service on 3615 LOCAT. Landlords often list a visiting time; prepare to meet hordes of other flat-seekers on the staircase and take supporting documents and cheque book.
Bureau de l'Information Juridique des Proprietaires et des Occupants (BIPO)

6 rue Agrippa-d'Aubigné, 4th (01.42.71.31.31). M° Sully-Morland. **Open** 9am-5pm Mon-Thur; 9am-4.30pm Fri. Municipal service provides free advice (in French) about renting or buying a flat, housing benefit, rent legislation and tenants' rights.
Centre d'Information et de Défense des Locataires
115 rue de l'Abbé-Groult, 15th (01.48.42.10.22). M° Convention. **Open** 9.30am-1pm, 2.30-6pm Mon-Fri (until 8pm Thur). For problems with landlords, rent increases, etc.

Repairs & Cleaning

Most department stores provide services, such as ticket sales, watch and jewellery repairs and printing. *See chapter* **Specialist Shops**.
BHV (Bazar de l'Hôtel de Ville) *Main shop: 52-64 rue de Rivoli, 4th (01.42.74.90.00). M° Hôtel-de-Ville.* **Open** 9.30am-7pm Mon, Tue, Thur-Sat; 9.30am-10pm Wed. *DIY shop: 11 rue des Archives (01.42.74.94.51). DIY tool hire annexe:* 40 rue de la Verrerie, 4th (01.42.74.97.23).
Credit AmEx, MC, V. The leading department store for camera cleaning and repair, photo-developing, photocopying, shoe repair, watch repair, car parts and tool hire.
Horloger Artisan/Jean-Claude Soulage *32 rue St-Paul, 4th (01.48.87.24.75). M° St-Paul.* **Open** 9.30am-noon, 3-7pm Tue-Fri; 9.30am-noon Sat. **No credit cards**. Watch and jewellery repairs and restoration.
Nestor Pressing *10bis rue Berteaux-Dumas, Neuilly-sur-Seine (01.47.69.74.15). M° Les Sablons.* **Open** 9am-9pm Mon-Fri. **Credit** AmEx, MC, V. Full-service cleaning, clothing repair, ironing, shoe repair for most *arrondissements* and western suburbs. Home pick-up 3-10pm. 48-hour and express service.
Rainbow International *40 rue Galilée, 77380 Combs-la-Ville (01.60.60.18.16).* **Open** 7am-9pm daily. **No credit cards**. Rainbow will clean carpets (around 25F/m²; 15m² minimum), sofas, leather, etc.

Emergency Repairs

Numerous 24-hour emergency repair services deal with plumbing, electricity, heating, locks, car repairs and much more. Most charge a minimum of 150F call-out and 200F per hour's labour, plus parts; more on Sunday and at night.
Allô Assistance Dépannage *(08.00.07.24.24).* No car repairs.
Numéro Un Dépannage *(01.43.31.51.51).* No car repairs.
SOS Dépannage *(01.47.07.99.99).* double the price, but claim to be twice as reliable. 320F call-out, then 320F/hour. 8am-7pm Mon-Sat; nights and Sun 400F call out, 400F/hour.

Smoking

Earnest official health campaigns have made only a slight dent in French lighting-up habits. Under a 1991 law, restaurants are obliged to provide a non-smoking area (*espace non-fumeurs*). However, you'll often end up at the worst table in the house. Unless you're seriously allergic to tobacco you'll probably find it more pleasant to sit amid the smoke with the rest. Smoking is banned in most theatres, cinemas and on public transport.

Study & Students

The University of Paris is split into numerous units around the city and suburbs, of which the renowned Sorbonne is just one. Anyone who has passed the *baccalauréat* can apply, so over-crowded facilities and huge drop-out rates (up to 50 per cent at the end of the first year) are perennial problems. The situation is different in the prestigious, highly selective *Grandes Ecoles*, such as the Ecole Normale Supérieure and Ecole Polytechnique.

Students at French universities study either for a two-year *DEUG* or for a *Licence*, a three-year degree course. Many students take vocational or business-oriented courses, and many do a *stage*, a practical traineeship, after or during their degree. Other study options include private colleges, whether to learn French or make the most of Paris' cultural opportunities. Meeting other students can be difficult as most students live with their parents and there are few organised social activities. Sport is one good way, as you can do free sports courses as part of your degree. There are cheap organised ski trips. Registration in Paris universities takes about three weeks; each course has to be signed up for separately, and involves queueing at a different office to obtain a reading list.
CROUS (Centre Régional des Oeuvres Universitaires et Scolaires) *39 av Georges-Bernanos, 5th (01.40.51.36.00/Service du Logement 01.40.51.37.17/19/21). RER Port-Royal.* **Open** 9am-5pm Mon-Fri. Manages all University of Paris student residences. Most rooms are single-occupancy (around 750F/month). Requests for rooms must be made by 1 April for the next academic year. CROUS posts ads for rooms and has a list of hostels, some of which overlap with **UCRIF**. In summer, university residences are open to under-26s (around 100F/night). CROUS also issues the ISIC card, organises excursions, sports and cultural events, provides information on jobs, and offers discount theatre,

cinema and concert tickets. It is the clearing house for all *bourses* (grants) issued to foreign students. Call the Service des Bourses on 01.40.51.35.50.

Exchange Schemes

Socrates-Erasmus Programme
Britain: *UK Socrates-Erasmus Council, RND Building, The University, Canterbury, Kent CT2 7PD (0122-7762712).*
France: *Agence Erasmus, 10 pl de la Bourse, 33081 Bordeaux Cedex (05.56.79.44.10).* The Socrates-Erasmus scheme enables EU students with reasonable written and spoken French to spend a year of their degree following appropriate courses in the French university system. The UK office publishes a brochure and helps with general enquiries, but applications must be made through the Erasmus Co-ordinator at your home university. Non-EU students should find out from their university whether it has an agreement with the French university system such as the US 'Junior Year Abroad' scheme via **MICEFA** (26 rue du Fbg-St-Jacques, 14th/01.40.51.76.96).

Cartes de Séjour and Housing Benefit

Centre de Réception des Etudiants Etrangers *13 rue Miollis, 15th (01.53.71.51.68). M° Cambronne.* **Open** 9am-4pm Mon-Fri. Foreign students who wish to qualify for housing benefit or to work legally during their course in Paris must get a *Carte de Séjour*. You need to present your passport or national identity card; proof of residence; an electricity bill; student card; student social security card; visa (if applicable); a bank statement, accompanied by a parental letter (in French) proving that you receive at least 2500F per month. Add to this three black-and-white passport photos and a 200F *timbre fiscal* (which you buy at the Centre or a *tabac*). Expect it to take around two months. Pick-up is at the Préfecture de Police at 9 bd du Palais (4th). You will then be eligible for the ALS (*Allocation Logement à Caractère Social*), which is handled by three CAFs (*Centres de gestion des allocations familiales*), depending on your *arrondissement*. They are open 8.30am-4pm/5.30pm Mon-Fri.
CAF *101 rue Nationale, 13th (01.40.77.58.00). 18 rue Viala, 15th (01.45.75.62.47); 67 av Jean-Jaurès, 19th (01.44.84.74.98).* Depending on your living situation, you may receive 600F-1000F a month.

Student & Youth Discounts

Despite Paris' expensive reputation, a wide range of student discounts

makes budget living possible. To claim the *tarif étudiant* (around 10F off some cinema seats, up to 50 per cent off museums and standby theatre tickets, 20 per cent in some hairdressers), you must have a French student card or an International Student Identity Card (ISIC), available from **CROUS**, student travel agents and the **Cité Universitaire**. ISIC cards are only valid in France if you are under 26. Under-26s can get up to 50 per cent off rail travel on certain trains with the *Carte 12/25*, or buy the *Carte Jeune* (120F from Fnac), which gives discounts on museums, cinema, theatre, travel, sports clubs, restaurants, insurance and some shops. Theatre, concert and opera deals usually work by buying discounted seats at the last minute.
SMEREP *54 bd St-Michel, 6th (01.56.54.36.34).* **Open** 9am-5.30pm Mon-Fri. A 140F *Carte Jeune* offers similar reductions to the Fnac card, including the Louvre and the RATP. Look also for the magazine *JAP* (*Jeune à Paris*), which has useful discount vouchers.

Student Accommodation

The simplest budget accommodation for medium-to-long stays are the Cité Universitaire or *foyers* (student hostels). An option, which is more common for women than men, is a *chambre contre travail* – free board in exchange for childcare, housework or English lessons. Look out for ads at accommodation offices, language schools and the American Church. For cheap hotels and youth hostels, *see chapter* **Accommodation**. As students often cannot provide proof of income, a *porte-garant* (guarantor) is required, usually a parent, who must write a letter (in French) declaring that he/she guarantees payment of rent and bills.
Cité Universitaire *19 bd Jourdan, 14th (01.42.53.51.44). RER Cité Universitaire.* **Open** offices 9am-3pm Mon-Fri. Foreign students enrolled on a university course, or current *stagiaires* who have done two years of career work, can apply for a place at this campus of halls of residence in the south of Paris. Excellent facilities (lawns, tennis courts, swimming pool, gym, theatre, library, an orchestra and student restaurant) and a friendly atmosphere compensate for rather basic rooms. Rooms must be booked for the entire academic year (Oct-June). Rents are around 1700F-2200F per month for a single room, 1200F-1625F per person for a double. Prices vary according to which *maison* you live in. UK citizens must apply to the Collège Franco-Britannique, and Americans to the Fondation des Etats-Unis.
UCRIF (Union des centres de

rencontres internationales de France)** *27 rue de Turbigo, 2nd (01.40.26.57.64). M° Les Halles.* **Open** 9am-6pm Mon-Fri. Operates several cheap, short-stay hostels in France, including four in Paris.

Resto-U

3 rue Mabillon, 6th (01.43.25.66.23). M° Mabillon. **Open** 11.30am-2pm, 6-8pm Mon-Fri. **No credit cards.** A chain of cheap university canteens run by CROUS. If you have a student card from Paris university you can buy a *carnet* of tickets at 14F per ticket (24F for ISIC cardholders).

Student Employment

Foreign students from the EU can legally work up to 39 hours per week. Non-EU members who are studying in Paris may apply for an *autorisation provisoire de travail* after one year to work a 20hr week.
CIDJ (Centre d'Information et de Documentation Jeunesse) *101 quai Branly, 15th (01.44.49.12.00). M° Bir-Hakeim/ RER Champ de Mars.* **Open** 9.30am-6pm Mon-Fri; 9.30am-1pm Sat. The CIDJ is mainly a library giving students advice on courses and careers, but also houses the youth bureau of ANPE (Agence Nationale Pour l'Emploi), the state employment service, which provides assistance with job applications. Many ANPE job offers are part-time or menial, but divisions exist for professional jobs.

Language Courses

Alliance Française *101 bd Raspail, 6th (01.45.44.38.28). M° St-Placide or Notre Dame des Champs.* **Fees** enrolment 250F; 1460F-3900F per month. A highly regarded, non-profit French-language school, with beginners and specialist courses starting every month, plus a *médiathèque*, film club and lectures.
Berlitz France *38 av de l'Opéra, 2nd (01.44.94.50.00). M° Opéra.* **Fees** 7714F-29,735F. Well known and effective classes, but pricey; mainly used by businesses.
British Institute *9 rue Constantine, 7th (01.44.11.73.73/70). M° Invalides.* **Fees** 1500F-6000F per term. Linked to London University, the 4000-student Institute offers both English courses for Parisians, and French courses (not beginner) in translation, commercial French, film and literature. It is possible to study for a three-year French degree from the University of London (details from Senate House, Malet Street, London WC1/0171-636 8000).
Ecole Eiffel *3 rue Crocé-Spinelli, 14th. (01.43.20.37.41/ fax 01.43.20.49.13). M° Pernety.* **Fees** 500F-2650F per month. Offers intensive classes, business French, phonetics and an au pair programme.

Eurocentres *13 passage Dauphine, 6th (01.40.46.72.00). M° Odéon.* **Fees** four weeks 7729F. This international group offers intensive classes for up to 15 students. Courses emphasise communication over grammar, and include an audio-visual *médiathèque* and lectures.

Institut Catholique de Paris *12 rue Cassette, 6th (01.44.39.52.68). M° St-Sulpice.* **Fees** *enrolment* 500F (*dossier* test); *registration* 3750F; 15-week course (6 hrs/week) 3780F. Reputable school offers traditional courses in French language and culture. The equivalent of a French *bac* is required, plus proof of residence. Students must be 18 or above, but don't have to be Catholic.

Institut Parisien *87 bd de Grenelle, 15th (01.40.56.09.53). M° La Motte Picquet-Grenelle.* **Fees** *enrolment* 250F; 990F-2900F. This dynamic private school offers courses in language (up to 25 hours per week) and French civilisation, business French, plus evening courses if there's enough demand. Except for beginners, you can enrol all year.

La Sorbonne – Cours de Langue et Civilisation *47 rue des Ecoles, 5th (01.40.46.22.11 ext 2664/75). M° Cluny-La Sorbonne/RER Luxembourg.* **Fees** 3450F-11,550F per half-year. Classes for foreigners at the Sorbonne ride on the name of this eminent institution. Teaching is grammar-based. The main course includes lectures on politics, history and culture, as well as language-lab sessions. Courses are open to anyone over 18, and fill up very quickly.

Specialised Courses

American University of Paris *Office of Admissions, 31 av Bosquet, 7th (01.40.62.07.20). RER Pont de l'Alma.* Established in 1962, the AUP is an international college awarding four-year American liberal arts degrees (BA/BSc). It has exchange agreements with colleges in the US, Poland and Japan. A Summer Session and Division of Continuing Education (102 rue St-Dominique, 7th/01.40.62.07.20) are also offered.

Christie's Education Paris *Hôtel Salomon de Rothschild, 8 rue Berryer, 8th (01.42.25.10.90). M° George V.* The international auction house offers a one-year diploma in French fine and decorative art (Sept-June; 55,220F), shorter courses and a Monday 20th-century art course (15,550F), based on a combination of lectures and visits (in French).

Cours d'Adultes *Information: Hôtel de Ville, pl de l'Hôtel de Ville, 4th (01.44.61.16.16). M° Hôtel-de-Ville.* **Fees** 160F-1000F. A huge range of inexpensive adult-education classes are run by the City of Paris, in town halls and colleges. To enrol, you need a *Carte de Séjour.*

Tourist information

Office de Tourisme de Paris

127 av des Champs-Elysées, 8th (08.36.68.31.12/recorded information in English and French). M° Charles de Gaulle-Etoile. **Open** *summer* 9am-8pm daily; *winter* 9am-8pm Mon-Sat, 11am-6pm Sun. Closed 1 May. Brochures and information on sights and events in Paris and the suburbs. It has a souvenir and bookshop, a bureau de change, hotel reservation service, and sells phonecards, museum cards, travel passes and tickets for museums, theatres, tours and other attractions. All staff are multi-lingual. Branch offices have more limited facilities. **Branches:** Eiffel Tower (01.45.51.22.15). Open May-Sept 11am-6pm daily. Gare de Lyon (01.43.43.33.24). Open 8am-8pm Mon-Sat.

Espace du Tourisme d'Ile de France

Carrousel du Louvre, 99 rue de Rivoli, 1st (08.03.03.19.98/from abroad (33)1.44.50.19.98). **Open** 10am-7pm Mon, Wed-Sun. Sleekly designed information showcase for Paris and the Ile de France, includes information on museums, châteaux, accommodation, gourmet weekends, golf and walking tours.

CIDD Découverte du Vin *30 rue de la Sablière, 14th (01.45.45.44.20). M° Pernéty.* **Fees** from 420F (for 4 hrs). Wine tasting and appreciation courses (some in English) from beginner to advanced.

Cordon Bleu *8 rue Léon-Delhomme, 15th (01.53.68.22.50). M° Vaugirard.* **Fees** 220F-4950F. Three-hour sessions on classical and regional cuisine, one-week workshops and ten-week courses aimed at those refining skills or embarking on a culinary career.

Ritz-Escoffier Ecole de Gastronomie Française *38 rue Cambon, 1st (01.43.16.31.43). M° Madeleine.* **Fees** 275F-172,000F. From afternoon demonstrations in the Ritz kitchens to twelve-week diplomas. Courses are in French with English translation.

Ecole du Louvre *Porte Jaugard, L'aile de Flore, Musée du Louvre, quai du Louvre, 1st (01.55.35.19.35).* **Fees** 1420F-1750F. This prestigious school runs art history and archaeology courses. Foreign students not wanting to take a full degree (*Licence*) can enrol (May-Sept) as *auditeurs* to attend lectures.

INSEAD *bd de Constance, 77305 Fontainebleau (01.60.72.40.00).* **Fees** 155,000F. Highly regarded international business school, with 520 students from across the world, offers a ten-month MBA in English.

Parsons School of Design *14 rue Letellier, 15th (01.45.77.39.66). M° La Motte-Picquet-Grenelle.* **Fees** 300F registration; 8 sessions 2000F-2500F. Subsidiary of New York art college offers full- and part-time courses in art, fashion, photography, computer, interior and communication design, in English.

Spéos – Paris Photographic

Institute *7 rue Jules-Vallès, 11th (01.40.09.18.58). M° Charonne.* **Fees** 450F-35,500F. Bilingual photo school affiliated with the Rhode Island School of Design.

Telephones

All French phone numbers have ten digits. Paris and Ile de France numbers begin with 01; the rest of France is divided into four zones (02-05). Portable phones start with 06. 08 indicates a special rate (*see below*). If you are calling France from abroad leave off the 0 at the start of the ten-digit number. To call abroad from France dial 00, then country code. Since 1998 other phone companies have been allowed to enter the market, with new prefixes (eg. Cégétel numbers starting with a 7).

France Telecom English-Speaking Customer Service *0800-ENG-SPK/08.00.36.57.75.* **Open** 9.30am-5.30pm Mon-Fri. Freephone information line in English on phone services, bills, payment, Internet.

Special Rate Numbers

08.00 Numéro Vert Freephone.
08.01 Numéro Azur 0.74F under 3 min, then 0.28F/min.
08.02 Numéro Indigo I 0.74F under 56 secs, then 0.79F/min.
08.03 Numéro Indigo II 0.74F under 41 secs, then 1.09F/min.
08.36 2.23F/min. This rate applies not just to chat lines but increasingly to cinema and transport infolines.

Public Phones

Most public phones in Paris use phonecards (*télécartes*). Sold at post offices, tobacconists, airports and train and Métro stations, cards cost

Women's Paris

Paris is essentially unthreatening for women, although the usual precautions of not going out alone late at night apply as they would in any other large city. The worst problems tend to be concentrated in the suburbs, although be careful in areas like Pigalle, the rue St-Denis, the Bois de Boulogne and Bois de Vincennes. Violent crime has been on the increase, but the majority of rapes go unreported, which makes figures hard to estimate. Nonetheless counselling and support services do exist. While French men refrain from whistling and bottom-pinching, many are not shy about trying to pick women up. The best brushoff is a withering stare, well-practised among streetwise *Parisiennes*. Legislation was passed in 1992 to punish sexual harrassment in the workplace, but prosecutions are rare. Flirtatious advances are commonly accepted as consistent with male machismo or chivalry. French women got the vote only in 1948, and the pill only in 1967, but a high proportion of women in the Ile de France work, although as everywhere in Europe salaries are lower than for male counterparts (by an average 25 per cent at management level). Despite some important female ministers and judges, there are few women in top civil service or business positions. For further information on associations, try also the Annuaire au Feminin website on www.iway.fr/femmes.

Maison des Femmes

163 rue de Charenton, 12th (01.43.43.41.13/ 01.43.43.42.13). M° Reuilly-Diderot or Gare de Lyon. **Open** 4-7pm Wed, Fri, Sat; café 7-10pm Fri.
Run with heartfelt enthusiasm, the strictly women-only MdF hosts a feminist library, a café, assorted women's groups including Ruptures, a feminist theory workshop, and SOS Sexisme, an anti-sexism group, and the ARCL lesbian archives (*see chapter* **Gay & Lesbian**). Counselling about women's work rights is also offered (*Conseil Juridique Droit du Travail*). Volunteers can guide on where to look for legal or employment advice or a rape crisis centre.

Librairie des Femmes

74 rue de Seine, 6th (01.43.29.50.75). M° Mabillon. **Open** 11.30am-7pm Mon-Sat. **Credit** AmEx, MC, V.
Paris' main feminist bookshop owned by Editions des Femmes has a gallery area and leaflets on events.

Alliance des Femmes pour la Démocratie

5 rue de Lille, 7th (01.45.48.83.80). M° Rue du Bac. This group militates against sexual discrimination, whether it be granting political asylum to feminist writers or opposing international prostitution rings.

CNIDFF

7 rue du Jura, 13th (01.42.17.12.34). M° Gobelins. **Open** 1.30-5.30pm Tue-Thur (*phone* 9am-12.30pm).
The Centre National d'Information et de Documentation des Femmes et des Familles offers legal, professional and health advice for women.

Service des Droits des Femmes

31 rue Le Peletier, 9th (01.47.70.41.58). M° Le Peletier. **Open** phone calls only 9am-5pm Mon-Fri. **Library** 9am-5pm Wed, Thur (by appointment only).

Sponsored by the Ministère de l'Emploi et de la Solidarité, the service promotes women's rights and oversees the implementation of programmes aimed at achieving equal employment opportunity.

Violence conjugale: Femmes Info Service

(01.40.02.02.33). **Open** 7.30am-11.30pm Mon-Fri; 10am-8pm Sat.
Telephone hotline for battered women, directing them towards medical aid or shelters, if need be.

Viols Femmes Informations

(08.00.05.95.95). **Open** 10am-6pm Mon-Fri.
A freephone in French for dealing with rape.

WICE

20 bd du Montparnasse, 15th (01.45.66.75.50). M° Montparnasse-Bienvenüe. **Open** 9am-5pm Mon-Fri. **Membership** 350F; 500F joint; 250F students.
American expatriate cultural/educational centre runs courses ranging from art history and literature to wine tasting. Membership benefits include discounts to certain shops and leisure facilities, and a library.

Contraception

To obtain the pill (*la pilule*), the coil (*stérilet*) or the morning-after pill, you'll need a prescription, available on appointment from the first two places below or from a *médecin généraliste* (GP) or gynaecologist. Note that the mini-pill is not reimbursed. Spermicides and condoms (*préservatifs*) are sold in pharmacies, and there are condom dispensing machines in Métros, club lavatories and on street corners. For sanitary products, supermarkets are your best bet.

Centre de Planification et d'Education Familiale *27 rue Curnonsky, 17th (01.48.88.07.28). M° Porte de Champerret.* **Open** 9am-5pm Mon-Fri.
Free consultations in French, on family planning and abortion. Abortion counselling on demand; otherwise phone for an appointment.

MFPF (Mouvement Français pour le Planning Familial) *10 rue Vivienne, 2nd (01.42.60.93.20). M° Bourse.* **Open** 9.30am-5pm Mon-Thur; 11am-4pm Fri. Phone for an appointment for contraception advice and prescriptions. For abortion advice, just turn up at the centre. **Branch:** 94 bd Masséna, 13th (01.45.84.28.25/ open Fri only).

Women's Accommodation

Union des Foyers des Jeunes Travailleurs *21 rue des Malmaisons, 13th (01.42.16.86.66). M° Maison-Blanche.* **Open** 9am-1pm, 2-5pm Mon-Fri. **Rates** per month 2500F (half-board). **No credit cards.** An organisation running around 30 *foyers* (hostels) in Paris, of which some 15 are specifically for women aged 18-25, who are either working or unemployed but looking for work.

Union Chrétienne de Jeunes Filles *22 rue de Naples, 8th (01.45.22.23.49). M° Villiers; 168 rue Blomet, 15th (01.56.56.63.00). M° Convention.* **Open** 9am-7pm daily. **Rates** *single room* per month 3150F (half-board). **No credit cards.** Individual and dormitory rooms for women aged 18-24. Breakfast and dinner are included. Shorter stays possible in summer.

40F for 50 units and 96F for 120 units. Cafés have coin phones, while post offices usually have card phones. In a phone box, the digital display screen should read *Décrochez*. Pick up the phone. When *Introduisez votre carte* appears, insert your card into the slot. The screen should then read *Patientez SVP. Numérotez* is your signal to dial. *Crédit épuisé* means that you have no more units left. Finally, hang up (*Raccrochez*), and don't forget your card. Some public phones take credit cards. If you are using a credit card, insert the card, key in your PIN number and *Patientez SVP* should appear. Continue as above.

Phone Books

Phone books are found in all post offices and most cafés. The *Pages Blanches* (White Pages) lists people and businesses alphabetically; *Pages Jaunes* (Yellow Pages) lists businesses and services by category.

Telephone Charges

Local calls in Paris and Ile-de-France beginning with 01 cost 74 centimes for three minutes, standard rate, 29 centimes/minute thereafter. Calls beyond a 100km radius are charged at 74 centimes for the first 39 seconds, then 1.14F per minute. International destinations are divided into 16 zones. Reduced-rate periods for calls within France and Europe: 7pm-8am during the week; noon Sat to 8am Mon. Reduced-rate periods for the US and Canada: 7pm through to 1pm Mon-Fri; all day Sat, Sun. France Telecom's **Primaliste** offers 20 per cent off on calls to six chosen numbers.

Cheap Rate Providers

There are several companies offering low rates for overseas calls, which usually involve you dialling an access number before the number you want to reach. Some require an advance payment to establish a credit limit. Some offer itemised billing to a credit card. The following providers offer competitive rates from France: Based in France, **AXS Telecom** *(01.53.00.37.10);* **BigBig Fone Co** *(01.46.98.20.88);* **First Telecom** *(01.46.98.20.00).* Good deals are offered in the UK by **AT&T Global Customer Service** and in the US by **KallMart**.

24-Hour Telephone Services

Operator assistance, French directory enquiries (*renseignements*), dial 12. To make a reverse-charge call within France, ask to make a call *en PCV*.
International directory enquiries 00.33.12, then country code (eg. 44 for UK).
Telephone engineer dial 13.

International news (French recorded message, France Inter), dial 08.36.68.10.33 (2.23F/min).
Telegram all languages, international 08.00.33.44.11; within France 36.55.
Time dial 36.99.
Traffic news dial 01.48.99.33.33.
Weather dial 08.36.70.12.34 (2.23F/min) for enquiries on weather in France and abroad, in French or English; dial 08.36.68.02.75 (2.23F/min) for a recorded weather announcement for Paris and region.
Airparif (01.44.59.47.64). Mon-Fri 9am-5.30pm. Information about pollution levels and air quality in Paris: invaluable for asthmatics.

Minitel

France Telecom's Minitel is an interactive videotext service available to any telephone subscriber, although it is gradually being superceded by the Internet. Hotels are often Minitel-equipped and most post offices offer use of the terminals for directory enquiries on 3611. Hundreds of services on the pricier 3614, 3615, 3616 and 3617 numbers give access to hotel and ticket reservations, airline and train information, weather forecasts and dozens of recreational lines that include 'dating' hook-ups.
For French telephone directory information, dial 3611 on the keyboard, wait for the beep and press *Connexion*, then type in the name and city of the person or business whose number and/or address you're looking for, and press *Envoi*. Minitel directory use is free for the first three minutes, 37 centimes per minute thereafter. Minitel directory in English dial 3611, wait for the beep, press *Connexion*, type MGS, then *Envoi*. Then type *Minitel en anglais*.

Television

Everyone derides French TV, but at least cable and satellite mean an ever-growing choice of channels.
TF1 The country's biggest channel, and first to be privatised in 1987. Game shows, dubbed soaps, gossip and audience debates are staples. Detective series *Navarro* and *Julie Lescaut* draw big audiences, as do old episodes of *Colombo*. The 8pm news has star anchors Patrick Poivre d'Arvor ('PPDA') and Claire Chazal.
France 2 State-owned station mixes game shows, documentaries, and serious cultural chat in Bernard Pivot's literary *Bouillon de Culture*.
FR3 The more heavyweight – and hence less popular – of the two state channels offers lots of local, wildlife and sports coverage, on-screen debating about social issues, and *Cinéma de Minuit*, late-night Sunday

classic films in the original language.
Canal+ Subscription channel draws viewers with recent films (sometimes in the original language), exclusive sport and late-night porn. *Télétubbies*, *The Simpsons* and amusing talk show *Nulle Part Ailleurs* with satirical puppets *Les Guignols* are available unscrambled.
Arte/La Cinquième Franco-German hybrid Arte specialises in intelligent, often themed, evenings. Arte shares its wavelength with educational channel *La Cinquième* (5.45am-7pm).
M6 M6 is winning the 20s and 30s audience, with imports like *Ally McBeal* and some excellent homegrown magazine programmes, such as *Culture Pub* (about advertising), finance mag *Capital* and voyeuristic *Zone Interdite*.

Cable TV & Satellite

France offers a similar range of cable and satellite channels to every European country. The basic package from Paris-Câble (01.44.25.89.99/160F per month, plus connection fee) includes **Paris Première**, excellent for fashion shows and *VO* films and the *Rive Droite-Rive Gauche* arts magazine, TF1's continuous news programme **LC1**, documentary channel **Planète**, history channel **Histoire**, **Eurosport**, **MTV** music television, **MCM** its French imitator, woman's mag **Téva**,, **Série Club** for vintage series, and **Canal Jimmy**, which shows British and American sitcoms in the original, such as *Friends* and *Ab Fab*. You have to go to the next package (from 194F/month) for **BBC Prime**, which shows up-to-date *Eastenders* and archaic comedy repeats, and **CNN**'s 24-hours news. Other packages offer film channel and pay-as-you-view options.

Satellite potentially offers better reception, lower (if any) subscription prices and a better-targeted *bouquet* of channels, but is opposed by most Paris and suburban local authorities. Operators include Eutelsat (channels from the rest of Europe and the Middle East), Canal Satellite (linked to Canal+), Astra, TPS and AB Sat.

Ticket Agencies

The following sell tickets for rock and classical concerts and theatre.
See also chapter **Theatre**.
Fnac *Forum des Halles, 1st* (01.40.41.40.00). *M° Les Halles/RER Châtelet-Les Halles.* **Open** 10am-7.30pm Mon-Sat. **Credit** AmEx, MC, V. Bookings in person only, or on 3615 FNAC or www.fnac.fr.
Branches: 136 rue de Rennes, 6th (01.49.54.30.00); 74 av des Champs-Elysées, 8th (01.53.53.64.64); 24 bd

des Italiens, 9th (01.48.01.02.03); 4 pl de la Bastille, 12th (01.43.42.04.04). **Ticket +** *(01.49.87.50.50).* **Open** 9am-9pm Mon-Sat. **Credit** MC, V. Telephone bookings linked to Fnac.
Virgin Megastore *52 av des Champs-Elysées, 8th (01.49.53.50.00). M° Franklin D Roosevelt.* **Open** 10am-midnight Mon-Sat *(billetterie by phone on 01.44.68.44.08);* noon-midnight Sun. **Credit** AmEx, DC, MC, V. Branch: Carrousel du Louvre, 1st.

Time & the Seasons

France is one hour ahead of Greenwich Mean Time (GMT). In France time is based on the 24-hour system so that 8am is *8 heures,* noon is *12 heures (midi),* 8pm is *20 heures* and midnight is *0 (zéro) heure (minuit).*

Average Temperatures

January 7.5°C (45.5°F); February 7.1°C (44.8°F); March 10.2°C (50.4°F); April 15.7°C (60.3°F); May 16.6°C (61.9°F); June 23.4°C (74.1°F); July 25.1°C (77.2°F); August 25.6°C (78.1°F); September 20.9°C (69.6°F); October 16.5°C (61.7F); November 11.7°C (53.1°F); December 7.8°C (46°F).

Video Rental

Prime Time Video *24 rue Mayet, 6th (01.40.56.33.44). M° Duroc.* **Open** noon-midnight daily. **Rates** 30F for three days; free membership. **Credit** MC, V. Rents English language videos. Branch: 12 rue Léance-Reynaud, 16th (01.47.20.50.01).

Visas

European Union nationals do not need a visa to enter France, nor do US, Canadian, Australian or New Zealand citizens for stays of up to three months. Nationals of other countries should enquire at the nearest French Consulate before leaving home; if they are travelling to France from one of the countries included in the Schengen agreement (most of the EU, but not Britain, Ireland, Italy or Greece), the visa from that country should be sufficient. For over three months, *see p339,* **Cartes de Séjour.**

Working in Paris

All EU nationals can work legally in France, but must apply for a French social security number and *Carte de Séjour.* Some job ads can be found at branches of the Agence National Pour l'Emploi (ANPE), the French national employment bureau. This is also the place to go to sign up as a *demandeur d'emploi,* to be placed on file as available for work and to qualify for French unemployment benefits. Britons can only claim French unemployment benefit if they were already signed on before leaving the UK. Non-EU nationals need a work permit and are not entitled to use the ANPE network without valid work papers.
CIEE *1 pl de l'Odéon, 6th (01.44.41.74.74). M° Odéon.* **Open** 9am-6pm Mon-Fri. The Council on International Educational Exchange provides three-month work permits

for US citizens at or recently graduated from university, has a job centre, mostly for sales and catering, and provides a three-month permit to those with a pre-arranged job.
Office des Migrations Internationales (OMI) *Service de l'Expatriation-BCO, 44 rue Bargue, 75732 Paris Cedex 15 (01.53.69.53.29).* The OMI provides work permits of up to 18 months to Americans aged 18-35 and has a job placement service. *Stagiaires* should pick up permit, which takes 8-10 weeks, in their home country.

Job Ads

Help-wanted ads sometimes appear in the *International Herald Tribune,* although the 'sophisticated personal companion' make up the bulk of them. The free publication *FUSAC* carries some job ads for English-speakers, mainly English-language teaching, bar work, secretarial/PA, telesales and child minding. Offers for English-speakers are sometimes listed on noticeboards at language schools and Anglo establishments, such as the **American Church**; most are for babysitters and language tutors. Positions as waiters and bar staff are often available at international-style watering holes. Bilingual secretarial/PA work is available for those with good written French, *see p353.*
If you are looking for professional work, have your CV translated, including French equivalents for any qualifications. Most job applications require a photo and a handwritten letter; French employers are very fond of graphological analysis.

Business Resources

Information

The best first stop in Paris for anyone initiating business in France is the **Bourse du Commerce.** Most major banks can refer you to lawyers, accountants and tax consultants; several US and British banks provide expatriate services. For business and financial news, the French dailies *La Tribune* and *Les Echos,* and the weekly *Investir* are the tried and trusted sources. *Capital,* its sister magazine *Management* and the weightier *L'Expansion* are worthwhile monthlies. *Défis* has tips for the entrepreneur, *Initiatives* is for the self-employed. BFM on 96.4 FM is an all-news business radio. *Les Echos* gives stock quotes on www.lesechos.com; Minitel service 3615 CD offers real-time stock quotes. Business directories *Kompass France* and *Kompass Régional* also give company details and detailed French

market profiles on 3617 KOMPASS. The standard English-language reference is *The French Company Handbook,* a list of all companies in the 120 Index of the Paris Bourse, published by the *International Herald Tribune* (01.41.43.93.00). It can be ordered for £50 from Paul Baker Publishing, 37 Lambton Rd, London SW20 OLW (0181-946 0590).
Paris Anglophone Directory lists 2500 English-speaking companies, professionals and organisations. It can be ordered for 98F plus 25F postage from Paris Anglophone, 32 rue Edouard Vaillant, 93100 Montreuil (01.48.59.66.58).

Institutions

American Chamber of Commerce *21 av George V, 8th (01.40.73.89.90/ fax 01.47.20.18.62). M° George V or Alma-Marceau.* **Open** 9am-5.30pm

Mon-Fri. The American Chamber has a library for members, hosts social events and has an active small-business committee. Its directory, listing Franco-American firms and organisations, is available to non-members (400F), as is its *Guide to Doing Business in France* (400F).
Bourse du Commerce *2 rue de Viarmes, 1st (01.55.65.55.65). M° Les Halles.* **Open** 9am-6pm Mon-Fri. This branch of the **CCIP** houses a wide range of services for new businesses, including L'Espace Création (01.53.40.48.50) and the Centre de Formalités des Entreprises (01.53.40.46.00).
British Embassy Commercial Library *35 rue du Fbg-St-Honoré, 8th (01.44.51.34.56/fax 01.44.51.34.01). M° Concorde.* **Open** 10am-1pm, 2.30-5pm Mon-Fri, by appointment. The library stocks trade directories, and assists British companies that wish to develop sales or set up in France.

Chambre de Commerce et d'Industrie Franco-Britannique

Promotes contacts in the Franco-British business community through talks, social events and seminars. It has three divisions: **Language Training Centre** *41 rue de Turenne, 3rd (01.44.59.25.10).* *Mᵒ Chemin-Vert.* **Open** 9am-7pm Mon-Thur; 9am-5pm Fri; 9am-1pm Sat. French and English courses in business communication.
Trade and Membership Department *31 rue Boissy d'Anglas, 8th (01.53.30.81.30). Mᵒ Madeleine.* **Open** 2-5pm Mon-Fri. Annual membership 1450F. Commercial enquiries library. The annual trade directory costs 375F.
Franco-British Educational Services *1 impasse St-Claude, 3rd (01.44.59.24.11). Mᵒ St Sébastien-Froissart.* **Open** 9am-1pm Mon-Thur; 2-6pm Fri; 9am-1pm, 2-5pm Sat. Administers language courses and Chamber exams.
CCIP (Chambre de Commerce et d'Industrie de Paris) *27 av de Friedland, 8th (01.42.89.70.00/fax 01.42.89.78.68). Mᵒ George V.* **Open** 9am-6pm Mon-Fri. A huge organisation providing services for businesses. In the same building is an information centre, and the best business library in the city (30F per day; 300F per year). Its publications *Business and Commerce Undertaken by Non-French Nationals* (for small businesses) and *Foreigners: Starting Up Your Company in France* (for large companies) in English, cost 48F and can be purchased at CCIP or at Presses Universitaires de France, 49 bd St-Michel, 5th (01.44.41.81.20). Trade, market and export information on Minitel 3615 CCIP and 3617 CCIPLUS.
US Embassy Commercial Section *4 av Gabriel, 8th (library 01.43.12.25.32/fax 01.43.12.21.72). Mᵒ Concorde.* **Open** 9am-6pm Mon-Fri, by appointment. Business library provides advice on US companies in France, as well as contacts, research and information. Minitel 3617 USATRADE will respond to enquiries within 24 hours (Mon-Fri).

Trade Fairs & Conferences

The leading centre for international trade fairs, Paris hosts over 500 exhibitions a year, from the Auto Show to the major fashion collections.
Foires et Salons de France *31 rue de Billancourt, Boulogne-Billancourt (01.48.25.66.55/ fax 01.48.25.04.55). Mᵒ Billancourt.* **Open** 9am-1pm, 2-6pm Mon-Thur (5pm Fri). Distributes the calendar *Salons Nationaux et Internationaux en France* (send a 6.70F pre-stamped envelope or pick one up in person). Consult Minitel 3616 SALONS.
CNIT *2 pl de la Défense, BP 321,*

92053 Paris La Défense (01.46.92.28.66/fax 01.46.92.15.78). Mᵒ Grande Arche de La Défense. Mainly computer fairs.
Palais des Congrès *2 pl de la Porte-Maillot, 17th (01.40.68.22.22). Mᵒ Porte-Maillot.*
Paris-Expo *Porte de Versailles, 15th (01.43.95.37.00/fax 01.53.68.71.71). Mᵒ Porte de Versailles.* Paris' biggest exhibition centre from agriculture to pharmaceuticals.
Parc des Expositions de Paris-Nord Villepinte *BP 6004, Paris Nord 2, 95970 Roissy-Charles de Gaulle. (01.48.63.30.30/fax 01.48.63.33.70). RER B Parc des Expositions.* Trade fair centre near Roissy airport.

Accountants & Lawyers

Many big UK and US accountancy and legal firms have Paris offices.
France Audit Expertise *148 bd Malesherbes, 17th (01.43.80.42.98/fax 01.47.64.03.92). Mᵒ Wagram.* **Open** 9am-6pm Mon-Fri. Handles companies of all sizes.
Levine & Okoshken *51 av Montaigne, 8th (01.44.13.69.50/fax 01.45.63.24.96). Mᵒ Franklin D Roosevelt.* **Open** 9am-6pm Mon-Fri. A specialist in tax and corporate law, with many US clients.
Shubert & Dusausoy *190 bd Haussmann, 8th (01.40.76.01.43/fax 01.40.76.01.44). Mᵒ St-Philippe-du-Roule.* **Open** 9am-4pm Mon-Fri. Law firm helps English-speaking business people set up in France.

Translators & Interpreters

Certain documents, from birth certificates to loan applications, must be translated by certified legal translators, listed at the CCIP (*see above*) or embassies. For French-English or English/French business translations of annual reports, brochures, etc, there are dozens of reliable independents.
Association des Anciens Elèves de L'Esit *(01.44.05.41.46).* **Open** by *phone only* 9am-6pm Mon-Fri. A translation and interpreting cooperative whose 1000 members are graduates of L'Ecole Supérieure d'Interprètes et de Traducteurs.
International Corporate Communication *3 rue des Batignolles, 17th (01.43.87.29.29/fax 01.45.22.49.13). Mᵒ Place de Clichy.* **Open** 9am-1pm, 2-6pm Mon-Fri. Translators of financial and corporate documents. Also offers simultaneous translation services.

Secretarial Services

ADECCO International *4 pl de la Défense, Cedex 26, 92974 Paris La Défense (01.49.01.94.94/ fax 01.46.93.03.44). Mᵒ Grande Arche de La Défense.* **Open** 8.30am-noon,

2-6pm Mon-Fri. This branch of the large international employment agency specialises in bilingual secretaries and office staff – permanent or temporary.
TM International *36-38 rue des Mathurins, 8th (01.47.42.71.00/fax 01.47.42.18.87). RER Auber.* **Open** 9am-6pm Mon-Fri. Full-time French-English bilingual secretarial staff.

Computer Equipment

Surcouf Informatique *139 av Daumesnil, 12th (01.53.33.20.00/fax 01.53.33.21.01). Mᵒ Gare de Lyon.* **Open** 9.30am-7pm Tue-Sat. **Credit** MC, V. An impressive computer superstore, with repair service and an English-language software stall.
KA *14 rue Magellan, 8th (01.44.43.16.00/ fax 01.47.20.34.39). Mᵒ George V.* **Open** 9am-7pm Mon-Fri; *technical service* 9am-6pm, Mon-Fri. **Credit** AmEx, MC, V. Sale and rental of IBM, Apple and Compaq.
Prorata Services *27 rue Linné, 5th (01.45.35.94.14/fax 01.45.35.19.13). Mᵒ Jussieu.* **Open** 9am-7pm Mon-Fri; 10.30am-6pm Sat. **Credit** V. Use Macs and PCs on the spot (1F/min) or hire a portable. Its graphic design studio, Studio PAO is at 15 rue Jussieu.

Couriers

Chronopost *9 rue Hérold, 1st (08.03.801.801). Mᵒ Sentier/RER Châtelet-Les Halles.* **Open** 8am-8pm Mon-Fri; 9am-3pm Sat. **Credit** AmEx, MC, V. This post office offshoot is the most widely used service for parcels of up to 30kg. International service.
DHL *59 av d'Iéna, 16th (08.00.20.25.25). Mᵒ Iéna.* **Open** 9am-8pm Mon-Fri; 9am-5pm Sat. **Credit** AmEx, MC, V. Big name in international courier services.
Branch: 6 rue des Colonnes, 2nd.
Flash Service *(01.42.74.26.01/fax 01.42.74.11.17).* **Open** 9am-6.30pm Mon-Fri. **No credit cards**. A local bike messenger company.
Relais Express *(01.42.05.18.26/ fax 01.42.05.39.82).* **Open** 8.30am-6pm Mon-Fri. **No credit cards**. Local courier service by bike or van.

Office Hire

CNIT *2 pl de la Défense, BP 200, 92053 Paris La Défense (01.46.92.24.24/fax 01.46.92.15.92). Mᵒ La Défense.* **Open** 8.30am-7.30pm Mon-Fri. The trade centre houses 800 firms and offers a data-processing service, video-conference facilities and offices and meeting rooms.
Jones Lang Wootton *49 av Hoche, 8th (01.40.55.15.15/ fax 01.46.22.28.28). Mᵒ Charles de Gaulle-Etoile.* **Open** 8am-7pm Mon-Fri. Britain's leading office-rental firm. **Branch:** 193-197 rue de Bercy, Tour Gamma B, 12th (01.43.43.60.61).

Essential Vocabulary

In French, as in other Latin languages, the second person singular (you) has two forms. Phrases here are given in the more polite *vous* form. The *tu* form is used with family, friends, young children and pets; you should be careful not to use it with people you do not know sufficiently well, as it is considered rude. You will also find that courtesies such as *monsieur, madame* and *mademoiselle* are used much more than their English equivalents. *See chapter* **Directory A-Z** for information on language courses and **Menu Lexicon** for help in deciphering menus.

General Expressions

good morning/good afternoon, hello *bonjour*
good evening *bonsoir;* **goodbye** *au revoir*
hi (familiar) *salut;* **OK** *d'accord;* **yes** *oui;* **no** *non*
How are you? *Comment allez vous?/vous allez bien?*
How's it going? *Comment ça va?/ça va?* (familiar)
Sir/Mr *monsieur (Mr);* **Madam/Mrs** *madame (Mme)*
Miss *mademoiselle (Mlle)*
please *s'il vous plaît;* **thank you** *merci;*
thank you very much *merci beaucoup*
sorry *pardon;* **excuse me** *excusez-moi*
Do you speak English? *Parlez-vous anglais?*
I don't speak French *Je ne parle pas français*
I don't understand *Je ne comprends pas*
Speak more slowly, please *Parlez plus lentement, s'il vous plaît*
Leave me alone *Laissez-moi tranquille*
how much?/how many? *combien?*
Have you got change? *Avez-vous de la monnaie?*
I would like… *Je voudrais…*
I am going *Je vais;* **I am going to pay** *Je vais payer*
it is *c'est;* **it isn't** *ce n'est pas*
good *bon/bonne;* **bad** *mauvais/mauvaise*
small *petit/petite;* **big** *grand/grande*
beautiful *beau/belle;* **well** *bien;* **badly** *mal*
expensive *cher;* **cheap** *pas cher*
a bit *un peu;* **alot** *beaucoup;* **very** *très;* **with** *avec;*
without *sans;* **and** *et;* **or** *ou;* **because** *parce que*
who? *qui?;* **when?** *quand?;* **what?** *quoi?;* **which?** *quel?;* **where?** *où?;* **why?** *pourquoi?;* **how?** *comment?*
at what time/when? *à quelle heure?*
forbidden *interdit/défendu*
out of order *hors service (hs)/en panne*
daily *tous les jours (tlj)*

On the Phone

hello (telephone) *allô;* **Who's calling?** *C'est de la part de qui?/Qui est à l'appareil?*
Hold the line *Ne quittez pas/Patientez s'il vous plaît*

Getting Around

Where is the (nearest) Métro? *Où est le Métro (le plus proche)?;* **When is the next train for… ?** *C'est quand le prochain train pour… ?*
ticket *un billet;* **station** *la gare;* **platform** *le quai*
entrance *entrée;* **exit** *sortie*
left *gauche;* **right** *droite;* **interchange** *correspondence*
straight on *tout droit;* **far** *loin;* **near** *près/près d'ici*
street *la rue;* **street map** *le plan;* **road map** *la carte*
bank *la banque;* **is there a bank near here?** *est-ce qu'il y a une banque près d'ici?*
Post Office *La Poste;* **a stamp** *un timbre*

Sightseeing

museum *un musée;* **church** *une église*
exhibition *une exposition;* **ticket** (for museum) *un billet;* (for theatre, concert) *une place*
open *ouvert;* **closed** *fermé*
free *gratuit;* **reduced price** *un tarif réduit*
except Sunday *sauf le dimanche*

Accommodation

Do you have a room (for this evening/for two people)? *Avez-vous une chambre (pour ce soir/pour deux personnes)?*
full *complet;* **room** *une chambre*
bed *un lit;* **double bed** *un grand lit;*
(a room with) twin beds *une chambre à deux lits*
with bath(room)/shower *avec (salle de) bain/douche*
breakfast *le petit déjeuner;* **included** *compris*
lift *un ascenseur;* **air conditioned** *climatisé*

At the Café or Restaurant

I'd like to book a table (for three/at 8pm) *Je voudrais réserver une table (pour trois personnes/à vingt heures)*
lunch *le déjeuner;* **dinner** *le dîner*
coffee (espresso) *un café;* **white coffee** *un café au lait/café crème;* **tea** *le thé;* **wine** *le vin;* **beer** *la bière*
mineral water *eau minérale;* **fizzy** *gazeuse;* **still** *plate*
tap water *eau du robinet/une carafe d'eau*
the bill, please *l'addition, s'il vous plaît*

Behind the Wheel

give way *céder le passage*
it's not your right of way *vous n'avez pas la priorité;* **no parking** *stationnement interdit/stationnement gênant;* **deliveries** *livraisons*
toll *péage;* **speed limit 40** *rappel 40*
petrol *essence;* **unleaded** *sans plomb*
traffic jam *embouteillage/bouchon;* **speed** *vitesse*
traffic moving freely *traffic fluide*
dangerous bends *attention virages*

Numbers

0 *zéro;* 1 *un, une;* 2 *deux;* 3 *trois;* 4 *quatre;* 5 *cinq;* 6 *six;* 7 *sept;* 8 *huit;* 9 *neuf;* 10 *dix;* 11 *onze;* 12 *douze;* 13 *treize;* 14 *quatorze;* 15 *quinze;* 16 *seize;* 17 *dix-sept;* 18 *dix-huit;* 19 *dix-neuf;* 20 *vingt;* 21 *vingt-et-un;* 22 *vingt-deux;* 30 *trente;* 40 *quarante;* 50 *cinquante;* 60 *soixante;* 70 *soixante-dix;* 80 *quatre-vingts;* 90 *quatre-vingt-dix;* 100 *cent;* 1000 *mille;* 1,000,000 *un million.*

Days, Months & Seasons

Monday *lundi;* **Tuesday** *mardi;* **Wednesday** *mercredi;* **Thursday** *jeudi;* **Friday** *vendredi;* **Saturday** *samedi;* **Sunday** *dimanche.* **January** *janvier;* **February** *février;* **March** *mars;* **April** *avril;* **May** *mai;* **June** *juin;* **July** *juillet;* **August** *août;* **September** *septembre;* **October** *octobre;* **November** *novembre;* **December** *décembre.* **Spring** *printemps;* **Summer** *été;* **Autumn** *automne;* **Winter** *hiver.*

Further Reading

History, Art & Culture

Beevor, Antony & Cooper, Artemis *Paris after the Liberation*
The city during rationing, liberation and existentialism.
Bradbury, David & Sparks, Annie *Mise en Scène: French Theatre Now*
Who's who in contemporary French theatre.
Christiansen, Rupert *Tales of the New Babylon*
The Paris of Napoléon III, from sleaze, prostitution and Haussmann's bulldozer to the bloody Commune.
Cole, Robert *A Traveller's History of Paris*
A useful general introduction.
Cronin, Vincent *Napoleon*
A fine biography of the great megalomaniac.
Fitch, Noel Riley *Literary Cafés of Paris*
Who drank where and when.
Horne, Alastair *The Fall of Paris*
Detailed chronicle of the Siege and Commune 1870-71.
Littlewood, Ian *Paris: Architecture, History, Art*
Paris' history intertwined with its treasures.
Lurie, Patty *Guide to Impressionist Paris*
Impressionist paintings matched to their location today.
Marnham, Patrick *Crime & the Académie Française*
Quirks and scandals of Mitterrand-era Paris.
Martin, Hervé *Guide to Modern Architecture in Paris*
An accessible, bilingual illustrated guide to significant buildings in Paris since 1900, arranged by area.
Mitford, Nancy *The Sun King; Madame de Pompadour*
Great gossipy accounts of the courts of the *ancien régime*.
Johnson, Douglas & Johnson, Madeleine *Age of Illusion: Art & Politics in France 1918-1940*
French culture in a Paris at the forefront of modernity.
ed Passek, Jean-Loup *Larousse Dictionnaire du cinéma.*
ed Rapp, Bernard, and Lamy, Jean-Claude *Larousse Dictionnaire mondial des films*
All that film buffs need on Gallic cinema and beyond.
Salvadori, Renzo *Architect's Guide to Paris*
Plans, illustrations and a guide to Paris' growth.
Schama, Simon *Citizens*
Giant but wonderfully readable account of the Revolution.
Toklas, Alice B *The Alice B Toklas Cookbook*
Literary and artistic life, and how to cook fish for Picasso, by the companion (and cook) of Gertrude Stein.
Zeldin, Theodore *The French*
Idiosyncratic and entertaining survey of modern France.

French Literature

Abaelardus, Petrus & Heloïse *Letters*
The full details of Paris' first great romantic drama.
Aragon, Louis *Paris Peasant*
A great Surrealist view of the city.
Balzac, Honoré de *Illusions perdues, La Peau de chagrin, Le Père Goriot, Splendeurs et misères de courtisanes*
Some of the most evocative in the 'Human Comedy' cycle.
Baudelaire *LeSpleen de Paris*
Baudelaire's prose poems with Paris settings from public parks and new Haussmannian cafés to squalid lodgings.
Céline, Louis-Ferdinand *Mort à crédit*
Remarkably vivid, largely autobiographical account of an impoverished Paris childhood.
De Beauvoir, Simone *The Mandarins*
Paris intellectuals and idealists just after the Liberation.
Desforges, Régine *The Blue Bicycle*
A vivid, easy-read drama of resistance, collaboration and sex during the German occupation. First of a trilogy.
Hugo, Victor *Notre Dame de Paris*
Quasimodo and the romantic vision of medieval Paris.
Maupassant, Guy de *Bel-Ami*
Gambling and dissipation.
Modiano, Patrick *Honeymoon*
Evocative story of two lives that cross in Paris.
Perec, Georges *Life, A User's Manual*
Intellectual puzzle in a Haussmannian apartment building.
Restif de la Bretonne, Nicolas *Les Nuits de Paris*
The sexual underworld of the Paris of Louis XV, by one of France's most famous defrocked priests.
Queneau, Raymond *Zazie in the Metro*
Paris in the 1950s: bright and very *nouvelle vague.*
Sartre, Jean-Paul *Roads to Freedom*
Existential angst as the German army takes over Paris.
Simenon, Georges The Maigret series
All of Simenon's books featuring his laconic detective provide a great picture of Paris and its underworld.
Vian, Boris *Froth on the Daydream*
Wonderfully funny Surrealist satire of Paris in the golden era of Sartre and St-Germain.
Zola, Emile *Nana, L'Assommoir, Le Ventre de Paris*
Vivid accounts of the underside of the Second Empire.

The Ex-Pat Angle

Gallant, Mavis *Home Truths*
Short stories juggling between Paris and Canada.
Hemingway, Ernest *A Moveable Feast*
Big Ern drinks his way around 1920s writers' Paris.
Littlewood, Ian *Paris: A Literary Companion*
Great selection of pieces by all kinds of writers on Paris.
Maugham, W Somerset *The Moon & Sixpence*
Impoverished artist in Montmartre and escape to the South Seas, inspired by the life of Gauguin.
Miller, Henry *Tropic of Cancer, Tropic of Capricorn*
Low-life and lust in Montparnasse.
Nin, Anaïs *Henry & June*
Lust in Montparnasse with Henry Miller and his wife.
Orwell, George *Down & Out in Paris & London*
Includes Orwell's stint as a lowly Paris washer-up.
Rhys, Jean *After Mr Mackenzie*
Life as a kept woman in seedy hotels.
Stein, Gertrude *The Autobiography of Alice B Toklas*
Ex-pat Paris, from start to finish.
Süskind, Patrick *Perfume*
Pungent murder in Paris on the eve of the Revolution.

The New Generation

Clémentine, Guillaume *Le Petit Malheureux*
A light-hearted, at times fantastical, life on the dole.
Darrieussecq, Marie *Truismes* (Pig Tales)
Ambiguously feminist. Woman becomes sow.
Dyer, Geoff *Paris Trance*
Bar crawls and literary ambitions of young expats.
Houllebecq, Michel *Extension du domaine de la lutte*
Epitome of the new nihilist novel.
ed Royle, Nicholas *Time Out Book of Paris Short Stories*
New fiction by British, American and French writers.

Index

Maps

Paris Arrondissements

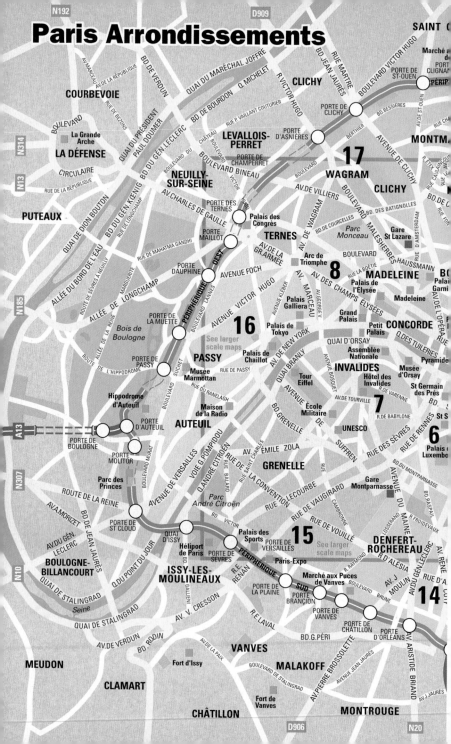

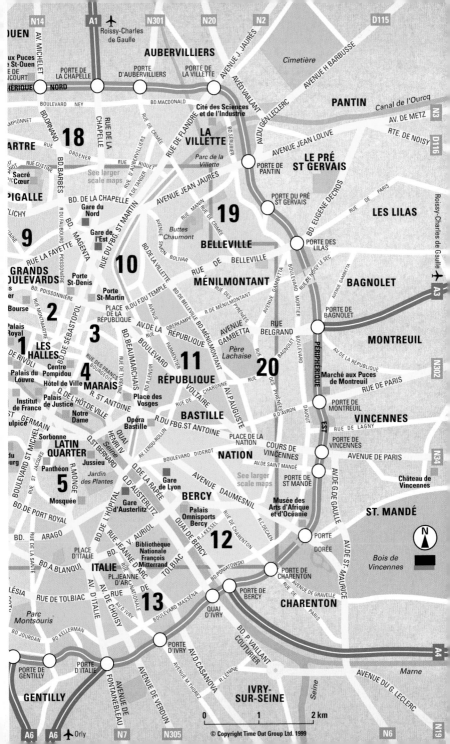

Street Index

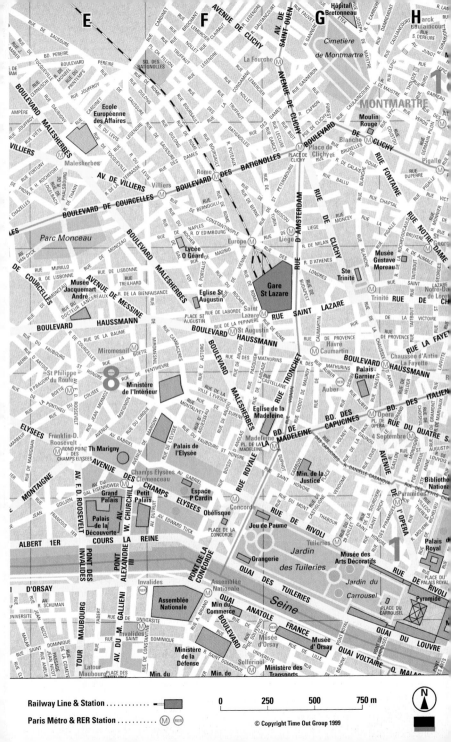

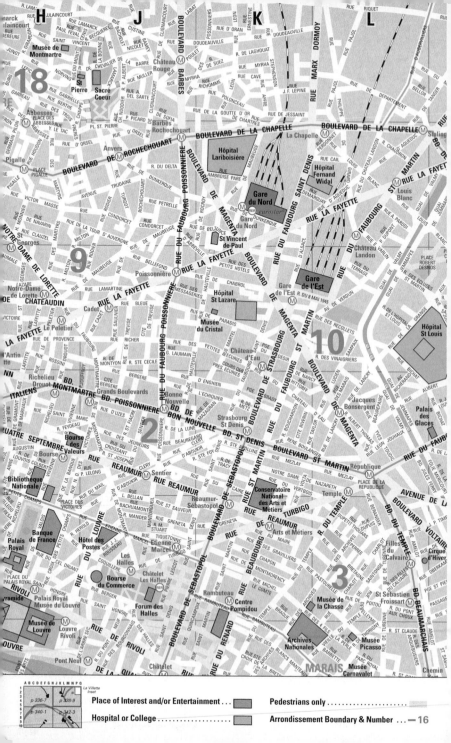

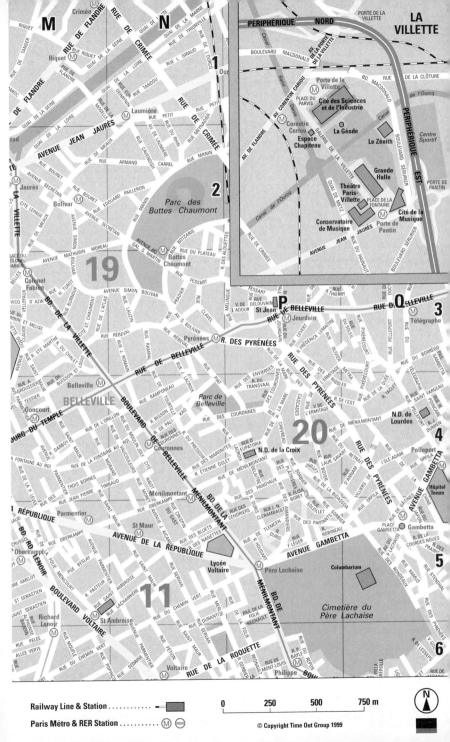

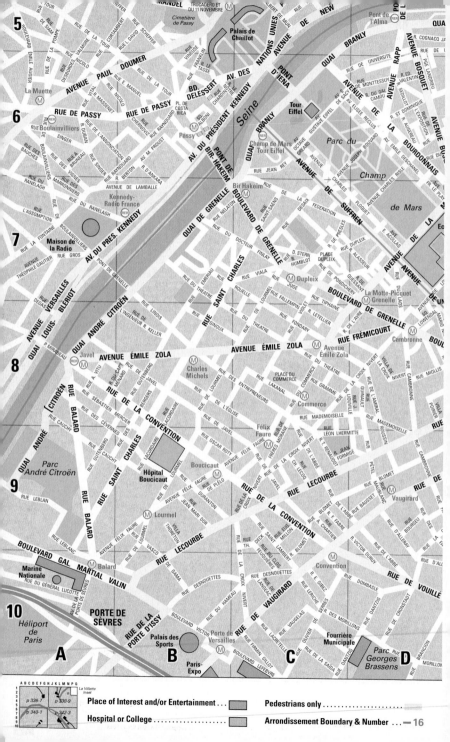

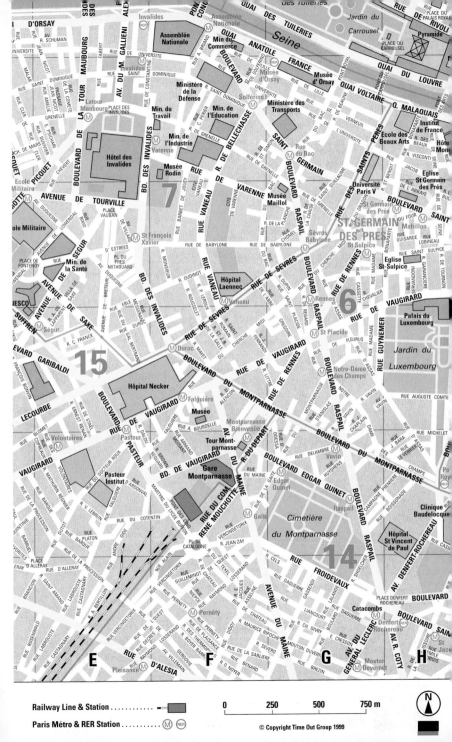

Railway Line & Station . . . .

Paris Métro & RER Station . . . . (M) (RER)

0   250   500   750 m

© Copyright Time Out Group 1999

N

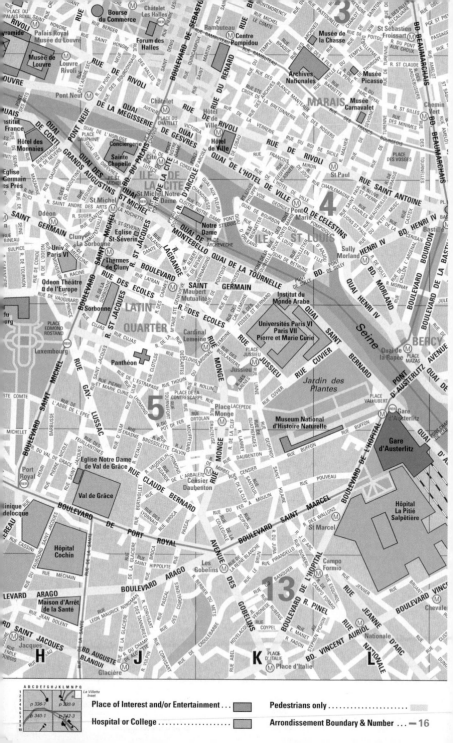

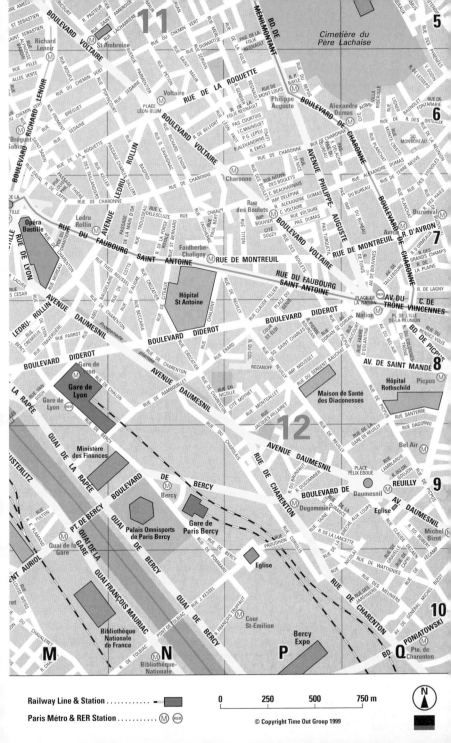

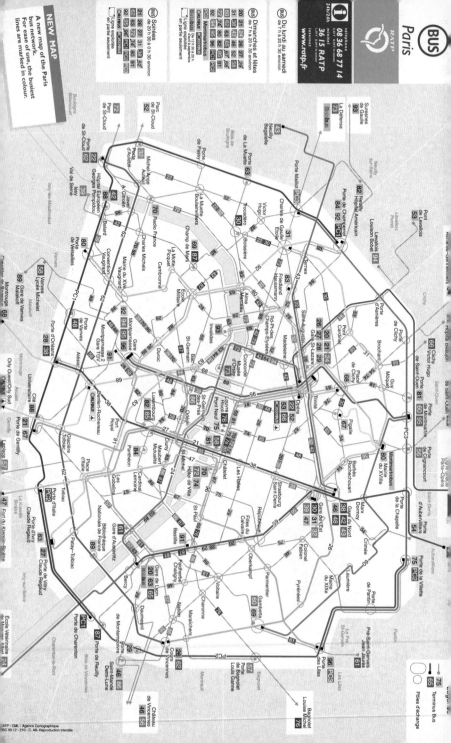

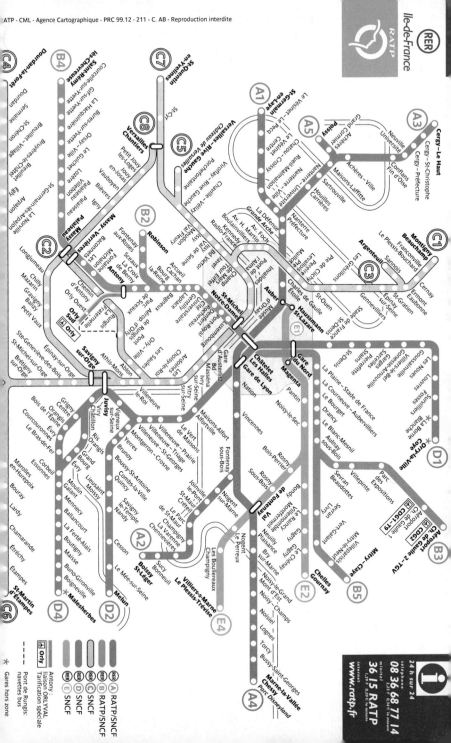

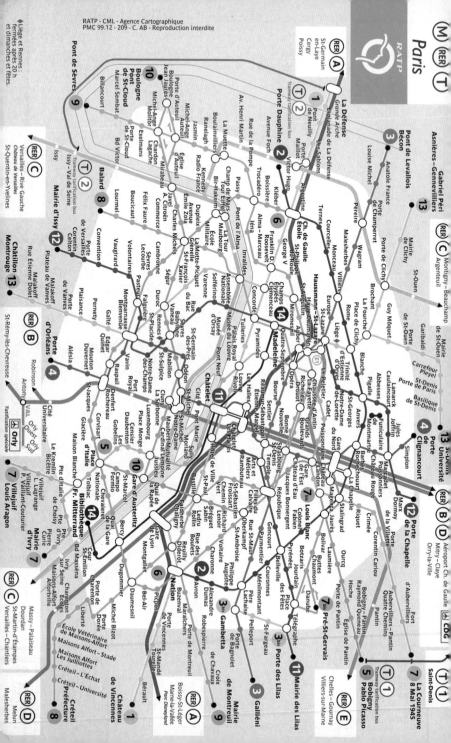